RUGGED INDIVIDUALISM RECONSIDERED

RUGGED INDIVIDUALISM RECONSIDERED

Essays in Psychological Anthropology

by Francis L.K. Hsu

THE UNIVERSITY OF TENNESSEE PRESS • KNOXVILLE

Copyright © 1983 by The University of Tennessee Press
Knoxville
All rights reserved
Manufactured in the United States of America
First edition

Frontispiece: Artwork from Chapter 16, "Eros, Affect and *Pao*"

Clothbound editions of University of Tennessee Press
books are printed on paper designed for an effective
life of at least 300 years, and binding materials
are chosen for strength and durability.

Library of Congress Cataloging in Publication Data
Hsu, Francis L. K., 1909–
    Rugged individualism reconsidered.

    Bibliography: p.
    Includes index.
    1. Ethnopsychology—Addresses, essays, lectures.
2. Individualism—Addresses, essays, lectures.
3. Kinship—Addresses, essays, lectures. I. Title.
GN502.H78   1983   302.5′4   82-13687
ISBN 0-87049-370-1
ISBN 0-87049-371-X (pbk.)

Contents

PART IV: Kinship, Society and Culture

PART V: Culture Change, Facts and Fancy

PART VI: Intercultural Understanding

Preface

Individualism, A Two-Edged Sword

By any standard of excellence the achievement record of the United States of America is one of which all its citizens can justly be proud. The stability of our government has withstood presidential assassinations. The change of our national administration has been regularly achieved by the ballot, not violence.

We have shown the greatest capacity for transforming science into technology, including the technology of business and industrial management. It is no accident that while only 7 percent of Americans till the soil, we not only feed ourselves exceptionally well, but give or sell large quantities of food to many peoples around the world, including the Soviet Union. Our supermarkets and franchises, such as McDonald's, are copied by most of the world.

It is not an exaggeration to say that two world wars, which threatened to return mankind to barbary, could not have been won without American participation. Our fundamental belief in the rule of law was given its highest expression when we dismissed an erring President from office. We entertain more people on earth with our movies and music than like products from any other society. Although the assembly line idea was first used centuries ago in imperial China, it was the Americans who practiced it in a gigantic way to give American industry its leading position during the twentieth century.

Our list of luminaries whose work has benefited all mankind is long: Franklin, Edison, Bell, Ford, Salk, Dewey, Oppenheimer, to name but a few. Up to 1980 a total of some 467 Nobel Prizes were awarded, 156 (or 33 percent) of them to citizens of the United States. Several of the American winners of this great honor were, of course, born and raised in other societies. But is that not indicative of the open doors of this society and its attraction to the rest of the world? In what other country could a non-native like Kissinger become secretary of state?

In their love of individual freedom and equality Americans are unrivaled. In no other society do we find so much attention and effort being expended on the individual, including the handicapped. Special ramps in public buildings for those in wheel chairs, elaborate equipment and trained monkeys for quadriplegics, and seeing-eye dogs for the blind are but a few examples. We can boast of more charitable and scientific foundations than any other country in the world.

It is no accident that the world has heard again and again about the American Dream, but never the Chinese Dream, the Japanese Dream, or even the English Dream.

There is, however, another side to our America, a side we cannot by any yardstick be proud of, a side we would like to disown and a side we often shrug off as being the work of a minority: deviants, mental patients, habitual criminals. "Teenage Robbers Erase Poor Family's Christmas"; "Diplomat, Beaten, Robbed"; "Man, 32, Accused of Raping Mother"; "Boy, 14, Held in Murder of a Neighbor." Such headlines are endless in our news media. In one segment of CBS's "60 Minutes" (October 1981) it was stated that one-fourth of the murders in Los Angeles in 1980 were committed by kids. Reporter Ed Bradley said that every police officer to whom he and his CBS associates talked told them that kids commit crimes more vicious and unpredictable than do adults.

In some instances the viciousness staggers one's imagination. "Youths Given Life Terms in Brutal S.F. Sexual Assault." "The woman, 24, was abducted at gunpoint by four youths ranging in age from 16 to 18 as she was unlocking her parked car on Second Street." She was held for four hours, raped, robbed, and kicked out of her car. "She was then shot twice before the young assailants drove her car over her and left her in the street" *(San Francisco Chronicle,* July 14, 1981). In others, the youthfulness of the offenders is astonishing. "Authorities sought a decision . . . whether to prosecute a 9 year-old boy who police say shot a 6 year-old playmate through the heart, then dragged the dying child outside and left him under a stairwell" *(West Oakland Tribune,* August 15, 1980).

But crimes of violence are not confined to any age, socio-economic, racial, or ethnic group; women commit them as well as men. Recently under the headline "A Tenderloin Regular Beaten Up By Women," the *San Francisco Chronicle* (August 11, 1980) reported an incident in which a ninety-two-year-old World War I veteran was not only robbed by two women, but "roughed up" as well.

A most amazing case was a robbery committed by a man in a wheelchair. "Danny Stettner rolled his wheelchair into the Friendly Freeport Gulf Station two blocks from his house, assembled a .22-calibre rifle in front of a startled attendant and demanded money. With about $200 crammed into his pockets, he turned around and rolled away, police said" *(San Francisco Chronicle,* December 10, 1981).

By every account, crimes of violence have become rampant in the United States, and their increase has been continuous. In 1970 there were 363.5 cases of violent crimes reported per 100,000 persons. By the first half of 1980, the corresponding figure jumped to 535.5 *(U.S. News and World Report,* October 27, 1980). The variety and bizarre natures of the crimes committed are dazzling, running the gamut from mass slaughter (Richard Speck, John Wayne Gary) to cannibalism (Edmund Kemper, III, who killed eight women, decapitated them, and ate the flesh of some of the victims, according to the *San Francisco Chronicle,* May 29, 1981).

Family members are vulnerable to each other. Various estimates tell us that two to four million cases of serious child abuse occur each year

(Helfer and Kempe 1968:24–25). Abuse of the elderly has reached "epidemic proportions." "Up to 2½ million cases may occur each year, rivaling child abuse in frequency" (according to a December 1981 newsletter from the Family Service Agency, San Francisco). Some authorities have also described the incidence of wife-beating and abuse as epidemic.

Some of our public schools have become veritable jungles. During a five-month period from September 1980 to January 1981, a total of 22,961 persons in California schools fell victim to violence and 912 of the cases involved the use of weapons. By far the largest group of offenders were students (19,315), and the largest group of victims next to students were teachers (1,783) *(San Francisco Examiner and Chronicle,* August 5, 1981).

According to more than one poll, fear of violence has become the number one preoccupation of most Americans, even topping inflation. "Fear Stalks the Streets," was the title of one *U.S. News and World Report* article (October 2, 1980).

Is this violence in our society a new phenomenon, brought on by more extensive industrialization, urbanization, and modernization? The answer does not seem to be in the affirmative.

The August 12, 1977, *Chicago Sun-Times* ran two reports. The first was about a modern-day series of murders in Texas involving two teenage boys who reported "getting paid from $5 to $200 for recruiting other boys for a 33 year-old man by the name of Corll, who tortured them, forced them into homosexual acts and murdered them." One of the teenage recruiters admitted assisting with some of the killings and later shooting Corll to death.

The other report in the same paper was about a nineteenth-century event headlined: "Mass Murder Record? 47 Told Here in 1896." "The mass murder uncovered in Texas last week won't eclipse a grisly record set in Chicago in 1896 when Herman Webster Mudgett (also known as H.H. Holmes) confessed to murdering 47. . . . In 1892, Mudgett constructed a building which later became known as the 'murder castle.' . . . The second floor was a maze of rooms without doors and doors without rooms. There were 30 windowless, airtight sleeping rooms laced with gas pipes controlled with valves in Holmes' (Mudgett's) bedroom. . . . A chute ran from the rooms to the basement where Holmes could send asphyxiated victims. In the basement was a dissecting table with a complete surgical set, a crematory built into a wall and three vats containing acid and quicklime. . . . Police found human bones in the basement stove, highly polished skeletons in boxes, bloody ropes, bloodstained garments and a torture rack. . . . When he was hanged, Holmes was 35 years-old."

What do our nation's artistic, technological, and political achievements have to do with the interpersonal violence that plagues us? It is my hope that the reader of the following pages will see that achievement and violence in fact spring from one common denominator: rugged individualism.

Reflect on one simple truth in the chemical world. H_2O is water that we drink, but H_2SO_4 is an acid that will severely damage our body if we come into direct contact with it. Even though two compounds contain some common elements, they may be totally different from one another and differ drastically in their manifestations. Likewise, rugged individualism in combination with the sciences or the arts has very different consequences than does rugged individualism in combination with frustration, anger, greed, lust, and so on.

A first step toward understanding the connection between achievement and violence is to recognize that all creativity is a form of deviation, a departure from the norm. Deviations of which we and our society approve we term creativity, but creativity of which we disapprove we term deviation. The more rugged the individualist, the more likely the individualist is to be creative in the drive toward goals, with or without regard for established rules, and the individualist is less inclined to concern himself/herself with whether successes are to be achieved at the expense of others. In fact, as Maccoby so ably demonstrated in his book *The Gamesman* (1976), the modern corporate executive is driven to organize winning teams, "to cut deals and to gamble," and even to separate ambitions from the "human feelings within himself." To succeed, the rugged individualist is "driven" to treat all other human beings as things, to be manipulated, forced, or eliminated if they happen to get in the way of his forward march.

John Addison Howard, one-time president of Rockford College, wrote in his foreword to a book, *Unto the Generations* (1968), by Daniel L. Marsh, one-time president of Boston University.

> The society in which we live is coming apart at the seams. A projection of the trends in public conduct presents a cruel spectre of an every-man for-himself, might-makes-right national community in the years ahead. . . . The wise and perceptive political philosopher, Montesquieu, observed that a form of government can operate only as long as the people behave in a manner which is suited to it.*

I submit that in spite of, or hand-in-hand with our spectacular achievements, we Americans are edging closer everyday to behaving in a manner that, by escalating the anti-social aspects of our society, is making our form of democratic government more and more difficult to operate.

Although Howard and Marsh are right in their diagnosis of American social trends, they erred in thinking that reminding Americans of what

---

*Marsh assembled in this book eight American documents ranging from the Mayflower Compact and Lincoln's Second Inaugural Address to Wilson's Road Away from Revolution and MacArthur's speech to his countrymen at the formal surrender of Japan.

their noble ancestors stood for would make them change their direction. For present-day Americans have merely escalated the same individualism that propelled their forebears. Changing requirements in contemporary business, industry, and government have made many Americans into what William Whyte called *The Organization Man* (1956). But on the psychological level, rugged individualism is very much alive. That is why Maccoby's corporate executive tends to be unhappy and dissatisfied even as he succeeds. Our society will continue to generate more geniuses and star performers who will excell in diverse fields, but it will also relentlessly foster more deviants and criminals whose anti-social creativity will reach more alarming proportions.

How far the line between criminality and socially applauded or glamorous behavior has been blurred in the public mind is graphically illustrated by the fact that Lee Harvey Oswald's mother was able to make a fortune after he was killed by selling his belongings and pictures, contributing personal stories about him to periodicals, and authorizing Oswald souvenirs. A paperweight inscribed "My Son, Lee Harvey Oswald, even after his death, has done more for his country than any other living human being" was priced at $250. When a prospective customer complained of the high price, Mrs. Oswald snapped, "Are you kidding? This is Lee Harvey Oswald" (as reported in *Newsweek,* December 4, 1967).

"America is fast becoming a nation living behind dead-bolt locks—with a gun tucked away in a closet" *(U.S. News & World Report,* October 27, 1980). People do not venture out at night in public parks or playgrounds. Unlike our primitive ancestors, we are well protected from wild animals but are mortally fearful of our fellow human beings. Confronted with increasing violence, the American response as a whole has been "how do *I* protect *myself?*"

Newspapers are attempting to answer the question. For example, "The Most Dangerous Streets of the City," was the headline of an article identifying the most mugging-prone and least mugging-prone districts of San Francisco *(San Francisco Chronicle,* October 19, 1981). Another article, "Two Muggers Tell Their Stories," provided graphic details of the activities of convicted muggers Tiny Tim Sims and Little John George. Both men say "the victims have only themselves to blame." Their advice? "Don't carry more than $50 to $100 in cash, don't wear fancy clothes or jewelry, take care of your business in the daytime, and avoid places where you have to show a lot of money" *(San Francisco Chronicle,* October 19, 1981). In the same paper, "Who Gets Murdered" was the headline of another article (December 15, 1981), based on a report compiled by the S.F. Police Department for the first eleven months of 1981. Its author tells us that the most likely murder victim is a "white male between the ages of 21 and 30," and that "a lot of it (killing) grows out of casual meetings, involving prostitution, vice and drugs." Finally, in the section of the *San*

Francisco Chronicle entitled "Living" came the inevitable "how-to" manual, "A Practical Guide to Personal Safety" (December 30, 1981). Its basic point is: "In public, the best way to avoid attack is to present yourself in a manner that discourages would-be assailants. . . . You must show yourself as someone with self worth, someone who cares what happens and who will mount a vigorous defense if attacked. . . . Also keep in mind that predictability can equal vulnerability. . . . For this reason, try to cultivate unpredicability in both your daily movements and special activities. . . . Many habits . . . are protective. Checking the backseat of your car at night before getting in is one example. . . ." The same guide then offers pointers in four contexts: "How to Avoid Danger on Buses and Trains," "Tools for Self-Protection," "Safety on the Streets," and "Precautions on the Road."

As solutions to violence, what do our politicians and public officials have in mind? A recent effort is a Task Force on Violent Crime created in April 1981 by Attorney General William Smith and co-chaired by former Attorney General Griffin B. Bell and Illinois Governor James Thompson. By June 1981 it had held public hearings in Washington, Los Angeles, and Atlanta. Its recommendations so far? "Help turn over abandoned military bases to states to ease prison overcrowding, upgrade the search for 42,000 violent fugitives, ask the Navy to help fight drug traffickers and urge that local police enter violence-prone public schools" *(San Francisco Chronicle,* June 15, 1981).

Although the final recommendations of the task force are not yet known, some public statements give us an idea of what is yet to come. When interviewed on ABC (August 16, 1981), Governor Thompson made three points: (1) get tough on criminals; (2) with federal help, establish more prisons in the states; and (3) get to the root cause, drug traffic. A couple of months later, Attorney General Smith "laid out President Reagan's ideas for a federal assault on crime" before the National Press Club *(San Francisco Chronicle,* October 23, 1981). Summarized, the main ideas are: (1) mandatory sentences for gun use; (2) compensation for crime victims; (3) a constitutionally sound death penalty; and (4) allowing courts to deny bail to persons "who clearly present a danger if released."

Similar to the federal task force was the twenty-two-member California State Commission on Crime Control and Violence Prevention, which completed its two-year search for "the root causes of crime" in January 1982. It came up with a long list of oft-repeated "causes," such as child-abuse, the decaying of the family unit, and racial tensions, but it added a new factor: "gentle births." "A positive birth experience—one that is gentle, loving, and non-traumatic—increases the likelihood of healthy child development" and less violent behavior *(San Francisco Chronicle,* January 28, 1982).

There is a curious parallel here between what we are doing about violence and what the Chinese throughout their long history did about their famines, epidemics, corruption, and oppression. The Chinese had known many rebellions. After each successful rebellion, its leader established himself as the new emperor of a new dynasty and ruled exactly as his predecessors before him. He offered no new ideology, no restructuring of the bureaucracy or the socio-economic ladder, no fresh incentives, and few, if any, changes in the judiciary, executive, and legislative processes. Chinese prisons were like hells, but the Chinese never instituted prison reforms. The Chinese approach to the problem was, "If you think it's bad, don't get imprisoned." The Chinese had foot-binding for women for over a thousand years, but they never had any leaders who championed the cause of liberating their mothers and sisters, wives and daughters from this terrible inhumanity. It may sound fantastic to my American readers, but I am not being facetious when I say that here, too, the approach of many Chinese was, "If you don't like it, don't be born a woman."

Strange as it may seem, I must observe that the American approach to crimes of violence, in contrast to its approach to technology and science, is characterized by the Chinese-style rebellion. Old administrations are replaced by new. Old scholars retire and are succeeded in our universities and research institutes by new doctorates. But their outlook remains the same. Being reluctant to touch the American "Sacred Cow" they continue to treat only the symptoms, seeing prisons, police, sophisticated alarm and surveillance devices, mace, whistles, guns, and the avoidance of dangerous situations as the only answers.

Rugged individualism is related not only to our problem of violence. It may prove to be a key, as some of the following chapters will show, to our understanding of a host of other matters, from our American way in religion, in psychiatry, in art and literature, and in sex to our reaction to other peoples—to why, for example, the Japanese have succeeded so well in industrializing themselves.

Is it not time that we took a revolutionary look at our sacred cow, and have rugged individualism reconsidered?

Acknowledgments

Students, colleagues, and friends who helped me in specific parts of the book are acknowledged in the individual chapters. I am also grateful to my wife, Vera, for her encouragement and to my son-in-law, Dr. Patrimpas Prapuolenis, for assistance in preparing the manuscript for publication and constructing the indexes; and to my daughter, Penny Hsu-Prapuolenis, for the drawings on page 175 and pages 266–67, one of which adorns the frontispiece. Finally I am indebted to the Wenner-Gren Foundation for Anthropological Research and its Director of Research, Mrs. Lita Osmundsen, for generous grants over the years which made the researches possible that went into several of the papers, and which has enabled me to put this book together in its final form. It goes, however, without saying that I alone am responsible for my opinions and conclusions.

Francis L.K. Hsu
Mill Valley, California
May 1982

RUGGED INDIVIDUALISM RECONSIDERED

1

Rugged Individualism Reconsidered

For some time our society has been engaged in a wave of self-examination. We are plagued by many problems for which there simply does not seem to be any easy solution: juvenile delinquency, racial tension, dishonesty in government and in business, but above all our apparent difficulties in competing with Russia in space exploration and in relations with the non-Western world. This self-examination has assumed urgent proportions since the collapse of the summit and the cancellation of Mr. Eisenhower's peace mission to Japan.

At the highest level it has been carried out by a Committee on National Goals appointed by Mr. Eisenhower and headed by Dr. Henry M. Wriston, President of Brown University. The results of this Committee's work can be gauged from a speech "Our Goal: Individualism or Security?" delivered by Dr. Wriston at Bowdoin College. I have not seen a more eloquent piece extolling the rugged individual. According to Dr. Wriston, the greatness of a country depends upon its leadership, and leadership cannot be stimulated and nurtured without rugged individualism. The popular importance attached to this speech is shown in the many excerpts or substances of it reprinted widely as featured articles in *Chicago Sun-Times* (June 5, 1960), *Wall Street Journal* (June 1, 1960), *Reader's Digest* (August, 1960), and elsewhere. The *Chicago Sun-Times* even endorsed Wriston's view in an editorial entitled "The American Way: Do It Yourself."

Wriston's views were soundly echoed by the former Lebanese Minister Charles Malik, who on June 11 delivered at Williamsburg, Virginia, another widely circulated speech commemorating the fifty-day prelude to Independence Day. Later Wriston's ideas were praised by most of the eight prominent men who contributed to *Life* magazine's series entitled "The National Purpose" (May 23 through the June 20 issues).

David Sarnoff's firebreathing piece asks us to intensify the cold war and speak up louder for the doom of the Communist countries. Billy Graham's sermon calls for the conversion of all individuals to God as a prelude to improving the world. As to the others, except for Lippmann, who emphasizes the necessity "to use our growing wealth wisely for public ends," there seems to be nothing but a similar reaffirmation of the essence or expressions of rugged individualism.

In my view, between the internal and external problems confronting us today, the internal ones are perhaps more fundamental and crucial, for it is

This chapter was originally published in the *Colorado Review*, Vol. IX, No. 2, 1960, pp. 143–62.

upon our ability to deal effectively with our internal problems that our ability to deal with our external problems depends. I am not suggesting that we should wait till we have completely solved our internal problems before tackling the external ones. Time alone makes that impossible. Rather, the internal and the external problems should be tackled simultaneously and with the same vigor. In my view, too, all of our major internal problems, from juvenile delinquency and corruption in government to racial and religious tension and prejudice, are traceable, directly or indirectly, to that much extolled virtue of our Founding Fathers, rugged individualism.

I fully realize that, in speaking of rugged individualism in this vein, I am liable to be regarded as blasphemous toward the sacred cow of America. But since I am a student of science, I take it to be my earnest duty to speak up as my scientific conscience leads me without fear and favor.

The most basic ingredient of rugged individualism is self-reliance. Most individuals in all societies around the world may be self-sufficient. That is to say, the individual is able to take care of his own physical and mental needs. But American rugged individualism means that one is not only self-sufficient as a matter of fact but he must strive toward it as a militant ideal. The individual should constantly tell himself and others that he controls his own destiny, and that he does not need help from others. He may have good or bad breaks, but "smile and the world smiles with you, cry and you cry alone."

A brief comparison will make the point clear. A man in traditional China with no rugged individualism as an ideal may not have been successful in his life. But suppose in his old age his sons are able to provide for him generously. Such a person not only will be happy and content about it, but is also likely to beat the drums before all and sundry to let the world know that he has good children who are supporting him in a style to which he has never been accustomed. On the other hand, an American parent who has not been successful in life may too derive benefit from the prosperity of his children, but he certainly will not want his friends and the rest of the world to know about it. In fact he will resent any reference to it. At the first opportunity when it is possible for him to become independent of his children, he will do so.

Therefore, even though we may find many individuals in all societies who are in fact self-sufficient and even though we may find individuals in America who are in fact dependent upon others, the important fact is that where rugged individualism is not an ideal, self-sufficiency or self-reliance is neither promoted nor a matter of pride. But where rugged individualism is an ideal, self-sufficiency and self-reliance are both promoted and are a matter of pride. In our society an individual who is not self-reliant is called a misfit. In fact a dependent character is thought to be in need of psychiatric help.

The rugged individual's self-reliance has two attributes. The first is fierce competitiveness. The rugged individual must advance or regress according to his own efforts and luck. When one individual advances, it necessarily means that others are regressing by comparison even though they have not slipped at all in absolute terms.

The other attribute is the high premium on aggressive creativity. Creativity has become such a popular word in the United States that when one wants to praise someone's work to the extreme, all one has to say is that the work is creative. For since each individual has to compete perpetually to defend his rugged individualism, he must forever find new ways of getting ahead of his fellow competitors. In fact he has to be creative to keep his place at all.

The consequences or correlates of self-reliance, with its twin attributes of competition and creativity, are many. The first concerns sex morality. I am not speaking of sex morality in any absolute and universal sense, because sex morality, like other kinds of morality, is relative among different peoples. What is considered to be moral in one society is often considered to be immoral in another and vice versa. I am speaking of it from the point of view of American social organization and ideal. According to American custom pre-marital intercourse, extra-marital intimacy between the sexes, mistress-keeping, prostitution, and the sale and viewing of pornography are all immoral. Yet, although these are considered forms of immorality in American society, they have been on the increase and will be more so as time goes on as a consequence of individual self-reliance and competition.

For example, the Postmaster General disclosed last year, "Mail order pornography and obscenity is a $500 million a year business that is growing in volume." The Postmaster General went on to say, "Defiant barons of obscenity . . . unquestionably are contributing to the alarming increase in juvenile delinquency and ruthless mail order merchants in filth are violating the homes of the nation in defiance of the national government." Of particular interest here are the reasons which the Postmaster General gave for this increase in smut sale. "First," he says, "the tremendous profits realized from a relatively small capital investment; second, the very broad definition of obscenity handed down by certain courts, including those in certain metropolitan areas notably Los Angeles and New York, where most of the mail order business in obscenity and pornography originates." (*Chicago Sun-Times,* April 25, 1959)

In my view only one of these reasons has any relevance, but its relevance is not what the Postmaster General thinks. It is perfectly true that smut sales can result in tremendous profits from a relatively small capital investment. But if a society enjoins the individual to compete by creative efforts for success on individual terms, what would be more natural for the individual than to try to gain tremendous profits from small capital investments? Isn't it true that the best American success stories have always included many in which small investments led to enormous profits? American business has always talked about giving the customer what he wants. And if consumer research services indicate a greater demand for sex-linked or sex-suggestive products, why is it not good business to provide more sex?

Smut sales are, however, only one kind of profit-making device through the use of sex. One Chicago paper, in its exposé against smut sales, quotes a minister, the Chairman of the Legislative Committee of the Churchman's Commission for Decent Publications, as observing that the tide of smut is "directly responsible for an alarming breakdown of moral fiber in this country." The minister said that he personally studied the content of some of the magazines on sale in Washington which "if read by any youth would give him a fairly accurate blueprint of the following: How to seduce a virgin; how to rape a girl; how to take advantage of the absence of a husband or wife in order to have illicit sex relations; how to prime a girl with liquor to make her receptive to sexual relations; how to use torture to heighten sex feelings, and so on." *(Chicago Sun Times,* August 12, 1959) But is it really necessary for youths to buy the smut the minister personally examined in order to learn these tricks? No, for they are daily exposed to hundreds of paper-back novels at every newsstand with half-nude men and women in suggestive poses on the covers and such titles as "No Bed of her Own." They also see hundreds of movies, the most blatant of which, "Gigi," even won many Academy Awards.

Think of the plot of "Gigi." Here a young adolescent girl is being groomed to serve as some wealthy man's mistress for a few months in exchange for maids, carriage, clothes, and houses. It was only due to a last minute change of heart that the playboy keeper of mistresses decided to marry her and this was regarded as being such a windfall by the girl and all concerned that it became an extremely attractive American story. Gigi is the heroine, and the mistress-keeper millionaire playboy becomes the hero. From the beginning to the end there is nothing but sex, sometimes blatant, sometimes thinly veiled with old Maurice Chevalier cheering the characters on. I understand that "Gigi" has been the rage among teenage and pre-teen girls and boys in the schools. In fact, we can easily find numerous other films which are at best exhibitions of sexual brinkmanship.

Besides learning from the movies, young people can learn from the highly publicized private love lives of many of the movie stars themselves. Their often clandestine sex lives are so publicized and so glamorized that they are often the very foundation for the sale and popularity of the stars' own movies. From the point of view of the movie stars and that of the producers these lives are simply means to motion picture greatness. If more display of sex seems to ring the cash register, why should they not reach for greater successes?

From this first correlate of self-reliance that concerns sex morality, we now go to another correlate, that of corruption or dishonesty. It is, of course, very difficult to obtain a precise statistical picture of the amount of corruption or dishonesty in any society. Furthermore, it is nothing new or unusual to find these in any large and complex society. What is unusual is that a country with the greatest expanding material prosperity in the world should experience so much criminal corruption and dishonesty. What is new is that while it has been taken for granted that crime is a consequence of poverty and misery, the late Dr. Edwin H. Sutherland's research on white-collar crime has proven this notion to be false.

What does Dr. Sutherland mean by white-collar crime? Here are some examples. Misrepresentation in financial statements of corporations, manipulation in stock exchanges, commercial bribery, bribery of public officials directly or indirectly in order to secure favorable contacts and legislation, misrepresentation in advertising and salesmanship, embezzlement and misapplication of funds, short weights and measures, misgrading of commodities, tax frauds, and misapplication of funds in receiverships and bankruptcies—all these are covered by what Al Capone would describe as "the legitimate rackets." *(American Sociological Review,* February, 1950, pp. 1–12. The substances of this article were also incorporated into Dr. Sutherland's book entitled *White Collar Crime,* 1949.)

According to Dr. Sutherland's investigations, white-collar crimes cost the society far greater financial and moral losses than armed banditry and thievery. A man may be sentenced to ten years to life imprisonment for armed robbery of a few hundred to a few thousand dollars, but the culprit who embezzles $100,000 belonging to a bank is often met with far less punishment, while the criminal who defrauds the government and the public out of millions in shady deals often gets off scot free. Dishonesty in income tax declarations is so common that it is considered neither a shame nor a crime. Fixing traffic tickets by the police is of such common occurrence that some parents brag about their smart actions to friends in front of their children.

It is indeed puzzling why the wealthiest nation on earth should be plagued with such blatant dishonesty. This fact will remain puzzling unless we recall that the rugged individual's self-reliance is bound up with competition and creativity. We think of competition as being governed by rules and chivalry, not realizing that for every lucky one who made it there are bound to be thousands who failed to do so and that when failure means loss of self-respect, the competition is often a matter of dog-eat-dog. We think of creativity in terms of scientific advances and artistic achievements, not acknowledging that another meaning of creativity is deviation from the norm, the custom, and the moral rule. When the rugged individual is forced to a corner by severe competition and threatened with a loss of self-respect, can we blame him for not remaining honest and true to his principles?

Once this is understood we should perceive the fundamental differences between corruption in the U.S. and that, say, in India. In the Eastern countries corruption is mostly committed by people who are threatened by their inability to keep themselves and their families in groceries. In America corruption is not founded on poverty. It is more frequently committed by people who are well fed and well-clothed but who must find creative ways to expand and enlarge their operations in order to compete with others for greater success.

Opponents of this view may retort that those who resort to corruption for greater success have misused creativity and competition. My answer to such a retort is that when individual success is given the only honored place in life, there is not much room left for any workable criteria by which wholesome creative and competitive efforts can be distinguished from unwholesome ones. The Fuller brushman who bribes a housewife with a little brush in the hope of inducing her to purchase a lot of his wares and the big-time businessman who bribes a White House aide with mink coats or Persian rugs or FCC officials with fancy air trips and luxury yacht cruises, in the expectation that the government's multi-million-dollar wheel of fortune may be so influenced as to stop at his number and disgorge a bit of its reward, are all after success in the same fashion.

Our former President Coolidge's famous saying "America's business is business" is by no means a forgotten sentiment, for there are many who insist today that even governments should run like a business. Business means creative efforts to exert influence on the customers and to find success in competition. And success in competition is measured by the size of the profit. Where is the psychological divider which will separate the businessman in government and his attitude toward it from the business-man outside of government and his attitude toward the general public? If he is accustomed to regard influence as his most precious asset in one situation, what is there to prevent him from desiring it and resorting to it in the other?

A third correlate of rugged individualism is conformity. This is in sharp contrast to the values of rugged individualism, and its presence is there-fore highly paradoxical. In fact the observed trait of conformity is so much in contrast to rugged individualism that it prompted David Riesman to suggest that Americans are changing from their original "Inner-directed" personality orientation to an "Other-directed" orientation (Riesman 1952). I think Riesman is wrong here. For there is a direct connection between rugged individualism and conformity.

We noted previously that the basic ingredient of rugged individualism is militant self-reliance. But it is obvious that no individual can be complete-ly self-reliant. In fact, the very foundation of the human way of life is man's dependence upon his fellowmen without which we shall have no law, no custom, no art, no science, and not even language. If an individual wishes to lead a human existence in this society or any other, he is bound to be dependent upon his fellow human beings intellectually and technological-ly as well as socially and emotionally. An individual may have differing needs from his fellow human being, but no one can truly say that he needs no one. It becomes clear then that the basic American value of self-reliance, by its denial of the importance of other human beings in one's life, creates contradictions and therefore serious problems, the most ubiquitous of which is insecurity.

This insecurity presents itself to the individual American in a variety of ways. Its most important feature is the lack of permanency both in one's ascribed relationships (such as those of the family into which one is born) and in one's achieved relationships (such as marital relationship for a woman and business partnership for a man). Its most insistent demand on the individual is to motivate him in a perpetual attempt not only to compete with his fellow human beings but also to belong to status-giving groups and, as a means of achieving these ends, to conform to the customs and fads of the peer group which are vital to his climbing and/or status position at any given time and place.

In other words, in order to live up to their ideal of militant self-reliance, Americans must often do exactly its opposite. Expressed in the jargon of science, there is a direct relationship between rugged individualism and conformity. That is to say, other things being equal, the stronger the emphasis on rugged individualism, the greater the individual tendency toward conformity. We noted the many public media, such as movies and literature, which influence the conduct of our young people today. But there are even stronger forces at work. In a summary report on the "Cornell Study of Student Values," which covers a total of 2,760 under-graduate men and women attending Cornell and 4,585 undergraduate men and women attending ten universities (U.C.L.A., Dartmouth, Fisk, Harvard, Michigan, North Carolina, Texas, Wayne, Wesleyan, and Yale), Edward S. Suchman concludes, "Much of the student's development during four years in college does *not* take place in the classroom. The conformity, contentment, and self-centered confidence of the present day American students are not academic values inculcated by the faculty, but rather the result of a highly organized and efficiently functioning extracur-ricular social system" (Suchman 1958: 119–20).

How does this "social system" bear on the sex mores of our students via self-reliance? Suchman gives no indication of this in his report. But on every college campus with which I have had any dealings and about which I have any information, sex figures as a major game in the sorority-fraternity controlled social life. Everywhere there is a highly conscious but un-heralded popularity contest going on among the girls. The popular girls do not simply date boys. They want to date those boys who are most wanted by other girls. To get a chance to do so they must first belong to the right campus groups. But even after this, the girls simply have to make more and more concessions in order to keep such boys interested. And the most popular girls in these campus jungles are not those who live up to the American moral orientation but those who can keep members of the opposite sex interested. There is no question in my mind that, on today's campuses, girls are by far the more aggressive of the two sexes, even though occasionally they still vaguely recall the fact that their intentions should be thinly veiled by coyness. Given rugged individualism, the development of a new strain of aggressive female is inevitable. Forced to compete for higher statuses among peers, the girls have no alternative but to compete on terms agreeable to the peer group at any given moment of time.

This leads us to the fourth correlate of rugged individualism, which is racial and religious prejudice. It has been a puzzling contradiction to many of us as to why a culture which extolls Christian love, freedom, equality, and democracy should also be plagued by so much racism and religious bigotry. This contradiction is easily resolved in the light of the connection between rugged individualism and the tendency toward conformity. The rugged individual, who must defend his self-reliance at all cost, unlike one who is taught to respect authority and external barriers, has no permanent place in his society. While he is always anxious to look above for opportunities to climb higher, he is constantly threatened by the upward encroachments from below. His must be a continuous effort at status seeking and maintaining. Since this process is like rowing a boat upstream, in which one has to keep rowing in order to stand still, the rugged individual is forced to conform to the custom of either the group to which he aspires to belong or the group of which he is already a member. Associating with members of a lower status group is a sure way of reducing one's own status. Conformity and the fear of losing status, rather than the alleged wickedness of the bigots, are thus the true backbone of the racial and religious prejudice in this society. The bigots may employ intolerance as a means to their own ends, but such individuals will achieve no success if intolerance has no psychological root among the general public which they try to inflame.

The fifth correlate of rugged individualism is the tendency toward unrealism in interpersonal relations and, by extension of the same psychology, to international relations. The rugged individual is bound to be self-centered. He is taught to shape the world in his image. He sets out to advance himself by overcoming all obstacles. He is prepared to gain his ends by submitting to conformity if necessary, but with reference to those deemed inferior to him, he demands conformity to his wishes, He may wish to take good care of his inferiors, help them and educate them, and he may often go to great trouble and expense in reforming them so long as they acknowledge their inferiority and do his bidding. The most intolerable situation to him is when those deemed inferior to him demand equality with him, or even worse, act superior to him. Since the ultimate aim of the rugged individual is superiority over all, he can neither accept defeat nor change in his position of superiority. He will refuse to admit that change. He will withdraw from active contacts. If necessary, he will certainly resort to violence to uphold his superiority. And he tends to build up reasons satisfying to himself as to why he is acting the way he does, regardless of whether his reasons are convincing or not to others. In interpersonal relations within the society among his fellow Whites, the rugged individual may acknowledge temporary inferiority as a matter of expediency, but in international relations the rugged individual cannot tolerate anything but his and his society's absolute superiority over all.

A small item of fact will perhaps make this point clear. Before World War II, I had often been asked by persons brought up in England and especially in America why they did not find Japanese (especially men) so congenial as the Chinese. The most vehement would simply say they hated the Japanese and loved the Chinese. I think part of this reaction is undoubtedly due to some differences between the national character of the Chinese and that of the Japanese, which we cannot enter into here, but part was undoubtedly due to the fact that Chinese as a people were then not competing with the West, indeed were not competent to do so, because China was politically chaotic, economically hopeless, and militarily prostrate, while the Japanese as a people presented severe challenges to American and European superiority in every way conceivable. This is why, as Harold R. Isaacs has shown in his able book *Scratches on Our Minds: American Images of China and India* (1958: 190–98), the American reaction to the new Chinese regime is so violent. Americans literally felt that they owned China, or protected her, or nurtured her, and now the ingrate is biting the hand that fed her.

Given the need of the rugged individual to be self-centered and to be superior, it becomes also psychological necessity for him to react to unpleasant developments and contrary facts which challenge his superiority by dream-like unrealism. This is one time when the rugged individual will fall back on the greatness of his past as justification for his unrealistic conduct of the present. For a United States of America occupying the kind of secondary world position envisaged by Henry Steele Commager, in which she will no longer be able to dictate terms to all, is most unacceptable to the rugged individual. Unrealism is but his mental device for self-protection.

The last correlate of rugged individualism we shall discuss leads to another paradox. This is organization. Of the pernicious effects of organization on man, I cannot name a better expositor than William H. Whyte (1956), with the bulk of whose book *The Organization Man* I thoroughly concur. But after having correctly analyzed the effects of the organization, Whyte concluded his stimulating book with nothing better than the suggestion that the individual fight the organization. How can the individual fight the organization without more organization? But of far more fundamental importance is Whyte's fallacy, a fallacy which he shares with many others, that organization and rugged individualism are diametrically opposed to each other. This is why he advised the individual to fight organization, for Whyte wants him to look to rugged individualism as the final guiding principle for all action.

There are obvious reasons why this supposed opposition between organization and rugged individualism is fallacious. Life in the human style is impossible without some organization. Rousseau's famous dictum that man is born free, but is everywhere in chains, is as unsound as the idea that the earth is flat. If we are truly free we will be like wild animals. Organization involves definite lines of demarcation of peoples and actions, most of which are necessary though arbitrary. We can find men and women living with each other out of wedlock who fulfill all requirements of marriage, but the society needs a clear distinction between those who are married and those who are not. We can find aliens who are more patriotic than citizens but the laws have to make precise distinctions between those who are citizens and those who are not. One is classified as legitimate or illegitimate, employed or unemployed, male or female, major or minor, and in a thousand other ways. These classifications may be arbitrary, but they are indispensable in any society.

However, over and above the minimum level of organization necessary for human existence, the amount of organization is in direct ratio to the complexity of the society and, within complex societies, in direct ratio to the emphasis upon rugged individualism. The first part of this formula is self-evident and needs no elaboration. The second part of it will become clear if we review our analysis of rugged individualism and its consequences.

Take our problem of literary obscenity, smut sales, and sexuality in show business. More severe competition will simply force the merchants, producers, and artists into more creative means of getting more trade. We are imperceptibly forced into more organizational means to censor, regulate, catch, and punish the culprits who have gone too far. The situation is exactly the same with reference to corruption and dishonesty. Given the conditions of severe competition, a majority of human beings and all corporations will be forced into more creative means in reaching greater success. Students in schools and colleges will seek new ways to get around regulations. Potential embezzlers and confidence men will seek new ways of defrauding the company or the public. Syndicates and corporations will hire experts to seek loopholes in the law and find new avenues of influencing public officials. The net result is that the government is forced to tighten and widen its organization to protect public interest and national welfare.

The most unusual development, yet most understandable in the light of our analysis, is that in religion. Our churches have taken on every characteristic of big business. This big business psychology has gone so far that we seem to forget that religion is a personal matter, a private relationship between the individual and his Maker. On the contrary, we seem to think that outside the organized church there is no salvation and only those who are members of some organized parish possess direct links with God. How far this big business mentality and organizational activities have permeated the church is indicated by a *Christian Century Magazine* survey of 1951 (based on the results of polling 100,000 ministers all over the country) to determine the "outstanding" and most "successful" churches in the United States. The results showed twelve to be deserving of such merit and praise.

One of these was the First Presbyterian Church of Hollywood. A report on this most "successful" church in the *Reader's Digest* (February 1952) describes the size of its membership, organization, budget, and physical plant; the numbers of its clubs, choirs, basketball teams; its radio and TV programs; cordons of prayer, push-button-like card files, and kitchen facilities, but little about the quality of the minister's teachings. The reporter concluded his article by saying, "When I asked Dr. Evans to explain the huge success of his church, he answered, 'I honestly don't know. Sometimes the spirit of God decides to do something somewhere, and does it. Perhaps that is happening here. Or it may be our use of prayer. . . .' " In other words, the "success" of this church seems to consist of the social and material endeavors of the parishioners that rebound to their benefit alone and a whirl of competitive activity which is inferentially equated with depth of spiritual faith.

As to the future, the reactions from different quarters may be somewhat instructive. In a previous publication (Hsu 1953) I quoted the national magazine's report on the most successful church and made substantially the same observations that I have made here. Lay scholars have so far raised no objections to observations I have made on this subject. But professional religionists, the few that have bothered to look at my book, apparently thought otherwise. One priest said I overworked my self-reliance just as Freud overworked his sex. One missionary characterized my views as biased. One theological professor accused me of basing my whole discussion on Christianity on only one newspaper report. So far none of these critics pointed to specific facts to indicate how I was wrong or biased. Furthermore, when I quoted some of these facts in a personal discussion to one of the best-known ministers heading one of the largest churches in the Chicago area, he expressed amazement and indignation, not at the facts, but at my pointing them out to him.

My intention here is not to criticize the church or even the ministers as such even though my remarks will inevitably be construed by some readers in that light. I merely wish to point out that when rugged individualism with its twin expressions of competition and creativity has so undermined the true foundation of religion, the churches and religionists have no alternative but to resort to organizations to keep people interested. Hence, organization is equated with church and the characteristics of the organization man come very close, however much it is denied, to those of the big churchman.

For purposes of this presentation, I have made no value judgments. I am certainly not against rugged individualism as such. My task is to point out the possible links between the much extolled rugged individualism and many facts which have never been so linked. Nor does it mean that because of rugged individualism a majority of the American people are active parties to the consequences just outlined. Even if all laws are thrown overboard, a majority of us will remain law-abiding citizens. But in such an eventuality the unlawful activities will increase and will make life less and less tenable for the law-abiding majority. The same is true of the effects of rugged individualism. A majority of the citizens of our society will remain decent, honest, and relatively independent in spite of cut-throat competition. But the blind promotion of rugged individualism with no reference to the social context in which it must operate will increase the pressure toward corruption, moral laxness, conformity, etc., so that our society will tend to be headed in the opposite direction from that which it plans to take.

Furthermore, besides the consequences enumerated so far, there are other correlates with which rugged individualism has always been firmly linked in the minds of scholars and the general public. I have not dwelt upon the latter kind of facts because rugged individualism has been glamorized so often and so much that our understanding of its true implications has become dangerously lopsided. But to round out this presentation let us note some of these other correlates of rugged individualism, such as idealism, science and technology, and organization. What has given the Western man his superiority over the rest of the world during the last three hundred years is not his religion or his romantic love but his ideologies, his science and technology, and his organization. It was his self-reliant ideology which led him to discard the shackles of paternal authority, monarchical power, and medieval magic in favor of wider organizations such as national states and universalist churches, mercantile fleets and industrial empires, totalitarianism and democracy. When the West met the East, it was the Western man's scientific technology and well-organized armed might which crushed the East. As late as 1949 in a *Harper's* magazine article, one high ranking U.S. official attributed civil war-torn China's plight to the fact that the Chinese were "organizationally corrupt." For over a century many Eastern societies pondered on the reasons why science and industrial revolution developed in the West and not the East.

It is instructive to note that today, the two giants of the West, *U.S.A.* and *U.S.S.R.,* are still most attractive to the rest of the world for their skill in scientific technology and in organization. In various parts of the world experts of the two Western giants are helping peoples of other nations to organize their educational systems, or their marketing arrangements, or their agricultural practices, or their industrial efforts, or their military capabilities, or their national finances, etc. Ideology, science and technology, and organization are three of the outstanding contributions of the Western man to the rest of the world. Unfortunately, psychological sources of these contributions are also the Western man's basic difficulty with himself and with his fellowmen, whatever their race or creed.

It may be asked, why can't we devote our energies to propagate only the desired results of rugged individualism and eliminate the undesired consequences of it? If rugged individualism worked the magic which catapulted the Westerners to their prominence in today's world, why can't it do the same in the world of tomorrow? The answer must be sought in an elementary anthropological discovery: that human beings, their ideologies, technologies and organizational methods operate in social and cultural contexts which determine not only their meanings but also their results. English individualism up to recent times was a limited thing. The demands for equality and freedom were primarily centered in the political sphere but far less in the economic and especially social spheres. Royalty, aristocracy, class, church tradition, and the local community served as brakes or ceilings against runaway individualism. Besides, the colonies absorbed the lives and energies of not a few would-be deviants. In other words, it was a qualified individualism and not rugged individualism.

Eighteenth- and nineteenth-century American individualism was indeed more rugged. The scope of equality and freedom was greatly widened from the political into the economic and social aspects of life. But although the aristocracy and publicly acknowledged class hierarchy were abolished, the church, the old world traditions, and especially the solidarity of the small local community remained as effective checks on irresponsible and wanton exercise of that rugged individualism. A person who had embezzled money from the local bank and served a prison term for it could never return to his community and re-establish himself.

The sociologist George Homans' analysis of a New England town in *The Human Group* (Homans 1954) shows exactly how greater mobility, spreading industrialism, and impersonalization of human relations led to disappearance of these forces of social control and how such a change led to the general lowering of ethical standards in the conduct of local affairs. What we have left not only in New England but elsewhere is rugged individualism without an effective social frame of reference which, if encouraged, as Dr. Henry Wriston and other thinkers would have us do, will only aggravate and compound our difficulties rather than reduce them.

Rugged individualism is a great ideal, but the conditions of life in which this ideal has served its ends effectively have changed. No ideal can operate without a social context. Honesty is certainly a fine ideal. But even honesty is not always the best policy, especially in diplomacy and especially for nations which are forced by circumstances mutually to spy on each other. What we must realize is that we need a new social framework into which our ideal of rugged individualism can be put to work. This new social framework is to be found in Walter Lippmann's suggestion (in the *Life* series referred to above) that we "use our growing wealth wisely for public ends," in John Kenneth Galbraith's emphasis that we need heavier investments in the "public sector" for such things as more school rooms instead of more tail-fins (1958), and in Henry Steele Commager's observation made [1959] at the University of Colorado that we must rearrange our thinking so as to help improve a world society in which there are not one or two but six or possibly more centers of power.

However, such a new social framework cannot be achieved by appealing to "altruism" or other noble ideals of the rugged individual. This individual must be shown that it is in his own interest or the interest of his children and his children's children for him to support this new social framework for future peace. To achieve this end we need much more stupendous research in the behavioral sciences. The world, thanks to Western natural sciences, has gradually emerged from the pre-modern notion of the magical nature of the physical universe. Man used to pray or recite incantations for rain where he now builds huge dams. Man used to engage priests and witchdoctors to cure illnesses where he now makes use of the X-ray and penicillin and speaks of Virus X's.

But man continues to react magically about human behavior and human relations. He considers it utter foolishness to build a skyscraper on sand but he still insists on building empires or alliances by forcing unwilling peoples to do his bidding. He would not think of cheating the aircraft or rockets he constructs by slipping in inferior chrome, but he often tries to pull the wool over the eyes of other humans by short-changing them, by misleading advertisements, or by propaganda efforts on an international scale.

Above all he is still addicted to the magic of words in human affairs. Two lovers under the moonlight can say a lot of magical words. But these words will retain their magic only if there is substance in their relationship as lovers. No amount of words can substitute for the magic of true love. Not recognizing this basic principle governing human behavior, man still thinks he can change a saucepan into a spade because he calls it a spade, a dictatorship into democracy by calling it democracy, or a lot of irreligious frivolities into religion by calling it worship of God.

It is necessary for us to realize and recognize that in human affairs no less than in the physical world everything has a price and we cannot get anything for nothing. The price may be money, energy, heartache, misery, revolution, war, or outright death; and it may be paid by ourselves or the future generations to come but it cannot be evaded forever. In family affairs men and women who show no respect and consideration for their own parents cannot later expect their own children to treat them with respect and consideration. In international affairs countries which have ruthlessly oppressed or enforced their superiority over other countries can hardly expect mercy or love from their former inferiors once the shoe is on the other foot. In a genuine sense the United States of America, as the most illustrious descendant of Europe, is paying and will be paying through the nose, not in money only, for the generations of international misdeeds perpetrated by its ancestors.

The only way to get out of this vicious circle is to break it now by a concentrated effort in the behavioral sciences to devise ways and means of liberating man from his magical mode of thought about human behavior. In my humble opinion efforts along these lines are much more relevant to the problem of our survival than the building of bigger atom bombs and the launching of more successful rockets to reach the moon. I do not mean that we can find one solution to end all problems. There is neither an easy nor everlasting solution to the problems of life. To live is to have problems. However, if we realize that no one has a permanent tenure in life, that neither oppression nor superiority is permanent, that all of us are mere transients in this world, that we come from we do not know where and we go to we do not really know where either; and if we realize that, in order to make our journey of life pleasant, it is necessary for us to make it pleasant for others, then perhaps there is some hope. I am a perpetual optimist, so much so that I often think I am a hopeless optimist. But as long as I live I shall hope. For to live is to hope.

Part I:

Behavior, Psychology and Culture

Introduction

One year, when I was a fifth grader in a small town in eastern Manchuria, there was a rash of theft in our school. We did not know whether the culprit was from outside or among us. During a period of about a month some of my schoolmates told about a way to catch the thief (or thieves), which I never heard of until that time. I was about eleven then, but in the absence of compulsory education, some of my fellow classmates were much older. Here was what a fifteen-year-old told me.

You take a cat, kill it, stick several sewing needles in his heart, and then put it in a rice and vegetable cooker (what the Cantonese call wok), half filled with water. As the fire underneath begins to make the water boil, the thief (or thieves) will experience piercing heartache. He will then be forced to confess his crime.

Nothing came of this. We did not catch the thief, but the epidemic of theft subsided, and I was not aware of any cat being boiled.

Later when I was in eighth grade, I began to read popular novels, including one entitled *Traces of Angels in Green Forests (Lu Ye Hsien Chung)*. The wife of a scholar became jealous because he spent all his time with a concubine. So she consulted a blind fortune teller who gave her a small wooden doll to put in her pillow. On its eyes was a blindfold, on its chest was attached a medical plaster, and on its back were inscribed her husband's birth year, month, date, and hour, which made the doll represent the wayward man. Before falling asleep on the pillow every evening, she was told, she should call out her husband's name three times and then ask him to return to her. The blindfold was to prevent her husband from seeing the other woman's beauty, and the plaster was to cause him to change his heart.

The upshot of the story was that the lady not only did not get her husband back, but she committed suicide when her plot was found out.

Outside of these two instances I had never heard of witchcraft or sorcery in all the years that I spent in north China, many parts of Manchuria and eastern China as student, social worker, visitor, traveler, and researcher. Between 1941 and 1944 when Japanese invasion forced the movement of some seventy million Chinese, including myself, to the then "Free China," I lived and worked in Yunnan province in the southwest as a field researcher and college teacher.

In that region of China as elsewhere there was no scarcity of ritual activities, of the periodical kind to celebrate gods' or goddesses' birthdays, or for emergencies such as an epidemic or drought. I even witnessed seances at which paid mediums "called forth" the souls of the dead to communicate with their survivors for one reason or another. But I never heard anymore about sorcery or witchcraft.

That was the extent of my knowledge about the black art until I accidentally came upon Kittredge's classical work on *Witchcraft in Old and New England* (1929) while I was a graduate student at the London School of Economics. From that book I went to anthropological publications on the subject. The results of this forage into the literature led me to realize that there were very sharp differences between Western and non-Western (including the Chinese) approaches to witchcraft and sorcery.

The literature on the black art sometimes uses the two terms witchcraft and sorcery interchangeably. In my article "A Neglected Aspect of Witchcraft Studies" (Chapter 2), I did not insist on any precise distinction between them either. Witchcraft refers to the black art when the accused may not even know that he (more usually she) has the powers and is using them, while sorcery refers to that practiced by some individual either by himself or herself or with the help of others, against one or more intended victims.

The principal burden of what I wish to say in the "A Neglected Aspect" article is that non-Westerners do not seem to fear the black art as much as Westerners, for they do not inflict such severe and absolute punishment as death against its perpetrators, intentionally or otherwise. But those scholars accustomed to the Western way of seeing and doing things have so far failed to perceive this basic difference.

Some fifteen years after the publication of the above article, I saw Chinese sorcerers in action for the first time in my life. It is called "beating the trouble makers," *ta siu yan* in Cantonese and *ta hsiao jen* in Mandarin. This is an old custom in Kwangtung (Canton) province which I had not seen elsewhere in China. On three recurrent days (the sixth, sixteenth, and twenty-sixth) in every lunar month, a large number of women, and more rarely men, old and young, would congregate in a hilly park with a protruding rock known as the Lover's Rock on Hong Kong Island. There, either with the help of an expert or on their own, they would individually "beat the trouble makers." But the same ritual may be performed on some streets, at crossroads, near a temple, or on the side of any hill.

Referring to "trouble makers" as *siu yan (hsiao jen* in Mandarin) and to their antagonists "benefit givers" as *kuei yan (kuei jen* in Mandarin) is universal in China. The trouble makers may be a rival in business or romance, a too exacting mother-in-law or an uncooperative relative, a friend who has betrayed one's trust or a co-worker who has sabotaged one's plans. Or the trouble maker may be a spirit, an unknown element or elements which have caused one misfortunes such as accidents and sicknesses, or prevented one from successes. The purpose of the ritual is to drive the trouble makers away and to attract the benefit givers to ensure one's welfare and to expedite one's progress toward advancement.

The procedure is as follows: The client brings foods (peanuts, walnuts, rice, eggs, and fat pork), various "command credentials" *(fu)*, paper-cut figures including that of the trouble maker (in black), and those of several benefit givers (in green or red), a variety of other papers with colorful figures of humans and animals printed on them, stacks of make-believe paper money in fifty million-dollar denominations, and candles and incense sticks.

The details of the ritual activities need not detain us here. The reader will find a careful description of them in Chien Chiao (1981). The most important ingredient of this ritual is the fierce physical pounding of the black paper-cut figure with the heel of a shoe while the beater chants:

> *So and so is beating the trouble maker.*
> *The trouble makers on streets,*
> *The trouble makers on roads,*
> *Male trouble makers,*
> *Female trouble makers,*
> *Foreign trouble makers,*
> *Beat the trouble makers and invite*
> *   the benefit givers,*
> *The benefit givers are invited with*
> *   their honorable horses,*
> *(Name of the client) gets what he wants,*
> *Thousand things are to his satisfaction.*

There was variation in the chant, and also in some cases the black paper-cut figure representing the trouble maker is stabbed with a knife and torn to shreds. After this the whole thing, including the make-believe money, is burned.

In case the client had a specific trouble maker in mind, the client would obtain the individual's birth data (the hour, day, month, year—the same as were inscribed on the wooden figure as described in the Chinese novel we saw before—and even the address). These were inscribed on a piece of paper to be wrapped together with the black trouble-maker figure for pounding, and then the entire bundle was burned. The whole thing might take from half an hour to two hours, depending on whether the client's grievances were few or many. On any of the recurrent days a visitor to the Lover's Rock Park in Hong Kong can count fifty to several hundred people, including peddlers operating snack stands or offering incense and other needed paraphernalia for the ritual. On such a day the park is like a small-scale public fair, a public fair of sorcery.

Two features stand out of this Hong Kong scene. The first is that the Chinese practitioners of sorcery do not as a rule aim at "killing" the trouble makers, who may be humans or spirits, but merely seek their removal or departure. That was why they also offer paper money and clothes and incense sticks, to induce the trouble makers to go away. This relativistic attitude of the non-Western practitioners of sorcery separates them from their absolutist Western counterparts.

The other feature is that the Hong Kong practitioners, instead of being lone victors over their intended victims, as their Western counterparts would have (or allegedly would have) desired, hoped, by the same rituals, to bind themselves closer to human or spirit helpers *(kuei yan* as distinct from *siu yan)*. This merely underlines the Chinese preference for inclusiveness and mutual dependence among human beings, in sharp contrast to the Westerners' preference for exclusiveness and self-reliance (see Chapter 14 in Part IV of this volume).

How a society treats sorcerers and what the practitioner of sorcery seeks (or allegedly seeks to accomplish in the case of witchcraft) are but part of each people's approach to the supernatural in general. The paper on "Christianity and the Anthropologist" (Chapter 3) deals with the failure of most anthropologists to study Christianity as it is practiced in the West. One consequence is that most anthropologists to this day have not really come to grips with the truly fundamental differences between the Western and Arabic monotheistic approach to the supernatural in contrast to the Hindu pantheistic approach, and the polytheistic approach of the rest of mankind including the Chinese and the Japanese.

In the monotheistic approach only one God is true, while all other supernaturals, including those invoked by sorceries, are false. Therefore, believers of one God cannot but be bent on the extermination of believers of others including sorcerers and alleged witches. Since action generates reaction, the severity of religious persecution and strife escalates with the strength of faith in any one supernatural.

"The Chinese of Hawaii: Their Role in American Culture" (Chapter 4) confirms the point that religious behavior differs profoundly among different peoples in spite of the fact that they call themselves Christians, or Buddhists, or Moslems. The same creed and even the same church hierarchy (e.g., of the Roman Catholic Church) simply do not manifest themselves in the same way behavior-wise in different societies. The crucial determinant in this variation is culture.

The Chinese, in spite of the fact that they are a minority in a society where the Western mode of Christianity prevails and in spite of the fact that they not unnaturally desire acceptance and status among their host people, have not changed their relativistic and inclusive ways in religion. Even though many of them are Christians, they simply do not allow church affiliation to separate them or to become cause for social tension or antagonism.

I think the lack of religious conflict or tension among the Chinese is due to two factors. First, they have too much attachment to their primary groups—the kinship and locality networks—to be free for more distant involvements. That is why the Chinese have not been known for crusades of the European kind. Second, not having been trained as rugged individualists who practice a philosophy of "cry and you cry alone," the Chinese are affectively not so isolated as to need such involvements.

Popular impression of the Chinese is that they practice strong emotional control. I suggest that, compared with Westerners, they simply possess a lower level of emotionality. This suggestion seems to find support in certain known facts about sex crime and adolescent crisis. In both areas we compare the Chinese with the Americans.

Chapter 5, "Sex Crime and Personality: A Study in Comparative Cultural Patterns," hypothesizes that this lower level of emotionality is probably a most important reason for rarity of sex crimes among the Chinese. In Chapter 6, "Culture Pattern and Adolescent Behavior," Blanche Watrous, Edith Lord, and I present some projective data as well as cultural reasons to explain why generation gap has little significance among the Chinese in Hawaii. In doing so we find their lower level of emotionality plays an important part.

The reader will note that because these papers were first published some time ago, many figures given in them are not current today. However, the trends they portrayed, instead of being contradicted by more recent developments, have simply gained momentum.

2

A Neglected Aspect of Witchcraft Studies

Witchcraft and witch hunting have been the subject of many papers, monographs, and books. To date there are at least three intensive anthropological inquiries (Evans-Pritchard 1937; Kluckhohn 1944; Africa 1935) and a number of shorter works (Cannon 1942; Krige 1947). The usual conclusions on witchcraft and witch hunting are that they are related to law and order, that witchcraft can have serious effect among people who believe in it, and that witch hunting is an outlet for psychological tensions. But such works remain partial analyses because none has highlighted the absolutistic attitude of the West toward witchcraft and witch hunting, as contrasted with the relativistic attitude of the rest of the world in this regard.

Witch hunting, as it occurred in Western countries, whether it be England, France, or Italy, had one outcome. Occasionally, the lives of some witches, confessed or alleged, might be spared, but more usually such persons were burned, hanged, drowned, or otherwise executed, because of their public offense. The estimates of scholars on the number of witches put to death in Europe vary enormously, from 30,000 to several million (Summers 1926). But even if we take the lowest possible figure given here, there is no match for it among the more populous Asia or the rest of mankind. There was no way in Western societies for such persons to redeem themselves or to compensate their victims for their alleged wrongdoing. There would certainly be no counter-witchcraft to which their alleged victims could safely and openly resort, for to possess counter-witchcraft would be maintaining traffic with devils, and hence the victims themselves would be subject to accusation and persecution as witches (Kittredge 1929).

In contrast, witch hunting as it occurs in all non-Western societies has usually the following relativistic characteristics unknown in the West:

1) The lives of witches or sorcerers,[1] even after conviction, can be spared if the guilty ones or their kinsmen make compensation to the victims. Sometimes public confession of guilt on the part of the witches is enough. In other instances, the victims take action with only the intention of getting retribution payments. After confession and/or retribution, the guilty one will return to his or her former place in society without further difficulty.

2) There are always counter-witchcraft measures or white magic which

This chapter was originally published in the *Journal of American Folklore*, Vol. 73, No. 287, 1960, pp. 35–38.

are essentially the same sort of acts as those employed by the witches (alleged) or sorcerers (actual), but which are greatly valued by the people (Wolfe 1954). Possessors of such counter-witchcraft measures may even achieve positions of influence (Browne 1929; Firth 1954; Hogbin 1934).

3) Where witches or sorcerers are reportedly "executed," they are more commonly put to death by angry private avengers related to the "victim" or by mob action. Even where there is a proper chieftainship with regular trial-conviction procedures, the penalty more usually befalls only those sorcerers who have killed by resorting to plain poison to aid their sorcery.

It seems that in this absolutist-relativist difference lies a most fundamental aspect of the witch phenomena which is yet to be explored. A possible retort to the suggestion that we compare the witch phenomena in non-Western and Western societies is that witch hunting and witch belief are historical matters in the West, while in nonliterate societies they exist today; and that, in any case, such phenomena were perversions of true Christianity. To this the following reply can be given:

The great Kittredge, in his monumental work on *Witchcraft in Old and New England* said:

> That the belief in witchcraft is still pervasive among the peasantry of Europe, and to a considerable extent among the foreign-born population in this country, is a matter of common knowledge. Besides, spiritualism and kindred delusions have taken over, under changed names, many of the phenomena real or pretended, which would have been explained as due to witchcraft in days gone by. (1929: 370)

Then, in his general conclusion, he said:

> The belief in witchcraft is the common heritage of humanity. It is not chargeable to any particular time, or race or form of religion. (p. 373)[2]

Though not entirely clear, I think scapegoating, which remains a recurrent phenomenon in the West, may be psychologically linked with witch belief. The forms have changed; the substance has not. This same witch fear expresses itself in the West during many a crisis. During World War I it was the German minority who were designated the "Huns." In most of post-World War I era the bearded, bomb-throwing Bolshevik took the place of the "Huns." In World War II it was the Japanese minority. And during the present period of the cold war tensions the smooth shaven, intellectual "Red" have been objects of a persecution which only the Russian Sputniks have helped to tone down. From this point of view we do not have to confine our attention to "peasantry of Europe" and "the foreign-born population of this country" as Kittredge put it, but have little difficulty in perceiving the wisdom of his more final conclusion that the belief in witchcraft is the "common heritage of humanity" which is not chargeable to any particular time, or race, or form of religion.

Perversion should by definition occur only occasionally, but the witch phenomena, like religious wars, occurred in the West with high frequency and over long periods of time.

When we speak of perversion of Christianity it is necessary to bear in mind that from the Protestant point of view the Mormon movement, the Amish faith, and even the Unitarian development, are probably all perversions. In other words, it seems hard to justify that witch belief is merely an oddity either in nonliterate societies or in the West; actually it forms an integral part of their respective social fabrics. As such, therefore, our knowledge of its true significance in human societies is hampered unless we seriously compare its state in Western societies and that in non-Western societies.

I know of no anthropological work on witchcraft thus far which makes such a comparison, and brings out the contrast between the absolutist, all or none Western approach and the relativist, more or less non-Western approach to witchcraft and witch hunting. Yet herein lies one of the most significant keys to the differences between the basic Western outlook and that of the rest of the world. The Western outlook is one in which compromise has little or no place while the outlook of most Asian and African peoples is one in which extremes, though they may occur now and then, have no prolonged persistence. This is why the Inquisition appeared only in the West, while it did not mar the history of the Orientals and Africans. This is why an American is designated a Negro if 1/64 of his ancestry was Negro. But on the reverse side of the coin, this is why the West led mankind in drastic political ideologies and changes and why the West excelled in scientific and industrial achievements, all of which ushered the entire mankind into the modern era. For the absolutist view has given rise in the West to a fervor and determination for the pursuit of truth and beauty and good, or untruth, ugliness and evil, depending upon the goal toward which the fervor and determination were directed. But in either direction these Western characteristics have rarely been matched by the rest of mankind.

To link psychological characteristics which have made the West great with psychological characteristics which the West, not unnaturally, has always consciously regarded as perversions, is bound to be distasteful to many. However, unless we try to examine and probe into this link, our scientific deliberations on witchcraft and witch hunting as social and cultural phenomena will always remain partial and lopsided.

NOTES

[1]In the Western world a difference has sometimes been made between witchcraft and sorcery. The former was generally associated with the intention of overthrowing the Christian belief while the latter aimed at practices for personal ends only. There was, therefore, greater condemnation against the former than

against the latter. An anthropologist made the distinction that sorcery consists of acts consciously practiced by the sorcerers with specific aims, while witchcraft results from actions of witches who may not even be aware of them (S. F. Nadel in *Africa,* op. cit.). But an examination of the pertinent literature fails to reveal any consistent distinction between these two terms. In Shailer Mathews, *A Dictionary of Religion and Ethics* (Chicago: Christian Century Press, 1922), we find the following: "Witchcraft—This word and sorcery refer to practically the same sort of beliefs and practices, namely the use of magic powers or spirit agencies for purposes, usually, though not always, private and malevolent. Witchcraft, in a narrower sense, refers to the arts of the female sorceress, or witch, while sorcery is a more general term covering the arts of both the sorcerer and sorceress. . . . Both the sorcerer and the witch are supposedly in control of secret powers, sometimes magical and sometimes spiritistic" (p. 474). *The Oxford Dictionary of the Christian Church* by E. Cross has no entry on sorcery, but only on witchcraft. In this entry no distinction is made between witchcraft and sorcery (pp. 1472–1473). In E. R. Pike's *Encyclopedia of Religion and Religions* (London, 1951) witchcraft is defined as "the exercise of supernatural power, usually malevolent, supposed to be possessed by persons in alliance with the Devil or evil spirits; also called sorcery, the black art, etc." (p. 397). In Hasting's *Encyclopedia of Religion and Ethics* (New York, 1921), under "sorcery," it says "see Magic, Shamanism, Witchcraft" (p. 694, Vol. XI); under "Witchcraft" it says "see Divination, Magic," (p. 749, Vol. XII); under "Magic," witchcraft and sorcery are both used interchangeably. It seems that magic is made to embrace both witchcraft and sorcery (pp. 307–311, Vol. VIII).

In the works of Montague Summers, op. cit., and *The Geography of Witchcraft* (London, 1927), the two terms are used without clear distinction (p. 137, 201, 384, 386, etc.). On the other hand, H. C. Lea's volumes give much more of a distinction between witchcraft and sorcery. In his view the Christian sense of the term "witchcraft" "had come to have a narrower meaning." Sorcery was "the dabbling of humans in the supernatural for merely earthly ends" and it was "a petty matter" compared with witchcraft which was the "presumptuous assaults of the human mind on the truth of God as taught and administered by his Church." He goes on to say that "the penalty of sorcery was seldom death, and when it was, could usually be escaped by adjuration, while from that ancient code which still lay at the base of all the Church's law rang still the divine injunction—'Thou shalt not suffer a witch to live' " *(Materials Toward a History of Witchcraft,* I [Philadelphia, 1939], xxviii–xxix). But in reality a review of the known cases of execution does not always bear out the fact that accused sorcerers were often spared. And Montague Summers opens his work on *The History of Witchcraft and Demonology* with the quotation, "A sorcerer is one who by commerce with the Devil has full intention of attaining his own ends" and then goes on to say, "it would be, I imagine, hardly possible to discover a more concise, exact, comprehensive and intelligent definition of a Witch" (p. 1). In this paper a distinction between witchcraft and sorcery was made only on one occasion according to the anthropological literature referred to. This distinction is of no importance to this paper.

²Felix Morrow in his "Foreword" to M. Summers' *The History of Witchcraft and Demonology* (1956 edition) shows how the Roman Ritual today contains a substantial section devoted to the liturgy prescribed for driving evil spirits out of possessed persons" (pp. xi–xii).

3

Christianity and the Anthropologist

Many scholars including anthropologists speak about "primitive" religion as a matter of course in contrast to some other kind of religion which must by definition be advanced or civilized.[1] When we seek a logical or consistent basis for such a dichotomy, we find it lacking. The facts simply do not warrant this distinction.

The Japanese, villagers and townspeople alike, use amulets and talismans that are identical in function with the Mephistopheles' Seal and other charms found in Continental Europe. Many magical practices prevail everywhere. Prayers for material reward and personal favors are held all over the world. Taboos on sex, food, and toilet, etc., are universal. Miracles are believed and expected by a majority of mankind regardless of creed. Almost everywhere there is a class of professionals or semi-professionals who enjoy a more privileged position than the ordinary believers with reference to the supernatural by virtue of their specialized knowledge or exalted ritual status. The enforcement of ethical values is common to many religions often termed "primitive." Even the fact of literateness, through which some religions are built on written and elaborate theologies and others are not, fails to enable us to separate the "primitive" from the "civilized." For all scientific purposes, the "primitive"-"civilized" dichotomy is useless (Bohannan 1963; Hsu 1964).

What new categories do we have to replace the abandoned dichotomy? Reflecting the classical dichotomy between tribal and large-scale religions, Bohannan has recently proposed the distinction between tribal religions (in which "participation is limited to a rather specific social group") and universal religion (which is "primarily independent of any specific social group or type of group") (Bohannan 1963: 328). It is clear that by these criteria Shintoism and Hinduism belong to the tribal group since one can only be a real participant in them through birth, while Buddhism belongs to the universal group since it crosses national boundaries along with Christianity, Islam, and Judaism.

A more scientifically versatile classification of religion will probably have to involve more categories than a simple dichotomy. However, the purpose of this paper is not to set up any definite new scheme of classification of the world's religions but to clear away one basic hurdle which has prevented social scientists in general and anthropologists in particular from even approaching such a classification and constructing a tenable

This chapter was originally published in the *International Journal of Comparative Sociology*, Vol. VIII, No. 1, 1967, pp. 1–19.

theory of the relationship between culture and religion. This basic hurdle is the failure to examine Christianity critically,[2] in contrast to the spirit with which scholars have examined the belief systems of some of the other societies.

Most scholars of comparative religion analyze religions only in terms of philosophical-theological ramifications or formal aspects such as size and organization. They usually conclude with noble sentiments on how different religious paths are different struggles of man with his inevitable destiny (a recent example of this is S. G. F. Brandon 1962: 384–385); or are too readily given to the tendency of demonstrating that different religions are really identical in their basic teachings (e.g. S. Radhakrishnan 1948: 21, 23, 32, 35, 63–65, 71). Most psychologists and sociologists, because of their lack of concern and knowledge of religions outside the Western world, usually do not touch on the difference between Christianity and other religions at all. They tend to develop their theories of religion and personality, or religion and social order, based on Judeo-Christian creeds as the latter have manifested themselves in Euro-American societies. Throughout such deliberations, occasional references to Buddha or Mohammed may be made almost as a matter of academic decoration (I speak of this without any derogatory intent; e.g. W. H. Clark 1958 and P. H. Benson 1960). The famous Max Weber is somewhat broader in his approach, basing his sociology of religion in Christianity, Judaism, Islam and Hinduism. The Chinese way in religion, and still less the Japanese way, play no real part in it. (Weber 1963). One sociologist, William J. Goode, expressly assumes the opposite course by writing an entire book on religion without touching Christianity or any of the so-called great religions (1951). Another sociologist, Milton Yinger, does take in a wider range of variables. For example, he takes up the usually ignored problem of schism in religion but after some discussion, the causes of schism are traced to a profusion of vague and large "causes" of religious differentiation due to "variations in personal religious needs and interests," in "economic and political interests," in "nationality," "social mobility and social change," and "differences that derive from the internal development of the religious system" (1957: 133–142).

It is not suggested that a simpler explanation must prevail over more complex ones even when the facts are complex. But the facts in the present case are not so complex, once we agree to examine them and do so in a truly comparative way. What Yinger does is to pass over the truly comparative facts:

> Most of the studies of the relationship between social differentiation and religious differentiation have been concerned with Christianity. Variation in Hinduism, the several divisions of sectarian Shinto, contrasts between the crude peasant gods Thor and Odin, the refined god of the nobility, the wide differences between the intellectualized beliefs of the upper classes of Ancient Greece and the mystery cults of the masses, the development of orthodox,

conservative, and liberal branches of Judaism, etc., have all been explored.   (1957: 134)

But the fact is "variation in Hinduism. . ." has not "all been explored," especially not in comparison with that in Christianity.

It is possible that Yinger, since half of his book consists of collected works by other scholars, is merely reporting the present state of research on religion. But it is not clear how he expects to construct a sound theory of religious schism, as he attempts to do, if he too fails to examine the facts that "most of the studies" have not been concerned with. The phenomena of religious differentiation and schism in the West and in the non-Western world have never been seriously examined in a truly comparative sense. The fact is that the extent of religious denominationalism is far less in the Asian and African worlds than in the Western world. Protestant Christianity has about 260 denominations in the United States, but in spite of its long history in China, Buddhism has not more than two score of sects. Moreover, and this is by far the more important point, religious differentiation is very different from religious schism. Asian sects and denominations, even where existent, tend to be non-separatist and non-exclusive.

ANTHROPOLOGISTS AND CHRISTIANITY

Western anthropologists have never studied Christianity, nor have they made any serious move in that direction. But their view of religion everywhere is the Western folk view of Christianity and religion. Consequently, as we shall show below, in discussing any question of change in religion anywhere, they at once tend to export Western notions of Christianity.[3] In fact, it can be said, though this is not within the scope of the present paper, that many anthropologists tend to employ the Western folk view of Christianity to analyze social change in general.

Hidden in the back of the minds of some anthropologists would seem to be the idea that religions in which one God alone prevails are higher (therefore more "civilized," "rational," or less "degenerate") than others in which this is not the case (which are therefore "primitive"). This, in my view, is why anthropologists from Andrew Lang through Wilhelm Schmidt to Paul Radin have been engaged in the futile attempt to search for a High God obviously rooted in and patterned after the monotheistic Christianity of Western man, or for the shadow of such a High God (due to degeneration [Schmidt], alternating irrationality [Lang], or realism [Radin]) in the polytheistic world of non-literate peoples. None of these scholars had anything relevant to say about the religions among the literate peoples of Asia in their schemes.

Recent anthropological literature on religion has made no advancement in this matter. It either omits bringing Christianity into any sort of serious discussion altogether (e.g. Herskovits 1948: 347–377, Keesing 1958: 321–341, Lessa and Vogt 1958, and Beals and Hoijer 1965: 566–603, Linton's *Study of Man* [1936] has no chapter on religion), or concentrates on discussions such as the link between ritual and guilt or ritual and anxiety in general (e.g. Mead 1964: 198–212, Malinowski 1925 [reprinted 1948,] and Radcliffe-Brown 1939),[4] or concludes that witch belief is a function of frustration and implies that witch persecution and execution are common to all societies (Kluckhohn 1944, Krige 1947, *Africa* 1935, and Howells 1948: 107–127), in spite of the fact that there is much evidence indicating that there is a fundamental difference between witch persecution in Western and non-Western societies (Hsu 1960), or repeats the same scientifically indefensible lines of Langian and Radinian thought with nothing new in concept, data, or analysis (e.g. Hoebel 1960: 553–554).

It is interesting that Beals and Hoijer express themselves in the following vein when they touch on Christianity:

> Religion functions importantly in reinforcing and maintaining cultural values. Though few religions apparently are as explicitly linked to ethics and morality as, for example, Christianity and Judaism, it is probably true that all or most religions tend, implicitly at least, to support and emphasize particular culturally defined standards of behavior. (1965: 599)

Here not only do the authors say nothing about denominationalism, persecution, and holy wars, but they create (unconsciously perhaps) a distinct impression that the two Western religions named are, by their allegedly more explicit linkage with ethics and morality, superior to the rest. No place in their treatment of religion do they even touch on Hinduism, Buddhism, or Islam.

One anthropologist—almost the only one—who has recognized one important element of the distinctions that our present essay tries to clarify was A. L. Kroeber in his discussion of religious asceticism:

> Puritanical aims are also ascetic; but the special quality of puritanism seems to be the wish to apply asceticism to others as well as to oneself, to enforce it socially. (1948: 598)

Unfortunately for the science of anthropology, he did not pursue the implications of this fleeting recognition. Kroeber had undoubtedly hit upon something most basic not only to Puritans but also to Western Christianity as a whole. The "wish to apply asceticism to others" is one expression of a general tendency to impose one's own idea of God on others through militant factionalism, spreading missionary activities, prolific theology, persecution, and even wars. The object to be imposed is not limited to asceticism, nor is the wish to impose confined to the Puritan variety of Christianity. The Puritans are merely an extreme current in a vast ocean of Christians who tend, instead of confining their own beliefs and practices to themselves, actively to "do unto others what you wish them to do unto you."

What we sorely need is not to touch on Christianity here and there but to scrutinize it as much as we would all religions; not to see it merely in terms of its ideals but also in the light of its practices. When this is done we shall find that (a) Christianity as most of the world knows it possesses certain characteristics which, taken as a whole, distinguish it from other creeds everywhere (except Judaism and Islam); (b) these characteristics are intrinsic to Christianity in the West but not to Christianity in the East—such as China, Japan, and India; and (c) the failure on the part of anthropologists to heed and take these characteristics into consideration has seriously hampered their analysis of religious and social change.

CHARACTERISTICS OF CHRISTIANITY

First, since Christians see their own supernatural as the only true God and their own theology as the only true or pure scripture, they are in essence intolerant of other views and practices. Christian writers are even prone to characterize the founder of Islam as an epileptic or hysteric (Charles J. Adams 1965: 293–294). When they speak of native Asian and other creeds, they obviously consider them as outright superstition or deviations from the true path (e.g. Henry Doré 1925). This attitude underlies even recent anthropological works. A 1959 publication on Tikopian social change speaks of "pagans" or "pagan beliefs," in contrast to "Christians" and "Christian beliefs" just as a 1964 publication on Tibetan religion uses such terms as "fabled Western Heavens," "idol," "idolatry," freely (Raymond Firth 1959a and Robert B. Ekvall 1964).

Thus, side by side with—or indeed, because of its universalistic aspirations—Christianity has been generative of internal divisions which are mutually exclusive. This divisiveness has led to great dynamism in Christianity with one major revolution (the Reformation of Martin Luther) and many lesser reforms. But it has also led to many denominations that are to all intents and purposes duplicates of each other, expressions of sheer factionalism, of the desire to exclude in order to achieve exclusiveness. By contrast, the believers of all Asian indigenous creeds are not even inclusive. Rather they tend to be indifferent. Since they see all supernaturals as equally true they have no need to quarrel over them; they do not argue over absolute truth or purity. There will be little tendency to exclusivist internal divisions and no internal impetus for reforms or revolutionary changes.

The second characteristic of Christianity is that it is prone to missionary activities while the believers of Asian and other creeds see no such need. The merit of this is to *care* about others. The Christian record of fighting against social injustice is more impressive than any other religion. Christian missionaries were among the first modern educators and medical men who worked hard among literate and non-literate peoples around the world. But for them, the fight against foot binding in China during the latter part of the nineteenth and the first part of the twentieth century would have enjoyed much slower success. But the greater the tendency to division, the greater is the necessity for bringing the "good tidings" to alien territory to win converts for the sake of aggrandizing one's own sect. The Asians are indifferent toward other creeds and potential believers since they see no threat to any one and only true belief. They suffer from what Western Christians describe as lethargy. I have heard more than a few sermons in Christian churches and lectures on comparative religion by Christian leaders that Confucius was more negative than Christ because the former said: "Don't do unto others what you don't wish them to do unto you." Of all the missionaries in the world, almost all are from the Christian West, while the lands which are much more overpopulated have not shown any such fervor.

The third characteristic is the extensiveness of its theology. Christians will continue to produce more and more explanations and expositions of their own creed as a means of defending themselves against encroachment by other creeds, and also of expanding their own sphere of influence. On the one hand, doctrines like the Virgin Birth, Original Sin, and the Crucifixion require many supporting doctrines to make them meaningful and plausible to the average believer. On the other hand, since their's is the only truth, they must eliminate other claims to truth from outside and from within. In this process, Christians have produced some of the most beautiful and profound music and literature in the world.

The non-Christian Asians, and Africans as well, have little interest in theology because they have no comparable need to defend or to expand. Their supernatural beliefs are usually close copies of reality. There are good spirits and bad spirits, who can be bribed, coerced, or prayed to for a variety of profane purposes. Gods when compared with each other are more potent or less potent, more kind or more vicious, more honest or more tricky, beautiful and vain or so unhappy about their ugliness that they hide all day and come out at night (as in the case of the Japanese God of Katsuragi). One supernatural may even enjoy such a super-ordinating position over the others that he is alone called by a term *(Kwoth in dit)* not applicable to other spirits, as in the case of the Nuer religion so intensively described by Evans-Pritchard (1956: 28–62). But all of these supernaturals are equally true and/or functional. They may or may not be related to or have anything to do with each other. Rituals for gaining better advantage with the spirits may multiply, but theories to explain the gods' will and intention are without utility. Consequently, a flourishing creed such as Japanese Shintoism has practically no scripture other than the very old Kojiki and Nihonsholi which had but a tenuous connection with the religion. The Hindus certainly are prolific in scriptures, but since they consider all supernaturals as expressions of the same God-head, subsequent theological creations made no attempt to resolve inconsistencies and conflicts with preceding ones. In this way, their profuse theological literature is merely additive and rarely integrative so that the end result, even in one volume, is usually like the Hindu epic *Mahabharata*—a patchwork of diverse, separate tales.

The scriptures of Buddhism which began in India became more and more neglected in China so that a majority of believers were ignorant of it. Furthermore, in contrast to the Western Christian worship in which a sermon is essential (especially in Protestantism), the Chinese temples do not have regular sermons (in fact rarely have them). A majority of Chinese and Japanese temple-goers look for and receive blessings, luck, and fore-knowledge of personal vicissitudes to come, instead of being showered with the truth from the Scriptures. Sermons and other regular means of explication in the West serve to reduce the gap of knowledge between the Great Tradition of the religious establishment (in this case represented by the clergy and the learned theologian) and the Little Tradition (in this case represented by the ordinary church or temple-goer). But the general lack of sermons in Japan and especially in China cannot but widen it.

The fourth characteristic follows from the previous three. Christianity has been prone to religious persecution, is highly persecution-conscious, and is often quick in supporting wars against what Christians think are "godless" peoples. The Inquisition, through which up to 200 Catharist heretics (also known as Albigenses) in Southern France were burned at the stake during one day in 1254, and the Crusades, which perpetrated war and destruction for many centuries, are matched, on the other side of the coin, as it were, by the fury, luridness, and crudity of the conspiracy and the orgies of the Black Mass among the organized witches in England and continental Europe (Margaret Murray 1921, George L. Kittredge 1929, H. C. Lea 1939 and Jay Williams 1957). These and the less spectacular but nevertheless real discriminations in daily life because of differences in faiths are as characteristic of Christianity as they are uncharacteristic of Buddhism, Taoism, and other Asian and African creeds. Religious wars are unknown in the Asian world except in connection with Islam. Such persecution of religious groups as occurred among them was always linked with struggles for favors—as when Taoist priests advised the T'ang emperors against Buddhists or with short-lived mob actions as in the case of the Boxer Rebellion, or with threat of outside encroachment as when Tokugawa closed Japanese doors against all foreigners. The T'ang emperors' suppressive measures against Buddhists are especially illuminating. What they wanted was to *limit* the number of Buddhist temples, monks, and nuns in the national and provincial capitals (the number allowed was in direct ratio to the importance of the locality), not their total elimination. Witch-hunting, a subject mentioned briefly above, must be seen in the same light. Witch persecution in the West has always been absolutistic, as contrasted to relativistic elsewhere among Asians and most other non-literate peoples, as well as possibly among most Africans. That is to say, convicted or even suspected witches would be killed in the West, while they often could buy or confess their way out elsewhere (Hsu 1960 and Middleton and Winter 1963). This was why no experts on counter-witchcraft would exist in Western societies (except the priests who professed orthodoxy or they would be treated just like witches) while in most of the rest of the world counter-witchcraft is a well known and well accepted activity (Hsu 1960).

Furthermore, among Christians, the religious motive is often injected into conflicts which have nothing whatever to do with religion. In the confrontation between Euro-America and Soviet Russia, an accusing finger is constantly raised at the latter for being Godless as though that were truly a basic issue.

The tendency in Christianity is not only exclusiveness but also to make one exclusive creed prevail everywhere. In fact, it is against not only those of rival creeds but also against the agnostic and especially the atheist. The terms "atheist" and "agnostic" are not found in Asia except in modern times through translation from the West. Furthermore, many Christians are not shy about resorting to some sort of force (legal, group pressure, or even military) to enforce their views. Consequently, though religion and religious institutions everywhere may be used to further political ends or as instruments of rebellion (a well known example is messianic movements among many peoples under colonialism), such connections are most frequently formed, hoped for, or suspected in Christianity. It is interesting that even today not only does the Ecumenical Council have to make so much effort in "giving" religious liberties for all peoples, but there is a significant minority in that very Council which is still voting against it (according to the reports in various papers in November and December 1965).

However, this readiness to impose their will on others is not unrelated to the fact that, in the long run, more Christians and Christian organizations than other religionists and religious organizations have shown their readiness to fight tyrants and tyranny. The fact that *The Deputy* became such a best seller in print and on stage is illustrative of this very point. It is an indictment against a very important religious leader for not having spoken up against the Nazi atrocities. So far as I know, no literature or drama with a similar intent exists in the literate Asian societies. Since the polytheists and pantheists make no claim to exclusiveness and have no desire to see any exclusive creed prevail anywhere, they are indifferent to those who doubt or firmly disbelieve. They are less easily moved to action.

The fifth characteristic of Christianity is that it will move more and more toward rationalism in its beliefs and practices, which is one of the mainsprings of its first characteristics mentioned above, namely, denominationalism, while Asian and African religions have no comparable tendencies. Christians need to have their creeds explained, prayers made intelligible, and rituals simplified. At any one time this tendency may not be clear to the person attending a Catholic, an Episcopalian, or even a

Presbyterian service. But over the decades and centuries the entire movement of Christianity from its early form, through Catholicism and Protestantism to Unitarianism, leaves little doubt in this matter, especially when
we contrast the development of non-Christian religions even including
Islam. Now the Catholic Church has begun to change its prayers from
Latin into the spoken language of the worshippers.

Shintoism developed few denominations and no significant movement
for the revision of its beliefs and practices over the centuries. The same
held true for Taoism. Hinduism developed many revisionist sects which
emphasized some particular aspects of Hindu beliefs and practices, but
none of these is strongly rationalistic and certainly none claimed to replace
all others. Japanese Buddhism has a very strongly denominationalistic
history as contrasted to its Chinese counterpart, but the whole tone of this
Japanese history is marked by more absolute personal attachment and
obedience of the disciple to the master (Nakamura 1960: 355–56). Neo-
Confucianism in China could indeed be considered symptomatic of a
trend toward more rationalism, but apart from the fact that Confucianism
cannot be considered a religion, Neo-Confucianism did not make a
"break" from old Confucianism.

In these characteristics Christianity, especially Protestant Christianity,
stands in contrast to all other religions in the world (except Judaism and
Islam, with some modifications). We have primarily contrasted the Christian characteristics with those of prevailing religions of Asian societies
because some elementary conditions under which these Asian religions
prospered, such as literateness, long histories, and national independence
make them more comparable with Christianity than are religions in non-
literate societies.

Christianity West and Christianity East

Let us now deal with the second problem we set out to deal with, by
asking the question, does Christianity exhibit the same characteristics
everywhere? That is to say, when Asians or Africans become converted to
Christianity, will these characteristics not also become those of a majority
of Asian or African Christians? My answer is in the negative. For the
characteristics I have so far advanced pertain primarily to Christians in the
West but not to Christians in the East.

Christianity is now regarded as a Western (Euro-American) religion in
light strictly of its developmental history and not of its origin. It originated
in geographical Asia. From Palestine it went eastward within the first
century A.D., while it went westward much later. The contrasting results in
the two worlds are colossal. First, numerically, while a majority of Euro-
Americans are Christians, only a very small fraction of the Asians can be so
designated. In India where the first missionaries arrived about 50 A.D., the
Christians come to about three per cent of the population. In China and

Japan the quantitative picture of Christianity is even more dismal—being less than one per cent of the population in each. I submit that this is a strong evidence that most Asians find Christianity incompatible. Second, an equally telling fact was already mentioned before: practically all the Christian missionaries of the world are Euro-Americans and not Asians. Regardless of the fact that there may be some who turned to missionary work for ulterior motives, the volume of Christian missionaries from any society is a fair indication of the seriousness with which most people in that society regard their Christianity. Third, while the European history of Christianity is replete with instances of a political leader (king or prince) who was a Christian convert impressing, coaxing, or forcing his subjects into conversion to the same faith, no such Asian example can be cited. When General Chiang Kai Shek was baptized a Methodist in the late 'twenties, at the height of his political popularity, missionaries—especially Methodist ones—were elated. Judging by Western historical antecedents, they anticipated, consciously or unconsciously, that the days were numbered before all China was Christianized. At least, some Westerners thought, Chiang would try to make all China Christian; of course, they were disappointed.

Japan was the only Asian country where a ruler (Tokugawa) executed and banished by law considerable numbers of missionaries and Japanese Christians for fear of foreign encroachment, just as at another time, the followers of the True-Pure Land Sect in the Satsuma Clan (southern Kyushu) were put to death for fear of political insubordination (Nakamura 1960: 313). But neither in Japan nor China was there any significant long-standing and popular movement for *rooting out* religious heresy or witch-hunting. The Chinese Boxer Uprising in 1900 was typically a short-lived mob phenomenon. Western missionaries were welcome by emperors and the people as long as they did not endanger the regime or create resentment of their privileged positions among a people with much obvious poverty. The sole place in Asia where the Inquisition existed for a considerable period of time was in Goa of India—instituted and carried out by the Portuguese colonial government.

There are *quantitative* and *qualitative* differences between a majority of Asian Christians and a majority of Euro-American Christians which cannot be explained away easily. It goes without saying that there are bread-and-butter Christians as well as holier-than-thou Christians anywhere. Between these extremes the majority of Christians in Asia and the West must be considered earnest souls who take their Christianity with usual seriousness. I submit that the attitude of this general body of Christians in each area is a fair indication of the quality of the faith in action. Among such Westerners, being Christian usually means definite membership in a given local, denominationalized church, exclusive adherence to its conventions as regards marriage, christening, funerals, and other rituals, some attendance at the Sunday services and other church functions, some knowledge of the Bible, a certain conscious or unconscious feeling of superiority over non-Christians, lack of ambiguity about religious affiliation, and the importance of this affiliation as a determining factor in marital selection and even social intercourse. Any suggestion that church membership is entered into for ulterior motives or that one man can at the same time be a Methodist or Presbyterian, not to say a Protestant or Catholic, will be met with disbelief, derision, or hostility. In this complex is also the American tendency to regard religion to mean, as Norbeck points out, "ideas, ideals or goals about which one feels strongly or desires intensely" (1961: 270).

The situation in Asia is quite different where most Christians also participate in ancestor worship, pay homage at temples or shrines, consult astrologers, celebrate duplicate wedding ceremonies (Christian and indigenous), or perform two contrasting funeral rites (to make two sets of relatives happy).

Two episodes are highly illustrative of the Japanese approach to Christianity. In a highly Westernized and affluent city between Osaka and Kobe, a music critic related to me his family history which is distinguished. It turned out that not only had he and his wife met romantically and married by free choice, but his wife's parents and his father's parents had all met and married on the same basis. In commenting on this situation, which is certainly unusual among any stratum of Japanese, the gentleman said as though by way of explanation: "We are all Christians." But when I later checked with this man as to his present church affiliation, he replied that he did not have any and added without hesitation: "I have graduated from Christianity." While he smiled in saying so, further conversation on this point indicated that he was not joking and fully meant what he had said. Being a Christian is to him a social condition which freed him and his forebears from certain traditional patterns of conduct but it has little or nothing to do with belief or disbelief in God as such.

A well-educated lady in a nearby community was known to be very active in her local church (Presbyterian). In fact, she was one of its pillars. When I asked her about the *butsudan* (Buddhist family altar for ancestors in her house) and the activities connected with it, she said, "I am bad . . . for a Christian. I make regular offerings of tea. . . ." It is evident that she knows what Christians in the Western model are supposed not to do. From the way she expressed herself so readily, I felt that though guilt was perhaps a small element among her feelings, she was not really embarrassed by my question or her answer. She was making clear to me a point of fact, and in so doing, her usual Japanese good form of self-deprecation came into play.

Incidents on the same theme but in different guises recurred again and again wherever I came upon Japanese Christians, in spite of the Japanese desire to Westernize obvious to every visitor from other lands. Furthermore, church membership in Japan has not increased since World War II. Probably it was similar facts as these that prompted a Catholic missionary, about two centuries ago, allegedly to observe that the Japanese were invented by the devil for the prevention of the spread of Christianity. Some protestant missionaries were even more specific. They thought that the Chinese tongue seemed Satan's master-devise to exclude the gospel (Pierson 1886: 89).

The missionaries had good reason to feel discouraged toward both peoples. The characteristic behavior of the Chinese toward Christianity before 1949 on the mainland and since then elsewhere is much the same as the Japanese. In 1947, residents of Peking were called upon by the editors of a large daily to write about their own true life experiences on "How to Conquer Poverty." One Mr. Liu wrote in some detail on how he did it by joining the Catholic Church where he found food and shelter for his family. He said in part:

> I would like to offer my own experience. About twenty years ago I was in a similar plight. Then the times were good. I had a big family. I had no selling skill and I was unfit as a heavy manual laborer. So a friend introduced me to the Catholic Church at———, where they have a Woman's Home. I took my wife and three small children to this Home to pledge their faith in the creed (Catholicism). I did some work elsewhere. I visited them once a week bringing them some gift every time. In that enclosure they studied characters, learned the scriptures, and worshipped God. At first they were very unhappy and bored. But after some days they felt all right. They got to know other inmates and fell in with the routine. The children no longer craved for home, since they had lots of other children to play with. They had three meals a day. The food was not too good, but having lived in poverty, that was not unbearable. Those women who had nursing babies usually got a little more food. Generally a person could be eligible for Baptism three months after admission. There was no male in the home. All teachers and other officers were nuns. Boys over six years of age were not admitted. Those admitted did not have to bring their own bedding.
>
> In short, this is one of the ways of meeting an emergency. Just get baptized and don't worry about the rest. The proverb says: "The Supreme Ruler of Heaven will not starve even a blind sparrow." He will certainly not starve us, who are human beings, the most exalted of all living creatures, and are all children of God.
>
> Another way out is to go to the Relief Department of the Bureau of Social Welfare of the Municipal Government.
>
> P. L. Liu
No. 68 Chiang Yang Fang
Fifth Police Area
Peiping (Hsu 1949a: 782–83)

The point here is not that a certain Chinese named Liu revealed himself to be a rice-bowl Christian. The most significant thing is that Mr. Liu thought it was perfectly natural to state his ulterior motives for joining the church, earnestly presented his case as a good example for others to follow, and gave his name and address at the end of his public letter without embarrassment. Moreover, in the days that ensued, no correspondent in this or any other paper even expressed mild disapproval of Mr. Lui's suggestions.

Mr. Liu's essential approach to religion was identical with that of a Chinese girl who applied for a scholarship at Northwestern University in 1952. In the space marked "Religion" on the application form[5] she wrote: "None at the present, but willing to be a Methodist." The University being originally founded as a Methodist institution, and still having an independent Methodist theological seminary occupying part of its campus, the Chinese girl was not being frivolous at all. From the Chinese way of thinking, the utilitarian side of the church is paramount. And neither Mr. Liu of Peking nor the Chinese girl at Northwestern University would be ashamed to speak about what they thought was the most logical and rational way of solving their respective problems.

These Japanese and Chinese attitudes toward Christianity are merely an expression of their essential approach to religion in general. They tell us much as to why religious persecution or witch-hunting could neither be significant nor widespread throughout Japanese and Chinese histories. Religion simply cannot be a burning issue as a basis for social discrimination if people go regularly from temples to shrines, or perform contrasting rituals from different belief systems as though they were partaking of different foods. Our usual thoughts about religious persecution is that there are bigots who want to persecute. What we must also realize is that in most true religious persecutions (as distinguished from the Nazi type of persecution of Jews) there must also be determined souls who want to be persecuted for the religious beliefs they hold. It is simply not probable for a majority of Chinese and Japanese to be so determined about particular religious creeds as to be willing to put themselves on the persecution block. They are not wont to persecute for religious reasons, they are not so persecution-conscious, and they rarely look for that kind of trouble.

Such facts make it logically ludicrous to designate groups of Japanese or Chinese as being Buddhists, Taoists, or Shintoists, as many Western scholars, as well as various year book and encyclopedia publishers, have done. They simply cannot be so classified because a majority of them tend to be non-exclusivist in their religious affiliation whatever the religion in question. Thus the characteristics of Christianity we have outlined in the first part of this paper are not characteristics of Christianity everywhere but its characteristics in the West. In order for monotheistic Christianity to maintain even a toe-hold in Asia and Africa, it has to seriously modify its Western characteristics.

How Christianity in the United States has undergone further transformation to render its ways somewhat different from its counterpart in Europe and Latin America is equally interesting. However, compared with the differences between Christianity in the West as a whole and Asia as a whole, the United States-Europe-Latin American differences are matters of detail. This has been dealt with elsewhere (Hsu 1953: 263–277). What we must also realize is that these Western Christian characteristics had extended pre-Christian roots, just as the Asian Christian characteristics are no great deviation from their traditional approaches to the supernatural. For even when they had many gods, the Greeks and especially the Romans, and before them, the Egyptians and the Hebrews, had also consistently shown most of the monotheistic pattern of religious behavior under Christianity. The Athenian trials of Pericles' mistress, Aspasia, and of his philosopher friend, Anaxagoras, as well as the trial and execution of Socrates were but a few of the examples. The Romans had their emperors who threw Christians to the lions. The Egyptian Pharoah Ikhnaton made Aton, the transformed Sun-god, the sole God of his empire and persecuted the old state god Amon and his followers. The Hebrews under and after the two prosperous kings, David and Solomon, made Yahweh their own God to the exclusion of all other deities. How the contrasting Western and Chinese approaches to religion are rooted in their respective patterns of psychocultural orientation has been explained in an earlier work (Hsu 1953: 217–277).[6]

Our analysis leads us to believe that the core and the existing conversion boundaries of Christianity among the presently literate peoples (about three per cent of Asians but about eighty per cent of Euro-Americans are Christians) are probably closest to the culturally permitted limits. Unless Christianity is drastically changed in its character so that most Western Christians will regard it as non-Christian, or at least as a travesty of Christianity, monotheistic Christianity will only prevail among Western peoples. It follows that though continually expansionistic through missionary activities, no monotheistic Christianity is likely to make comparable headway through conversion among the presently literate but non-Christian peoples as it did among the Europeans.

COMMON GROUND AMONG LITERATE AND NON-LITERATE PEOPLES

Under the domination of a Christian colonial power, or continued intensive activities by Western Christian missionaries, and without the aid of written histories of which they could be proud (whether justified or not), the peoples of non-literate societies may conceivably be more prepared to accept Christian conversion than are their Asian brethren. The fact that the black African population, according to various estimates, is about fourteen per cent Christian may be an indication of this. Polynesia seems to be an example of a group of peoples who are willing even more than other non-literates to accept conversion to Christianity. The Hawaiians broke their own taboos and accepted Christianity so abruptly that Kroeber invented the not-too-useful concept of "culture fatigue" to describe their condition (1949: 403–405). The Togans and the Tikopians, two other Polynesian peoples, seem to be equally willing to become

Christians. According to Raymond Firth, Tikopia became overwhelmingly Christian by 1952.

It is not our plan here to deal with facts relating to Christianity in all the non-literate world. This cannot be done in a short paper. However, enough can be ascertained to show that there is a basic and qualitative gulf between the Polynesian's Christianity and the Western man's Christianity which cannot but confuse the anthropologist who fails to perceive it and vitiate his analysis. The following types of statement on social change in Tikopia, based on what are probably the most detailed field work and most exhaustive analysis known to our discipline, illustrates this defect:

> It might seem that the influence of Christianity would have appeared particularly in marriage preferences. Since in *other* societies it is common in Christian circles for objection to be made to the marriage of Christian with pagan, one might have *expected* this in Tikopia. No doubt the Mission hierarchy had views on this matter. But in practice the Tikopia did not seem to pay great attention to this point. In general, the religion of a wife tended to agree with that of her husband. There was no case known to me of a husband who was a practising Christian having a wife who had remained unbaptized and a practicing pagan. But there were in the 1952 census ten cases of a husband who was a pagan having married a Christian wife, who then in effect abandoned her cult in order to follow his. Of these, most notable was the case of the wife of the Ariki Taumako. She was a Christian girl, a daughter of the late Christian chief of Tafua in Faea. Alleged to have been one of the mistresses of the Ariki Taumako, she was said to have risen in the night from her home and come over, in Tikopia style, to the other side of the island to marry her lover. It was alleged also that she was instigated to this action by her father for political reasons. Yet her husband, the chief, was stalwart in his paganism in 1952 and she participated fully in the traditional religious affairs of Uta. Here again, Christianity in Tikopia was not *yet* strong enough—or deep enough—to overcome the exercise of personal choice in spouses. For a few women it could not wholly control even ritual procedure, in outward conformity to the rules of the accepted faith. But for the most part, by 1952 Christianity was so widespread in Tikopia that *religious difference in marriage was not of great statistical weight.* (Raymond Firth 1959: 204–205. Italics mine.)

Three observations can be made at once. First, while the statement that "in other societies it is common in Christian circles for objection to be made to the marriage of Christian with pagan" conveys the idea that Christians elsewhere tend to object to marriage with non-Christians, the facts as we have seen them prove otherwise. It is indeed common for *Western* Christians to do so but it is not at all common for Asian or other Christians to do so. There is no scientific basis for Firth to have "expected" the former in Tikopia.

Second, the statement that "Christianity in Tikopia was not yet strong enough or deep enough. . . ." means that one day in some unspecified future time Christianity will so progress in Tikopia that it will be strong enough—and deep enough to do what it has done and is doing in the West. Again, this is an error due to lack of wider knowledge. In a real sense the anthropologist's predicament here is like that of Malthus in the latter's famous prediction of population growth based on nineteenth-century data. There were unavoidable reasons why Malthus was so myopic, but there is far less reason for the twentieth-century anthropologist to be the same. This lack of concern to look at readily available facts for broadening his perspective is best illustrated in Firth's discussion of the need for the student to assume an "as-if attitude," by "accepting at face value the phenomena of the religion they study." Firth says that he borrowed this concept of "as-if attitude" from Forberg who lived about 160 years ago (Firth 1959b: 137, 147). Had Firth glanced over Herbert A. Giles' translation of Confucius' *Analects* he would have noted that Forberg was antidated in this regard by quite a few years:

> He sacrificed to the dead, as if they were present. He sacrificed to the spirit, as if the spirit were present. The Master said, I consider my not being present at the sacrifice, as if I did not sacrifice.   (Confucius 1960 reprint, I; p. 159)

Third, the statement that by 1952 Christianity was so widespread in Tikopia that "religious difference in marriage was not of great statistical weight" shows how figures as such are deceptive. The basic purpose of the social sciences (especially anthropology) is not merely to count heads and find out how many persons in a given population have *professed* to be this or that, but to understand the deeper significance of this surface acceptance in terms of more substantial matters. The pertinent question is, what difference does such outward affiliation to a universalistic creed mean in the Tikopian's life, in the decisions that he will have to make with reference to important problems and crises from birth to marriage to making a living and to death? From Firth's account we must say that profession of Christianity has made relatively little difference to the Tikopian, especially when contrasted to the patterns of Christian behavior in the West.

When this is understood and when we also see how African and other nonliterate Christians mix indigenous practices and beliefs with Western originated Christian rituals and theology, we should realize that the patterns of Christianity among non-literate peoples are essentially similar to or even identical with those of literate Asians. Figuring very largely in these patterns are, among others, the following elements: a polytheistic (or pantheistic) approach to the supernatural in which all gods are equally valid, non-division among believers, absence of missionary spirit, non-acquaintance with theology or lack of regard for it, absence of religious persecution, non-exclusive and tenuous church affiliation, and no rationalistic or reformistic trend except under severe pressure from outside. In this complex is also the absence of critical examination of religious beliefs, and the tendency to "accept foreign practices of supernaturalism as additional techniques for mastery of the universe like the civilized housewife who collects recipes" (Norbeck 1961: 271). These are the same elements which characterize indigenous religions among a majority of non-literate peoples and Asians.

In this circumstance we should realize that when Malinowski theorized that magic fills the gap of science (1925) he was simply seeing the facts from the Western point of view. Under the rationalistic Western cultural orientation, "science" and "empirical reality" are the accepted notions of life and magic (or magico-religion) has to try to enter into the picture to fill any gap in that matrix of Western life characterized by them. But the picture actually might have seemed to the Trobrianders (as Malinowski's ethnographic description and analysis leave no doubt in the matter) and to the Asians and the non-literate peoples in the world very different. Magico-religion is so much intertwined with their accepted notions of life for centuries that what the Western man regards as "science" and "empirical reality" (as expressed in the Western man's Christianity, medicine, and gadgetry) have to try to enter into the picture to fill any gap in that matrix of traditional way in which magico-religion figures largely or is undistinguished from "science" and "empirical reality." In short, where the Western man sees magic as filling in the gap of science because he has taken science for granted, the non-Western man may see science as filling in the gap of magic because he has been so used to magic as part of the order of nature. This point has very important implications to our understanding of social change in general (for detailed analysis of this point see Hsu 1952a).

Under the impact of Western monotheistic Christianity, the defensive actions of some Asian religionists seem to run along two lines. On the one hand, believers of polytheistic Hinduism tend to claim that their faith is really monotheistic, as the following statement indicates:

> However, a vast majority of the economically poor Hindus approach God through traditional simple methods using the ways of devotion *(bhakti)* and of performances *(karma)* rather than the path of pure knowledge *(jnana)*. It is the continuation of these methods that is responsible for the mistaken belief not uncommon in the West that Hinduism is a polytheistic religion. If the doctrine of the Brahman is not understood, this is an easy mistake to make, for, in popular Hinduism, God is worshipped in different forms.   (Sen 1961: 20)

In view of our analysis, Sen's "defense" is misplaced. Except for the belief that all forms of supernatural are manifestations of the same Godhead *(Atma)*, on which point the Hindu differs from his Japanese and Chinese brethren, Hinduism is as inclusive, tolerant, and lacking in missionary zeal as Western Christianity is exclusive, intolerant, and mission-oriented in theory and practice.

On the other hand, the believers in many Asian and African religions tend to attempt some innovations in their indigenous religious practices. Regular Sunday services, YMBA (Young Men's Buddhist Association), hymnals written in Western music, a single Buddha figure adorning each of certain Japanese Buddhist temples, mixed social clubs, even a few missionaries in the United States and Europe, are but some of them. These usages are adopted for self-preservation or social status. But anyone who cares to observe the Vedanta Society in action in Chicago, or a Buddhist Temple in Honolulu, will realize that these are but token missionary activities when compared with those of Christianity throughout the world, and there is no indication at all that they will spread as Western Christianity did before them.

In thus placing together religions in non-literate and Asian societies we do not mean to deny the differences between them. Taoism, Buddhism, Shintoism, and Hinduism are creeds nurtured in literate societies which produced especially learned men who more or less systematized the theologies, accumulated them to a degree through many generations, and achieved sometimes organizational complexities and artistic heights unknown in the non-literate societies. The religious specialists of the Trobrianders, the Tungus, the Kalinga, or the Navajo Indians obviously did not have such capabilities or opportunities. However, although it has been customary among scholars and laymen to refer to some of these Asian creeds as "great" religions but not so to any of those indigenous nonliterate religions, our analysis shows that this distinction between these "greats" and the "non-greats" is far less significant than those between all indigenous Asian and African creeds on the one hand and Western Christianity and Islam and Judaism on the other.

Nor do we negate the differences among the monotheistic Christianity, Judaism, and Islam, or those among the various polytheistic non-literate religions. The many fine differences among religions in diverse non-literate societies (such as between those with impersonalized and personalized techniques, between those with or without a special class of religious functionaries, etc.) (e.g. Edward Norbeck 1961) may well prove important for the anthropological theory of religion and culture and will continue to engage the attention of some anthropologists. But before the physical anthropologist classified hominids into races, he had first to clarify the differences among apes, fossil protoanthropoids, and existing human beings. In such a composite group of biological creatures there exist many more pronounced and significant differences between species which cannot be understood by means of the conceptual details of race. If an analogy is permitted, it seems that the differences between Western monotheistic Christianity (and Islam and Judaism as well) and the other religions in literate and non-literate societies are in the order of those among species, the differences between indigenous Asian religions and non-literate religions are in the order of those among races, while the differences among non-literate religions are probably in the order of those among sub-races.

NOTES

1. The author is indebted to Paul J. Bohannan, Robert C. Hunt, Thomas Rohlen, Edward Norbeck, and John F. M. Middleton for reading the manuscript and giving critical suggestions.

2. Islam and Judaism belong here too, but they cannot be considered in a short paper such as this.

3. Edward Norbeck has made this point on different ground (Norbeck 1961: 269–71).

4. The hypotheses of Malinowski and Radcliffe-Brown have been admirably reconciled and improved upon by George C. Homans (1941).

5. Northwestern University has since eliminated this question from its application form.

6. There are also noticeable differences in religious behavior between the Chinese and Japanese. How these differences are correlated with their respective ways of seeing the world have been examined in my book *Iemoto: The Heart of Japan* (Cambridge, Mass.: Schenkman Publishing Co., 1975, Chapter 11).

4

The Chinese of Hawaii: Their Role in American Culture[1]

I

The racial composition of Hawaii's population today is roughly as follows: Caucasian, 32 per cent; Japanese, 32 per cent; Hawaiian and part-Hawaiian, 15 per cent; Filipino, 10 per cent; Chinese, 6 per cent. The remaining 5 per cent is made up of Puerto Ricans, Koreans, and others. These percentages have been substantially and relatively the same during the last twenty years, except that for Caucasian, which has doubled itself during this period. Over 95 per cent of the Chinese are situated on Oahu Island, of which Honolulu is the principal city.

The bulk of the original Chinese in Hawaii came in the latter part of the nineteenth century, as illiterate, indentured laborers on the plantations. Their initial contract usually provided for a period of three years of work in the island in exchange for free transportation, food and lodging, and a wage of about three dollars a month. Most of them were drawn from one district near Canton. Some 10 or 15 per cent were from four neighboring districts.

Today, most of the Chinese in Hawaii are second, third, and fourth generation Americans. They have spread over the entire economic and social ladder of the territory. In 1882, about fifty per cent of the workers on the sugar plantations were Chinese. In 1934, though the total number of workers on plantations had increased by about four and one-half times that of 1882, only 1.5 per cent of the workers were Chinese. In 1890, about 11 per cent of Chinese males gainfully employed were engaged in "preferred" occupations. In 1930, the corresponding figure was 50 per cent. In 1890, only 3 per cent of gainfully employed Chinese females were engaged in "preferred" occupations. In 1930, the corresponding figure was 70 per cent.

Residentially, Chinese are found in every census tract of Honolulu. This picture was already true in 1920 and is certainly true today. Even in 1930, only 47 per cent of the population of the so-called "Chinatown" of Honolulu were Chinese. In that year, only 30 per cent of the population in areas adjacent to Chinatown were Chinese.

In school attendance records, the Chinese in Hawaii topped all racial groups. In 1930, 75.8 per cent of Chinese five to twenty-four years of age were in school, as compared with 60.3 per cent of Hawaiians, 57.7 per cent

This chapter was originally published in the *Transactions of the New York Academy of Sciences,* Ser. II, Vol. 13, No. 6, 1951, pp. 243–50.

of Caucasians, and 71.5 per cent of Japanese in this age group. In 1940, the Chinese retained their first place in school attendance record. Today, most Chinese in Hawaii speak excellent English and live in American style. They promote boxing and play American football. They are found in elective offices, such as territorial senators and representatives, and in professional ranks, such as doctors and lawyers.

II

By the usual standards, then, the Chinese of Hawaii are very American, except that they are not white. However, if we look closer and deeper, we see patterns of behavior among the Chinese of Hawaii, today, which differ in a number of ways from those which characterize Americans. Most Americans, as well as the majority of Chinese in Hawaii, will object to this statement. It is, however, the purpose of this paper to show that, while it is impossible for any people with a distinct cultural background to erase that background within a matter of three or four generations, especially if they live in a more or less circumscribed area, such as an island, these differing characteristics carried by the Chinese, far from being undesirable, may become, contrary to the usual assumptions, a foundation for some invaluable contributions of the Chinese to American culture and society as a whole.

What are some of the characteristics of the Chinese in Hawaii today? First let us look at religion. Practically all Chinese born and raised in Hawaii in recent years have become Christians. Yet they do not seem to care if they are not all Protestants. In fact, there seem to be as many of them Catholics as Protestants. The activities among Chinese Catholics are certainly as evident as they are among Chinese Protestants. In addition, there are a large number of Chinese Mormons and some Chinese Bahaians.

This poses a very interesting question: Without any Christian background when they came, how did it happen that they took to Catholicism and Mormonism as much as they did to Protestant denominations, especially since Protestantism has the dominant religious value in American culture? Two further facts are to be noted in this connection: (1) It is a rule, rather than an exception, for members of the same family to have different religious affiliations, such as, for example, a Catholic father, a Methodist son, and an Episcopalian daughter, while the mother retains her custom of worshipping at Chinese temples. (2) Differences in religion do not seem to hamper Chinese family solidarity. Frequently, Christian Chinese have told me that if and when their mothers asked them to go to Chinese temples they would do everything the elders requested. They did not see any conflict with their own church activities.

What is observable in religion seems to be evident also in the organizational activities of the Chinese in Hawaii. In the first place, most Chinese belong to organizations traditionally Chinese in nature. These organizations are based upon territorial ties (such as district and village), kinship ties (such as clan), occupational ties, or recreational needs (such as boxing and music). A relative minority of Chinese belong to modern organizations, such as the women's clubs or university men's or women's clubs, or organizations in support of the Community Chest, a cancer fund and information, or Chinese schools.

In the second place, very few of even the modern organizations are based upon a definite cause. Most of them are mere social clubs. Apart from the cancer and some temporary China relief organizations, there is nothing comparable to the Society for the Prevention of Cruelty to Children, the Society for the Prevention of Cruelty to Animals, the Anti-Vivisection Society, the Conference of Christians and Jews, or the Women's Christian Temperance Union.

The family among the Chinese in Hawaii is equally interesting. All the second, third, and fourth generation Chinese in my experience consider freedom of choice in marriage essential. Teen-agers, as well as older students, use terms like "dating" and do go out with members of the other sex freely. But the courtship lacks many essential American qualities. For one thing, Chinese boys seem to complain that Chinese girls are far too cocky and far too concerned with their own dignity rather than with popularity with the boys. Several boys told me that when they went out with Chinese girls to a dance, their dates often went off and danced with other boys most of the night. Then, Chinese boys agree that one can't "make" a Chinese girl, as one can girls of other races. In general, Chinese men and women in courtship seem to lack the ardor, demonstrativeness, and ecstatic devotion common among young American lovers.

In the marital relationship, the Chinese in Hawaii have something equally distinct. The vast majority of Chinese families, judging by census reports and personal observation, would seem to consist of a husband, wife and unmarried children. But the relationship between the spouses and between parents and children is much less marked by individuation and much more by a pattern of taking each other for granted. There is little question of "wooing your husband or wife anew each day," and parents have little private life from which their children are excluded.

One other thing of interest is connected with names. Practically all Chinese born and raised in Hawaii have non-Chinese first names. However, they do not only have Harry Wongs, or Mary Chongs, but they also have a large number of non-Anglo-Saxon looking names. The extreme examples are Maysevene, for a girl who was born on May the seventh, or Worldster, for a boy whose father was interested in the unity of mankind.

III

What is the meaning of these characteristics among the Chinese in

Hawaii? I think they can be understood best if we introduce a hypothesis which I have elaborated elsewhere (Hsu 1949b). The hypothesis poses the Chinese as being situation-centered in their personal and cultural orientation and the American as being individual-centered. A situation-centered pattern tends to produce individuals whose main attempt will be to find a satisfactory adjustment with the external environment of men and things. The chief concern of such a psychology will be to fit in or harmonize with what exists. The individual-centered pattern produces individuals whose main attempt will be to find ways and means of fulfilling their own mental requirements. The chief concern of that psychology will be to bend the external world of men and things according to their predilections. The situation-centered personality is more realistic and works toward compromise, but the individual-centered personality has greater emotional intensity and aims at all or none.

In spite of this contrast, however, competitiveness enjoys a high value in both cultures. This quality explains such things as the economic successes of the Chinese in Hawaii and their lead in school attendance, but it is the contrast between situation-centered and individual-centered orientations in Chinese and American cultures which explains the most distinctive characteristics of the Chinese in Hawaii.

First, religion. In China, in spite of centuries of missionary work, less than one per cent of the population today is Christian. Being members of the American society, in an environment where Christianity has a much higher degree of social importance than in China, the Chinese in Hawaii naturally embrace it. But they have neither the militant Christian spirit characteristic of pioneer Americans, nor any feeling of superiority toward non-Christians. This is perfectly consistent with a situation-centered outlook. This outlook, in contrast to the individual-centered outlook, is inconsistent with a religion in which the major emphasis is on a personal, direct, and introspective relationship with God and in which all other gods are false and therefore must be eliminated.

Given this background, it is easy for the Chinese of Hawaii to embrace not only different sects of the same religion, but even different religions, within one family. The high proportion of Catholics is of especial interest. One of the outstanding private schools in Hawaii is Saint Louis College for Boys. Many Chinese are Catholics because they studied or graduated from this school, which happens to offer excellent training in commercial arts, such as bookkeeping. To a people with a situation-centered orientation, but without an emotional intensity which will make a personal religion of overwhelming importance, the external advantages, such as those offered by Saint Louis College, are likely to be of much importance. In China, too, of the very small number of Christians, 90 per cent are Catholics and 10 per cent are Protestants. In China, also, over the centuries, the only group that created disturbances of a religious nature consisted of the monotheistic Mohammedans. To the Chinese, religion is a means through which an individual will find his place among men or gods. Even if he accepts monotheism, he is far too reasonable to be hostile to other beliefs.

The Chinese way in organization is no less illuminating. In general, two things stand out. The Chinese organizations in Hawaii, whether traditional or otherwise, tend to be inclusive rather than exclusive, in contrast to the usual American way.

The simplest expression of the American psychology of exclusiveness is found in the so-called restricted neighborhoods. When a number of well-to-do families moved into one end of a lower income street in a Connecticut town, they renamed their half of the street. The widest expression of this psychology is racial discrimination. This is a fact too well known to need documentation. In fact, one of the most important aspirations of the average American is locked in a paradox. On the one hand, he wants to be one of the fellows. On the other, he takes pride in being a member of an exclusive group, from which others are excluded.

On the contrary, even the new organizations of the Chinese in Hawaii fail in this characteristic. Even the now-famous American-Chinese Club tends to be more interested in its business possibilities (such as having its hall rented for entertainment purposes, at a profit, and declaring a dividend among its members toward the end of the fiscal year), rather than in making the club inaccessible to aspirants. I have often been told by members of this club that it was started in reaction to some of the restrictive attitudes on the part of some of the Haole[2] clubs, yet the American-Chinese Club has no scruples about admitting anyone who is part-Chinese.

The second thing to be observed about Chinese organizations in Hawaii is that they have little of the crusading spirit. This is so even with the two so-called secret societies, which allegedly began as an attempt to overthrow the Manchu Dynasty in China. It is to be recalled that in the history of the WCTU movement in the United States there were a number of outstanding women who individually went out of their way to smash up saloons. This spirit is utterly alien to Chinese organizations. There are some Chinese organizations to help cancer research or the Community Chest, but these are minor. One may argue that the Chinese in Hawaii do not need a WCTU movement because alcoholism is not a problem among them, but as will be evident below, there certainly is a need for something which might be called the "Chinese Society for the Prevention of Gambling." No such organization exists, however. In other words, there are, in the normal course of events, hardly any Chinese organizations, whether in Hawaii or China itself, whose aim is to do something for people, to reform or improve them, whether they want to be reformed or improved or not, or to annihilate other people or groups.

Lastly, let us look at the family. Given the opportunity, Chinese youngsters like to choose their own mates and set up their independent households, and name themselves and their children in accordance with the fashions of the times and place, but they are not likely to insist upon these things regardless of consequences. They do not have the one-mindedness which is fostered in the American culture so that they will insist on all or none. They are much more prepared to accept a compromise situation so that in a matter of choice of a mate they will consider the wishes of their parents almost as much as they will be motivated by their own desires. In their sexual love for each other, they will be concerned over what other people say as much as they are conditioned by their own preferences; and in their marital adjustment they will safeguard their individual happiness as much as they will be affected by the permanence of their marital ties once the wedding bells have been rung. For these reasons, the Chinese in Hawaii are not yet afflicted by two of the most vexatious American problems today. (1) The Chinese in Hawaii have no problem of the aged. This is so, not because the Chinese support their elders more, but because they are not given to the idea that old people are a stumbling block to the happiness of the young. According to the Chinese situation-centered culture pattern, the old have merely advanced to another stage of life in which they have a new significance. Being old is not synonymous with becoming useless or being relegated to the background. Therefore, the old can age gracefully and with dignity. They do not have to "refuse" to get old, nor do they have to hold onto the young for fear that once they let go they will have no respected place in the scheme of things. (2) The Chinese in Hawaii are not troubled by adolescent difficulties. Both police files and interview material with social workers and Chinese parents show that the problemed adolescent is an exception rather than the rule. This is at least partly related to the lack of old-age problems. Since the old do not have to hold on to their young with great emotional intensity, there is little reason for the young to react to the old strongly. Since children and parents maintain little privacy of activities, the adolescent is far too realistic to want to abandon all his social ties because of some momentary pleasure or hatred.

IV

It has often been argued that Orientals are masters of self-control and therefore, inscrutable. This is sheer popular misconception. No people can control their emotions permanently and in every direction. If the Chinese in Hawaii have merely engaged in more self-control than the majority of Americans, then we should also have some indication of this fact in their inevitable breakdowns, such as crime, suicide and mental illness; but the facts are quite contrary to such an assumption.

For purposes of this paper, three kinds of crime are distinguished. They are: (1) rape, assault with intent to rape; assault with intent to ravish; and attempt to commit rape,—all sex crimes[3]; (2) manslaughter, robbery, burglary, larceny of all kinds, auto theft, forgery and embezzlement; and

(3) gambling. Honolulu police reports for random years (1917–18, and 1925 to 1940 inclusive) and records from all courts of Hawaii for sixteen years were examined. It was found that the number of Chinese in these reports, compared with Whites,[4] is not only disproportionately smaller in the sex crime charges and convictions, but also disproportionately under the manslaughter, etc., charges and convictions. Under the category of gambling, however, the positions between Chinese and Whites are reversed. Here the Chinese figure is disproportionately above that of the Whites.

The connection between sex crimes and runaway emotions is obvious. Even manslaughter and burglary, etc., would also seem to require much overpowering of reason by emotion. On the other hand, gambling is undoubtedly the least emotional of all the ways of getting into trouble with the law.

Next, material on suicides and attempted suicides was examined for the years 1936 to 1950 inclusive. The overall suicide rates for Chinese for the 15 years were, in proportion to the population, about half of that for Whites. But if suicide and attempted suicide cases are combined, the difference is even greater.

For the Chinese, suicide is a very serious business and they must have good reasons for taking that road. Being of a calm nature, they can make sure of succeeding; but being situation-centered, they do not easily take the road of desperation, not only because of their greater consideration for the people that surround them, such as family, relatives, neighbors, and friends, but also because they do not have emotions which easily disturb them. The Whites, on the other hand, are more pressed by emotion and less hampered by situational considerations. For them, success is a greater individual triumph, but failure is correspondingly a greater personal misery. They are, therefore, likely to feel desperate much more frequently than the Chinese and they take rash actions. Being more disturbed emotionally, they are often unable to be sure in their methods of suicide.[5]

These contrasts stand out even more strongly when sex is considered as a factor. The ratio of suicides to attempted suicides among Chinese males is about 1 to 1. Among white males, the ratio of suicides to attempted suicides is 1 to 2.3. Females of all racial groups seem more often to attempt suicide than actually accomplish suicide; but while the ratio of suicide to attempted suicide among the Chinese females is 1 to 4, the corresponding ratio among the White females is 1 to 11.6.

What has been said about crime and suicide is corroborated by some data on the racial incidence of known cases of mental illness in Hawaii. The difficulties involved in the classification of mental illness are obvious, but when two different sources agree, and when both sources are again in agreement with other aspects of life, we have reasonable grounds for taking them with some scientific seriousness. In one study, an analysis of the admissions figures for the year 1947 to the only receiving hospital for psychiatric disorders in Hawaii shows the incidence of mental illness per

100,000 population to be highest among the Whites and lowest among the Chinese (Wedge and Abe 1949). The rate of organic psychoses, however, remained constant in all groups.

These results are matched by figures on "new registrations by race" supplied by the Bureau of Mental Hygiene of the Board of Health of Hawaii, for the years 1947, 1948, and 1949. Here the rates for Whites, though not the highest of all, were double that for Chinese, which again was the lowest.

So whether we look at the normal activities, such as religion or organization, or at abnormal situations, such as mental illnesses or crime, the data are consistent with one another, and with the patterns of competitiveness and situation-centered orientation of life.

This analysis leaves something to be desired, however. It fails to explain why the Chinese will not, at least outwardly, take on all ways of life according to the prestige standards in American society. For example, the highest prestige in America accrues to the white Protestant. If the Chinese in Hawaii are competitive and oriented toward a satisfactory place in the external situation, they should at least want to be Protestant even if they cannot be White.

Again, being an American means to speak good English, to exhibit American manners, and generally to belong to the proper age and status groups. Two investigators in New York City have independently informed me that they have great difficulty in getting college or high school students who have European-born parents to tell them something about their homes or to introduce them to their elders because they are ashamed of the old folks and their ways of life. If the Chinese in Hawaii are competitive and oriented toward a satisfactory place in the external situation, they should at least reject their elders or attempt to do so, like the children of some New York immigrants, especially in view of their own physical differences from white Americans.

These seeming paradoxes will become comprehensible if we introduce a new factor. This is the attraction of the Chinese family and, through it, certain phases of Chinese culture, to the individual. The Chinese kinship organization offers the individual a primary sense of belonging, permanence, and security. It will take a great pull elsewhere to make the individual forego the advantages of being a member of such an organization. That is partly why there is not only little inducement for breaking with the older generation, but there is little crime committed against members of the family.

The advantages are, of course, not without their darker side. Because of the desire to harmonize with the external world and a lack of incentive to break with the older generation, the younger Chinese in Hawaii have little tendency to leave the beaten paths, to be adventurers, to explore new ground and to blaze a new trail, which qualities have, to date, been the mainstay of America's greatness.

V

Having placed some cultural characteristics of the Chinese in Hawaii in perspective, we must now ask two questions. Will the Chinese in Hawaii, in the generations to come, lose their present characteristics? If that should be the case, will it be the most desirable thing for American culture as a whole?

Our answer to the first question is simple. All behavior characteristics which distinguish one people from another are traceable, as far as the science of man has revealed, not to blood, but to cultural history and social organization. As the latter change, the behavior characteristics will change rapidly or more slowly. If a Chinese child is raised entirely in a white home, a white neighborhood, a school of white children, and a society of white individuals, there is little likelihood that he will develop any of the Chinese characteristics portrayed above. On the other hand, as the Chinese in Hawaii live today, their departure from their cultural background is likely to be slower. But with each new generation, the original Chinese characteristics will probably diminish.

This answer leads us to the second question, the answer to which is more complicated. When the term "Americanization" is used, consciously or unconsciously, it refers to two things: One, the process whereby the individual acquires the Anglo-Saxon characteristics of American culture, speaking English, being like Whites in racial characteristics, and embracing Protestantism in religion; two, an emphatic hatred toward all things foreign to the above. For example, a recent refugee from Austria proudly told people that he would not eat anything that he could not order in English and that, as a result, he got along for weeks on doughnuts and coffee. This man might have a personal reason to exaggerate his contempt for his foreign heritage, but his militant attitude toward things foreign is by no means unusual in America. Americans, generally, acknowledge themselves to be bad linguists. But it is not often understood that the root of this apparent lack of ability in foreign languages is to be found in the life in American schools. School children of any foreign background do not dare, for fear of ridicule, speak any other language than English. All enlightened Americans are troubled by racial difficulties in the United States, but it is not often pointed out that the usual attitude toward Americanization is at the root of this intolerance. Since culture, no less than the mind, has an essential unity of its own, it is hardly possible for Americans to be racially tolerant as long as being an American is such a militant fact and as long as all foreign peoples and things are explicitly or implicitly regarded as inferior.

From this point of view, it will be a great loss to American culture if the coming generations of Chinese of Hawaii should lose all their distinctive characteristics; for these characteristics may possibly serve as a moderating factor within the context of American civilization. This is not to minimize the significance of American cultural heritage so far. Without the spirit embodied in the creed of the Protestant pioneers of America, American civilization could hardly have risen to its present height and the American people, as a whole, could hardly have achieved their colossal material prosperity. Chinese cultural characteristics, with their emphasis on harmony with the external world and lack of crusading zeal, could not have done these.

However, what America needs today is not only more physical and industrial conquests, but also more consolidation of the physical gains in human relationships, not only within the United States, but also with the rest of the world. For this purpose, an individual-centered orientation, with its high emotionality and emphasis on all or none, will not fill the bill. If we can understand and accept this fact, and can make some of the qualities of the Chinese in Hawaii truly and actively a part of the great American heritage, we may yet achieve a greater America, as the nation which will offer to mankind not only the technical know-how, but a social architecture which will form a solid foundation for the peace and prosperity among mankind as a whole.

VI

Having concluded that there is a need for a synthesis of some kind between the cultural characteristics of the Chinese in Hawaii and those of America is one thing. How to bring about this synthesis, in face of the present-day tense social climate of America, because of international developments, is quite another. We may have to modify our views on Christianity to achieve this synthesis. We may have to change some of our attitudes toward Americanism. We may have to tell our children that Americans do not necessarily have the best of everything in the whole wide world. Finally, we may have to admit that there are great men in every land, just as there are George Washingtons and Abraham Lincolns in America. These will be difficult things to do and to speak up for; but as long as we can discuss the question freely, we have hope.

NOTES

1. Based on a field work sponsored in 1949 by the Social Science Research Council, the Viking Fund, and the Committee on Research of the Graduate School of Northwestern University. In securing material for the paper, the author acknowledges indebtedness to Chief Justice S. B. Kemp and Associate Justice L. Le Baron of the Supreme Court of the Territory of Hawaii, Judge G. R. Corbett of the First Circuit Court, Chief Dan Liu of the Honolulu Police Department, Professor

C. Glick of the University of Hawaii, and Dr. John G. Lynn IV, of the Bureau of Mental Hygiene of the Territory.

2. Hawaiian term for Caucasians, excluding Portuguese.

3. Usually, in police and court files, the term "sex crime" also includes such other things as adultery, seduction, etc. In this paper, the term refers to the above-named categories only.

4. The term "White" here includes the "Portuguese" and "other Caucasians" in this and other reports.

5. In the corresponding figures pertaining to the Japanese in Hawaii, the contrast to Whites is even more pronounced.

5

Sex Crime and Personality:
A Study in Comparative Cultural Patterns

News reports of sex crimes appear so frequently in the United States today that authorities in diverse fields—psychiatrists, jurists, and police—are deeply concerned. J. Edgar Hoover, for one, has termed sex crimes "a major threat to the women and children of the nation."

How are we meeting this threat? The remedies proposed so far—stricter laws for incarceration of the offender, or more psychiatric services for early identification and confinement of "constitutional psychopathic inferiors"—will not improve the situation as a whole. Those in favor of harsher laws need only remember the failure of Prohibition. That unsuccessful experiment proved that the most thorough police methods will fail to enforce any law to which people do not wish to submit. Those who emphasize the early discovery and treatment of "insanity," so often a defense in murder trials, ignore the fact that actual criminal psychopaths are responsible for but a fraction of all sex crimes. Here is what Dr. Edward Kelleher, chief of the Municipal Court Psychiatric Institute of Chicago, stated last spring: "Our experience shows that the sex offender can be any one, or any kind of a person. Only one-half of one per cent were found to be actual criminal sexual psychopaths. The group of sex offenders as a whole varies as widely in intelligence and stability as any other segment of society."

It seems we must re-examine our entire approach to the problem of the sex criminal, and such a re-examination should begin by realizing that sex crimes are not equally prevalent in all societies. For instance, throughout years of residence and research in China, I found sex crimes to be as rare there as they are prevalent in the United States. In China, such crimes came with military disorder. They resulted from a total social upheaval that was also accompanied by large-scale looting and wanton shooting. Any brief survey of Chinese newspapers printed in peacetime will illustrate this point. You may read there numerous stories of murder, larceny, assault, kidnapping, robbery, brigandage and adultery. But rarely will you see a report of rape and sex murder.

This contrast between China and America is even more striking when we consider the life of the majority of Chinese. Chinese farm and city workers often live on the premises of their employers. These wage earners

This chapter was originally published in *The American Scholar,* Winter 1951–52, pp. 57–66.

do not see their families for months or years at a time. Older Chinese immigrants living in the continental United States carry this pattern to the extreme. Many of them have not seen their families for twenty years or more.

EMOTION OUT OF CONTROL

Recently proposed legal and psychiatric measures to combat sex crimes are inadequate because they place these crimes in a class by themselves. Such suggestions assume these crimes are distinct from all others. They are not. They share a common denominator with hundreds we can remember in yesterday's headlines: the murder of a girl by her jealous twin sister, the torture of a woman by her sadistic man friend, the strangulation of a father by his angry son, or the shooting of a baseball star by a girl he never knew but who decided that, if she could not have him, "nobody else will." The common denominator, to put it simply, is emotion out of control.

The relative vehemence of emotional expression in American patterns of life, and its relative weakness in Chinese patterns, is striking. This is evident in the art of the two nations. Emotions are as conspicuous on American canvasses as they are scarce on Chinese rice papers. When American artists treat humans, they tend to portray humor, reverie, distress, agony, lovesickness, or wretchedness of the soul. Chinese artists, on those rare occasions when they portray the human form, either leave it as a tiny dot in a vast landscape or treat it so that the body is hidden behind heavy clothing and there is no clearly defined facial expression. In American art, emotions are important even in a still-life drawing; in Chinese art, inner feelings are inconspicuous even when human beings are the subject matter. The emotions become still more explosive in modern American painting.

The contrast is equally evident in literature. As a rule, Chinese novels deal with what the characters *do*. American novels are more concerned with what the characters *think* and *feel*. There are, it is true, a few exceptions. But the comparison of any famous Chinese novel, like *The Romance of the Three Kingdoms* or *All Men are Brothers* (both have been translated into English, the second work in full by Pearl S. Buck), with almost any widely hailed American novel, will reveal the absence of introspection in the former and its relative abundance in the latter. No traditional Chinese novelist tells the whole story through the eyes of one character. (The limited point of view, however, is a regular technique of the American novelist.) The American love story usually treats the union of the hero and his girl as the climax of the book. The Chinese novel's treatment of sexual love is not only casual and frank, but union between the lovers ordinarily occurs fairly early in the narrative. The balance of the story tells how the hero marries the heroine *properly* and with what rectifying wedding ceremony.

The contrast in novels is a telling reflection of the actual patterns of life. In the West, a man and woman "fall" in love without (in theory, at least) rhyme or reason. One is at once "mad" about the other, and both parties are pleasantly doomed. When two lovers appear in public with their arms around each other, the rest of the world can go by. On the other hand, modern Chinese youths, though attracted to many American ideas and practices, conduct their love affairs quite differently. The majority want freedom of choice in marriage. But their greatest concern remains the opinion and feeling of their parents.

The letters to Chinese "Dorothy Dixes" are interesting in this respect. Not only are Chinese young people sensitive to parental interference, but also to that from brothers or sisters. Even an incomplete education may cause serious concern, but rarely have I seen a letter raising questions of compatibility between the two young persons. This is in line with the public attitude of Chinese lovers toward each other. They regard all public intimacy between the sexes as indecent. An American in love asks the question: "How does my heart feel?" A Chinese asks: "What will other people say?" American men and women marry because they are "crazy" about each other. But an age-old Chinese adage says of a woman's marriage:

She'll go, she'll go;
For meals, for clothes.

The differences go further. People who clutter up the matter of choosing a mate with so many practical considerations are not likely to be as ardent lovers as those who depend primarily upon their own feelings. Love and hatred come from the same psychological forces and the intensity that applies to one applies also to the other. The Chinese, when he does hate, tends to fall short of the American's intensity, determination and finality. Not only are sex crimes rare in China, but all crimes motivated by runaway emotions are equally unusual.

The murder of a man by his wife occurred occasionally in the olden days because this was a married woman's single road to freedom. But murder because of hatred, despite the many difficult problems of adjustment within a Chinese household, was almost unheard of. Murder, in Chinese saying, is "taking life because of the desire for wealth." And practical motives were most certainly behind the numerous tortures in Chinese prisons not so long ago, or the bloody intrigues among the aristocrats during the dynastic days.

This remains true in modern cities where the crime of passion is still the exception. When an angry son hurled a knife and killed his father in 1946, shocked newspaper editors vehemently denounced him. In another case, the emotions involved were not even powerful enough to sustain the attacker through his acts. In 1945, a jilted college student slashed his girl's wrists and shoulder several times with a knife and then jumped into a shallow lake. Both recovered, and the youth who had attempted the murder-suicide faced a barrage of editorial castigation. One professor characterized the affair as a "dirty and ugly business." We should remember that both cases were sensational simply because of their rarity.

So whether we look at art, literature, romance or actual family relations, the same contrasts obtain:

1. In American life, strong emotions and their individual expression stand out; in Chinese life, lack of strong emotions and a sensitivity to social opinion are important.

2. The centering of American attention on individual emotions tends to intensify them; Chinese concern for the reactions of others tends to moderate the emotions.

This is why Chinese feel that Americans are unpredictable, while Americans say Chinese are "inscrutable," masters of self-control. Americans are not so predictable as Chinese because they follow their individual predilections more than Chinese do. More vehement emotionally, they may explode where the Chinese will not. Chinese are noted for their impassivity because they heed the dictates of external circumstances more than Americans do. Less overtly emotional, they feel at ease where Americans do not.

CONTRASTING PATTERNS OF FAMILY LIFE

What is the origin of these contrasting American and Chinese personality characteristics? The most obvious factors are seen in those phases of family life in which America and China consistently differ.

To begin with, while the average size of the Chinese family is smaller than popularly imagined, it usually consists of more than one married couple and more than two generations living under one roof. Very early in life, therefore, the Chinese comes into *constant* contact with a larger number of relatives than the American does.

Far more important are the respective patterns of family behavior. First, the basic tendency of the American family is toward rugged individualism. Each new generation replaces the old, and old age is synonymous with being relegated to the background. The Chinese family, on the other hand, emphasizes loyalty to the lineage. Old age leads to a more respected status. Secondly, American parents are the sole agents of control over their minor children. Even when grandparents exercise authority during an emergency, they merely follow the rules laid down by the parents.

Partly because of their fear of being replaced, American parents are likely to be jealous of any infringement on their right to sole control. Chinese parents, lacking such fear, are less touchy about interference with their authority. The liberty taken by most Chinese relatives would break up the majority of American homes. Furthermore, while most American children do not assume adult roles until they are legally of age, Chinese

children are delegated mature responsibilities as soon as they are physically and mentally ready.

The results of these broad differences in family patterns are far-
reaching, and once begun, they are bolstered by many forces in the
respective societies. The more exclusive and omnipresent parental control
in America makes the parental image stand out above all else in the mind
of the young. A child's attitude, whether of dependence or rebellion,
becomes focused upon the parents, since they are the sole sources of
reward or punishment. The American family pattern thus nourishes a
personality marked by strong emotions and preoccupation with the self.

The diluted and less final parental control in China evokes early in life
an appreciation of the differences between changing external circumstances. Since parents are not the sole determinants in punishment or
reward, they do not become the chief oppressors or only gods. Therefore,
there is a less turbulent opposition or paralyzing attachment between
parents and children. The parental image in the mind of the individual has
its proper place with those of other relatives. The Chinese family pattern is
thus the source of a personality characterized by more moderate emotions
and a desire for harmony with the external world.[1]

MARTYRDOM, BIGOTRY AND ORGANIZATIONAL STRENGTH

However, the American personality has certain qualities the Chinese
personality does not possess. Chinese, with their comparatively placid
reaction to the world, are usually difficult to stir up. Americans, stronger
emotionally, are more easily touched by men and events. The Chinese
personality is essentially conservative; it tends to be cautious and works
toward compromise. The American personality is potentially more progressive; it tends to drive toward given ends without remorse. The Chinese
personality blunders less, but the American personality accomplishes
more.

Thus, while there is a small minority of Americans who commit violent
crimes of passion, the great body of Americans are given to spontaneous
acts of kindness, kindness on a scale and with a promptitude scarcely
equalled elsewhere in the world. A girl trapped underground kept the
whole nation in suspense. Another girl disfigured while rescuing her
brothers and sisters was showered with countless gifts from every part of
the country. Similarly, while many Americans have been easy prey for
organizations like the Ku Klux Klan, the Bund, and the Christian Front,
many more Americans have vigorously supported the March of Dimes,
domestic charities, CARE and other international relief agencies.

Largely as a result of difference in personality orientation, the histories
of social organizations in the two countries are very dissimilar, despite the
fact that Chinese and Americans have qualities in common. Both are, for
example, suspicious of public officials and regimentation. The old Chinese

dynasties ruled not by active control over the people but by the people's passive acquiescence.

But there are vital differences in the social organizations of China and America that reflect the peoples' different personality orientation. Though tensions are not unusual in American corporations, associations and unions, these groups have a longer life and a greater vitality that leads to expansion. Most Chinese organizations make an auspicious start and then peter out. The only lasting organizations in old China were those based in concrete relationships such as a village, district or trade. Enthusiasm for an abstract ideology or the remote possibility of greater things to come was rare. Americans support a particular government or political party with determination and solidarity, even though quarrels are common; but at the height of the Nationalists' popularity in China, the party suffered from serious defections within its own ranks.

There is no mystery in all this. Emotional intensity enables Americans to combine with each other when they are aroused. The lack of this quality causes the Chinese to be less perseverant because their emotions ebb easily. Furthermore, with their self-preoccupation, Americans are likely to be more concerned with their individual responsibilities. Chinese, being sensitive to external circumstances, tend so to exaggerate any slackening of effort in the next person that a general stampede and a collapse of the entire organization often result.

That is why in America a change of political allegiance by any prominent person is a matter of public censure, while the few bureaucrats in Chinese history who have refused to serve under a new dynasty have been hailed as the greatest of the great. This is also why, during the present period of change, there has been little voluntary exodus from China comparable to that from Russia after 1917, and it is unlikely that the emerging administration will be drastically non-Chinese.

This does not mean that voluntary martyrdom is absent from Chinese culture. Many famous Chinese have given their lives for causes which were of no profit to themselves or their children. For example, in 1519, numerous high officials chose execution or exile rather than support the emperor's wish to leave his capital on a pleasure trip. Such a display of courage is not an isolated example. But the objectives which Chinese martyrs opposed were those that violated certain traditions, ways of behavior that must be observed in the manner of the forbears who set them. Americans, however, characteristically have fought to defend the Constitution not for tradition's sake but in the name of liberty and freedom for themselves and the generations to come. In other words, Chinese have most often interpreted the present in terms of the *concrete* past. Americans have strong feelings about the present in terms of the *imagined* future.

Bigotry is the extreme negative expression of the American personality type; opportunism is the Chinese complement. As extremes are rare, the vast majority of each society merely incline toward one or the other pole of their respective strengths or weaknesses. But the consequences of these inclinations cannot be overestimated. If this analysis is at all correct, the higher incidence of crimes motivated by runaway emotions in America must be linked to the same sources of energy which have made America great. Such crimes are, therefore, one of the prices for American civilization.

THE PERILS OF SELF RELIANCE

The question we now face is: Can the sources of such crimes be reduced without at the same time doing serious damage to the mainspring of American civilization? Many contributing factors come to mind. We need, for example, to re-examine the role of Puritanism in American culture. A more realistic approach to certain sex problems is in order. We need, also, to question the wisdom of an exaggerated pattern of romantic love in marriage. The emotional upheaval of disappointment should be reduced. Most important of all, however, is the need to reevaluate the meaning of self-reliance as it is encouraged in American homes, schools, and the society as a whole. Self-reliance has two facets. On the one hand, it consists of a strong emphasis on individual differences. On the other, it involves an exaggerated feeling for the self.

There is no doubt that, except for identical twins, no two individuals are biologically alike. Nor is there any doubt that, in a democratic society, the maximum realization of all individual potentialities is of great consequence. It is no accident that in America intelligence tests, which purport to reveal individual differences, and psychoanalysis, which deepens and intensifies the feeling for self, have both achieved great popularity. The prevalence of the "scientific" view, carried to an extreme in progressive schools, that infants and children "know best" for themselves, must be understood in the same light.

However, like all good things, self-reliance can be overstressed. When educators reiterate the necessity of encouraging in youngsters a natural sex attitude, they often forget that, to be completely natural, man must return to the caves. When parents, hoping to fit their offspring for life in a democratic society, encourage them to be independent and aggressive, they should recall that excessive independence leads to anarchy. When people point to huge American enterprises as examples of what unflinching individual efforts can accomplish, they will do well to note also that crimes of passion spring from the same uncontrolled individual predilections.

Furthermore, no society will survive if self-reliance is exaggerated to the point where it overshadows common interests and co-operation. In times of war, the men who play the most important roles must be alike not only in their attitude and action, but also in their dress and much of their private life. Even in the absence of an emergency, the basic fact about modern life is man's increasing dependence upon society and culture to aid him in his struggle against natural and social obstacles, for the preservation of his freedom and the realization of his potentialities. The more complex the society and the culture, the greater the dependence of the individual upon his group.

It is true that minimizing self-reliance will have a moderating effect on American life in general. But American society, having reached its present height, today needs more social consolidation, so that people can take time out to appreciate what they have and to appreciate each other—not more industrial and commercial conquests in the course of which people hurriedly live and hastily die. This need is not satisfied by the relatively temporary sense of solidarity accompanying an emergent crisis, which Americans have always been able to achieve. Much more nearly permanent, it will require a considerable modification of the prevalent fundamentally personal outlook. The present international difficulties make this outlook more imperative, not less.

A society with an overdeveloped pattern of group conformity runs the danger of stagnation, but a society with an overdeveloped pattern of individualism tends ultimately to destroy itself by internal explosions. In the latter type of society, unless the pattern of life is modified in time, crimes motivated by runaway emotions will increase as frontiers diminish. The place of an ideal society is somewhere between the extremes.

In the light of the foregoing, we shall be unrealistic if we expect the psychiatrist or the policeman to be a sufficiently effective check on sex crimes. Psychiatrists may straighten out some aberrant individuals; the police will protect some possible victims: neither can stem the tide flowing from a pattern of life.

NOTE

1. The contrast made here has nothing to do with the popularly known concepts of *introversion* and *extroversion*. Both Chinese and Americans may be introverts, persons who deal with reality by thought. Or they may be extroverts, persons who deal with reality by action. But the Chinese tends to mobilize his thought or action for the purpose of *conforming* to the reality, while the American tends to do the same for the purpose of *making* the reality conform to him. The business man who talks about creating a demand for goods he wants to sell is an example of American extrovert personality. An old time Chinese business man, on the other hand, would be interested merely in filling existing needs.

6

Culture Pattern and Adolescent Behaviour

The attention focused on adolescence in this country during the past decade and a half is probably without parallel in human history. The psychiatrist, the educator, the juvenile court officer, the business man, the newspaper reporter and, frequently, bewildered parents have all contributed to this emphasis on teenage problems and behaviour. The increased concern with every facet of adolescent life is apparent from the many conferences, including those in the White House, on juvenile problems and by counting the number of articles related to teenagers in the *Readers Guide to Periodical Literature*. From 1955 to 1957 there were fifty-one articles on the subject, as compared with sixteen in the years 1941–43, and only three in 1919–21.

Although much of the emphasis on this transitional period between childhood and maturity lies in the realm of sensationalism related to pathological behaviour—to the 5 per cent or so of deviant adolescents who are "acting out" their frustrations in an unhealthy manner—the increasing trend in the U.S. towards juvenile violence, with concomitant emotional disturbance, is a matter of realistic concern to social scientists. Psychologists and sociologists generally assume that adolescent stresses stem from major biological and social adjustments, which seem to be an unavoidable part of the transitional period. Cultural anthropologists, on the other hand, are less pessimistic. They have been interested in certain cultural factors which may be linked with relatively low incidence of violence among adolescents, as well as those cultural factors which appear to make the process of growing-up less traumatic than others.

THE RORSCHACH FINDINGS

In 1949 one of the co-authors of this article carried out a seven-month period of field work among the Chinese in Hawaii.[1] Part of this field research was to collect Rorschach protocals.[2] Of the 115 Chinese tested, the records of 28 boys and girls, aged 14 to 19 years (mean age 16.03 years), are examined. These individuals, selected on a random basis from two high schools, one public and one private, were estimated by their teachers to be "fairly good" students of average to high average intelligence with no outstanding academic or emotional problems.

This chapter was originally published in *The International Journal of Social Psychiatry*, Vol. 7, No. 1, 1961, with Blanche Watrous and Edith Lord, pp. 35–53.

The records were first scored, according to Klopfer, and analysed by Edith Lord.[3] To facilitate comparison with the Thetford, Molish and Beck study of personality structure in normal American adolescents (1951), they were re-scored by Watrous, according to Beck's system, to determine the amounts of organizing activity (total Z score) and the incidence of autistic fantasy (M -).[4]

Hawaii Adolescents Males 19, Females 9

Total No. of subjects..............28
Age range...................... 14–19
Mean range 16.0
Total R........................ 84.3
Mean R........................ 30.1

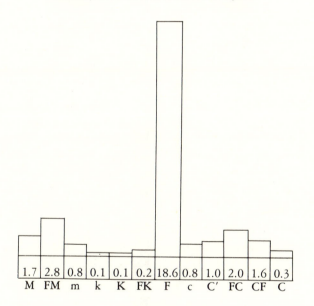

1.7	2.8	0.8	0.1	0.1	0.2	18.6	0.8	1.0	2.0	1.6	0.3
M	FM	m	k	K	FK	F	c	C′	FC	CF	C

Figure 1

Table A
Mean W = 8.4; W% 28
Mean D = 14.3; D% 47
Mean d = 2.9; d% 10
Mean Dd = 3.8; Dd% 13
Mean S = 0.3; S% 1
Mean Dd + S = 4.1; Dd + S% 14

Table B
Mean F% 62
Mean A% 40
Mean εC 3.1
Mean M:εC 1.7:3.1
Mean W:M 8.4:1.7
Mean P 12 (actual No., 3.8)

The composite psychogram (Fig. 1) gives the immediate impression of a predominantly healthy personality structure. The number of responses is within the average range (30.1), the intellectual approach (W-D-d-Dd+S%) suggests that these adolescents have good ability to integrate experience and to evaluate their environment with common-sense judgment and sensitivity. The Hawaiian Chinese adolescents have a healthy respect for reality with a slight tendency to over-rationalization (F%). Their greater response to external than to internal stimuli (M: Sum of C) might indicate that they are "doers" rather than "dreamers." At the same time their emotions seem smoothly integrated into their total personality functioning. Adaptivity (A%) and conventional conformity (P) are again within normal range. This psychogram compares favourably with Beck's Spiegel sample for "normal" American adults (Fig. 2).

Chicago Adults and Hawaii Adolescents

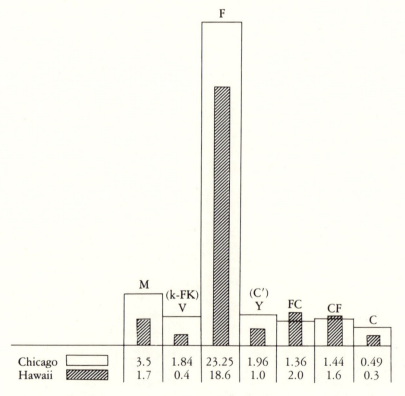

	M	(k-FK) V	F	(C') Y	FC	CF	C
Chicago	3.5	1.84	23.25	1.96	1.36	1.44	0.49
Hawaii	1.7	0.4	18.6	1.0	2.0	1.6	0.3

Figure 2

Lord, who analysed the adolescent records before, observes: "We therefore may state . . . that the healthy emotionality . . . is not a function of youth or age but is a part of the Chinese personality. Chinese, including adults, have in their personalities a considerable portion of animal-spirit; they tend to retain the habit of problem-solving—associated with youthfulness in the Western world—by action rather than by fantasying. The tendency towards over-rationalization persists but is less intense among the adults. . . . There is a slight increase in the amount of internal living. Also, intellectual life slightly outweighs emotional life with the adult population" (Edith Lord: personal communication). This observation is seemingly not shared by Richards, who says that "it would be close to impossible to pick up a Rorschach record and identify the subject as belonging to a group designated by Dr. Hsu as Hawaiian Chinese." (T. W. Richards, 1954, analysed 35 Rorschach protocals of Hawaiian Chinese adults from the same 115 collected by Hsu.)

We agree with Richards to the extent that psychograms alone are not an infallible means of distinguishing his Hawaiian Chinese adults from white American adults. But when our adolescent records are compared with those in the Thetford, Molish and Beck study (1951), certain significant differences as well as similarities stand out. In the following pages, for the sake of brevity, the subjects in the Thetford, Molish and Beck study will be designated as "Chicago" group or "Chicagoans," and the subjects in the Hsu study as "Hawaii" group or "Hawaiians." The 24 adolescents in the former study are among 155 Chicago public school children selected with the same criteria used by Hsu: "normal intelligence, freedom from overt behaviour problems discernible by their teachers, and an average academic achievement." Even the ages of the two groups of subjects are nearly identical, as shown by Table 1.

Table 1
AGE OF ADOLESCENTS

	Total No.	Boys	Girls	Age Range	Mean C.A.
Hawaii	28	19	9	14–19 yrs.	16.03 yrs.
Chicago	24	14	10	14–17 yrs. 11 mos.	15 yrs. 8 mos.

Let us now compare the characteristics of the two sets of records. In total productivity (R), the Chicago youngster possesses a considerably greater amount of intellectual energy than do the Hawaiians:

Table 2
PRODUCTIVITY (R)

	N	Mean	SD
Hawaii	28	30.10	19.80
Chicago	24	41.35	15.00

The Hawaiian adolescents seem to be typically cautious, constricted, and conventional when faced with a new and threatening situation. On the first Rorschach card, more than half the Hawaiian adolescents gave only 1 or 2 associations and almost one-half showed marked rigidity (F% 100).

(a) Intellectual approach

Intellectually, the Hawaiians exhibit a fairly well-rounded approach (Fig. 1) with W% 28, D% 47, d% 10, Dd S% 14. This percentage of whole, large detail and small detail responses conforms to Klopfer's optimum—with a slightly greater per cent of tiny detail and white space percepts than is considered desirable. The average number of S, 0.84, for the group is low; only 7 boys and 2 girls used white space for the location of percepts. The Hawaiians, therefore, seem conspicuously lacking in oppositional tendencies or in feelings of self-assertiveness.

Although the Hawaiians cannot be compared directly with the Chicago adolescents in terms of intellectual approach, because of differences in the Beck and Klopfer scoring of location areas (see Note 4), the degree of organizing activity (Z) sheds some light on the similarities of the two groups with respect to intellectual functioning. Beck has advanced the Z score "as an index to the organizational aspects of intellectual functioning as revealed by the Rorschach test," (Thetford et al. 1951: 61) postulating that "drive and intellectual level are the two personality components most closely related to this ability." The ability to organize meaningful environmental elements is similar to the ability to produce whole responses. As noted below, the Hawaiian adolescents show slightly greater organizing activity than the mainland groups:

Table 3
ORGANIZING ACTIVITY
Z Score Total

	N	Mean	SD
Hawaiians	28	31.60	22.10
Chicagoans	24	28.90	23.00

Thus, while the Chicago group shows greater quantity of intellectual energy (R), the Hawaiians may use their drive more constructively. The large Standard Deviations in both groups indicate, of course, in statistical terms, that the intra-group variation is greater than inter-group variation. This fact does not, however, negate the importance of the overall inter-group differences.

A striking difference between the two groups lies in the high ratio of W to M (whole responses to human movement percepts) given by the Hawaiians. Twenty-seven of the 28 tested gave a higher ratio of W:M with only one male showing a ratio of W:M, 1:2; another male gave a ratio of W:M, 17:1, while others gave ratios of 22:2, 9:0, 8:0, 8:1 (Hertz and Margulies 1943).

(b) Fantasy

The average quantity of fantasy production, as noted above, is 1.7 M. Although this average is too high to suggest marked repressive emphasis, there is some reluctance among the Hawaiian adolescents to use fantasy as a personality defence. Twenty-five per cent of the subjects tested gave no M response, and only one subject (with an extremely high Sum C) gave 5 M associations or 8 per cent of his total output. The quality of the fantasy is particularly significant in assessing Hawaiian personality. Only one-fourth of the total number of 47 fantasy percepts are extensor—connoting active, striving imagination or suggesting an unconscious effort on the part of the subject to free himself from restraints.[5] No subject had more than 1 extensor M. The predominant adolescent-fantasy, on the other hand, is flector M, related to the need to submit to the stresses of the environment, to accept passively, to be submissively resigned to one's difficulties. It is also interesting to note, in terms of this passive adjustment, that the infrequent extensor M occurred only in records containing flector or static M. Typical expressions of Hawaiian fantasy appeared in card III. They are ones such as "two people trying to carry something," "two persons struggling to lift . . ." etc., which are clearly flector in quality, or the Hawaiians use static fantasy, with people "talking," "standing," or "looking." Thus, the Hawaiian adolescents do not appear "ambition-ridden." Their goals are probably those which are realistic of attainment. They do not fight against their environment but accept environmental stresses passively—as suggested by both the low incidence of oppositional tendencies (S) together with the submissive quality of the fantasy.

Table 4
PERCENTAGE DISTRIBUTION OF M-

Number of Responses	Hawaiian Adolescent %	Chicago Adolescent %
3 (or more)	0	0
2	0	4
1	10	25
0	90	71
Mean	0.10	0.33
SD	0.39	0.56

In absolute number, only one Hawaiian gave one M-. Thus, the Hawaiian adolescents would appear, only minimally, to resort to this potentially pathological personality defence as compared to the greater incidence of such behaviour in the Chicago group.

Male Adolescents; N = 19; Age 14–19; Mean Age 15.84
Female Adolescents; N = 9; Age 15–19, Mean Age 16.22

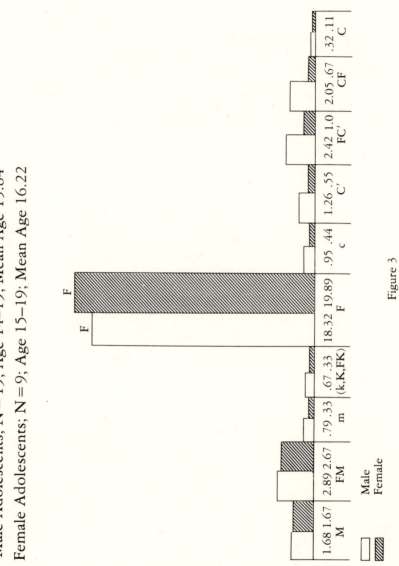

Figure 3

The re-scoring of Hawaiian M responses according to Beck (Note 3) shows the near absence of autistic or highly personal fantasy (M -) among these adolescents. Beck has related this finding in anxious, non-schizophrenic adolescents to "the loss of a parent for purposes of support to the child" (Beck 1952: 53); the parent is failing to provide the needed warmth of feeling. Beck has also noted these Rorschach test associations in schizophrenics of all ages.

In terms of purely formal control, the Hawaiians could be considered somewhat constricted (F% 62). But the males with a mean of 59% appear to be more relaxed and less cautious when compared with the females with a mean of 71% F (see Fig. 3). Likewise the males show more ability to engage in generalized thinking whereas the females show more practical judgment.

Table 5a

Male Adolescents

N	19	(H + A) : (Hd + Ad)	
Mean R	31.6	3.26 + 10 : 2.26 + 3.67	
Mean F%	59	13.26 : 5.93	
Mean A%	40	(FM + m) : (Fc + c + C')	
Mean εC	3.74	(2.89 + 0.79) : (0.95 + 1.26)	
Mean M:εC	1.68:3.74	13 : 6.93	
Mean W:M	9.26:1.68		
Mean P	3.7		
Mean W = 9.26 W%	3.0		
Mean D = 14.0 D%	45		
Mean d = 3.26 d%	11		
Mean Dd = 3.58 Dd%	11		
Mean S = 0.84 S%	3		
Dd + S = 4.42%	14		

Table 5b

Female Adolescents

N	9	(H + A) : (Hd + Ad)	
Mean R	28	(3.0 + 8.67) : (2.55 + 3.78)	
Mean F%	71	11.67 : 6.33	
Mean A%	40	(Fm + m) : (Fc + c + C')	
Mean εC	1.34	(2.67 + 0.67) : (0.44 + 0.055)	
Mean M:εC	1.67:1.34	3.34 : 0.99 X	
Mean W:M	6.67:1.67		
Mean P	3.9		
Mean W = 6.67%	24		
Mean D = 14.89%	53		
Mean d = 2.11%	.8		
Mean Dd = 4.22%	15		
Mean S = 0.11	0.4		
Dd + S = 4.33%	15		

A rough comparison of Beck's vista response (FV) among the Chicago adolescents, whose mean FV is 1.87, with the Hawaiian adolescents, whose mean is 0.2 FV (FK), points up the fact that the latter have fewer self-appraisal tendencies and less self-consciousness than the former. Similarly, despite the fact that Hsu specifically inquired for shading responses (C'), the Hawaiian mean in this category is much less than Beck's mean, 1.0 FY (C') versus 2.50 FY. Thus, the Chinese seem to have not only fewer feelings of intellectual inadequacy than the American adolescents but possibly fewer dysphoric feelings as well, although these interpretations should be considered with caution because of the limited nature of the research.

(c) Emotionality

The total response of the Chinese adolescents to bright colour, as noted below, is strikingly similar to that in the Chicago group:

Table 6
SUM OF COLOUR (SUM OF C) RESPONSES

	N	Mean	SD
Hawaiians	28	3.10	1.64
Chicagoans	24	3.03	3.02

The Sum of Colour is considered an index to the amount of affective energy available for coping with the external environment. Among the Chinese adolescents only 3 subjects, all girls, gave no associations with bright colour determinants (10%). When the colour responses are differentiated as to form-colour (FC), colour-form (CF), and pure colour (C), there are certain interesting contrasts between the Chinese and American adolescents:

Table 7
FC RESPONSES

	N	Mean	SD
Hawaiians	28	2.0	3.14
Chicagoans	24	1.13	1.67

Table 8
CF RESPONSES

	N	Mean	SD
Hawaiians	28	1.67	0.94
Chicagoans	24	1.92	2.08

Table 9
C RESPONSES

	N	Mean	SD
Hawaiians	28	0.30	0.82
Chicagoans	24	0.33	0.62

When the ratios FC:CF of the Hawaiians and Chicagoans are compared, the former's ratio of 2.0:1.67 suggests a more mature emotional rapport than the latter's ratio of 1.67:1.92. This greater degree of identification with others and greater responsiveness to the needs of others again are both consistent, as we shall see later, with the varying childhood emphases of the two groups. On this basis it could be predicted that the Hawaiian adolescents would not temporarily regress into emotional outbursts and stormy explosions as frequently as would teenagers in Chicago.

(d) Content

There are other significant differences between the Hawaiians and the Chicagoans. The animal response (A) is considered an index of adaptability. According to Beck the mean A% of his control group is 46.87, and its standard deviation, 17.58 (Beck 1952: 15). The mean A of the Hawaii adolescents and that of the Chicago group are both similar to Beck's control group, except that the Hawaii group is slightly more flexible and less stereotyped than the Chicago group, the figures being 40.0% for the former and 44.50% for the latter.

The ability to perceive whole human associations (H) is interpreted as an index of empathy with other people. Beck speculates that perception of H varies directly with intelligence: the greater the number of H, the greater the degree of intellectual liberation. The perception of the part human or human detail (Hd) suggests less liberation of this kind of energy. The mean H response of the Hawaiian and Chicago groups is almost identical:

Table 10
H RESPONSES

	N	Mean	SD
Hawaii	28	3.43	3.35
Chicago	24	3.50	3.06

There are, however, differences in the Hd responses:
Table 11
Hd RESPONSES

	N	Mean	SD
Hawaii	28	2.25	3.18
Chicago	24	4.16	3.98

The higher Hd than H mean of the Chicago group as compared with the Hawaiian sample raises several questions. Thetford, Molish and Beck (1951: 65ff.), comparing their Chicago children's findings with the adult (Spiegl) findings, reported in the literature that the adults show higher whole human than part human (H:Hd). They also found that among the Chicago children the mean Hd increased at each of the three developmental stages investigated, leading them to speculate as to whether inhibitory processes were operating in childhood and adolescence. When the H and Hd of the adult and Hawaiian adolescents are compared, the same ratio of higher H than Hd obtains:

Table 12
HAWAIIAN H AND Hd RESPONSES

	N	Mean H	Mean Hd
Adults	39	4.56	2.18
Adolescents	28	3.43	2.25

These findings lead us to suggest that while among the Hawaiians as among the Chicagoans the number of H responses varies directly with intelligence, the ratio of higher H than Hd responses among the Hawaiian adolescents indicates a greater degree of mental freedom.

Acculturation among the adolescent Hawaiian Chinese apparently proceeds far more smoothly than among many groups subjected to the influence of alien cultures. That this process is achieved without disruption of pre-existing goals and ideals is apparent in the similarity of "normal" American and Hawaiian psychograms, and by the absence of conspicuous psycho-neurotic behaviour. These youngsters show neither autistic fantasy activity nor uncontrolled emotionality. There is no serious imbalance between their inner living and their response to the external environment. Although the adolescents are sensitive to their social environment, they do not appear hypercritical or suspicious. Their degree of wariness appears normal (H + A:Hd + Ad = 12.33:6.13). They are certainly not overly concerned with bodily anxiety (low mean At [anatomy] response). The genral range of their content is healthy. Most significantly, their reality testing is at a healthy level, and their occasional uncritical thinking seems benign in nature.

From Rorschach findings the overwhelming feature in the personality pattern of the adolescent Hawaiians appears to be the retention of the Chinese traditional psychological orientation in alien soil. The traditional respect for the father figure, acceptance of authority symbols and, inferentially, of paternal traditions remain—particularly among the males. There is little rebellion on the surface and there are few rebellious strivings within. The conflict of generations is not superficially apparent. These adolescents are socially adaptive, for the most part emotionally unperturbed. The boys do not seem overly anxious about their masculine rôle, and the girls do not seem to reject their femininity. These youngsters have apparently no passionate wish to change; no felt need to alter their environment. They tend to accept their rôles and they seek goals within their grasp. It is doubtful if they will become "big achievers," or will be flamboyantly successful by American standards. It is equally doubtful that they will become "discontents" or that their ego organization will become disruptive. A more detailed comparison of the Hawaiian adolescents with the Thetford, Molish and Beck study of 24 normal Chicago adolescents yields the following similarities and differences:

(1) The intellectual approach of the two groups is roughly similar, with the Chicago youth having a greater amount of intellectual energy at their disposal, but with the Hawaiians exploiting their mental resources in a somewhat more constructive, ambitious manner.

(2) Both quantity and quality of Hawaiian fantasy depart from the white American pattern. The Chicago youth show greater dependence upon inner living, with the Hawaiian adolescent more reluctant to internalize stresses; Hawaiian fantasy, when expressed, is predominantly passive in nature, suggesting submissive acceptance of the environment. The incidence of creative imagination among the Hawaiians is, however, optimally proportionate to their level of drive. Also significantly, the Hawaiians show a lower incidence of autistic, pathological fantasy than the American youth.

(3) The Hawaiian Chinese seem to have fewer self-appraisal tendencies and fewer dysphoric reactions than the Chicago group.

(4) The two groups show a surprisingly similar quantity of affective energy. However, the Hawaiians exhibit less emotional immaturity, more empathy and greater sensitivity to the needs of others. The affect expressed is less egocentric than among the Chicago group.

(5) Both groups show healthy intellectual adaptivity. However, the Chicago sample suggests more inhibitory, more wary behaviour with respect to other individuals than the Hawaiians.

THE WIDER CULTURAL PERSPECTIVE

Margaret Mead was the anthropological pioneer who first pointed out that adolescent turbulence, regarded as universal by the Westerners, was absent in Samoa (Mead 1928). The Chinese in Hawaii are also rarely troubled by adolescent difficulties. In racial composition the Chinese make up a little less than 6 per cent of the total population in Hawaii. The majority of the original Chinese migrated to the islands during the latter half of the 19th century. Today most of the Chinese in Hawaii are second, third and fourth generation Americans, spreading over the entire economic and social ladder of the state. Even by 1930, 50 per cent of the males and 70 per cent of the females were engaged in "preferred" occupations. In 1949 there were no Chinese hand laundry establishments in the islands. Instead there were Chinese banks, department stores, and a wide variety of business and industrial establishments. A majority of the Chinese live outside the bounds of "Chinatown" in Honolulu. By 1949, the Chinese had a greater percentage of school attendance than all other racial groups. Most Chinese speak excellent English and live in American style. According to the usual standards, the Chinese of Hawaii, except for physical type, seem very American. Certain cultural differences from the average American are, however, apparent: though most present-day Chinese in Hawaii have become Catholics or Protestants, there are also Chinese Mormons, Chinese Bahaians and Chinese Buddhists. As a rule, rather than the exception, members of the same family have different religious affiliations: for example, there may be a Catholic father, a Methodist son, an Episcopalian daughter, while the mother continues to worship at Chinese temples. Differences in religion do not seem to affect family solidarity, and Christian children frequently go with their elders to Chinese temples—seeing no inconsistency in this behaviour. The relationships between marriage partners and between parents and children appear more casual and less intense than among white Americans. But their adolescents are family oriented to a much greater degree than the average teenager on the mainland of the U.S. It is not that the Chinese boys and girls in Hawaii do not desire independence. They do, but, at the same time, they accept parental injunction and control in general. For example, the adolescents prefer to choose their own mates, set up their independent households, name their children and themselves according to prevailing fashion. However, if parental wishes are opposed, they tend to be less insistent upon these prerogatives than would most young white Americans. They seem to be less sensitive about parental interference. They are more inclined to accept a compromise situation, reconciling the wishes of their parents with their own preferences, even in the matter of mate selection. The most striking difference, in fact, between the Chinese American adolescents in Hawaii and white American adolescents on the mainland is the absence of overt rebellion against authority. The "big fight" with parents is lacking. The Chinese in Hawaii are simply not troubled by adolescent difficulties. Both police files and interviews with parents and social workers suggest that the "problem adolescent," when found, is an exception. It is a common fact among Chinese parents in Hawaii that, while white Americans anticipate more problems as their children approach adolescence, they expect less and less problems as their children progress in age.[6]

All these observations bear out our Rorschach findings. We must ask, then, what are the factors which make for a relative lack of adolescent turbulence among Chinese Americans and a relative abundance of it among white Americans?

Our hypothesis is that the Chinese way of life is situation-centred and that of the Americans is individual-centred. (The hypothesis and its application which follow were developed by Hsu, with which Watrous and Lord do not necessarily concur.) The situation-centred way of life encourages the individual to find a satisfactory adjustment with the external environment of men and things, while the individual centred pattern enjoins the individual to find means of fulfilling his own desires and ambitions. The individual-centred man tends not only to view the world in absolutist terms, but also to insist on standing or falling alone. As a result he is likely to experience much emotional conflict. His triumphs are moments of effusive and public ecstasy, and his failures are moments of deep and secret misery. In neither can he really share with others, especially the latter. Never being sure of his human relations, he has a perpetual fear of failure, though he jealously guards his privacy, however dear that privacy costs. The situation-centred man tends not only to view the world in relativistic terms, but also consciously to seek mutual dependence with circles of fellow men. As a result he enjoys a great deal of mental ease. His triumphs are never solely a vindication of his own noble qualities, for his parents, relatives and departed ancestors have all generously contributed. Similarly, his failures are never a complete proof of his own inability to make the grade, for his parents, relatives and departed ancestors share the blame. Securely anchored in his primary groups, he is always protected from being a complete failure, though often he suffers from too many relatives. (A complete statement of this hypothesis and extensive qualitative documentation of it are given in Hsu, 1953).

In order to show how this hypothesis can help us to explain the psychological contrasts between our Hawaii and Chicago adolescents we propose to examine four factors bearing on the life of the adolescent: (*a*) childhood experiences; (*b*) parental attitudes; (*c*) the rôle of the peer group; and (d) the demands of the wider society.

Childhood Experiences

Before two years of age Chinese children have, as a rule, a secure environment. Among both the wealthy and the poor the customary Chinese practice is to feed the baby, or heed it in some other way, whenever it cries. The wealthy parents do so with the aid of wet nurses and servants. The poor mothers carry their young ones on their backs when they go to the fields. As soon as the child is weaned the picture is, however, somewhat different. In matters of food and clothing, the basic pattern remains one of complete and nearly unregulated satisfaction. The children of the poor may be forced to undergo uncertainty and want by necessity, but that is not the intention of their parents and the little ones can see it for themselves. The children of the rich can get anything they want. They are constantly spoiled by servants. But in social and ceremonial matters the attitudes of the Chinese parents are less tolerant. In the first place, children are praised and rewarded, or rebuked and punished, in direct proportion to their ability to measure up to adult behaviour standards. Chinese parents do not seem to worry about frustration or security in their children. They are much more concerned with the question of social and ritual propriety. While in every society it is the wealthy families who try to conform to the culturally upheld ideal, the weight of this Chinese pattern was often even felt by the children of the comparatively poor. There is a widely circulated and dramatized folk-tale which, though extreme, is nevertheless revealing. Once upon a time there lived a man with his sickly mother, a wife and son. The family being poor, he soon found that he could not support all four. With the consent of his wife he decided to bury his son alive. But as soon as he dug into the ground, quantities of gold came up with his spade. Heaven was moved by his filial feelings, so that a would-be tragedy concluded happily for all. In real life, whenever warranted by economic necessity, it is not unusual for grandparents to be served at the expense of grandchildren.

In the second place, infantile or childish behaviour, though often providing amusement for adults, is not emphasized, nor idealized, nor played up through research. Up to the time of World War II there were few toys, and little academic effort at understanding the psychology of children. In fact, Chinese parents do not seem to assume the existence of a children's world qualitatively different from that of the adults. Children are regarded as little adults who will become adults after adult models. The traditional Chinese terms for education, when translated into English, approximate the words "instruction," "restraint," "learning."

In the third place, the maturing Chinese child will experience a good deal of inconsistency in his social relationship. Chinese, especially the mothers, are not too concerned about consistency in discipline. Even if the mother wants such consistency, various relatives will make her discipline inconsistent. The child's grandmother is always there ready to go over his mother's head. Aunts, uncles, older cousins and grandfather tend all to feel free about giving the child some forbidden articles while his mother is not looking. The customary family ideal is such that even if parents object to such interferences it would appear socially unreasonable for them to make an issue of it. In other words, Chinese parents are seldom the absolute and exclusive masters within the four walls of their homes.

Fourth, and above all, the growing Chinese male is initiated into the adult world imperceptibly. The inconsistency in his early experiences would have already given him a head start in this direction. Then he begins to participate in adult activities as early as he can manage it. By accompanying his father to business meetings, temple fairs and on social calls he becomes almost effortlessly, and at an early stage of his development, acquainted with his place in society. Except in matters pertaining to sex, parents make little effort in keeping their own affairs from the male child. If the family has just suffered a major catastrophe the parents do not discuss among themselves whether they should let Johnny know. Johnny suffers with them right away.

From ten or twelve years of age onwards, Chinese males do not experience any sudden change of status. The same gradual initiation into their adult rôles continues.

Like the Chinese children, American children also suffer from few significant frustrations before weaning. But between the time of weaning and the legal age of 18 or 21, the circumstances surrounding the average American child tend to be drastically different from those within the experience of the average Chinese child. Like Chinese parents, American parents emphasize adequate satisfaction in food and clothing for their children. But while the lots of the wealthy children and the poor differ widely in China because of necessity, there is less discrepancy of this sort in America. There are few American parents who have to starve their children because of dire want. But in other matters the differences are more intensive and far-reaching.

First, with the possible exception of the very poor, or fresh immigrants from southern and eastern Europe, Americans from middle classes upward tend to apply themselves diligently toward giving their children a qualitatively different world from that of themselves. Nearly ideal conditions prevail in this world of the young. It is further buttressed by Santa Claus, tales about the love and sorrow of animals, a nearly complete correlation between reward and good conduct on the one hand and between punishment and bad conduct on the other. In time of family distress artificial behaviour on the part of the parents keeps the children away from the shock of reality. Many parents send their children to Sunday schools when they have doubts, in order to bring their children up "right." In time of want children are more likely to be served than parents. The many arms of the Society for the Prevention of Cruelty to Children in America, when contrasted with the many societies "for Saving Papers With Written Characters On" or societies "for Giving Away Free Coffins" in China, make the differences of the two cultures very apparent.

Secondly, infantile and childish behaviour is endorsed by American parents, constantly boosted by American business and permanently played up by American research. One of the major duties of the American parents is to enable their children to play and see that they do. The over $800 million a year toy industry, the myriad of commercialized juvenile literature, and the variety of occasions and days during the year on which gifts are expected and given are all strong evidence indicating who are centres of the society.

Thirdly, American parents as a whole emphasize consistency in discipline to an extent unknown among Chinese parents. It is not supposed, of course, that in their actual day-to-day life American parents can be as consistent as they wish to be. But their difference from the Chinese comes first from the ideal they emphasize (and which their family counsellors and child psychologists tell them to emphasize), and secondly from the fact that they live in individual families where few occasions for interference of grandparents or other in-laws exist. Furthermore, even when grandmothers take over during an emergency the older lady is only supposed to administer things according to laws laid down by the younger woman. This consistency tends to suppose a complete or nearly complete correlation between reward and good conduct on the one hand, and punishment and bad conduct on the other.

Lastly, from an early date American parents encourage their children to be self-reliant. When they are a little older, the label of "sissy" or "cry-baby" will shame most youngsters into reacting promptly. Here again we are aware of the fact that many American children do in fact fall back on their parents when the going is tough and the hands of their parents, especially those of their mothers, are very heavy. In fact, Irene M. Josselyn, a practising psychiatrist and psychoanalyst, describes vividly how difficult this struggle for independence is for many youngsters and how one young 14-year-old girl resents her mother for dictating what she should wear and for letting her choose what she desires to wear. In other words, independence is both desired and feared. Clinical psychologists can usually confirm the impression that they see an inordinate number of cases in which the problems of children are rooted in the heavy hands of their mothers. It is to be expected, in a culture where self-reliance is equivalent to self-respect, most of those individuals who are in need of clinical help to be those who have failed in some way to measure up to the accepted pattern of self-reliance. The reason why some American mothers' hands are heavy will be discussed in the next section. In three years of work, first as a medical social worker and later as a psychiatric social worker in Peking Union Medical College Hospital between 1934 and 1937, Hsu did not find the type of mother-child problem known to American clinicians. From Hsu's experiences in China, both as an individual and as an anthropological field worker, he can state that, among Chinese children, the type of struggle for independence described by Josselyn was rare.

All these are understandable once we appreciate the high American premium on self-reliance as contrasted to its low esteem in the Chinese situation. Furthermore, American parents foster this sense of self-reliance by separating their children from the adult world. In this culture, children have no social rôles in the adult world except for being children. Besides family visits to grandmothers or aunts or during vacations, children are not involved with affairs of the parents. Parents frequently see their friends after having put their children to bed or in the charge of a sitter. Youngsters have their own playmates, whom the parents may not know, and their own jargons, which often take the adults by surprise.

The results of these differing childhood experiences are far-reaching. A majority of Chinese youngsters grow up equipped with a much more realistic view of life and the world around them than their American counterparts. Theirs is a world in which basic satisfactions often intertwine with frustrations, in which principles are frequently affected by compromises, in which hypocrisies and circuitous means of getting out of trouble are not uncommon. Adolescence is a time when the Chinese youngsters have already become acquainted with, and in many cases initiated into, their roles in society. The shortcomings of the greater world do not give

Chinese adolescents any sudden emotional trauma; they have sampled many of them before. The intricacies of the adult society fail to cause them confusion and bewilderment. They have long known differences between what adults do and what they say, and have nearly perfected the art themselves.

The majority of American youngsters grow up, in contrast to the Chinese, equipped with an idealistic attitude towards life and the world around them. Theirs is a world in which light and shadow in human affairs are crystal clear, in which God invariably punishes the bad and rewards the deserving, and in which hypocrisies are banished and frustrations at a minimum. The imperfect world of which American youngsters become aware at adolescence is therefore full of sudden emotional shocks. They are confused because the rules they have been used to often no longer apply. They may refuse to heed their parents at this time simply because they are disillusioned by what they had been told thus far and what they have now found.

Parental Attitudes

The Chinese parents, having never been complete masters of their children in the first place, do not feel especially rejected as the youngsters become more independent. Furthermore, the nature of the Chinese way of life has been such that age, far from being a liability, is a premium. To the Chinese parents, maturity and independence of the children mean only an assurance of a more permanent place in life for themselves.

The American adolescent is a person who has physically grown into the adult world, but with his social and cultural development lagging behind. Having been taught to be self-reliant and aggressive, he is now ready to explore on his own. Facing this, the American parents' attitude towards their children is a seeming paradox. When they say they want Johnny to be independent they mean he can wash his own hands, turn on the light or take the bus by himself, but they decidedly do not mean that Johnny can refuse to eat of his own choice. So when the adolescent is physically ready to explore this confusing world on his own, the parents, accustomed to being complete masters of their children, suddenly find themselves incapable of control. American parents feel the danger of rejection more vividly than the Chinese parents because, in America, once the children become independent parents will have few honored places in the scheme of things. They therefore want to retain their parental power as long as they can. This is why, as we saw above, the hands of American parents on their children, especially those of American mothers, tend to be heavy. To the American adolescent this is often unbearable. The infant at birth can be satisfied with a bottle. At three or four he gets excited about being dressed like Daddy. He will demand to be thrilled by more and bigger things as his physical power grows. According to psychologists children are most suggestible at the age of eight or nine, after which the suggestibility decreases. Seen from the present analysis, this climax of suggestibility is probably a time when American children find their best adjustment between parental restraint and their own physical capability, after which the latter has outgrown the former.

In this way the Chinese adolescent has less desire to rebel against parental authority not only because his process of initiation into the wider society has begun much earlier in life but also because his parents have little psychological need to hold on to him. The American adolescent experiences more difficulties not only because his life so far has had little reference to the wider society but also because his parents have the strong urge to hold on to him.

The Rôle of the Peer Group

It is a foregone conclusion that human beings, in order to be human, must lead their existence in a human group, not only for food, sex and language but also for a sense of affiliation and importance. Elsewhere Hsu has classified these latter needs into sociability, security and status and examined how this classification is preferable to that of some others and can help to explain the qualitative and quantitative differences in human behaviour in different societies. But whether scholars agree on these categories, we do not believe that there is any doubt that all human beings, in one manner or another, seek group affiliations. However, while the Chinese situation-centred orientation of life stresses mutual dependence between the generations, the American individual-centred orientation of life emphasizes reliance upon the self. The Chinese, with their ideals of filial piety and reverence to tradition, authority and the past, enjoin their youngsters never to sever their relations with their elders. The Americans, with their ideals of freedom, equality, and drive for creativity and for future, encourage their youngsters to be independent of the adults almost from the beginning of life. In the last section we saw how this independence on the part of the young affects the thinking and behaviour of parents when their children really grow up. The same independence affects the young as soon as they go to school. Independence from parents simply means that they must seek affiliation with peer groups. The greater the sense of independence from parents, the more urgent the need for affiliation with peer groups. In other words, the Chinese youngsters have greater relationship along the vertical line with their elders, but the American youngsters are more deeply involved along the horizontal line with their peers. The resulting psychological difference is significant. The individual who has chiefly to maintain horizontal relationships, must make greater exertions than those who have mainly to deal with vertical relationships. For, from the children's point of view, parents, whether in China or the U.S., can almost be taken for granted but peers cannot. In fact, while parents in all societies tend to express their affection for their children and, in most societies, work hard to make sure their children are affectionate toward them even when harshly treated in return, peers nowhere have any great love for each other. In fact, peers whether in highly individualistic societies or not, always compete with each other, and therefore one must be continuously on the look-out for trouble with them, trouble which might lead to rejection.

The American adolescent is therefore likely to be far more under the tyranny of his peers than his Chinese counterpart. This gives the former far greater reason for anxiety, for conformity, for violent gestures, including immoral acts and even murder and mayhem, if these are dictated by his needs for retaining or improving his status in his peer group.[7]

Among those who operate within the legal bounds, the extent to which American youngsters are tied to their peers may be gauged from a "Cornell Study of Student Values," which covers a total of 2,760 undergraduate men and women attending Cornell and 4,585 undergraduate men and women attending ten universities (U.C.L.A., Dartmouth, Fisk, Harvard, Michigan, North Carolina, Texas, Wayne, Wesleyan and Yale). Suchman, in a summary report on this study, concludes that "much of the student's development during four years in colleges does *not* take place in classrooms. The conformity, contentment and self-centred confidence of the present-day American students are not academic values inculcated by the faculty, but rather the result of a highly organized and efficiently functioning extracurricular social system" (Suchman 1958). We do not have a comparative inquiry conducted among the Chinese in China or in Hawaii. However, it is well known that, even as late as 1949, Chinese high schools rarely had any kind of intra-school organizations besides athletic ones, and in Chinese colleges and universities there mostly flourished "native place" organizations, each composed of youngsters from the same province. A recurrent complaint by many observers was that all such voluntary associations did not last, for the students lacked lasting interest in them. In fact it has often been said, by Chinese and Westerners, that the Chinese were like loose sands which do not stick together. In the light of our analysis here, the Chinese youngsters lacked the urge to cohere with their peer groups because they had a far more tenacious relationship with their elders on the vertical plane. Hawaii's high school and college in 1949 had more American type of peer organizations. In the University of Hawaii there are even Chinese fraternities and sororities. But, as reported elsewhere (Hsu 1951), they entered into the affairs of their elders in a manner and to an extent unknown among other Americans in the U.S.

The Demands of the Wider Society

Adolescence, particularly later adolescence, is a time when the individual is well within range of the adult in physical capabilities. We have seen that in the Chinese situation the adolescent's physical growth is accompanied by a corresponding process of his gradual entry into adult society, while in the American situation it is not. However, regardless of whether he is or is not initiated into adult society the adolescent, with his increased mobility, contact and perception, cannot help but be influenced by the dominant patterns of culture governing the society. In America the most desired position of the individual is a combination of *(a)* economic and social independence and *(b)* success to this end with speed. Economic independence means to find a job and that one must no longer live on an allowance. That achievement in turn helps him to establish social independence which includes, among other things, full control of one's own hours, movements and activities. As to success with speed, nothing expresses the sentiment better than the recent proposal by Grayson Kirk, President of Columbia University, to shorten our college education from four years to three years, and the enthusiastic and favourable comments this proposal has received so far (Kirk 1960). The increasingly lowered age of dating is an indication of the same thing. Coupled with these is the fact that individualistic competitiveness has increasingly driven adults to indiscriminate and irresponsible use of any means to pursue their own selfish ends, the high ethical standards preached in the society becoming increasingly a mockery both to the adults but especially to the youngsters.[8]

The American adolescent, confronted with these forces in adult society, often does not know how to cope with them. He may try to take social independence first, or he may seize upon the idea of speed first. When easy outlets are not available he may be driven to unusual ones such as those of the criminal, or to express himself in quarrelsomeness, family explosions, hostility and sulkiness against parents and other adults. These same forces in adult society tend to affect the Chinese adolescent far less than they would the American, even though the two live in the same society and are subject to the same demands of that society. In the first place, at adolescence the Chinese is likely to have become wise in adult ways because of his gradual transition from childhood to adulthood. In the second place, being more oriented towards vertical relationships, he is less involved in and affected by forces prevailing in the wider society than is his horizontal-relationship-bound American counterpart.

In every culture individuals vary, so that not all Chinese adolescents are free from difficulties and not all American adolescents present problems. But forces current in each culture tend to dispose the youths of that culture in one or another direction, so that we are in a better position to appreciate why adolescence presents far less of a problem to the Chinese than to the Americans. In fact, before contact with the West the Chinese had no term meaning adolescence. The individual went from childhood and puberty straight to adulthood. But there are more concrete evidences which we can briefly examine. In inter-societal comparisons we are, of course, limited by the availability of data and by the comparability of the data if found. But a comparison of adolescent crime during the best years of the Nationalist administration in China with that of a corresponding period in the U.S. yields the following interesting points (the Chinese data are taken from police files of fourteen capital cities—*Ministry of the*

Interior Year Book, 1936 (National Government of China 1936). The American statistics are taken from *Uniform Crime Reports* (U.S. Government 1931, 1932, 1933). Both sets of facts pertain to the years 1931, 1932 and 1933):

(*a*) American males between 16 and 21 committed more felonies than misdemeanours; Chinese males between 13 and 20 committed more misdemeanours than felonies.

(*b*) American males between 16 and 21 committed more crimes than all other seven-year groups under 51; Chinese males of 13 to 20 committed fewer crimes than all other seven-year groups under 51.

These contrasts are startling when we realize that both Chinese and Americans are subject to the same biological changes, but that during the first half of the century Chinese youth lived in an environment far less socially, politically and economically secure than the Americans. These contrasts become understandable, however, when seen in the light of our hypothesis and analysis so far.

Theoretically, as the Chinese in America become more integrated with the host society and more acculturated to its way of life, they are likely to experience the same sort of adolescent difficulties which seem to form part of the American way of life. This expectation is a logical sequence of our view that adolescent turbulence is basically a function of culture pattern and not heredity or poverty or lack of playgrounds. But the Chinese in Hawaii have up to date been able to keep some of the essential content of their culture pattern alive among them. This is due probably to two reasons. First, their family system, which as among all peoples is the cradle of their culture from generation to generation, is of prodigious strength which exerts a strong centripetal influence on the individual. Secondly, being on an insular island of small size, they tend to keep close touch with each other through their associational and other activities, though they mix freely with persons of other ethnic stocks. (Over 80 per cent of the total population of Hawaii are found on the island of Oahu, where Honolulu is located.)

CULTURE PATTERN AND ADOLESCENT PSYCHOLOGY

We can now see how our Rorschach findings fit in with the wider cultural perspective. We can understand the reason why, psychologically, and compared with the Chicago adolescents, the Hawaii adolescents have a smoother transition from childhood to adulthood, less rebellious strivings on the surface and within, fewer signs of autistic fantasy, less uncontrolled emotionality and bodily anxiety, more empathy, greater sensitivity to the needs of others and more submissive acceptance of their rôles.

However, adolescent difficulties generated by American culture are not altogether a disadvantage, just as their relative absence in Chinese culture is not altogether an advantage. In the Rorschach findings we noted that the Hawaiian adolescents have no passionate wish to change, no felt need to alter environment, and that they are unlikely to become "discontents." Put differently, this means they are not often stirred by issues and not easily moved enough so as to strive for reform.

The white American youth, because of discontinuity between their early and later experiences, sometimes come to the position of responsibility with an idealism far less known among their counterparts in China. American youths tend to go out to improve things, to fight towards a better living, or at least to do things differently from their parents and to explore unknown possibilities. This is one of the secrets of strength of American culture. The Chinese youths, because of their early initiation into the world of their elders, cross the threshold of adulthood like old rogues who know all the ropes. They tend to follow well-beaten paths, to talk wisely and to compromise. This is one of the reasons why for the last twenty centuries Chinese social and political institutions and technology, while remarkable in their own right, have shown little change.

The evolution of a culture may come about by way of internal forces or external pressure. External pressure for change is exemplified by contact between different nations. Internal pressure for change is present when there are differences in outlook between successive generations. The greater the latter differences, the greater will be the tendency to change.

However we look at it, adolescent unrest is simply one of the prices of the American type of culture. By wise manipulation we shall be able to reduce the price, but we cannot eradicate it. To eradicate the price means to eradicate much of the potentialities of the culture.

NOTES

1. The field work was undertaken by F. L. K. Hsu, under the auspices of the S.S.R.C. and Northwestern University's Graduate Committee on Research, between May and December 1949. For some aspects of the Chinese in Hawaii, see F. L. K. Hsu, 1951 (Chapter 4, this book).

2. The Rorschach tests were administered in 1949 by Francis L. K. Hsu as part of a more inclusive field-work project among the Chinese in Hawaii. The 28 protocals were first scored and analysed by Edith Lord. Later they were reanalysed and in part rescored by Blanche Watrous according to Beck to facilitate comparison with a study of Chicago adolescents. Hsu and Watrous are responsible for the writing and final interpretation of the Rorschach findings.

3. Lord points out that some possible sources of error may occur when records are obtained by one examiner and scored by another. For example, Hsu, the administrator of the tests, inquired of each subject specifically for C' (black), sex responses and the absence of C', whereas he tended not to inquire for texture (c). This may have led to spuriously high C' and sex responses. It should also be

pointed out that when these records are compared with Beck's "normals" (Thetford, Molish, and Beck 1951), the M responses may seem low because certain FM responses would have been scored as M responses in the Beck scoring system.

4. Beck's criteria for scoring W are somewhat more restrictive than those of Klopfer, who scores the cut-off W or incomplete W as a whole response. The Z score includes W and adjacent or distant details seen in relation to each other. Beck's scoring of M to include movement found only in human content and animals in anthropomorphic stances is sufficiently different from Klopfer's scoring of M to necessitate re-scoring in order to compate M- response. Beck's scoring of M includes movement found only in human content and animals in anthropomorphic stance, but excludes movement of human body parts (for example, "a finger pointing"). This varies sufficiently from Klopfer's to necessitate re-scoring according to Beck to compare M-. The minus scoring derives from perception of form.

5. M is scored extensor when the direction of the human activity is centrifugal, or away from the centre, as contrasted with flector M where the direction is centripetal or towards the centre (Beck 1946).

6. During the last ten years there have appeared in the newspapers (last one to come to my notice: The *Washington Post,* April 17th, 1960) and some magazines (such as *Look,* 1958) reports indicating the absence of juvenile delinquency in Chinatowns in the U.S.A. Such reports, though interesting, are not scientific evidence for the conclusion they draw. Rose Hum Lee (1952) pointed out rightly that the picture of Chinese delinquency in the San Francisco Bay region remains unclear because of the small size of the juvenile in proportion to the total adult population, due to U.S. immigration restrictions up to 1940. Up to about that time the Chinese population in the San Francisco Bay area and elsewhere had a drastically unbalanced sex ratio, in some instances over ten males to one female. But the Chinese population in Hawaii has exhibited relatively normal ratios for many decades.

7. In 1952 an adolescent in Michigan assaulted one nurse and killed another. Subsequent investigations showed no "obvious" motive for the crime. A whole series of articles on this crime was written by John Bartlow Martin in the *Saturday Evening Post.* It turned out that the boy in question wanted to prove to his gang that he was "good" enough to belong. A recurrent finding in adolescent crimes has been the absence of "obvious" motives—"obvious," that is, to the investigators and writers.

8. Studied analyses of these conditions are available: see L. K. Frank (1950) and Edwin Sutherland (1949). It will have been evident to the reader, however, that the interpretation of adolescent crime and difficulties we have presented in this paper is very different from that given by Sutherland. The crux of Sutherland's theory of crime is differential association. "Criminal behaviour is learned in association with those who define such behaviour favourably and in isolation from those who define it unfavourably, and that a person in an appropriate situation engages in such criminal behaviour if, and only if, the weight of the favourable definitions exceeds the weight of the unfavourable definitions" *(ibid.,* p. 234). What this theory says is that the social context of the individual determines his tendency to criminality or otherwise. This view agrees with findings in modern social sciences but it does not go far enough. What we have tried to show in this paper is the *forces* which propel the youngsters in the Chinese culture pattern to give greater weight to their vertical associations and which, in turn, lead to lesser adolescent difficulties and criminality, and those which propel the youngsters in the American culture pattern to be more tied to the horizontal associations which in turn lead to greater adolescent difficulties and criminality.

Part II:

Anthropology and Psychoanalysis

Introduction

Anthropology has greatly benefited from its association with psychiatry and especially psychoanalysis. Anthropologists have attained many new insights and opened up many new areas of research in human behavior and culture patterns wholly or partially as a result of this association.

The clinical disciplines have not, in my view, been similarly affected in this process. There is evidence that, instead of seeking out new understanding of human behavior, most psychiatrists and psychoanalysts who have bothered with anthropology at all have been preoccupied with finding intersocietal or cross-cultural confirmation of their Freud-centered theories.

The essays in this section of the book begin with "Taboo" (Chapter 7), the origin and significance of which Freud had much to say. Freud was not quite right, however, and his error included his invention of a primeval horde; but stimulated by his ingenious ideas, anthropologists have become more fruitful in their views of it.

Freud was the first to develop extensively the idea of repression as a basic psychic mechanism in human development. Following that lead some anthropologists have developed the notion of shame and guilt cultures which contrast, in my view, is better expressed as "Suppression versus Repression" (Chapter 8). Instead of seeing this contrast as the sole explanation for differences between whole cultures, however, I try to show that other factors are operative. In this way we can better perceive differences between China and Japan, where suppression overshadows repression, and those between Germany and the United States, where repression overshadows suppression.

Some readers may see my statements herein concerning sex and homosexuality as outdated, since this paper was written several decades before the advent of gay and sex liberation in America. However, although homosexuals have gained a degree of public acceptance in some areas and sex is openly discussed and even flaunted on television, I must caution my readers against hastily declaring that the American society and culture have undergone any fundamental change. Changes are certainly visible, from fashions to computers, and Americans glorify change. But many changes are more apparent than real. For when we take a deeper view, as we shall do in the latter part of the book, especially Chapters 12, 14, and 16, sex repression of the traditional West and sex explosion in today's America are but two sides of the same coin namely, preoccupation with sex.

In "Anthropology or Psychiatry: A Definition of Objectives and Their Implications" (Chapter 9) I tried to point out the inadequate evidence presented by students in both fields who emphasized the overwhelming importance of early childhood experience in personality formation—a Freudian precept. From that I went on to explore the differing roles of anthropology and the clinical disciplines. But since the publication of this article in 1952 I have come to the realization that, in spite of the inadequacy of the evidence so far presented, the great importance of early childhood experience in human development is undeniable. The reason is the predominance of affect patterns, which one acquires in infancy and childhood, over role capabilities, which one continues to learn through adolescence and adult years. The penetrating observations, such as those of Hostetler (1976), Hostetler and Huntington (1967, 1968) and others (e.g. Peters 1965, Bennett 1969) on the socialization process among the Hutterites in North America, are extremely convincing.

A major point of this paper, however, is the suggestion of a working and practical definition of the difference between the mentally healthy and the mentally ill. The former will be better able to adapt themselves to later circumstances in spite of unfavorable early experiences. But the latter will tend less able to do so. They tend to be scarred by their early experiences for life.

The last paper in this section, "An Anthropologist's View of the Future of Personality Studies" (Chapter 10), has two objectives. The first is to show the fallacy of the overuse of individual depth psychology in gauging cultural characteristics of a whole society. The other is to emphasize the need for students of cultures (whether they be psychoanalysts or anthropologists) to scrutinize their own culture by birth or adoption for comparative purposes. For example, had Erickson carefully analyzed the American culture he would probably not have resorted to his absurd explanation that German anti-Semitism was rooted in the fear of castration which the Jews aroused in other peoples who did not practice it. He would also have realized the similarity between his description of the German attitude toward the imagined or actual Jewish male contamination of the purity of German womanhood and the white American stereotype of and attitude toward the Blacks.

7

Taboo

The word "taboo" for most people evokes a picture of an "ignorant and primitive savage" obsessed by unreasoning fears and customs. This certainly could not be applied to a civilized society like our own.

Or could it?

One of the insights which the study of anthropology brings is the ability to look at one's own society with the "ethnological eye." Many features taken for granted by the ordinary citizen then appear in a new light, and one discovers irrationalities just as numerous as those in any "primitive" group. Let's apply this insight to taboos.

Primarily, taboo concerns the avoidance of some action. If the avoidance isn't accomplished it will lead mysteriously, in the minds of men, to punishments not explainable by common sense or the principles of science. These punitive results may not come about each time a taboo is violated. Their severity varies from taboo to taboo; and not all taboos of any society are observed by all its members. But the test of a true taboo is that failure to observe it excites such horror or apprehension in the minds of the culprit and some of his people as to demand they do something about it.

The word "taboo" originated in Polynesia, where its system was highly developed. It is *tapu* in Samoa, and *kapu* in Hawaii. But the Tongan *tábu* (anglicized taboó) came to be best known.

A taboo commonly met with today—as long ago—concerns a common necessity, food. The Australian Bushman will not eat foods which are made taboo by the tribal elders from time to time. A violator will suffer severe punishment whether he is caught or not. If caught he will be put to death. If not, he will become sick and die. A counterpart to this Australian custom is the taboo against eating pork among Arabs and Jews, beef among the Hindus, meat on Friday among the Catholics. The punishments for violating their meat taboo are less severe than among their Australian brethren, but they are nonetheless considerable. Furthermore, the manner in which these taboos can be lifted is similar: among the Bushmen it is in de-tabooing by the elders; among the Arabs, Jews and Hindus, expiation by sacrifice under the direction of the priest; among the Catholics, papal dispensation.

The Toda tribe in South India has sacred days, called *Madnol,* when feasts cannot be given, funeral ceremonies may not be performed, people

---

This chapter was originally published in *What's New,* Summer 1958, No. 206, pp. 12–15. Reprinted by permission of Abbott Laboratories.

may not bathe or cut their nails, clothes cannot be washed, nor can rice be cooked with milk, and nothing may be taken from the village. The ancient Greeks made the feast days of the gods sacred and on these days all work was taboo. Plato rationalized that "gods, pitying the toils to which our race is born or undergo, have appointed holy festivals, by which men alternate rest and labor." To the Hebrews, the Day of Atonement was the *Sabbath Sabbathon,* when no work might be done. According to Leviticus, a violator of this taboo was threatened with death.

We have so much of the same heritage that there are still many state laws in the United States prohibiting work on Sundays. Not so many years ago when the governor of one state tried to force the repeal of these obsolete and inoperative laws, he failed; instead, he himself was almost tossed out of office. Other well-known taboos we share with the world include the incest taboo, segregation taboo, and the taboo on cannibalism.

The Chains of Danger

Why do men observe taboos? Many explanations have been advanced. Sir James Frazer saw a basic unity in magic and science: both assume immutable laws. In the mind of man both magic and science are based on cause-and-effect associations. The empirically tested associations are science while the false associations are magic. In Sir James' view, then, taboo is negative magic: the idea behind it is that avoidance of certain acts will avert certain definite and adverse consequences.

This theory engaged the attention of anthropologists for a long time. But it fails to explain man's adherence to taboos for two reasons. It fails to underline that the mental process behind science is experimental: it is ready to change the formula when results continually disprove it. The process behind magic and taboo is dogmaticism: the same formula will be continued even if disproven. More fatal to this theory is that it presupposes the disappearance of taboos as science progresses. This is not the case. We live in a world which is scientifically a far cry from those of our jungle and Roman ancestors. Yet we see no end to our taboos.

The theory of Bronislaw Malinowski as it applies to taboo is an improvement. To Malinowski, taboo—as a form of magic—fills the gaps in man's knowledge. Since life must go on regardless of these gaps, magic provides us with actions or attitudes that will tide us over by giving us a pattern for action and mental security. In a way, this theory suffers from the same defect as that of Sir James; namely, if taboo is a poor substitute for knowledge, then as knowledge advances taboo must disappear. A more serious flaw in Malinowski's theory is that taboo, instead of providing security, may actually be the cause of anxiety by nonobservance. What gap of knowledge does the parent-child and sister-brother incest taboo fill? The knowledge of this taboo excites horror in the violators instead of security.

A theory better known to physicians is that of Sigmund Freud. Freud thought that the incest taboo originated in the Oedipus situation of the family triangle. The rebuffs and frustrations to the child's infantile sexual attraction to the parent of opposite sex lead to repression but not to extinction of the impulse. Incest taboos and the horrors attached to their violation are "reaction formations" to the repressed impulse. But in *Totem and Taboo,* Freud specifically accounted for the origin of the ban—he presupposed the existence of a primeval horde, ancestral to all mankind, in which the father dominated all his sons and exercised exclusive right to all the women. The sons' resentment became so strong that one day they secretly killed their father and ate his flesh to partake of his strength. After this act the sons were seized with deep remorse and guilt. They made a pact of secrecy among themselves and returned to install an "animal" as a father-substitute totem. Then they forbade all to eat its meat, and banned sexual intercourse within their circle of close relatives.

The basic fallacy of this theory has long ago been pointed out: there was simply no evidence of such a primeval horde. The "facts" were merely theories proposed by the Australian anthropologist, Atkinson. Besides, the theory does not explain the wide extension and diversity of incest taboos outside the individual family, nor a multitude of taboos on objects other than food. But Freud's theory, though based on unproved suppositions, has, like its predecessors, helped our understanding of taboo.

A scientific theory which will explain any taboo must explain all of them, for it is the essence of science that it must explain more and more things with fewer and fewer theories. In the present instance it is important to realize that although taboos have a tremendous variety, they pertain to a few basic matters: food (including cannibalism), sex, life's crises (such as birth, initiation, marriage and death), sacred persons and potent things. What is common to these categories?—DANGER. These are objects or occasions of danger to the individual and danger to the society of which the individual is a member. Since each human being must carry on the human way of life with others, it is redundant to say that the two dangers are really one.

It is not hard to see how these common matters of taboo evoke feelings of danger. Food can give life, and the wrong food can take life. Sex is the origin of life (even the Trobriand Islanders, who reportedly are ignorant of physiological paternity, believe that the father has to open the way). All over the world sex jealousy is a source of tragedy since it may lead to murder and mayhem. The sexual act is followed by a period of weakness, a weakness that may be carried over to the religious rite or to the actions of daily life. It was for this reason that the ancient Romans, as many peoples in the world, forbade worshipers to have sex relations before a religious festival. The Festival of the Ambarvalia in Rome was one of these. It is for this reason, too, that many societies use only children for some religious ceremonies because they are pure. David Mandelbaum actually received verbatim replies from the Kotas of India to this effect. Our own use of choirboys in Sunday services and flower children in weddings are other familiar examples.

As to life's crises, each of them is a major or minor transition that demands rearrangement and realignment of men and events. They involve either addition of new members to the whole group or a part of it, or subtraction of old members from it. Sacred persons are invested with spiritual or earthly powers, or both, and hold the fate of their fellow men in their hands. Potent things may affect one's life or luck. They may be strangers, or strange objects and materials seen by any people for the first time, numbers, times, names, plants, animals, corpses, places, rites, temples and natural calamities. As to cannibalism, its practice has never been as widespread as the taboo against it. Furthermore, even among cannibalistic peoples the practice is taboo within each tribe. No group can exist as a corporate body if cannibalism is permitted within it.

All these are matters of greatest concern to every individual and his society. Each society, in order to safeguard the individual and the group, has a particular set of symbols with which to express its corporate concern in the problems of existence. This concern has two facets: the solidarity of the group at any moment; the survival of the group through time. In essence, this is the theory of Radcliffe-Brown of Oxford.

LANGUAGE, HAMBURGERS AND SEX

The basic symbols of all mankind are called language. Each society has a symbol system for everyday use; language serves this purpose. But more intense symbols are needed to buttress its solidarity and continuity; these symbols are sacred and taboo. Sanctity covers symbols which underline the positive elements of social solidarity and continuity. Taboo attaches to symbols which do the same job in a negative way. They are two sides of the same coin. Sanctity is primarily a matter of duties to be performed; taboo is always a matter of actions to be avoided. It does not seem possible for any human society to rally and maintain itself without the cementing forces of sanctity and taboo.

With this theory all taboos can be explained. We cannot serve hamburgers to our best guest. Nor can we belch after dinner or slurp the soup during it. As respectable members of our American society we are not only restricted as to what we eat but how we eat. Only "low-class people" or "the uneducated" or "foreigners" do those things. Observance of these symbolic marks thus distinguishes members of one group from those of others.

We have greatly played down our funerals. We rarely see pompous funeral processions in our cities today. But nonetheless we have many observances. It is not good for the widow to wear gay, colored clothes and appear frivolous, nor is it seemly for the mourners to present anything but a grave mien. These acts do not help the dead. They may even be against the wishes of the living. But they are acts which symbolize grief over loss of members, transition, and reintegration of the group.

Our weddings are still full of taboos. The maid of honor should be unmarried. The bride should wear white only if she is being married for the first time. I once witnessed a wedding in which the groom dropped the ring when he was putting it on his bride. The repercussion of that little mishap was unhappiness between the couple for many days. Practically speaking, none of these should have anything to do with the success or failure of any marriage. But even now, the notion is still current that a formal church wedding tends to give the union a better start than a civil marriage. Carrying out the acts is to fulfill sanctity. Breaking them is a matter of taboo.

The sex taboo is still basic to our modern culture. Not only do we have incest taboos like other peoples, but as the Kinsey reports show, we also have strict taboos on how and where the sexual act is to be carried out. We have taboos on sex in television and film. We have taboos on the use of sex-linked words in mixed company. We even have taboos on words which have an indirect and remote relationship with sex. For example, the public toilet was called W. C. (water closet) thirty or forty years ago. Within the last several decades it went through the following changes of name: lavatory, washroom, restroom, men and ladies, kings and queens. In the South, I have seen outhouses renamed "convenience houses." It should surprise no one if the futuristic name for our toilets is headed in the direction of plus-minus signs. This is not due simply to our desire for a change. As a people we resist changes in many things, either fundamental or trivial; but our willingness to change in the present instance would seem to be an expression of the Puritanic aversion to sex which was necessary for the solidarity and the continuity of the Puritanic social organization.

There are many taboos on objects. The sanctity of our national flag needs no repetition here. Its destruction is taboo because it symbolizes our national greatness. For men and women their respective clothes are taboo to each other. They cannot put on the other's clothing because that taboo dramatizes the importance of male-female division of our society and solidarity among each sex. This is the same reason why there are clubs for men from which women are excluded.

We can see that each of the previously mentioned scientists contributed to this latest theory of taboo, of group solidarity and continuity. Sir James Frazer brought out that taboos are not capricious fantasies of man: they serve a real purpose. Malinowski led his fellow anthropologists to look behind the external manifestations and into the psychology of human behavior. Radcliffe-Brown supplemented and completed the series of anthropological endeavors by pointing out the symbolic meaning of taboo to the whole society. But Freud's deeper probing into the mystery of the human mind was not in vain. For though the anthropologists have shown that the father of psychoanalysis started from no "facts" when he spoke of the primeval horde and patricide, they have to concede that his psychological insight was an invaluable aid in solving the riddle of taboo. The anthropologists can disect the diverse ramifications of taboo symbolism in every variety of cultural context. But without Freud's insight into the Oedipus situation they can hardly explain why the parent-child and brother-sister incest ban is practically the only universal taboo, and why violation of this taboo seems to give rise everywhere to the greatest of all horrors. Symbolically, the parent-child and brother-sister incest taboo safeguards the solidarity and continuity of the nuclear family, everywhere the basic unit of human existence. Psychologically, Freud's explanation of "reaction formation" to a repressed impulse goes far to elucidate the horrors associated with its violation.

It's apparent that in modern society taboos keep a stronghold no less than in other societies. What happens is that the forms of taboo come and go, but the psychosocial needs for security and group solidarity in taboos will act at all times to generate or take over new taboos. The very first taboo among early men might have started when a group of them instinctively, like all animals, and for the sake of self-preservation, cringed from the approach of strangers or strange things. This became a habit, and being able to communicate, they told each other about it; later their children were indoctrinated. This became a taboo and a symbol for solidarity of the tribe. Even for the Romans, strangers and strange materials were taboo. For example, because the Romans used bronze, iron became taboo in all Roman religious rites after it was first introduced into daily life.

But as time goes on, the later generations of descendants in any society may observe the same old taboos without knowing the original reasons for them, or transfer the same old need for taboos to some new objects of taboo. The latter was the reason why age-old taboos were once discarded wholesale by the young Hawaiian King Kamehameha II. What he did was not to discard taboo as such. He simply replaced taboos his people had with those they did not have when he and his people were converted to Christendom.

In any given period, the intensity of taboo observances and the chances for new taboos are in direct ratio to the individual's need for security and his society's fear for its lack of solidarity. Most Oriental villages will observe more taboos and enforce old ones with greater thoroughness during an emergency such as earthquake, drought and epidemic. The ancient Romans did the same before their soldiers went to war and during a siege. This is also the case in our culture today. In war or near war conditions our national flag tends to be more taboo than usual; we have increased suspicion against strangers, and forebodings about strange things; we tend to submit ourselves to greater leadership strength. Some of our war leaders attain, in the minds of their followers, nearly the quality which Max Weber has described as *charisma*. A challenge to such persons tends to bring out hostility patterns from their followers quite similar, for instance, to those that are evoked whenever the divine chiefs of Samoa or the sacred cows of India become endangered.

For the plainest demonstration of this principle examine any military organization. At all times the avowed purpose of such an organization is war now (emergency) or some time later (future emergency). Accordingly, it is in the armed forces that we find more numerous "don'ts" (taboos) and "insignia of power" (sacred things) than in any other area of life. Subtract these symbolic "don'ts" and "insignia of power," which demand unquestioned adherence by all concerned, and we shall have no military organization and no strength for self-defense. In the latter event both the individual and his society will be in peril.

For several decades now we have had a struggle between communism and dictatorship on the one hand and capitalism and democracy on the other. Accordingly, we have had a ban (also close to a taboo by all anthropological criteria) on communists and especially communism. The question is not that some of our attempts in this direction have been misplaced nor that many of our popular notions about communism may be fallacious. The visible fact is that we as a people feel there are men and women who are communists and ideas which are communistic, and that both are dangers to our individual security and group survival. The psychology for taboos in this direction has become so severe that the word communism cannot be mentioned in public without denunciation, and communism as a form of philosophy cannot be touched on in schools. Furthermore, those with alleged communistic thoughts and even some who happened to drink coffee with communists, however unintentionally, have been penalized exactly as in another era when those who unwittingly associated with violators of taboos were believed to be as guilty as the sinners.

Understanding the reasons for taboos does not make some of the punishments for their violation less harsh. But it does tell us that we will have less stringent taboos in any area of life if that area is beset with less danger to the individual security and group survival. It is not likely, however, that we shall ever reach a state when we can dispense with taboos altogether. The reason is that as long as man exists he will have individual and group problems which are either insoluble (such as death and love at all times) or beyond his ability and even comprehension at a given moment (such as space control today). The more people we have and the wider our contacts and operations, the more complex becomes the dynamic process of individual security and group survival.

Taboos are one set of man's fixed points of reference in his ever-changing life and world studded with surprises. In this sense, many taboos are not only good but essential to the human way of life, so long as the taboos we have do not blind us completely to our vision of reality. If we could encourage more feeling for sanctity in weddings and give less play to the personal pleasures of the honeymoons which follow them; and if we could pay more attention to the spirit of some taboos in our family behavior and foster less desire for informality, we may yet see fewer divorces and fewer problem children.

8

Suppression versus Repression:
A Limited Psychological Interpretation of Four Cultures

THE PROBLEM

The word "repression" is used here in the Freudian sense, namely "the exclusion of painful and unpleasant material from consciousness and from motor expression."[1] According to this definition, materials that are repressed are buried deep in the unconscious. The word suppression is used here in the common everyday sense: namely, the restraint from certain actions because of external circumstances, the thought of such actions, however, not being necessarily excluded from consciousness. As a rule the materials that are suppressed are not buried in the unconscious and can be called forth very readily and unwarped. The much-discussed feeling of guilt, which according to Freud is traceable to the infantile sexuality of the person in relation to one or another of the parents, is an illustration of repression. On the other hand, the fact that many motorists drive within specified speed limits because of police patrol or fear of accidents may be a case of suppression. After long years of driving, a motorist may appear to obey automatically the various road signs; but few motorists, when directly questioned, will fail to see the relationship between speed limits, the law, possible accidents, and the unfortunate consequences which might result from unwise actions.

Every society is bound to impose some restraint on its members, whether in the earlier years of the individual or later. Since no individual is fully conscious of all the restraints of his society that are applicable to him and since repression usually begins as suppression, it is evident that, in the normal course of events, the individual in every society is subject to some forces of suppression and some of repression. However, some cultures employ more suppression as a mechanism of socialization, while others employ more repression for a similar purpose. In a culture which emphasizes suppression as the mechanism of socialization, external controls will be more important to the individual than internal controls. In a culture which emphasizes repression as the mechanism of socialization, internal controls will be more important than external controls. In the former the

This chapter was originally published in *Psychiatry,* Vol. XII, No. 3, 1949, pp. 223–42. Copyright © 1949 by The William Alanson White Psychiatric Foundation, Inc.

basic pattern of life tends to be situation-centered. In the latter the basic pattern of life tends to be individual-centered.

It will be clear at once that this thesis is somewhat similar to that advanced by the late Dr. Benedict in her book on Japan:

> True shame cultures rely on external sanctions for good behavior, not, as true guilt cultures do, on an internalized conviction of sin. Shame is a reaction to other people's criticism. A man is shamed either by being openly ridiculed and rejected or by fantasying to himself that he has been made ridiculous. In either case it is a potent sanction. But it requires an audience or at least a man's fantasy of an audience. Guilt does not. In a nation where honor means living up to one's own picture of oneself, a man may suffer from guilt though no man knows of his misdeed and a man's feeling of guilt may actually be relieved by confessing his sin. (Benedict 1946:223)

Three things will, however, make the present paper materially different from Dr. Benedict's treatment of the subject. First, Dr. Benedict speaks of a contrast between Japan on the one hand and America or the West on the other, while in the present paper four cultures will be selected for analysis: Germany and the United States are selected as examples in which repression as a mechanism has greater weight than suppression; Japan and China are selected as examples in which the order of the two mechanisms are reversed. Furthermore, it will become plain later that there are differences—between Germany and America on the one hand and between Japan and China on the other—which cannot be explained on the basis of her theory. Second, it will be shown that shame or guilt are only symptomatic of the basic socialization processes undergone by the individual. The total range of facts may be more adequately covered by the concepts of suppression versus repression, leading respectively to greater sensitivity on the part of the individual to external sanctions or to internal controls. The behavior of an individual brought up under a primary emphasis on suppression may range from using different kinds of language for different occasions—which are not necessarily contradictory one to another—to so much shame that he has to commit suicide; just as the behavior of an individual brought up under a primary emphasis on repression may range from all kinds of internally satisfying rationalization within himself to an actual feeling of guilt. Thirdly, the social origin of the Japanese character envisaged by Dr. Benedict, though superior to that envisaged by Dr. Gorer (1943) is inadequate and even wide of the mark. For, as the ensuing analysis will show, what accounts for a large part of the basic Japanese character must also be applicable to that of the Chinese, and Dr. Benedict's picture of growing up in Japan does not fit China.

Attitudes Toward Sex

As a point of departure I might begin with a form of fine art: namely, painting in the four cultures. In European painting, of which both German and American paintings are examples or descendants, one of the predominant subject matters is woman. (For purposes of the present paper, the fact that European painting is essentially Latin in origin is beside the point, just as the fact that Christianity originated from Palestine, as we shall see later, is not vital to a discussion of Christianity in Europe. In each case the particular material in question must be examined against a number of other things which enter into the pattern of the culture in which the material has been found.) The basic search is for the most beautiful female form. The angel, the wife, the mother, the prostitute, the flower peddler, the sea bather and so on and so on, are represented in diverse poses, situations, and different degrees of suggestiveness and temptation. The basic idea, however, is to mask the suggestiveness and temptation so that they will not turn into what is commonly regarded as obscenity. On the other hand in Chinese and Japanese painting, the female form as subject matter is comparatively rare in what is commonly acknowledged as respectable art. When women appear in the picture, they are usually either minute dots in a vast landscape or are heavily clad so that the natural form of the body is almost completely covered.

In general, the famous Chinese painters are known for their treatment of subjects like tigers, horses, insects, flowers, landscape, birds, fish, and so forth. A few have become famous through their skill in treatment of human subjects, male and female alike, but these artists were rarely among the great ones. A similar situation prevails in Japanese art. Though still life is of some importance in American art, the majority of Western-European and American masters have not achieved fame through their treatment of that subject.

In both China and Japan, pornographic drawings or pictures have had a long history. Here women do not appear in suggestive poses. They and their sexual partners dramatize the facts of life in the minutest detail. In traditional China the artist who made a good living by making pornographic pictures was not publicly acclaimed; but such pictures by a famous artist have been known to become fairly valuable as antiques.

Furthermore, the way these pictures were appreciated is important. The literati-bureaucrats, who formed the most respected class, would not have enjoyed the pornographic pictures openly; their public life would be free from this sexual element. But most, if not all, of them would have no qualms about examining the frankest pictures with their wives, their concubines, or with prostitutes, in the privacy of the sleeping chamber. They might not make a practice of perusing pornography, but most of them would have no serious objection to looking at pornographic pictures if the occasion warranted. To a Puritan or even to any average middle-class American, examining such pictures in the privacy of his home but evincing no interest in pornography publicly would connote leading a double life; but the traditional Chinese literati-bureaucrat would simply laugh at any suggestion that in this way he was leading a double life.

A similar if somewhat more intense dichotomy of life into discreet, but not surreptitious, provinces is applicable to Japan.[2] The basic pattern in Chinese and Japanese art is one in which either no sexual aspect of life is presented or sex is given the fullest representation in the form of pornography.[3]

What then, in terms of the hypothesis given in the first part of this paper, is the meaning of the differences in painting between China and Japan, and the Anglo-Saxon-Teutonic cultures? Briefly, these differences represent the direct versus the devious manner of approach to sex; they also show the compartmentalization of sex versus the disavowal of it. Sex presumably is one of man's most fundamental urges. In a culture which employs repression as the chief mechanism of control, the forces which tend to eliminate the sex urge from consciousness only serve to make it appear in diffused and indirect fashion. The basic pattern of approach to sex tends to be one in which men try to get at women without, at the same time, getting too near to the sexual act. In a culture which employs suppression as the chief mechanism of control, the regulations are external and, therefore, less omnipresent and all-pervasive. The sex urge tends to be channelled into specific areas of life where it can appear directly and without mental chains. The basic pattern is likely to be that sex is completely absent in some areas while it appears in the socially allowed areas in concentrated doses.

I would like next to examine written literature. It is a commonplace that since the rise of Romanticism one of the more powerful themes in fiction in the Anglo-Saxon-Teutonic world has been the love life of men and women. (There are, of course, a large number of European and American writings such as Thomas Mann's *The Magic Mountain,* or Thomas Wolfe's *Look Homeward, Angel* which have treated problems and situations that are not concerned with the love life of men and women.) On the other hand, apart from pornographic novels, like *The Plum of the Golden Vase*[4] in China, Chinese and Japanese fiction has been much less concerned with this aspect of life. The vast majority of Chinese novels which have acquired great popularity are ones like *The Romance of the Three Kingdoms;*[5] *All Men Are Brothers;*[6] *The Story of T'ang Dynasty* (there are a number of novels based roughly upon the various dynasties); *The True Story of Chi Kung, the Mad Monk; The True Story of Pao Kung, the Wonderful Official;* and so on—novels which touch upon little or no love life. *The Dream of Red Chamber,*[7] *Western Chamber,*[8] and *Strange Stories from a Chinese Studio*[9] are a few of the others which are primarily stories of love life between the sexes. Japanese fiction, according to some students of Japan,[10] is even less concerned with the love life of men and women. The majority of Japanese novels depict the drama of loyalty to masters, or of a conflict of loyalty to two or more masters. There are many instances in which a wife expresses her loyalty to her husband by releasing him from obligation to her so that he might be free to serve his masters.

However the differences go far beyond the quantitative level. The

Western European novel that is built upon the love theme usually treats of the union between the hero and the heroine as the highest point of achievement or climax. Not infrequently the entire book is based upon the pursuit, the difficulties, the misunderstanding, and the interferences, all leading up to the point where the two chief characters are physically united, but, as in a painting, the actual union is left undescribed in the novel. Most of the time the authors describe the burning desire on the part of one character for the person of the other sex as though that very desire were unrelated to the sexual act.

The Chinese novels, wherever they touch upon women, speak of the male's pursuit of the female in the same way as his pursuit of other worldly goods, like gold or jewelry. In pornographic novels the sexual acts of the characters are, of course, frequently described in detail throughout many parts of the story. But even in other novels the sexual union is treated with a degree of frankness which one finds only traces of in portions of Whitman's *Leaves of Grass*.[11] In *The Dream of Red Chamber* the hero, although never sexually united with the heroine, had sexual relations with a number of other women, including maids, while at the same time wooing his ideal sweetheart. In addition he also had erotic relationships of varying degrees with a number of other women and a homosexual relationship with an actor. The developments in *Western Chamber* are characteristic of the majority of popular traditional novels which, though never reaching the same literary height and reputation as *Western Chamber,* were enjoyed by a much wider audience through the village and town storytellers all over China. In *Western Chamber,* the hero and heroine overcame the initial obstacle and met in a back garden, and their sexual union was at once described. The rest of the plot concerned what the hero had to do to marry the heroine properly and what they had to do to obtain proper social status. In many colloquial novels the hero and the heroine sexually unite much sooner than in *Western Chamber,* and the sexual episode is passed over like numerous other episodes. During the usually brief pursuit period, sexual congress as the aim was never very much veiled, so that when the hero and heroine met no reader would be surprised at the outcome. Certainly no words are wasted on the exaltation of women, nor on abstract description and analysis of the agony of the soul in its yearning for the object of love.

The contrasts obtained by comparing the literature of the two Eastern cultures with those of the two Western cultures is consistent with that obtained in connection with painting. First, Western novels are much more engrosssed than Eastern novels in sex life as the major theme. Second, Eastern novels treat sex as one aspect of life, so that when sex life is depicted it is done with much greater frankness; but when the depiction of sex life is not the primary objective of the novels, it is merely noted and the plot goes on to other things. Third, Western novels often treat of the union of the two sexes as the chief climax; for, according to notions of romantic love, the supposedly permanent desire and perhaps compatibility of the two specific people for each other is the entire concern. In Eastern novels the main problem is more commonly what happens after the two specific people have sexually united; for marriage is not construed as a matter for the two specific people alone, but actively involves the whole society in general and their respective kinship groups in particular. This last contrast is not entirely lacking in painting. There is no doubt that, as a whole, Chinese and Japanese painting emphasizes much more the total situation of the individual characters than the moods and thoughts of the individual characters themselves. When repression is emphasized in socialization, the main areas of tension are more internalized than externalized; and the main psychological needs are centered around an internal balance rather than one of harmony with the outside world. On the other hand, when suppression is emphasized in socialization, the main areas of tension are centered around one's relation with one's fellowmen; and the psychological needs are expressed more as a desire for harmony with the outside world rather than as a desire for an internal balance. While neither category is exclusive of the other, the comparatively greater of the two emphases in any one culture gives shape to the expressions of the majority personality needs which find their way into art and literature.

The two outstanding points of contrast thus far stand as follows: First, in Chinese and Japanese art and literature, sex is compartmentalized; whereas in Anglo-Saxon-Teutonic art and literature, sex tends to be all-pervasive. Second, in the former the approach to women is comparatively direct, while in the latter it is comparatively indirect.

These two points of reference are applicable to a wide range of facts pertaining to the actual sex life in the two types of cultures. In Anglo-Saxon-Teutonic cultures the two sexes have never been segregated, although the rules for their meeting may have been more stringent formerly than in more recent times. In Chinese and Japanese cultures, on the other hand, the exclusion of females from a large number of areas of life is a very ancient usage. In Anglo-Saxon-Teutonic societies women have traditionally played parts in government and international politics; any cursory glance over European history will make this evident. In Japanese society women have rarely reached great heights. In China the few women who by personal ability and a fortunate concatenation of circumstances have been able to wield power in government have been regarded as examples of human aberration; in Chinese and Japanese history the female role is comparatively insignificant.

In religion, too, the female role is much more significant in Anglo-Saxon-Teutonic than in Chinese or Japanese cultures. Christianity in its basic precepts certainly did not conceive of woman as being an equal of man. Rather, women, as members of the weaker sex, were to be protected and supervised, like all other weaker persons. But gradually and consistently the position of women with relation to church affairs became more significant. With the Reformation and the rise of Protestantism the place of women in religion has been further enhanced. It has often been erroneously stated that Christianity raised the position of European women. The position of women before God, from the viewpoint of the present author, was raised in spite of the church, and the subsequent effect of Christianity on the position of women in other lands comes from the fact that the gospel of Christ was spread largely by Anglo-Saxon-Teutonic peoples who amalgamated their own cultures with their missionary messages. In China up to the nineteenth century and in Japan up to World War II, although men and women could often worship in the same temples, there was no question of equality between the sexes in religious affairs. Women remained the ritually unclean sex, and before the gods their position remained one of subordination to men.

But while the Anglo-Saxon-Teutonic cultures encourage association and equality between the sexes, their approach to women, when compared with Chinese and Japanese cultures, must be described as indirect. Such etiquette as kissing the hand, and permitting embraces between men and women not husbands or wives, nor lovers, and such slogans of chivalry as "ladies first," are generally expressions of this indirectness in approach. A cartoonist captured this basic contradiction, almost ambivalence, not many months ago in a short cartoon strip which appeared in *The New Yorker*. Two men in bathing suits are seen on a beach very much engaged by the sight of a young lady clad in a long flowing gown through which her slim form can be seen. Then she walks away, only to come back in the briefest of bathing suits, settling herself nearby. Neither of the gentlemen even raise their heads from their books. The cartoonist might have had the idea that gowns are rare on a beach and that rarity attracts more attention. More probably he was epitomizing the fundamental psychological contradiction of wanting to get at women without getting too close.

An excellent illustration of this contradiction is in social dancing. It is not the purpose of this paper to trace the origin of social dancing. But the popularity of the custom in given cultures seems to be correlated with the question of whether sex is repressed in general or compartmentalized. Social dancing permits a high degree of diffused intimacy between people who otherwise are not allowed such intimacy. Yet the manner of such contact is more or less rigidly defined by custom. Seen in relation to my analysis of art and literature, the popularity of social dancing in the West is perfectly in order. On the other hand the rejection, or at least the failure of a whole-hearted acceptance, of social dancing in China is equally in order. Since the middle of the nineteenth century, many Western institutions, usages, customs, and technological achievements have been accepted in China. Some of these have achieved great popularity at once. Others were resisted and failed. In the light of the science of culture these acceptances and resistances are perfectly understandable. But a contradiction not easily explainable otherwise concerns freedom of choice in marriage, and social dancing. The former is at once accepted and at once becomes a chief point of tension between the older and the newer generations;[12] but the latter has up to date been taken up by some moderns, and rejected by others, or taken up during one short period of time but rejected during a subsequent period of time. In different cities it has been cursed as one of the reasons of the downfall of the Chinese society, because it has brought about immorality. But the same critics of modern social dancing never marshalled the same amount of fire at public prostitution, or at the old institution of concubinage which still persists in diverse ways. And when one realizes that the modern generation of Chinese—although many have won the battle of freedom of choice in marriage with their parents—have very often been badly curtailed in the realization of their victory because of lack of regular channels for meeting members of the opposite sex, the rejection of social dancing becomes even stranger.

The strangeness of the case will greatly diminish if one thinks of the two basic points of references; namely, the indirectness of approach to sex in Anglo-Saxon-Teutonic cultures, and the compartmentalization of sex in Japanese and Chinese cultures. To the former, social dancing is valued because it combines intimacy with distance in a diffused manner. To the latter, social dancing threatens to confuse the several social categories. Physical contact with prostitutes similar to that involved in social dancing as a preliminary to sexual congress is understood; but as an end in itself or as part of the family life it becomes bizarre.

Another area of life which may be of importance in this connection concerns sexual anomaly, such as homosexuality. In American life much light has been thrown on the subject by the publication of the Kinsey report. First, let us consider the sources of orgasm among the U. S. population as a whole; although masturbation decreases with age and heterosexual intercourse increases with age, homosexual outlet remains more or less constant from adolescence to forty years of age. Second, while homosexual outlet as a source of orgasm is chiefly found among *unmarried* males, as one would expect, it is also significant enough to rate among *married* males. Furthermore, while among unmarried males of all educational levels masturbation decreases with age, among the same group, homosexual outlet, like heterosexual outlet, increases with age. At the same time among married males—especially those with college education—homosexual outlet as well as masturbation increase slightly as they grow older (Kinsey, Pomeroy, and Martin 1948: Figs. 126, 128–133; pp. 488–93). These facts are very interesting. But of greater significance are the attitudes towards homosexuality and the passive or active nature of the homosexual experience. Among all college and other students with whom a few of my students and I have discussed the subject, we found a strong and immediate reaction of disgust against homosexuality or any suggestion of it. The Kinsey report does not indicate the nature of homosexual activities involved where the authors discuss homosexuality as an outlet, but in connection with mouth-genital contacts in male homosexual situations two categories of activities are differentiated: "male active" and "male passive." Without exception the "male passive" incidence is, in every age group from 16 to 40, more than double the "male active" incidence (Kinsey et al. 1948: 370–71).

There is no comparable quantitative data for China or Japan but certain qualitative observations may be made. Benedict said of Japan:

> Homosexual indulgences are also part of traditional "human feelings." In old Japan these were the sanctioned pleasures of men of high status such as the samurai and the priests. In the Meiji period when Japan made so many of her customs illegal in her effort to win the approval of Westerners, she ruled that this custom should be punishable by law. It still falls, however, among those "human feelings" about which moralistic attitudes are inappropriate. It must be kept in its proper place and must not interfere with carrying on the family. Therefore the danger of a man or a woman's "becoming" a homosexual, as the Western phrase has it, is hardly conceived, though a man can choose to become a male geisha professionally. The Japanese are especially shocked at adult passive homosexuals in the United States. Adult men in Japan would seek out boy partners, for adults consider the passive role to be beneath their dignity. The Japanese draw their own lines as to what a man can do and retain his self-respect, but they are not the ones we draw.   (Benedict 1946: 187–88)

The most striking thing about this passage is its close similarity to circumstances and attitudes which one would find in China. First, in China as in Japan, one would certainly not encounter any comparable emotional attitude of disgust toward homosexuality as such. As a person who has been educated in China up to the university level, I can report from personal observation that, among the students, there is a gradual reduction of the degree of consciousness of homosexuality or of frequency of suggestions about homosexuality, from primary school upwards. Among higher primary school male students (comparable to U. S. fifth to eighth grades), in a non-coeducational situation where the total range of age differences was very wide,[13] homosexual relations between the bigger and smaller boys was constantly suggested and joked about in general. An actual case of homosexuality provided material for hilarity rather than disgust. In fact disgust was not found at all. In my secondary school, which was again a boy's school, gossip about and suggestions of homosexuality were about as frequent as on the previous educational level. In my senior middle school years (corresponding to U. S. 11th and 12th grades), there were two recognized homosexual pairs in my class. One pair consisted of a married man in his early thirties (wife living at home about three hundred miles away) and a rather feminine looking unmarried young adult of around eighteen to twenty. It was generally recognized that the former was the active party and the latter, passive. The other pair consisted of two young adults, both in their twenties. One of them was married at the time (wife also about two hundred miles away), and was somewhat older than the unmarried one. But unlike the usual pattern among homosexuals, in this case the older married person was the physically stronger but passive party.

From the point of view of a comparison the interesting thing is that neither the active nor the passive parties to these cases of homosexual attachments entertained any strong feeling of embarrassment indicating either guilt or shame, as the following illustrative material will show. One day the active party of the first homosexual pair was very much emotionally upset because of some trouble with the school authority. As he was a sort of leader among the student body, his many friends expressed concern but he could not be pacified. Some of the latter went without much ado to his passive homosexual partner and asked him to go and comfort the older man. The manner of their request and the polite but warm language they used made the sexual element involved clear to everybody, in the context. The younger man hesitated for an instant but subsequently went and spoke softly, in the presence of others, to the older man. They held each others' hands. In the other case the older but passive partner to the attachment was more active socially and even made active homosexual advances to another boy younger and weaker than he; but whenever his long-time active sexual partner was involved in a quarrel with others, he would defend the younger person without restraint and would willingly submit to the latter's curses and rebukes. Twice he even submitted to a public beating by his younger friend without offering any self-defense except hysterical cries of agony.

In both cases the active parties showed feelings of triumph and satisfaction. They were objects of envy, much in the same way that the man who won the affection of many girls in my college years was envied. The passive parties were usually ridiculed in the beginning of the attachment. When such an attachment was suggested the passive one would usually strongly deny it; but once the initial situation was over the later reception of such a person among the student group depended very much upon his position in general. In the second case of homosexuality described above, the passive partner, who was the older and stronger one of the two, happened to be a good scholar and a fairly good basketball player. He was on the reserve list of the school's basketball team. There was amusement about his particular homosexual behavior, but there was no visible ostracism nor disgust against him in general. This remained so even after two instances in which he was publicly kicked around by his active partner, who was smaller than he. After each event many students made remarks and privately gossiped about his hysterical cries and nonresistance, but the attachment and the man's personal relations went on much as they did before.

In the first case, the active partner was handsome and inactive in public affairs. The passive partner, who was younger than his active friend, was more of an object of sexual curiosity than anything else. In the sense that boys would like to boast that they were active partners to homosexual unions, he had nothing to boast about. But once the situation was established he was accepted without enthusiasm, but without disgust. In college life, where coeducation was the rule and not the exception, homosexuality as a subject for conversation, gossip, or jokes definitely became rare. Here the overwhelming interest was in the heterosexual direction. Homosexuality, as it cropped up occasionally, was laughed off, and the person who showed evidence of engaging in passive homosexuality was an object of ridicule.

In the wider society very much the same pattern toward homosexuality exists. There is no disgust toward the active homosexual, but ridicule and contempt are shown the passive one, especially if the passive one is a professional homosexual. In the late Manchu dynasty, Peking, the national capital, had a number of legal male brothels where the bureaucrats entertained and otherwise had a good time very much in the same way as they did in whore houses. The accounts of this period show that there was contempt for and amusement at these professional passive homosexuals, many of whom were married and who chose to do what they did largely because of poverty; but in any case the contempt was not differentiable from that levelled against female prostitutes in general. It was the contempt of a person of some status for persons of low or no status. Actors and actresses, chiropodists and attendants in houses of prostitution were looked upon with equal contempt.

Thus, while in all the cultures under discussion homosexuality is not regarded as being the normal way of sex gratification, the presence of strong repressive history against it, indicated by the presence of strong disgust, necessitates its being approached by an indirect rather than a direct method in America. Similarly the absence of such repression due to compartmentalization of sex activities makes it possible for such matters to be approached directly and without strong emotion in the two Eastern cultures.[14]

The differences between the two camps, however, go deeper than have been made apparent by the analysis so far. In China the indications are that the incidence of homosexuality tends to decrease with age, while in the U. S. it tends to persist in spite of strong feelings of disgust. Then, homosexuality in the two types of cultures is qualitatively dissimilar. In the East the active male homosexual suffers from little or no social pressure, while the passive male homosexual is usually an object, more or less, of shame. Accordingly, apart from those who are hermaphrodites, children who have been sold or put into positions of servitude or disadvantage, or male prostitutes who engage in the practice as a matter of trade, the usual male homosexual in China takes the sexually active role. The situation in the U. S. seems to be quite otherwise: where, for example, as we have seen before, in mouth-genital contacts the "male passive" incidence is, in every age group from 16 to 40, more than double the "male active" category. Of all the pornographic literature commonly known to Chinese students I have never read or heard about one which involved homosexuality between males of the mouth-genital contact variety which was engaged in because of desire on the part of the passive party. In pornographic pictures I have never seen a single one of this type of activity whatsoever. While some of the aforementioned specific classes of persons might carry on a passive male role in mouth-genital contact because of their disadvantageous positions or economic necessity, the majority of them would stop doing it as soon as circumstances warranted it. Yet heterosexual mouth-genital contact, usually with the female performing fellatio on the male, was common in both pornographic novels and pictures.

In order to explain these differences one might resort to the Freudian theory that the core of homosexuality is correlated with rejection of the persons of the opposite sex because of some deep-seated repulsion or fright (Oedipus influence), or of unconscious identification with the parent of the opposite sex (associative homosexuality) (Fenichel 1945). This hypothesis is, if true, chiefly applicable to a culture with strong repressive mechanisms and not applicable to one with suppression as the chief method of socialization. The emphasis on repression, which is commensurate with an individual-centered pattern of life, is conducive to strong repulsions or attachments between individuals; while the emphasis on suppression, with its situation-centered pattern of life, is not. For this reason such deep-seated repulsion or fright which according to Freud would result in rejection of persons of the opposite sex, or unconscious identification with the mother, would be much more common in the Western than in the Eastern cultures under discussion. The presence of such deep-seated emotions, or unconscious identification with mother, would lead males into *homosexual craving* of the passive as well as the active variety; but where they are absent, or only present to a minor degree, homosexuality is a mere substitute for heterosexuality, and the overwhelming interest of such a male would naturally be the active role.

As pointed out before, repressed material tends to go deep into the unconscious and become omnipresent in the life of the person; such bottled-up psychic energy and emotions tend to blow up at a more or less unpredictable time and place. On the other hand suppressive mechanisms are generated by a person's comparatively immediate external environment and tend to remain on the layers of the mind nearer reality; in the latter situation, since there is less bottled-up psychic energy and emotions, there is less opportunity for individual conflagration. The external environment allows more room for change and for maneuver. It is in this light that one may understand many facts about sex crime. For example, in the U. S. rape is a common crime in peacetime. In China and Japan the picture is otherwise. A brief survey of the newspapers in the respective countries will leave little doubt on the matter. Raping is concommitant in China and Japan only to war or civil disorders; then it tends to occur on a large scale, like looting and wanton shooting, because of the lack of external restraint. Similarly, while in Anglo-Saxon-Teutonic cultures verbalization of sex is forbidden in general among the middle and upper classes, there is much in the language of everyday life which may be said to have a veiled sexual flavor, such as the reference to reaction to genital stimuli under certain conditions as "leaving a bad taste in the mouth" (Hendricks 1934: 38). In Chinese and Japanese culture there is no such strong taboo against certain types of usages in general, but the type of language is much more determined by the company. Among the elite and on religious occasions all profanity is to be avoided; the language used is one full of literary allusions. However, children and rustic folk think nothing of reviling enemies with strong language chiefly centered around sex. When such is the occasion, the language is not ever veiled and the most commonly heard epithet is "I have sexual intercourse [using the word in the male active sense] with your mother." Even highly placed bureaucrats and Confucian scholars have been known to speak in such a vein privately, especially when they were aggravated by their inferiors.

RELIGION AND OTHER ASPECTS OF CULTURE

The material of this paper has thus far been confined chiefly to sex. When many non-sex activities are examined in these two kinds of cultures, they seem to be equally consistent with the major thesis of this paper. From the point of view of any modern anthropologist, the origin of certain religions, such as Christianity, Mohammedanism, or Buddhism, is a historical problem and cannot, therefore, be reasonably accounted for in personality-psychological terms. However, the influence and spread of one or another form of religion in given cultures—provided that there is agreement that forms of religions are subject to scientific treatment—are very much dependent upon their acceptability or unacceptability according to the personality characteristics generated by the pre-existing cultural norms. From an analysis of novels it is apparent that there are certain differences between the two camps in the approach to sex. The actual differences are, however, far wider in scope. If the differences in Eastern and Western novels can be characterized, it might be said that the latter usually emphasize introspection or searching for the soul as well as the inner meaning of life, while the former usually interest themselves in the opposite direction, namely, the external equilibrium or searching for the individual's proper places in the most appropriate social situation. From this point of view it is easy to see why Christianity has taken much deeper root in Europe and America than in either Japan or China. The personality-culture pattern which is developed out of repressive mechanisms emphasizes the individual, which in turn looks for one all-pervasive god. The personality-culture pattern which is developed out of suppressive mechanisms emphasizes the external relationship of the individual which in turn looks for satisfactory adjustments with a number of gods, each for a specific purpose.

In the same way it becomes easy to see why Protestantism had to replace Catholicism in Western Europe. Catholicism, with its many saints and a priestly hierarchy as well as numerous and complicated rituals which are considered necessary parts of the total function of individual worship, is less soul-searching and less introspective—in a sense much closer to polytheism than monotheism—than Protestantism, with its simplified rituals, absence of saints, and emphasis on direct communication with God. Furthermore it is no accident that Christianity, in spite of many centuries of Western missionary work and a desire on the part of the East to imitate the West, has made scarcely any headway. Up to the present less than one percent of the Chinese population is nominally Christian, while roughly the same proportion is reported for Japan.[15] Furthermore, the most interesting thing is that of the about 3,000,000 to 4,000,000 Chinese Christians, only about 400,000 are Protestants and the rest are Catholics.[16]

Thus repression versus suppression translated into the realm of religion may also be seen to be related, respectively, to religious intolerance versus religious tolerance. In Anglo-Saxon-Teutonic cultures religion is a matter exclusively of individual souls; in China and Japan it is a matter primarily of the spiritual station of the individual. In the West the search for inner peace and balance is primary; in the East the search for suitable rapport with the world of spirits is primary. In the West religion concerns itself with individual guilt and salvation; in the East it concerns itself with group responsibility and individual salvation within the group. For this reason condemnation to hell is believed to be irreversible in the West, while the misfortune of the dead in China may be alleviated by the good deeds of those family members who are alive.[17]

Let us next examine certain basic psychological attitudes in the two types of cultures. The best exposition of this is that of Dr. Benedict on guilt and shame. To quote:

> The strong identification of circumspection with self-respect includes, therefore, watchfulness of all the cues one observes in other people's acts, and a strong sense that other people are sitting in judgment. "One cultivates self-respect (one must jicho)," they say, "because of society." "If there were no society one would not need to respect oneself (cultivate jicho)."
>
> True shame cultures rely on external sanctions for good behavior, not as true guilt cultures do, on an internalized conviction of sin. Shame is a reaction to other people's criticism. A man is shamed either by being openly ridiculed and rejected or by fantasying to himself that he has been made ridiculous. In either case it is a potent sanction. But it requires an audience or at least a man's fantasy of an audience. Guilt does not. In a nation where honor means living up to one's picture of oneself, a man may suffer from guilt though no man knows of his misdeed and a man's feeling of guilt may actually be relieved by confessing his sin. (Benedict 1946: 222–23)

Dr. Benedict was, of course, speaking only of Japan when she spoke of shame culture. In terms of the present paper, guilt occurs most readily in a culture that is obviously based upon repression as the chief mechanism of social control; while shame occurs most readily in a culture that is obviously based upon suppression as the chief mechanism of social control. One does not have to go far to look for evidence of guilt in Anglo-Saxon-Teutonic cultures. Even the recent House bill which changed immigration laws affecting Japanese was passed in terms of retribution for a wrong committed by the United States.[18]

On the other hand, in China and Japan, shame, an embarrassment arising out of the fact that one is suddenly out of tune with one's social relationship, is very much in evidence. The sense of shame is applicable to a wide range of life's activities. It applies to national affairs no less than it does to personal affairs. It applies to serious business relations no less than it does to casual social encounters. The appropriate clothes for the appropriate occasion, the suitable manners for the suitable situation, the commonly recognized deference and subordination between superiors and inferiors—a mistake in any of these or other conventions—may be a grave cause for the rise of the sense of shame. A traditional Chinese scholar who has misused or given the wrong stroke to a word in a public document or even a letter, will have a hard time living the experience down. In the same way a slip of tongue in public is a much more serious matter in Japan than in the United States.

It is in this sense of shame that one must look for the meaning of the concept of "face." It is a popular misconception that "face-saving" is peculiar to China and Japan. Anybody who has made even a cursory observation on American public and private affairs will realize that this is untrue. On numerous occasions "face" and "face-saving" are equally an American concern. But what distinguishes "face" in the East from that in the West is that it is much more inclusive in the former than in the latter. A person brought up in a culture with suppression as the major mechanism of social control tends to concern himself much more with what he does in the presence of others, and in many more connections, than a person brought up in a culture with repression as the major mechanism. For this reason form has much greater meaning and importance in the East than in the West. For the same reason the relationship between superiors and inferiors, such as male and female, bureaucrat and commoner, employer and employee, conqueror and conquered, tend to be more rigid and more without humor in the East than in the West.

Using the same key of suppression versus repression certain new light could be thrown on the so-called "racial problem." Race prejudice has been explained on the basis of a frustration-aggression theory (Dollard, Miller, Doob, Mowrer, and Sears 1939: 151–56; Dollard 1937), but such a theory alone cannot explain why such prejudice is a common problem in Germany and the United States, but nonexistent in China and Japan, or at least not in the form which is found in the West. In a culture which is based upon suppression and therefore a satisfactory external relationship, the different statuses are adequate for purpose of handling the situation involving contact between two ethnic groups. The Chinese traditionally called all non-Chinese groups barbarians but as barbarians they were to be left alone, once the acknowledgement of political superiority was made. In fact the conquests against non-Chinese groups in Chinese history were chiefly done at the whim of the autocratic emperors. Once the conquest was accomplished, the people had little interest in the conquered. Many aboriginals in China achieved distinction in the imperial examinations and bureaucracy. This group and their descendants were at once accepted because of their statuses in the existing scheme of things. They were respected or laughed at according to their literary achievement, the same as if they were Chinese scholars.

The treatment of conquered peoples like Koreans, Chinese, Europeans, and Malays in modern times by Japan has often been exceedingly harsh at first, when the battle dust was still not settled. The Japanese, because of their treatment in the first place in the hands of Westerners, wanted revenge and also wanted to show that they were far above the other Asiatics. They usually wanted the conquered peoples to show them extreme external signs of subordination. Take Korea for example. At first, extreme external obedience was exacted from all Koreans. There were many forms and instances of harsh persecution of the Koreans in Korea. But as the Japanese position in Korea became more secure, the Koreans who took over Japanese clothing, language, and manners were more and more accepted by the Japanese. Many Koreans I know complained about the fact that some upper class Koreans would rather be Japanese than Koreans. Many of them did make the change, including marriage to Japanese women.[19]

This is not the case in Germany or the United States. In each of these cultures, because of its emphasis on repression as a mechanism and therefore on inner balance, external passive accommodation between the dominant and the subordinate castes—Jews in Germany and Negroes in the United States—is not enough. Negroes who are "uppity" in the South have been lynched. In spite of isolation in ghettos or otherwise restricted spheres, the Jews in Germany were continuously objects of pogroms.

It is true that there were outstanding Negroes who were not only accepted but also nearly idolized by British society in the eighteenth century (Little 1948: 199–202), but it took less than half a century for various forms of prejudice to rise (Little 1948: 207–209). There was also the Chinese Boxer Rebellion of 1911 in which the chief objects of attack were European missionaries and later all Europeans. However, in discussing the racial problem of the Anglo-Saxon-Teutonic world one has to remember that the direction of persecution in each culture was first of all given by its historical background. In the United States it is only the Negro who is an object of nation-wide persecution, while the other minorities such as Chinese, Japanese, Mexicans, Indians, and so on, are not so historically related to the mass hysteria. Furthermore, many American landladies and restaurant-keepers have been known to accommodate Negroes from Jamaica and elsewhere, while at the same time refusing to have anything to do with Negroes with a southern accent, who are their compatriots. In Germany, persecution only befell the Jews and not other groups. Britain of the eighteenth century simply had no historical condition for racial prejudice against the Negroes. The Chinese Boxer Rebellion against European missionaries must be understood as a temporary mass hysteria under conditions of general poverty, ignorance, obvious

Western encroachment, and misconduct on the part of many missionaries. It was certainly neither deliberately planned nor carried out, and it did not last. Furthermore, the hysteria only hit the north and west. In a number of southern provinces the governors rigidly forbade the activities of the Boxers, and the movement did not spread. Lastly, the movement was not only against European missionaries but also against Chinese ministers and Christians in general. All in all the outbursts—whether the object was racial or otherwise—in the Eastern cultures lacked the deliberation and permanency which such outbursts had in the Western cultures.

CHINA VS. JAPAN, AND AMERICA VS. GERMANY

From the foregoing analysis it may have seemed that there is a complete similarity between Chinese and Japanese culture on the one hand and American and German culture on the other. Nothing would be further from the truth. The similarity appears only because one factor has been examined: suppression or repression as the chief mechanism of social control. When a second factor is added, the picture at once changes. This second factor is the presence or absence of a unified loyalty to the wider society or state. When this factor is added it will be seen that there are vast differences between Japan and China, and again between Germany and the United States.

Here again the analysis must be begun with the understanding that the origin of German loyalty to the abstract symbol of the state and Japanese loyalty to her emperor are both historical facts the origin of which cannot be explained simply on the basis of the projective system of the individual. However, given this loyalty or its lack, combined with the mechanism of repression or suppression, certain features will tend to appear in one or another culture in given situations, such as constructive effort in peace, or revitalization after defeat.

The presence or absence of a strong sense of a unified loyalty to the wider symbol of state could largely be held to account for the differences in modernizing developments in Japan and China. Although both Japanese and Chinese societies emphasize suppression and therefore proper external relationship of the individual as the goal of life, the existence of a strong sense of loyalty to the emperor means that each individual attempts to fulfill his obligations not only in his immediate but also the widest possible social environment under the emperor. This makes for a smooth and thorough national organization which is capable of effective and quick action. Japanese industrial and military advances in modern times, with no change in her traditional social and political structures, is an outstanding illustration of this point.[20]

In defeat, once the situation is clarified, the Japanese, because of the traditional emphasis on proper stations under the emperor, will have overwhelming and genuine enthusiasm and love for their conquerors. The individual has merely changed his object of loyalty a bit, especially when the old nominal symbol has not been altered. There will be no sense of shame anymore. All the individual has to do is to accommodate to a new situation with somewhat modified statuses. Because of the individual conditioning to suppression as a mechanism of social control, the changed situation, once established, causes no deep resentment, simply because the individual is not psychologically hurt. A conditioning to proper external relationship merely calls for a readjustment of that external relationship when the necessity comes. Because of the loyalty to a wider national symbol, the Japanese are not likely to be so resistant to such customs as social dancing (as the Chinese will, regardless of what happens), if the custom is endorsed by the new conquerors, which is the power behind the throne. Once the conqueror-conquered statuses are clarified and well established, what is good for the wider nation will be good for the individual.

The case of China is similar to Japan in one respect and different in another. Chinese culture emphasizes suppression as a mechanism of social control, but China traditionally has no permanent symbol of loyalty to the wider state. It is significant that while in Japanese history there has been only one dynasty which claimed its descent from the Sun Goddess, who in turn was the creator of the universe, in Chinese history there have been nearly twenty dynasties which were unrelated and which replaced one another. Certainly none would be considered as the originator of the universe, or even of Chinese society as a whole. The emperor, though equipped with absolute power while the dynasty lasted, was nevertheless regarded by the people functionally and could be removed by revolt. In place of a permanent loyalty to the emperor and his descendants, the Chinese believe in permanent affiliation to a kinship group. The descendants of emperors of a fallen dynasty were soon forgotten by the people; but among the ordinary families even the remotest kin member would be traced in genealogical books. Many wealthy and powerful families boast of descent from some famous ministers, legendary or real, who supposedly existed in Chow or Ch'in dynasty, about two thousand or more years ago.

This being the case, when the need for modernization arose in China as it did in Japan, China was unable to take quick and effective action in order to meet the challenge of the West, because the organization of the wider society was neither smooth nor thorough. The loyalty of the individual was to the family group, and the most important goal of an individual was in achieving proper status within that group. As a result Chinese large-scale industrial enterprises, which started more or less at the same time as large-scale Japanese industrial enterprises, and with equal advantage in capital and equipment, deteriorated into nonentity, while their Japanese counterparts went ahead by leaps and bounds. The respective histories of the Chinese Merchant Navigation Company and the Japanese Nippon Yosen Kaisa provide us with one of the many illustrations on this point.

In defeat and under conditions of conquest, the Chinese, like the

Japanese, will not be deeply resentful, because the individual is psychologically unhurt; but the allegiance to kinship ties will cause the average person to be without enthusiasm for the new regime set up by the conquerors. In this respect the Chinese will be unlike the Japanese. Furthermore the conquerors of China will be opposed if they do not leave the people alone. Throughout Chinese history those alien dynasties which remained in power the longest were those that knew how to leave the Chinese alone. On the other hand indigenous dynasties were short-lived if they did not leave the people alone. The opposition of Chinese to conquest is more likely a result not of any deep-seated feelings against the new rulers but of hatred for external inconvenience.

If left alone, the average Chinese attitude toward conquest or a new regime will be one of indifference. They will not effectively form large non-kinship groups, or participate actively in such groups, unless the basic kinship pattern has been in some way modified. So far whatever modification there has been in kinship pattern has usually occurred in large urban centers and even there slowly (Hsu 1949a). New elements of culture from the West, especially where it pertains to the virtues involving kinship groups, will be accepted, if at all, with reserve.

Germany and the United States present two different combinations of the factors analysed in this paper. German culture emphasizes repression as a mechanism of social control, and therefore, individualism; but this individualism is combined with a desire for loyalty to the widest possible culturally defined group, the sate. This flare for some wider structural framework of reference is clearly seen in German scholarship for the last several hundred years. Germany is, as far as I know, the only Western European society in which, as in Japan, the sanctity of the family and the female sexual function could be exploited to suit the purposes of the state without serious opposition from the people. Nevertheless, because of the fact that this emphasis on the wider social and political framework is combined with repressive mechanisms and individualism, in German culture there has always been a conflict between these two poles. It was no accident that Hegelian dialecticism, with its thesis and antithesis, first arose and gained popularity in Germany.

This extreme emphasis on the place of the individual with reference to the state enables the German people to make smooth and thorough organization on a large scale for effective and quick action in time of peace and stress. The fact that Germany, a comparative late-comer in the Industrial Revolution, should have been able to catch up with England, in terms of expansion, output, and productivity, is good evidence for this observation. Once defeated, and subject to a situation of conquest by alien rulers, the German will not only have no enthusiasm for the conquerors but will intensely hate the outsiders, because his internal emotional balance is badly hurt. Before a new political and social framework is established, the individual, because of lack of any real social anchorage, will feel lost and aimless; but he will soon converge toward anything which will suggest the rise of a wider framework with an indigenous German appearance: this may be Naziism or its modified form; anti-semitism; or something new. The important thing is that the new framework desired will have to be wide, on a state scale, and it will also have to look German. In this connection it is very interesting to contrast the external attitudes of Japan and Germany toward conquerors. The Japanese, as a whole, are afraid that the United States will leave; they find comfort in having United States support and authority for, at any rate, an indefinite period of time. On the other hand, Germans, as a whole, are anxious for the departure of the controlling powers. Recent reports show that Western Germans are suspicious of the new German government set up there, because it is not sufficiently German. In both cases the desire for a wider allegiance is present; but the people brought up in a culture which emphasizes internal emotional balance cannot react in the same way as another people brought up in a culture which emphasizes external harmony with the powers that be.

America represents a situation different from any of the foregoing three, because here the cultural tradition emphasizes no unified allegiance by the individual to any single group, from family to the state. As aptly observed by many scholars, Americans are suspicious of any single group exerting overwhelming control, and the entire constitution as well as the power structure of the various levels of government are based upon the principle of check and balance. The social groups claiming allegiance of the individual are many, but most of them are neither permanent nor necessarily in harmony with the whole. As a matter of fact the typical picture of American social groups is one in which there are all kinds of inconsistencies, contradictions, conflicts as well as accommodation. The over-all cultural emphasis is still stark individualism, based upon repression as the chief mechanism, and the age-old philosophy that if each works for his own good the end result will be the most good for the largest number.

In time of peace the constructive efforts will be slow. In spite of her superabundance of resources, tremendous mechanization and the highest standard of living in the world—floods, droughts, the dust bowl, hurricanes, tornadoes, poorly equipped and staffed schools, and so on will continue to affect one sector or another of the American nation. There will be little or no coordinated effort to deal with some of these basic problems and the colossal production and economy will move on with tremendous waste.

In time of national distress, of defeat, and under conditions of conquest—from which Americans have fortunately never suffered—the American people would be deeply disturbed and would resist the conquerors, regardless of whether the latter left them alone or not. There would certainly be no enthusiasm for any alien regime, not even a passive acquiescence. Allegiance to idealism would make any external accommodation with conquerors very difficult. The individual in such a situation would have less feeling of being lost or aimless like the Germans, but would be able to look around for some positive lines of action, simply because Americans have been used to managing for themselves and not to being told to do one thing or another. The lack of any permanent traditional allegiance to any single group, such as the Chinese kinship structure or the German and Japanese state, coupled with historical experience of organization from chaos, would enable an American to enter into much wider associations of resistance, and with much greater speed than, for example, the Chinese.

A DISCUSSION ON ORIGIN

The foregoing analysis is really only a first approximation of the problem. In a paper of this kind it is impossible to treat the subject exhaustively. Furthermore, any discussion of the wider national issues in personality terms is bound to be limited in application and value. However the question of the origin of the patterns of suppression or repression in the two types of cultures must also be examined, and the personality characteristics correlated with each.

In Dr. Benedict's attempt to explain the origin of the Japanese character, which from the Western point of view is full of contradictions, she says:

> The contradictions which all Westerners have described in Japanese character are intelligible from their child rearing. It produces a duality in their outlook on life, neither side of which can be ignored. From their experience of privilege and psychological ease in babyhood they retain through all the disciplines of later life the memory of an easier life when they "did not know shame." They do not have to paint a Heaven in the future; they have it in their past. They rephrase their childhood in their doctrine of the innate goodness of man, of the benevolence of their gods, and of the incomparable desirability of being a Japanese. . . .
>
> Gradually, after they are six or seven, responsibility for circumspection and "knowing shame" is put upon them and upheld by the most drastic of sanctions: that their own family will turn against them if they default. The pressure is not that of a Prussian discipline, but it is inescapable. In their early privileged period the ground has been prepared for this development both by the persistent inescapable training in nursery habits and posture, and by the parents' teasing which threatens the child with rejection. These early experiences prepare the child to accept great restraints upon himself when he is told that "the world" will laugh at him and reject him. He clamps down upon the impulses he expressed so freely in earlier life, not because they are evil but because they are now inappropriate. He is now entering upon serious life. As he is progressively denied the privileges of childhood he is granted the gratifications of greater and greater adulthood, but the experiences of that earlier period never truly fade out. In his philosophy of life he draws freely upon them. He goes back to them in his permissiveness about "human feelings." He

reexperiences them all through his adulthood in his "free areas" of life. (Benedict 1946: 286–87)

This lucid theory, which would account for contradictions in Japanese personality by the sharp contrast between early and later childhood experiences, is inadequate simply because it fails to apply to China. In many respects Chinese culture does not carry as many or as extreme contradictions as does Japanese culture. But from the Western point of view Chinese personality is equally full of contradictions. What can be more contradictory than for an educated and respected bureaucrat-scholar to talk earnestly on the evil of licentiousness, while he himself may have a thoroughly good time with his male friends at a brothel with no qualms at all? What can be more contradictory than for a people to forget about various gods until the occurrence of an emergency like a cholera epidemic?[21] Yet the same discontinuity in training between early and later childhood which Dr. Benedict observed for Japan does not hold true in China (Hsu 1949). Furthermore, a kind of sharp discontinuity between earlier and later experiences is very evident in the life of an American (Hsu 1952a).

That there is no consistent correlation between infant care and personality in all cultures studied thus far has been admirably demonstrated by Orlansky (1949). On the other hand, I believe that the factors responsible for, or correlated with, the basic contrast in the mechanism of socialization—suppression versus repression—between the two Eastern and two Western cultures may be sought in the broader aspects of the family life. These factors are considerably different from those given by Dr. Benedict for Japan alone.

If one looks at the family in China and Japan on the one hand, and Germany and the United States on the other, he sees that there are quantitative as well as qualitative differences. First the quantitative differences: The family in China and Japan is, as a whole, the larger joint family with more than one married couple and more than two generations living under the same roof. In contrast the family in Germany and the United State is, again as a whole, the smaller conjugal family with only a married couple and their unmarried children as the sole occupants of one unit of the living quarters. This being the case, it is obvious that the Chinese and Japanese individual in the process of growing up, as compared with the German and American individual in the same condition, is likely to have a much larger number and more categories of persons who have meant something to him from every period of life. This could mean in terms of the present suppression-versus-repression theory, two things. First, in the mind of the developing Chinese or Japanese child the parental image, in the normal course of events, is likely to be adulterated with that of a number of other relatives who, in one way or another, enter into the picture. This means a more diffused source of disciplinary power from the very start. The reverse, again in the normal course of events, is true of the developing American or German child. Second, because of the much larger family unit, the child in the two Eastern cultures early learns to appreciate the importance of different categories of relatives who mean something to him and to his parents. This sets the beginning of the sensitivity to external harmony, because, not only the child's life but the parents' attitude and behavior tend to be more or less seriously influenced by the presence or absence of one or another of the members of the joint family. The American and German picture is again the reverse.

However, compared with the qualitative differences, these quantitative differences are of minor importance. For if the average size of a family in the two Eastern cultures is compared with that in the two Western cultures, it is at once clear that the differences are not as tremendous as one would imagine. While there are many families in China of 30 or more people, the average size of the Chinese family is only 5.3 while that of America is between 3 and 4. The average family size in Japan is equally not tremendous. But if one examines the ideal and even actual patterns underlying the behavior of the individuals of the family in the two kinds of cultures, the differences are found to be truly great. First, even in premodern times, the family in Europe and America tended to atomism—except that modern America has carried the trend farther than the rest. The basic pattern of the Euro-American conjugal family is that each new generation ruthlessly replaces the old. And as the old no longer has any place in the existing scheme of things they, among a few other classes of people, are the ones who will suffer the greatest amount of psychological misery. On the other hand, China and Japan, even in modern times, emphasize loyalty to the family group as a whole, except that in China the picture is much more complicated and uneven. The basic pattern of the family is that age leads to new and more respected statuses and greater significance. True psychological misery does not, therefore, befall the aged. Misery is the lot of those who have no descendants or are otherwise without place in any existing kinship structure.

The matter goes beyond a mere question of atomization versus loyalty to the whole. Probably as a result of the tendency to atomization, and the stark fact that each new generation ruthlessly replaces the old one, parents of the Anglo-Saxon-Teutonic family tend to exert complete control over their children, the other relatives having no disciplinarian importance even if they live in the family. In such a family a person has little escape from parental control before maturity. On the other hand, lacking such motivation, parents of the Japanese-Chinese family have less determination to exert complete control over their children. Even if they wanted to do so, other family members like grandparents, aunts, and in-laws can exert effective interference with their authority in one way or another.

The implications of these differences are, in terms of the present theory, both far-reaching and obvious. The more exclusive and severe parental control in the Western family is consistent with the importance of repressive mechanisms in socialization and therefore with greater or more severe

internalization of the parental imago and other restrair
individual. The less exclusive and severe parental con'
family is consistent with the importance of suppress
socialization and therefore with smaller or less seve'
the parental imago and other restraining forces i'
pointed out at the beginning of this paper, although both ᵤ
repressive mechanisms are present and operative in an averagᵤ ,
regardless of his culture, the individual in the two Western culturᵉˢ
discussed here tends to look more to internal forces for guidance of his
actions, while the individual in the two Eastern cultures tends to look more
to external circumstances for guidance. This makes the difference between guilt and shame. This also makes the difference between individualism and what in the absence of a better term may be termed situationalism.
Finally, it is easier for the individual to tolerate contradictions in the
external situation by treating each situation more or less separately, than
for the individual to reconcile contradictions in the internal psyche—since
the functioning mind has to be much more closely knit than the functioning society or culture; thus the behavior of the Eastern individual is, from
the point of view of that of the West, naturally rife with obvious contradictions.

SUMMARY

The present paper is primarily an attempt at explaining certain culturally
determined aspects of personality in terms of suppression-versus-
repression theory, in two types of cultures. Four cultures have been
selected for analysis: Japan and China represent the cultures in which
suppression is the more important mechanism of socialization of the
individual; America and Germany represent the cultures in which repression is the more important mechanism of socialization of the individual.
Certain serious differences between Japanese and Chinese cultures and
also between American and German cultures are explained on the basis of
an additional factor—namely, loyalty to a wider political framework, state
or the throne. No claim is made that these factors—suppression or repression, and loyalty to the wider state or the lack of it—explain the whole of
the four cultures. They only explain a number of selected phenomena
which are, I think, essential to these four cultures.

In the same way no all-inclusive claim is made that the quantitative and
qualitative differences between the family patterns in the two types of
cultures can explain the origin of everything. I have tried to demonstrate
the possible connection between the Chinese-Japanese type of family and
suppression as the major mechanism of socialization; and the possible
connection between the American-German type of family and repression
as the major mechanism of socialization. But these family differences will
not explain the origin of loyalty to the wider state of Germany and Japan,

he lack of such loyalty in America and China. In fact I believe that
ctors bearing on the latter differences certainly must be sought in a wider
field, including historical developments.

NOTES

1. William Healy, A. F. Bronner, and A. M. Bowers, *The Structure and Meaning of Psychoanalysis,* New York, A. Knopf, 1930, p. 218. The use of the word "unpleasant" in this connection has been criticized by Robert R. Sears in "Survey of Objective Studies of Psycho-analytic Concepts" [Social Science Research Council Bull. No. 51 (1943); 156 pp.; see p. 105]. However, the criticism has no vital importance to the present paper in which one could just as well substitute the word "certain" for "unpleasant."

2. See Benedict 1946, chapter 9. Dr. Benedict's description of Japan on this point is similar but not identical with the above. She says: "They fence off one province which belongs to the wife from another which belongs to erotic pleasure. Both provinces are equally open and aboveboard" (p. 184).

3. One may argue, of course, that pornography is not art. But if by art one means a kind of reproduction of experiences of life by visual or auditory means, he will have little reason to exclude pornography as a whole from art. Like any work of art, there are more artful works of pornography as well as less artful ones.

4. *The Plum of the Golden Vase (Chin p'ing Mei)*: with an introduction by Arthur Waley; London, John Lane, 1939. English translation by Bernard Miall from the abridged version by Franz Kuhn.

5. Translated by C. H. Brewitt-Taylor; Shanghai, China, Kelly and Walsh. Limited, 1925.

6. Partially translated by Pearl S. Buck; New York, For Members of the Limited Editions Club, 1948.

7. Translated by C. C. Wang, Garden City, N. Y., Doubleday, Doran and Co., 1929, preface by Arthur Waley.

8. *The West Chamber: A Medieval Drama,* translated by Henry H. Hart; Stanford Univ. Press, 1936. For another translation, see *Hsi Hsiang Chi, The Romance of the Western Chamber: A Chinese Play Written in the 13th Century,* translated by S. I. Hsiung; London. Liveright, 1936.

9. Partially translated by Herbert A. Giles; Shanghai, Kelly and Walsh, Limited, 1908 and 1916.

See also *Chinese Ghost and Love Stories,* translated by Rose Quong; New York, Pantheon, 1946.

10. I am indebted to K. Colgrove and M. K. Opler for much information on the Japanese novel. It agrees with the author's personal impression derived from his limited acquaintance with Japanese fiction through Japanese works which have been translated into Chinese and published in China.

11. This book was publicly burned in Philadelphia in the late nineteenth century.

12. Inquiries among students on various levels of education show that the freedom of choice in marriage is very high on the list of positive values. See Olga Lang, *Chinese Family and Society,* Yale Univ. Press, 1945. See also A. L. S. Chin,

"Some Problems of Chinese Youth in Transition," *Amer. J. Sociology* (1948), 54:1–9.

My own survey (unpublished) of the letters to editors in two great North China cities (Peiping and Tientsin), between 1945 and 1949, also reveals that the question of freedom of choice in marriage is the subject most frequently mentioned.

13. The range of ages among primary and secondary school pupils in China has been wide because there was no compulsory education. Therefore, in the same higher primary school class the age range often could be from 10 or 11 to 25. In my higher primary school there were a couple of boys who were 29.

14. From what little I know about it, homosexuality and the attitude toward it in Germany would seem to represent a kind of cross between the two Eastern cultures and Anglo-American cultures. While a man like Hans Blüher could write and publish a whole work on the importance of homosexuality as a sexual outlet, homosexuality has been forbidden by law.

15. Douglas Haring, "Japan and the Japanese" in Ralph Linton (ed.), *Most of the World,* New York, Columbia Univ. Press, 1949, p. 858. John Embree's figures are lower, about less than half of one percent of the population (*The Japanese Nation,* New York, Farrar, 1945, p. 218).

16. In Japan the proportion of Catholics is the smaller of the two, being about one-fourth of the Protestants. See John Embree, reference footnote 22, p. 219.

17. For a discussion of Chinese religion and its main differences from Christianity, see F. L. K. Hsu, *Under the Ancestors' Shadow,* New York, Columbia Univ. Press, 1948. See also Hsu, "China," in Linton, reference footnote 22, pp. 775–85.

18. See report in *Chicago Tribune,* March 2, 1949.

19. John Embree has given an excellent account of Japanese national attitudes towards various foreign groups (reference footnote 22, pp. 237–58). Some discriminatory attitudes and measures against native peoples in Japan, Korea, China, and so on, have been described, but the over-all picture one gets is consistent with the present thesis. Only one large scale outburst against Koreans in Japan has been reported. That was during the 1923 earthquake (p. 246).

20. A similar observation has been made by both Dr. Hu Shih ["The Modernization of China and Japan," in Ruth Nanda Anshen (ed.), *Freedom, Its Meaning,* New York, Harcourt, Brace & Co., 1940, pp. 114–21] and Dr. Ruth Benedict (reference footnote 2, pp. 78–79 and later chapters of the book). The argument presented here is, however, closer to that of Dr. Hu and farther from that of Dr. Benedict. The latter emphasized the fact that the rapid advances of Japan were "rooted in traditional Japanese character" the main attribute of which was "taking one's proper station" (Benedict, p. 79). From the analysis presented so far, it becomes apparent that that which Dr. Benedict regarded as "traditional Japanese character" was generally common to traditional China as well. If one follows Dr. Benedict's argument entirely, he would expect the Chinese to make comparable advances in industrial and military fields, as Japan did during the last century. This, however, China failed to do, and in my view it was the lack of a traditionally sanctioned symbol of loyalty to the wider society in China which made the difference.

21. For a description and analysis of measures taken by a rustic community against a cholera epidemic, see F. L. K. Hsu, *Religion, Science and Human Crises,* 1952a.

9

Anthropology or Psychiatry:
A Definition of Objectives and Their Implications[1]

INTRODUCTION

The importance of many psychiatric assumptions and findings to anthropology is well known. The reverse relationship, namely the adoption of anthropological assumptions and findings in psychiatry, has also been noticeable, though not so pronounced. The extent to which the two disciplines have crossed one another may be attested to by the many important works by Mead, Gorer, Benedict, Kardiner, Roheim, Du Bois, Linton, Dollard, La Barre, Honigmann, Haring, and others. The list is not large, but it is impressive and is growing.

The most important result of this cross-fertilization had been the appearance and growth of a new subject generally called *Culture and Personality*[2] in college catalogues and on title pages of books. And the most fundamental of the theoretical positions emerging from this new discipline has been not only that culture is important in shaping personality but also that the early years are crucial. There are three interrelated reasons at the basis of this position, namely, (a) infancy comes first, (b) the earliest years are the most plastic, and (c) that which has been done (e.g. canalization) cannot be undone.

Mowrer and Kluckhohn (1944) have given one of the best expositions of the relationship:

> The utility which the accumulated inventions, knowledge, and values of past generations have for modern man is clearly attested by the prodigious amounts of time and money that go into the task of *education*. However, the human animal accepts the burden of this heritage only under protest and may, in some instances, find it altogether intolerable. When this happens, one commonly discovers that the educative process . . . has been pushed too fast or too far, with the result that such individuals require special *reeducation* if they are to be put back on the path of normal development and function. Unwise *teaching* thus creates or at least importantly contributes to the need of *therapy*. . . .
>
> In this and the remaining sections of this chapter, the dilemmas of growing up and living in a modern civilized society will be traced, with one eye on the individual as *pupil* and the other on him as potential *patient*. . . .
>
> It is a commonplace that the period of infancy and early childhood is of

---

This chapter was originally published in the *Southwestern Journal of Anthropology*, Vol. 8, 1952, pp. 227–50.

peculiar importance in personality formation. Just as the first few weeks of foetal life are crucial in determining whether an individual will be psychically normal or a monstrosity, so also are the first years after birth uniquely fateful in establishing personality trends.

For optimum development, it would appear from our theoretical consideration that a newborn child should be as continuously satisfied as possible during the first few months of extra-uterine life. This means answering every cry or indication of want with such rewarding care as feeding, warming, rocking, stroking, drying, etc. Keeping the infant's anxieties and tensions at a minimum improves gastro-intestinal function which is so important for the processes of maturation. . . . As important as this is, responsively answering the child's expression of need should have equally desirable behavioral consequences.

Just as a century ago no biographer would be satisfied without some reference to heredity, so John Gunther in his (latest) book (1950) entitled *Roosevelt in Retrospect* says:

Roosevelt had an abundantly happy childhood; the grim, biting distresses that afflict most children passed him by. There were few, if any, abrasions from the outside world—he was as sheltered as if behind a Chinese wall—and few harrassments discontents at home. So far as we know today he was never severely punished; he lived in an atmosphere almost totally devoid of conflict. Perhaps this helped give him his confidence in later life, and perhaps too it may have contributed to his touchiness and sensitiveness to criticism.

Roosevelt left the womb of Hyde Park at fourteen when he was packed off to Groton. But the influence of this early childhood environment was ineradicable, and to the end of his days he loved every tree he had known as a youngster, every rise of meadow, ripple of lawn, and fall of brook. Most of us, the psychologists tell us, are stamped forever with the imprint of our own childhood; F. D. R. was no exception. (167, 170)

CONTRARY FACTS

But there are dissenting voices and contrary facts, some of which come from the very scientists who, at one time or another, emphasized the importance of early training. The following are a few instances.

(a) Wayne Dennis (1947)—After observing Navaho and Hopi infants, who are used to being tied to cradle boards for anywhere from six months to over one year after birth, this student concluded that, whatever influence this may have later on, there is no observable difference in behavior between white American and Indian children within one year.

Every one of the responses of white infants was observed among the Indian infants and no response was observed among Indian infants which has not been noted commonly among white subjects. (44–45)

(b) D. Leighton and C. Kluckhohn (1947)—These authorities found wide discrepancies between Navaho childhood experiences and their adult personality. They asked themselves:

> How can anxiety level be so high among a people where infants are nursed whenever they want to be, where childhood disciplines are so permissive, where there is so much affection for children? . . . In spite of the fact that Navaho infants receive a maximum of protection and gratification, when they grow to be adults they are very moody and worry a great deal.

And their own answer to this question was:

> The explanation is probably not that the theorists are utterly wrong but that they claim too much for the earliest years and do not pay enough attention to later events and to the total situation in which the mature person finds himself. Infantile indulgence probably does constitute the firmest foundation upon which, if later circumstances are reasonably favorable, a secure and confident adult personality can be developed. But it affords only a possible basis; it does not, in and of itself, promise fulfillment.   (110–111)

(c) Abram Kardiner (1945)—In the introductory portion of his book *Psychological Frontiers of Society* showed that the "basic personality structure" is dependent upon a hierarchy of systems, beginning with those "projective systems" determined in infancy and early childhood, through "learned systems," "taboo systems," "pure empirical reality systems" to "value systems and ideologies." He summed up his views on some Alorese male character structures as follows: "In short, it is the summation of influences in a culture and not one specific detail which is responsible for character formation" (34, 224).

(d) Karen Horney (1937)—Horney pays rather little interest to early childhood. She was among the first to develop in detail a description of some of the effects of cultural pressures in producing neurosis. She concludes:

> The sum total of childhood experiences brings about a certain character structure, or rather starts its development. With some persons this development essentially stops at the age of five. With some it stops in adolescence, with others around thirty, with few it goes on until old age.   (152)

A prominent psychiatrist sums up Dr. Horney's position thus:

> In short, her emphasis is almost entirely on how the current neurotic trends work and produce difficulties, and she shows little interest in how such trends developed in the first place.   (Thompson 1950:201)

(e) Harold Orlansky (1949)—Orlansky has made the most extensive survey to date of current literature on the mutual influence between anthropology and psychiatry. He examined the reports on features of infant and child care in different cultures, such as breast vs. bottle feeding, length of breast feeding, self-demand vs. scheduled feeding, weaning, thumb sucking, mothering, sphincter training, restraint of motion, and their specific consequences. Then he looked into the same literature to match these specific experiences with specific character consequences. He concluded that "the events of childhood and later years are of great importance in reinforcing or changing the character structure tentatively formed during infancy."

> It appears that the effect of a particular discipline can be determined only from knowledge of the parental attitudes associated with it, the value which the culture places upon that discipline, the organic constitution of the infant, and the entire socio-cultural situation in which the individual is located. In short, it is contended that personality is not the resultant of instinctual infantile libidinal drives mechanically channelled by parental disciplines, but rather that it is a dynamic product of the interaction of a unique organism undergoing matura- tion and a unique physical and social environment. (38–39)

(f) Erich Fromm (1949)—According to Fromm, the "social character," or the character of all or the majority of the members of a society sharing the same culture, does not come from any single cause. Its origin is rooted not only in the interaction of "economic, ideological and sociological factors," but also to be referred to the nature of man expressed in the form of basic human needs such as those for "happiness, for harmony, for love," and "for freedom" (Sargent and Smith, eds. 1949: 6).

Enough has, I think, been given to indicate some of the dissatisfaction with the more orthodox Freudian position on personality development. Ralph Linton (1949), M. E. Fries (1947), Gardner Murphy (1947), Esther Goldfrank (1945), Robert Winch (1950), and others have expressed similar thoughts.

Apart from the conclusions of Dr. Dennis, however, which do not purport to show more than the insignificance of infantile experiences on babies within one year of age, some questions may be raised in connection with the position of each of the several authorities quoted. For example, Leighton and Kluckhohn, while admitting that the theorists have claimed too much for the earliest years, do not indicate how much is "too much." It is one thing to say that "infantile indulgence probably does constitute the firmest foundation upon which . . . a secure and confident adult personal- ity can be developed," but it is quite a different matter to develop an operational mechanism so that we can find what this "firmest foundation" means to Navaho society and culture as a whole. Lacking such a mechan- ism the two authors merely observed that "the high degree of tension observed among adult Navahos may be traced partly to the exceedingly grave pressures to which Navaho society is at present subject, and also to the conflicts caused by weaning, other experiences of later childhood, and beliefs about supernatural forces," and brought their book, *Children of the People* to a close. They made no attempt to relate these observations to the cultural material contained in their other book, *The Navaho,* except to indicate that certain witch and ghost tales current in Navaho society relieve "the shocks and emotional wounds that occur during the training of the Navaho child" (Kluckhohn and Leighton 1947:135–36).

From Kardiner's statement quoted above, one should have no doubt about his awareness of the importance of total cultural influences to personality structure. But when one looks into his actual *interpretation* of the field material at his disposal, one finds a different story. Here, in spite of the principle emphasized, Dr. Kardiner holds infantile experiences to be supreme. The case of the Alorese illustrates this point well. Kardiner concludes that the Alorese hate their mothers and have no effective personality structure for constructive action. As children the Alorese spew premasticated food; they have more intense temper tantrums than children of an unnamed number of other societies; they use violent epithets to imprecate their elders; and they tell nasty folktales about their fathers and mothers (Kardiner 1945:147, 150–51, 133–34). As adults they have no affection toward anybody; they have dreams indicating a desire to steal from Dr. Cora Du Bois, their ethnographer; they have no real conscience; they are stingy; they suffer from general insecurity because "there is the characteristic unwillingness to waste anything though there is actually no food scarcity"; they possess many words in their vocabulary indicating deception; their women have a customary history of running away from their husbands and will not return or yield to male sexual advances till the men have paid up, which shows that love is mixed with hatred, etc. (152, 176, 153, 164, 137, 202–203).

Where are all these characteristics derived? *Extremely poor maternal care.* "From the 14th day onwards maternal care is sporadic, inconsistent and undependable"; there is no parental affective solicitation; infants trying to walk get little help; infants being weaned are slapped and pushed away; their discipline lacks deliberateness and consistency; they therefore hate their mothers and, throughout life, they cannot love without the desire to deprive (147 et seq.).

Now apart from the fact that many of these items of evidence will fail to support Kardiner's major thesis,[3] he has even misread some items of the original data, and unintentionally omitted others contrary to his thesis. For example, of the two tales which he used to show the "deep and lasting impression such harsh and unorganized parental care creates" (133–134), one actually reveals an unexplained warmth toward the grandmother and no antagonism toward the wife; and the other may be found in a good many other cultures including America. In the second tale the boy got rid of his misbehaving mother but reunited with his wife. And from the way the tale ended they evidently lived happily ever after.

A more serious misreading of Dr. Du Bois's data is found in Kardiner's allegation that youngsters use epithets to revile their elders. This is held to be an evidence for not only the lack of idealization of the mother, but also the "preponderance of hatred and agression toward her" (150–151). But the actual data on which Kardiner based his conclusion read as follows:

> The children imitate their elders by using obscene words in anger. Words for genitalia are common epithets of derogation. Violent cuss words are: "Sleep with your mother; your father can't."   (138)

Now this is certainly different from Kardiner's impression. What the Alorese do is actually to revile their enemies' mothers and *not their own mothers*. One reviles the mother of one's enemy because it hurts one's enemy—and the more the enemy cares for that mother, the more the epithet is going to hurt. Incidentally, this phenomenon is common among Chinese, Russians, and the Italians. A further fact, which is diametrically opposed to Kardiner's interpretation but which has no place in his interpretation, is that the Alorese children address their "cries of distress to the mother" (132).

Kardiner suggests, as another source of poor maternal care, that the Alorese child, though it

> probably gets enough food as measured in terms of calories . . . lacks the consistent image of one person with whom it can associate relief of hunger tension. . . . The breasts of three women under such conditions are not as effective as one, because the whole relaxation conditioning becomes confused by nipples of different shapes, breasts of different size and consistency, and various body odors. (147)

This may be so but from what we know about children, it is probably not unfair to raise the question as to who is more confused: the Alorese child or the American psychiatrist. Dennis' study, quoted above, should leave little doubt that infants can get used to widely divergent conditions under which they are brought up. I certainly know of Chinese children who have, from the beginning, gotten used to nipples of more than one woman.

Kardiner, however, did recognize variations among the Alorese. Two of his male biographees[4] (Fantan and Rilpada) have a more effective personality and suffered less from obstructed development because "paternal support took up the slack," but in both cases "notwithstanding" their individual "advantages, the culture caught up" with them. Here Kardiner employs a most obviously circular procedure. For how do we know that the culture has caught up with them? Because "their character . . . is not so very unlike the others," although the "sequences cannot be established from the material submitted" (Kardiner 1945:223). But what is this so-called "norm" of Alorese character based upon? It is based upon the life pattern of two other males and four females on whose character *poor maternal care* has been written all over.

No student of humankind should minimize Dr. Kardiner's brilliant contribution to the subject, but one must ask if there cannot be a better matching between the data exhibited and the conclusions drawn.

Dr. Karen Horney's contributions have been great. Her books are of great influence today. I can, however, best raise a question in the words of another eminent psychiatrist, Dr. Clara Thompson (1950): "In her enthusiasm for her new approach, Dr. Horney has often given the impression that she considers the past life of the patient of no consequence in itself," and that, in therapy, "the exclusion of the past . . . gives a one-sided picture, a kind of structure without a foundation" . . . and that "to attack a defense system before the patient, through study of the past, has developed enough understanding of its origin to free him from guilt about it, must produce . . . either panic" or an attempt at reform by covering up "his former defense mechanism with a new defense more acceptable to the analyst and those about him" (200–202).

Orlansky's conclusions, though seemingly logical, may in fact lead nowhere. They are so inclusive that they exclude nothing and leave us exactly where we started. It is like saying that in order to understand the French Revolution we have to know not only everything about the French physically, geographically, socially, economically, politically and religiously, past and present, but also everything about the earth and all other peoples inhabiting it. The natural consequence of such a view is the position to which Orlansky was inevitably led: that "personality is . . . a dynamic product of the interaction of a *unique* organism undergoing maturation and a unique physical and social environment" (1949:39). Thus Orlansky pointed out, on the one hand, the undue emphasis on the importance of early experiences (not their unimportance), and on the other, the great power of later events; as a result, he stressed the importance of everything. As the biological composition and the total experiences vary from individual to individual, the natural conclusion is that every personality is *unique*.

No one can deny that the personality of every individual is different from that of every one else. Many scholars *begin* their treatises on personality by pointing out this fact.[5] Nor can anyone deny that all dogs no less than all stones differ one from another. Even physicists have agreed that certain phenomena, such as the behavior of the electrons, are subject to a good deal of individual variation not accounted for in its entirety by physical laws. But a science of biology, geology, or physics is made possible only because the similarities among the phenomena in question are stressed, not their individual *uniqueness*. By *emphasizing* the uniqueness of each personality Dr. Orlansky will not only negate the science of man, but will even change psychiatry or any systematic study of personality into an art which can, in an old Chinese saying, "only be felt but not explained."

Fromm has offered the most ingenious reconciliation between early and late experiences to date. His position is, in one respect, similar to that of Orlansky. He stresses the fallacy of any single formulation of causation and the need for taking into account both the total environment and the biological drives.[6] But he goes further. He asks the question:

> Is not the assumption that the character structure is molded by the role which the individual has to play in his culture contradicted by the assumption that a person's character is molded in his childhood?

He answers his own question in the negative.

> We must (Dr. Fromm proceeded) differentiate between the factors which are

responsible for the particular *contents* of the social character and the *methods* by which the social character is produced. The structure of society and the task of the individual in the social structure may be considered to be the *psychic agency of society,* the institution which has the function of transmitting the requirements of society to the growing child. . . . Methods of child training are significant only as a mechanism of transmission and they can be understood correctly only if we understand first what kinds of personalities are desirable and necessary in any given culture.   (1949:6–7)

But one basic difficulty remains: namely the former may have no reference to the latter. Even in a relatively stable society, such as China before 1840, it could not be shown with any certainty that certain kinds overall infantile and childhood experiences will lead to certain kinds of overall social roles.

Thus there is an apparent contradiction: on the one hand, psychologists, psychiatrists, and analysts find it imperative to examine infantile and childhood experiences. Some psychiatrists and anthropologists keep writing (and selling) books showing that marriages and divorces are predestined in the nursery (Bergler 1949) or that the Russians behave like Russians because of the way they are swaddled as infants (Gorer 1949). Now some Russian scholars have finally seen the light. One of them contends that the "neurotic aggressive American personality" is a result of the "commercial diaper service".[7] On the other hand, many clinicians and anthropologists are equally impressed by the fact that human conduct cannot be understood or predicted by a knowledge of a few infantile experiences such as diaper control or even of everything that occurs during the infantile or childhood years.

The result is, as shown above, that some authorities do an elaborate study of the infantile and childhood experiences of people, then point out, in general fashion, that these experiences do not really mean as much as they have been supposed to, and leave the subject just where it becomes interesting. Some authorities have insisted on the importance of later experiences as reinforcing or altering forces, but there is little indication in their actual interpretation of the field material that this insistence is much more than lip service. Other authorities have emphasized the present situation to the virtual exclusion of early phases of life. Still other authorities have pointed out the importance of everything, from birth to death, and from biological peculiarities of each individual to the entire culture history of the society, which, as I have indicated, if it will not annihilate any *science* of man altogether, will certainly make such a science out of the question for the foreseeable future.

Proposed Solution of the Dilemma

I have taken much space to state the problem because I hope to avoid any possible criticism that I have tried to set up a straw man and then, with a flourish of discovery, knock it down. There is a real problem, perhaps even a dilemma, which awaits solution.

The solution I propose is simple enough. The basic contradiction and the uncertain generalities on the part of the authorities quoted above come from a failure to recognize—or if recognized, failure to conceptualize—the differences in objectives between anthropology and psychiatry. That both disciplines are concerned with human behavior is a truism. That each can learn and benefit from the other is a foregone conclusion. But psychiatry is essentially concerned with single individuals who are ill and are in trouble with their environment. Anthropology is essentially concerned with whole groups of individuals who are normal, functioning members of their society.[8]

At this point some scholars and practitioners will point out that the line of demarcation between the normal and the abnormal is not so clear, but the matter is by no means as simple as that. The outstanding pitfall of anthropologists who have adopted psychiatry, and psychiatrists who have invaded anthropology, would seem to be for both groups to discuss their entire subject matters in terms of psychiatry, namely from the point of view of the individual: if not the individual-individual, it is the individual in a relational whole. But the first thing to be noted is that psychiatry deals with individuals who are more or less trying to live by themselves, while anthropologists deal with individuals who live as performers of different socially and culturally approved roles. That is to say, person X may like to perform role A more than role B. But the situation may be such that person X can only carry on with role B and not role A. All functioning members of every society *have* to do many things repeatedly, from making public addresses to embracing their aunts, which they would rather not do (but *cannot* do many things again and again, of an equally wide range, which they would rather do). On the other hand, all persons that are attended by psychiatrists are those who only do, or wish only to do, the things which they are predisposed to do but not the things which they, according to their culture, are supposed to do. In other words the subject of the psychiatrist is a person who actually cannot get along with his/her social roles and culture environment while the subject of the anthropologist is one who can.

The second thing to note is that, while individual differences are endless and multitudinous, roles in any society are relatively limited. Thousands of individuals of different societies could, for purpose of scientific study, be classified as doctors, bus conductors, teachers, garbage collectors, bureaucrats, politicians, grocers, bar tenders, seamstresses, fathers, sons, neighbors, white-collar workers, Protestants, Brahmins, and so on, but one has yet to see a classification of individual personality types which can make comparable claim to scientific usefulness.[9]

The differences may be explained as follows. Individuals differ physically and experientially *much more* than do social or cultural roles. That is to say, we can duplicate a role with a *higher* degree of assurance of accuracy than we can the personality of any one individual. In any society we can hope to make a more or less adequate inventory of its roles that will provide us with a fairly good idea of the structure of the society and the composition of its culture. But in all societies, even small ones like that of the Alorese, we shall have a much harder time trying to make an inventory of personality types which will give us a comparable idea of the psychological depth of the majority of the individuals making up the society.

Neither of these two propositions is in any sense new or original. Both can be understood by common sense. Our common sense tells us that to be accepted by our families, our friends, and in our place of work we have to do many things that we do not want to do and forego many things which we want to do. Our common sense also indicates that members of any group, club, or occupation, however homogeneous, are individuals whose personal character cannot but vary.

NORMAL VERSUS ABNORMAL

We must proceed to the next distinction, namely that between individuals who are psychologically sick (who are the proper subject of psychiatrists) and the normal functioning members of society (who are the chief concern of anthropologists). There is strong indication that the difference in outlook and reaction to the environment between these two groups of mankind is tremendous.[10] The pathological person is one who clings consciously or unconsciously to the past much more than she does the present. He still hates his father because the elder never gave him enough pocket money when he was a child. He despises his brother because the sibling always got more attention than he did before their hometown relatives. He broods over some humiliation that he suffered in the kindergarten or high school. To such a person past experiences, especially frustrations, are much more important than present ones, even satisfactions.[11] In other words, by this definition he is one who is suffering from a sharp dislocation between his present environment and his past experiences, and thus is in need of psychiatric help toward readjustment.

On the other hand the normal functioning member of any society is one who is dependent consciously or unconsciously upon the present much more than she is upon her past.[12] Her father might have whipped her unfairly when she was young, but she glows over the fact that the elderly person can no longer do so now. More likely she does not even reflect upon that at all. She might have been constantly picked on by the neighborhood girls, but she can now look at their lack of achievement and be proud of her respected position. She might even once have lived in a house that was struck by lightning, which shocked her badly, but she knows now how electricity works and can see no cause for worry when it thunders and rains. To such a person present situations, whether frustrating or satisfying, are much more important than past delights or grievances. In other

words the normal functioning member of a society is one, by this definition, whose attitudes and roles more or less correspond. All human beings
may have all kinds of internal tensions and stresses, but all normal functioning members of all societies are not in serious psychological trouble
with their environment since they usually can face and solve their difficulties as these difficulties occur.

Two points must be clarified at this juncture. First, I am aware of the
much quoted thesis of the late Professor Ruth Benedict (1934), which is
given in her article *Anthropology and the Abnormal.* Although Dr. Benedict
never intended to say in this essay that absolute criteria for mental abnormality will forever be impossible, her thesis has given rise to the general
impression that psychopathology is invariably relative to culture, that what
is abnormal in one culture may be normal in another. Fortunately this
confusion of thought has been clarified by Wegrocki (1948). Extending
from Benedict's arguments, Wegrocki distinguished between two kinds of
individuals. Those whose behavior looks "analogous" to that of the
psychotic but is "not homologous" to it because their behavior is "socially
sanctioned and culturally determined." In this category would be the
Haida chief who, upon the death of a member of his family, would vent his
tension by "causing" the death of someone he suspected. This is not
abnormal behavior in the psychiatric sense of the term at all.

On the other hand, there are those whose behavior shows fixed symptoms of the true psychopath, which represent a change in the personality
when a tension-producing situation arises. The "quintessence" of this true
"abnormality" is defined "as the tendency to choose a type of reaction
which represents an escape from a conflict-producing situation instead of a
facing of the problem.[13]

The question of a definitive, a clear-cut differentiation of all true
psychopathic behavior from all culturally determined "psychopathic-
looking" behavior in all societies remains open because our descriptions of
different peoples are far from being systematic. But it should be noted that
Wegrocki's definition of true abnormality is essentially the same as the one
which emerged from our discussion above. That is to say, psychopathic
persons, in their attempts to escape from conflict-producing situations,
will usually cling or fall back onto their past, since the latter is the basis of
their personality. But a normal, functioning person is one who will face the
tension-producing situation and attempt and succeed in solving it in some
presently practical and culturally accepted way. All human beings, President Franklin Roosevelt not excepted, must have had grievances and
ecstacies as infants, children, and adolescents, but a relative minority in
any society are bothered by or cling seriously or regress to these past
experiences so much that they are unable to act their present roles.
Normal persons so defined are ones who, even if they have had gross
trauma in the past and tremble every time they encounter anything remotely suggesting trauma, can still find enough satisfaction in their present circumstances to fulfill their roles.

The second point to be clarified follows the first. We may ask, will the normal functioning members of a society, as defined in this paper, ever break down? The answer is undoubtedly in the affirmative. Dr. Yacorzynski, associate professor of clinical psychology of Northwestern University Medical School, tells me that while some individuals are more susceptible, everyone has potentialities for breakdown, if the environmental situation becomes tough enough. The best indication of this may be seen in the now famous Guadalcanal case in World War II. A contingent of United States Marines in this sector of war was thrown into the firm belief that they were expendable and that the prospect of sudden violent death for every one was certain. When this group of soldiers was finally relieved, it was found that every one of them was suffering from a war neurosis not hitherto known. In the words of one observer:

> We are not sure whether we are seeing a new disease entity, appreciating that similar cases have been seen in the past. We do believe, however, that never before in history has such a group of healthy, toughened, well-trained men been subjected to such conditions as the combat troops of the U.S. Marine Corps faced during the days following August 7, 1942. The strain and stress experienced by these men produced a group neurosis that has not been seen before and may never be seen again.[14]

While the Guadalcanal results throw much light on the limits of personality organization, they are no contradiction to the thesis of the present paper. The Guadalcanal kind of human situation is so unusual in the family of societies that, for purposes of the anthropologist, it is of little consequence[15].

Some of the ablest people I have known and worked with in Hawaii and elsewhere have shown drastically different kinds of personality characteristics. From the point of view of the practitioner, one or another of them may even need psychiatric attention. But from the point of view of the anthropologist, all of them have apparently been able to arrange their many relationships so that they not only merely fulfill their roles but also make their performances highly successful.

The psychiatrist can argue that one or another of these individuals or other apparently functioning members of any society could become mentally unbalanced in short order if their environment drastically changed. The mental unbalance may occur in some individuals even without an upheaval of their surroundings. This is perfectly possible. But the answer of the anthropologist will have two facets. On the one hand the importance of the individual in every society comes from the fulfilling of roles as a functioning member of one's society. On the other hand it has not been shown that the vast majority of the functioning members of any society, even faced with some disasters like the Great Depression or the Black Death, will all go off the deep end. The majority of the Guadalcanal soldiers, after treatment, returned to normal life. The reason is simply that, faced with the destruction of some previously established satisfaction system, the vast majority of the normal, functioning members of any society will probably be able to locate new inducements to life in the present situation. They will undoubtedly try to look for things to which they are accustomed. But if unable to duplicate what they have had before, they will probably accept substitutes.

Conversely, it has also often been said that individuals who are mentally ill and in need of care in one society may become perfectly normal, functioning members of another society. This is also theoretically not impossible. But the anthropologist also has an answer. It has scarcely even been demonstrated that the vast majority of diagnosed mental cases of any society, by the definition used in this paper—namely, individuals whose particular pasts bother them more than their present satisfies them—will ever be capable of becoming permanent functioning members of another society[16].

In this way the contradiction of the early versus later experiences may be resolved: to the mentally deranged person earlier experiences mean much more than later or present situations; to the normal person the order of importance is reversed. For the psychiatrist, who tries to understand the troubles of one sick individual at a time, the early experiences of his/her patient are vital keys in their treatment. What is more, for effective results the psychiatrist will also have to look into the patient's physical conditions. On the other hand, for the anthropologist who tries to describe and analyse the life patterns of groups of normal individuals or whole societies, infant and childhood experiences are of much less consequence than the roles, structures, and cultures of the societies in question. At best the early training of the individual may be used as a symptom of some of the cultural emphasis. With few exceptions, anthropologists in field work have held the biological conditions of all peoples to be constant as a whole[17].

But this does not seem to exhaust the potentialities of the present formulation. There are at least three other difficult problems on which a definitive and, I think, scientific stand may be taken. First, the question of individual security versus insecurity. Psychiatrists for a long time, and some anthropologists more recently, have talked about a patient or a group of individuals as being *secure* or *insecure.* It will be pertinent to ask the question, how secure is really secure? secure enough for what? how can one measure complete security in human personality? Some scholars and practitioners will probably answer that a person or a group may be "relatively secure." But the further question is, relative to what? relative to whom? to the psychiatrists or the anthropologists?

As far as I am aware, the answer to this crucial question has always been taken for granted. Both anthropology and psychiatry have been engaged in searching for something that has neither been defined nor demonstrated to exist. An example of the dangers in this state of affairs is to be found in some views of Professor John Gillin (1948). According to him,

the cultural definition of life for adults in many primitive societies is relatively simple, [that] essentially one type of person, sex, and age considered, will fit the bill in a simple society. The culture is relatively homogeneous; the social subdivisions are few; the differential functions or specialties expected of adults are scarce and do not demand the entire personality; classes, subdivisions, each with its own subculture and its own general personality type, do not exist in the average primitive or simple rural society. Thus in . . . such society it is possible to trace in detail the relation between the constellations of childhood and the personality traits of the adult. The two fit together nicely, for the institutions and custom-complexes of adult life are stable, relatively few and comparatively well integrated. [In contradiction to this kind of society] the society which we know as North American is greatly diversified and under a constant strain of change. The opportunities for the individual are so various, the statuses and roles which the individual may assume in adult life are so diverse, that it is far from easy to decide the type of childhood training and conditioning which may fit the individual for successful interaction in so complex an arena.

Now, continues Gillin,

There are two more or less opposed poles around which an individual's security system can be organized: On the one hand is the dependent type of personality organization, which is oriented toward outside sources of support (such as kinship, material possessions, and magico-religion). On the other hand is the independent type of personality, which utilizes external resources, but which is organized about a firm core of inner potentialities calculated to furnish the bases for satisfactory solution of whatever problems may confront the individual. . . . [The individual] must be trained in adaptability, in the ability to analyse new situations and to respond to them successfully; . . . [he] must be educated to realize the relativity of the external "absolutes" and to recognize the underlying requirements of both personal and social integration.   (169–172)[18]

Apart from the fact that personality adjustment in "primitive" societies may not be as simple as it looks, Gillin's thesis has one basic defect. On the one hand it will be difficult to conceive of the widespread realization of his ideal American personality, for,

The individual of our time and of our society must be acquainted to the fullest possible extent with the content of our culture, for this is the material with which the new synthesis must be started. But, more than this, he must be aware of the principles of culture in general—what will and what will not work—if he is to avoid for himself and his descendants a period of ferocious personal and social maladjustment, he must know that culture patterns may be planned, that they are capable of manipulation one to another, and that new patterns and new configurations can and will be taught to upcoming generations, either by conscious training or by trial-and-error. There is nothing inexorable in the traditions which support the culture patterns of a society, any more than there is anything foreordained in the course of an infectious disease which is amenable to medical manipulation and cure. The time of change is upon us, and it is a wise child who knows his own father, for in this time the child should be far wiser than the father, far more sophisticated regarding the cultural conditions of his existence, far more capable of choosing among the alternatives which may and undoubtedly will be presented to him before he dies.   (Gillin 1948:173)

On the other hand, his thesis, if carried out, will only intensify the consequences of one basic aspect of American philosophy of life, namely the emphasis on the individual and self-reliance. This aspect of American philosophy rose to great height with the expanding frontier. And it goes on even after the frontiers are no longer expanding. The widespread interest in psychoanalysis, and now in the so-called science of dianetics, is symptomatic of it. The naked result of this phase of Ameican cultural pattern is a tendency which may be expressed in somewhat exaggerated form by the answer that Mr. Casper Milquetoast of the comics received when he asked a youngster if the latter would not mind raking up his yard for a consideration: "What I gotta do and how much is in it?"

But Dr. Gillin is not aware of this danger when he says:

> The problem is essentially this: to train the members of the next generation to rely upon their own inner resources as distinct from external props for the solution of life's problems, but at the same time to develop personalities capable of social cooperation and sufficiently flexible to appreciate the values of, if not to originate, new cultural patterns of a more permanent functional value than those we now possess.   (Gillin 1948:172)

The question is, if individuals are trained to depend on their own inner resources how can they at the same time develop personalities capable of social cooperation? Do human beings ever cooperate in the abstract, for the sake of cooperating? Dr. Gillin speaks of "primitive peoples" and "the simpler cadres of" American society as being primarily reliant upon external resources for security, but do anthropologists and psychiatrists of today, who are certainly not among the "simpler cadres" of any society and who should, in addition, know culture and some of its pitfalls, cooperate among themselves or with each other simply because of the ideal of social cooperation?

The truth of the matter is that since no human potentialities can be realized without interacting with the external resources, there are simply no human beings who can only or even chiefly rely on their inner resources. The only such individuals are fanatics and inmates of asylums. The rest of all humankind are bound to rely more or less on external resources as much as on inner resources. The Anglo-Saxon stream of Western culture (including that of the United States) emphasizes more of the inner resources than the external ones. The order of emphasis in most other cultures is the reverse.[19] But no society can survive if it has a culture pattern that teaches the individual to rely only upon inner resources.

From this point of view the question of security or insecurity must be answered in terms of a suitable balance between inner and external resources. By this criterion an individual is secure if she is a normal functioning member of his/her society, achieving a suitable balance between inner and external resources as prescribed by his/her society and culture. By the same token she will be insecure if she/he fails to do so. The validity of the criterion has the de facto recognition of the psychiatrist because that is what doctors strive to achieve with all patients.[20] It also has the support of many anthropologists because their object of study consists of the society and culture and the position of the individual with reference to society and culture.

A second problem is the extent to which infancy and childhood experiences of the individual can be correlated with adult roles. Is it right that in "primitive" societies "the constellations of childhood and personality traits of the adult . . . fit together nicely"? (Gillin 1948:169). The correct answer is probably no. Any society, however simple its organization and however crude its technology, is bound to contain individuals whose expectations cannot find satisfaction in their own society. The fact that there were marginal Alorese, who sought to gain prestige in their own society by working with Dr. Du Bois (1942:191), is a simple but effective substantiation of this point. In cultures under more intense European pressure, such as many parts of Africa, Melanesia, and Malaya, there is not the slightest doubt that infancy and childhood experiences may be even diametrically opposed on many counts to adult patterns of life (not psychology). Hallowell's work on the Saulteaux Indians in their acculturative situation is particularly illuminating on this subject (Hallowell 1942). In large Oriental societies such as China and India, this picture today is equally true. Under such circumstances there may be complete dislocation between the family pattern and the patterns of behavior within the larger whole. The family cannot, as such, be regarded as the "psychic agency" of the society, although its broad influences are the originator of the general personality tendencies of the individual.[21] There is nothing unusual about the fact that the infancy and childhood in some societies seem to be out of line with the adult personality of that society.

A third problem is the relationship between the personality characteristics of a people and their culture. It has been shown that, among the normal functioning members of a society, there need not be continuity between infancy and childhood experiences on the one hand and adult behavior patterns on the other. That is to say, there can be many adult activities that are not traceable to the projective systems based upon earlier experiences. The question may now be posed: How far can a correlation be established between infancy and childhood experiences and the culture of a society? Or how far can the latter be regarded as projections of the former?

Some scholars seem to have little doubt on the matter. Dr. Bateson (1942) suggests, for example, that the British and American attitudes toward their respective colonies are extensions of their respective parent-child relationships. The American parents encourage their children to "certain sorts of boastful and exhibitionistic behavior while still in a position somewhat subordinate to and dependent upon the parents," while in England, the parent-child relationship is characterized by "dominance and succoring." The American parent-child relationship "contains within itself factors for psychologically weaning the child, while in England, among the upper classes, the analogous breaking of the succoring-dependence link has to be performed by . . . the boarding school." Since "colonies cannot be sent to a boarding school," therefore "England has very great difficulty in weaning her non-Anglo-Saxon colonies, while these colonies have had corresponding difficulty in attaining maturity—in sharp contrast with the history of the Philippines" (76–82). Dr. Geoffrey Gorer is equally daring in his analysis of the American culture. He maintains that the sibling relationship in the American family is of no great importance with only one "important exception" (Gorer 1948).

> [This] occurs when two children of the same sex, particularly two boys are born within a short interval of each other. . . . The elder brother is likely to introduce the younger brother into his play groups, and later his gang. . . . The younger brother is a member of a group in the majority older than he is, and with standards of daring and accomplishment beyond the level of his years. Fired by the standard he is set, the younger brother becomes extravagantly rash in his words and action, confident that he will be saved from the dangerous results of his behavior by his older brother's protections, by his superior strength and wisdom.

He concludes; "This situation is common enough to have several analogues in adult life. The most striking is to be seen in Congress, where the House of Representatives often acts most irresponsibly, in the confidence that its elder brother, the Senate, will save it from the worst aspects of its folly (97)."

There does not seem to be the slightest scientific justification for making this kind of observation. This is merely argument by analogy. But this is not to say that one should completely shift to the opposite position, namely that culture is superorganic, that it originates and changes upon laws of its own, with little or no reference to human beings.[22] While there is much to be said for the superorganic school of thought, a fact that is hard to ignore is that personality tendencies of a people can exert a tremendous amount of influence over their culture patterns. This is particularly clear when we look at areas of the world where two peoples with different cultures are suddenly thrown into close contact with one another. The Mongols of the thirteenth century, when they conquered all of China, seriously considered the possibility of killing off all of the Chinese so that there would be enough pasture for their sheep and horses. The Chinese of today, even though accepting thousands of items from Western cultures, have so far resisted social dancing. An analysis of the Chinese personality characteristics will show further that it will be a long time, if ever, before Christianity and psychoanalysis, even of the dianetics brand, will gain any kind of popularity in that country. Each of these is an instance in which the incoming patterns of culture have conflicted with preexisting personality characteristics.

But there are many other phenomena in any culture that cannot be correlated with any common personality characteristics of the people sharing that culture. No amount of study, it seems, of the Chinese personality characteristics can explain the presence in Peking, between 1911 and 1926, of the two houses of parliament; just as no research on the English character is ever likely to elucidate the birth of Christ in Palestine and the subsequent crystalization of Christianity as a church. Numerous other examples could be added, but this is hardly necessary. What is important is that, once the difference in objectives between anthropology and psychiatry is recognized, it will be clear that the development of culture cannot be entirely accounted for on the basis of individual psychology or psychopathology. The development of culture is a complex process, in which the historical as well as the psychological factors are very important.[23]

Conclusions

The main purpose of this paper is to show (1) that a degree of confusion of thought exists concerning the relative importance of earlier and later experiences; (2) that this confusion is caused by confounding the objectives of anthropology with those of psychiatry; and (3) that a clarification of these different objectives is helpful not only in viewing the early versus later experience tug-of-war, but in establishing a more workable view concerning such vital concepts as security versus insecurity, the continuity or discontinuity between childhood experiences and adult personality characteristics, and the role of the individual in shaping culture.

The basic procedure underlying the study of humankind is similar to those of all sciences. As a beginning there must be description and classification. Next comes the work of finding any relationship between two or more factors within the phenomena in question. Then comes the task of prediction; namely, if the relationship between two or more factors can be established, will this relationship occur again in some other or similar contexts? Lastly, through prediction human beings hope to exert influence or control over the phenomenon in question. That our knowledge about ourselves and our doings is less exact than a chemist's knowledge about matter and that students of human life do not have any real laboratory methods need not lead them astray from these basic points of reference.

Anthropology and psychiatry, in spite of their differing objectives, deal with the same general subject matter and have to resort to the same fundamental procedures. Each discipline has benefited from the other. The loss to anthropology of today would have been very great if, for example, Freud's teachings and the work of his followers were totally unavailable. But each discipline, in its work toward prediction and control, must aim at factors which are most likely to lead to such prediction and control. The psychiatrist, whose aim is the restoration of the mental and social health of one sick individual, has to take into account not only infancy and childhood experiences, adult characteristics, and all data concerning the social organization and culture wherever they affect the patient, but also the latter's organic conditions as well. The anthropologist, on the other hand, whose aim is ultimately to direct or redirect a whole society or societies, not only takes in general the biological equipment of the people under scrutiny for granted, but must also consider a study of their infancy and childhood experiences as being of secondary importance. For a knowledge of these experiences, like that of the biological composition of a human being, will not enable one to predict much, like a magical key, about adult roles and even less about the pattern of culture of the society as a whole.

Psychoanalysis and psychiatry do not have well proven theories of human behavior either of individuals or of groups. They merely have a number of working hypotheses. Instead of taking these hypotheses as finished products, anthropologists should utilize them as added points of reference, to grope, together with the medical scholars, toward a firmer knowledge of personality, society, and culture. In doing so it will be well for the anthropologist not to lose sight of (1) adult experiences and personality characteristics, (2) social organization, and (3) culture. The anthropologist must realize that while the content of the second and third factors may be strongly influenced by personality characteristics, their origin, development, contact, and change are the result of a multitude of factors including those that are historical. The anthropologist need not neglect childhood experiences altogether. But s/he must keep in mind that childhood experiences may have significance only if seen against the other factors involved. Anthropologists have for long discarded the racial theory of culture. If we are not careful we shall be in danger of drifting into a nipple-diaper theory of humankind that will be equally dangerous and absurd.[24]

NOTES

1. This article was first read at the Viking Fund Supper Conference, New York, October 1950. The author does not wish to convey the impression that the works of all the scholars he criticizes here are on the wrong track. In fact the present paper is truly, though partly, and outgrowth of the very works criticized. His indebtedness to all those whom he criticized is, therefore, great. Nor does he claim this article to be an exhaustive treatment of the entire field of culture and personality. Its main purpose is to thresh out certain fundamental problems which are the common interest of some student of humankind. For this reason no attempt will be

made at a complete summary of all scholarly works on the subject. Mans omissions are therefore inevitable.

In preparing this article for publication the author is specifically indebted to Drs. Robert French, Robert Winch, M.J. Herskovits, Ralph Linton, John Embree, Doublas Haring, G.K. Yacorzynski, Tom Richards, A.I. Hallowell, Walter Dyk, Otto Klineberg, Richard Wang, Hortense Powdermaker, John Gillin, William A. Hunt, Joseph Casagrande, and Paul Fejos. Not all of these scholars, however, agreed with all of the arguments and views expressed here; for the last two the author is alone responsible.

2. Kluckhohn and Murray consider this to be a misnomer. The prefer *Personality in Nature, Society, and Culture,* which is the title of a book under their editorship (New York, 1948).

3. For example, are there no American women who will leave their husbands because their men show *public* signs of inattention or because they value their money more than their wives? How many words are there in the American vocabulary indicating deception?

4. The word "biographees" is coined to denote the subject of a biography.

5. See Gordon W. Allport. *Personality: a Psychological Interpretation* (New York, 1937) or Gardner Murphy, *Personality: a Biosocial Approach to Origins and Structure* (New York, 1947).

6. One wonders how some of the drives which Fromm specifies were discovered. For example, about any postulated drive "for freedom," one may ask: Freedom from what?

7. Ivan Pelionok, *Childhood Rearing and the Neurotic Aggressive American Personality* (1950; reviewed in the New Leader, June 17, 1950). Dr. David Olmstead informs me that the name Pelionok means "diaper," and the whole thing may be a hoax.

8. It it true that there are a few psychiatrists whose aim goes beyond the therapy of single individuals. But it is also true that there are some physicists/ornithologists who have schemes for saving humankind. If the work of the vast majority of anthropologists is compared with that of the vast majority of psychiatrists, there will be little doubt about the validity of the statements made here.

9. For summary discussion see e.g, Kimball Young, *Personality and Problems of Adjustment* (New York, 1947), ch. 13: "Types of Personality", pp. 301–36, or Otto Klineberg, *Social Psychology* (New York, 1940), ch. 15: "The Problem of Personality," especially section on "Personality Types," pp. 227–36. William Sheldon's efforts on the relationship between physique and mental abnormality are interesting (see his *The Varities of Human Physique,* New York, 1942). But the applicability of his findings to such a phenomena as juvenile delinquency and to other behavior remains to be seen (see his *Varieties of Delinquent Youth,* New York, 1949).

10. In this discussion I am excluding organically-based mental illnesses. Recent studies on glandular imbalance in connection with cases of schizophrenia and such a well-known phenomenon as paresis show that, in the long run, it may become possibte to cure such individuals by ordinary medical means. Oneirophrenics studied by Meduna of the Illinois Medical School show all the symptoms of true schizophrenics but will recover quickly by medical reduction of their blood sugar level.

11. The mentally ill person may, of course, *create* a past to which to cling (e.g., the hysterical women observed by Freud who all confessed having been seduced

by their fathers) instead of the actual past. However, all memories of, or unconscious reactions to, the past usually involve addition to or subtraction from it, so that created past and the true past in the minds of the individuals concerned are not qualitatively different. Another thing is that some mentally ill persons are said to be going through a process of regression so that, instead of clinging to the past they may have fallen back on the past when present going become difficult. This again is not qualitatively different from the views expressed in the text. The question of apparently normal persons becoming mentally ill will be touched upon below.

12. This is, of course, an unproven assumption the usefulness of which is upheld because of the absence of anything better.

13. Wegrocki, in Kluckhohn and Murray, eds., *Personality in Nature*, p. 560. Wegrocki distinguishes a third category of people, namely those whose behavior is simply devious from the norm of his society and culture, which they also accept. In this category are certain homosexuals. These people are simply delinquents. This is, however, not germane to the present discussion.

14. E. Rogers Smith, *Neurosis Resulting from Combat* (American Journal of Psychiatry, vol. 100, no. 1, 1943), p. 94. For more detailed information on this group of men see also A.A. Rosner, *Neuropsychiatric Casualities from Guadalcanal: I. Persistent Symptoms in Three Cases* (American Journal of the Medical Sciences, vol. 207, pp. 770–76, 1944) and others.

15. On the other hand, the Guadalcanal case may be compared to the case of the human body in general. All human beings have the potentiality of being physically disintegrated by diseases, but the majority of them is usually not so attacked.

16. The place of martyrs, prophets, and great men like Socrates is relevant in this connection. But these are social deviants and should certainly not be confused with the mentally ill. This question will be dealt with in another paper.

17. A notable exception was the work of Leighton and C. Kluckhohn among the Navaho. They examined the *Children of the People* from a number of points of view, including intelligence and physical health (Part II, pp. 117–82). William Sheldon's work remains outside of current anthropological thinking (see footnote 8 above).

18. Dr. Gillin is, of course, aware that individual differences do exist in nonliterate societies. See his article, *Personality in Preliterate Societies* (American Sociological Review, vol. 4, pp. 681–702, 1939).

19. For a discussion of the relative reliance upon inner versus external resources in some cultures see F.L.K. Hsu, *Suppression versus Repression: a Limited Psychological Interpretation of Four Cultures* (Psychiatry, vol. 12, pp. 223–42, 1949. Ch. 8 of this book).

20. In this connection psychiatrists and clinical psychologists resort, as far as the author can ascertain, to a rule of thumb. For them the insecure person is one who is suffering from insecurity more than others who live in the same culture.

21. Such as a higher degree of reliance upon external or internal resources, or of emotionality (see Hsu, *Suppression versus Repression,* Ch. 8 of this book).

22. For an exposition of this theory see Leslie White, *The Science of Culture* (New York, 1950). White seems, however, to carry the theory to an extreme that was probably not intended by Kroeber (see A.L. Kroeber, *Anthropology,* rev. ed., New York, 1948, pp. 253–54).

23. The word "historical" here refers to those events which cannot be explained from internal reasons, such as those that are fortuitous, extraneous, or accidental.

24. A view closely similar to mine was expressed by the late John F. Embree in a brief communication to the American Anthropologist (vol. 47, p. 636, 1945).

The present paper was written and read before Alfred R. Lindesmith and Anselm L. Strauss published their excellent article *A Critique of Culture-Personality Writings* (American Sociological Review, pp. 587–99, 1950). Their paper and the present one cover certain amount of common ground, and they also make some similar criticisms, such as the inadequacy and nonrepresentative nature of the data used by some writers or the lack of factual support for the much emphasized importance of infancy in personality formation. But their paper aims admittedly at negative criticism while the present paper emphasizes the positive and the differing roles of the psychiatrists (and analysts) and especially the anthropologists.

10

An Anthropologist's View of the Future of Personality Studies

The alliance of anthropology with psychology was not accidental. By the first quarter of the present century, students of anthropology had come to a point where descriptions of fact led to few meaningful generalizations, and the old concepts like diffusion and evolution were already worn out. The need for some conceptual tools to marshall the materials together and to delve below the surface of things was acute. Psychology, in its many forms, answered this need.

Specifically, anthropologists owe much to Malinowski for his brilliant exposition of the idea that different parts of a culture are not haphazard collections, but are intrinsically related to one another; that this interrelatedness of the parts is centered in what he described as the primary needs of man, such as sex and food. But Malinowski never defined his primary needs beyond sex and food; and he made no attempt to explain differences between cultures. What Malinowski must have known was that sex and food were needs which men share with animals and that a science of human behavior must explain not only differences between men and animals, but also those between one human society and another. The works of Mead, Benedict, *et al.* have furthered the conception of societies and cultures as wholes and have shown how societies differ in their orientations. They have at least indicated the beginnings of how we may answer such questions as: "Why do they behave like Kwakiutl Indians and not Japanese?"

A recurrent criticism of the works of Mead and Benedict has been that in their emphasis on the society and culture as wholes they have neglected the human beings, and, hence, individual variations. The contributions of Linton, Kardiner, DuBois, Dollard, Gillin, Hallowell, Kluckhohn, Henry, Erikson, Honigmann, Lewis, *et al.,* have considerably revised the picture. These students have one and all made us not only of the usual anthropological techniques of observation and participation, but also of life histories, psychoanalytically inclined or otherwise, and projective tests, especially the Rorschach and the TAT. Through these efforts, we have come to perceive not only how different peoples behave as wholes or in public, but to understand something about the individual's secret worries, excesses, hates, and fantasies, and the origins of some of these worries, excesses, hates, and fantasies in different societies.

This chapter was originally published in *Psychiatric Research Reports 2,* American Psychiatric Association, December 1955, pp. 155–68.

There are, however, certain serious difficulties in the current trends of culture and personality studies which need re-examination. The first, in my view, is the tendency on the part of some students to make what may be described as psychoanalyses of whole cultures. Their main preoccupation seems to be a search for documentation for Freudian doctrines. Geza Roheim, who has exercised, and still exercises, a tremendous influence, is an outstanding example of this approach. What Roheim has done is to locate data among many non-Western peoples which suggest or give support to psychoanalytic theories such as the Oedipus complex, or the meaning of certain dream symbols, or sibling rivalry, or the castration fear, etc. When he has found some evidence for these, he is satisfied and goes no further. For example, Roheim (1950) thought that he had effectively refuted a point made by Clyde Kluckhohn when he showed that, whether it be in Navaho or Patagonia, the individual tends to dream and employ certain universal dream symbols when pressed by a loaded bladder in their sleep.

"A middle-aged Navaho informant several times married and father of many children related the following dream:
'I milk my cow and I am *half way through milking.* Then I cannot finish because it begins to move around. I have a *rope* around her neck and I keep jerking her with that rope. I look at the *cow's feet* several times. Its feet look like a donkey's, but it has bags of milk here (shows stomach). Milking is easier now. I started feeding the milk to a little calf. It will not take it because it is scared. I *smell* the milk, it is *sour.* I *pour it out.* The cow has disappeared. While I am looking for the cow I *find a big creek,* like *mountain water,* and pulling up my pants I wade in. I see little fish in the water and try to catch one with my hands. The cold feeling of the water wakes me up!'
"At this point I told the informant that when he woke up he had to urinate. He confirmed this. Now, how did I know that? Urethral waking dreams are characterized by representing the pressure of the urine in the form of various fluids (milk, sour milk, clean water). The emphasis on the smell and then the opposite emphasis on cleanliness also indicate the same thing. The other element in these dreams is that (a) delaying factors are represented (cannot find the bathroom, etc); (b) the flow or urine is symbolized as already taking place, sometimes as water or as some other fluid.
". . . The point is, the urethral symbolism in the dream of *the Navaho is exactly the same as in the dreams of any European or American patient."*

But granted that the Navaho and the Chinese share similar unconscious psychological mechanisms; we are still at a loss as to why a Navaho and a Chinese behave differently in spite of it. The Roheim type of research leads to the same impasse which many analysts and psychoanalytically inclined social scientists "discover": that the reason for war is to be found in our infantile aggression against our parents. Since all human beings have parents, and since all human beings must, in the process of their socialization, necessarily be frustrated again and again, leading to at leat some hostility toward their parents or parent surrogates, war becomes inerradicable. There is little wonder, then, some of our leading analysts speaking on the subject of international aggression could think of no better method of preventing it than the fear for all-out atomic destruction or even invasion from Mars.[1]

Yet a shift of focus and an examination of the different forms of societies and their historical developments lead to quite a different story and perhaps some hope. We find that while religious differences are found in all societies, only certain societies have been plagued with religious wars and religious persecutions. We find that while most peoples have moved from one habitat to another, only certain peoples are too eager to emigrate under very little pressure while others tend to resist emigration even in the face of a lot more pressure. And we find, too, that while many civilizations have become extinct (according to Toynbee (1947)), most of those which suffered from such fate tended to be of one variety while others fared better.[2] These are differences which can be understood, not on the basis of food and sex needs, and not on the basis of Oedipus complex, castration fear, and other allegedly universally valid psychological mechanisms, but on the basis of cultural differences (Hsu 1953).

A second difficulty in current trends of culture and personality studies concerns the lack of any successful effort to meet the challenge of inadequate coverage. For example, Dr. DuBois (1944) obtained life histories of eight somewhat misfit Alores and thirty-seven Rorschach protocols of others in a population of less than 600. Dr. John Honigmann (1949) registered among the Kaska Indians not more than six brief life histories and only twenty-eight Rorschach protocols among a population of one hundred and seventy-five. How can we be sure that the conclusions based on so few examples of each people are valid for any people as a whole?

To be sure, in some instances this defect could be and has been somewhat remedied. Thus Redfield's conclusions on the Mexican Tepoztlan have been in some respects drastically revised by the much fuller coverage and more intensive inquiry carried out by Oscar Lewis (1953) seventeen years later. Other anthropologists in larger teams, working longer than DuBois and Honigmann in the respective fields, may certainly obtain better coverage in the same way. But can the Oscar Lewis restudy of Tepoztlan really be considered statistically adequate? There were about 4,000 people in the village in question at the time of restudy, but he and his students obtained usable Rorschach protocols on 100 individuals and intensive data on 7 families. And what do we do when we come to larger societies, such as those found in certain African regions, each of which numbers one or several millions? Or huge Oriental or Occidental societies such as China, India, or the United States, where the population of each comes to hundreds of millions? Can we ever hope to get satisfactory, or even reasonably adequate, coverage beyond the most surface matters such as those that can be taken care of by polling techniques?

My suggestion for meeting this difficulty will seem at first to some to be cavalier, but I think it has intrinsic merit. At the outset, it is necessary to recognize that adequate sampling in a pure statistical sense for any but the smallest societies is usually impossible. We do not have to come to large populations numbered in millions. This is inevitably true even with reference to societies such as the Alores, where the basic unit consisted of 600 individuals or the Tikopia, with its community of less than a thousand. There is first the difficulty of the investigator's time and energy. Investigators go singly or at most in teams of two, and the time limit is usually one year or two. There are only a certain number of hours a day, and there are definite limits to the psychological and physical endurance of man. It is simply unrealistic to expect one or two individual investigators to pry open the private and public lives of six hundred or a thousand individuals in such short durations.

In this regard there are other difficulties even more forbidding. Except in a situation of superior to subordinate, or the conquerer to the conquered, or the doctor to the patient, the social scientist has no way to make sure that all the individuals whom he deems it necessary to get in touch with will cooperate fully or even cooperate at all. It is easy enough to "bribe" the poor, the shiftless, and the lowly in status. But let us reflect on the chances of success of an outside investigator hoping to study the mental and social life of the Commander in Chief of the Armed Forces of the United States, or the Chief Justice of the Supreme Court, or the boss of the soft coal miners, whose positions correspond to those of big chiefs and small chiefs in non-literate societies. He does not even have to be as ambitious as that. He may begin by trying to get the average American business executive to submit to an hourly interview about his private life every other day, or even every week, in his anthropological tent. I think the anthropologist is more likely to fail of his objectives than to succeed.

Fortunately our knowledge of the relationship between the individual personality and the society and culture as a whole tells us that these difficulties are not fatal. To the extent that every action of the individual tends to be governed by, or at least related to, the unconscious or conscious material of the individual accumulated from his past experiences, it would appear reasonable that there could be no better key to the understanding of human behavior than a psychoanalytic understanding of the individual's past. As every analyst can testify, psychoanalytic histories, though summarizable in broad terms, must vary in detail from individual to individual. It is almost a truism that no two individuals are completely alike in personality, and, in this regard, the psychoanalyst has no need for the kind of crusade on behalf of individual differences now and then engaged in by the anthropologist. The latest of such efforts is illustrated by a paper by C. W. M. Hart (1954). What must be said, however, is that no individual, in the normal course of his living as a member of any society, uses all his inner resources or expresses all his inner stresses. In fact, on the one hand he has no need to do so, and on the other hand, he cannot do so even if he so desires. He has no need to do so because some of his personal experiences are outside the scope of his interaction with other human beings. He cannot do so because since his relationship with other members of the society depends upon the establishment of a rapport, he must find a common ground with them, and this common ground precludes the exercise or expression of many or most personal peculiarities.

From this point of view we may regard individuals in every society as falling into two categories. There are those who will not only remember their individual pasts but must compulsively hold on and react to their pasts irrespective of the present. An individual in this group will react to every employer as though he were dealing with his father's authoritarian hand; and he will react to every girl who has anything to do with him as an object of his vehement infantile fantasy. There are, on the other hand, those who do not act in this way. They suffer from inner stresses and are often pressed by deepseated urges, both of which are undoubtedly traceable to their past experiences, or glandular activities, etc., but in one way or another they are able to control, warp, or sublimate these tendencies, or their personality traits are such as to make many people tolerate their peculiarities, or even consider them cute. In any case, they are able to maintain their rapport with the people and events which matter to them. The first group we must describe as abnormal, or on their way to abnormality, while the second group must be described as normal. Therefore, while the therapist must explore everything about the abnormal patient, from his childhood experiences to his glandular activities, the student of social sciences has no need for deep individual analysis of the Freudian type in order to comprehend and predict the behavior of the normally functioning personality in any given society. In fact, if he wants to arrive at an accurate picture of human behavior and its prediction, he must know how to overlook individual psychological peculiarities and concentrate on those which are most likely to help him predict the direction of the individual personality operating as a functioning unit in any given society. For the latter purpose, a systematic inquiry, description, and analysis of the culture pattern as a whole remains the basic necessity. This picture of the culture may be supplemented by some individual life histories and psychological tests to obtain depth, but the latter type of data are no substitute for the former, and do not need to be very extensive to be useful.

There is nevertheless a question as to what constitutes an adequate description and analysis of a culture. As pointed out before, the idea that different aspects of a culture are interrelated is not new. Furthermore, this relationship is not a random one, but presumably predictable in terms of one or a few integrated aims of the society as a whole. But many scholars have not always exercised scientific caution and astuteness in attempting to establish this intrinsic relationship between the parts and the whole. There is a tendency to stop when a correlation between, say, the economy and the form of government is found. There is another tendency to argue by analogy. This has been discussed by Lindesmith and Strauss (1950) and myself (Hsu 1952b). It was with these in mind I attempted to work out what seems to me a new kind of analysis of two large national cultures, those of the Americans and of the Chinese (Hsu 1953). I dare to make my modest claim to a certain novelty on the basis of the fact that, in pursuance of a particular hypothesis, I had perhaps gone farther into the life among the two peoples than did most of my predecessors by whose works I had nonetheless profited. In this work I stopped at no tabooed subjects and observed no boundaries of respectability, but ruthlessly pursued the same thesis with reference to all materials available to me, however diverse and incongruous. For this reason, one reviewer had criticized me for literally attempting to cover the universe. What I have done is in accordance with a very simple and generally accepted scientific doctrine: namely, to try to explain more and more facts with fewer and fewer theories. The accuracy of each theory must be tested by asking whether or not it can predict the personality trends in given cultures. From my analysis of the Chinese and American culture patterns, I came to the conclusion, for example, that more Americans will be given to alcoholic excesses, and more progressively so, than I believe will be the case for the Chinese. Similarly, my analysis of the two cultures has convinced me that for a long time to come more Americans will continue to insist and look for romantic love than, I believe, will Chinese. Finally, from the same analysis, I decided that even if subjected to more intensive missionary influence for much longer periods of time, a majority of Chinese are not likely to be given to some monotheistic faith such as Christianity but that conversely, even if not being endowed traditionally with Christianity or Judaism, a majority of Americans cannot but be identified with some other form of monotheistic creed. Furthermore, those Chinese who become Christians will be more inclined toward Catholicism than Protestantism, while their American brethren will be exactly the reverse (Hsu 1953).

Exactly which individual or individuals in American or Chinese society will indulge in alcoholic excesses, or go overboard for romantic love, or take up the cross and become a zealous missionary remains a matter for the students of the individual to diagnose or to determine. These specialists, be they social workers, clinical psychologists, psychoanalysts, or psychologists of individual differences, not only will have to probe into the deep psychological states of the individual, but also to examine his physical conditions from every point of view. But my predictions on the behavior of the two peoples as a whole are not based on the study of their respective depth psychologies. In fact, I believe that deep analysis is not only unnecessary but will possibly be misleading. For, as we have noted before, most individuals in any society do not, as a rule, in the normal course of events, act on their deeper impulses, yearnings, and frustrations. On the contrary, a majority of them will be flexible enough to find a *modus vivendi* so positive in most areas of life that they will enjoy it in spite of their deep personal differences.

The third difficulty in the culture and personality field seems to me to be more crucial than either of the two discussed so far. This concerns the

question of criteria against which the scientist can make his generalizations, especially those which it is impossible to make except by comparison. On this point, I find no explicit statements in our literature. This is
especially obvious in some of the studies of the German character during
and since World War II (Brickner 1943; Levy 1948; Kracauer 1947;
Keoskemet and Leites 1945; Monez Kyrle 1951; Rodnick 1948).

In general, these authors either elaborate the idea, implicitly or explicitly, that German society and culture are, with no reference to the rest of the
West, bad, or that their badness is expressly described in contrast to the
goodness of the democracies, giving much to support the former but little
more than a few hasty notes to the latter. The more extreme of these
authors frankly describe German society and people as suffering from
some variety of psychpathology, such as "compulsiveness." In this connection, the work of Eric Erikson (1949) would seem to be more objective,
but even he is not entirely free from one-sided exaggeration of the
"badness" of Germany. Erikson does not describe the Germans as pathological in their support of the Nazi movement. But he speaks freely, for
example, of their aggression, political immaturity, racial prejudice, etc.,
with not the slightest indication as to how aggressive, racially prejudiced,
or politically immature is "too aggressive," "too prejudiced," and "too
immature." Even more serious perhaps is the fact that Erikson has failed to
note the close similarities between Germany and the rest of the West. For
example, Erikson has ignored, intentionally or otherwise, the fact that
there is hardly anything he said of the character of the Germans that is not
also, in one way or another, true of that of the Americans.

He describes the Germans, among other things, as being characterized
by an adolescent stubborness, refusing to give in on anything, and emphasizing that youth is the master of its own destiny. He derides Hitler's
tirades, which were focused on single foreign leaders such as Churchill or
Roosevelt, calling them "feudal tyrants" or "senile fools." He castigates
Hitler for making "fanatical cries" of "Germany, Germany, Germany,"
and imploring the German people to believe in a "mystical national
entity." He speaks of the Germans as believing in the "purest white and
blackest black" and as looking upon the world as either "vastly superior in
age and wisdom, the goal of eternal longing and *Wanderlust,* or as a mean,
treacherous, encircling encampment of enemies living for one aim: namely, the betrayal of Germany."

But are these not all true of Americans? Is youth not the master of its
own destiny in America? Does not our science of pediatrics even seem to
support the idea that infants and children have all the answers? Is not the
belief and insistence on unconditional surrender and eternal victory
dangerously close to adolescent stubbornness? Characteristically, is it not
an American habit to attack Nazism or Communism in terms of the
dictator's wishes (whether they be Hitler's or Stalin's), or at most the evil
designs of a core of hardened "criminals"? As to our attitude toward the

entity America, it is doubtful if a majority of us who, in our firm belief that the American way of life is the most superior of all ways of life, have a precise idea as to what we mean. It is common knowledge that many incongruous and incompatible things have somehow been lumped together and justified in the name of Americanism. The belief in purest white or blackest black is so American that it seems superfluous to elaborate it. In fact, to the average American there is hardly any middle way: it is always an "either . . . or" proposition. This is why a person with one thirty-seconds of Negro blood is a Negro. Ths is why India, in her attempt to be neutral, is so intolerable to us. This is why we had to intern all Japanese on the West Coast, regardless of citizenship, in World War II. Finally, Erikson should have perceived the close American parallel to what he speaks of as conflicting attitudes towards this world in the German: There is on the one hand the world of Thoreau, who found in nature and seclusion an incomparable source of pleasure and wisdom, (which world many Americans erroneously believe to be a matter of the past yet which is still actively expressed in the American dream of a house in the woods and the American love of camping); and there is, on the other hand, the world of those Americans, statesmen and common people alike whose daily concern would seem to be the ferreting out and the destructon of the ever-present enemy who is bent on the betrayal and destruction of America. In fact, the parallel between Germany and America in this regard is more obvious than that: at the height of Hitler's power there were anti-Nazis (which must have accounted at least in part for persecution within Germany), exactly as in America no matter who is in power, there is always opposition to the established government.

All these underline but one point that is of the greatest importance to Erikson's entire analysis which he did not perhaps foresee: either German Nazism was rooted in none of the features he describes, or the rise of American Nazism in the future is a foregone conclusion. That these conclusions may come to Erikson as a total surprise will make them no less important and true. For a science of the ways of man must be built by comparing facts wherever they occur.

Here I would like to make a proposal which I hope will at least be considered by my colleagues in the sciences of man. This is that the student of culture and personality must know the way of life of his own society and the values that are prevalent in it; these he will employ in his studies of other ways of life as a comparative basis from which to draw generalizations. He should not merely have a rough idea about his own way of life and its dominant values. He must study them as thoroughly as he may the way of life of any other people. In fact, since anthropologists have concentrated so much energy on non-literate societies, it will probably be a good idea if much of our energies are devoted for the next two decades to our own society, especially if the society happens to be a Western one. The results of such a shift of research focus will not only do much for the social scientists whose concern is with normally functioning individuals in groups, but also for clinicians whose views about their own way of life are as a rule derived from psycho-pathology.

Apart from the obvious requirement of all sciences for comparative data, this conclusion should deserve the special consideration by research psychoanalysts and psychoanalytically inclined anthropologists. It has been an established practice that psychoanalysts must be psychoanalyzed themselves before they can successfully analyze other human beings. The rationale for this, as I understand it, is that the psychoanalyst, in order to have a rational understanding of his clients' problems, must have first of all a rational understanding of his own prejudices and impulses. Doesn't it seem a matter of common sense, then, for the scientist who wishes rationally to understand other societies and their ways of life to acquire first a rational understanding of his own society and his own way of life?

I am pretty certain about what such a step can do. It will at least enable the student of man to see man in a wider perspective. Had Erikson taken this step, he might have been forced to come to a very different understanding of the German prejudice against the Jews. He might have realized that it is scientifically erroneous to theorize about German prejudices without looking into prejudices in the United States, South African Union, and the rest of the world, wherever this phenomenon is outstanding. Had he done so, he almost certainly would have seen that his description of the German stereotype of Jews, and German attitude toward the imagined or actual Jewish male contamination of the purity of German womanhood came really close to much of the American stereotype of, and attitude toward, the Negroes and other non-white peoples. He would have also seen, too, the absurdity of his explanation that German anti-Semitism is rooted in the fear of castration which the Jews arouse in other peoples who do not practice circumcision. If that were so, what then, we must ask, is the reason why the Arabs, who practice circumcision themselves, also persecute the Jews? Conversely, why is it that the Chinese, who do not know circumcision, are not intolerant towards the Mohammedans?

What Erikson should have seen is that, given the cultural tradition of persecution against the Jews, *some* individual Germans will inevitably use it to elaborate their own personal problems, such as fear of castration, exactly as some individual Americans hate Negroes in terms of economic competition. But neither fear of castration nor of economic competition is the basic force underlying religious or racial prejudice. In fact, we see a picture that is usually the exact opposite in the case of racial and religious prejudice. For while such prejudice is severe in all parts of the industrialized and wealthy West, it is generally absent in the entire agricultural and impoverished East. In the latter, active persecution of an acculturated racial minority was historically and is presently exceedingly rare. Religious wars were completely unknown. Even the Hindu-Moslem riots in India are of a very recent origin, beginning a few decades ago. Racial and religious prejudices of the kind demonstrated by the German Nazis are as characteristic of all the West as they are foreign to all the East. We thus come upon an apparent paradox which will be no paradox at all if we go beyond local and superficial matters, such as the fear for castration or economic competition, and understand the basic force behind all prejudices. The paradox consists of the fact that prejudices seem to be more prevalent and intense in societies where the value of the individual as well as individualism as a living philosophy are rated high. The basic key to solve the paradox lies in the following chain of facts: greater individualism leads to less permanent human relations because of freedom, equality and competition; less permanent human relations and more competition lead to greater fear of losing one's place among fellow human beings; this fear will cause most individuals to climb at all costs, but as, in the normal course of events, only a relatively few can get to the very top while a majority have to lag behind, many individuals have to resort to means other than climbing to compensate for their fear of loss of place; pushing other people down by refusing to associate with them, by excluding them from clubs, neighborhoods, occupations, or even persecuting them by physical violence, are the inevitable compensatory devices, all of which spell prejudice.

Racial and religious prejudices are present in all parts of the West. But they are infinitely more tenacious in Protestant Germany or England than in Catholic Italy or Spain. In the northern countries, there is literally no way in which a Jew or a persecuted minority can escape the onus by readjustment of his status or belief. Conversion means little and economic position means less. When a Jew has neglected or sought actively to negate his Jewish ancestry by assimilating all that is dear and important to the gentile, his Jewish ancestry will be thrown back in his face. At best there is always a question of his social acceptance. But in the southern countries, an individual member of a minority has a much better chance of improving himself and of working up to a status of social acceptance through achievement, conversion, or acculturation. This becomes particularly clear in intermarriage. The children of a foreigner who marries Italians or Spaniards become Italians or Spaniards and are accepted as such, especially if these children think, act, and are dressed like Italians or Spaniards. The children of similar unions in the northern countries remain outside the pale of respected society and there is never complete acceptance.

The inherent differences in racial attitudes within the home societies became more pronounced in the colonial areas, past or present. Except in New Zealand, the more individualistic colonies (usually Protestant) from Australia through Africa to North America are one and all more intensely prejudiced than the less individualistic colonies (usually Catholic) from the Orient through East and Central Africa to Mexico and South America. The intrinsic difference in racial prejudice is not in the presence or absence, or the comparative frequency, of lynchings and pogroms and other forms of violence, but in the day to day attitude of the every-man. In the Protestant colonies, a member of the minority remains minority, whatever station he achieves. This is so even in North America, the relatively most enlightened of them all, especially if he is a Negro. As to interracial marriage, there are not ony various legal attempts at banning it, but, even when these legal barriers are removed, the popular pressure against it is prohibitive. It is a well known fact that while some American educational institutions may hire Negroes as teachers, such employment is out of the question if the otherwise employable Negroes have white wives.

Catholic colonies present a different picture. Here there are also such things as color bars and hostility toward Jews in most areas, especially in Africa and sometimes in the Orient. But as a matter of general practice, the French and the Portuguese African policy differentiates between, on the one hand, Africans who are educated and can speak French or Portuguese and can think like the masters, and, on the other, other Africans who are the majority and who cannot do these things. To the former is applied the term citizens, or acculturated Africans, and on them are conferred recognition like that accorded the European French or Portuguese. These favors are held back from the rest of the subject peoples. The number of the former category may be very small, but the point is that once having achieved those distinctions they are treated as equals and will be given places of power and honor and complete social acceptance regardless of birth and origin. As to Protestant portions of the New World, racial and religious tolerance is so much more pronounced and obvious than other parts of the West that more descriptive material becomes unnecessary.[3]

This understanding, that stronger prejudices are more likely to be associated with patterns of life with a stronger stress on individualism, freedom, and equality than with patterns of life in which the latter stress is weaker would have been impossible to attain without subjecting the pattern of prejudice in Nazi Germany to a wider comparison. When that is done, we shall also find Erikson's entire analysis of the rise of Nazism in Germany to be lacking in perspective and therefore lopsided. In the wider perspective, Nazism is but one of the many strands of totalitarianism which recurs in the Western way of life, in contradiction to democracy, which is also but one of the several expressions toward individual freedom and equality and which equally recurs in the Western way of life. Throughout Western history, this polarity and irreconcilable struggle takes many forms: between good and evil, orthodoxy and heresy, established governments and revolutionaries, etc., exactly as it is symptomatized today in the entire West by the war between Communism and Capitalism, and within many a major society of the West by the hostile positions between the extreme internationalists and the extreme isolationists, or the ultra-conservatives and the ultra-liberals. Since most or all of the principal characteristics which Erikson attributed to the Germans are in one way or another attributable to the rest of the West, the problems of Germany and the German orientation are more accurately problems of the West and

Western character. German culture, including Nazism, no less than Russian culture, including Communism, are integral parts of the West. Unless there is some change in the intrinsic orientation of the Western way of life beyond particular societies like Germany, in my view all efforts to relieve tensions among men will be in vain, however hard our present efforts to eradicate German Nazism and however smashing our future victory over Russian Communism.

In this paper, I have attempted to recapitulate and to assess the gains and the shortcomings of the study on culture and personality as seen by an anthropologist. The contribution of the anthropologists are in their emphasis on culture and its patterning as the forces shaping the individual personality. But the anthropologists have benefited tremendously from the contributions of those scientists whose initial orientation deals with the individual: the psychologists, and, particularly, the analysts and psychiatrists.

Because the field of personality is relatively new and is therefore ill defined in scope and methodology, there have been certain unfruitful trends. There is a trend in which both the anthropologist and the analyst have gone overboard for individual psychology. In this regard, the principal effort of some of the most prominent of our analysts seem to be concentrated in the direction of ascertaining the universal existence of the Oedipus complex, universally valid dream symbols, and the like. All human beings in all societies live under certain common conditions known as the universals of culture. This, added to the universal existence of the individual family, with parents and unmarried children, makes it reasonable to suppose that certain universal elements of human psychology could result. But to have done so, to have shown that all human societies have e.g. the Oedipus complex, is little more than to have demonstrated that all human beings also need food and sex. Food and sex are needs that human beings share with all animals. The Oedipus complex may eventually turn out to be a factor common to the personality of all human beings. But a science of man must look into the common elements of human modes of existence as well as those elements which make them different. And the outstanding factors which have made groups of human beings different from one another are cultural differences. Animals may fight and kill because they want food or because they are propelled by sex. It is apparent that human beings do not live and fight just for these motives. They have ideas and ideals, traditions and taboos, which often cause them to be most irrational when a reasonable analysis of their circumstances will gain them more practical benefit; and they will go to war of mutual extinction when a more logical re-examination of their premises should lead to a more peaceful solution that is beneficial for all. There are human beings who could have eaten better if only they had agreed to adopt better seeds and better tools. There are human beings who would be less plagued by epidemics if they would only apply themselves to a more rational control of bacteria. There are human beings who could have avoided starvation if they had only agreed to emigrate. Others love nothing better than blind expansion regardless of the consequences. For a solution of these and many other problems that are inherent in the differences in the ways of man, but are beyond food and sex as well as the Oedipus complex or the universal dream symbols, we must rely on a more thorough and systematic understanding of all aspects of given cultures, and not on the psychoanalysis of this and that individual or symbol or society.

Our view of the first defect helps us to remedy a second. There is no doubt that science proceeds from the qualitative to the quantitative; as the science of man develops, it has more and more to rely on the quantitative approach. It is pointed out, however, that in the foreseeable as well as the unforeseeable future, no scientific apparatus or methodology is ever likely to be devised so as to adequately fathom the depth of the psychology and past experiences of a large number of individuals in any large or even small society. This difficulty is not insurmountable. The nature of man and his manner of existence are such that to predict the behavior of a majority of the normally functioning members of any society, deep psychological techniques which fathom the individual's past are unnecessary. A majority of the normally functioning individuals, in order to live effectively, are governed by their own insights, which prove to them that the best policy is to come to terms with society and to find rapport and a community of interest with fellow members of the same society. For such purposes, the individual's deeper resources and strains are usually irrelevant. It is only those who are abnormal, or those on the verge of becoming abnormal, who will cling to the past or some other compulsive point of reference. For the purpose of therapy or correction, we need deep analysis. But with reference to such individuals, the therapist cannot stop at deep analysis. He must also have a complete physical examination as well as an adequate test of intelligence. Therefore, the student of personality, whether he be an anthropologist or an analyst, if he deals with the movements of an entire society and the prediction of the behavior of a majority of the members of such a society, has no legitimate concern for being unable to secure adequate psychoanalytic histories from and projective testing results on most individuals.

The third problem in our current approach to personality is the most important, and deserves our scrutiny. This is the tendency on the part of the student of personality to generalize freely on peoples other than his own without consciously and rationally knowing his own culture pattern, values, prejudices, and fears. To remedy this defect, I propose that every student of man acquire an adequate understanding of the way of life of his own society first.

NOTES

1. For example, this would seem, crudely speaking, to be the general opinion reached at a private conference in 1947. But similar views were aired later elsewhere.

2. With the exception of Mayan and Inca civilizations, all which fell were Occidental. Toynbee artificially broke the Chinese civilization into two. It is obvious, however, that the Chinese civilization had never experienced extinction in the sense that Babylonian civilization did.

3. For a more comprehensive treatment of the origin of prejudice, see F. L. K. Hsu (1953, Chapter XIII; 1961a, Chapter 7). Dr. Remy Bastian, an anthropologist from Haiti, in commenting on this paper, pointed out the following local fact which contradicted the generalized picture presented here: the German immigrants to Haiti tend to marry Haitians and raise families while the French immigrants tended to refrain from doing so although some of them took mistresses. However, to judge the true significance of why some individuals vary, we need fuller information on the particular circumstances of these immigrants. The picture depicted in this paper refers to the majority, and, like all generalizations on human groups, is not intended to be 100 percent true.

Part III

Affect, Personality and Culture

Introduction

The importance of affect in human affairs needs to be investigated and understood more thoroughly than we have done at present. Social scientists, reformers, and clinicians who deal with nonliterate peoples or peasants in societies where industrialization is a minor factor have often spoken of the irrationality (or at least the nonrationality) of the objects of their inquiry or charge. They fail to see that peoples, each guided by particular patterns of affect, do not share with the outsiders looking in the same feelings about the self, about each other, and about the rest of the world.

In other words, they may be just as rational as the outsiders, but their rationality is based on premises other than those of the observers. As a result the insiders and outsiders can have very different basis for rationality because what the one feels to be right is felt by the other to be wrong.

Consider the case of treatment of dogs. The American way with dogs looks irrational to the Chinese. Why should a society with some 10 percent of its citizens living below the poverty line lavish so much of its resources on dogs? From the Chinese point of view, getting rid of dogs who compete with humans for food is natural. That was why the Communist government succeeded in eliminating the animal in the urban areas without much resistance. As to the Vietnamese, raising dogs for meat is like raising cattle for the slaughterhouse to the Americans.

The first paper in this section, "Role, Affect and Anthropology" (Chapter 11), may seem to end in a pessimistic note. But where affect dominates, as between the Catholics and Protestants in Northern Ireland, strife between peoples with even minor cultural differences seems to last forever. The possibility that cultures will maintain and escalate their differences once they began to branch out should certainly be explored.

In contrast to scientific theories and technology, which have undergone enormous changes in human history, art and literature tend to be eternal. We continue to enjoy Michelangelo's masterpieces and Homer's epic poems and Shakespeare's dramas, but we no longer pay comparable attention to Aristotle's science or Galileo's astronomy. Why? Because the latter are matters of usefulness (role) while the former are those of feeling (affect). We love, hate, seek loyalty, and shun betrayal as did the ancients, and they, were they alive today, would have been able to relive the joy and agony of our relations with our parents and children, spouses, employers and employees, friends and others. However, how peoples with unlike cultures love, hate, and agonize, but especially what make them love, hate, and agonize, differ enormously. These differences lead to enormously dissimilar consequences.

The second paper in this section, "Mirrors of Life" (Chapter 12), contrasts the art and literature of the West with those of China, including the China under Western pressure and invasion. This paper deals more extensively and comprehensively with some of the facts already touched on in some of the preceding pages (Chapter 5, Sex Crime and Personality and Chapter 8, Suppression versus Repression.

The final paper, "Kinship is the Key" (Chapter 13), spells out a sociocentric model of man . . . Psychosocial Homeostasis (PSH). The individual's need for affect, to receive it and to give it, is central to this model. But unlike the individual-centered Freudian model, PSH begins with the premise that the most essential ingredient of human existence is the *interpersonal nexus*. (For another and more extensive exposition of the PSH model see Francis L.K. Hsu 1971b:23–44.) It goes on to detail some of the PSH's behavioral ramifications.

11
Role, Affect, and Anthropology

Not so long ago my wife and I were invited to a luncheon by the wives of some educators and businessmen, to brief them on China. They and their husbands were soon to take a three-week tour of the People's Republic. The ladies were busy studying guide books, short histories of China, and geography. They knew that tips were out in China, but what gifts should they give the guides in appreciation? And how could they avoid offending their Chinese hosts or hostesses?

One of the ladies had a friend with a China connection, who claimed to speak Chinese fluently and who gave her advice in a letter, which was dittoed and circulated. It is too lengthy to quote in full, but some excerpts follow:

> I am thrilled for you and wish I were packing for China instead of Switzer-land. It was an emotional trip for me two years ago for I was actually seeing the sights and streets of my childhood . . . I am sure you have been deluged with suggstions so the following may be very repetitive . . . Glue—take a small bottle or tube . . . as most of the stamps are glueless and their glue is awful. Paper matches—they have only the bulky little wooden matches and they are hard to carry. (You can gauge the sophistication and standard of living of a country by their matches.) Bob . . . reports that most underdeveloped countries have wooden matches.

The correspondent went on to list some other items to bring, from tea bags and instant coffee to soap and Kleenex. She concluded with what she meant by her "emotional" relationship with China:

> Since we were there for business purposes they (the Chinese) were far more anxious for us to see modern China but my interest was in the old since I had tender memories of tap dancing with my sisters at the Altar of the Sky at the Temple of Heaven so I insisted on several sentimental journeys.

We anthropologists will undoubtedly agree that the author of this letter is not a reliable source on China and the Chinese. Her relation with the Chinese is not unlike that between many a white hunter in Africa and his "beaters" or even his victims whose stuffed heads would later adorn his living room walls at home.

This chapter was originally published in the *American Anthropologist,* Vol. 79, No. 4, December 1977, pp. 805–808.

It is interesting that such a letter was taken seriously by highly placed Americans about to visit China.

Later my discomfort grew when I reflected on the similarity between what this letter writer says about the Temple of Heaven and some of Malinowski's thoughts during his Trobriand days as revealed in his diary.

> I went for a walk along the foot of the hill. There was a fairy-like view on the mountain side, now filled with the rosy light of sunset, and on the bay. Overcome by sadness, I bellowed out themes from *Tristan and Isolde* [1967:52].

This one entry would have told us nothing at all of Malinowski's relationship with the islanders but for the fact that other entries in the diary show it to be no accident. Malinowski roared out "a Wagnerian melody" when he was caught in a rainstorm (p. 230), was stirred by the Prize Song, Marche Militaire and Rosenkavalier, longed "for music, for *Tristan and Isolde, . . .* [it] seemed to me I was actually hearing it. Yesterday, for instance, the Ninth Symphony" (pp. 63–64), and wished he had a piano so that he might be able to compose (p. 192). On one occasion he even sang the words "Kiss my ass" to a Wagnerian melody "to chase away" flying witches when he was a little nervous walking with some natives at night (p. 157). Throughout the diary there is only *one* entry in which Malinowski expressed pleasure with a native melody accompanying a dance, *tselo* (p. 37).

Being a trained anthropologist, Malinowski gave us a wealth of data about the life of the Trobrianders, including their *kula* ring, their preference for father's sister's daughter marriage, and their garden magic. Unlike our American lady Malinowski would never have been so naive as to link wooden matches with cultural sophistication. But the puzzle of their similarity fascinated me. Malinowski himself seemed to have supplied the key to it later in the diary (1967:167):

> As for ethnology: I see the life of the natives as utterly devoid of interest or importance, something as remote from me as the life of a dog. During the walk, I made it a point of honor to think about what I am here to do. About the need to collect many documents. I have a general idea about their life and some acquaintance with their language, and if I somehow "document" all this, I'll have valuable material.—Must concentrate on my ambitions and work to some purposes.[1]

Malinowski differed from the American woman in that he collected more systematic information about what the natives did and the material world they lived in. But what he and she shared was the lack of truly *human* relations with the natives—the Chinese or the Trobrianders.

What do we mean by truly *human* relations? I suggest truly *human* relations are characterized by affect (or feeling) in contrast to the not-so-human relations, characterized by role (or usefulness).

We know role in terms of skilled or unskilled labor, white-collar workers or blue-collar workers, dentists or diamond cutters, homemakers or politicians. As our society has grown in complexity, the number and variety of roles have grown with it. In fact, role differentiation is the major concomitant of the growth in societal complexity.

On the other hand, while our roles have evolved in number and proficiency with the complexity of the industrial society, we still have the same kind of feelings as out ancestors who lived many thousands of years ago: love, hate, rage, despair, endurance, hope, anxiety, forbearance, loyalty, betrayal. The list is not long and many of the descriptive terms are similar to each other. That is why, in contrast to old books of science and technology, which become obsolete rapidly, great literature (fiction, poetry) and great art (painting, sculpture), and even great philosophy and ethics survive the ages, for we moderns can relive their creators' lives through what they have left to us, and they, too, were they alive today would have been able to discuss with us our problems with our children and parents, friends and enemies, employers and employees, sweethearts and spouses.

Role and affect are not mutually exclusive. But they are easily distinguishable from each other, as when we say "business is business," or "you can't buy friendship with money." Role is what we are busy doing, but affect influences what roles we choose (if there is a choice) and how well we perform them. Role activities may get us riches and fame but affect patterns determine how well we enjoy the riches and the fame, and the meaning of our work and our very existence. Machines increasingly replace humans as role performers. But who and how many among us accept robots as mates, friends, or parents?

However, while Westerners may experience love, hate, and despair the same as the others, how they express love, hate, and despair, and especially what makes them love, hate, or despair, possess distinct characteristics that are different from these of others. For example, although such objects as pottery horses from Tang tombs or masks from Africa have value as curios, non-Western fiction and music are the concern only of Western specialists. They find no honored places except in specialized libraries and collections. The difference in patterns of affect was why peoples with unlike cultural heritages—from the American woman who spent her childhood in China to Malinowski who labored for four years in the Trobriands—failed to develop truly *human* relations with their hosts.

Today anthropologists have, of course, come a long way from Malinowski, who was only one of our intellectual ancestors. But have we addressed ourselves seriously to the question of whether we can understand the peoples we try to study—how they feel about themselves, about each other and about the rest of the world—without developing truly *human* relations with them?

Why do we still so freely use the word "primitive," referring not only to economics and technology but to nearly everything else in most of the

Third World? Is it not because we cannot modify our feeling of superiority deeply ingrained in the Western mind? Why do we still regard, explicitly or by implication, industrialization (or some other material factor, e.g., poverty or ecology) as the primary force that will change the cultures of the world in the Western model? Is it not because we tend to seek some other form of world mission where once the West thought Christianity would do?

Merchants in Chinatowns throughout the world stage lion dances to celebrate the Chinese New Year, as the Chinese University of Hong Kong does Parents' Day and New Students' Week, and the communes in the People's Republic do the arrival of barefoot doctors. Recently the inhabitants of Taipei greeted a Chinese airman who defected in a MIG19 with firecrackers, and their counterparts in Peking did likewise the news of restoration of Teng Hsiao-Ping to power. Might these not be external symptoms of deep-seated affective patterns which persist in spite of role changes?

Most of us are familiar with the figure of a cultural tree Kroeber offered us in his *Anthropology* (1948) with its branches crossing and rejoining each other to symbolize cultural diffusion. I think Kroeber was at least partially wrong. Cultures borrow much from each other in role matters such as foods, artifacts, etiquette, theories of nature, and tools for control of human beings and things. But there is little evidence that people change in any fundamental way, and, as a whole, their patterns of feeling about themselves, about each other, and about the rest of the world.

Maybe the cultural tree is not unlike its biological counterpart after all, with one minor difference.

In the biological world elephants do not try to be friends with fleas. The branches of the biological tree all go their separate ways, continually diverging. In the cultural world individuals constantly associate with each other across cultural boundaries. Not only that, throughout history societies with different cultures have formed alliances to fight other alliances. We now have a sort of world alliance, the United Nations. The branches of the cultural tree in our new diagram should, therefore, be made to bend toward each other, though never merging into each other.

Some may decry pessimism. But is our shift from the Melting Pot concept of America to that of Cultural Pluralism built on pessimism?

NOTE

1. This or similar expressions are repeated quite a few times in the diary, e.g., pp. 227, 229, 278, 291. In Ch. 23 I will deal more extensively with Malinowski's diary and its meaning for anthropology.

12

Mirrors of Life

ASPECTS OF ART

The art form to be discussed here is restricted to painting. There are, of course, many technical differences between Chinese and Western painting. Western artists use a wider variety of media, such as oil, crayon, water color, pastel, charcoal, casein, and etching. Chinese artists have limited themselves more to water colors or brush and ink. Western artists paint upon a variety of materials—canvas, cardboard, glossy papers, wood surfaces, walls, metal, and glass. The Chinese have resorted more exclusively to papers and silk. Perspective in Western painting is achieved by shading and by contrast; in Chinese painting, like that of the ancient Greeks, this is done by superimposing one object on another.

However, there is a far more basic difference that sets them apart from each other: human subjects are as conspicuous on Western canvases as they are relatively scarce on Chinese papers. Moreover, the conventional paintings that circulate widely in the West and in America seem to deal more with females than males, and they reveal, more than anything else, the mental state of the subject. Some, like the paintings of da Vinci and Van Dyck, often express a happy emotion. Others, like those of Van Gogh and Munch, tend to portray a bleaker side of life. In the majority of these paintings, the background on the canvas—such as a house, furniture, trees, or sky—is important only insofar as it adds color to the human beings portrayed. This pattern is so strong that even when a still life or a landscape is the subject, such as in Winslow Homer's and Andrew Wyeth's works, the painting—be it land or seascape, grapes or bananas—contains an emotional quality that the artists instills in inanimate entities.

Even when Chinese artists do portray the human form, they either treat it as a minute dot in a vast landscape, or so heavily clothe it that the body is hidden. The facial expression of such figures is nil. The viewer obtains a much better idea of the status, rank, prestige, and other social characteristics of the subjects portrayed than he does of their personalities.

Furthermore, Chinese painters throughout the last two millennia have excelled in depicting tigers, horses, flowers, landscapes, birds, fish, and even insects. But there are few indeed among the artistic greats who have

---

This chapter was originally published in *Americans and Chinese: Purpose and Fulfillment in Great Civilizations,* by Francis L.K. Hsu, New York: Doubleday and Co., 1970, pp. 17–41.

focused their attention upon human subjects. The drama, the emotional vehemence, and the conflicts of the human heart, which are normal in paintings considered great in the West, are uncommon in Chinese art. In fact, when we do see human faces in Chinese paintings, their blankness bears a remarkable resemblance to the expressionless figures portrayed in "Daughters of the American Revolution." However, the absence of expression in the Chinese faces results because the Chinese artist is not concerned with personality, whereas the very blankness of the features in Grant Wood's work is intended by the artist as a satiric representation of character.

The two life styles are thus reflected clearly in the two nations' paintings. In Western art the focus is on man or woman as an individual. In Chinese art the important thing is the individual's place in the external scheme of things. In addition, American art often reflects the inner tension of the individual; this concern is practically absent from Chinese art.

However, the differences go much deeper. A basic search in much of Western art has been for the most beautiful or ideal female form in the person of the angel, goddess, madonna, wife, mother, prostitute, flower girl, or sea bather on a September morn. Yet, the Western artist, in his effort to realize this ideal, usually combines two opposing forces: the depiction of the temptation and the effort to partially conceal this very temptation. Western art abounds with suggestive sexuality.

Sexuality is almost totally absent from all Chinese art except pornography. In the latter genre, men and women do not appear in suggestive poses as is common in Western art; rather, they dramatize sexuality in the most minute detail. One may argue, of course, that pornography is not art. But, if by art one means a kind of visual reproductin of experience, whether literal, interpretative, or symbolic, there is little reason to exclude pornography. As in all categories of art, there are more artful pornographic pieces and less artful ones. It is certainly true that pornography is not absent in the West. Not only in France and the other Latin countries, but in England and the United States where such things are legally banned, pornographic drawings are readily available to those who look for them. If the Western ones that I have seen are any indication of the whole, they are certainly not any less revealing than their Chinese counterparts.

Although both countries have laws against pornography, the contrasting patterns of the two peoples' personal reactions to pornography are a truer guide to their differing psychologies. No respected Chinese, especially the Confucian scholar-bureaucrat, and even the man on the street, would openly admit it, but few Chinese would have any qualms about privately viewing the frankest pictures together with their spouses, sweethearts, or prostitutes.

To a majority of Americans, with their puritan background, the matter is more complicated, for their personal guilt and social ostracism are forever associated with pornography. Furthermore it may lead to much more serious consequences. I have seen quite a few letters to modernday Dorothy Dixes written by irate, anguished, or perplexed wives or mothers who have unexpectedly discovered pornographic material hidden by their husbands or sons. Frequently these letter writers were told that their men need psychiatric help.

Every society must have rules to regulate behavior. In the individual-centered puritan tradition of America, sex is regulated more by restraints within the individual than by external barriers. Conversely, in situation-centered China, sex is controlled more by external barriers than by internal restraints. Where the emphasis is on internal restraints, man is enjoined not only to avoid sinful action but also to eliminate sinful thoughts. It is interesting that there is no Chinese counterpart to the biblical injunction, "But I say to you that every one who looks at a woman lustfully has already committed adultery with her in his heart" (Matthew 5:28).

Yet sex, being one of man's most fundamental urges, can hardly be eliminated from thought. Where attempts are made to eliminate it from consciousness by condemning it as bad, it merely takes refuge in the deeper layers of the mind, a condition Freud described as repression. Where the purpose is merely to regulate it, sex is simply channeled into specific areas of human association where one need not feel reserved. In the former approach, sex becomes a sin which may be justified by circumstances such as man's need for self-perpetuation. While this ideal is hard to live up to in actuality, it is interesting to note that the Virgin Birth and the Immaculate Conception remain active theological doctrines of the West. Furthermore, although the origin of the alleged founder of Taoism was also associated with the same myth, the Chinese never made any virtue of it. For in the Chinese attitude, sex is a natural urge of man, like eating, to which, according to Mencius, expression must be given in the right place and with the right parties.

Consequently, repression of sex is correlated with the generalized interest in it in Western art, where sex appears very frequently but in the form of diffused suggestiveness. Compartmentalization of sex, on the other hand, causes it to be practically absent from Chinese art in general, but concentrated without restraint in pornography. Except where sublimated, the desirability of sex increases in reverse ratio to its availability. Hence the emotional energy directed toward sex often outweighs that toward all other subjects of Western art while it is without comparable significance in Chinese art.

Those who are familiar with American developments may insist that the central characteristic of American art is its variety. Superficially, this seems to be true. Even a brief look will enable us at least to identify many American trends, most of which have their own well-known artists, such as the early portrait tradition (Gilbert Stuart, Thomas Sully, Samuel F.B. Morse, John Singleton Copley), the Hudson River School (Thomas Cole, John Kensett), the *trompe l'oeil* school of still-life painting (William Harnett), cubism (Stuart Davis, John Marin), expressionism (Marsden Hart-ley, Hans Hoffman, Willem de Kooning, Wassily Kandinsky), and reactions against emotionalism (pop art, op art, Mark Rothko, Marisol, Andy Warhol, etc.). Different students may classify the artists and their works differently (and agreement is difficult) but there is no doubt about the variety.

Although belonging to the same artistic tradition, European and American styles of art possess some noticeable fine differences. For example, American art makes less use of overly sexual subject matter than its European counter-part. However, to my knowledge the following American artists are known for one or more paintings of nudes or of lightly clad women of evident sexuality: James McNeill Whistler, John Sloan, Willem de Kooning, Reginald Marsh, Yasuo Kuniyoshi, and Ivan Le-Lorraine Albright. Diffused sexuality, however, is by no means rare in the works of others.

Another more typically American development is the proliferation of new schools or trends, each of which seems to be a reaction to some more established school or trend: the precise realism of Grant Wood and Andrew Wyeth as reaction to expressionism; the pop and op art of Mark Rothko and Marisol as reaction to expressionism. An earlier example of this trend would be the Armory Show where the exhibition of paintings by Duchamp, Sloan, Glackens, Henri, and others, which had been gradually purged from the more acceptable exhibitions, created a furor so violent that police had to be called in to protect the more controversial pictures.

In fact, this tendency to proliferate is so great that charges of "that's not art" and extensive explanations of what makes this or that art are extreme-ly common. In form and substance, Western art in general and American art in particular have undergone enormous changes through time. Be-tween the works of Michelangelo and Jackson Pollock there does indeed seem to be no link.

However, if we examine the basic approach of Western artists we shall find in it no fundamental change in spite of a common assertion that "Modern art . . . differs radically from any art which has preceded it" (Clark 1963). The cubists, the expressionists, the dadaists, the pop and op artists (in time there will be more innovators) concern themselves, as did their Western predecessors, with individual feelings. The difference be-tween them and their predecessors is that, whereas the latter depicted the feelings of their individual subjects (or projected their own feelings into their individual subjects), they now tend to express the feelings (or the feelings against the expression of feelings) of their individual selves. Therefore while human figures or landscapes by Western classicists or romanticists would, in the non-artist's eyes, bear some resemblance to these subjects, this need not be so in the case of the contemporary artist. Since the modern artist seeks to express only his own feelings, objective arguments are irrelevant. There is no need to justify the validity of a square wheel (or a forest that looks like an empty tool shed, or a stenographer represented by a decimated notebook beside what looks like a deformed and dancing baby whale). Jackson Pollock's works seem to represent the most extreme American trend of atomization, since they aspire to freedom from all external restraints. It is said that many of his paintings are twenty-two feet long only because that is the length of his studio wall.

A particular artist is merely expressing his own private feelings and imagery, which need not meet the requirements of objective agreement. The viewer will simply find his own meaning, very much as if he were reacting to an ink-blot test. The only difficulty is that much explanation is often necessary for many works of the newer Western art to be appreciated as art at all. American art, by its greater radiation of trends and "schools," has merely intensified the Western concern for and elaboration of one's individual feelings. Such an intensification and elaboration of the artist's own feelings will inevitably lead to vitality and inventiveness without depth.

Franz Schulze, an art critic, though noting correctly that vitality and inventiveness are "encouraged" in the American society while depth is "not so much discouraged as out of the question," interprets wrongly why most Western moderns have proceeded onto their present path:

> Perhaps because it is now so nearly impossible to find any steady, believable, profound, and clear-cut meaning in the contemporary world—hence it is impossible to interpret that world in depth—these artists seek to reproduce their only certain and reliable reaction to the world, which is that of undifferentiated sensation extracted from it . . . .
>
> That [Schulze is speaking of the works of Jordan Davies, Arthur Green and Raymond Siemanowski in Chicago] the symbols have more to do with comic strips and billboards than with apples, madonnas, sunsets, or even abstract volume analysis, suggests that when traditionally sanctioned subjects seem exhausted and meaningless, traditionally discredited ones appear at least worth a try, even if it is a tongue-in-cheek try. (1967)

Had Schulze examined the real lives of diverse peoples outside America and Europe, he might have seen the error in his judgment. The truth is not that the contemporary world is so bereft of "steady, believable, profound, and clear-cut meaning," but that the intensification of each individual's feelings can only lead to his increasing isolation and lack of commitment to anything. Such individuals will inevitably find *their* world bereft of "steady, believable, profound, and clear-cut meaning."

Chinese art, on the other hand, has undergone little change in historical times even after contact with the West, neither in form and substance, nor in approach. Historically, the Northern School concentrated on exact details while the Southern School used broadly expressionistic brush strokes. There were, of course, individual masters who differed in some minor ways from the others; but there were no innovations by some artists which were repudiated by other artists (much less which met with a kind of furor even remotely resembling that reported in the West) and there simply was no significant discussion on what was or what was not art. The similarity between Chinese masterpieces of the ninth century and those of today is so evident that they present no problem of understanding—in sharp contrast to the history of Western art.

The Western method of painting came to China with the introduction of Western schools, noticeably as early as the turn of the present century. Those who paint with that method use cardboard, canvas, Western water colors, crayons, and oils. But for those who paint in the Chinese style the traditional media such as Chinese ink, color, paper, shell, and woodcut remain prominent. A sort of "marriage" between the two art traditions was effected when a few Chinese-style painters introduced Western-style perspective and a greater degree of expressiveness than their predecessors. In the main, a majority of Chinese painters stuck to their Chinese tradition, and the much smaller group of Wester-style painters were assiduous disciples, at a distance, of Western Classical and Romantic masters.

Since 1949 the political imprint has been heavy on artistic as well as other activities of mainland China. However, it is the *purpose* for which art is created that has changed, not its structure, content, or general approach. The traditional animals, flowers, and scenery are still common, but humans mostly in non-traditional situations now figure much more prominently than before. We now see "Eighth Route Army Soldiers Being Welcomed by Civilians," "The Iron and Steel Plant at Paotow," "Sheep and Shepherd on the Slopes of the Ningsha Hui Autonomous Region," papercut figures of "Brother and Sister Planting Trees," etc., as well as shell pictures of "Heavenly Angel Spreading Flowers" and a "Crane Standing Beside Pine Trees" (both the latter are traditional subjects). Art is now used to propagandize for social and economic development under the guidance of an all-powerful state instead of being an object of mere enjoyment to the artist or consumer.

In Taiwan the question of the seeming stagnation of Chinese art in contrast to the proliferation of Western "schools" and trends recently resulted in a heated newspaper debate. When David Kwok, a Chinese artist known in the United States, argued the need for change, other artists challenged him. As yet no real change is visible. The reason Western art has produced such extensive change in form and substance while Chinese art has remained constant is discussed elsewhere (Hsu 1970:352–81).

FICTION

These basic contrasts in Chinese and Western art are equally obvious in fiction. Chinese traditional novels usually concentrate on what the characters do in their roles as emperors or common men, while Western novels[1] are much more concerned with what the characters *do, think,* and *feel* as individuals. There are, of course, a few exceptions. But compare any Chinese novel which has remained popular throughout several centuries such as *The Dream of the Red Chamber* (Tsáo 1929) or *All Men Are Brothers* (Shih 1948) with any widely read American novel such as *The Grapes of Wrath* or *Elmer Gantry* or *The Deere Park*. The absence from Chinese novels of excursions into the mind of a character is as pronounced as their abundance in American fiction. No traditional Chinese novelist tells the whole story from the point of view of one character, a common technique of his American counterpart.

Among the works of Chinese fiction with which I am familiar, the deepest an author has penetrated into the workings of a character's mind was when a hero, confronted by an enemy, calculated that if he did a certain thing he would surely defeat or outwit the villain. The height of Chinese imaginative authorship seems to have been reached in *Hsi Yu Chi* or *Western Journey* (Wu 1930), a fantasy about an arduous trip to India by some Buddhist monks in the early seventh century A.D.; *Tale of the Mirrored Flower,* a satire on human relations; and *A Record of Adventures into the Western Ocean,* a fictional account of the historical exploits of the eunuch admiral, Cheng Ho, between 1405 and 1438.[2]

No less revealing is the way love is handled in the two types of novels. In the American love story, the union of the hero and the heroine is usually the climax. Not infrequently, an entire book deals with the pursuit of romance, the agony, the misunderstandings, the stumbling blocks that must be hurdled before the two chief protagonists join each other and the book comes to an end. Even where love is not the primary emphasis, as in *The Grapes of Wrath* or *The Jungle* or *Of Mice and Men,* the American novel pulsates with strong emotions. The Chinese novel, even when it deals with romance, does so with a casualness or frankness that may well be distasteful to many American readers. Sexual union usually occurs early in the narrative; it is never the climax of the story. The balance of the novel is concerned with how the hero goes about marrying the heroine properly, with the rectifying wedding ceremony tediously described to the last detail. Mutual attraction between an individual man and woman is not enough. Their personal feelings are never more important than the sanctions and assistance of the family and the society. This Chinese cultural pattern remains true even in novels which superficially employ the complex plots common in Western novels.

Brief synopses of two Chinese novels of love—*Hao Ch'iu Chuan (The Story of an Ideal Marriage)* and *Yu Chiao Li (The Strange Romance of the Beautiful Pair)*—will give the reader a clearer idea of this contrast. Although the two plots involved appear to have all the complications— mistaken identity, odd coincidences, narrow escapes—of *Tom Jones* or *A Tale of Two Cities,* nevertheless it will be seen that the emphasis is still on family arrangements and approval rather than on individual romantic initiative and personal emotions.

In the first novel, the hero is the son of a member of the imperial censorate whose duty is to impeach corrupt officials. Worried that his father's strictness in his work was making him many enemies in high places, the hero urges his father to be more cautious. On the way to the national capital where his father has his official residence, he encounters the family of the beautiful heroine who through a forged imperial decree was nearly trapped into marrying a villain. The son exposes the plot and saves her, and she falls in love with him. When he falls ill, she nurses him back to health. After overcoming further difficulties perpetrated by the villain, he and the heroine are finally married with the emperor's approval.

The other novel, *The Strange Romance of the Beautiful Pair,* begins with an aged minister in the imperial court who is devoted to his only child, Red Jade, a beautiful poetess. Another high official asks for the hand of the poetess on behalf of his son, unsuccessfully because the latter failed the informal literary test arranged by the girl's father. In hatred, the boy's father arranges matters in court so that the poetess' father is ordered to embark on a difficult mission in Mongolia. The plot thickens with mistaken identities, plagiarism in poetry, the girl travelling disguised as a man, and a secret proposal to marriage until the hero Meng-li is happily married to Red Jade.

The familiar theme of love overcoming obstacles has made these two novels most appealing to Western readers. They were each in part or whole translated into Western languages several times and commanded the attention of such notables as Goethe, Schiller, and Carlyle.[3]

The marriage of the young poet to two girls, depicted in the second of these novels, was in accord with traditional Chinese custom. Clearly then, Chinese and American novelists describe two very different kinds of romantic characters. With few exceptions, such as the warrior in *Captain from Castile,* the advertising executive in *The Hucksters,* or James Bond, Mike Hammer, and other super-spies and detectives, the conventional romantic American hero and his lady are devoted to one another. In particular, there is a tendency for the male characters to exalt their female idols in thought, words, or action.

A Chinese hero, on the other hand, pursues his female love object and revels in her beauty in the same way that he strives to gain control of other worldly goods or prestige. In *The Dream of the Red Chamber,* the hero, although never sexually united with the heroine, has illicit relations with a number of other women, including servant maids, while never abandoning his ideal sweetheart. In addition, he also has erotic connections of varying degrees with a number of other women and homosexual relations with an actor. To American readers such a characterization probably befits that of a rogue or villain unless he has other redeeming heroic qualities or is able to repent. But Chinese readers do not condemn this character. Lacking the Western, individualized approach to sex, they have referred to him and his girl as great lovers for many decades.

These contrasts are not confined to only a select handful of Chinese and American novels. Among other popular Chinese novels are *The Romance of the Three Kingdoms; The True Story of Chi Kung, the Mad Monk; The True Story of His Eminence Pao, the Wonderful Official; The Golden Lotus; Western Chamber;* and *Strange Stories from a Chinese Studio.*[4] Any reader reasonably well acquainted with American fiction could prepare a similar and extensive list of novels.[5]

Concern with what the characters do in their social roles as contrasted with what they do, think, and feel as individuals is only one of the Chinese-American differences. Another is the nearly universal preoccupation with sex in American fiction and its segregation into a separate area in Chinese fiction. Love today, as at all times, is the most important theme of native American novels as well as of other Western novels which have enjoyed wide acceptance in this country. There are, of course, a number of great European and American works, such as Thomas Mann's *The Magic Mountain,* Thomas Wolfe's *Look Homeward, Angel,* Feodor Dostoevski's *Crime and Punishment,* John Hersey's *A Bell for Adano,* Sinclair Lewis' *Babbitt* or *Main Street,* Nordhoff and Hall's *Mutiny on the Bounty,* and Marjorie K. Rawlings' *The Yearling,* which have treated problems and situations that are not concerned essentially with love. Too, there are famous authors like Mark Twain, Herman Melville, and Jack London, whose writings have scarcely touched upon romance. I doubt, however, that anyone would choose to contend that the vast majority of Western novels do not deal with love.

With reference to love and sex, the most popular Chinese novels have been of three kinds. There are those which do not deal with the man-woman relationship at all, or only deal with it hurriedly as a minor matter; there are those which devote their entire attention essentially to one romantic affair like the two which were summarized, but which do not discuss sexual relations on a biological level; and there are pornographic novels.

The Romance of the Three Kingdoms is a typical novel in which romance is merely a bypath of the main route of the story. A synopsis of one brief section of this ten-volume work will indicate to what extent "romance" figures in Chinese novels of this variety. This novel was based upon that period of China's history, about A.D. 200, when the country was divided among three warring factions.

At one point, the mastermind of the Eastern faction, the kingdom of Wu, designs the following strategy to destroy the head of the Western faction, the kingdom of Shu. The ruler of Shu needs a wife, and the king of Wu has a beautiful sister. The story is spread that the king could marry this desirable woman if he came in person to the court of Wu. The strategist's idea is to kill the wife-seeker at a reception in his honor. The king of Shu, reluctant to accept the invitation, hesitates until his chief strategist advises him to go, accompanied by one lone warrior. What the Wu strategist fails to foresee is that the mother of the king of Wu would insist on attending the banquet to inspect her prospective son-in-law. The elderly dowager at once develops a liking for the king of Shu. She decides that he is the right man for her daughter. So he is married to the beautiful woman with all the ceremonial pomp due a king, against the wishes of the Wu strategist.

Having lost the first round, the unruffled Wu strategist works out a second plan. The king of Shu is showered with all kinds of gifts. A palace is built for him and his new bride, furnished with all manner of luxuries, and staffed with a host of servants and beautiful girls. Here he is entertained lavishly. The Wu strategist's idea is that, having lived in such ease and comfort, the king of Shu will be unwilling to leave his gracious surroundings. He also counts on the princess's persuading her husband to stay on indefinitely.

Unfortunately for the kingdom of Wu, the Shu strategist is one step ahead. He foresees this latter eventuality and provides his master with a plan to deal with it. The upshot is that the Wu princess, far from persuading her husband to stay, insists on going with him to his kingdom. A second attempt at assassination is out of the question because this would widow the princess. The pair could not be separated because the princess remained loyal to her husband. Result: the king of Wu loses the battle of strategy as well as a beautiful sister. The outcome so humiliates the Wu strategist that he eventually dies of anger, which, I suspect, is the common American disease—high blood pressure.

There are only a few other romantic episodes in this novel. The ruler of the Northern faction, the kingdom of Wei, is routed in battle because he neglected strategy while dallying with another man's wife. This is a typically Chinese piece of didacticism in which romance is no more than a vehicle for the moral—that the fulfillment of personal fancies runs a poor second to other considerations, and the failure to heed this injunction has disastrous consequences. In another instance, a great general, serving under the ruler of Shu, wins a wide expanse of territory after refusing romantic advances from an exquisite widow. But the remainder of the ten volumes is devoted to events that have nothing to do with romance.

Chinese pornographic novels do not portray romance, as Americans understand the term: the existence of a mutual devotion beyond the sexual plane, a situation where sexual congress between a man and woman is the catastasis. Chinese pornography describes the plain externalized pleasures of sex in blatant detail, and it is interspersed throughout with homosexuality and other forms of perversion. One of the few American novels which can faintly compare in frankness is Henry Miller's *Tropic of Cancer.*[6] Even in this book (formerly forbidden in this country but now permitted to be sold in bookshops only because of a court decision), the author merely uses some artless four-letter words over and over again, relying upon the usual devices of shadow, sound implication, or dialogue to portray the sexual act.

Almost all other Western literary pieces, whether banned or not, deal with sex by nuance. James T. Farrell's *Studs Lonigan,* Edmund Wilson's *Memoirs of Hecate County,* William Benton's *This Is My Beloved,* James Jones's *From Here to Eternity,* and Erskine Caldwell's *God's Little Acre,* are not to be excepted. The hundreds of paperbacks found in newsstands, air terminals, train stations, and other bookstalls, in spite of their inflammatory titles such as *Big Bunny, Tell No Man,* and *Beside Lover Boy,* and their often livid covers featuring nearly nude men and women, follow the same pattern. The relatively hesitant writers will leave a man and a woman at the chamber door. The bolder ones will step as far as the bed. But the Chinese authors who deal with this matter go relentlessly forward from that point where many of their Western brethren take leave of the scene.

Some illustrations will make this clear. For example, in James Jones's *From Here to Eternity,* the author describes a scene in which a soldier in Hawaii spends the night with a prostitute. The two are lying in bed, their nakedness covered by a quilt:

> "But why? Why will you remember me?"
> "Because," he said, "because of this." And smiling, he took a corner of her quilt and flipped it off her and looked at her lying there.
> She did not move and turned her head to smile at him. "Is that the only reason?"
> "No. Also because you touched me when Angelo was here."
> "Is that all?"
> "Maybe not all. But a lot."
> "But not because of talking to me?"
> "Yes, that too. Definitely that too. But this also," he said looking at her.
> "But the talking too?"
> "Yes. The talking too. Talking is important."
> "To me it is." She smiled contentedly at him and took a corner of his quilt that he was still lying under propped up on one elbow looking down at her and flipped it off of him, like he had done to her.
> "Why, look at you," she said.
> "I know. Ain't it shameful?"
> "I wonder what caused that."
> "Can't help it. Does it every time."
> "We really ought to change that."
> He laughed and suddenly they were talking, bed talking, as they had not been at all before. And this time it was different.
> Afterwards, grateful, he bent his head down for her lips.

Here not only the sexual act is veiled, but also feeling of love—"I know I'll remember you," "this time it was different," he was "grateful"—are added to the episode. Once the act of intercourse is completed, his attempt to kiss helps to sanctify the preceding, but unreported, coition. For in the American way of life, sex relations can only be justified within the terms of romantic love.

Henry Miller, in his *Tropic of Cancer,* is supposed to be more frank:

> As I watch Van Norden tackle her it seems to me that I'm looking at a machine whose cogs have slipped. Left to themselves they could go on this way forever, forever grinding and slipping without ever anything happening. Until a

hand shuts the motor off. The sight of them coupled like a pair of goats without the least spark of passion, grinding and grinding away for no reason except the fifteen francs, washes away every bit of feeling I have except the inhuman one of sating my curiosity. The girl is lying on the edge of the bed and Van Norden is bent over her like a satyr with his two feet solidly planted on the floor. I am sitting on a chair behind him, watching their movements with a cool, scientific detachment: it doesn't matter to me if it should last forever. It's like watching one of those crazy machines which throw the newspapers out, millions and billions and trillions of them with their meaningless headlines. The machine seems more sensible, crazy as it is, and more fascinating to watch, than the human beings and the events which produce it. My interest in Van Norden and the girl is nil; if I could sit like this and watch every single performance going on at this minute all over the world my interest would be even less than nil. I wouldn't be able to differentiate between this phenomenon and the rain falling or a volcano erupting. As long as that spark of passion is missing there is no human significance in the performance. The machine is better to watch. And those two are like a machine which has slipped its cogs. It needs the touch of a human hand to set it right. It needs a mechanic.

I get down on my knees behind Van Norden and I examine the machine more attentively. The girl throws her head on one side and gives me a despairing look. "It's no use," she says. "It's impossible." Upon which Van Norden sets to work with renewed energy, just like an old billy goat. He's such an obstinate cuss that he'd break his horns rather than give up. And now he's getting sore because I'm tickling him in the rump.

"For God's sake, Joe, give it up! You'll kill the poor girl!"

"Leave me alone," he grunts. "I almost had it that time!"

The language of *The Tropic of Cancer* is not any more explicit than in later examples such as Robert Grover's *One Hundred Dollar Misunderstanding,* which once more is about a prostitute and her customers (1961). Except for the added risqué element because the prostitute is Negro and the customers are white, Grover's description follows the same pattern of veiling the sex act with non-sexual phrases and nuances. This, in spite of the fact that the narrative of the sex act is given in two dialects: negro American and white American, each being hardly intelligible to the speaker of the other. The following two excerpts deal with the same episode:

(1) I wash him real nice an soff, counta him bein so awful tickledingus, and then I gits t'work. Time I start in, I got me so many worryful considerins t'do, I can' hardly pay no mind t'teckneek. Workin an considerin, and wonnerin does this dum Whiteboy know what t'do wiff that thing fer the other haff o'his haff and haff, I find I done me too dam much considerin.

Nex, I ain been at him a minit, an pop, off he go!

Kee-ryess! (p. 35)

(2) But different—that's my point. For instance (and this will be difficult to tell without becoming obscene) this colored professional prostitute had the same inclination that Margie has, except she went about it . . . . Well, she went about it *more* so than Margie ever did. I mean, she just acted as if it was quite natural, as

I suppose, in view of her status, it was. Though I found her manner of approach more than slightly disquieting. I mean, it was so professional, so undramatic and lacking in the necessary preliminaries. It was startling, almost sickening for gosh sakes!

I suppose, however, that never having been to a house of ill repute, I had acquired certain misconceptions about how such women behaved—based on my natural, normal experiences. Experiences unpaid for, is what I mean.

In fact, I was so surprised by her manner of approach (and also by a couple of unlikely intrusions by some other paid professional colored girl, who kept opening our door and sticking her head inside, first while mine was gone, and then later) that I reached my first (if you'll pardon the expression) climax a bit too hastily. (I should also add that the surroundings I found myself in had something to do with the above.)   (p. 45)

Tropic of Cancer and other novels such as *Lady Chatterly's Lover* are believed by many to be the extreme in literary directness, and a variety of "realism" over which writers, literary critics, police, judges, purity committees, and the general public all fiercely once contended (and in places still do). Yet these books as well as *The One Hundred Dollar Misunderstanding* do not compare in frankness with material to be found in the well-known Chinese novel, *The Golden Lotus.*[7]

Before it was light, Golden Lotus, still hungry for more, fondled his weapon with her slender fingers till it was ready once more for action.

"Darling," she said, "I want to lie on you." She climbed on to him, and played the game of making a candle upside down. She put her arms around his neck and wriggled about. She asked him to grip her firmy by the waist. Then she lifted herself up and dropped herself again: mox in mulierem penis capulo tenus iniit, nec ulla par extra manebat nisi quam fibula tenuit.

"Darling," she said. "I will make a red silk belt for you, and you can keep in it the medicine the monk gave you. And I will make two supports which you can tie at the root of it and fasten around your waist. When they are tightly tied, molliserit et totus inibit. Nonne putas id praestar huic fibulae quae tam dura et molesta est?"

"Yes, my child, make it by all means. The medicine is in my little box. Put it in for yourself."

"Come back to-night," Golden Lotus said, "and we will see what it is like." (Vol. III, pp. 318–19)

In spite of the fact that the descriptions of sexual intercourse in American literature are invariably much less bold than those in Chinese writings, American public reaction to these passages has consistently been more severe. The publishers of *God's Little Acre* were sued on the grounds of immorality by the New York Society for the Suppression of Vice. Whitman's *Leaves of Grass* was publicly burned in Philadelphia just before the turn of the twentieth century. The legal battles over *The Tropic of Cancer* are still comparatively recent. Some reviewers persistently charged that such works as *Two Adolescents* and *From Here to Eternity* were pornography in disguise. Many respectable libraries either do not keep such books as *Memoirs of Hecate County* or leave them in a locked press. Developments in the second half of the twentieth century may seem to cloud the observation here but I think future reaction against the liberalizing trends cannot be ruled out. On the other hand, *The Golden Lotus* is regarded in China as one of the greatest masterpieces of the empire. In the 1930's governmental organs, influenced by the West, attempted to have the franker paragraphs of this and similar works expurgated, but they met with little success. The new government in mainland China, in its determination to promote social and industrial progress, has eliminated sex as an important element in the fiction since 1949. But I think it also possible that future reaction against the totalitarian trends may once again accentuate sex in Chinese terms.

So we see sex is more widespread in American than Chinese fiction but it tends to be less explicit. The reader's imagination is stimulated by suggestive words and phrases, just as it is aroused by certain lines or poses in art. In contrast, sex either receives but scant attention in a lengthy Chinese novel or it is relegated to a separate novel. The majority of novels are not concerned with the love lives of men and women, but those which do deal with sex do not do so by subterfuge.

Furthermore, in no Chinese novel is sex as such ever condemned. The sexual urge leads to undesirable results or punishment only if it appears in improper places and is indulged in excessively or between improper parties. Thus the previously mentioned ruler of Wei suffered defeat following his adventure with another man's wife. And the hero of *Golden Lotus* died of his inordinate ventures in sexual pleasures.

In the American novels where pornographic or nearly pornographic passages are present, they usually are accompanied by the message that the events described are matters for condemnation or are, as in the episode from *From Here to Eternity,* associated with affection approaching true love. Accordingly, bold descriptions are most often restricted to relationships outside of wedlock, often between prostitutes and their customers, or between notoriously "loose" women and their similarly unprincipled companions. Yet the majority of American popular novels exalt love, divorced from the sexual act, as something magnificent in itself. Individual feelings being most important, the moral or immoral nature of the affair usually depends upon whether the love is "ture," or whether the partners are "happy." If it is "true," then love will find a way. If it is not "true," then separation between husband and wife is justified and so also is a liaison between a man and a woman either or both of whom are married to someone else.[8]

Some readers may be wishing now for an opportunity to ask me this question: Since, as you yourself stated, the majority of Chinese do not read and write, how can the novels have anything to do with them? Isn't the contrast you have described here no more than one between what is read by a very small group of Chinese intellectuals and what is popular with the majority of the American people?

The question is not hard to answer. While many Americans learn child-training, psychoanalysis, poetry, novels, drama, religion, and international affairs through schools, churches, clubs, and the mass media, the majority of their illiterate Chinese brethren are informed how ancient emperors ruled, famous warriors conquered, statesmen outwitted each other, and the handsome beggar married the daughter of the prime minister, through storytelling, shadow plays, classical operas, and regional operettas.[9]

Storytelling is one of the most ubiquitous forms of entertainment in China. Storytellers are found in every market place and temple fair, and in all cities and towns. They are in great demand during the ancestral festival of the Seventh Moon and the Spring Festival at the end of the Chinese year. They are frequently hired to entertain guests at a wedding, funeral, or birthday celebration. They tell their tales in different ways: some by talking; others by interspersing their talk with singing, since most of the popular novels are also available in lyric form. They may recite a single episode or they may be commissioned to tell an entire novel from beginning to end.

As a matter of fact, storytelling most decidedly antedated written fiction in the vernacular in China. The first fiction was a kind of prompt book to aid the storyteller's memory, each containing a synopsis of the narrative, called *hua pen* or "story roots," which were the first rudimentary novels. The earliest surviving *hua pen* comes from the archives of the famous Buddhist caves in northwestern China, and probably was in circulation in T'ang dynasty (A.D. 618–907). Five of the earliest speciments of these ancestors of Chinese fiction are today available in the government library in Japan. These prompt books retained their popularity with story tellers long after the full-fledged development of Chinese fiction (Ch'en 1961:467–497).

Shadow plays and colloquial operettas are always performed on a permanent or improvised stage. The average company's repertoire contains dramatized versions of the great novels, in whole or in part, and additional pieces based on unwritten folk tales often to be found in *hua pen*. The classical operas are much more formal than the shadow plays and operettas. They are more expensive to stage and to attend. Much of these troupes' repertoire is based on such novels as *The Romance of the Three Kingdoms,* and the opera may take from half an hour to several days to perform.

Of these media, storytelling reaches the widest audience, for there is no Chinese town or village unexposed to it in one way or another. The classical operas, while less widespread, are performed in the provincial capitals and other large cities, and are enjoyed by literates and illiterates alike.

The themes of these stories, operas, operettas, and shadow plays are similar to those of Chinese fiction in general. While most novels, movies, operas, and operettas which enjoy popularity among adult Americans are usually strung together by love affairs, Chinese themes can easily be classified into those which have to do with romance and those which do not. Romance is rare in the classical operas and in shadow plays, and it is only slightly more in evidence in the colloquial stories. In local operettas, romantic and non-romantic plots seem to be equally popular.

What has become of Chinese fiction since Western contact and especially since 1949? One big change is that, since about the 1900's, the Western-style product has become more dominant in fiction than in art. The traditional Chinese-style novels were still being written and read: the historical, the detective, the "Robin Hood," the supernatural, the romantic, and the mixed forms. But it is of note that the most important recent book on "modern Chinese fiction" deals exclusively with the Western-style Chinese novelists from Lu Hsün to Eileen Chang, but entirely ignores, with some justification, modern writers of traditional works such as Chang Hen-sui or P'ing Chiang Pu Hsiao Sheng (pen name) (Hsia 1961). In these Western-style Chinese novels the themes of individual struggle and the technique of first person narrative have become prominent. However, with few exceptions, notably Shen Ch'ungwen, the modern Chinese novelists' chief concern has been the hypocrisy, decadence, cruelty, or oppressiveness of traditional Chinese life, or the failure of the Republican Revolution.

The True Story of Ah Q (1941) by Lu Hsün (1941) one of the few modern Chinese stories to have attained an international reputation, is a good example. Ah Q, the hero, is among the very poor in a village and embodies all the characteristics of a Chinese national malady. His time was about the end of the Ch'ing dynasty when China was suffering from one humiliating defeat after another at the hands of powerful foreign nations. Ah Q deceives himself about having gained "spiritual victory" when he is bullied (which is often) and loses no time in bullying those weaker than himself. He gets into the company of a gang of city thieves and becomes their fence for stolen goods in the village. While doing this he brags about the anti-Manchu revolution (of which he heard rumors) as though he were personally a part of it. By this means he intimidates the village gentry and others who mistreated him before. However, the revolutionary forces that finally come to the village refuse to accept him as a comrade. Instead they ally themselves with the village gentry and execute him for his alleged role in a robbery. During the trial the bewildered Ah Q can only profess his vague envy for the revolutionaries. On the way to the execution ground he imitates a defiant shout like a traditional doomed convict for the benefit of the watching crowd because he feels this is expected of him.

Other modern Chinese novelists before 1949 said more about love or sex than did Lu Hsün in *The True Story of Ah Q*. But except for a few like Shen Ch'ung-wen they were preoccupied with the ills of the larger social and political situation. Even the works of Shen Ch'ung-wen who is regarded as "the greatest impressionist in modern Chinese literature" (Hsia 1961:208), exhibit, at one extreme, the need for "abiding by the wisdom

of the earth and enjoying a realistic sense of contentment which redeems
. . . [a man's] animal existence" and, at the other extreme, "a feeling of
quietness, a mood of poignant sadness completely objectified in the
helplessness of all the characters in their automatic motions of work and
play, in the small talk which fails to dispel gloom, and especially in the
contrasting views of the dingy house and the loveliness of spring outside"
(201, 210). This is not to say that there is no variation among noted
modern Chinese novelists. Mao Tun is distinguished for his gallery of
heroines and his psychological drama, while Lao She who is best known to
Western readers through his *Rickshaw Boy*,[10] eschews romance and de-
votes most of his literary energy to men and their actions. Pa Chin is
especially famous for his massive *The Love Trilogy* (1936) and *The Torrent:
A Trilogy* (in three separate books: *Family* 1933; *Spring* 1938; and *Autumn*
1940). He believes that the social system alone is to blame. Chang T'ien-i
is primarily a master of short stories and of satire. But he exercises his
satiric skill on all individuals regardless of class: their tensions, snobberies,
struggles, insults, and injuries. Eileen Chang[11] is a young author of *Romances,* unique for her "astonishing combination—a Chaucerian gusto for
life and all its little enjoyments plus an adult and tragic awareness of the
human condition" (Hsia 1961:392–393). But Ch'ien Chung-shu is "a
stylist of unusual distinction" (Hsia:457) and perhaps makes more use of
symbolism than most other Chinese writers. Furthermore, instead of
using satire as "a mode of protest against the evils of soceity," as is common
in modern Chinese literature, "Ch'ien turns the tables on the writers and
exhibits them as one of the major components of social and cultural
decadence" (Hsia:434).

Yet when all this is granted, three basic features mark most or all of the
better modern Chinese fiction.

The first is the "inability" of the characters . . . "to find in the purely
erotic sphere any meaning as personal assertion or of self-indulgence."
Ai-li S. Chin, who makes this observation, is speaking of three categories
of modern Chinese short stories in her study sample: those between 1915
and 1949, those in Taiwan, and those on the mainland between 1962 and
1966. In the first group "romantic" love loses some of the romance as it is
fitted into the lives of a generation intent on remaking society. Taiwan
examples are marked by "intensity of negative feelings between father and
son" but not by "the kind of emotional intensity which means positive
individual satisfaction or personal indulgence." As for the Communist
stories, "the underplaying of private emotions in the boy-girl and husband-wife relationship is obvious," and Chin concludes,

> The Chinese self therefore has had his center of gravity more exclusively in
> social relations and less solidly in himself. (1966:88)

A second basic feature of modern Chinese fiction is the tendency to
scrutinize the ills of contemporary Chinese life, with strong emphasis on

external realism but little interest in exploring the mind. Hsia, from whom we have drawn heavily in this discussion on modern Chinese fiction, characterizes this condition as "psychological poverty" and observes,

> In view of the absence of tragedy in traditional Chinese drama and of the strong satiric tradition in Ming and Ch'ing fiction (the distinguished exception is the tragic novel, *Dream of the Red Chamber*), one may legitimately wonder whether the study of Western literature has in any significant manner enriched the spiritual life of the Chinese.   (Hsia 1961:504)

The last basic feature common to modern Chinese fiction is the nearly complete absence (with rare exceptions) of any influence from the Western symbolist movement. Except for Eileen Chang, nearly all the noted writers of modern Chinese fiction before 1949 were already involved in or sympathetic with the Communist movement in China. Most of them have been more or less active since then. The major change after 1949 has been the increasingly "rigid organization of writers into arbitrary regional units" ... and "the imposition upon them of harsh discipline almost immediately afterwards" (Hsia 1961:470).

According to some students, the literary products in mainland China suffered both qualitatively and quantitatively even before the most recent purges accompanying the Great Cultural Revolution wrecked the literary careers of some of the writers.

Whatever the future portends, it is clear that these new developments have not changed the basic common features of Chinese fiction outlined here. Under the new regime there will not be merely greater emphasis on depiction of external ills of contemporary Chinese life but on a uniform direction of their solution; not merely little interest in the individual mind, but stronger pressure for all minds to dwell on similar thoughts. The main difference between the purgers and the purged in the recent Great Cultural Revolution is not in the basic direction of Chinese fiction but in who has deviated from it and how deviously. In this framework the Western symbolist movement becomes even less relevant than before.

Hsia's explanation of the Chinese lack of interest in psyche and in Western symbolism leaves much to be desired. He is on sound grounds when he points out that "... in appropriating the Western tradition, it is only to be expected that Chinese writers should accept and make use of what they find most congenial and meaningful" (504). This principle is valid for all societies and cultures, including those of Americans and of Chinese. But he errs in believing it to be due to Chinese rejection of traditional religions in favor of nineteenth-century absolutes of democracy, science, and liberalism. The Chinese have never been interested in the deeper workings of the mind even when traditional religions were in full swing. Hsia also errs in equating Confucian rationalism with Western rationalism, thereby alleging that, since traditional religions no longer "kept Confucian rationalism in check," Confucian rationalism precluded any possibility of Chinese interest in symbolist movement. There is no historical indication of Chinese interest in symbolist movement in the first place.

Religious creeds or scientific philosophies or political isms, no less than art and fiction, cannot as such cause the interest (or its lack) in mind exploration or symbolism in American fiction or modern Chinese fiction. Such creeds or philosophies or isms are subject to patterning by the approach to life of whatever people that originate or receive them. They, too, will be accepted or magnified or rejected or modified by different societies and cultures depending on their congeniality and meaningfulness. The particular Chinese situation-centered approach to life makes particular patterns of art congenial and meaningful to a majority of the Chinese. These patterns emphasize external realism, not exploration of the mind; and the place of the individual in the environment, not the struggle against it. Similarly, in the particular Western (including American) individual-centered approach to life, the objectives tend to involve emotions, the seeking of the original and the unseen or unseeable, and the struggle of the individual to assert and find himself by way of anti-orthodoxy and proliferation of new trends. This focus on individualism occurs not merely in art and fiction, but also in business, religion, and political and social behavior.

NOTES

1. In this discussion we shall confine ourselves chiefly to novels of American origin except where noted.

2. *Western Journey* and *Tale of the Mirrored Flower* are Chinese fantasies comparable to *Alice in Wonderland* or *Gulliver's Travels*.

3. Fragmentary translations into English and Portuguese of *the Story of an Ideal Marriage* were first brought back to England in 1719. These were edited as *Hao Kiu Chuan* or *The Fortunate Union* by Thomas Percy and published in 1761. *The Strange Romance of the Beautiful Pair* was first translated into French in 1826, and later into English and Dutch. It was widely read and admired in Europe. (Ch'en, Shou-yi: *Chinese Literature: A Historical Introduction* [New York, 1961] pp. 493–97. Ch'en's brilliant book provides more detailed synopses for most of the Chinese novels mentioned in our discussion.) Ch'en suggests that the two romances were widely appreciated in the West because "there is usually a sufficient portrayal of the social usages and mores of the Chinese people to make a novel of this category interesting to foreign readers (Ch'en 1961, ibid., p. 494). Our interpretation of their popularity in the West obviously differs from Ch'en's. Our interpretation is further supported by the fact that other novels such as *The Golden Lotus* or *All Men Are Brothers*, which also contain much "portrayal of the social usages and mores of the Chinese people," were not introduced into the West till much later and even then they never commanded as much attention of Western literary men. The reason for this differing Western treatment, I suspect, is that *The Golden Lotus*

deals with physical sex too blatantly while *All Men Are Brothers* practically does not deal with love at all. Both are, consequently, less acceptable.

4. *The Romance of the Three Kingdoms* by Lo Kuan-chung was partially translated by C. H. Brewitt-Taylor (Shanghai, 1925). There are two translations of Chin Ping Mei, one being *The Golden Lotus* by Clement Egerton, London, 1939, in four volumes. An English translation by Bernard Miall from an abridged version in German by Franz Kuhn, was published under the title *The Plum of the Golden Vase* (Introduction by Arthur Waley) (London, 1939). *Western Chamber* was also translated twice: Henry H. Hart (Stanford, 1936), and S. I. Hsuing (London, 1936). *Strange Stories* was translated in part by Herbert A. Giles (Shanghai, 1908 and 1916), and also in part by Rose Quong, under the title *Chinese Ghost and Love Stories* (New York, 1946).

5. We are speaking primarily of the widely read "popular" novels found as book club selections and on paperback book racks in drugstores. Those authors generally considered by university professors and other intellectuals to be of high literary merit and significance and which are the subject of classes in American literature—Hawthorne, Melville, Mark Twain, Faulkner, Hemingway, Nathaniel West, Norman Mailer, James Baldwin, John Barth, Saul Bellow, etc.—do not necessarily conform to this pattern.

6. Others which would fall in the same category are Reag's *The Story of O*, Southern's *Candy*, Mailer's *The American Dream*, Updike's *Couples*, Donleavy's *The Ginger Man*, and Sutton's *The Exhibitionist*.

7. In the translation of *The Golden Lotus* (Clement Edgerton, translator. London, 1939) all pornographic passages from their Chinese original are rendered in Latin, as in the paragraphs quoted below. The explanation for this is given by the translator in his introduction to the book. Referring to the novel's Chinese author, he said, "If he had been an English writer, he would have avoided some subjects completely, skated over thin ice, and wrapped up certain episodes in a mist of words. This he does not do. He allows himself no reticences. Whatever he has to say, he says in the plainest of language. This, of course, frequently is acutely embarrassing for the translator . . . . But it could not all go into English, and the reader will therefore be exasperated to find occasional long passages in Latin. I am sorry about this, but there was nothing else to do."

8. After the book had gone to press my good friends Frank and Dora Kuo called my attention to two books: Frank Harris' *My Life and Loves* (1963) and an anonymous autobiography, *My Secret Life* (1966) (both published by Grove Press, New York). The former was first published in Germany in 1922–27, and the latter was privately printed in an eleven copy edition at the author's expense in Amsterdam around 1882. Privately circulated erotica of this kind was not unknown in the West for centuries before modern times. Even in secrecy or under disguise these were in the main confined to French and Italian languages. But Grove Press of New York City is able to publish them in the U.S.A. for the first time becaue, since 1959, American laws governing sex matters in books and other public media have been liberalized through court decisions. These books even surpass their Chinese counterparts in frankness.

However, this new development does not negate our arguments advanced here. While Chinese writers treat erotica as part of a larger social context, their Western brethren see it as an end in itself, unrelated to other aspects of life. Consequently, these Western writers are preoccupied with the variety of sexual conquests and of sexual acts, of its sensations and of details of sexual organs to an extent unknown among Chinese writers of comparable interest. The entire *My Secret Life* is saturated with sexual episodes of every variety. It has no other substance. *My Life and Loves* is concerned with four things: adventure, ideas, men and events, and sex. But as its editor observes, "no matter what his subject, Harris' person and his vanity permeate every page" (p. xv).

The last observation, the fact that the author of neither book cared for any lasting intimacy (one of them mentioned brief marital interludes while the other never touched on marriage at all), and the preoccupation with varieties of sexual conquest as well as sexual sensation, betray the individual-centered approach very well. Frank Harris and the writer of *My Secret Life* merely exemplify the extremes to which some of those raised in that approach can go. But such extremes are even more interesting when we read about a more basic reason why Frank Harris wrote as he did. This reason is found in his own "Forward" to *My Life and Loves*. Several executive and judiciary decisions against his publications in the U.S. caused Harris financial embarrassment. So,

> If America had not reduced me to penury I should probably not have written this book as boldly as the ideal demanded. At the last push of Fate (I am much nearer seventy than sixty) we are all apt to sacrifice something of Truth for the sake of kindly recognition by our fellows and a peaceful ending. Being that "wicked animal," as the French say, "who defends himself when he is attacked," I turn at length to bay, without any malice, I hope, but also without any fear such as might prompt compromise. I have always fought for the Holy Spirit of Truth and have been, as Heine said he was, a brave soldier in the Liberation War of Humanity: now one fight more, the best and the last. (pp. 1–2)

It is clear that for Frank Harris, quite apart from his personal fondness for sexual variety and sensations, the frankness of his writing was the instrument of an antiestablishmentarian and a revolutionary, an attitude so characteristic of the individual-centered West and so alien to the situation-centered Chinese. So repression of sex in literature and blatant erotica are at once two sides of an irreconcilable tug-of-war in individual-centered West. It contrasts sharply with situation-centered China, where no comparable polarization is discernible.

In this light, the challenge that Grove Press uses to induce enthusiasm for its erotica publications is well chosen. It must strike a responsive chord in the individual-centered mind. The advertisement begins: "Do you have what it takes to join the Underground?" (Advertisement for subscription to *Evergreen*, insert in *My Secret Life*).

9. Since 1949 the mainland Chinese authorities have consciously utilized and encouraged most of these media for the dissemination and arousal of public enthusiasm for Communist ideology and national goals.

10. *Luo-tuo Hsiang-tzu*, 1938, translated by Evan King as *Rickshaw Boy*, (New York, 1945).

11. Two of her novels have been translated by herself into English: *The Rice-Sprout Son*, (New York, 1955) and *Naked Earth*, (Hongkong, 1956).

13

Kinship Is the Key

One of the most urgent needs in the social sciences and, by extension, in at least three of the clinical sciences—psychiatry, psychoanalysis, and clinical psychology—is knowledge of the underlying assumptions rooted in cultures other than those of the West. We need to explore these cultures for solutions to problems besetting our own society. As long as we remain culture-bound in our definition of problems, we cannot take advantage of feasible solutions extraneous to the Western tradition.

Consider our approach to air piracy, which is certainly one of the major forms of violence. In an hour-long Columbia Broadcasting System program on hijacking (October, 1972), a psychiatrist, Dr. David G. Hubbard, director of the Aberrant Behavior Center in Dallas, Texas, who has also served as consultant to federal prisons and to the Federal Aeronautics Administration, offered his conclusions after interviews with forty-eight culprits in jail. These men are schizophrenic paranoics, he said. They are suffering from a sense of failure, e.g., inadequate masculinity. They have dreams of glory, and they are interested in death but do not wish to die by their own hands. And they consider any of the following outcomes of their action as success: touching the one-hundred-thousand-dollar ransom (or whatever amount) even though they may lose it five minutes later; dying themselves after causing the death of others; ending up in a foreign jail after having forced the plane to land where they command it; and even taking the plane out of its authorized ramp.

Given this approach, it is only natural that our major attempts to prevent air piracy have been chiefly in the form of detection (electronic devices, search of passengers before boarding, personality profiles, etc.); force (sky marshals, sealing of rear exits of the planes, guards and fences around airports, etc.); and the elimination of sanctuaries for hijacked planes (agreement with Cuba). The astonishing thing is that Dr. Hubbard, after concluding, in a *Life* interview, that "the hijacker is unique, he should be treated as such," admits there are an estimated eight million Americans with the psychiatric syndrome he describes. Add to this the hundreds of thousands who bought sweatshirts bearing the sentiment, "D. B. Cooper, where are you?"[1] and countless others who catapult songs eulogizing the criminal's exploit into financial successes, and we come up with considerably more than eight million potential air pirates.

This chapter was originally published in *Center Magazine,* Vol. VI, No. 6, November/December 1973, pp. 4–14.

Is it not unrealistic to think we can successfully deal with such a large number of potential air pirates by electronic detection and guards? Has not the time come for us to scrutinize some of the fundamental premises of American culture?

Since we are confined by our traditional American thinking about social problems (and I do mean "traditional," though the usual American way is to relegate the patterns of thinking of other cultures into the category of "traditional," while equating American ways with "modern"), it is not unnatural for America's top university research people who are concerned with the air piracy problem to be as myopic as the general public. Thus a professor of psychology on the C.B.S. program concluded that the reporting of air piracy cases stimulates more hijacking. I do not dispute the notion that wide reporting of "how to" may have some escalating effects in all areas of crime; people looking for success without regard to social consequences are bound to seek lessons for the perfect crime. I am merely appalled by the low level on which our scientific talent and support are focused.

However disrespectful it may seem to compare the dignified work of eminent scholars with the view of a suburban Chicago police chief after a rash of recent murders, their similarity is striking. The working "theory" of the suburban Chicago police is that heavy and continuous rains drive some unbalanced individuals berserk, hence the high frequency of murders.

If we look at the prevailing approaches to drug abuse, we find the same picture: detection and punishment of the pushers, explanation of the pitfalls of addiction to the young, and treatment of addicts by physical and psychological means—but nothing about the more fundamental causes of the persistence of the problem, which surely must be the conditions of society. Under the impact of the West, China had a drug problem for over half a century. But our scientists interested in the problem have not even noted the fact that Chinese drug addicts were mostly old while their American counterparts today are predominantly young. They have failed, too, to note that, despite the fact that China before 1949 was plagued by hundreds of thousands of opium and other drug addicts, there was no Chinese movement for the use of drugs as a pathway to truth. There simply was no Chinese Timothy Leary or his kind of follower. These differences say something basic about systems rather than individuals being the cause of the problem.

The same culture-bound myopia has prevented social and clinical scientists from coming to grips with other serious problems, from alienation to the bloody carnage on our highways, from religious and racial tensions to juvenile delinquency, and from the sagging morale of Detroit auto workers to shoplifting. We may stop air piracy by the most thorough airport security system in operation, but creative Americans will undoubtedly find other antisocial areas in which to exercise their talents. Under the circumstances, antisocial acts seem to outpace our defensive, curative, or preventive methods of dealing with them. Perhaps it is this seemingly hopeless picture that prompted Billy Graham to suggest castration of the rapist as a way of stopping sexual assaults on women. "That would stop him pretty quick," he said. In another era some kings and tribal chiefs used to punish pickpockets by chopping off their hands. These pre-modern rulers, also, must have said something like "That will stop them pretty quick."

Billy Graham shares one thing in common with clinicians and social scientists: they are all firmly wedded to individualism. Consequently they look to the individual for the basic sources of his achievements as well as the roots of his troubles.

I submit that the beginning of doing something about our failures is to move from an individual-centered Western model of man to a more universal sociocentric model. I begin with the observation that the most essential ingredient of human existence is the *interpersonal nexus,* not the individual, in spite of Henry David Thoreau, the lone Hindu meditators in the Himalayas, and certain Christian ascetics. If Thoreau was really so much in love with solitude, why did he write his many journals? The conclusion is inescapable that his real intention was to start a club of solitude lovers. As to Hindu gurus, I have the impression that most of them would not mind the hardship of coming to Madison Square Garden to save us rather than remaining in the Himalayas. Finally, even Carthusian monks, in spite of their silence, form a monastic order. Given this premise, we shall see the inadequacy of not only Freud's focus on intra-psychic function of the ego vis-à-vis id and superego, but also Erik Erikson's revisionist view, when he adds the extra-psychic emphasis of a strong ego with "an individual core, firm and flexible enough to reconcile the necessary contradictions in any human organization, to integrate individual differences, and above all with a sense of identity and an idea of integrity." Erikson, and others who follow in his footsteps, may concede a greater role to interpersonal factors, but they offer us only a slightly enlarged version of the individual-centered model of man.

A sociocentric model of man is shown in the diagram on the next page. In the absence of a better model, I have represented the elements in eight irregular concentric layers, 7 to 0. Layers 7 and 6 represent Freudian "Unconscious" and "Preconscious," which have become so well known in Western culture that they need no elaboration. Layer 5 is the "Unexpressed Conscious." Its contents are largely kept private to the individual himself either because he is afraid to communicate them (for example, some girl cannot even tell the boy she loves that he has halitosis); or because others will not understand or care (for example, can one get on a bus and at once tell its conductor what his mother did to him this morning?); or, he can only feel it but has difficulty in explaining it (for example, can we always tell why we do not like someone?); or, he is ashamed to divulge it (for example, can any one of us measure up to the high standard set by Jesus when he said, ". . . that whosoever looketh on a woman to lust after her hath committed adultery with her already in his heart"?).

The hallmark of Layer 4, the "Expressible Conscious," is that its con-

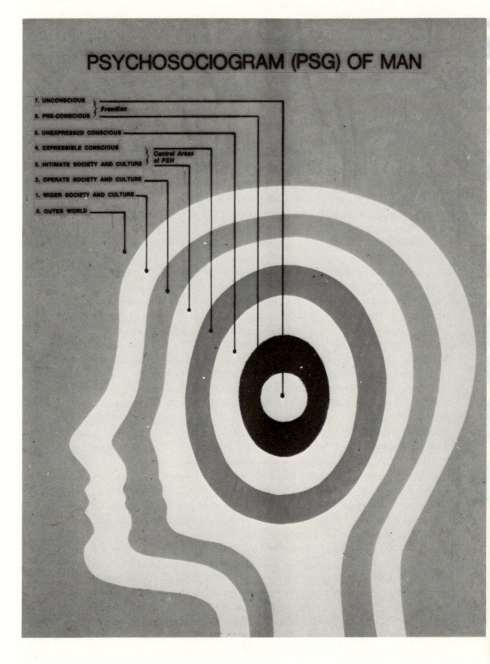

tents can not only be communicated easily to others but can be understood and responded to by others without any great difficulty: love, greed, vision, fear, grief, and knowledge of the correct and unacceptable ways of behaving according to moral, social, and technical standards of each culture. Some of the contents here are so public that we don't have to use real language. Body gestures or para-language will do—that is what we mean when we say of a girl that she is acting provocatively.

Layers 4 and 3 are separate. As such they represent the inside world of the individual and his outside world. Layer 3 contains humans, ideas, gods, and things that make up eveyone's "Intimate Society and Culture." The hallmark of Layer 3 is that we relate to all its inhabitants and contents by bonds of *affect*. We feel strongly about them. The loss of, departure of, or infringement upon them create emotional problems for us. For its human inhabitants this means intimacy— or a condition in which one can be off guard, can dare to reveal one's worst without the fear of being rejected, and can afford to receive help and sympathy without bearing the onus of charity. The non-human inhabitants of Layer 3 are some of the individual's most beloved pets or cherished possessions and/or ideals. Dogs, for example, are so important to many Americans that they incorporate them in wedding processions and insist on burying them in segregated cemeteries. The idea of privacy is definitely part of Layer 3 for a majority of Americans, but that of exceeding the speed limit or even taking a shopping cart from a supermarket is not. Jesus is part of Layer 3 for most Christian Americans but the Buddha is not; bedroom furniture is, but park benches are not.

Layer 2, "Operative Society and Culture," consists in the first place of humans whom we relate to by *roles*. Among these are the individuals we employ or by whom we are employed, from whom we buy or to whom we sell. They are most of our neighbors, teachers or students, leaders or followers, preachers or congregation. If you are a teacher, you must have students; and if a student, you must have teachers. If you aspire to be a leader, you must have people willing to be led. In order to play out our roles, we need each other. The inhabitants of Layer 2 are useful to us and we to them, but we do not feel strongly about them, or perhaps feel anything at all. When they depart or we lose them, no emotional problems are created for us. We may, of course, be inconvenienced, but there is no need to mourn their loss. The owner of a giant enterprise does not grieve for the death of one of his employees. He merely advertises for someone else. Nowadays it is fashionable for Western theologians to discuss comparative religion by invoking the tenets of Buddhism or Islam. But how many of them are prepared to defend the teachings of Buddha or of the Koran the way they would the Bible or the Torah? Public parks and zoos and roads are definitely part of Layer 2. We need them for our enjoyment and convenience. But we litter them and even vandalize them because we do not love them at all.

Layer 1 contains people, gods, ideas, and things that exist as part of our culture but apart from us. We neither use them nor feel for them. For example, most white Americans had very few black Americans as co-workers, employees, neighbors, or friends before World War II. White Americans saw American Indians either as obstacles to white progress or as hapless inmates on reservations. Today most Americans have heard of the Tennessee Valley Authority, but most of us have nothing to do with it. Even about things we use daily and persons in whom we have great interest, we may remain quite ignorant. How many of us, for example, know anything about the theory of the internal combustion engine of the automobile? I, for instance, do not even know how to change a tire—I leave that to the specialists.

Layer 0, "the Outer World," contains humans, gods, ideas, and things that are not even nominally part of us. For a majority of Americans, "inscrutable Asia" and "darkest Africa" are part of Layer 0.

One difference between Layers 0 and 1 is that we may suddenly find ourselves linked with the contents of Layer 1 without intending to be, but not so easily with those of Layer 0. Americans abroad may be asked about the T.V.A. or about the Zuni Indians because they come from a society where these are present. I was asked many questions about the Great Wall after I came out of China. Somehow I was expected to be an expert on the Great Wall.

Another point to be noted is that cultural and societal boundaries do not entirely coincide. Thus for most Americans the ways of life of Western Europeans may be in their layers 1, 2, or even 3, instead of Layer 0. Before the Meiji Restoration, the Japanese used to be proud of their cultural and racial affinity with Chinese. *Dóbun-doshú"* (same written language and same race) was a common phrase then. After the Meiji Restoration up to the end of World War II, they repudiated it. After Premier Tanaka's 1972 visit to Peking the Japanese are once again not unhappy with their Chinese connection.

If we regard the Psychosociogram (PSG) as the "anatomy" of human existence, then the Psychosocial Homeostasis (PSH) to be explained next is the "physiology" of human existence. The core idea of PSH is indicated by the shaded area of the diagram. It covers layers 4 and 3, with the shading slightly running into Layers 2 and 5. I borrowed the term "homeostasis" from physiology. This shaded area is the central substance of man as a social and cultural being. It is the *human constant,* within which every human individual seeks to maintain a uniform, beneficial stability within and between its parts.

The basic features of the operation of PSH are these: every individual needs the affective relationships of Layer 3 and, in the normal course of events, employs little more than the contents of Layer 4 as his psychic basis for interaction and communication. With reference to humans, affect creates the condition of intimacy. This intimacy makes every individual's existence meaningful. The need for it is as important as the requirement for food, water, and air. Basically it gives the individual his sense of well-being. To lose it suddenly may be so traumatic as to lead to aimlessness or suicide. The cultural rules and artifacts residing in Layer 3 also figure largely in the equation. Changes in them, too, are hard to tolerate. In the short run, that is what we mean by culture shock. In the longer run, if such changes are forced on the individual over a period of time, without alternatives for the individual to transform and reintegrate his PSH, they may lead to serious mental disorders or loss of interest in life.

However, although both humans and non-humans may be objects of affect, humans are preferred over the non-humans. Consequently, the process of Psycosocial Homestasis is primarily one of seeking and maintaining affective relationships with humans and, when necessary, substituting one set of humans for another. Only when humans are not available for affective links do we entertain some such sentiment as Mark Twain once sourly expressed: "The more I look at humans the more I like dogs." Furthermore, even if non-humans have substituted for humans in our Layer 3, we never give up our need for humans.

There are many possible modes of PSH. Some cultures make maintenance easier than others. The mode most characteristic of a majority of the Chinese in their traditional society and culture is by way of the kinship network and is relatively the easiest. Almost every human being begins life in the basic kinship configuration consisting of parents and children. His parents are the first occupants of his Layer 3. Here is where a majority of mankind experiences boundless affect. For the Chinese and others like him, whose culture says his self-esteem and future are tied to his first group, parents, siblings, and other close relatives are the permanent inhabitants of his Layer 3. They share his glory and they are his principal resources in time of distress and need. As a result, the non-human elements in the pre-1949 Chinese individual's Layer 3 tended to be knowledge, artifacts, and rules of conduct centered in the kinship sphere. Filial piety was the cornerstone of all morality, attachment to ancestral-land was a foregone conclusion, and all customs and usages discouraged the individual from being adventurous toward the rest of the world.

The Chinese individual could satisfy the requirements of his PSH without moving far afield into the outer layers. Intimacy was readily and continuously accessible to him. If, for reasons beyond his control (such as war or famine), he got to the outer layers at all, he was likely to seek previously unknown but existent ties, namely kinship or locality ties; to develop kinship-like ties; to continue his ties with his kinship and local group at home; and to perform the role activities necessary for him to find his place in the non-kinship setup but not to initiate dissent or rock the boat, for his affective needs were satisfied elsewhere. Hence the Chinese have never supported a missionary movement or experienced significant religious dissension and persecution, and have had few secondary groups outside the kinship and local spheres. Their famous travelers were either in imperial service or were devout followers of the Buddha bent on obtaining the complete teachings of the Lord to bring them back to China.

China has produced no counterpart of Florence Nightingale, Saint Francis Xavier, Lawrence of Arabia, or Carry Nation, all of whom set out to remake the world. No Chinese imperial conquerer was ever interested in spreading a religious creed or the Chinese way of life.

Although parents and siblings are also the first inhabitants of the Western individual's Layer 3, he is expected to evict them from it. His culture tells him that his self-esteem and future prospects depend upon how well he can stand on his own two feet. That does not mean that all adult Americans are separated from their parents, but after they marry or reach legal age they have to alter the nature of their relationship with their elders. Furthermore, given a society where manhood and womanhood are defined as independence from parents, the drive for such independence begins long before the ability to do so is attained.

But relationships with peers are drastically different from relationships with parents. Parents are like dogs: we kick them in the teeth and they still come back for more. We cannot take our peers for granted that way. They are likely to be competing for the same things that we are. Our desire for mastery over them is matched by theirs over us. This is the basic condition for the intense loneliness which many have tried to link with drug abuse. This initial pattern of hazardous links with peers sets the tone of the Western man's approach to his fellow men for the rest of his life.

As a result, the Western man's problem of PSH is far more strenuous than that of his Chinese opposite number—a difficulty which has contributed to the internal dynamism of Western society and culture in contrast to the internal static quality of their Chinese counterparts. The Western man has to resort to a variety of ways to solve it. To mention a few of them, the Western man may explore Layers 2, 1, or even 0 for new frontiers and new peoples (preferably what he calls primitive peoples) on which and on whom he can lavish his affect; he must convert or incorporate some or all of the inhabitants in these layers into his Layer 3 so that he can find his own identity and fulfillment; he can accomplish this as a great missionary in the style of Livingstone or Albert Schweitzer—or he can attempt to revolutionize the world by bringing to all "backward" peoples the message and know-how of industrialization, democracy, or whatever.

Lest it be thought that such expansive tendencies developed in the West as a result of Christianity or industrialization we must note that the conqueror Alexander the Great led the way. After being forced to retreat from the Indus River to Persia, the Greek king decided to organize the "marriage" of ten thousand of his followers to Iranian maidens and stage one last vast banquet in which all joined him in a symposium and the drinking of a "loving cup" to the union of mankind and universal concord. According to at least one contemporary observer, that was how Alexander the Great hoped to unite East with West. No Chinese conqueror ever expressed such a wish, even in his fantasies.

In dealing with the problem of scarcity of PSH resources, the Western man may also pursue the opposite course by going inward to explore his own inner self for definition and guidance, with accent on his own anxiety, fixation, and other aspects of the unconscious. Here, too, the Western way is in sharp contrast to that of the Chinese.

For example, as we noted in Chapter 12, most Western fiction is concerned with its characters' psychic tensions and interplays as well as the variety and intensity of personal sensations, while Chinese fiction deals with externally perceivable actions and their consequences. This Western emphasis on the psyche has gone so far that even a scholar of Chinese origin, Dr. Chih-ts'ing Hsia, in surveying *modern* Chinese literature for American audiences, characterized it as suffering from "psychological poverty."

As to the search for variety and intensity of personal sensations, it is reflected even in pornography. The Chinese have quite a few pornographic novels; some are of the pulp type and others have become classics. They feature homosexual liaisons, oral-genital connections, and other erotic modes. But the passive partner in homosexuality is invariably a servant, an apprentice, or other person of low status serving a licentious master. The oral-genital connections were invariably one-sided, the partner of lower status providing for the gratification of his superior. There was no question of the roles being reversed. The social barrier tended to outweigh any desire for personal sensuality. Hence the sexual episodes are usually part of a larger plot involving family affairs, bureaucratic intrigues, or even war.

The links which bind the members of any society together are generally of two kinds: role and affect. Shorn of sociological jargon, which often obscures rather than clarifies, role is basically a matter of usefulness: what one can do for another in terms of services and goods. It may be a case of you scratch my back and I will scratch yours; but ultimately the most widely accepted form of usefulness is what money can buy. Affect is feeling: how much I care for you and how much that feeling is appreciated. Whether or not one's feeling for another is reciprocated, it certainly cannot be bought and sold. If it is, we call such liaisons disparaging names, especially if they involve persons of the opposite sex.

In any society, role and affect overlap. Through role relationships, members of each society get things done, skilled and unskilled, heavy tasks and light chores, deployment of weapons against the enemy, or mobilization of resources to wipe out locusts. But it is love, devotion, loyalty, and patriotism which really bind a society's members together so that they will, in the long run, support each other, protect each other, work for each other beyond the call of duty, even die for each other. There is no society in which everyone does everything for love; but a society in which no one will do anything except for money is in serious trouble.

The Western routes to Psychosocial Homeostasis lead not only to the separation of role from affect but also to escalation of role relationships and a dangerous shrinkage of the areas where affect can be and is operative.

To begin with, whether by outward expansion of Layers 2, 1, or 0, or by inward exploration of Layers 5, 6, or 7, the yield of interpersonal intimacy is precarious or scarce. Outward expansion by the individualist brings about a kind of asymmetrical affect. The inividualist who has no affective links at home needs to shower affect on the object of his outward exploration. But the trouble is that the objects of his affect do not need him for their PSH the way he needs them for his PSH. He may live among them but they are not intimate enough with him for affective sociability. He may be their friend, but they are too enmeshed in other intimate concerns to provide him with affective security. And while they may marvel at his weapons and fear him like the plague, they do not accord him any affective status. They treat him in role terms when in fact what the individualist really wants is reciprocated affect.

This state of affairs cannot be improved by the individualist's efforts to convert the objects of his affect to his way of looking at things, to give them some of his style of education, to uplift them to his moral standards, and save them from witchcraft and paganism. In the end, the expanding individualist man's affect is often lavished on the idea of his mission and conquest and how successes in ventures of his design prove his own manhood, rather than on the human beings who are supposed to benefit from them. Should the objects of his affect refuse the benefit of his ventures, he may even declare, like Linus of "Peanuts" fame, "I love mankind but hate human beings."

With reference to inhabitants of Layers 2 and 1 (i.e., people of his own society) the individualist's problem of affect is even more acute. Since the individualist and his peers are in sharp competition with each other, each of them needs to stake out a human "territory" for himself in order to safeguard his own precarious PSH. Since they must compete with each other for the same people as instruments for their separate affective establishments (PSH), they find it difficult to coöperate with each other even in role terms. This is why free associations or clubs, based on countless number of causes, have prospered and grown in America. This, too, is why many of the associations or clubs are at war with one another.

The inevitable next development is for the individualist man to substitute non-human elements (such as wealth, ideas, machines, or animals) for the humans he cannot possibly reach. This pattern of PSH has some advantages. Non-humans can be controlled with far greater certitude than humans. The individualist can lavish affect on them in a manner to suit himself; he does not have to concern himself with the problem of non-reciprocity; nor does he have to worry about negative affect such as suspicion and hatred on their part, should he decide to discard or replace them. The individualist man can have all his own options open. That is why dogs are so important in American life: we can control them and take for granted their boundless affect.

Since our basic premise is that the most essential ingredient of human existence is the interpersonal nexus, not the individual alone, it is logical for us to expect that the individualist man will not stop at mere control of things such as wealth. He is bound to see the latter as a means of getting closer to his fellow men, even though control over non-humans may keep him busy enough to camouflage his lack of intimacy with humans. The man of wealth cannot be sure how those who dance around him really feel about him. In the end he must be satisfied with fulfilling his PSH requirements with the non-human, such as material success, and defend himself with such ideas as "business and sentiment don't mix" or, "the more wealth I create the more people I will benefit by giving them employment."

The net result is the escalation of role activities. It has led our society to become enormously complex, in the same way a modern jet liner, which contains some two million parts, is complex. This complexity is due primarily to the number and variety of jobs, of patents, of books published, of sensuous experiences to be had, of crimes committed, as well as of detection and prevention devices invented, of laws and government agencies; but it has little or nothing to do with devotion, loyalty, love, kindness, or sympathy. That is why Detroit auto workers find their jobs so unsatisfying and show their dissatisfaction by low productivity and shoddy performance. In 1972 a record twelve million cars were recalled. A 1973 Gallup Poll tells us that, of the representative sample of wage-earners questioned, "half say they could accomplish more each day if they tried, with three in five in this group indicating they could increase their own output by twenty per cent; the percentage who say they could get more work done is highest (sixty-one per cent) among workers aged eighteen to twenty-nine." The same survey also revealed that job satisfaction is the key factor in productivity. "Among those who say they are 'very satisfied' with their jobs, less than one quarter say they could increase their output at least thirty per cent. In sharp contrast, among those who say they are 'very dissatisfied' with their jobs, about four in ten say they could do at least thirty per cent more work a day."

The shrinkage of the interpersonal applicability of affect necessarily increases the intensification of one's preoccupation with oneself. The individualist man cannot but be interested in expansion of the self: outward and inward. When he expands outward he is bent on changing the minds of his contacts; when he expands inward he desires more converts to his way of mind-expansion. Both are not ends in themselves but merely means to augment his PSH resources.

In the light of this hypothesis, Freudian psychology and psychoanalysis fall into proper perspective. Without intending to disparage Freud and psychoanalysis (I have learned much from them), I see psychoanalysis as one way for the individualist man to achieve and maintain his PSH. It compensates for his lack of intimacy with humans in less artificial circumstances, in conditions under which he can be off guard, dare to reveal his worst without the fear of rejection, and receive help and sympathy without the onus of charity.

Regrettably it is a relationship for which he must pay and which, from the point of view of the analyst, is marked by role and not affect; consequently it is an asymmetrical relationship. But it is not different from the case of other patients who have to pay for oxygen tents, artificial kidneys, or spectacles. T-Groups and Esalen and the Maharishi Mahesh Yogi's Transcendental Meditation are variations on the same theme. Societies where the requirements for PSH are more easily satisfied and maintained have less need for psychoanalysis and T-Groups, just as individuals with stronger kidneys or lungs or sight, so to speak, probably have fewer chances of ever needing artificial kidneys, oxygen tents, or spectacles.

By the same token, societies where PSH requirements are more easily satisfied and maintained will be not only less expansive and adventurous (exploration of Layer 1 and 0) but also less acquisitive: their members have less need to prove themselves by conquering frontiers or by substituting material wealth for human intimacy. This is not to deny that people of non-Western societies enjoy travel for sheer sensory pleasure, or trade to make money. But the individualist man is far more moved by the constant pressure of lack of human intimacy; therefore his acquisitive activities tend to be limitless. The difference between the two approaches is similar to that between regular eating due to hunger and compulsive eating due to some deep-seated emotional needs. In one case, once the hunger ceases, the action of eating will stop; in the other, the action is endless since emotional needs are much harder to satisfy.

Arnold Toynbee recently characterized inflation as a "child of greed." I do not pretend to know the causes of inflation but I surmise that they are more complicated than that. When role has greatly escalated at the expense of affect, money becomes the primary symbol of appreciation and of being appreciated, of fulfillment and of status. In that event, why would employees of corporations not insist on higher and higher wages and benefits, and why would corporations not insist on higher and higher profits and dividends?

However, here we are compelled to see some wisdom in the adage that "money does not buy happiness." For the individual, money is at best a substitute for happiness just as saccharin is only a substitute for sugar. For the society as a whole, our unprecedented wealth has not brought us greater interpersonal harmony and mental health, not even to speak of happiness. When affect is absent in most or all interpersonal links, people will not stop at demanding higher wages and higher profits. They will take other antisocial roads, either because they do not care or in order to vent their frustrations for their all-too-precarious PSH. Five thousand glasses, twelve thousand spoons, and ten thousand food trays disappeared during 1972 from the cafeteria of the Pentagon; the John F. Kennedy Center was stripped bare by visitors shortly after it opened; recently the Bayside Cemetery of Brooklyn was vandalized, coffins taken out and corpses violated; universities have felt it necessary to employ female decoys and armed guards to protect their coeds from rape; citizens fear to walk the streets after dark and refuse to open doors for callers; corruption or violation of public trust is rife in all phases of government. These things have not happened because our society is poor. The crimes, violent or nonviolent, white-collar or blue-collar, adolescent or adult, spectaculars like airplane hijacking or quiet ones like the use of drugs, seem, rather, to be escalating drastically with the increase of wealth. Moreover, they seem to keep pace with, if not actually outstrip, methods and techniques of detection, prevention, apprehension, and detention. This paradox is sharpened when we realize that we are looking at a society which proclaims itself Christian, where the Church as an institution is still important.

Yet, while money does not buy happiness, neither is it the source of our many social ills, as some recent observers of the generation gap and adolescent crime would have us believe. Only the other day I heard a network commentator say that the Watergate venture was due to the fact that one political faction had too much money. That really was stretching a point. Money is not the cause of happiness or unhappiness, of moral conduct or immoral conduct. When more and more people not only regard trickery as normal but also do not know when and where to stop, it is because they want to get ahead, relentlessly doing bigger and better jobs, asking no questions. Thus, the compulsive acquisitiveness, the widespread interpersonal violence, the escalation of new models of crime, from stealing to robbery to murder, and the proliferation of new pleasures, new foods, new inventions, new pressure groups to fight the expansionist tendencies of other causes, and fresh efforts to seek new frontiers, all spring from the same causes. They all have a great deal to do with the scarcity of natural human intimacy, which leads to a more precarious PSH process in the West than in many non-Western societies, and which makes Westerners as a whole and Americans in particular unable to live at peace with themselves and with the rest of the world.

When natural human intimacy is scarce, PSH will be precarious and role relationships will greatly escalate at the expense of affective relationships among human beings, since non-human connections will increasingly be substituted for the unreliable human connections. The inevitable result is the treatment of human beings as things (role), the game plan will become the name of all human relationships, and all we can look forward to, then, are the kind of dehumanizing horrors Alvin Toffler described in *Future Shock*.

That is why whenever our thinkers and social planners talk about the quality of life and its improvement, they cannot rise above physical things—more safeguards to cushion automobile crashes, more laws and regulations to control violence and corruption. But can marital harmony be legislated? With all our child-protection agencies and laws do we have any less a generation gap than other societies where these are absent? In this context, psychoanalysis, by inciting people to delve ever more deeply into Layers 6 and 7 of their psychic stores, will surely exacerbate the pitfalls of individualism, by justifying deviation on the ground of hidden psychic pressures and needs, and creating dissatisfaction in others so that they will search for or demand their share of what they thought they had missed.

I am not suggesting that psychoanalysis has no function for mental sufferers, any more than I would suggest that medicine is useless for those in need of artificial kidneys, oxygen tents, or spectacles. But let us face the fact that the more desirable state of affairs is not for more people to need artificial kidneys, oxygen tents, and spectacles, but fewer. Wouldn't it be wrong, and indeed unethical, for medical practitioners to go on the assumption that everyone needs them?

I realize that tension is at the root of creativity and that creativity is indispensable to social and cultural progress. If we reduce the precariousness to PSH, will we not also reduce the conditions for creativity and social cultural progress?

My answer is yes, but I still favor its reduction; and my justification is that another name for creativity is deviation, and that uncontrolled development may lead not to social and cultural progress but to social and cultural destruction. When role relationships drive out affect relationships, all humans will treat each other as mere things. But since human beings are not things but creatures equipped with intelligence and imagination and affect, they may prefer to treat other people as things but they will definitely resent being treated as things by others. The PSH failures will thus lead to so much more mutual mistrust, suspicion, and hatred that our society will find it hard to stay together.

I do not presume to know the exact optimal limits of tension which enable any society to achieve a beneficial balance between the forces for destruction and those for genuine progress. But I feel strongly that our society has already gone too far, and that we need to retrace some of our steps.

What can we do to increase the natural human intimacy in American life and make the individual's PSH process less precarious? First, the solution will involve some modification of our values from an individual-centered emphasis to a more socio-centric direction. Up to now this need has not even been recognized. In 1960, Dr. Henry Wriston, then president of Brown University, delivered a speech at Bowdoin College entitled "Our Goal: Individualism or Security?" (see Chapter 1). I do not know a more eloquent piece extolling the rugged individual. According to Dr. Wriston, the greatness of a country depends upon its leadership, and leadership cannot be stimulated and nurtured without rugged individualism. The popular importance attached to this speech was shown by how widely it was reprinted or editorialized (e.g., in the Chicago *Sun-Times,* June 5, 1960; the *Wall Street Journal,* June 1, 1960; *Readers Digest,* August, 1960).

Now, thirteen years later, another university president has spoken in the same vein. This time it is the Reverend Theodore M. Hesburgh, president of the University of Notre Dame. "I have long believed that a Christian university is worthless in our day unless it conveys to all who study within it a deep sense of the dignity of the human person, his nature and high destiny, his opportunities for seeking justice in a very unjust world, his inherent nobility so needing to be achieved by himself or herself, for oneself and for others, whatever the obstacles." Father Hesburgh's ideas first appeared as an article in *The New York Times* which has been republished in the Rockefeller Foundation magazine, *RF Illustrated*.

Wriston's speech was more vehement in its promotion of rugged individualism, but Hesburgh's article hardly moved away from that position. When Hesburgh refers to the interpersonal nexus at all he uses the expression, ". . . for oneself and for others. . . ." But the emphasis of his article is on how to transmit the cherished values, while Wriston's was not. And Hesburgh's idea is that the principal vehicle in the process is the teacher-educator. "Values are exemplified better than they are taught, which is to say that they are taught better by exemplification than by words." I agree that what the teacher-educator does is more important than what he says, but I maintain that the teacher-educator has but a very minor part in the PSH pattern of the individual. The teacher-educator primarily helps the individual with his role activities (Layer 2 and beyond), not his affect activities (Layer 3 and inward); for when the teacher-educator meets his pupil it is already too late—the pattern of the latter's feelings about himself and his relations with fellow human beings and the rest of the world, is likely to be set. The teacher-educator in the university has even less influence in this matter. Besides, with the shrinkage of affect, to which the American teacher-educator as well as his American pupil are equally subject, the chances of any affective link are slim.

It is to the pattern of our kinship that we must urgently turn our attention. For it is the family which nurtures, transmits, and escalates the affective component of the individual from generation to generation. Here is where parents ought to remember that what they do is more vital than what they say. Here is where parents must realize that if they do not respect their own parents they can hardly expect respect from their sons and daughters. Here is where the precariousness of the parents' PSH pattern cannot but be carried on in the generations to come. The task before us is not to ask more impossibles of the teacher-educator, but to reorient the parents toward a greater awareness of the pitfalls of individualism, and to design ways and means as to how best to bring up their progeny under this new awareness. The kinship system is the psychic cell of every society. It holds the key to social and cultural development in the same sense that the germ cell holds the key to the biological organism and provides us with some idea of what the unfolding animal is going to be like.

However, once we see the need for a more sociocentric view of man, we might also see that the secrets of restructuring the kinship machinery cannot be unraveled via the traditional Freudian concepts rooted in Western individualism.

NOTE

1. The first successful hijacker, who got away with two hundred thousand dollars by parachuting out of a Northwest Orient plane, gave his name as D. B. Cooper.

Part IV

Kinship, Society and Culture

Introduction

Leaders of all religious movements and political ideologies seem to pay the utmost attention to youth. In order to enlarge and consolidate their organizational strength, they promote Sunday Schools, Little Red Soldiers, and young adult groups. In May 1981 it was reported that even the Ku Klux Klan has a new organization, Klan Youth Corps, for recruiting school age adherents. Leaders of such movements, as of all governments, intuitively know the value of indoctrination in the individual's early years. Traditionally the Chinese even spoke of foetal education. In the American educational system, the lower the grades the more the curriculum is guided and controlled by authorities outside the school walls.

But it was Freud and some of his disciples who systematically explored the early socialization process in terms of repression, parturation trauma, oral and anal characters, id, Oedipux Complex, libido, reaction formation, and so on. Under their influence other students of socialization have elaborated many theories of personality development by focusing on many single points of reference such as the consequences of breast feeding versus bottle feeding, demand feeding versus scheduled feeding, or mother-infant sharing or not sharing the same bed.

Given the socio-centric premise outlined in the previous chapter, I employed the concepts of Dominant Dyad and Dominant Attributes in kinship for gauging the broader psychological links between the individual's interpersonal orientation and the web of kinship which nurtured him or her.

"The Effect of Dominant Kinship Relationships on Kin and Non-Kin Behavior: A Hypothesis" (Chapter 14) tries to accomplish this task in three steps. First, it shows that not only one kinship relationship (dyad) may exert influence on another, but one relationship can be so dominant (Dominant Dyad) that its influences give shape to the entire kinship system. Second, the influences of the Dominant Dyad do not simply change any other relationship into a secondary version of it. Instead it tends to bend the quality and pattern of interaction of the other relationships in its direction. This is why Chinese husbands and wives do not relate to each other the way their American counterparts do. Finally, the influences of the Dominant Dyad do not stop at the kinship boundary. They extend far and wide into behavior patterns of the rest of society.

The second paper (Appendix to Chapter 14) is a brief exchange of views on the Dominant Dyad hypothesis with two University of Cambridge scholars.

The third paper, "Variations in Ancestor Worship Beliefs and Their Relation to Kinship" (Chapter 15), demonstrates a close correspondence between a society's beliefs concerning deceased ancestors and the dyadic dominance in its kinship system.

Although we have established a link between kinship and ancestral belief, however, we must now proceed to see how kinship has any relevance to other aspects of the same culture as well as different cultures. In his *Civilization and Its Discontents* (1962) Freud says:

> At one point in the course of this inquiry I was led to the idea that civilization is a process which mankind undergoes, and I am still under the influence of that idea. I may now add that civilization is a process in the service of Eros, whose purpose is to combine single human individuals, and after that families, then races, peoples and nations, into one great unity, the unity of mankind . . . . These collections of men are to be libidinally bound to one another . . . . But man's natural aggressive instinct, the hostility of each against all and of all against each, opposes this programme of civilization. This aggressive instinct is the derivative and the main representative of the death instinct which we have found alongside Eros and which shares world-dominion with it. And now, I think, the meaning of the evolution of civilization is no longer obscure to us. I must present the struggle between Eros and death, between the instinct of life and the instinct of destruction, as it works itself out in the human species. This struggle is what life essentially consists of, and the evolution of civilization may therefore be simply described as the struggle for life of the human species. (Freud 1962:69)

This elegant statement explains, I think, the civilizational process of the West quite well, but it falls short where some other societies, notably China, Japan, and India, are concerned. It is the Western way for children to be opposed to parents, for adherents to one religious creed to be against those to others, and for supporters of one cause to be fighting those of others. Christianity, the main religion of Western man, holds the world's championship in internal division by denominalization. In fact it is not uncommon for ardent Western supporters of one cause to turn around to become its vehement opponents, as have many former communists. There is an obvious incongruity in a society that has lionized Herman Melville and his *Moby Dick* but also has promoted "save the whales." The utmost irony came to me in May 1981 when a group guarding the welfare of whales was led by Gregory Peck, who played Captain Ahab in the movie.

Freud's analysis does not apply to the Asian societies, especially China and Japan, because he had no knowledge of cultural differences. Like most of his followers today, Freud frankly thought that what he saw of the West was universal. His myopia made it impossible for him to see that Eros does not have the same importance in the Asian kinship system as it occupies in its Western counterpart.

Some sort of affect (or feeling) is necessary to join human beings together into families, clans, clubs, nations, or United Nations. But what Freud failed to see is that affect may be eros based or *pao*-based. Perception of this basic distinction, which hopefully the reader will do via the last article in this section, "Eros, Affect and *Pao*" (Chapter 16), presents us with a surprising new vista of the intricate links among kinship, society and culture.

14

The Effect of Dominant Kinship Relationships on Kin and Non-Kin Behavior: A Hypothesis

The concept of kinship extension was first explained by Radcliffe-Brown. He observed "the tendency" among the Bantu tribes and Nama Hottentots of South Africa to develop patterns for the mother's brother and the father's sister by regarding the former as somewhat of a male mother and the latter to some extent a female father (Radcliffe-Brown 1924 and reprinted 1952:19). He concludes as follows: "In primitive society there is a strongly marked tendency to merge the individual in the group to which he or she belongs. The result of this in relation to kinship is a tendency to extend to all members of a group a certain type of behaviour which has its origin in a relationship to one particular member of the group" (1952:25).

Radcliffe-Brown's use of the term "primitive" is unnecessary. The kind of behavior he spoke of cannot scientifically be used to separate mankind into "primitive" and "civilized." In fact the very dichotomy of "primitive" versus "civilized" is to be questioned (Hsu 1964). However the idea of extension of patterns of behavior characteristic of one kinship relationship to that of another has been the basis of much valuable field research. Thus Fred Eggan, among others, has shown that the Hopi not only class mother's mother's mother and the mother's brothers as "siblings" but also extend "the sibling relationship to all the members of one's clan and phratry who are of roughly the same age or generation and also to the children of all men of the father's clan and phratry, including the clans and phratries of the ceremonial and doctor fathers regardless of age" (Eggan 1950:43–44).

However, all of these works, including those aided by precise models such as those of Lévi-Strauss (1949) and White (1963) deal merely with the modification of one kind of kinship relationship by another, the degree to which kinship categories are applied to non-kins, or the bearing of these phenomena on kinship or kinship-connected behavior such as avoidance of intimacy but particularly mate selection. Where the question of relationship between what goes on in the kinship sphere and what goes on outside it is concerned, two approaches have been apparent. The first is the personality-and-culture one, which attempts to relate certain child-rearing practices which are little or unrelated to forms of kinship (such as swaddling, permissiveness, sibling rivalry, length of breast-feeding, alleged or real sudden changes in parental attitude when the child reaches a certain age, etc.) to the personality of the individual or culture of the society. The other is that of students of social structure which either

This chapter was originally published in the *American Anthropologist*, Vol. 67, No. 3, 1965, pp. 638–61.

ignores the question or tries to explain social development without reference to kinship at all (Lévi-Strauss 1953:534–35 and Hsu 1959:792–93).

Our present hypothesis is designed to do a number of things. First, we
hope to go beyond Radcliffe-Brown and others by showing that not only
the influences of one kinship relationship upon another is a general
phenomenon, but that these influences can originate from one relationship and extend to all other relationships so as to shape the entire
kinship system. Second, when these influences exert themselves thusly,
the effector relationships do not simply change into secondary versions of
the affector relationship, as Radcliffe-Brown and others have observed so
far, and the kinship systems in question make no assumptions of such
formal changes either. Instead, what occurs much more generally is that
the qualities and patterns of interaction in the effector relationships have
assumed characteristics similar to those of the affector relationship so that,
e.g., the husband-wife relationship or father-son relationship *as husband-
wife or father-son relationships* in one kinship system appears drastically
different from that in another. Third, we hope to show that the same
influence becomes visible in the qualities and patterns of behavior among
those other members of the same society who are not related through
kinship, acting in non-kinship roles. In other words, we hope firmly to link
interaction patterns in a kinship system with the characteristic modes of
behavior in the wider society of which that kinship system forms a part. In
doing so we hope to convince, on the one hand, many students of psychological anthropology that it is the broader aspects of interpersonal interaction patterns in the nuclear family and not merely certain limited child
rearing practices which are crucial to human development and, on the
other, many students of social structure that they have unnecessarily
restricted the scientific fruitfulness of their efforts by ignoring psychological anthropology. Last, in order to carry out these tasks we have to
scrutinize kinship relationships in terms of their attributes, for it is then
that we can not only trace their influences where human beings are
structurally linked through terminological or other kinship-connected
categories but also identify their ramifications outside the kinship organization, far beyond their boundaries throughout the society.

Dominant Relationships and Dominant Attributes

Before going into the hypothesis it is first necessary to define four basic
terms: Relationship and Attribute, and Dominant Relationship and Dominant Attribute.

I first dealt with the importance of distinguishing between the structure
and content of social organization in a paper entitled "Structure, Function,
Content and Process" (1959:790–805).[1] In the present exercise we must
distinguish between relationship and attributes, and see structure as consisting of a combination of relationships and content, a combination of

attributes. A relationship is the minimum unit into which two or more individuals are or may be linked. In the nuclear family eight such relationships are basic. These are: father-son, mother-son, father-daughter, mother-daughter, husband-wife, brother-brother, sister-sister, and brother-sister. Attribute refers to the logical or typical mode of behavior and attitude intrinsic to each relationship. The words logical, typical, and intrinsic are crucial to this definition. By them we mean that the attributes of each relationship are what David Schneider describes as "constants" (Schneider 1961:5) because they are universally the potential and inherent properties of that relationship.

The easiest example for aid in understanding this is perhaps that of the employer-employee relationship. The intrinsic attributes of this relationship are, for example, functional considerations, calculated obligations and rewards, and specific delineations in duration. A man enters into such a relationship generally because he has work he wants done or he desires wages or their equivalent. Furthermore, the length of time during which the relationship lasts is likely to be understood or made specific in advance. The details vary from society to society but these intrinsic attributes can be found wherever an employer-employee relationship is said to exist. On the other hand, these attributes intrinsic to the employer-employee relationship do not obtain in the case of a romantic relationship. The intrinsic attributes of each relationship are the basic ingredients and determinants of the interactional patterns between parties to that relationship.

No nuclear family would seem to give equal prominence to all its eight basic relationships. What actually occurs is that in each type of nuclear family one (or more) of the latter takes precedence over the others. When a relationship is thus elevated above others it tends to modify, magnify, reduce, or even eliminate other relationships in the kinship group. Such a relationship is designated in our hypothesis as the *dominant relationship* while others in the system are *non-dominant relationships*. For example, if the father-son relationship in the nuclear family is the dominant one, it will increase the social importance of the father-son relationship at the expense of other relationships such as husband-wife so that the father and mother will have more to say about their son's future wife than the son himself. In such an eventuality the kinship group or kinship team as defined by Naroll (1956:696 and 698) tends to extend itself far beyond the nuclear family of parents and unmarried children because of its inclusion of a variety of other consanguineal relatives and their wives and children. Conversely, if the husband-wife relationship is dominant, it will alter the parent-child relationship into a temporary arrangement to be replaced or discarded when the child grows into adulthood. In such a case the kinship group tends to correspond to the nuclear family at all times because of the exclusion of all consanguinal relatives as soon as they are married.

The intrinsic attributes of the dominant relationships are designated in our hypothesis as the *dominant attributes* while those of the non-dominant relationships in the system are designated *non-dominant attributes*.[2] In each form of nuclear family the dominant attributes will so influence the non-dominant attributes that the latter tend to converge in the direction of the dominant attributes.

The dominant attributes prevail over the give shape to all the non-dominant attributes. The sum of all the attributes converging toward the dominant attributes in the kinship system is designated its content, just as the sum of all the relationships under the influence of one or more dominating relationships is its structure.

The interrelationship may be roughly represented in the following diagram:

Kinship System

Structure   Content

Dominant Relationship————————— Dominant Attributes

Non-Dominant Relationships————————— Non-Dominant Attributes

THE HYPOTHESIS

Having defined the terms we are then ready to tackle the hypothesis which, in skeletal form, is as follows: *the dominant attributes of the dominant relationship in a given kinship system tend to determine the attitudes and action patterns which the individual in such a system develops towards other relationships in this system as well as towards his relationships outside of the system.*

We shall explicate this hypothesis in three parts: first, an examination of four basic kinship relationships and their attributes; second, the effect of dominant relationships on other kinship relationships in the same kinship system; third, the effect of dominant relationships on non-kin relationships.

Six points should be made clear at the outset. First, the different relationships overlap to a certain extent in their attributes. For example, discontinuity is common to husband-wife, mother-son, and brother-brother relationships. It is the particular combination of attributes, not single attributes, which differentiates one relationship from another. Second, the differences between attributes are rarely if ever absolute, but as a rule used in a comparative sense. Continuity versus discontinuity, or inclusiveness versus exclusiveness are illustrative of this view. In the geometric sense of a line being a set of points, continuity is made up of a set of discontinuities. Third, when an attribute is listed for relationship A but not for relationship B it does not mean that it is entirely absent in the latter. Thus the attribute authority is not entirely absent in the mother-son

Four Relationships and Their Attributes

Relationship	Attributes	Definition of Attributes
Husband-Wife	1. Discontinuity	The condition of not being, or the attitude of desiring not to be, in a sequence or connected with others.
	2. Exclusiveness	The act of keeping others out or unwillingness to share with them.
	3. Sexuality	Preoccupation with sex.
	4. Volition	The condition of being able to follow own inclinations, or of desiring to do so.
Father-Son	1. Continuity	The condition of being, or the attitude of desiring to be, in an unbroken sequence, or connected with others.
	2. Inclusiveness	The act of incorporating or the attitude of wishing to be incorporated.
	3. Authority	Personal power that commands and enforces obedience, or the condition of being under such power.
	4. Asexuality	The condition of having no connection with sex.
Mother-Son	1. Discontinuity	(Already defined above)
	2. Inclusiveness	(Already defined above)
	3. Dependence	The condition of being or the attitude of wishing to be reliant upon others.
	4. Diffuseness	The tendency to spread out in all directions.
	5. Libidinality	Diffused or potential sexuality.
Brother-Brother	1. Discontinuity	(Already defined above)
	2. Inclusiveness	(Already defined above)
	3. Equality	The condition of being or the attitude of wishing to be of the same rank and importance as others.
	4. Rivalry	The act of striving, or the attitude of wishing to strive, for equality with or excellence over others.

relationship, but this attribute tends to be so overshadowed by one or more others, or embraced by them, that it is not independently significant. Fourth, some attributes, such as authority and sexuality, are opposed to each other, while others, such as authority and dependence, are intimately related to each other. Fifth, the list of attributes given for each relationship is not exhaustive. Further analysis may yield new ones. Lastly, in this and later analyses the reader should bear in mind the contribution of Parsons in his essay on "Family Structure and Socialization of the Child" (1955a:35–131). Some of our attributes are similar but not identical with some aspects of Parsons' "role structure" of the nuclear family and their differentiations. These will be pointed out as we progress. More pronounced differences between our analysis and Parsons' will occur in later sections of this paper.

Let us examine the links between these relationships and their attributes. The attributes of the husband-wife relationship are discontinuity,[3] exclusiveness, and sexuality. It is discontinuous because, and here I must ask leave for elaboration of the obvious, every husband is never a wife and every wife is never a husband. Every husband-wife relationship is a unit by itself, independent of all other relationships. There is no structural necessity for any husband-wife relationship, as such, to be related to other husband-wife relationships. It is exclusive because, while marriage in every society is a public affair, every husband and wife must universally carry out by themselves alone some activities which are crucial to the conjugal relationship. This remains true regardless of the form of marriage. It is a well known fact that in most of the polygynous societies of Africa each wife in the polygynous situation has her own hut where live her own children and where her husband visits her. It is also well known that the wife in the few known polyandrous societies receives her husbands separately and each of the several husbands usually establishes some kind of individualized ritual relationship with a particular child.

Among these exclusive activities, sexuality occupies an obvious, central place, which is the third attribute of the husband-wife relationship. The connection between sexuality and husband-wife relationship needs no elaboration. Of all the eight basic relationships the husband-wife relationship is the only one in which sexuality is universally an implicit and explicit constant.

The attribute of volition is commensurate with both exclusiveness and sexuality. Of all the eight basic relationships in the nuclear family, that of husband-wife relationship alone is one which, by virtue of sexuality, involves a kind of need for individual willingness unknown or not required in the others. Even in societies where caste or other customary rules exclude individual choice, individual preferences enter into the making, continuation and termination of the relationship. Sometimes the volition may be exercised by parents, or family heads and not the man and woman entering or forming the relationship. But that is a kind of freedom of choice nevertheless which is not naturally true in the other basic relationships in the nuclear family. Furthermore for the male at least there is universally more room for personal manoeuvre no matter what the kinship system he lives in.

The basic attributes of the father-son relationship are continuity, inclusiveness, and authority. It is continuous because every father is a son and every son, in the normal course of events, is a father. Therefore every father-son relationship is but a link in an everlasting chain of father-son relationships. It is inclusive because while every son has only one father, every father actually or potentially has many sons. Therefore the relationship between the father and the son is inherently tolerant rather than intolerant toward sharing with others. The attribute of authority comes from the fact that every father is many years older than his son and is inherently in a position of power over the younger man.

A closer examination will reveal that the several attributes intrinsic to each of the two relationships are mutually commensurate with each other. Take the attributes of the father-son relationship first.

Continuity means relatively lengthy existence of that relationship in time. With normal birth and marriage more lengthy existence in time means greater chances of involvement of others who were not previously in the picture. Thus two bachelors may develop a friendship. If the friendship lasts more than a few years there are chances of each of them being married to a woman. If their friendship had ended before they were married, there would have been no question of inclusion in their friendship of the two women who came later. But if they continue their friendship after marriage, it is reasonable to expect that the new wives will be involved in the relationship. If their friendship continues still further, there is the likelihood of their having children who are also likely to be involved in some way in the friendship of the two older men.

However, the widening of the circle of involvement as this friendship continues is not restricted to birth and marriage. One member of the friendship team may move away, due to business or other reasons, to another locality where he will meet new people and make new friends. If he discontinues his friendship with his older friend, then indeed his circle of friendship need not be more inclusive than before. But if he wants to continue the older friendship, then it becomes obvious that the circle is inevitably enlarged. Thus we may generate the following subsidiary hypothesis: the more continuous a relationship, and the longer it lasts, the more inclusive it will become of other individuals who were not previously in that relationship.

Authority can be exercized generally in one of three ways. First by brutal power on the part of the superior over the subordinates. Second through what Max Weber would designate as charisma or what is popularly known in the United States as sex appeal of the superior. Third by conviction on the part of the subordinates of the superior's right, duty, or privilege to exercise authority just as it is their right, duty, or privilege to obey it. It is obvious that the first two ways of exercizing authority are likely to be less permanent than the third. In the first, resentment is likely to occur among those who are subject to the authority so that they may revolt or attempt to get out from under the authority at the first opportunity. In the second way, authority is likely to be disrupted as soon as there is a reduction of charisma on the part of the superior or of his sex appeal through old age or loss of capacity in some manner. At any rate, death is likely to end his position of authority once and for all. In the third way, since the subordinates are taught to respect the superior's role of authority, revolts are much less likely.

The lines separating these three ways of authority are relative, but the third way is more likely to characterize authority in the father-son relationship especially since the attribute of continuity enables the sons to cooperate, because they themselves expect to exercise it in the same way when it is their turn to do so. In this situation the idea of authority permeates the relationship and is not tied to the accident of the brutal power or the special qualities of a single person. Under such circumstances authority does not disappear with the death of the person in authority; it tends to continue after his death in the form of the cult of the dead (in the kinship sphere) or worship of the past or tradition (in the society generally). Furthermore, on the basis of what we said before of the relationship between continuity and inclusiveness, we can say that the more continuous the worship of the ancestry of a kinship group or tradition of a society, the more inclusive that authority is likely to apply to wider circles of human beings.

In the same light we may see the attributes of the husband-wife relationship. Discontinuity is more commensurate with exclusiveness and inclusiveness. Going back to the same friendship example discussed before, it is obvious that the shorter the duration of friendship, the less the chances of involvement in friendship with others who are not originally part of that friendship. Sexuality and exclusiveness are necessary for each other because no matter how widely distributed the sex appeal of a single individual, the core of sexuality, that is the sexual act, is universally carried out between two individuals. There are many forms of self-eroticism such as masturbation which can be restricted to one individual alone, and there are other forms of sexual practices which can involve more than two individuals, but there is no question that the sexual act between one man and one woman is the universal norm.

Sexuality as a physiological phenomenon necessarily waxes and wanes even during that period of the individual's life when the sex drive is strong. Then as the individual grows older the sexual drive diminishes and recedes. There are known differences between the male and the female in this regard and there are also known individual differences. But there is no question that sexuality recedes and then disappears as age advances. Furthermore, death concludes it. Unlike authority, which can be exercised many centuries after a man's death, sexuality cannot be exercised in absentia. Consequently sexuality in contrast to authority is much more commensurate with discontinuity than with continuity.

Turning now to the mother-son relationship we find five differentiable attributes: discontinuity, inclusiveness, dependence, diffuseness, and libidinality. In common with the husband-wife relationship it is discontinuous because no mother is a son and no son is ever a mother. But the next two attributes are more particularly its own. These are dependence and diffuseness, built on two closely related facts. First, since the mother comes into the new born child's life at the earliest possible moment, she caters to its wants at a time when it is at its most ineffectual. For the infant, the mother is the principal agent for all satisfaction. She is his answer-all. Second, the mother's relationship with her infant involves more interaction of an unstructured nature than that of the father's since, as some psychoanalysts would put it, the "mother normally achieves identification with her infant through libidinally charged processes which permit her to become a child with her child again. . . . The identification with the baby permits her to enjoy her 'regression' and to repeat and satisfy her own receptive, dependent needs" (Alexander 1952:104 and 106).[4]

Therefore, though dependence is not entirely absent in some of the other kinship relationships, it is the outstanding ingredient in the mother-son relationship (as it is also naturally in the mother-daughter relationship). Dependence obviously enters into the father-son relationship. But there it is greatly modified by the fact of growth. Intensive interaction between a father and his son usually occurs some months or years after the son's birth when the latter is less ineffectual and helpless than when he first began life with his mother. In Parsons' terms (1955a:47–55) the father-son relationship is one step farther in the process of role differentiation from that of mother-son. This means not only far less dependence, but that dependence when it occurs has changed its nature from one due to sheer inability to comprehend or perform any task to one in which the need is for guidance, channelling, wisdom of experience, or punishment. In Parsons' terms these are characteristic of "instrumentality" rather than "expressiveness" (1955a:45).

In the mother-son situation dependence is found in its pristine state but in the father-son situation dependence is only an element of what can better be described as authority (Parsons' "power"). The attribute authority includes a degree of dependence but it is much higher on "instrumentality" and on "power." Conversely though "power" and some "instrumentality" are not totally absent in the mother-child relationship, these (especially "instrumentality") tend to be overshadowed by other more characteristic attributes. This enables us to understand why diffuseness is an attribute of the mother-son relationship but not of others. Diffuseness is related to lack of differentiation and therefore of specialization. Of the eight basic relationships in the nuclear family, those of mother-son and mother-daughter are the least structured and differentiated in role because the younger member of the dyad is, to begin with, so completely helpless and dependent.

The last attribute, namely libidinality, associated with the mother-son relationship is present whenever the partners of the relationship are not of the same sex. But this attribute is likely to be stronger in the case of mother-son relationship than that of father-daughter or brother-sister because of greater physical intimacy at a time when the son is least differentiated with reference to his place in the social system. In general our libidinality is related to what Parsons designates as "expressiveness" insofar as the latter contains a sexual component, but his concept would seem to embrace our attributes dependence (partially) and diffuseness (entirely).

However, although we derive the term libidinality from the Freudian term libido, it is not identical with the latter in significance. Freudian libido is conceived as the raw material of a sexual nature which is the fountainhead of all psychic energy and which, through socializing mechanisms such as repression or sublimation, becomes greatly modified, warped, diverted, or its sexuality driven from consciousness. It is strictly a matter of personality dynamics. Libidinality in our sense may undergo repression or sublimation in the individual but it is primarily characteristic of general patterns of interpersonal interaction in a society so that it expresses itself throughout the culture in diverse ways in its native state without significant modification or at least with the sexual component still visible.

On the other hand, the attribute libidinality is very different from that of sexuality which is exclusive to the husband-wife relationship. Sexuality involves a specific and recognized urge and motive with relatively clearly defined objects for its satisfaction, while libidinality is more nebulous, undifferentiated, but usually without clearly defined objects for its satisfaction as sexuality. The attraction between two lovers is characterized by sexuality but that between certain types of entertainers and their public, between the temple lingam (male phallic representation) and their worshippers, and even between certain pieces of art and their viewers, contains libidinality in our sense.

The brother-brother relationship is discontinuous because solidarity among brothers marks each generation out from the last and the next. Each set of brothers has no structural connection with the brothers of the generation above or the brothers of the generation below. The brother-brother relationship is inclusive for the same reason that father-son and mother-son relationships are inclusive, for there are likely to be more than two brothers. Brother-brother relationship is not a dyad intolerant of the inclusion of other parties.

Two attributes, equality and rivalry, are peculiar to the brother-brother relationship. Of all the relationships in the nuclear family, brothers are more likely to be equal age-wise and occupy more nearly equivalent positions in the social system than others. Husbands and wives may be more similar in age to each other than some brothers but they seem to be universally complementary in function and differentiated in work. A greater degree of general equality tends to obtain between brothers than between all other related persons in the nuclear family. With greater equality comes greater chances of rivalry. Competition can occur in any situation wherever there are individuals who think they ought to at least be as well situated as others. But it is between equals, within a structural arrangement where they are more equal among themselves than between themselves and others in that configuration, that competition becomes most intense.

The link between equality and rivalry in the brother-brother relationship would seem to suggest that all the attributes intrinsic to this relationship are mutually compatible with each other. This is not the case. While the attributes of father-son relationship are mutually supportive of each other and those of the husband-wife relationship are also mutually supportive of each other, the attributes of mother-son relationship and again those of brother-brother are not always harmonious. In the mother-son relationship dependence is commensurate with diffuseness and libidinality, but it is not always supportive of inclusiveness because the dependent may be so jealous of the person on whom he depends as to be intolerant of other parties. This incompatibility may be moderated by the fact that, since it is usually the depended upon and not the dependent who provides the initiative, the dependent is necessarily tied down in his decisions by the preferences of the depended upon and therefore cannot exclude with as much ease as an independent. But dependence is highly incommensurate with discontinuity because by all psychological evidence, one who is dependent will normally seek the continuation of the relationship in time rather than its breakage. The problems of weaning and of first separation from parents are but two of the most common illustrations of this fact. Finally, discontinuity is also incommensurate which inclusiveness because the two undercut each other. Viewing all five attributes of the mother-son relationship as a whole, we find discontinuity alone to be specially discordant, which must create serious problems for the predominantly dependent.

In the case of brother-brother relationship, the attribute of equality reinforces inclusiveness. It is under such ideals as "all men are brothers" or "all men are created equal" that universalistic religions or political philosophies are usually based. Similarly the attribute of rivalry reinforces discontinuity. The essence of rivalry expresses itself in the effort to excel over others or even the desire to annihilate the others. Therefore it is separatist in consequence no matter what rationalization is used to soft pedal it. One of the most universal signs of status or achievement is separation from the others. Yet these very links between discontinuity and rivalry on the one hand and inclusiveness and equality on the other pit these two sets of attributes against each others. For the former is centrifugal while the latter is centripetal. Not only is discontinuity incompatible with inclusiveness, but rivalry and equality are usually at odds with each other, for, as we noted before, rivalry heightens itself with greater equality.

THE EFFECT OF DOMINANT KINSHIP RELATIONSHIPS ON OTHER KINSHIP RELATIONSHIPS

Our next order of business is to examine the way in which the dominant relationships in a kinship system affect other relationships in that system.

Since it is impossible in a single paper to analyse the complicated possible effects of each dominant relationship on all the other relationships in a system, we shall illustrate our points by confining ourselves to the effects of the dominant relationship on primarily one non-dominant relationship in each instance. We shall begin with a system where the father-son relationship is the dominant one. Previously we noted in passing that in such an eventuality the parents will have more to say about their son's future wife than the son himself. In the light of the respective sets of attributes intrinsic to the father-son and husband-wife relationships, this means that the attribute of exclusiveness intrinsic to the husband-wife relationship is greatly modified in favor of the attribute of inclusiveness characteristic of that of father-son. Hence married partners in this system seem aloof to each other, for they often place their duties and obligations towards parents before those towards each other. Custom will strongly disapprove of any sign of public intimacy between spouses. Instead it enjoins them to exhibit ardent signs of devotion to their (especially his) elders. In case of a quarrel between the wife and the mother-in-law, the husband must take the side of the latter against the former, especially in public. Polygyny with the ostensible aim of begetting male heirs to continue the father-son line is a structural necessity.

Yet in spite of all this the marital bond in a father-son dominated system tends to endure. Divorce is possible but rare. The attribute of continuity and the attribute of authority militate against the dissolution of the marital bond. Continuity means that all bonds including the marital bond are likely to last once they are formed. Authority, with all that it implies toward the past and the superiors, means that the pleasures or displeasures of the married partners are less important considerations for staying together than those of their elders or of the kinship group as a whole according to tradition.

This form of kinship is likely to be associated with a strong cult of ancestors[5] and a maximum tendency for the development of the clan.

Where the husband-wife relationship is dominant we should expect the father-son relationship to be temporary. In all likelihood that relationship tends to end or nearly so upon marriage of the younger man, after which the father will no longer have strong authority over him. The cohesion between a husband and wife takes precedence over all other relationships and mate selection is at least theoretically entirely in the hands of the prospective spouses. Not only will the father or mother have no right to initiate divorce for his daughter or son, but any over-intimacy between a son and his parents against the objections of his wife is likely to lead to serious marital disharmony. In such a situation monogamy is the only form of marriage possible to satisfy the exclusiveness of the husband-wife relationship. Discontinuity makes for lack of respect for old age, tradition, and the past in general. Therefore there will be sharp gulfs between the generations and no true ancestor cult of any kind.

The attributes of sexuality and exclusiveness make public exhibition of marital intimacy (by such things as terms of endearment and kissing) easy and almost imperative, for in the ardency of their exclusive feelings for each other, they need to pay no attention to the rest of the world. In spite of all this, the marital bond is brittle. Divorce is likely to be far more common than in a father-son dominated system. The attribute of discontinuity and the attribute of sexuality are both conducive to this. Discontinuity means that all relationships including the marital one are not really forever since there is little concern for the past. Sexuality adds to this impermanency since its emphasis means that marriage is likely to be precarious, as sexuality waxes and wanes during any period of time and throughout life. Therefore, while in the father-son dominated system the marital bond is not endangered by long periods of separation, in the husband-wife dominated system even separation of a moderate duration creates great marital hazards.

But a dominant husband-wife relationship has other effects on the father-son relationship than making it temporary. The father-son relationship in a husband-wife dominated system is likely to be imbued with sexuality and exclusiveness. Parents insist on exclusive control of their children, are likely to be extraordinarily sensitive about their rights over them, and resent all advice from grandparents and other relatives (the inclusiveness intrinsic to parent-child relationships is lost). Furthermore there is even likely to be competition between the parents for the affection of the youngsters. Add to this the attribute of sexuality and we have then a most fertile soil for the Oedipus Complex. Since the resolution of the Oedipus Complex involves such mechanisms as repression or sublimation, I submit that it is not at all fantastic to suggest that modern day emphasis on sex education on the part of parents is a devious expression of the repressed or sublimated sexuality rooted in a husband-wife dominated kinship system. By contrast, sex as a subject cannot even be touched upon casually between parents and children in a father-son dominated kinship system.

In a mother-son dominated kinship system the father-son relationship tends to exhibit discontinuity rather than continuity. For one thing the father-son tie is not eternal so that the cult of ancestors, even if it exists, tends to be minimal (according to our scale, see Chapter 15). Authority of the father will be greatly reduced so that the father is less a strong guiding, channelling, and punishing figure than a nourishing, supportive, and succoring one. Furthermore, the father image is blurred so that there tends to be the need for the son to seek other "father" figures, not to replace the real father but to assure himself of adequate sources of nourishment, support, and succor. In fact, the line of distinction between the father figure and the mother figure is often unclear.

The attribute of inclusiveness of the mother-son dominated system, like that of the father-son dominated system, is not incommensurate with polygyny, for the marital bond needs not be exclusive. But lacking the attribute continuity, the custom is not primarily for the purpose of maintenance of the patrilineal line as it would be in the father-son dominated system. Rather it seems to be strongly related to the attribute of libidinality or diffused sexuality, and therefore the mother-son dominated system is likely to be associated with more than just polygyny. If the attributes of exclusiveness and sexuality are commensurate with monogamy, and those of inclusiveness and continuity are in line with polygyny, then those of inclusiveness and libidinality or diffused sexuality favor plurality of spouses in general, including polygyny and polyandry, as well as other practices such as cicisbeism defined by Prince Peter as "an arrangement between the sexes, wherein one or more of the male partners is not related to the woman in marriage" (Prince Peter 1963:22), or conjoint-marriage in which polygyny is combined with polyandry, enabling several males (often related) to be married to several females, or a passing connection between one woman and more than one man for several reasons, including insemination of the childless female by a male other than her husband with the latter's consent.

In a brother-brother dominated society there will be strong tensions between fathers and sons. Rivalry among brothers will spill over to the father-son relationship and the attribute of equality will seriously affect the authority of the old over the young. In fact, these attributes are conducive to sexual competition between fathers and sons. At any rate, the possibility of such emulation is real enough to produce many forms of hostility such as suspicion or witchcraft accusations against each other. Therefore the cult of ancestors is likely to be either non-existent or minimal, and even when some form of ancestor cult may be said to exist, the central effort will be directed toward preventing the spirits of the departed from punishing or performing wrathful acts rather than showing concern for the ancestor's comfort and respect.

In the husband-wife relationship calculatedness tends to rise above everything else. Rivalry and equality reduce the need for protection of one sex by the other. In fact they tend to make the "weaker" versus "stronger" sexes dichotomy superfluous. The complementary element between the sexes is so greatly diminished that the question of devotion, fidelity, and sentiments between married partners are unimportant or subordinated to considerations such as calculated advantages and disadvantages. Their relationship may be marked by a contest of power, economic or otherwise, rather than a depth of intimacy. Polygyny, instead of being rationalized in terms of the need for continuing the family line, as in the father-son dominated systems, is practiced primarily as the man's sign of status or wealth. On the female side a sort of polyandry is practiced, not necessarily fraternal from the point of view of economy among the males, but primarily as the woman's symbol of ability and affluence. This is the only kind of kinship system in which exists the condition for true male concubinage. One feels almost compelled to term it female polygyny (as distinguished from the usual polyandry). In addition, premarital and extra-marital relations are likely to be common in theory and practice. The custom of surrogate fathers whereby a childless woman is inseminated by her husband's brother or someone else is not likely to be rare. For sex is apt to be used as a means for conquest or for other gains rather than as an expression of emotional or moral or social commitment. The marital bond tends to be weak. We can expect divorce to be common especially where it is not mitigated by plurality of spouses or lovers in one form or another.

In an earlier paragraph we noted the observation of Radcliffe-Brown (1952:19) that among the Bantu tribes and Nama Hottentots of South Africa the mother's brother is a male mother of a sort and the father's sister is somewhat of a female father. In the light of the effects of the dominant relationship in each system on some other relationships in that system, we may say with a good deal of justification that husbands in a father-son dominated society are younger fathers, mothers in a husband-wife dominant society tend to be older wives, fathers in a mother-son dominated society tend to be male mothers, while wives in brother-brother dominated societies are to some extent female brothers. However, such observations tend to miss the point and obscure the truly significant effects of each dominant relationship on non-dominant relationships. The fact is *not* that the husband-wife relationship under the dominance of the father-son relationship is changed, in terms of that kinship system, or in the minds of the individuals concerned, into a father-son relationship. What occurs is that *the intrinsic attributes of the husband-wife relationship are so influenced by the intrinsic attributes of the father-son relationship that the characteristic qualities and modes of interaction of the husband-wife relationship in that system, as husband-wife relationship, are very different from those in other systems where the father-son relationship is not dominant.* Furthermore, if our hypothesis is correct, the characteristic qualities and modes of interaction of the husband-wife relationship (or any other basic relationship) in any kinship system become predictable once its dominant relationship is known. Conversely, knowing something of the characteristic qualities and modes of interaction of the husband-wife relationship (or any other basic relationship) in any kinship system will guide us to its dominant relationship (or relationships).[6]

Similarly, for those in husband-wife dominated systems, the male in the father-son dominated society would seem to suffer from lack of ambition; for those in the father-son dominated society, the male and female in the husband-wife dominated system would seem to be over-sexed; for those in both of these systems, the male in the mother-son dominated society would seem to be unsure of his sex identity; while for those in all three systems, the male and female in the brother-brother dominated society would seem to be too callous or calculating with reference to the matter of sexual attachments and too lacking in concern for fidelity. Sex seems to be a commodity to be satisfied or conquered through almost commercialized means. But these "problems" from the point of view of outsiders reared in kinship systems with other dominant relationships may be no problem at all in the minds of those persons who exhibit the characteristic behavior in question.[7] Until we appreciate the role of dominant kinship relationship of each system in shaping the other relationships in that system, our understanding of human behavior will hardly be cross-cultural.

THE EFFECT OF DOMINANT KINSHIP RELATIONSHIPS ON NON-KIN BEHAVIOR

Had space permitted we would have considered the equally telling effect of each of the dominant relationships on other relationships; however, we must proceed to the next task. In considering the effect of dominant kinship relationships on non-kin behavior we will once more confine ourselves to a limited exercise. We shall only comment upon one cluster of facts: the problem of authority.

Reviewing the four kinds of kinship systems dealt with above, we should expect authority to be less problmatic in societies with father-son and mother-son dominated kinship systems than those with husband-wife and brother-brother dominated kinship systems. Authority is a major attribute of the father-son relationship. Nurtured in this attribute, both the father and the son are attuned to its necessity. The superior does not have to disguise his power because he knows this is his due, and the subordinate has no need to disguise his obeisance since it is not necessary to be ashamed of it. Authority and compliance to authority are therefore carried out openly and elaborately with no qualms on either side. Difficulties may arise if the superior becomes too oppressive, but the salvation of the oppressed lies in finding individual relief from it, not in challenging the entire social structure in which such oppression occurs. The individual reared in the father-son dominated system will have no resentment against benevolent authority; in fact, he will love it.

In a mother-son dominated kinship system, authority is a major component of dependence; therefore, its exercise and compliance to it are also undisguised. However, while in the father-son dominated system the child is already conditioned to achieve a good deal of autonomy so that he can proceed independently once the specifications are given, the child in the mother-son dominated kinship system tends to retain more of his undifferentiated outlook and therefore needs continuous guidance, supervision, and restraint in order to conduct himself within the specifications desired by the authority. In a mother-son dominated society authority must be much more elaborately implemented with heavy reliance upon minute negative barriers to make this type possible at all. There will be challenges to authority, but the challenges will be ineffective and have little real impact on the society and culture. The central problem for the leader is not merely to urge his followers to action, but to get them to sustain their efforts toward specific, positive goals without being sidetracked by diverse or unrelated issues.

It is in societies with husband-wife and brother-brother dominated kinship systems that the problem of authority is most acute. In neither system is authority a dominant attribute, or a major element of a dominant attribute. The individual who is a product of such a system tends to resent authority or regard it as an obstacle to be overcome by all means. The difference between these two types of societies in this regard is, however, considerable. In the husband-wife dominated system the complementary nature of sex, pregnancy, and the care of the young provides the basis for two related developments. On the one hand there exists a certain amount of inevitable authority of the male over the female which came from man's primitive past and which, as far as we can see, may last indefinitely into the future. This is a kind of authority to which the female has to submit by voluntary cooperation for her own satisfaction. On the other hand, there is the idea of protection of the weak and the helpless which is at the root of chivalry or noblesse oblige. Therefore the authority can be exercised and maintained, in spite of the waxing and waning of its basis, as long as there exists functional inter-dependence between superiors or leaders and subordinates or followers. However, in exercising and maintaining their authority, the superiors or leaders must disguise their position by minimizing external signs of authority in their interaction with their subordinates or followers, buttressing their own decisions with public opinion, or resorting to other devices which tend to make them appear to be at most authority-transmitters but not authority-originators. Since chivalry is so obviously linked with women and children, adult males welcome the status of being protectors of the weak but resent that of being protected.

In the brother-brother dominated society authority is not an element of any of the attributes. It is true that the older brother can physically coerce his younger brothers but there is no need on the part of the latter which must be satisfied through some inevitable cooperation with the authority-attempting older brother. Consequently the exercise and maintenance of authority is inclined to be brutal (for there is no idea of chivalry to encourage saving or protecting the weak) and easily subject to rebellion and opposition (for the desire for power is widespread). The divisive tendency is extremely apparent. Superiors or leaders will be contantly in fear of harm from their followers and subordinates by assassination or, more diffusedly, by witchcraft. The problem of succession will be most difficult to solve in these societies, for rival claims are not silenced except by force. Yet, in contrast to husband-wife dominated societies, superiors or leaders in such societies do not have to disguise their power to originate decision since being dependent or under protection is a matter of expendiency rather than of admission of basic weaknesses as in the other system.

Our analyses of authority in the four systems enable us to question the cross-cultural validity of certain sociological findings concerning the incompatability of "task" and "emotional" functions. A number of sociologists have dealt with this problem (Marcus 1960; Kahn and Katz 1960; and Blau and Scott 1962). Bales has presented evidence from small group experiments to support the position that differentiation between task (our attribute, authority) and emotional functions of group gives stability. Taking five-men groups, Bales gives subjects problem solving tasks requiring cooperation. The researchers, behind a one-way mirror, observed and recorded interaction. (See Bales 1950 for methodology). Some of the findings are as follows: (1) the task leader (best idea and guidance man) was most disliked by other members whereas the emotional leader was most liked; (2) the emotional leader was least likely to be a task leader; and (3) through a series of problem solving sessions, the emotional leader was less likely to be chosen as task leader (over time). In contrast, the task leader was less likely to be chosen as emotional leader through successive trials (Bales 1953:111–161). Our analyses above give us reason to suspect that these findings are probably characteristic of the husband-wife dominated society where authority is resented and where the attribute of exclusiveness makes it additionally necessary to have sharp differentiation and separation of roles as well as everything else, but will not hold true for the father-son, mother-son, and even brother-brother dominated societies. In father-son and mother-son dominated societies submission to and dependence upon authority are not resented and therefore present no conflict with affective relationships between the superior and the subordinate. Furthermore, in both of these and in brother-brother dominated societies the attribute of inclusiveness will make separation of roles far less mandatory.

Our hypothesis on the effect of dominant kinship relationships on non-kin behavior can equally well be applied to illuminate other clusters of facts, from the nature of friendship, sexuality and associations, to forms of economy and patterns of social development, but these exercises can only be attempted in later publications.[8]

THE QUESTION OF PERSONALITY DYNAMICS

To the extent that our hypothesis is built on the basic premise that early experiences of the individual, especially those associated with members of his nuclear family, are extremely important in shaping the way he relates to the wider world, it is Freudian in orientation. There is no doubt, from what we now know about the dynamics of individual personality, that every person as he goes through life resorts to past experiences to deal with present and future problems which confront him. Since the nuclear family in which he grows up provides him with the structure and content for social action to begin with, the experiences in his early years cannot but serve as the basis for action in the wider human arena.

But here our hypothesis and Freudian psychology part. Freudian psychology puts overwhelming emphasis on the parent-child triad; our hypothesis stresses the fact that, depending upon the social system, the relationship of central importance may be one other than that triad.

Furthermore, the dominant relationship in the nuclear family, whether it be that of father-son or brother-brother, may seriously alter the very nature of that triad, as our analyses show, so that no universal Oedipal situation such as Freud and his followers conceived can be assumed. Exclusiveness and sexuality are indispensable attributes inducing the Oedipal problem; this combination is characteristic only of the husband-wife relationship. The father-son and the brother-brother relationships have neither attribute, while the mother-son relationship has diffused sexuality but not exclusiveness. In the brother-brother dominated system with its frequent and obvious rivalry between father and son even over sex, there will be many sentiments and expressions which, to observers familiar with the Freudian theory and reared in a husband-wife dominated society, easily suggest the Oedipal situation. According to our hypothesis, on the other hand, there is a distinct possibility that the latter type of observation will, on closer inspection, prove to be wide of the mark. For sexual rivalry between fathers and sons in a brother-brother dominated society is likely to occur when the sons are already adults; it is not likely to be resolved in the Freudian fashion if resolved at all; and it is merely one of many forms of rivalry in a social system where rivalry is a dominant attribute.

There are other differences between our hypothesis and the Freudian position. These particularly bear on the manner in which the individuals in different social systems tend to make use of their early experiences. In the husband-wife dominated society the individual makes use of them by their rejection, suppression, or repression because the dictates of his kinship system encourage him to depart from his parents as quickly as possible and to reject their authority as he grows up. When he chooses a wife because he needs his succoring mother, or cannot tolerate his boss because the latter reminds him of his authoritarian father, he is indeed being affected by his early experiences. But the operation of these early experiences, whether he wants to go back to them or get away from them, is likely to be denied because they are resented or unconscious.

In the father-son dominated society the individual makes use of early experiences by their deliberate maintenance, application, or extension, because the dictates of his kinship system encourage him to remember and cultivate his roots—his parents and his forebears. When he enters into ritual brotherhood with his business partners, or addresses his teachers as fathers, he is also affected by his early experiences. But the operation of these early experiences is likely to be spoken of openly because they are desired and conscious.

In yet another aspect, our hypothesis is different from both the relatively orthodox and certain revised Freudian positions. The relatively orthodox Freudians focus their attention on the influences which come to the individual by way of the erogenic zones. Others primarily deal with developmental problems connected with dependence and aggression (Whiting and Child 1953: Chapter 4; Erickson 1950: Chapters I and II;

and Whiting et al 1958). Our hypothesis, though it is not unconcerned with sexuality, dependence, and aggression, addresses itself far less to individual personality dynamics or its genesis than to that intricate but broad area of social and cultural life where different individuals meet and interact, the patterns of that interaction, which can be scrutinized independently of the actors involved, at least in analytic terms (Chapple and Arensberg 1940: 24–25), and the genesis of those patterns. To do so is not to deny the existence of unconscious motives on the part of the individual in any system.

Finally the reader who has come this far probably realizes that our hypothesis is also very different from that of Parsons (1955a & b). Our hypothesis and that of Parsons begin with the universal elements of the nuclear family. We have seen how some of our attributes and Parsons' differentiated roles are identical or related to each other. But our hypothesis becomes very dissimilar to that of Parsons when we go beyond the universal elements of the nuclear family and see the circumstances under which the same universal elements can help to give rise to *different* intra-kinship and extra-kinship patterns of interaction. For example, Parsons observes that although power (our attribute, authority) is a basic element in both father-son and mother-son relationships, a "critical change" in the evolution of the personality organization of the child occurs later when "the instrumental-expressive distinction comes to be differentiated out from the power axis" (1955b:135). Our hypothesis leads us to suspect that the extent of the differentiation of parental roles may vary greatly from one kinship system to another depending upon its dominant relationship and attributes. In a father-son dominated society the power or authority role of the father is likely to be greatly accentuated at all stages of personality development. His authority role is accentuated not merely because he wishes to exercise power but also because his sons tend voluntarily to concede it to him. Furthermore, while, according to Parsons, the mother's role is "disassociated" at the stage of "second fission" from power or authority (Parsons 1955b:135), our hypothesis suggests that the mother's role in a father-son dominated society is not likely to be easily separated from the power or authority element. In fact, as she grows older she is ingested with more power or authority rather than less. Consequently the kind of binary differentiation that Parsons discusses as occurring between the roles of the father and of the mother, respectively, into "instrumental" and "expressive" varieties tends neither to be so clear nor so final. In such a society both the father and the mother tend to lean toward "instrumentality" rather than "expressiveness." Following the same line of reasoning our hypothesis will lead us to believe that in a mother-son dominated society where dependence and libidinality (rather than authority as such) are dominant attributes, both the father and the mother tend to lean toward "expressiveness" rather than "instrumentality," while in the brother-brother dominated society both parents tend to be less "instrumental" and "expressive" than in either the father-son or the mother-son dominated societies, because of the greater impact of the sibling relationship. Parsons' analysis fits well with a husband-wife dominated society where, according to our hypothesis, differentiation of parental roles tends to be most pronounced.

THE ROLE OF FACTORS OTHER THAN KINSHIP

This hypothesis does not attempt to deal with the roles of geography (e.g., isolation or topography), diffusion through historical contact, size of population, political or military conquest, human or natural catastrophe, or hereditary endowment in human affairs. It aims at probing primarily the role of human beings in shaping each other, and within that scope kinship occupies a uniquely central place.

Our hypothesis does not, of course, say that, e.g., any form of marriage or sexual connection will *definitely* occur under the dominance of a certain kinship relationship. What it does say is that certain dominant relationships are compatible with certain forms of marriage or sexual practices, and that, if such a form of marriage or sexual practice is already in existence in a given geographical region for any reason whatever, it has a better chance of continuation with one dominant relationship rather than another.

ANTECEDENTAL EVIDENCE FOR THE HYPOTHESIS

The bulk of the data in support of this hypothesis from the qualitative point of view is to be found in *Clan, Caste and Club* (a comparative study of Chinese, Hindu, and American ways of life [Hsu 1963]). In this work my main effort was directed toward the relationship between the forces in the kinship organization and the development of what I term "secondary groupings" in the larger society outside of the kinship organization. The present hypothesis identifies the principal of these forces in the kinship organization as dominant relationships and dominant attributes. This hypothesis leads us to expect that these forces affect the behavior patterns within and without the kinship organization, in diverse ways including the development of secondary groupings. The American, Chinese, and Hindu kinship systems fit the picture well if we assume the first to be dominated by the husband-wife relationship, the second by father-son relationship, and the third by mother-son relationship.

Some antecedental evidence on our postulation for the brother-brother relationship is to be found in the African portion of "Kinship and Ways of Life: an Exploration" (Hsu 1961b:400–56). It is also to be found in a very interesting article by Melville and Frances Herskovits entitled "Sibling Rivalry, the Oedipus Complex and Myth" (1959:1–15). If we assume many African societies of the patrilocal type to be dominated by brother-brother relationship we shall find many central features of African life understandable.

In addition, unexpected support for our hypothesis on the mother-son dominated society is found in a recent book by Prince Peter of Greece and Denmark titled *A Study of Polyandry* (1963). It will be recalled that, according to our hypothesis, the mother-son dominated kinship system structurally favors plurality of spouses in different combinations in contrast to the father-son dominated kinship system which structurally favors polygyny, and the husband-wife dominated kinship system which structurally favors monogamy. Our hypothesis also leads us to believe that the brother-brother dominated kinship system tends to be similar in this regard to the mother-son dominated kinship system except to a lesser extent.

According to Prince Peter's survey of a total of 18 societies practicing true polyandry, 11 are to be found in India or nearby such as among the Kandyans of Ceylon and the Tibetans, while three are found in Africa. Of a total of 27 societies practicing some form of cicisbeism,[9] 15 are found in India or nearby, while five are found in Africa. Of a total of four societies where the rule is passing connection between one woman and more than one man, three are found in or near India. Of a total of four societies practicing a combination of polyandry and polygyny, three are found in or near India (Prince Peter 1963:506–11).

Prince Peter's survey does not, obviously, cover the Eskimo and the Chukchee custom of wife-lending as a matter of hospitality. But his figures are highly suggestive for one portion of our hypothesis. The hypothesis in part and as a whole, needs rigorous testing not only by intense field and library analysis but also by cross-cultural statistical research.

NOTES

1. A revised and augmented view of the same subject was given in "Kinship and Ways of Life" (Hsu 1961b) and in *Clan, Caste and Club* (Hsu 1963).

2. Among physical scientists the term "property" is generally used in place of our term "attribute." In the original article I used the term "recessive" to designate the non-dominant dyads and attributes.

3. The term discontinuity used in this paper is not idential with the term discontinuity which Parsons regards as one of the basic discoveries of Freud in analyzing the socialization process (Parsons 1955a:40). As our analysis will show, our term discontinuity refers not to an absolute break in the child's socialization process but to a quality of interpersonal relationships in comparative terms throughout life. This relationship is either very long and measured by decades and therefore more continuous, or very short and measured by a few months or a few years and therefore more discontinuous. However, sharp breaks in the socialization process are probably more likely to occur in a social system where discontinuity is one of its dominant attributes than in other systems where it is not.

4. In this presentation we will resort to some specific psychoanalytic observations on parent-child relationships but we do not follow any particular psychoanalytic theory of personality development.

5. Some sort of cult of ancestors is to be found in different parts of the world. So
far, the term "ancestral cult" or "ancestor worship" has been applied in anthropological literature to such facts without precision. A research project at Northwestern University attempts to examine the existing ethnographic literature bearing on
the subject with greater precision (See Chapter 15).

6. In my earlier publication distinguishing kinship content from kinship structure (Hsu 1959), I accepted the fact, based on Murdock (1949:226–228), that the
Eskimos and the Yankees of New England have a similar kinship structure. What I
tried to demonstrate in that article was that the contents of their two kinship
systems made their behavior patterns so different. In view of our present analysis,
it should become obvious that the Eskimos and the New England Yankees do not
even share a common kinship structure. In fact the Eskimo pattern of kinship does
not belong to any of the four forms analyzed in this paper. Whether the concepts of
dominant kinship relationships and attributes defined here or some other factors
must be resorted to in order to explain Eskimo behavior is a problem to be tackled
by future intensive field research.

7. According to Whiting: "In societies with maximum conflict in sex identity,
e.g., where a boy initially sleeps exclusively with his mother and where the
domestic unit is patrilocal and hence controlled by men, there will be initiation
rites at puberty which function to resolve this conflict in identity" (Burton and
Whiting 1961:90. See also Whiting *et al.* 1958). The situation of Hindu India fits
this picture of maximum conflict, but as far as can be ascertained, no initiation rites
exist other than the donning of the sacred thread at puberty or before. The
initiation rites in Whiting's studies predominantly comprise hazing, genital mutila-
tion, seclusion from women and tests of endurance. There is nothing like them
connected with puberty in Hindu India. The sacred thread rite has no trace of
overt sex symbolism and is primarily restricted to Brahmins and only occasionally
extended to lower castes such as the Pancha Brahma of Shamirpet, Hyderabad,
Kayastha of Bengal, or (in modified form) the Lingayat of Deccan, for caste raising
purposes. Yet projective materials indicate that Hindu males would seem to have
uncertainty of sex identity. Presuming Whiting's hypothesis to be correct, our
inference is that this seeming uncertainty is more of a problem to the outside
observer than to the Hindu. The fact that a majority of Hindu males undergo no
initiation rite, and that those who do regard it primarily as a matter of caste status, is
an important evidence in support of our inference. Whiting's hypothesis on
initiation rites has recently been challenged by Yehudi Cohen (1964), whose
grounds for the challenge do not, however, eliminate the possibility that initiation
rites may be at least partially related to the problem of sex identity in many
societies. On the other hand, the Hindu rite connected with the donning of the
sacred thread obviously is consonant with Cohen's idea of the need for the society
to manipulate "the child in relation to the boundaries of his nuclear family and kin
group in order to implant a social emotional identity and values consonant with the
culture's articulating principles." In the Hindu case the boundary is that of caste
instead of kin group and the principle is hierarchy as explained in our hypothesis.

8. For some of these covariations see Hsu 1961b but especially 1968, and
Chapter 15.

9. "So-called boarders in the U.S.A." (quoted by Linton) is listed as one case in
Prince Peter's compilation of cicisbeism. This case is dropped from our count.

Appendix to Chapter 14

DOMINANT KIN RELATIONSHIPS AND DOMINANT IDEAS

Francis Hsu's article (1965:638–661) on the effect of dominant kinship relationships on kin and nonkin behavior contains a large number of interesting suggestions for the study of covariation in kinship systems. Perhaps it will prove of most value in enabling us to put labels on social systems with different emphases within a single broad cultural area. For instance, in the New Guinea Highlands, it is not hard to recognize the Mae-Enga as a father-son dominated society (Meggitt 1965), while the Kuma (Reay 1959) would appear to fit the brother-brother dominated system in a number of respects. Rather less plausible, however, are the ways in which Hsu leads into his hypothesis.

(1) As a unit for study he chooses the nuclear family, containing the eight dyads that he lists. The assumption here presumably is that these provide the full set of primary kin relationships. But where the coresidential household unit is a pair of brothers-in-law or a mother's brother and his sister's children, would it not be necessary to treat the relationships resulting from these arrangements as primary for socialization purposes within that society? To analyze such a system in Hsu's terms one would then need to draw up a list of intrinsic attributes for these relationships too. Hsu's choice of his eight relationships is reasonable, but it is a certain extent arbitrary if he means to imply that they are *the only* basic ones and so provide an absolute baseline for his discussion.

(2) The same arbitrariness can be seen in his notion of "intrinsic attribute." This he says (p. 219) "refers to the logical or typical mode of behavior and attitude intrinsic to each relationship"; and he quotes an apparently similar pronouncement by Schneider (1961). In this definition is the "or" intended to indicate that logical and typical are here exclusive in distribution, or is "typical" meant as another way of saying "logical"? We are not sure what distinction is intended but shall take it that it is the first alternative. In that sense we can see that some of the attributes he sets out can be regarded as logical, while others are typical and neither logical nor illogical. Discontinuity/continuity and inclusiveness/exclusiveness are logical axes of comparison, based on formal definition, of the four relationships he takes. The others, authority, sexuality, and so on, are descriptive and typical.

This appendix is a critique by Andrew and Marilyn Strathern and the subsequent rejoinder by Hsu were originally published in the *American Anthropologist*, Vol. 68, No. 4, 1966, pp. 997–1004.

How does the author derive these typical attributes? He simply arrives at them and states them. There are difficulties for this even within the terms of the author's own scheme, since in any given particular social system the intrinsic attributes of all the kin relationships will presumably be modified by external factors and perhaps by the dominance of one relationship within the set, so that we could not hope to observe attributes in a pure state anywhere. Yet the author writes as though he means some of his typical attributes to be empirically derived (e.g., from examples of the arrangements for polygynists' wives in Africa). Some of the attributes are obvious enough—like sexuality in the case of the husband-wife relationship, although this is not how we would define the relationship structurally—but others, such as diffuseness in the mother-son relationship, seem to require more justification. Some of the attributes seem to be based on psychological theory, while others are sociological, like authority. But if authority is said to be universally a dominant property of the father-son relationship, does not this require prior demonstration from ethnography? And as soon as we went to ethnography, we would realize that our problem depended on the old difficulties of the distinction between *genitor* and *pater*. Which is Hsu talking about in his article?

Attempts to extend the proposed scheme to other relationships in the set of eight also show up difficulties. We might wonder if some New Guinea societies are brother-sister dominated. In terms of Hsu's logical axes the attributes of the brother-sister relationship are discontinuity and inclusiveness. For the typical attributes we may suggest desexuality—"the condition of repression of sexuality"—and libidinality. We derive the latter from Hsu's maxim that all cross-sex relationships are characterized by libidinality, but is it as plausible here as it is for the mother-son relationship? (Hsu himself notes his reservations on this point.) The first is derived from the near-universal sibling incest taboo ("repression" here begs a number of questions, but that is another argument), that is, it is taken straight from comparative ethnography, by which it stands or falls, not by any inherent logic of its own. Further, in terms of Hsu's hypothesis, how could we know that the taboo was not the result of some other kin relationship's being dominant and affecting the brother-sister relationship so that its "intrinsic" attributes remained always hidden? If our observation of the intrinsic attribute of a relationship depends either on its being dominant within its system or on no relationship's being dominant, it is clear that such observation will be difficult, for how are we to decide in advance which situation exists? It seems that we can only operate the scheme if we already know, as Hsu does, what the intrinsic attributes are!

(3) The Hypothesis does not attempt to state why, in any given case, one of the primary relationships should be dominant over the others. Had the author considered this, he might have taken into account external variables connected with economics, adaptation to environment, and so on as influences on primary kin relationships. But this would have militated against the direction of the variables he is proposing. Would he look on

these external factors only as intervening variables that modify the effect of otherwise-derived dominant kin relationships on nonkin behavior, or would he agree that they could affect kin behavior itself?

(4) After using "predictive" language in his title and in most of the paper, the author adds a covering caveat at the end: that he has been talking about "compatibilities" only. But it seems fair to take it that he means his characterizations to be to some extent predictive. If this is so, we can point out that the predicted effects are of two types: (a) institutional forms, which we may call structural effects; and (b) attributes of and attitudes to relationships involving authority, etc., which we may call cultural effects. The prediction is less convincing for the first than for the second type. For instance, Hsu suggests that in a father-son dominated society, polygyny to continue the male line is a "structural necessity," and that "this form of kinship is likely to be associated with a strong cult of ancestors and a maximum tendency for the development of the clan" (p. 228). Does he here see ancestor worship and the (presumably patri-) clan as interdependently growing out of this dominant father-son relationship with its attribute of authority? If this is so, the hypothesis would certainly require testing, but how would we set about testing it (as it is presumably a diachronic one)? It would seem that the hypothesis would have greatest predictive value for effects of type (b), for attitudes derived from relationships within the nuclear family could affect the reaction of an individual in his various institutional roles outside the family—for example, in his attitudes to authority, as Hsu points out.

We ask two main questions, then: (1) How are the "intrinsic" attributes discovered by the analyst? (2) How does one relationship become dominant over the others? By these criticisms we mean to suggest not that the attempt to set up generalized statements of the content of kin relationships is entirely fruitless, but only that the source of one's statements should be made clear. Is Professor Hsu a Platonist or an Aristotelian?

Andrew Strathern
Marilyn Strathern
University of Cambridge

Rejoinder: A Link between Kinship Structure Studies and Psychological Anthropology

Andrew and Marilyn Strathern's comments on my article (1965:638–661) are very helpful in that they enable me to explain some basic points that I was not able to do there. The purpose of that article was not only to further our study of covariation in kinship systems, as the Stratherns aptly observe, but also to point to a new conceptual framework for establishing more scientifically meaningful links between kinship systems on the one hand and culture and personality on the other. It is my view that the term "structure" has been used too indiscriminately by anthropologists, so that it has become an umbrella to embrace everything that goes on in a social or kinship system. As long as we continue this undifferentiated usage either we shall have no effective means of dealing with social organization comparatively or, if we do try, we shall be beset by meaningless conclusions such as that the Eskimos and the New England Yankees have the same kinship structure (Murdock 1949; Hsu 1959:792). To improve our analysis of kinship and its significance in social development, the most important new conceptual tools I propose are content and attribute, in contrast to structure and relationship.

Now to deal with the specific points raised (my numbers correspond to those in the Stratherns' comments):

(1) Although only eight dyads are listed in my paper, I made no claim that "these provide the *full* set of primary kin relationships" in the nuclear family. (If it seemed to some readers that I did, I am sorry and hereby correct the impression.) Obviously even in the terms in which I framed it, there are at least nine other relationships distinguishable in the picutre: father-child, mother-child, parent-son, parent-daughter, sibling-sibling, older sister-younger brother, older brother-younger brother, older sister-younger sister, and older brother-younger sister. These are not obscure and can be ascertained by a moment's reflection. I began with the first eight dyads, and I have only been able to clarify my hypothesis in connection with four of the eight. The work on the significance of content and attribute of kinship has just commenced, and how this conceptual framework will apply to other relationships, such as those of brother-sister and sister-sister, as well as to a host of other problems from divorce to authority is now being inquired into by some of the 18 participants to a Symposium on Kinship and Culture (August 20–29, 1966, at Burg Wartenstein, Austria[1]), to which I am going with great expectation. My inclusion of only eight dyads for an initial statement of the hypothesis and of analysis in some detail for only four of them is not entirely arbitrary, as the Stratherns would put it, but because (a) I happen to know more about the kinship systems that in my view are dominated by them and (b) these eight dyads (especially the four analyzed in deatail) seem to be more common as the dominant relationships in kinship systems of the world than that between two brothers-in-law or mother's brother-sister's child, which the Stratherns point out. In the wider applications of the hypothesis we hope to deal with many nonkinship relationships, including those of employer-employee, priest-parishioner, etc. Without intending to be presumptuous, I think the question may well be asked as to whether Mendel was "arbitrary" in beginning with peas to demonstrate his hypothesis on heredity rather than with horses, apes, and human beings at the same time.

(2) The notion of "intrinsic attribute" was borrowed from the physical sciences, and the term "dominant" in my dominant relationship is borrowed from biology. The Stratherns ask whether they are supposed to be "typical or logical," question their validity because we cannot "observe"

them "in a pure state anywhere," and insist on the need for "prior demonstration from ethnography" before we can use them as intrinsic attributes. The Stratherns' basic problem here comes from their misunderstanding of the nature of hypothesis building. Few hypotheses in any discipline are ever built on elements all of which are exactly known and proved. And even if we use only elements that have been previously proved, the relationship between the elements must be unknown or only vaguely known; otherwise there is no need to make much ado about any hypothesis concerning them. We construct a hypothesis because we want to develop a clearer knowledge about the relationship, and in order to do so we have to make various suppositions as if the relationship were (or that it were composed of) x or y or z or whatever you wish to call it. The test of a hypothesis resides not in its origin (for example, it may come simply from the mind of one scientist), but in its fruitfulness in regard to new data.

The mark of a scientifically worthwhile postulate (as distinguished from a wild guess) is that it must be based on some antecedent evidence, but the source of the antecedent evidence can be logical or typical, or even hunches that are only felt to work. However, in the present instance the Stratherns are probably right in objecting to my use of the terms "typical" or "logical." What I have in fact done is to use what might be termed a common-sense approach in which I am trying to get at rather difficult and enormously complex phenomena by simplifying along the way in an informed but still common-sense manner, i.e., by drawing on my own knowledge and the kind of logic that flows from it. But the fact that the attributes are not derived through consistently logical or empirical sources is no reason for denigrating their value in hypothesis building. If the new postulates can produce interesting new relations and send some of us out in a direction away from identifying kinship with social structure, or confusing kinship structure with kinship content, then they deserve our serious attention.

The fact that "we could not hope to observe attributes in a pure state anywhere" is no permanent stumbling block either. Our knowledge about most of the physical universe began with phenomena in their nonpure states. But each refinement in analysis or success in experimentation brings us closer to the pure state. The elements in medieval conception, such as water, fire, earth, and wind, are less pure than atoms; atoms are less pure than electrons and neutrons, just as cells, chromosomes, genes, and DNA form a sequence in which each succeeding postulate is purer than the last. But if the biologists and physicists had waited until all their postulates could be seen in a "pure state" or be empirically verified before they constructed their hypotheses, they would not have made much progress.

In the present instance some of my postulated attributes are based on more obvious grounds and are therefore easier for all to accept. The applicability of the attribute "libidinality" to the brother-sister relationship is indeed subject to some reservations; this and the whole question of incest taboo (whether between siblings or between parents and children) are indeed worthy of some intensive exploring from the point of view of this hypothesis and cannot be dealt with summarily in short communications such as the present exchange.

(3) In my hypothesis I specified that I was not considering "*why,* in any given case, one of the primary relationships should be dominant over the others." I also specified that I was not considering external factors such as geographical conditions, economics, or the influence of an acknowledged superior civilization (such as China to Japan before A.D. 1860 or ancient Greece to Rome and "northern barbarians"), but I do not deny that these may be of importance in influencing kin behavior. If one were to consider all possible variables at once, one would be bogged down in a hopeless mishmash from which no scientifically meaningful or testable hypothesis could emerge. What I prefer to do is to (a) seek a new conceptual means for examining the determinants of kin and nonkin behavior within the nuclear constellation of man, rather than outside it, and (b) assume the validity of my postulates for this operation because kinship is of paramount importance to human development on a priori grounds. If we begin getting confirmations to some of the connections posited by this hypothesis, then we should sit down and ask some of the other "whys."

(4) When I used the word "compatible," it was in connection with factors outside of the kinship universe, the appearance or nonappearance of which cannot be predicted from the factors operating within the kinship or social system. No amount of analysis of the Navaho kinship system could have predicted the appearance over two centuries ago of the European immigrants who thereafter established a particular form of society called the U.S.A., any more than a careful scrutiny of the Chinese kinship system could have predicted the aggression of Japan against her since the beginning of the 20th century. What my hypothesis specifically aims at doing is to say that certain dominant relationships, which shape the kinship system toward a certain type of content, are compatible with certain kinds of externally originated forces that influence the society. I argue in the same fashion with reference to forms of marriage or sexual practices. "What it does say is that certain dominant relationships are compatible with certain forms of marriage or sexual practices, and that, if such a form of marriage or sexual practice is already in existence in a given geographical region for any reason whatever, it has a better chance of continuation with one dominant relationship rather than another" (Hsu 1965:657). But the use of the concept of compatibility is not intended to be a "covering caveat" or an escape hatch. On the contrary, compatibility is in line with prediction, which is the ultimate aim of any hypothesis. But in the social sciences we had better be more modest and speak of compatibility. Some social scientist speak only of correlation and of ascertaining whether it is high, medium, or low. Indicating compatibility is therefore a milder form of saying predictability, for the first leads into the second unless some hitherto unknown significant variable comes in to disturb the flow of

events. In discussing the reaction of a kinship system to an externally originated factor that affects it, it is obviously far wiser to speak of compatibility than of predictability.

The Stratherns are quite right in pointing out that there are two types of predicted effects that can flow from my hypothesis: institutional forms, or structural effects, and attributes of and attitudes to relationships involving authority, etc., which are cultural effects. But I cannot agree with their view that the prediction (or expectancy of correlation) for the first type is necessarily less convincing than that for the second primarily because we cannot test the former. Surely the Stratherns would not disagree with the view that structural changes can lead to changes in attributes of and attitudes to relationships, just as changes in the latter can also lead to changes in the former provided that sufficient time lapses for mutual influences to occur. In particular I disagree with the Stratherns' view that the connection between ancestor worship and the patriclan under a dominant father-son relationship cannot be tested because it is "presumably a diachronic one." The distinction between diachronism and synchronism is really useless. The usual view is that everything in this universe is more or less diachronic, but that for purposes of scientific analysis we have to see the phenomenon under investigation as though it were synchronic. But we do *not* have to look at things as if they were synchronic, and it is the structuralist's concern with the synchronic, following Radcliffe-Brown and much British social anthropology of the 1940's, that has led to the idea that "diachronic" studies are somehow different. If we understand the nature of the event system, and the nature of psychic pressures on culture and the fact that action is a result of psychically perceived and often unconsciously motivated pressures, and that action always precedes "values," which are little more than a means for justifying action—then we can see that the distinction is useless. Worse, it blinds us.

Furthermore, if we obtain a high correlation between societies with the highest grade of ancestor worship (in the way I have defined this expression [Hsu 1965:659, Note 5]) and patriclan and societies with the dominant father-son relationship in a significant number of social organizations, we shall certainly have good reason to suspect that there is a connection among them. These are easy variables to operationalize, and statisticians and others are working on methods for obtaining causal statements precisely from similar kinds of materials.

(5) I have dealt with all the points raised by the Stratherns, but I would also like to point out a problem that they have not raised. This is the question, "how does a field worker know which relationship in a kinship system is dominant?" This question is being dealt with by several of us who are working on models for the identification of the dominant relationship or relationships in given kinship systems.[2]

What I have tried to offer is not a finished product. As I pointed out in the beginning of this rejoinder, the term "structure" has been used as an umbrella by students of social organization, generalized to cover everything. My hypothesis says that under this enormous umbrella we can analytically separate structure from content. In order to do so, we have to see structure in terms of relationships only, and content in terms of attributes. The two sets of phenomena are related in the sense that anatomy and physiology are related. At some points they are mixed, but it is my opinion that if we separate them analytically, we can arrive at some new understanding of what it is that kinship systems do in social development.

At the end of their comment, the Stratherns ask, "Is Professor Hsu a Platonist or an Aristotelian?" My reply is, "Yes and no." I am a Platonist-Aristotelian and a Confucian as well, in the sense that I have learned from all of them. It was Confucius who gave overwhelming emphasis to the individual's place among his fellow human beings, in contrast to both Plato and Aristotle, and this may have something to do with my preoccupation with the importance of kinship to social development. But I am not a monotheistic follower of any of them. I take my intellectual supplies where I can find them.

Francis L. K. Hsu
Northwestern University

NOTES

1. Under the sponsorship of the Wenner-Gren Foundation for Anthropological Research, New York. The results of the symposium appeared as *Kinship and Culture*, edited, by Hsu, 1971.

2. See Hsu, 1971d. pp. 489–491.

15

Variations in Ancestor Worship Beliefs and Their Relation to Kinship

Variation in attitudes toward ancestors among different peoples is tremendous. There are peoples such as the Nuer and Tiwi who do not care where their dead are buried (Evans-Pritchard 1940; Hart and Pilling 1960). By contrast, others such as the Tikopia bury their dead in their living rooms and make some offering to their ancestral spirits before every meal (Firth 1936). In addition to gross dissimilarities there are deeper differences which must also engage our attention. For example, there are cultures in which beliefs in ancestral spirits have an important place in the cosmology and "religious" practices, and those in which such beliefs are relatively unimportant (irrespective of the actual nature of the beliefs). Traditional Chinese are like Nupe, in that ancestral spirits are believed never to harm their own descendants; yet concern for the ancestors occupied the central place in Chinese religious practices while the cult is unimportant among the Nupe (Nadel 1954).

However, even when they touch on ancestor worship, most anthropologists seem to do so casually or to content themselves with finalistic observations such as: "Where ancestor worship is a prominent feature of religion, as in many African Negro societies, it may operate indirectly as a force toward conformance with ideals of behavior" (Norbeck 1961: 172), or ancestor worship is linked with "particularistic morality," especially in African societies (Schapera 1937:270).[1]

The first example is too vague to be scientifically useful, and the second is plainly misleading. The notion that ancestor worship is linked with "particularistic morality" is not untrue. The problem is that "particularistic morality" is not confined to ancestor worship, and ancestor worship has more attributes than can be described by "particularistic morality." Most religions contain injunctions as to right and wrong, good and bad. And all religions tend to re-inforce, to some extent, the ideals of behavior. But to point this out is no more than to observe that food does something for the human body.

Nutrition as a science did not progress until its students began to note which components in meat and vegetables are good for which aspects or processes of bodily growth. The science of anthropology cannot move forward by remaining at the level of general statements. We should try to ascertain what elements of ancestor worship are relevant to what sorts of ideals of behavior.

This chapter was originally published in the *Southwestern Journal of Anthropologist*, Vol. 25, No. 2, 1969, with Terrence Tatje, pp. 153–72.

VARIETIES OF ANCESTOR CULTS AND VARIETIES OF HUMAN BEHAVIOR

The purpose of this paper is to explore some specific links between varieties of ancestor cults and varieties of human behavior. But instead of regarding the cult as "a force toward conformance with ideals of behavior" (as those accustomed to proselytizing religions such as Christianity would seem to perceive it), we hypothesize that *ancestor worship is an essential expression of the inherent rules of behavior of the kinship system in the first place and of the society in general.* In this work we draw some inspiration from a few scholars who have studied ancestor worship with respect to its association with social structure but depart from them in very important ways. Radcliffe-Brown, who described the specific "social function" of ancestor worship cults as the maintenance of social group solidarity in societies organized on the basis of lineages and clans (1945:37ff.), was the pioneer among these few scholars. Without considering the differences in cult beliefs and practices from one case to the next, referring generally to certain South African societies, Radcliffe-Brown (1945:38) noted:

> The effect of the impact of European culture, including the teaching of the Christian missionaries, is to weaken in some individuals the sentiments that attach them to their lineage. The disintegration of the social structure and the decay of the ancestral cult proceed together.

While stressing that *social structure alone does not dictate the content of the religious beliefs,* Middleton and Tait likewise suggested that "ancestral cults" are especially likely to be found in societies where the political groupings are based primarily on unilineal descent groups. They discussed segmentary lineage systems of the type found among the Lugbara, Nuer, and Tiv as follows (Middleton and Tait 1958:24ff., italics added):

> *The form of the cults is segmentary, but their contents vary widely.* On the whole they reflect cultural and ecological conditions of the society, in particular the sense of dependence upon human and social forces or else upon non-human natural forces, and the control or lack of control of the environment which determines such features of the world-view. The Lugbara, for example, have an elaborate ancestral cult. But the Nuer and Dinka have little regard for the ritual aspects of the ancestors and their main cult is that of God: sacrifices are made to refractions of God associated with the various segments of the society (Evans-Pritchard 1956). This may reflect their greater ecological insecurity, their sense of dependence upon extrahuman forces and their realization of the weakness of human power to influence nature in general; whereas the Lugbara are very conscious of the importance of human effort in their productive agricultural economy. The Tiv have no ancestral cult, but their beliefs about *tsav,* essentially a representation derived from human ability, again reflect the self-confidence which infests their view of the relations of man to nature in agriculture and other pursuits (Bohannan 1953).

Swanson's analysis of ancestral spirit beliefs in *The Birth of the Gods* is the most systematic and extensive to date. Using a sample of 50 non-Western societies, Swanson divided ancestral spirit beliefs into four operational categories derived from ethnographers' statements:[2] (1) "inactive," (2) "active," (3) "aid or punish," and (4) "invoked." He concluded: There is a positive and significant relationship between the presence in a society of sovereign kinship groups other than the nuclear family and a belief that ancestral spirits are active in human affairs" (1960:108). That is, "ancestral cults" are significantly more likely to be found in societies organized on the basis of clans or lineages than in societies not so organized. Swanson's data also indicated no correlation between beliefs in "active ancestral spirits" and the presence of unorganized or nonsovereign kinship aggregates (e.g., phratries, kindreds, etc.).

However, there is a basic difference between the number of categories into which Swanson separated ancestral spirit beliefs and those which he used in the actual statistical tabulation of the data. In the latter operation Swanson combined the second, third, and fourth categories into a single class. Thus, his analysis utilized only a dichotomous coding for ancestral spirit beliefs: "inactive" versus "active in some fashion" (1960:103ff.). This is perhaps inevitable since his second, third, and fourth categories are not mutually exclusive; the second is clearly a residual category.[3] But the dual classification is not scientifically justifiable, because beliefs concerning ancestral spirits are much more complex than can be handled by a simple dichotomy.[4] This failure prevented Swanson from pursuing the theoretical significance of variation in beliefs about "active" ancestral spirits.

TYPES OF ANCESTOR CULT

We offer a more differentiated scheme consisting of 7 types of beliefs about spirits of the dead, based on ethnographers' statements, and suggest specific theoretical links between the range of variation in beliefs and the differences in kinship systems. The 7 types are:

(1) *Absence of Spirits*—general absence of beliefs in the existence of human "spirits," "souls," "ghosts," etc.

(2) *Neutral Spirits*—general belief in the existence of spirits of the dead, but such spirits are not believed to have any active influence on the affairs of the living.

(3) *Undifferentiated Spirits*—general belief in the existence of spirits of the dead as a potential source of help or harm to the living, but no specific importance is attached to the spirits of ancestors of close kinsmen; if worshipped at all, spirits are worshipped generally without specific reference to ancestors of departed kinsmen.[5]

(4) *Malicious-Capricious Ancestral Spirits*—general belief in the existence of ancestral spirits and in their importance to the descendants' affairs; accompanied by fear of arbitrary harm from them.

(5) *Punishing Ancestral Spirits*—general belief in the existence of ancestral spirits and in their importance to the descendants' affairs; these spirits will punish neglect or serious moral or ritual transgressions but do not actively help their descendants.

(6) *Rewarding-Punishing Ancestral Spirits*—general belief in the existence of ancestral spirits and in their importance to the descendants' affairs; these spirits are as a rule helpful to their descendants but will also punish neglect or serious moral or ritual transgressions.

(7) *Benevolent-Rewarding Ancestral Spirits*—general belief in the existence of ancestral spirits and in their importance to the descendants' affairs, but with no fear of harm or punishment from them. They are believed to give help whenever possible and to reward good without punishing the bad.

Inherent in the definitions of these types are five belief elements. These are shown diagrammatically in Table 1.

We have tried to define the seven categories in such a way that any variety of beliefs about the spirits of the dead may be classified in one of them. Societies which are normally regarded by anthropologists as practicing "ancestor worship" fall only in types 4, 5, 6, or 7. But the first three types are necessary to reveal the entire range of such beliefs.

ETHNOGRAPHIC EVIDENCE FOR THE SCHEME

Examples of societies holding each of the 7 types of beliefs about spirits of the dead are given in Table 2.

DOMINANT KINSHIP DYAD AND ANCESTOR CULT

Having defined the range of variation in ancestral spirit beliefs, we are now prepared to examine how it is related to patterns of social behavior by way of kinship systems. We do not presume complete identity in any culture between its kinship system and its pattern of social behavior in general. But we do presume a fundamental and ascertainable continuity between them. The kinship system of each society is its human factory which produces the appropriate psychological orientation for relating to the living *and for approaching the ancestral spirits.*

The link between the kinship situation and the religious system was first intimated by Margaret Mead (1930:70) nearly 40 years ago in her work on the Manus:

> It is also interesting to note the relationship between early childhood conditioning, the family situation, and the religious system. The Manus attitude toward the spirits is a composite of the attitudes of the child towards the father and of a man towards his children.

Table 1
Defining Criteria for Typology

	Existence	Neutral	Important	Normative	Positive-Negative
(1) Absence	1	0	0	0	0
(2) Neutral	2	1	0	0	0
(3) Undifferentiated	2	2	1	1	1
	2	2	1	1	2
	2	2	1	1	3
	2	2	1	2	1
	2	2	1	2	2
	2	2	1	2	3
(4) Malicious-Capricious	2	2	2	1	1
	2	2	2	1	2
(5) Punishing	2	2	2	2	1
(6) Reward-Punish	2	2	2	2	2
(7) Benevolent-Rewarding	2	2	2	2	3
	2	2	2	1	3

Column 1: "Existence"
  1 = no existence of spirits
  2 = existence of spirits
Column 2: "Neutral"
  0 = not applicable
  1 = no influence on living
  2 = influence on living
Column 3: "Important"
  0 = not applicable
  1 = no special importance of ancestors
  2 = special importance of ancestors
Column 4: "Normative"
  0 = not applicable
  1 = non-normative behavior
  2 = normative behavior
Column 5: "Positive-Negative"
  0 = not applicable
  1 = negative behavior only (malicious or punishing)
  2 = positive and negative behavior (capricious or rewarding-punishing)
  3 = positive behavior only (helpful or rewarding)

More recently Fortes (1959:30) expressed the same view in his work on Tallensi religion:

> In the most general terms, therefore, the ancestor cult is the transposition to the religious plane of the relationships of parents and children; and that is what I mean by describing it as the ritualization of filial piety.

It is interesting to note that, except for putting the link in a somewhat more specific focus, Fortes' observation has not advanced our investigation into the connection very far. We submit that the reason for this is that Fortes (as did Radcliffe-Brown, Middleton and Tait, and Swanson) has concentrated on kinship *structure* to the neglect of its *content*.

The meaning and significance of content and its component attributes, as distinguished from structure and its component dyads, are detailed in 3 papers concerning our Dominant Kinship Dyad hypothesis (Hsu 1961, 1965, 1966) and one forthcoming book (Hsu 1971d). Briefly, a dyad consists of two individuals, each standing in some role *vis-à-vis* the other. Examples of dyads in the kinship sphere are those of husband-wife, father-son, and so forth. Each dyad has certain intrinsic and characteristic qualities of interaction. These qualities are termed attributes. Examples of attributes are continuity (the tendency for a relationship to last a long time for no functional reasons), inclusiveness (the tendency for parties to one tie to tolerate or welcome sharing it with others), and so forth.

In many a kinship system one or two dyads are dominant, being more important than the other dyads. When this occurs, the inherent attributes of the dominant dyad(s) tend to prevail over the attributes of all other dyads in the system and beyond it. The overall organization of the attributes of all the dyads under those of the dominant dyad is the content, in contrast to the overall organization of the dyads, which is the structure. Content gives orientation to the system; structure provides the support for it.

We submit that viewing kinship systems in terms of their content, using our analytically derived attributes, can enable us to extend our understanding of the role of ancestor worship in human society and culture much further than has hitherto been possible.

For example, according to our Dominant Kinship Dyad hypothesis (Hsu 1965) a father-son dominated kinship system will exhibit strongly the attributes of continuity, inclusiveness, authority, and asexuality. By our definitions the first three of these attributes are expressive of an approach to life characterized, among others, by maintenance of ties with the past, close links between generations, high value accorded to and respect for age, the normality of intervention by elders in the affairs of the younger members, and duties and obligations between superiors and subordinates. Therefore, we expect a kinship system dominated by the father-son dyad to be associated with a strong and positive ancestral cult (type VII beliefs), since respect and idealization of the dead, ritual attention to ancestral spirits, and the notion of their benevolence to their descendants are logical extensions of their behavioral characteristics among men.

Conversely, according to the same Dominant Kinship Dyad hypothesis a husband-wife dominated kinship system will exhibit strongly the attributes of discontinuity, exclusiveness, volition,[6] and sexuality. Again, by our definitions the first three of these attributes are indicative of an approach to life characterized, among others, by flimsy ties with the past, the notion that each generation replaces the last, devaluation of old age,

Table 2
Societies Classified by Type of Spirit Beliefs

Type of Beliefs	Society	Statements
Type I: Absence of Spirits	Modern Western atheists	The basic tenet of the atheists' position is the denial of the existence of gods and supernatural beings in general.
	BaMbuti(?)	Turnbull suggests an absence of beliefs in spirits of the dead among the Pygmies of the Ituri Forest (1926:36, 40–45, 137–138, 147, 167, 225–239).
Type II: Neutral Spirits	Western Christian generally	With the possible exception of the saints of the Roman Catholic Church, Christian theology does not admit the direct influence of departed souls in the lives of the living.
	San Blas Cuna	The Cunas believe that after death the *purba* (soul, spirit) of the dead proceeds to "the afterworld" and has no influence on the living (Stout 1947:39–44; Nordens-kiöld 1938:338, 356–357, 454–455).
Type III: Undifferentiated Spirits	Kung Bushmen	The spirits of the dead are generally feared; those of dead kinsmen are not differentiated from others (Thomas 1958:127, 150–151, 248–249).
	Bella Coola	"They [ghosts] are always dreaded, and anyone who hears their whistling or their tongueless chatter cowers in his house, and hopes they will pass by. . . . The sight of such an apparition causes almost immediate death. . . . An unpleasant habit of ghosts is the throwing of stones at the living. . . . Even near approach to ghosts is sometimes dangerous" (McIlwraith 1948:449, 501; also pp. 446–449).
Type IV: Malicious-Capricious Ancestral Spirits	Apache (Mescalero, Chiricahua)	"Fear of the dead, and fear of the dead relatives particularly, does not have to be inferred. Instead its existence is asserted and emphasized by the natives" (Opler 1965:424). "Although ghosts of nonrelatives may and do cause fear and illness, it is far more common that the disease be the result of an encounter with the ghost of a deceased relative" (Opler 1965:425).

Alorese	"Late childhood is undoubtedly the period when individuals acquire their fear of supernatural beings. . . . These supernatural spirits are everywhere. . . . It is practically impossible to avoid their habitations; all one may hope is not to offend them" (DuBois 1944:68). "The interesting point is that these potentially malignant dead are always one's most immediate kin" (DuBois 1944:161).
Type V: Punishing Ancestral Spirits	
Gusii	"The people of Nyansongo view their religion as a set of demands made on them by the ancestor spirits. . . . The ancestor spirits are simply the dead members of the lineage who in the postmortem form continue to take an interest in the affairs of its living members. . . . The attitude of the living toward them is one of fear and deference, involving unquestioning obedience to their demands" (LeVine and LeVine 1966:56–57). "When a diviner diagnoses death or disease as punishment by ancestor spirits, she always names a misdeed of the patient as the ultimate cause. Sexual offenses, homicide (other than magical), and perjured oaths are the most serious of such offenses. Another misdeed invariably punished by the ancestor spirits is the neglect of proper mortuary rituals or the omission of a sacrifice for a dead ancestor" (LeVine and LeVine 1966:100).
Type VI: Reward-Punishing Ancestral Spirits	
Lugbara	" 'Our ancestors' are benevolent and wish well for their descendants, whom they protect and guide, but punish for sins" (Middleton 1965:64). "Ancestors are important only to their living kin, in particular, members of their lineage; they have no significance to other people" (Middleton 1965:65).
Tikopia	"External spirits are of many kinds. . . . Some, such as ancestors, are clearly benevolent, but may harm people if offended" (Firth 1967:296).
Type VII: Benevolent-Rewarding Ancestral Spirits	
Chinese	"They are always well disposed and never malicious toward the members of the families to which they are related. . . . The ancestral spirits will help their own descendants whenever they can. . . . They are never offended by their descendants, and they never cause disasters to befall the coming generation" (Hsu 1949a:241).

the idea of self reliance, and minimization of differences between superiors and subordinates. Consequently, we expect a kinship system dominated by the husband-wife dyad to be associated with no ancestor cult (type
I or II beliefs), since these behavioral characteristics are incompatible with
the requirements of such a cult.[7]

The attribute of sexuality in husband-wife dominance expresses itself in
male-female closeness, which enlarges the separation between the generations just as asexuality in father-son dominance abets the ties between the
generations. Sexuality, therefore, contains elements indirectly opposed to
an ancestor cult, in contrast to asexuality which contains elements supportive of it.[8]

We expect a mother-son dominated kinship system to be associated
with beliefs in "undifferentiated spirits" (type III). This prediction follows
from the attributes of discontinuity, inclusiveness, dependence, diffuseness, and libidinality intrinsic to the mother-son dyad (Hsu 1965). Dependence is similar to authority and inclusiveness, and, to that extent, the
effect of the mother-son dominance is similar to that of the father-son.
However, discontinuity cuts down the link between generations, and
diffuseness spreads out the directions of dependence so that the object of
dependence is not as clearly channeled as in the case of the father-son
dyad. For this reason ancestral spirits are likely to be merged with (or
undifferentiated from) all other sources of dependence in the spirit world.
The attribute of libidinality is more diffused than sexuality, but to the
extent that it is similar to the latter it will reduce cross-generational ties.

The attribute of dependence expresses itself in the attitude of wishing to
be unilaterally reliant upon others, and the attribute of diffuseness (aided
in this case by inclusiveness) expresses itself in the tendency to extend this
desire in all directions. Under these conditions it seems likely that the
general attitude of reliance on others (dependence) will be expanded to
the dead as well as the living. Further, it is likely that the spirits of the dead
will not be differentiated into kinsmen and unrelated persons (diffuseness), but instead all ancestral spirits will be treated as equally likely
sources of dependence (inclusiveness). The fourth attribute of the
mother-son relationship, discontinuity, probably weakens the ties between the living and the dead.

The situation is more complicated in societies where the mother-
daughter dyad is dominant in the kinship content. Like the mother-son
dyad, this kind of kinship system has dominant attributes of inclusiveness,
diffuseness, and dependence. However, unlike the discontinuous mother-
son dyad, the mother-daughter relationship has the attribute of continuity
(as does father-son). On the basis of these attributes alone, we would
expect similar attitudes toward spirits of the dead as in the mother-son
dominated case, but with greater importance accorded to ancestors because of the attribute of continuity, i.e., more strongly held beliefs in
"undifferentiated spirits" (type III beliefs).

However, another crucial factor enters into the situation. Of the basic kinship dyads considered, the mother-daughter dyad alone does not include a male role as part of the dominant relationship (sister-sister systems are not considered here). Usually mother-daughter dominance is found in social systems where institutional features undermine the authority position of males. These features, coupled with the fact that continuity in the female line enhances the importance and authority of women seem to be at the root of male ambivalence. Mother-daughter dominance occurs in many parts of the Caribbean where males are frequently absent from the household or have low economic status (Smith 1956; Solien 1959, 1961; Otterbein 1965). The same factors are associated with female dominance in lower class Negro American households (cf. Frazier 1966; Drake and Cayton 1962:564–657). Negro males from female dominated households may exhibit strong ambivalence toward the family group and toward authority in general, beginning in early adolescence (Tatje n.d.).

Mother-daughter dominance also occurs in some matrilineal societies and in some bilateral societies with matrilocal residence. Boyer (1964) presents a strong case for the dominance of the mother-daughter relationship in the kinship system of the Mescalero Apache, for example. Where matrilocal residence is found, in-marrying males find themselves surrounded by their wives' kinsmen and subordinate to their authority. Often the husband's subservient position is dramatized by strict rules of avoidance and other elements of respectful behavior. Among the Chiricahua Apache a man must strenuously avoid any direct contact with his parents-in-law as well as with other of his wife's close consanguineal relatives (Opler 1941:163–181). Chiricahua women do not observe similar rules *vis-à-vis* the husband's kinsmen (Opler 1941:184). Opler describes these avoidance patterns as formal behavioral declarations of respect for the authority of the matrilineal kin group.[9] Since Chiricahua and Mescalero individuals are rigorously trained to be independent and self-reliant, Opler is justified in seeing male ambivalence among both Apache tribes in terms of the underlying hostilities generated by the subordination of males to the authority of their affinal kinsmen. He suggests (Opler 1965:432), further, that hostility is normally displaced from the actual group to the ancestral ghosts, who are invariably feared as potentially malevolent sources of illness and death:

> The resentment, which could not normally be expressed in everyday life if the solidarity and unity essential to the health of the society were to be maintained, emerged in the guise of a mysterious terror of the dead relatives and a puzzling dread of the power of living relatives.

The reader may immediately ask why ambivalence of males is an important factor where the dominant dyad does not include a male role, but possible female ambivalence is not suggested for the opposite situation, i.e., where the dominant dyad does not include a female role (e.g., the father-son and brother-brother). The answer is that these are not parallel situations. The fundamental role of females as females—the bearing of children—is not seriously altered in the latter cases. But in the former, that of males, the exercise of authority is affected. Hence, we may reasonably expect male ambivalence in mother-daughter dominated kinship systems and expect it to lead to an equally ambivalent, perhaps hostile, attitude toward the departed spirits. For this reason, we also suggest types IV (malicious-capricious) and V (punishing) spirit beliefs as likely possibilities under this kind of kinship.

We expect a brother-brother dominated kinship system to be associated with beliefs in "punishing" and "rewarding-punishing" ancestral spirits (types V and VI). This prediction comes from the attributes of discontiuity, inclusiveness, rivalry, and equality. Equality is compatible with horizontal inclusiveness; rivalry complements inter-generational discontinuity. Given these sets of attitudes, intergenerational rivalry is a likely feature of brother-brother dominated kinship content. And each generation of brothers is likely to regard its father's generation with a good deal of ambivalence. This would account for the projection of negative (punishing) behavior toward ancestors. On the one hand the older generation is the source of benefits and status; on the other, it is the agent of control and discipline, and is reluctant to relinquish its power and authority. The result is an ambivalent attitude toward the spirits of the dead. Their importance is recognized, but they are still seen as potentially hostile rivals who may seek revenge or at least continue to act as agents of social control who punish their descendants' transgressions.

In short, based on the reasons given above, we suggest that societies in which the husband-wife dyad is dominant in the kinship system are most likely to be associated with type I or II spirit beliefs; mother-son dominant systems with type III beliefs; mother-daughter systems with types III, IV, or V; brother-brother systems with type V or VI; and father-son dominated kinship systems with type VI or VII spirit beliefs.

These predictions, based on a consideration of the intrinsic attributes of the respective dominant kinship dyads, are summarized in Table 3.

CAUTIONS AND CONCLUDING OBSERVATIONS

We do not intend to imply that kinship content is the only factor related to beliefs about the dead. It is not. Nor do we intend the predictive statements made above to be taken as causal ones. They are, rather, statements of relative probabilities. That is, a strong, positive ancestral cult is more likely to be found in a society where the father-son relationship is dominant than in one where the husband-wife dyad is dominant *because such beliefs are more compatible with the attributes stemming from the former kind of kinship than from the latter*. Finally, we are not trying to refute *in principle* the findings of Radcliffe-Brown, Middleton and Tait, or Swanson concerning the relationship of social structure and ancestral spirit beliefs. Their views and ours are complementary, not conflicting; but ours go farther than theirs. Indeed, there is a high degree of correspondence between kinship structure and kinship content. This does not mean that all societies with patrilineal descent and formally organized patrilineages or patri-clans will necessarily have kinship content dominated by the father-son dyad. It does mean that a society with patrilineal descent and the formation of lineages or clans is more likely to exhibit father-son dominated kinship content and, consequently, is also more likely to develop a more positive ancestral cult in our terms. In short, certain kinds of social structure and beliefs about the dead are more compatible with some kinds of kinship content than they are with others.

Table 3.

Predicted Associations Between Types of Spirit Beliefs and Dominant Kinship Relationships*

Dominant Dyad	I	II	III	IV	V	VI	VII
Father-Son						X	X
Brother-Brother					X	X	
Mother-Daughter			X	X	X		
Mother-Son			X				
Husband-Wife	X	X					

* An "X" indicates an expected association.

It goes without saying that the predicted association between the types of beliefs about ancestral spirits and kinds of kinship content is not a perfect one. In addition to the fact that kinship content is not the only variable affecting a people's belief system, there is also variation in degree of dyadic dominance in different social systems (see fn. 8). For example, if more than one dyad is dominant, more than one set of attributes will naturally become dominant. In that event the expected beliefs must be somewhat different in direction. For example, co-dominance of the father-son and brother-brother relationships will lead to a more positive attitude toward ancestral spirits than dominance of the brother-brother dyad alone—because the added father-son attributes of continuity and authority tend to counter those of discontinuity, equality, and rivalry. On the other hand, it can be expected to have a "less positive" attitude than one where only the father-son dyad is dominant.

For a quantitatively oriented testing of our hypothesized links between specific types of kinship dominance and patterns of belief about and treatment of ancestral spirits, we have devised an alternative method of analysis. This involves the rating of societies on the basis of the presence or absence of 26 specific elements of behavior connected with departed ancestors. This method together with some results will be given in a later publication. The major aim of this paper is to present a more precise scheme for, and a more productive approach to, the study of ancestor worship than those which have so far appeared.

NOTES

1. Other examples are Lowie (1924:174–75), who states simply that ancestor worship is a widespread phenomenon in Africa, Siberia, and China but is generally not found in aboriginal North American cultures; and Wallace (1966), who describes it merely as one of several kinds of "cults" in "communal religions." Norbeck (1961) makes but 3 passing references to the subject in his book, *Religion in Primitive Society*.

2. By way of explicating the basis for his categorization, Swanson (1960:102) stated: "We shall classify the activities of dead ancestors in our sample into four categories. There are some cases in which the observers do not report that the dead influence the living. There are situations in which the deceased's influence is portrayed in such vague terms as bringing misfortune or playing pranks, but not further described. There are societies in which the departed aid or punish their descendants, implying that the living merit this assistance or punishment. Finally, we find societies in which the dead are invoked by their descendants. In this fourth case, the descendants have some claim upon, or power over the deceased relatives which they can exercise to guide the actions of the dead."

3. Cases come easily to mind which belong in *both* the third and fourth categories: "aid or punish" and "invoked." Among the Lugbara of East Africa, elders frequently invoke the help of their ancestors in maintaining their ritual and secular authority; but the Lugbara also believe that the ancestral ghosts act on their own to punish transgressions and to aid their descendants (Middleton 1960, 1965). Similar beliefs obtain among the Tallensi of West Africa (Fortes 1959) and among the Tikopia (Firth 1967).

4. This difficulty leads us to question some of Swanson's actual codings. For example, he codes the Nuer and Tiv as having beliefs in active ancestral spirits who "aid or punish living humans" and the Tallensi as having beliefs in active ancestral spirits that "are invoked by the living" (Swanson 1960:216). Yet Middleton and Tait (1958:24), state that ancestral cults are unimportant or non-existant among the Nuer and Tiv. Conversely, while it is true that the Tallensi do call upon their ancestors for assistance (Fortes 1959:64), it is equally true that they believe that the ancestral spirits act independently to aid or punish (Fortes 1959:43–46, 51–54, 56–59).

5. These spirits may act normatively or non-normatively. In either case they may also be positive or negative.

6. In the original statement of the Dominant Kinship Dyad hypothesis (Hsu 1965) this attribute was termed "freedom." This term has since been changed to "volition" because the latter term is freer from popular connotations.

7. Our hypothesis does not presuppose that kinship dominance is necessarily a feature of all human societies. It is possible that in some societies the dominant social relationships is not a kinship one. For example, from existing ethnographic data we receive the impression that perhaps no one family relationship is dominant

in the society of the Kung Bushman, since all social ties are rather unstable. If we shift our concern slightly from kinship *per se* to a consideration of the *dominant relationship in the individual's environment in determining his characteristic interpersonal behavior,* we may be able to hypothesize that here the dominant relationship is one between the individual Kung and the harsh environment of the Kalahari Desert. The physical environment does not allow permanence or the development of strong interpersonal ties (Thomas 1958:87). The band is necessary for survival, and the overriding need for co-operation makes any friction within it intolerable. This results in the frequent fission of social groups and family ties among the Kung (Thomas 1958:10–11, 86–87, 157–58, 224).

The possible effect of the material environment on social relationships is interesting and has been pursued by some anthropologists (Foster 1965, with respect to peasants, and Lewis 1959 and 1966, with reference to urban poor). But those interested in the effects of the material environment have so far concerned themselves only with its harshness and limitations but never with its over-abundance and over-affluence. What is extreme wealth doing to contemporary human relationships in the United States? How far is the Kwakiutl preoccupation with status through destructive potlatches related to the ease with which they can acquire worldly goods?

However, looking over the known societies and cultures the case of the Kung Bushman can at best be regarded as an aberrant one, for typically man's most important preoccupation is with his social relationships, not his physical environment (see n. 9 below).

8. The extent to which the attributes of the dominant dyad prevail over those of nondominant dyads may vary from one social system to another. At this stage of our research on the Dominant Kinship Dyad hypothesis we have found two major sources of variation: (A) the attributes of some dominant dyads are mutually supportive while others are not; husband-wife and father-son dyads happen to be examples of the former while mother-son and brother-brother are examples of the latter (see Hsu 1965:647–48); and (B) where not one but two dyads are dominant, or where one dyad is dominant but another one occupies the position of subdominance, there is likely to be a "blending" of the dominant attributes, as in the Japanese system where father-son and mother-son dyads occupy respectively the position of dominance and sub-dominance (Hsu 1969a). Though we do not yet have all the facts and definitive conclusions, our survey of the ethnographic data up to this point indicates that the phenomenon of kinship dominance may be separated into the following classes: (1) single dyad dominance, (2) dual dominance, (3) one dyad dominance with subdominance by other dyads, (4) multiple dominance, and (5) no dominance. From this angle we may question the validity of the statements of those writers who stress the effect of physical environment on patterns of social relationship. The possibility at least exists that, for example, the supposed effects of the harsh environment on Kung Bushman society (mentioned in n. 8 above) are due to the fact that the kinship system had no dominant dyad and therefore had no strong orientation in the first place to guide the people in their quest for life and fulfillment. The observable fact among mankind is that there are different approaches to success and happiness just as there are to failure and misery. European mercantilism and industrialization were preceded by poverty and oppression among European peasants no less grinding than that of their traditional Chinese counterparts. But such poverty and oppression did not serve as Chinese incentives for comparable Chinese economic development.

9. This interpretation agrees with Sweetser's (1966) analysis; avoidance rules are interpreted as signs of respect and recognition of group authority in situations where the undermining of such authority would be socially disruptive. Avoidance rules are found to be most common where unilineal kinship is emphasized (either patrilineal or matrilineal), and where residence groups are small and impermanent. Though the Apache are bilateral, these criteria otherwise fit their case.

16

Eros, Affect and Pao

In "Kinship and The Associational Aspect of Social Structure" Parsons has introduced an illuminating analogy (1971:409–438). He compares the role of the erotic element in kinship and its ramifications in human relations at large with that of gold (or some other precious metal) in economy.

If eros in human relations is comparable to the metal gold in economic relations, affect is in my view comparable to the legal tender money. In the economic arena gold is the crude material; money is what most societies have made of it. The reality (and value) of the former can be cross-societal even without prior agreement and negotiation between the societies concerned, but the reality (and value) of the latter is strictly dependent upon the politico-economic power and ability of each society that issues it, and can only be used cross-societally through agreement, negotiation, the flow of goods, confidence, or even cultural direction (e.g., some societies want to join some regional common market, while others do not).

Until gold (or silver or cowrie shells) is transformed through legal fiction into money, its circulation is limited. Even traditional Chinese type of commercial and industrial differentiation, and certainly large scale transactions of the modern world on regular bases would be difficult if not impossible. In other words, the crude metal gold (or silver or whatever) cannot serve as the agent to bind large numbers of people or peoples together for common goals intrasocietally and intersocietally.

This is precisely the role of affect with reference to eros.[1] The crude sex urge will remain important on the personal level but it can at best unite a few individuals (two lovers, a man and his harem, several men and their common wife, and the children of such unions). When it is transformed into affect, it is then more heavily regulated by law and custom and channelized into common expressions by culture (e.g. the rules concerning marital fidelity and incest), and may eventually even serve as an agent to bind different societies together (e.g., matrimonial alliance between two or more tribes or castes; or the spread of the Western pattern of equality between the sexes in many societies which have gone about changing their law and customs accordingly).

The economy of every society has to have some gold (or silver or cowrie shells, etc.) as valuables and media of exchange. Some societies have

This chapter was originally published in *Kinship and Culture*. Francis L.K. Hsu (Editor), Chicago: Aldine Press, 1971, pp. 439–76. Reprinted by permission of Wenner-Gren Foundation.

confined themselves to such basic materials as the medium of exchange. But the network of exchange spreads more widely in those societies where money or some sort of legal tender exists than in others where it does not. The former societies are more likely and able to participate in international trade than others. The societies which stick only to some basic valuable such as gold do not go far in social, economic and political development.

The human network (kinship and beyond) composing every society has to have some eros as the commodity for binding some people together and for its continuation. While all presently known human societies transform eros in some degree into affect (that is to say, no society exists where sex and its immediate consequences [infant children] are the sole agents for joining individuals together), some societies have transformed this basic commodity into affect more than others, and some have even moved affect still farther so that it operates independently of eros. The question of how eros, affect, the network of human relationships and culture patterns are linked with each other awaits clarification.

FOUR WAYS OF EROS AND AFFECT

However, the parallel between gold-eros and money-affect is not a straightforward one. We must deal with the complexities of each culture separately. In our present exercise we shall examine how the differential relationships between eros and affect are linked with differences in kinship. Here we are not speaking of the primeval origin but simply regard kinship as the human "factory" which manufactures in each new generation of individuals the psychological elements (or orientations) by means of which they approach their traditions (past), problems (present) and solutions (future).

One basic channel of expression for every culture is its religious symbolism. If we compare the latter in Chinese, Hindu, Japanese and Western cultures we obtain the following:

A. China—Eros is irrelevant to affect. (No need for active attempt to separate eros from affect. Eros and affect each has its own separate areas of relevance as a matter of course.)

B. Japan—Eros enters into some aspects of affect but often does so in disguise.

C. Hindu India—Eros and affect mingled.

D. West—Eros is being actively separated from affect.

This four-way comparison may be graphically illustrated by the following four reproductions of religious symbolism: Plates A, B, C, and D.

Plate A is a common Chinese representation of the God of Longevity. It is found in numerous Chinese books and paintings. It adorns the ceremonial wall of many a Chinese home whenever the birthday of an old man or old lady is being celebrated. Plate B is a common Japanese representation of the same god. The most unusual feature in the Japanese version, from the Chinese point of view, is the enormous elongation of the god's bald head.[2]

Plate C is a Hindu representation of the *Lingam* (phallis), or the god Shiva. This is the form found in Gudimallam, Madras 1st century B.C. (according to Basham 1954: plate facing p. 105). Later representations of the *lingam* in Hindu temples are not usually so realistic, except in the great Shiva temple in Banaras. They tend to be simple rod-like forms on top, similar to the Japanese God of Longevity's head. But as a rule they also each have the female sexual organ *(yoni)* at its base, so that the two elements together are supposed to symbolize male and female principles in congress. The Nativity scene represented in Plate D is familiar to all Christians. It symbolizes the Virgin Birth.

To the Chinese, whose kinship system is marked by the absence of the attribute of sexuality or of libidinality, the sexual element is not a point of contention, to be glorified, denied or disguised. Consequently it has either no place in religious representations (as in Plate A) or is present as a matter of course, as when some gods have spouses. The Chinese Kitchen God is usually associated with his wife, and both are objects of worship. But most Chinese gods (of War, of Literature, of Wealth, etc.) have no spouses.

The Japanese, Hindu and American symbols increasingly concern themselves with the erotic element. In the Japanese kinship system libidinality is only a subordinate attribute (Hsu 1971); the Japanese phallic symbol is but the elongated head of an old god borrowed from China (as in Plate B), who cannot by any stretch of the imagination be associated with sexual prowess. In the Hindu kinship system libidinality is a dominate attribute; the sexual reference in the Hindu representation is obvious or even glorified but not complete (as in Plate C). The *lingam* is a symbol. Even when the *lingam* and the *yoni* are given together, they are but two principles in interaction, and bear no indication of the consequences of the union.

The Western representation (as in Plate D) signifies not only Western preoccupation with sex but also its result.[3]

Furthermore, a most interesting point which emerges from this comparison is the fact that, while the Chinese God of Longevity and Japanese God of Blessing grant pure blessing without further complication, the *Lingam* and the Virgin Birth are associated in India and in the West with destruction as well.

In the Hindu case Shiva is not only known as the Creator and the Destroyer at the same time, but he also suffers from obvious aggression from his wife, the Mata of Mother Worshippers. When Shiva's consort appears in the ferocious form of Kali, the latter has a black face and a garland of human skulls around her neck, and her husband's naked body under one of her feet. Hindus say that is why Kali is invariably also represented as having her tongue hanging out, for she was astonished by what she had mistakenly done (stepping on her husband).

The West has gone much farther in this association. Virgin Birth is not

A

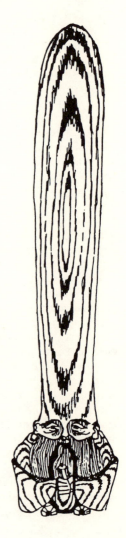

B

C

D

enough. But Christ has to be destroyed for Him to atone for the sin associated with the birth of all men.

Eros in the West

We shall recall that the husband-wife dominated Western kinship embodies, in my hypothesis (Hsu 1965), the attributes of discontinuity, exclusiveness, volition (freedom), and sexuality. Exclusiveness leads to the all or none approach, either one or the other (with reference to eros this attribute exposes itself in Virgin Birth and celibacy of clergy or orgy and Existentialism, etc.). When affect is thus lifted from eros, the probability is very high for nationalistic solidarity (within each society) or for universalistic solidarity (at least in ideals). But it also contains the seeds of perpetual disruption of that unity (intra- or inter-societally). This is because exclusiveness tends to separate those who want only affect versus those who want only eros, and those who want affect to combine with eros versus those who want one or the other alone to triumph.

This process of constant disruption is greatly aided by the attributes of volition and discontinuity. Volition means the individual is encouraged to value the status of making his own decisions and being his own master (individuation, the need for every individual to find himself, high value of privacy, etc.). Discontinuity means that he has less worry about deviation from the past, if his own will dictates it. He must, of course, find justifications for his deviating ways (inefficiency of the old methods, "it's time for a change," or the incongruity of the results with the overall social framework—e.g., "In a free society we must have more sex education"). But all the justifications will be based on ideas in line with the attributes of volition and discontinuity.

The separation of eros from affect forces eros into two divergent expressions. The first is its restriction to marital relations. The attributes of discontinuity but especially of volition and exclusiveness make strict monogamy the only legally accepted form of marriage. Therefore, though mistress-keeping and other forms of extra-marital liaisons were common and accepted among European aristocracy and the upper crust before modern times, concubinage was never legalized in the West. This was why Henry the VIII had no other recourse than execution of his wives. This condition is in sharp contrast to China where, though not a majority occurrence, concubinage was until recently a legalized institution, and where a concubine ws a secondary wife and her offspring were legal (albeit second class) children of her husband. Plurality of wives was legal in Japan and India.

It is this fact, that eros is customarily and legally restricted to a single marital bond, which made the Western husband-wife dyad so qualitatively different from other husband-wife relationships and from all other Western human ties. In that relationship we have eros, maximum affect, intimacy, and permanent commitment.

Under the dominant husband-wife dyad the attributes exclusiveness and discontinuity foster in the Western parent and child relationship a high degree of affect, intimacy and commitment second only to those in husband-wife relationship. However, the effects of these attributes on the parents and on their children are asymmetrical, because while the parents are already mature and in full control of their powers, the children are immature and not yet well developed in their powers. Consequently, parents have complete control of their children, but children have to regard their parents as the ultimate source of reward and punishment.

Under such circumstances the effective functioning of the sphere of kinship as kinship tends to be perpetually small. On the one hand, since eros is restricted to the husband-wife relationship, the rest of the genetically related persons tend to merge with a vast majority of other individuals to whom one is either bound by affect or not. On the other hand, just as exclusiveness and discontinuity have separated parents from parents, so they will also separate children from their elders. As the children grow this separation becomes more and more apparent. And it is in the West and not in China, Japan or India that we find laws declaring the legal and economic (and by implication social) independence of the children at somewhere around age 20. This latter fact makes what Parsons speaks of as the "concentration of the kinship system on the area of intimacies" (1971) inevitable.

The effects of this separation between parents and their growing children are also asymmetrical: now the grown up children tend to be less interested in (and in need of) their parents than their parents are of them. Under the influence of the attributes exclusiveness and discontinuity children have been the private possession of their parents and the parent-child intimacy is only second to that between spouses. There are several factors which make this separation harder for the parents than for the children. It is an observable fact of life that humans do not easily give up their exclusive possessions. To do so at a time when the parents are getting to middle age or beyond is even more arduous. Also, since eros is restricted to the marital relationship and since minor children are such an intimate part of that relationship, parents are likely to be tempted to find compensatory sources of erotic gratification in their children of the opposite sex for any significant deficiency in its satisfaction from their married partners. This is an aspect of Oedipus Complex. Adding to this strain is the attribute of sexuality which undoubtedly renders the resolution of this inverse Oedipus Complex more difficult.

However, with the attributes exclusiveness and discontinuity, the growing up children will only hasten their separation from their parents. And if the parents seem to retard or refuse the inevitable, the children must reject the elders. At a time when the children are blooming physically and mentally, meeting all kinds of new people in an ever widening horizon, this process of separation from parents becomes for them more and more natural. Here the attribute of sexuality will increase the urgency of the youngsters' need for members of the opposite sex far beyond what Freud saw as normal development after resolution of the Oedipus Complex (Freud 1943:295). Here the attraction of a peer of the opposite sex is both the more realistic love-object and the more desirable one than a parent of the opposite sex.

In an earlier paragraph we observed that the separation of eros from affect forces eros into two divergent lines of expression. We have so far analyzed its role in the marital relationship and its consequences. The other expression of eros is its diffusion throughout Western culture. For while every society to a certain extent separates eros from affect, and more or less depends upon affect but not eros for cementing social relations in general, Western society, with its attributes exclusiveness and discontinuity makes this separation very absolute and relies heavily upon affect for cementing social relations. Reaction to this absolute separation is aggravated by the attribute sexuality, which makes it impossible for Westerners to treat eros as a mere biological need in a class with food. Therefore the tendency to its complete denial tends to be countered by the tendency to its complete indulgence. It is this combination, and not merely the "process of establishing new bases of solidarity centering on the mechanism of affect" that has given rise to the "modern preoccupation with things erotic" (Parsons 1971) which includes also such fads as sex education, prize-winning movies like "Blow Up," "A Man and a Woman," "Georgy Girl," "Chelsea Girl," and countless others, and the ever increasing demand for enjoyment of sensuality and sex quite apart from moral rules or the marital bond. The word "modern" in Parsons' statement quoted above seems therefore to be misplaced. It should be replaced by the word "Western" to conform to the facts.

This Western configuration of human problems and their solutions is characteristic of the Western civilization from time immemorial. Even the dominance of the husband-wife dyad in the Western kinship system was as old. For example, when Noah learned of the impending flood from God as a punishment for the wickedness of men, his solution was to pack up his wife, his three sons and their wives, and pairs of all animals into a ship to escape the disaster. When the flood subsided they landed on Ararat. After thanking the Lord by appropriate rituals, Noah and his wife apparently lived for a while with his sons and their wives together. Then Noah drank the wine he made and, while under the influence of liquor he masturbated in his tent. Ham, seeing his father engaged in self-eroticism, told his two brothers about it, who were all disgusted with Noah. There ensued some kind of quarrel, and Noah then played favoritism by blessing Shem and Japheth and cursing Ham and condemning Ham's son Canaan and his future descendants into slavery.[4]

This Western treatment of this legend provides us with the most clear indication of dominance of the husband-wife dyad, with all its attributes. When the flood came Noah was 600 years old and his own father Lamech had died five years before. But Noah merely took his own wife, three sons and their wives to the Ark, and we have no indication as to what happened to his widowed mother. In those legendary times people lived long. Lamech died when he was 777 and Noah did not die until he was 950. Is it not reasonable to suggest that Noah's mother might have survived his father for a little over five years. The fact is that neither he nor the narrator of the legend concerned themselves with her.

Noah and his group did not remain in the soil where they were born and lived till the flood came. Instead they emigrated to some totally new place (Ararat) by means of the Ark. If they did not intend to emigrate they would have at least tried to return to their old home. But they did not even make any gesture in that direction. And Noah and his sons did not remain together long. They quarrelled and each son then went his own way with his wife. These are clearest expressions of discontinuity, exclusiveness, and volition (on the part of the sons) as well. And the source of trouble which caused their dispersion was sexuality.

The legend of Noah's approach to the flood and its aftermath thus inevitably set the tone of the husband-wife dominated kinship system of the Western man.

Eros in Chinese Society

Here we must also begin with the Chinese father-son dominated kinship system. This is also an old, old pattern, the psychocultural stage having been set long before the First Emperor of Ch'in politically consolidated the country into one empire at 221 B.C. The Chinese legendary treatment of the primeval flood was in sharp contrast to its Western counterpart.

The Chinese account is briefly as follows: Emperors Yao and Shun (said respectively to have reigned 2357-2258 B.C. and 2258-2206 B.C.) were great and moral rulers. In Yao's old age a terrible flood devastated the country. Yao appointed an official to control the flood but the official was unsuccessful. Yao decided to appoint the able and popular man Shun as his successor to the throne. Emperor Shun exiled the official who failed to control the flood and appointed the exile's son Yu in his place. Yu worked for many years, going all over the country, and succeeded in finally eradicating the flood. During his many years of duty he passed by his own house three different times (during the first year of his absence his wife gave birth to a son) but he was so mindful of his duty that he did not enter it even once. After his success, Yu was appointed the next emperor by a grateful Shun, obviously also in response to the people's will.

We can see at once how the Chinese approach is different from the Western one and how it is commensurate with the attributes of the father-son dyad: continuity, inclusiveness, authority and asexuality. The Chinese legend did not name any chosen person (as Noah was) to be favored by God and spared from the disaster; instead all Chinese were to be saved from it (inclusiveness). The Chinese legend did not carry the theme that the Chinese (or some of them) should take refuge in a boat or flee the country to somewhere else; instead they remained where they were born and lived (continuity). There was no question of sons going in different directions from their fathers; instead Yu worked hardest to succeed in what his father failed, thus vindicating his father's name (authority, continuity, and inclusiveness). Finally, Yu did not even once visit his wife during his many years of work even though he could conveniently have done so three times (asexuality).

In the Chinese configuration, eros is merely a reality to be dealt with, like man's need for fire or food. Man has to take precautions so that it is used properly, and is prevented from its destructive effects. It may be bought; it may be used for material or other gains; it gives pleasure; it is part of the marital relationship; it is necessary for continuation of the patrilineal ancestral line. It may be combined with a particular kind of affect (that between a man and his wife or concubine or mistress), but it has no intrinsic relationship with affect in other areas or in general. For example, in the Chinese concept of *hsiao,* or filial piety, a man is enjoined to devote his all to his parents, for their wishes and pleasures, at the expense of his marital and other relationships. If there is a conflict between his wife and his mother or father, there is no question about whose side he should take to make himself respectable in the eyes of society (albeit he may do so unwillingly or he may decide to be bad and not follow the socially acceptable way). There is no doubt that many Chinese took the side of their parents, even to the extent of divorcing their wives in consequence. Some great stories and poems have been left to posterity on this.

In "Suppression versus Repression: A Limited Interpretation of Four Cultures" (Chapter 8), I analyzed the differences between two basic ways of dealing with sex. For the Chinese, sex, like everything else, has its place, time, and partners with whom it can be resorted to. In the wrong place, at the wrong time and with wrong partners it is absolutely forbidden. Thus between a Chinese father and his son sex as a subject cannot be touched upon at all. (Just as the business spirit, expressed by the American phrase "business is business," is inapplicable to Chinese parent-child, sibling and teacher-pupil relationships; among these one should "give" and maybe later accept "gifts" or "favors" but one should not be calculating at all.)

Eros can combine with affect in whole (rare for men, more common for women) or in part; eros and affect can be irrelevant to each other; or affect (a particular kind) can reign so supreme that it eliminates everything else including eros. But there is no need to *deny* the existence of eros in order to mobilize affect, any more than there is need to deny the existence of business in order to mobilize friendship, or to deny the existence of filial piety to parents in order to mobilize loyalty to the emperor. Each kind of commodity (or joiner or element) is relevant to a particular human configuration and not to others. In terms of the gold-money analogy, the Chinese situation can be described as gold-money parallelism. There is no need for *protestation* in favor of pure gold or pure money. With this pattern the dominant attributes continuity, inclusiveness, authority and asexuality originating from the Chinese kinship system articulate well.

Inclusiveness makes it unnecessary for the Chinese to approach the world in terms of all or none, absolutely black or absolutely white. Even in philosophical ideals, the Chinese have never had the conception of the absolute virtue as opposed to the absolute evil. Instead the Chinese have developed the complementary principles of *yin* and *yan* (darkness and light, or female and male). The attribute continuity makes sharp breaks difficult. In this it finds additional support in the attribute inclusiveness as well. Since what has begun tends always to exist anyhow, its denial will do no good. Instead a more workable solution is either complete incorporation by designing a scheme large or vague enough to tolerate all, or situation-centeredness (the positive side of suppression) in which the prominent element in one human setting is not that in another one. The same actor can be involved in different settings different times where different (or opposing) dramatic roles and emotions are required of him.

That this situation-centered approach was the socially accepted norm in China is partially indicated by the very low status (in fact a sort of outcast status) traditionally assigned to Buddhist monks. Monks were men who left their families of origin, remained celibate, and never for the rest of their lives used the first or last names they had before entering monkhood. Chinese monks, in contrast to their Western counterparts, were always treated like the scum of the society. The famous *Chu Tze Chih Chia Ke Yen* (or *Precepts For Administration of the Family*) by the Confucianist, Chu Pe-lu (1627–1678 A.D.) contains an injunction against inviting monks and priests into one's home. Even today the author of an article in the Central Daily News published in Taiwan (1967) begins his general statement about different classes of human beings by lumping monks and priests together with prostitutes, actors and actresses, roaming traders and porters.

Chinese Buddhist monks completely discarded eros and even affect following the doctrine of non-attachment in Chinese terms. Conceptually they were extreme in their abstention and negation. But instead of being respected and adored for it they were objects of contempt and had no active or effective role in the society. The clergy never was at any time of Chinese history in a position to contend even mildly for political power.

As we pointed out above, in the Chinese conception, eros can be combined with affect in whole or in part. When the daughter of a wealthy and nobleman father ran away with a lowly foot soldier, eros and affect indeed operated wholly together. When many a filial son tried to please both his wife and his father, the two were combined in part. But many a rich old man married young girls for gratification or for sons, and the girls lived out their part of the bargain because their poverty-stricken parents needed the fat bride-price for existence. And a few times in Chinese history powerful empress-dowagers had male consorts not treated as husbands or even sweethearts. These were examples of eros without affect. The same was even more true with prostitution. The latter was such a legally and socially accepted institution in traditional China that prostitutes could be summoned into the homes of wealthy merchants for entertainment by song and dance, conversation, or spending the night. It was not unusual for a local official to offer a prostitute to a house guest whom he wanted to please as part of his hospitality. Some members of the literati might frown upon this, but even a majority of them would not (and did not) condemn it. If they did not do it (and did not approve of it) themselves, they certainly realized that it was not uncommon among wealthy merchants and bureaucrats. Most of them would not (and did not) strenuously object to being at the receiving end of such hospitality.

Prostitution and the marriage of a rich old man to a young concubine for gratification or for sons also exemplify how eros can be obtained by money. From the point of view of a girl born to poor parents, she would be lucky if she got to marry a rich husband as concubine. The extreme of this pattern was when a eunuch, after achieving power and wealth in the court, retired from service and "married" a wife. This happened more than once in Chinese history. As a matter of fact, a number of wealthy eunuchs, after the fall of the Manchu dynasty in 1912 and their discharge from the palace, married. Between 1934 and 1936, as medical social worker in the Peking Union Medical College Hospital, I met quite a few of these eunuchs and their wives. Some had adopted children.

Finally, the central concern among traditional Chinese with reference to proposed marriage was not "love" (eros or eros and affect) of the prospective partners but non-romantic qualifications such as ability, money, health, family reputation, severity or kindness of the boy's mother, etc. Physical defects which would prevent either spouse to function sexually was part of this package, but only a part. That was why some girls in traditional China insisted (and the society encouraged them in this) on "marrying" their dead fiances by going through all the wedding rituals after which they became full-fledged members of their dead husbands' clans.

Previously we noted that traditional Chinese society had a case of gold-money parallelism. There is in this pattern no inseparable relationship between the two, and effective functioning of one is not necessarily dependent upon the other. Money could be based on gold, but it does not have to be, if faith in the government which issued it is strong. The Chinese confidence in the collective Chinese way of life was so great that an overwhelming majority of its members did not wish to pull out or take actions calculated to jeopardize it (see Chapter 19).

For this reason, the society could afford to assume a relatively rational posture about eros, since it is not considered to be its foundation or root. So on the one hand the time-honored Chinese philosophy expressly states that sexual congress in marriage is one of the major relationships *(lun)* of mankind (the term *lun* is the same one used in designating the Five Cardinal Relationships, *Wu lun)*. In fact Mencius went farther and even simply spoke of sex and food as two *ta yü,* or great desires, of all human beings. On the other hand, the Chinese society is replete with proverbs and stories and aphorisms on the bad consequences of over-indulgence for the individual and his kin group or for the society as a whole. At least two traditional operas I know of and many popular stories and novels are based on the theme of reward to or reverence for men who were able to resist the temptation of eros and keep their minds on weightier matters, such as passing the imperial examinations. A good Chinese young man is one who concentrates on his career tasks at the expense of eros. In fact the previously recounted story of the Chinese mythological hero who conquered the primeval deluge bears this theme. A Chinese husband who works hard at his office or in his school room does not have to worry about neglecting his wife at home.

That the Chinese culture only looks askance at sex if it is resorted to improperly but not at sex itself is indicated by the fact, already explained before, that it considered celibacy to be no virtue. On the contrary, avowed celibates had exceptionally low status in Chinese society.

In this light we can say that the Chinese culture makes it possible for affect to function without eros. Here the Chinese culture truly distinguishes itself. One can observe without the fear of exaggeration that the Chinese culture was most highly developed affect-wise, just as Western culture as a whole is today most highly developed industrially. My criterion for "development" is, in either case, the degree of differentiation of the central substance involved (means for joining humans together in the case of China, versus means for production in the case of the West), and the productivity of this differentiation (different kinds of human relationships in the case of China, versus different kinds of goods in the West).

The Five Cardinal Relationships *(Wu Lun)*

The five cardinal relationships in Confucian China were lord and subject, father and son, husband and wife, brother and brother, and friend and friend. It is at once apparent that four of the five pertain to affect and not eros. Lest it be said that the father-son may not be entirely free from eros (Freud), we have to note that the Chinese traditional justification for marital relations is filial piety. For Mencius said that of the three unfilial acts, lack of heir is the worst. Thus even eros is pressed into the service of filial piety.

However, the Chinese emphasis on affect at the expense of eros is not merely expressed in the five cardinal relationships. The same relationships are also recognized in the Western culture though not seen in that order. The truly Chinese characteristic is that four of the five relationships have each a specific variety of virtue assigned to it. To the father-son relationship is assigned the virtue of filial piety *(hsiao)*; to the brother-brother relationship, fraternalness *(ti)*; to the lord-subject relationship, loyalty *(chung)*; to the relationship between friends, faithfulness *(hsin)*. These are four of the much extolled Eight Virtues, the others being courtesy (or propriety) *(li)*, righteousness (y*i*), integrity (or clear discrimination) *(lien)*, and self-consciousness (or sense of shame) *(ch'ih)*. It is of note that the virtue of harmony, normally assigned to the relationship of husband and wife, did not make the list.[5] Nor did it make another list of five virtues, which combined two others—kindness (j*en*) and wisdom *(chih)* with righteousness, propriety and faithfulness.

We must note three features peculiar to the Chinese situation. First, all of these virtues have as their primary objectives the cementing of interpersonal relations, but not such virtues as bravery and creativity, which center only in the individual. Second, in contrast to the Western world, an overwhelming amount of Chinese literary and moral energy was spent in discussing, analyzing, amplifying and exemplifying them. In the U.S. a few famous essayists dwelt on self-reliance (Emerson), solitude (Thoreau) or frugality (Franklin). But all of these American virtues discussed are individual-centered ones. Third, many Chinese virtues are so specific to particular relationships that they even tend to be non-transferable to other relationships.

The Chinese sages recognized that fraternalness can support filial piety (a man who is brotherly toward his siblings is likely to be filial toward his parents), and the Chinese classics often speak of *"yi hsiao cho chung"* (transfer filial piety to parents into loyalty to the emperor as when a man sacrificed his life for the throne). But filial piety is inapplicable to the relationship between friends, and fraternalness is not applicable to the relationship between lord and subject. Finally, eros is irrelevant to all these. It is particular to the marital relationship and certain well-defined extra-marital situations such as prostitution, and to nothing else.

If we think of two of the basic characteristics of industrial development as differentiation and productivity, we must observe that the Chinese have achieved a high degree of development in affect through differentiation, which in turn was linked with high productivity in human relationships in quality and quantity.

Previously we mentioned how eros was mobilized according to Chinese precepts in support of affect (marital relations were part of one's filial duty to parents). But there were two other ways that signified separation between eros and affect much more clearly.

One of these was the fact that where there was a conflict, eros must be sacrificed in favor of affect within the primary kinship grouping. We already noted that if a man's wife was in disharmony with his parents there was no question as to whose side he should take. One of the traditional

Chinese grounds for divorce was the displeasure of the husband's parents. One of the famous "Precepts for the Administration of the Family" already cited was that a good man would not allow his wife to instigate quarrels with his brothers.

The other way of separation between eros and affect was to be found in the marital bond itself. The usual phrase for marital harmony was "the husband sings and the wife harmonizes." But a somewhat less common phrase was for them "to show respect to each other as guest and host." These were high ideals, but there were men and women who not only lived up to but exaggerated them. According to the Biography of Liang Hung of Han dynasty, in *Book of Later Han Dynasty (Hou Han Shu)*, Liang was a wage laborer, hulling rice from house to house. "When he returned home every day his wife gave him dinner. (She respected him so much that) she did not dare to raise her eyes in front of his face. She raised the tray containing the dishes and bowls to the level of her eyebrows." Ever since then the phrase *chu an ch'i mei* (raising the tray containing dishes and bowls to the level of the eyebrows) has been used to eulogize utmost respect between married partners.

Later in Yuan (Mongol) dynasty a rags-to-riches opera greatly embellished this tale. According to the opera a girl Meng Kuang was betrothed to Liang. Before they were married, Liang's family became poor and the girl's father planned to select a different husband for her. She insisted, and her father reluctantly accepted Liang as a son-in-law into his house matrilocally since he was so poor. Later the father-in-law chased both her and her husband out. So the dispossessed couple found refuge in the house of a Mr. Wu. The girl Meng Kuang respected her husband so much that she "raised the tray with dishes and bowls to the level of her eyebrows" before serving it to him. When her father heard about this he "realized" that Liang was "not an ordinary man" (meaning that he really had "class"). (Here the text does not clearly indicate whether or not the father-in-law thought both his daughter and son-in-law were "not ordinary.") So he secretly sent his daughter's wet nurse to give his son-in-law some travelling funds and to encourage him to take the imperial examinations. The opera ended with Liang achieving the highest honor.

The pattern of marital adjustment between Liang and his wife in Han times was even more graphically exaggerated by a high official in Hupei province and his wife in the last century. This couple lived in separate parts of the same family courtyard. Before he visited her he would first send a messenger boy with his calling card. And when they met they sat on opposite sides of a low tea table (Chen 1935:Vol. 2, 695).

Reverting to our previous observation that the Chinese culture had a case of gold-money parallelism, we may now go one step farther and say that gold (eros) was used very little in the Chinese human economy. But money (affect) was the main instrument for its very high level of development. The development was so high that some of the tools (affect) were highly differentiated and not always easily transferable (the Eight Virtues, the Five Cardinal Relationships, etc.). We are, in this regard, reminded of the differences between primitive workshops and modern industrial enterprises. In the former not ony the processes of manufacture but also the sale of the products are likely to be in the hands of only one or a few persons. In the latter, the division of labor is likely to be high, and tools and techniques appropriate to one part of the process cannot be easily adapted to fill the requirements of another part in the same factory without more or less drastic rearrangement and reorientation. This same limitation also applies to changing over from one specialty to another. For example, sales personnel will have great difficulty in switching over to manufacturing, and textile mills cannot easily be used for auto production, etc.

CREDIT INSTRUMENT AND RECIPROCITY

However, we have not quite exhausted our analysis. Money is more efficient than gold in economic development because it fits a greater variety of requirements, both industrial and commercial, and also because it can circulate more widely with less encumbrance. But an even more efficient tool which can link even larger circles of producers, manufacturers, traders and consumers is some sort of credit instrument. Through this instrument we are able to carry on industrial and commercial transactions without the trouble of counting coins, dollar bills and even checks, of worrying about the authenticity and quality of the coins and notes and checks, of the problem of physically transporting the coins and notes and checks, of the risks of theft and embezzlement, etc.

If gold and money in economies are respectively likened to eros and affect in human relations, what is the element in the latter which may conceivably correspond to some sort of credit instrument in the former? I submit that in Chinese society that element is the concept of p*ao* or roughly, reciprocity.

Some sort of reciprocity is indispensable for the continuation of all human societies. Its importance was long ago demonstrated by Malinowski (1922) and by Mauss (1922–23). But the Chinese culture has given it such a special place that it has become an active motivator in Chinese behavior. It may be regarded as the most generalized ingredient undergirding even relation-specific virtues such as *hsiao* (filial piety) and *chung* (loyalty).

The most comprehensive statement of the properties of the concept of p*ao* is to be found in Lien-sheng Yang's "The Concept of *Pao* as a Basis for Social Relations in China" (Yang 1957).

According to Yang, although the term p*ao* has a wide range of meanings that which is most relevant to social relations in China is "response" or "return."

The Chinese believe that reciprocity of actions (favor and hatred, reward and punishment) between man and man, and indeed between man and supernatural beings, should be as certain as a cause-and-effect relationship, and, therefore, when a Chinese acts, he normally anticipates a response or return. Favors done for others are often considered what may be termed "social investments," for which handsome returns are expected . . . in China the principle is marked by its long history, the high degree of consciousness of its existence, and its wide application and tremendous influence in social institutions." (Yang 1957:291)

Yang sees the concept of *pao* as expressing itself in Chinese society in two major forms. For a majority of *hsiao jen,* the common men, the central expectation is equivalence in time: the doers of favor will be recompensed by a return from the recipient later, or the inflictor of injury can be sure that retaliation awaits him in time. Fearing endless chains of retaliation wise men and government often spoke against revenge or blood feuds.[6]

On a higher level stand the *chun-tsu* or gentlemen who will extend their help without seeking reward and give to others without regretting or begrudging their liability (Yang 1957:305). Yang explicates Mencius on this subject as follows:

As for a gentleman, in the words of Mencius, "If he treats others politely and they do not return his politeness, let him turn inward to examine his own (feelings of) respect," in other words, to make sure whether his own outward politeness came from true respect. For this inward examination, Mencius gives a lengthy illustration which may be summarized as follows: If a gentleman who is benevolent and observant of propriety is treated by a man in a perverse and unreasonable manner, the gentleman will first reflect upon himself, asking whether he himself has been wanting in benevolence or propriety, and also whether he has been failing to do his utmost. After he is satisfied with himself, if the man still repeats his perversity and unreasonableness, the gentleman will say, "This is a man utterly lost indeed! Since he conducts himself so, what is there to choose between him and a brute? Why should I go to contend with a brute?" (Yang 1957:305)[7]

Yang is of the opinion that the two approaches outlined here are quite different, but contends that since "in any period of Chinese history there were more small men than gentlemen," "reciprocity" was "the normal standard" for behavior as a whole (Yang 1957:309). This contrast in approach between the gentlemen and the common men does not negate the fact that for both, the concept *pao* was basic to all human relations. Filial piety was usually spoken of as repayment to parents for their pains in giving their children life and raising them. In fact one of the spurious Buddhist scriptures of Chinese origin is *Ta Pao Fu Mu En Teh Ching (Scripture on the Repayment of Parents' Kindness).* Loyalty to the emperor was invariably couched in terms of repayment of the latter's benevolence. The psychology was so deep-seated that quite a few eulogies of animals (e.g., dogs who saved their masters from drowning) centered in the anthropomorphizing theme of how the beasts gave their lives to repay their masters' kindness.

The difference in approach to *pao* or reciprocity between the common men and the gentlemen is nevertheless of a great deal of consequence. This difference was a two-fold one. On the one hand, the gentlemen would not "seek" (but not reject) reward for favors done, or "regret" or "begrudge" his liability "if he had benefited an ungrateful or wicked man" (Yang 1957:305). On the other hand, the gentleman would seek to benefit others more than he was recompensed in return. This approach is not only limited to those who are actually gentlemen according to Chinese custom but also those who aspire to that status. As I observed elsewhere:

> Whether we look at China, India or other societies in the world, including the Apollonian Zuni described by Ruth Benedict and the "effeminate" and cooperative Arapesh documented by Margaret Mead, we find some ambitious individuals who wish in some ways to excel over or differ from their fellow human beings. In the Chinese way of life the ambitious ones strive to become the most illustrious "sons" of the family and the clan, and, in so doing, make their clan more illustrious than other clans. The primary way of doing this is to upset the balance of long-run equality between obligations and rewards, by making one's obligations much bigger than one's rewards. In the same sense as a departed ancestor shading his descendants like a tree, a living man who can spread his personal shade to cover a large number of clansmen (and others if he is in a position to do so) is a more important man in the kinship group than another man who is unable to do so.   (Hsu 1963:167)

As we shall see later, this tendency on the part of aspiring gentlemen will become quite a problem in Chinese society today.

EROS AND *Pao*

The Chinese pattern of a highly differentiated affect without eros, and the extension of this differentiation by means of the concept of *pao* or reciprocity so that eros is even farther removed from it, has found ample expression in Chinese philosophy, art, novels, and poetry. In a previous publication (See Chapter 12) I demonstrated the contrast between Western and Chinese art and fiction in terms of the individual-centered versus situation-centered dichotomy. The locus of the former is the individual himself: his anxieties and fears, desires and aspirations, loves and hates, all of this leading either to the triumph of the individual or his destruction. The locus of the latter is the social situation in which the individual finds himself: he is a filial or unfilial son; he is an upright or corrupt official; he is rewarded with success in imperial examinations because he refused the advances of another man's wife; he fails in business becaues he usually short changes his customers; and so forth. It is not his own impulses which he can follow. It is the social group or groups of which he is a part that he must come to terms with.

We can see now how *pao* or reciprocity is intrinsic to the Chinese situation-centered orientation as eros is to the American (Western) individual-centered orientation. The more the emphasis is placed on the individual, the larger role eros is bound to play, for the social life is always close to its organic base. In such circumstances affect will have to be strenuously promoted, in the process of which eros will have to be strenuously excluded (repressed) to make larger groupings possible and durable. Eros by its very nature is exclusive and invariably will tie a few people together. It stands ready to pull the larger groupings asunder. But the individual-centered emphasis unavoidably encourages the individual to place individual satisfaction above the requirements of the group. That means the eternal danger of ascendance of eros over affect.

On the other hand, the more the emphasis is placed on the social situation of the individual, the more eros can be relegated to its restricted area of operation, for the commodity most required in social life is not so close to the organic base. The important criteria of correct behavior reside in the nature of the interpersonal link, not the desires and wishes of the individual. In this case affect can be effectively utilized for joining human beings together without the ever-threatening spectre of eros. Eros and affect each has its own sphere of direct relevance. Each needs not impinge upon the other and the most relevant situations to each one tend to be well defined. Even affect is also greatly differentiated according to the situational requirements. The utmost of this line of development leads to the concept of *pao* or reciprocity, which is the group basis of affect, as contrasted to eros, which is rooted in the individual.

In this chart the two patterns are seen as forming a continuum, with the Westerners always returning to the individual, which view is inevitably tied to the organic base of man (eros), and the Chinese always emphasizing the place of the individual in a human network, which view is inseparable from the duties and obligations characteristic of the group (*pao*). Both societies need affect: in the case of the West for joining more than a few members together; and in the case of the Chinese for differential cohesion and solidarity within the larger and more impersonal framework of *pao*.

In the former, the individual is trained and encouraged to make his own life and to feel that he is free to make his own arrangements for it. The expressions most commensurate with his approach to the world are: "I love to . . . "; "It is exciting. . . "; or "This interests me . . . ." His ideals will include such values as freedom, progress, initiative, independence, struggle against authority, all of which can be grouped together under the term autonomy in Western psychiatry.

In the Chinese situation, the individual is trained and encouraged to follow the established order of things and to feel that he will do best for himself if he follows authority. The reasons he most frequently gives himself for acting or not acting are: "I owe to . . ."; "I can't face my

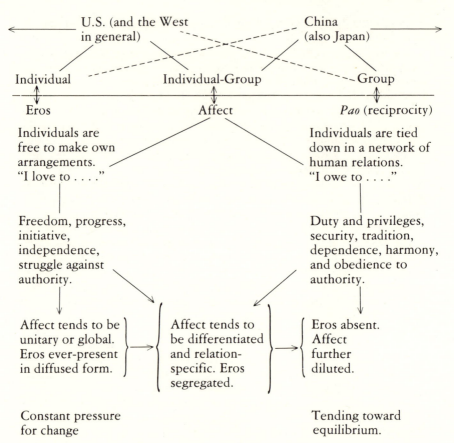

Constant pressure   Tending toward
for change   equilibrium.

ancestors . . ."; "My parents will be pleased . . . ." His ideals will include
such values as duty and privileges, security, tradition, dependence, harmony with fellow human beings and obedience to authority.

Probably this contrast is why Freud, a Western sage, thought that libido
is behind all human motivations and activities, and that civilization means
serious obstruction of individual psyche;[8] while Confucius, a Chinese sage,
laid so much emphasis upon *li* or propriety and said: "If the meat is cut
improperly one should not eat it" *(ke pu cheng pu shih)*.[9]

It is also interesting that these last characteristics in the relationship
among eros, affect, and *pao* are still analogous to that among Gold, money,
and credit instrument. Gold is the commodity relatively freest from
society and culture, and its holder has the most possibility of concluding
private transactions as he sees fit, regardless of the society and culture in
which he finds himself. That is why refugees prefer gold (and other
valuables), and peasants all over the world consider gold as the best hoard
if they feel insecurity.

Money is more tied to a particular society and its international valuation depends upon where that society stands economically with reference to a number of other societies, each of which also has currency of its own. In emergency the money of certain countries not seriously affected by any crisis (such as Swiss francs in Europe and U.S. dollars in various parts of the world) may be sought after as eagerly as gold, but the possibility of making absolutely private transactions with money is definitely more restricted than with gold. For one thing many illiterate peasants can recognize gold but not U.S. Dollars. The conversion of money into gold inevitably involves some institutional mechanism, and cannot be done in the final analysis between two private parties alone.

Any credit instrument is most absolutely tied to some institutional mechanism, and cannot be made use of without reference to it. In contrast to money, a credit instrument (such as drafts, letters of credit, etc.) is usually made in some sizeable denomination and not in a few dollars and cents. One cannot as a rule use it to pay retail shops. Even personal checks, which are half-way between money and full credit instruments cannot be freely used except when secured by personal acquaintances, check cashing agencies or certificaton. In other words credit instrument users are least free to engage in private two-party transactions. One cannot run away with it and use it with anyone at will.

DIFFERENCES BETWEEN *Pao* AND CREDIT INSTRUMENTS

However, here the parallel between eros-affect-*pao* on the one hand and gold-money-credit instrument on the other ends. The superiority of the credit instrument over gold and even money is that it can with efficiency link large groups of mankind economically. Its full use is both generative and an expression of a high degree of active economic unity within a society, and also among a group of participating societies in some larger economic structure (the most advanced results of which are such things as the Sterling Area, the European Common Market, etc.). If our analogy holds completely we should expect the Chinese, with their concept of *pao,* to show a much higher degree of unity and solidarity than Westerners, among whom no corresponding concept ever achieved such philosophical and ideological importance.

From one point of view this expectation is fulfilled. For example, compared with Hindu India, the Chinese society has achieved and maintained an impressive degree of political unity and solidarity through historical times (Hsu 1963:72–78). Furthermore, if we contrast the histories of the continent of Western Europe and of the continent of China, we find the latter to be marked by long periods of political unity and solidarity, while the former by disunity and internecine wars. This contrast is especially notable when we reflect on the fact that the racial and ethnic origins of what we call the Chinese today were probably at least as diverse as those of their present-day European brethren.

However, there are some drastic differences between the Chinese and the Westerners which cannot be accounted for by the factors discussed so far. For one thing the relationship between Chinese emperors and their subjects was always a negative one. When the emperor went anywhere, all windows along his route had to be shut tight, and no one except those in his entourage could appear on the street. To a lesser extent this calculated distance prevailed in a graded way between higher and lower officials, and between all officials and the people. This contrasts sharply with the kind of highly positive and emotional relationship between Western rulers and their subjects. I simply cannot think of any single ruler in Chinese history who enjoyed the kind of triumphal return that Richard the Lion Heart in front of his adulating subjects: men, women, and children, nor of one who was ever criticized by his official as was Queen Victoria at the hands of Gladstone, after the death of Prince Albert, for not appearing in public. There were few outstanding instances of officials who were devoted to their rulers to such an extent that they defended a falling dynasty to the death: Wen T'ienhsiang at the end of Sung and Shih K'e-fa at the end of Ming are two most famous examples. But there were many more who simply became high instruments for the new dynasty or retired from active work altogether. And once a dynasty or leadership seemed to be on the verge of collapse, a majority of the contenders for power or supporters of the existing regime tended to throw in their lot with the emerging new dynasty or leadership in order to be assured of a place under the sun. I regard this as strong evidence of lack of positive solidarity. This tendency was also helped by the fact that the new leaders usually ruled in the same way as the old: the personnel of the administration changed from time to time, but the nature of the administration did not. For this reason, I think, before 1912 China had no revolution, only revolt.

Side by side with this tendency was the fact that the Chinese never developed any significant cause-oriented groups or movements. Nearly all of their non-kinship groupings were local in nature. This included the most numerous *hui kuan* which Ping-ti Ho terms *landsmanns* organizations (Ho 1966). The only real exception is the organization of gangsters, such as the *Hung Pang* (Red Group) or the *Ch'ing Pang* (Blue Group). Occasionally these had been joined or formed by the *yu-hsia* or knights-errant mentioned before and occasionally they worked toward the restoration of a fallen dynasty. Dr. Sun Yat-sen's 1912 Revolution was materially helped by some of these groups in China and in the United States. But more often these were no more than gangstering in purpose, which sometimes took to violence for protection of their vested interests. The Tong wars of the early 20th century known in the United States were predominantly for the latter.

The gangster or knight-errant organizations shared the next characteristic of all Chinese non-kinship groupings: lack of missionary zeal. None of these organizations ever was primarily interested in improving some part of the society or of the traditional way of life. The knights-errant righted some individual wrongs from time to time. Some gangster organizations did side with rebels or revolutionaries. But none had developed a central philosophy or an ideology that it wanted to see prevail in all China or all the world, a fact we already examined in some detail in Chapter 3. Christianity and the Anthropologist. At best it was a restoring or holding operation. Usually it was not even that. And these were always outside the main stream of Chinese society.

Finally, even when the scholar-officials banded themselves together they hardly did better. The Tung-Lin movement of the late Ming dynasty was just such an example. It was dissatisfied with the way the government went but it did not have any clear-cut program (Hucker 1957:157). It discussed and objected. But above all it lasted less than twenty years (counting from 1604 A.D.). Only two other somewhat more clearly formulated but even briefer movements or controversies existed in Chinese history, each centered around an outstanding personality: Fan Chung-Yen (989–1052) (Liu 1957) and Wang An-Shih (1021–86), both of Sung dynasty.

Much has been written about Chinese religion in Western terms: so many Buddhists, Taoists and Confucianists, so many sects of Buddhism, etc. In fact a majority of Chinese cannot be described as Buddhists, etc. for they "belong" to no formal religious organization or temple. They will visit different places of worship or sacred spots as they feel the need to do so. The "sects" of Buddhism have no meaning to them for they hardly make any theological or even ritualistic differentiation when they do worship. The only religion that is common to all Chinese (except the small group of Christians but including most Moslems) is ancestor worship, membership of which is naturally limited to those related by patrilineal kinship. The few instances of religious persecution in China were different from their counterparts in the West both in quality and quantity (see Chapter 19, Chinese Kinship and Chinese Behavior). The fact is that few Chinese ever cared to die for such extra-kinship affiliations or causes and few Chinese in power found them relevant enough to the maintenance of their authority. Here again some esoteric religious practitioners, like the knights-errant, found it convenient at times to join in some rebellion. The Boxer Uprising which lasted less than one year was an outstanding example.

Contrast this picture with that of the West, with its Christian Movement, Protestant movement, seven Crusades, the nursing movement initiated by Florence Nightingale, the Inquisition and Witchhunting and burning, the democratic movement beginning with Magna Carta, Nazi and Fascist Movements, Communist Movement, Anti-vivisection Movement, Feminist Movement, Abolition Movement, nationalistic movement, etc., etc. All of them have spanned over long periods of time, and most of them can claim numerous martyrs and memberships of a magnitude no historical Chinese movements could even remotely match. Furthermore, sorcerers (sometimes designated witches, as in Witches Sabbath) were known to be organized with the express purpose of destroying orthodox creed and church, mostly Christianity. Is there any explanation for this enormous contrast?

DIFFUSION OF EROS

I submit that one basic factor for this contrast is to be found in a fact already mentioned previously, that, though affect has to be lifted from its erotic base for purposes of joining larger numbers of members in the Western society, eros cannot but be diffused in it. The extreme attempt to eliminate eros to the extent of its complete denial through the unnatural Virgin Birth is aimed at affect without eros. This is commensurate with a kinship content with exclusiveness as one of its dominant attributes. However, as we noted before, this complete denial is incompatible with a pattern of social life which is so close to the organic base because it centers in the individual. So what complete denial has done is to drive eros unerground so that the latter appears in disguise everywhere: in art, in literature, in drama, in social intercourse, in leader-follower relationship: "I am crazy about my boss"; "I love Kennedy." Even in the stronghold of this complete denial, namely the Christian church, nuns are said to be "married" to Jesus.

However, under the same impetus of the dominant kinship attribute of exclusiveness, eros is not likely to remain underground. In human relations no less than in relations among elements of the physical world, action generates reaction. The counter-movement of eros without affect has only in recent decades begun to erupt. A wholly new kind of sex-for-sex's-sake movies and plays and literature have now taken over the markets. We noted that this trend is more than the desire to establish "new bases of solidarity centering on the mechanism of affect"(Parsons 1971:427). In this configuration the role of the dominant attributes of sexuality in the Western kinship system has reinforced in each new generation of Westerners the Western preoccupation with eros. The attributes of volition and discontinuity facilitate the self-seeking activities of the individual especially when he attempts to negate or break with the past. A host of positive and related cultural values such as creativity, initiative and independence provide this orientation with ample support.

On the Chinese side their dominant kinship attribute of inclusiveness never was commensurate with absolute denial of eros in favor of affect. What it encouraged was proper human contexts for eros and for affect. In the prostitute-patron relationship naked eros is "natural." In the concubine-husband relationship naked eros may have a shared role with affect. In the wife-husband relationship naked eros tends to be overshadowed by affect, since the relationship between the married couple and his parents is more important in the Chinese scheme of things than all else.

Given its proper places where it can operate, in excess if the individuals choose to do so, eros has no necessity to go underground, nor to stage strong reactions toward a pattern of eros without affect. The Chinese dominant kinship attributes of authority and continuity do not encourage initiative, creativity, independence or a break with the past whether with reference to eros or to economic enterprise. And the attribute of asexuality has made it easier for the Chinese not to be troubled by sexuality where it is irrelevant. The Chinese "respect" their superiors, are "filial" to their parents, and do not consider eros to be an impediment to a normal relationship with the supernatural.[10] The question of "love" simply did not arise. Their gods did not "love" them, nor did they "love" their gods. "Marriage" to a god even in a symbolic sense was so absolutely incongruous in Chinese thought that such a suggestion would be ludicrous. Confucius' reply to a disciple who asked him to comment about gods and spirits was that one should "respect gods and spirits, but keep them at a distance."

Thus, for the Western man diffused eros is likely to be involved in any relationship however remote from it. The presence of diffused eros disables him from ever completely weaning affect from it. Consequently, affect in the Western world has remained global and not well differentiated because it is always more or less tied to its organic root. On the other hand, affect in the Chinese world has differentiated itself so greatly that in its extreme form, affect is thinned into pure *pao,* because they have been able to separate eros from it through the clear structuring of human relationships. Their affect tends to be much more removed from its organic root.

However, differentiation has its drawbacks. It can lead to specializations which are irreversible or at least difficult to interchange with each other. In biological evolution many species became extinct because they had painted themselves into a corner so to speak, by being over specialized in some direction so that they were no longer able to deal with changes in the physical environment or challenges of rival species. Although one cannot always speak with assurance of extinction or survival in the psycho-cultural sphere, in my view the relationship-specific differentiation of affect and further separation of affect into *pao* in the Chinese system possibly represents just such an example.

Since affect tends to be global and since eros is ever present, affect in the Western configuration can be more readily mobilized in any direction, and the diffused eros can always provide its direction with strong tendency to opposition or commitment. The global or unspecialized nature of affect enables the individual more readily to cross or to be freed from existing boundaries, and the ever-present eros propels him, once he has decided on his goal, with great emotional force. Therefore, he tends to be free to champion new causes, or to find new ways of championing old causes in or outside of his own society, with determination and a singularity of purpose that is truly astonishing to the non-Western man. If he cannot find Utopia he is likely to try to mold the world in his image, which means to build his own Utopia. This was why an aristocratic Beatrice Webb could decide to serve a period of apprenticeship in the squalor of East London, why a high-born Florence Nightingale could decide to face the hazards of the battlefield to care for the wounded in Crimea, why so many Spanish old settlers in Mexico could decide to join forces with the Indians to fight Spanish newcomers in a war of independence from their own society of origin, and why so many Westerners could decide, before steamships and planes made their travels easy and Western armed might secured their safety, to become missionaries in far away hostile lands for converting heathens to their God. I cannot help but see the tremendous hand of eros in the following account of St. Francis Xavier's arrival in Goa:

> The Society of Jesus has generally been noted for the erudition of its members, but it was founded by two men, Loyola and Xavier, who were essentially ecstatics, men of tremendous emotional force, for whom vision had a much greater value than learning. Both of them had been through a spiritual crisis, after which they abandoned the life of hunting, society, and war to which, the one as a Spaniard, and the other as a Basque, aristocrat, they had been born, and conceiving of the idea of the regeneration of Catholicism, menaced by its own internal weaknesses, the rise of the new learning, and the appearance of new heresies, they founded in 1540 the Society of Jesus, thereafter dividing the work, Loyola selecting Europe as his field, and Xavier Asia. The conversion of the whole Orient was Xavier's ambition, and he felt within him a sufficient force of soul to accomplish this miracle . . . . As Papal Nuncio he disembarked at the wharf of Goa in 1542. Many dignitaries of the Church were there to meet him and a large crowd. As he stepped ashore it was noticed that he was barefoot, that his gown was ragged and his hood of the coarsest stuff. Refusing to enter a palanquin and go in procession to the lodging prepared for him in the Archbishop's Palace, he desired them to point out the direction of the then hospital, a primitive institution compared to the later Jesuit hospital. Then motioning them to follow, he led the way on foot, his face turned up to Heaven, his lips moving in prayer. He had black eyes and a black beard and an air of wild happiness. When he came to the hospital, he began at once to wash the sores of the lepers. (Collis 1943:28–29)

The Chinese have produced no great religious man like St. Francis Xavier, nor any comparable to lesser Western missionaries and religious martyrs. In fact the Chinese for their great numbers and their long history of wars, conquests, expansion, turmoils, enormous influence and philosophical productivity, are spectacular for their complete absence of missionaries. Even their martyrs, for any cause whatever, were few and far between. In modern sociological jargon one might say that if in Western history the yield of missionaries and martyrs was at a rate of 100 per 100,000 population per year, the yield of missionaries in Chinese history would be at a rate of zero at any time, and its yield of martyrs would be at a near zero rate.

Since affect tends to be differentiated and since eros tends to be absent in most of its operating spheres, affect cannot be so readily mobilized in any direction, and the absence of eros tends to moderate any energy even after it is mobilized, so that attachment and commitment to non-traditional objectives (such as in non-kinship groupings and causes) will be mild. The relationship-specific affect simply cannot be easily conducted into channels in which they did not flow before. The absence of eros in such areas deprives the individual of the necessary emotional energy for urgency, and he tends to be cautious and therefore more rational. Large groupings can be formed by rulers and by force of territorial contiguity or livelihood, and the dominant kinship attributes of continuity (which favors prolongation of any relationship once it began), inclusiveness (which favors multiple affiliations) and authority (which favors no sharp break with the past) keep the society supplied with men who agree to play their part. But there is not likely to be great solidarity within such large groupings because the affect is not diffused with eros and therefore not so highly emotionally charged as in the case of the West.

The individual under such circumstances is much less free to champion new causes, or to find new ways of championing old causes or to seek Utopia by leaving his own society. He will not have the urge to make the world in hs own image. Instead he will try to find his best place in it. He would treat non-Chinese with respect if their conduct measured up to Chinese standards. But he is not likely to treat them with obvious contempt even if they do ot, for why should he bother with people whom he does not care to know better? In his relation-specific affect he is not much concerned with those who are very different from him. Not having rejected his parents, he does not have to avoid vertical relationship and seek only peers. He can view those lower than him with no urgency for their uplift in the same way he is seen by those whose station is above him. There is little personal involvement in others not covered by relation-specific affect.

This is why so few Chinese ever were seafarers and ever emigrated.[11] This is why Chinese rulers and public officials and heroes did not have to possess sex appeal, and were as a rule poor public speakers. This is why the age-old Chinese motto was "each man should only sweep the snow from in front of his own house." This is why the Chinese have never been known for missionary activities for the spread of Chinese religious creeds or of the Chinese way of life.

The network of *pao* or reciprocity can extend itself widely over large territories and sizeable populations as well as between societies. But it tends to become more and more a matter of pure business: exchange without sentiment. The central focus will be the correct thing to do since *pao* is socially required and its standard is culturally determined. It is inevitable that, in time, the correct thing to do tends to substitute for true sentiment on the part of the individual. The result is tremendous numbers and varieties of motion and of exchange, motivated by *pao* but little or no real involvement or zeal among the parties to the exchange. Lacking diffused eros the Chinese individual tends to confine his most intense involvement to kinship and a few other core relations. The following essay entitled "Drama and Human Life" from a recent issue of a major Taiwan newspaper confirms this analysis and even goes beyond it.

Last week at an evening party in honor of the delegates of the National Assembly, Delegate Yen Hsi-chen and her husband Mr. Hou Ch'ung-hsiu performed together the drama of Wu Chia P'o. (This is part of an opera which features prominently a hero who, after eighteen years of absence from home, returned to his patiently waiting wife. It is one of the most popular operas in China.) Miss Yen acted as the wife Wang, and Mr. Hou played the role of her husband Hsueh. The acting and singing were good and correct, and they became objects of much favorable comment afterwards.

After seeing this performance, many friends talked about it in the following vein: The acting of a husband and wife in real life, performing the roles of a husband and wife on stage, naturally would be good because the stage roles are identical to their real roles. These friends considered that this wa the most important reason why their performance was such a great success. At that time I only listened to these comments, but I did not enter into the discussion. Long afterwards, however I reflected on this matter on several occasions.

If we look at it in abstraction, drama on the stage is life, and life is also drama on the stage. The actual situation is that drama is compressed life, while life is drama prolonged. I have often seen movies recording track races. If the move is run at a higher speed, the human beings participating in the race run as fast as horses; but if the same movie is run at a slower speed, the human beings in the race look like snails. One is fast and one is slow, but this difference in speed is no more than that difference between drama on the stage and life as we actually live it from birth to death.

In the drama we have different roles: there are the roles of *sheng* (the male role), *dan* (the female role), *ching* (various kinds of warrior or petty official roles), *me* (auxiliary roles), and *ts'ou* (clown roles). Among the various roles in actual life we find *chun* (emperor, head-of-state, or chief administrator-of-organization), *ch'en* (subordinate official and secretary), *fu* (father), *tse* (son), *hsiung* (older brother), *ti* (younger brother), *fu* (husband), *fu* (wife), and *p'eng yu* (friend). The stage for performing drama is found in a theater. The stage for the performance of life is on the earth. The time span for a drama is usually one evening. The time span for the human drama of each man is one life. Actors and actresses describe what they do on stage as acting. Human beings describe what they do in life as reality. However, if we raise our sights and look at the world from a higher level, what real differences are there between the various roles of actual human life and the various roles of a drama? Is there a real difference between the earth and a theater? Is there any real difference between one lifetime and one evening? Is there any real difference between living and play-acting? Therefore, when I say that human living is play-acting, I think I have not made a big mistake.

If you want to make the drama good, you must have good actors and actresses who will each play male, female, military, auxiliary, or clown roles according to the requirements of his or her role. The singing and the acting must all be done exactly according to the requirements of the stage-craft and the song-craft. The beat and the rhythm and the rhyme must all be exactly correct. In the same way if you want harmony in human life, you must have the head administrator, the subordinate officials, the father, the son, the older brother, the younger brother, the husband, the wife, and the friends each acting according to his duties and obligations, and each expressing his sentiments as required by custom. It is said in the classic *Chung Yung* [often translated as the doctrine of the mean, but E. R. Hughes, the English student of Chinese philosophy, objected to it and prefers the title "the mean-in-action"] [Hughes 1943:1]: "To have emotions of pleasure and anger and sorrow and joy surging up, this is to be described as being in a state of equilibrium. To have these emotions surging up, but all in tune, this is to be described as a state of harmony. This state of equilibrium is the supreme foundation, this state of harmony the highway, of the Great Society (?civilization). Once equilibrium and harmony are achieved, heaven and earth maintain their proper positions, and all living things are nourished" [Hughes 1943:106]. This shows that even in the wider universe all heaven and earth and a myriad of things will be in their proper places and be productive if each part will act according to its role and the accepted rhythms and rules. How can a relatively small matter of a drama and a relatively short matter of a human life compare with these great events that occur in the entire universe?

Since human life is a drama, birth is then like the lifting of the stage curtain, and death is just like the closing of the stage curtain. In every drama, after the curtain is lifted, all performers must act according to the theme of the drama and in harmony with the rhythm and the beat—each acting his or her part out to the best of his or her ability as dictated by the dramatic role. No performer can be out of tune or out of step with the other performers or with the orchestra and go on his own. Also, each performer does not have to worry about what he physically cannot do or intellectually cannot reach. All each performer has to do is to carry out what he is supposed to do, according to the prearranged emerging drama. When he has done his best in this capacity, he is a great success and can bow to the audience and retreat behind the curtain with no regret.

The attention of a really good performer will be most concentrated on how he can do his best on the stage. He will not become pessimistic because of the tragic theme or tragic turn of events in the drama. His whole attention is on how in his performance he will execute just the required harmony, make just the expected gestures, and take just the correct steps according to the plan of the drama, but he will not become sorrowful just because the play is about to terminate. That kind of pessimism is misplaced. Those people who, in daily life, constantly worry about life and death not only do not understand human life, but they do not even understand drama.   (Shih Huan [pen name], in Chiung Yang Jih Pao [Central Daily News], Taipei, Taiwan, March 7, 1965)

The Western counterpart of this Chinese development is the continuous proliferation of closed groupings side by side with the great popularity of universalistic philosophies and creeds. Superficially these two are contradictory to each other. In fact they spring from the same source: affect underlined by diffused eros. This kind of affect ties the Western man to a romantic view of life in which the world must be all good or all bad. He must ally himself with all those who feel like him against all those who feel against him. He is happiest therefore when he participates in large, universalistic movements. But as his grouping grows larger and larger, he will be dissatisfied with its impersonality because he desires the personal touch (eros). So he seeks out some of those within the larger association with whom he can achieve a more intimate rapport. The result is a situation marked by perpetual fissionary tendencies and struggles in which all causes do not lack promoters with personal involvement or zeal. The Western man prides himself on "living," or "giving his all" to, whatever cause he is promoting. Having no kinship base where he can relax in security, he finds new "homes" as he moves along. The extraordinary popularity of counsellors and psychoanalysts in the West for individuals who cannot find personal fulfillment in life or in work bears witness not only to the large number of people who fail to find "homes," but also to the large number who never had an opportunity to develop a talent for close personal attention (eros). Any society, especially ones made up of millions of people, must be organized in terms of broad structures and functions which inevitably put its members into broad categories. The latter can never satisfy the needs of all or most individuals whose orientation is always close to the oganically based self.

Runaway Eros and Runaway *Pao*

The present trend in the West of indulgence in erotic thoughts and things is a reaction against its complete denial under Western Christian thought in general and the puritanical strain in particular. Such a counter movement is but one facet of an essential and recurring Western phenomenon: orthodoxy has always been countered by anti-orthodoxy in whatever field. In the present instance it may be properly described as a situation in wich eros has run away. It has run away not because "of the process of establishing new bases of solidarity centering on the mechanism of affect" (Parsons 1971:427) but because of the desire for eros *without* affect.

For a number of years the age for dating and going steady and marriage has been progressively lowered in the U.S. A number of factors have combined to induce this phenomenon, chief of which is the need for the security of having a group of one's own by giving one's declaration of independence from parents some substance. In a husband-wife dominated kinship where the attributes exclusiveness and discontinuity combine to make parents more intimate with each other than with either their own parents or their children, the latter are forced to find human security of their own and, in so doing, they cannot but be heavily influenced by the examples of what their parents have done with their grandparents.

The attribute of sexuality assures, of course, the continued importance of eros in their interaction, but that the more recent trend of "preoccupation with things erotic" is not due to "the process of establishing new bases of solidarity centering on the mechanism of affect" is clear from several points. First, as we already noted, in Western thought, especially Western Christian thought, solidarity through affect has always expressed itself in terms of denial of eros. Second, solidarity is not central to the recent trend of preoccupation with things erotic because the propagators and the practitioners of the new trend want *individualized experiences,* not group solidarity. Their extreme representatives are the hippies who look for experiences or happenings, whether via sex or lsd, unrelated to other experiences and happenings or individuals. The fact that often these people congregate together and seem to form some kind of groups is often an artifact of the non-hippies (including law enforcing agents) who usually see and treat them as a group.

Finally, it is highly inefficient to seek the maximization of eros through affect. Affect inevitably leads to larger social involvements so that other responsibilities (not the least of which are children and respectability) will inevitably curtail eros. Those who are preoccupied with eros, ancient or modern, have never been known for their devotion to marital or family life.

In Western history mistress keeping and other forms of extra-marital erotic activity (e.g., those of Boswell as depicted in *Boswell's London Journal)* were by and large the privilege of the leisurely upper crust.[12] Some of the less fortunate might frequent cheap houses of prostitution now and then, but they had not the time, the *savoir-faire,* and the financial means for achieving such erotic sophistication as drinking wine out of a cup inserted in the ballerina's slippers. In modern times we read about the activities of the international jet-set and of well-known characters in the world of show people. But the democratic process means that whatever once were the prerogatives of the few tend to diffuse among the many, by way of imitation and of demand, especially since the economic life of a majority has become so affluent. Eros has seemed to run away because the majority has now felt they should enjoy some of the things once limited to the few and they also have the time, the *savoir-faire* (thanks to mass media), and the economic wherewithal to make it possible.

The Chinese counterpart of runaway eros is runaway *pao* or reciprocity. The Chinese have always prided themselves on giving high value to *jen ch'ing wer* (human feelings). What they actually practice may not, as we have seen before, be calculated to satisfy individual human feelings but rather the requirements of *pao* or reciprocity. We also noted the fact that those who aspire to higher statuses usually try to outdo others by getting more people obligated to them and/or by more ample return gifts so that the recipients of their gifts become more obligated to them than they are to the recipients.

In traditional times those who were able to do this were limited to a minority of Chinese: those who fitted the gentleman class and a few others who were in a position to aspire to that status. Under the Western type of democratizing process the Chinese trend will inevitably be one of escalation of the circles and especially the burden of *pao* of reciprocity.

Here political accidents have presented us, at least for the time being, with two different Chinese societies: one on the Chinese mainland and the other in Taiwan. As yet we cannot say too much about the development in mainland China in this regard because it is new and because we have insufficient access to it. But what little we already know about it indicates that the overwhelming effort in the field of social reorganization centers in the direction of eliminating all forms of private *pao* (reciprocity) (e.g., by reduction or elimination of wedding, funeral, birthday and new year celebrations and of kinship duties and obligations; by making promotion through individual ties difficult) in favor of one form of public *pao,* first to the Communist Party and then to Chairman Mao Tse-tung (see Chapter 19). I make no claim that this hypothesis of what is developing in China is the only truth. I merely emphasize that if we make this hypothetical assumption we shall find the profuse public homage to Mao and the near sacred importance accorded his little red book more understandable.

In Taiwan, a similar form of public *pao* is first claimed for the Kuomintang or Nationalist Party and then to President Chiang Kai-shek. It is not generally realized by Westerners that whenever Chiang is mentioned in newspapers and magazines he is not referred to by his full name but always as "President Chiang" or the "President" or the "Leader" and this designation is always given an elevation in the text. Furthermore Chiang's birthday and his late mother's birthday are both occasions for national celebration. All of these usages are in line with traditional Chinese homage accorded to the emperor.

One problem is that the social organization as a whole in Taiwan has not been under the kind of attack or process of drastic reorganization as it has been on the mainland. The public *pao* therefore goes hand in hand with myriad forms of private *pao* among the individual citizens.

A degree of democratization inevitably goes on in every country of the post-World War II world regardless of the form of its government.[13] With it more individual citizens in any society tend to want more of whatever the upper crust of that society enjoyed before the process began. Some of these rising demands may be totally contrary to democratic ideals, or uneconomical. For example, in Hindu India lower castes who used to take widow remarriage as a matter of course have been known to forbid such remarriage as a caste-raising device. Other low castes who had not practiced the crushing dowry system for their daughters (instead some of them used to require bride prices from the families of the grooms) have now decided to institute this practice which was the economic downfall of many a Brahman family (Hsu 1963:20–22). So more Chinese in Taiwan today aspire either to a wider personal circle of *pao* or the position of having others more obligated to them than they are to the others.

On top of all this, the latter process is aggravated by the fact that two million or more mainland evacuees who came to Taiwan after 1949 have left most of their relatives and others in their *pao* circles behind so that they tend to look for substitutes for these vacant roles.

The combined result of these factors is an enormous escalation of the burden of *pao,* as expressed in the following essay entitled *"Li* (Propriety) Means Reciprocity" from Taiwan's *Central Daily News:*

Recently we have a new term in our society: *"hung huo"* (red disaster). Every inhabitant in the metropolis as a rule receives several red invitations every month. Some receive more, and others receive less. In particular the white collar workers and bureaucrats in large organizations often have to expend their entire monthly salaries on *ying ts'ou* (maintenance of propriety). This is most likely true during an astrologically propitious month when all kinds of happy events take place. Of course, those who are on the receiving end of gifts must invoke the old Chinese saying *"ch'ueh tzu pu kung"* (it is impolite to refuse); but those who are at the giving end often have to act according to the Chinese proverb *"yin ch'ih mao liang"* (spending salary not yet earned). For the wealthy this is not serious. The old Chinese proverb is, "One becomes enamored of propriety after getting wealthy." But for those who are not so affluent this is disastrous. What else can they do except to go around declaring how they love to be hit on the head?

Formerly, although people were in the habit of sending many invitations for numerous purposes, they still observed some rules. Now the situation has developed in such a way that invitations are dispatched to those with whom the sender has spoken only once upon a time a few words somewhere by chance. Furthermore, if a man is getting married himself and he sends out the invitations, this is still excusable even to those whom he has met briefly just once. But invitations are now sent on the pretext of the marriage of one's sister's daughter, or of one's mother's brother's son. Even worse are those invitations for tea which will take place in Kao Hsiung to people located in Taipei (a distance of about 200 miles). The addresses of old acquaintances who have not been seen for ten years will be tracked down, and invitations sent. In truth, one gets the feeling that between Heaven and Earth there is literally no escape. For those who have received the invitations, the dilemma is a bad one. They do not really want to send a gift. On the other hand they also are afraid of offending the senders by not doing so. After long deliberation, what they must do is eat less food so that they can manage a small gift even when they know that they have no chance to enjoy the dinner or tea that is indicated on the invitation because it is given so far away.

The Chinese people are well known for their propriety *(li)*. They like to talk about it. They also love face. Especially if a man wants to operate successfully in the society and being much in demand he must maintain this propriety everywhere. Superficially, exchange of congratulatory and condolence gifts is certainly in accordance with traditional custom, a custom which indicates that human beings feel deeply for each other. In reality, those whose sole income is supplied by salaries cannot bear the burden and must go outside of their regular sources for supplementary cash. This then imperceptibly becomes a major stumbling block to the abolition of corruption in bureaucracy. The result is that instead of being a custom symbolizing strong human feelings, the human feelings get thinner every day.

The ancients say, "Propriety means reciprocity—when you only receive and do not give this is not propriety; when you only give and do not receive, this is also not propriety." There is no question that those who have received gifts in the past must reciprocate with gifts when future occasions arise. Among close relatives and very dear friends, it is reasonable to reciprocate with money. Also, in the case of friends who are really poor—who need, for example, money for the funerals of their parents or money to help out with their daughters' dowries—gifts are not ony reasonable, but also necessary. Outside of such circumstances, we really should follow the Confucian dictum that, "in the matter of propriety, extravagance is not as good as frugality."

Our Ministry of Interior once proposed a kind of "form letter of propriety" for precisely the purpose of taking the place of the gifts on such occasions, since gifts have become such a difficult problem to so many people. But it never worked. It has not checked the tide of this terrible custom. Maybe many people feel that their face is much more important and that therefore they do not want to appear to be so cheap as to respond to such invitations merely with a letter of propriety expressing their congratulatory or condolence sentiments, but send no gift. We might actually follow the example of the Americans. Let us manufacture many different kinds of beautiful cards which can be used for marriages, for funerals, for birthdays, for promotions, for births of babies, for graduation, for a variety of expressions of sympathy, etc. We can have all kinds of cards printed. What we should do in the case of all those people who have no special relations with us is to respond with a card. In this way we shall not have to suffer from economic wounds, and we shall also have taken care of the Chinese custom of "propriety means reciprocity."

Those who want to dazzle other people by the size of their circles of social intercourse can put these cards into albums. They can also show everybody those albums whenever they have an occasion to do so. Those who want merely to exchange greetings with friends, such cards can show that they are both well. To deal with those who want to use such occasions for collecting money, these cards can express the respondent's sentiment that "my heart is willing, but my flesh is weak." Even those who want to use such occasions for conspicuous consumption may be satisfied. After mailing the card, the respondent and his entire family can descend upon the celebrant's house for a feast. I am sure that they will all be pleased.

In this way maybe we can keep the "red disaster" somewhat in check. I hope that the Ministry of Interior and the printing merchants will give this suggestion some earnest thought.   *(Central Daily News,* June 11, 1965)

This writer speaks only about what escalation of *pao* does to the individual economically and barely alludes to its link with bureaucratic corruption. The latter is but a part of a larger configuration of its consequences in which valuable time and energy are expended on unproductive ends while all kinds of private and public needs (not the least of which is efficiency in governmental machinery) remain unmet.

INTERNAL IMPETUS TO CHANGE

So democratization of eros has led to the profuse and widespread preoccupation with things erotic and demand for pornography, near-pornography, and for such self-gratification devices as LSD in the name of depicting the reality or of expanding inner freedom. But democratization of *pao* has led to suffocating social relationships with their endless rounds of feasting, gift-making, courtesy calls, etc. which run the danger of stifling all initiative in the name of propriety or the concern for human feelings (*jen ch'ing wer*). In each case the end results follow the initial premise, and no amount of attack on the latter is liable to change the course of its development unless something is also done about the former.

However, social reform is outside the scope of our analysis. One last point that may be of interest to the reform-minded concerns differential implications of the eros orientation versus the *pao* orientation with reference to social cultural change. Over the centuries every society or culture has undergone more or less change. The differences among them in this regard are:

(1) Some societies and cultures have changed at a faster pace than others;
(2) Some societies and cultures have responded to external pressures by adaptation more expeditiously than others; and
(3) Some societies and cultures have exhibited more internal impetus to change than others.

What concerns us here is the third of these differences.

While all societies and cultures must rely upon affect as the chief agent for social solidarity to deal with stability or change, we have seen that Western society tends to press it toward the eros end of the spectrum while Chinese society tends to press it toward the *pao* end of it.

If Parsons' Freudian based main thesis is on the right track, as we have good reason to think that it is, that the role of erotic impulse in socialization and the brother-sister incest taboo are the two basic ingredients at the very origin of human society and culture, then those societies and cultures which are closer to the eros end cannot but possess greater internal potentiality for reform and change than those which are closer to the *pao* end.

Organized power or tyranny may be able to initiate large projects and movements and force the outward compliance of sizeable populations, but the execution, continuance and especially expansion of such projects and movements must depend upon the willing skill and wholehearted commitment on the part of a majority of the individuals in their support. Otherwise the projects and movements will inevitably dwindle and disappear as happened to those begun by many a despot in world history.

A society and culture with its affective base of solidarity leaning toward eros will not only supply more individuals ready for active and zealous involvement in projects and movements begun by others, but even more individuals who will initiate with determination new projects and movements themselves. In this process the husband-wife dominated kinship system is a suitable human machinery to produce and reinforce the psychological orientation for it generation after generation. This kinship system perpetually ejects the individual from his family of origin so that he has to find new groups for his social needs.

The father-son dominated kinship system of the Chinese is equally a suitable human machinery to produce and reinforce the psychological orientation for a society and culture with an affective base of solidarity leaning toward *pao*. While this system will supply more individuals ready and willing to maintain the status quo and to intensify whatever maintenance of that status quo requires, it will not produce many dissidents, even fewer who have new ways to offer and are willing to go to extreme lengths to fight for their realization.

Escalation of eros may generate violence, crime, and dislocation but also continuous pressures for reform and change. Being extremely strong by nature and having been nursed in a kinship system with exclusiveness and discontinuity as two of its dominant attributes, these pressures will lead to authoritarian tendencies and thereby generate authoritarian tendencies in its opponents for self defense.

Escalation of *pao* may impress outsiders by its flurry of ostentatious courtesy and gestures of conspicuous solicitude, but also lead to stultifying intensification of existing customs with little opportunity for true innovation. Being imbued with no eros and having been associated with a kinship system with inclusiveness and continuity as two of its dominant attributes, the intensification merely generates a similar intensification all around.

Eros, since it is at the very core of the human psyche, can be counted on to be a fountainhead for new demands for continuous evolution of culture. There will not be many dull moments. In the last analysis the human psyche must be regarded as the origin of all human culture in the first place.

On the other hand *pao*, since it is far removed from eros, is not the center of human creativity. It can serve to maintain the status quo, to intensify it or to proliferate it, but not to change its course. Probably this is why so many elements in the patterns of life of the eros-oriented culture of the West have been so attractive to so many individuals reared in cultures not so oriented, including the *pao*-oriented ones of China and Japan. Of course Western power of conquest has had a great deal to do with this attraction since the latter part of the 18th century. But when the colonizer-colonized relationship is terminated the fascinating thing is that many Western cultural elements have diffused so widely. In this picture we are not merely speaking of material products such as automobiles, electrical appliances, box-spring beds and central heating, although these also have made the life of many an individual (the organic base) in the non-Western world more comfortable than what his own culture provided. Even more impressive is the spread of universal education (which gives more people a chance of getting what was available before only to the few), the ideas of freedom and equality (which enable the underdogs to stand up to their superiors), the "Folk-Rock" music, chaotic and individualistic dances from the old "Twist" to the newer "Fish" and the "Swim," and of course the fashion of self-choice in marriage.

With reference to the last point one anthropologist observes:

Very few societies leave it to individuals who are to be married to decide for themselves. The near-anarchy of American practice in this regard is most exceptional, although it represents a discernibly *increasing trend* in many parts of the world, as the acids of "modernity" corrode the "old kinship bonds." (Hoebel 1966:344) (italics mine).

In the light of our analysis, the most important element in that nebulous complex "modernity" is probably eros and the most important element in that well-known anthropological complex "kinship bonds" is *pao* or some sort of reciprocity. When *pao* meets eros, there is a good probability that eros will win in the long run.

NOTES

1. According to Western usage the terms eros and sex are often distinguished. This is rooted in a Western cultural peculiarity which we shall attempt to clarify. For the time being the reader is asked to treat these two terms synonymously.

2. In China this deity is one of the household gods together with the Kitchen God, Gate Gods, God of Joy and Bliss, etc. I am not aware of any special temple dedicated to him. In Japan this deity is commonly known as Fukurokuju or Fukurojin (old man of blessing) and as one of the Shichi Fuku Jin (or Seven Gods of Blessing). The other six are: Daikoku, Ebisu, Bisamon, Benten (the only female in the group), Hotei, Jurojin. I am also not aware of any shrine specially dedicated to Fukurojin. On the other hand Daikoku, but especially Ebisu, is honored in many shrines. The latter is variously thought to be God of Prosperity, of Trade, of Sailors, of Fishing, etc. One of the largest shrines dedicated to this god is the Ebisu Jinja in Nishinomiya, near Osaka. A set of statues of Shichi Fuku Jin is placed next to the Butsudan in many households.

3. The central theme of the Virgin Birth is, of course, a denial of both. But the psychological link between explicit denial of and preoccupation with the same object may be amply illustrated by the following Chinese tale. A poor farmer suddenly came to a fortune of 300 ounces of silver. There being no banks or safety deposit boxes in the village, he dug a deep hole in his backyard and buried them. Still fearing that someone would discover the treasure he put this sign beside the hole: "There are no 300 ounces of silver here."

4. The passage concerning Noah's self-eroticism is generally deleted or changed into more neutral statements in the modern versions of the Bible containing such expressions as "and became drunk and lay uncovered in his tent," "And Ham . . . saw the nakedness of his father, and told his two brothers outside." If these newer statements were correct, we should be greatly puzzled as to why the brothers should be so very ashamed of their father's naked body and why Noah should be so very angry with Ham, who merely told his two brothers about his nakedness, which they covered with a garment.

5. Two even more restricted virtues are *chen* and *chieh*. Both of these are virtues specific to a wife toward her husband, but not vice versa. The former concept refers to a woman's faithfulness to her husband; the latter to a widow who will not remarry.

6. A Chinese saying is: "If injury is recompensed with injury, when will mutual retaliation come to an end?" (quoted by Yang 1957:293).

7. Outside these two forms there is the approach of what Yang describes as knights-errant (*yu hsia*) who, amongst other characteristics, may "even rejct" any reward for favors given. But these knights-errant were generally outside of the main stream of Chinese society.

8. Some Western psychiatrists and analysts have considered Freud to be wrong in this.

9. Confucius made very little reference to sex and never said anything positive about it. His most famous disciple, Mencius, who paid much more attention to "human nature" (*hsing*) stated in a formal interview that food and sex are perfectly natural desires. For this and other reasons I. A. Richards comments that "it is possible that Mencius anticipates some of the educative prescriptions of Freud" (Richards 1932:75). Creel reports having heard a "practicing psychiatrist comment, after reading some of Mencius' psychological passages, that he seemed to have anticipated some of the theory of modern psychiatry" (Creel 1953:89). I can confirm the latter from the views of several psychiatrists. However, even Mencius' main thrust was fundamentally different from that of Freud. Mencius believed in the goodness of human nature. And he laid great emphasis upon the proper relationship between ethics and psychology.

10. Women are not supposed to go to temple worship during their monthly period. Many women wash themselves from head to toe before going for such an occasion. During a cholera epidemic when the help of all gods is urgently prayed for, the whole village or community is supposed to abstain from sex, meat and entertainment. But all this either has to do with cleanliness or with impressing the supernatural with the sincerity of the immediate request.

11. Superficially this statement seems questionable, since the Chinese populations in Malaya, Thailand, Indonesia, Philippines and Vietnam are considerable. However, when we measure the number of Chinese abroad in terms of Chinese in China we find the ratio of the former very small indeed. On the other hand, the number of Europeans outside Europe is larger than that in Europe. See Chapter 19.

12. It may be, of course, that they were also the only ones who kept journals.

13. Here I am strictly speaking in comparative terms. For example, the Russian society under the Communist regime is much more democratic than under the Czarist regime, though the former is not as democratic as the United States society under either major party.

Part V

Culture Change, Face and Fancy

Introduction

During the nineteenth century, Westerners saw China as a prize example of the unchanging East. Many good-hearted Europeans and Americans who cared at all tried to assist China and the Chinese toward some change. And quite a few Chinese themselves, especially the elite, were no less concerned with or did something about changing her traditional ways.

The imperial Manchu dynasty was toppled. In its place came a republic in 1911, with its two houses of parliament. A constitution and a new system of legal code and new courts were promulgated and instituted. Footbinding and slavery were abolished; coeducation and self-choice in marriage were introduced. But the changes were not easy in coming, nor did they spread in all parts of the country at the same pace. In the 1940s, when most women under forty-five had natural feet in urban areas and the coastal provinces, I saw little pre-teen girls with bound feet in the districts of Yunnan province bordering Tibet and Burma.

"Some Problems of Chinese Law in Operation Today" (Chapter 17) describes and analyzes the distance between the spirit of the new laws and the ideas in the minds of the people. "A cholera Epidemic in a Chinese Town" (Chapter 18) is a case study of a different kind of distance, that between the scientifically ascertainable reality and a community's preference. For even though surefire methods of Western origin for the prevention and cure of the killer sickness, the local people still carried on their own age-old ritual activities to counter it. Some of them did take to the new measures, but the latter only coexisted with the ritual activities, not replacing them.

The cholera epidemic central to this case study occurred in 1942 in interior China. But over thirty years later (1972) I found essentially the same ritual activities (albeit on a much larger scale) in the New Territories section of Hong Kong for another killer epidemic—bubonic plague. The difference between the two events? Whereas the earlier ritual activities were staged during a raging epidemic, the later ritual activities were staged some one hundred years after it. The residents of New Territories promised the gods who helped them to eradicate the bubonic plague a century ago that they would stage the same ritual activities in gratitude every ten years ever afterwards. And 1975 happened to be the end of one such ten-year cycle—this, in spite of their much higher literacy rate, far better public health conditions, many more easily accessible clinics and hospitals, and instant communication with any part of the world (see Hsu, *Exorcising the Trouble Makers: Magic, Science, and Culture,* 1984).

The Communist Revolution of 1949 appeared to have brought about many abrupt changes on many fronts. In fact while some Westerners were impatient about the lack of change in China before it, others have since

1949 complained that China moved too fast. A well-known philosopher expressed this Western concern in the following vein:

> The Communists have done their best to make the time in which we live a desperate and tragic one. For how tragic it is that these glorious civilizations which are Asia and Islam, now in resurgence, cannot draw at their leisure in their own way upon the equally glorious civilizations of the Hebrew-Christian, Greco-Roman, modern liberalized West, and even Karl Marx's original thought, without having their hands and our hands forced by Moscow and Peking Communists.　(F.S.C. Northrop 1952)

The philosopher obviously forgot that it was the industrialized and aggressive West which first began the hand forcing of China and the rest of the world. But that is beside the point here. "Chinese Kinship and Chinese Behavior" (Chapter 19) shows that although more drastic changes have occurred in China since 1949, they still fall short of the desired goal of national greatness via rapid industrialization.

The main stumbling block is the Chinese kinship system that so much more easily satisfies the individual's PSH requirements (see Chapter 13) than its American counterpart. This pattern leads to three consequences. First, most individuals find it unnecessary to forge strenuously ahead on their own for a feeling of fulfillment. Second, therefore, compared with Westerners as a whole, most Chinese tend to be less venturesome, less curious about the larger world around them and less likely to be involved in distant causes, especially abstract causes.

Finally, even if some exceptional Chinese individuals are more venturesome, more curious, and more desirous of involvement in distant causes, their concern for their kin and community—and above all their privileges, duties, and responsibilities—cannot but restrain them. For example, the Honorable Wang Yun-wu, one-time premier in the nationalist government under Chiang Kai-shek, gave the following detail in an autobiography about his youthful years. As a young man he came into contact with the revolutionaries, then underground and led by Sun Yat-sen, for the overthrow of the Manchu government. But after due consideration he decided not to endanger himself by joining its ranks because his widowed mother was old and he was the only son. The psychology of this distinguished modern Chinese was consonant with what happened (actual or legendary) at the beginning of the first century A.D. when Kuang Wu was fighting rival claimants to the throne. The widowed mothers of several of his best lieutenants reportedly committed suicide so that their sons could devote themselves to Kuang Wu's cause, who then successfully defeated all opposition and became the first emperor of the later Han Dynasty (25–220 A.D.).

The kinship system was the primary reason of why the Chinese society has throughout its long history not developed any significant secondary groupings outside the kinship and locality domains. Consequently an infra-structure to link the individual with the nation was absent when

Western invasion made industrialization and nationalism imperative. The basic problem of China under the new government since 1949 has been to create and nourish such an infra-structure. And the new government's answer was the urban and rural communes. The communes are new, without precedence in Chinese culture. Whether they can generate adequate loyalty and devotion to wean the individual psychologically away from his traditional loyalty and devotion to the kinship and locality remains to be seen.

From the Western point of view, the kinship systems of Japan and China are similar in their extent and intensity. This is understandable since most Westerners, under the ideology of individualism, usually grow up to look for freedom from all restraints, especially those of their parents, not to speak of other kinsmen. In fact Western students tend to see India's kinship system in the same light. It is only when we resort to careful comparisons between China and India (Hsu 1963) and China and Japan (Hsu 1975) that the finer but vital differences among them emerge.

A systematic assessment of the kinship systems of China and Japan and how their differences are related to the growth of the *iemoto* in Japan is not our concern here. Suffice it to say that *iemoto,* in my view, gave Japan the infra-structure to make her transition from a traditional economy to large-scale modern industrialization with much greater ease and rapidity than China. Chapter 20, *"Iemoto* and Industrialization," explains and demonstrates this hypotehesis.

The impetus for large-scale modern industrialization came from the West to Japan, as it did to China. But in contrast to China, Japan had an indigenous human organization to serve as its operating basis.

The exogenous science and technology for large-scale modern industrialization were new, but the nature of the human links and the affect that nourish, maintain and expand those links were old.

Finally in Chapter 21, "Roots of the American Family: From Noah to Now," we find evidence that in spite of rapid technological, economic, and social changes—including escalating divorce rates and galloping crimes of violence—there is an intrinsic continuity between the America of today and that of long ago.

The fundamental link is the American affective pattern that guides American views of the world as well as human relations. From the initial insistence on independence from parents, Americans have come to glorify change. That psychology leads Americans to equate improvements in our physical environment with those of the human arena. Since the former are more easily effected, and at any rate more obvious (higher GNP, new consumer goods, more powerful accelerators, landing on the moon, and so forth) than the latter (reduction of marital breakdown, prevention of violence, elimination of racial and religious prejudice, tension and strife, and so forth), Americans often regard successes in the physical world as evidence or cause for social improvement.

What we have yet to see is that rugged individualism makes the American human scene transitory (for the transitory nature of American human relationships, see Warren G. Bennis and Philip E. Slater, *The Temporary Society,* 1968, and Philip E. Slater, *The Pursuit of Loneliness,* 1970). That transitoriness makes it imperative for the individual to be bent on ruthless exploitation of and acquisition in the physical world for his psychosocial homeostasis (PSH). The changes in the physical world (new technologies, more lethal weapons, space) are indeed new, but the changes in the human scene are old, in fact as old as between the biblical Noah and his sons.

17

Some Problems of Chinese Law in Operation Today

I

It is easy to follow some of the popular misconceptions current in certain quarters of the western public and say or write something in the nature of the following (Fitzgerald 1941:77–78):

> In practice . . . the law is never invoked, and not being called upon to act, the officials take no steps, even when the facts are well known, the subject of gossip on all sides, and the offender and his would-be bride living at hand within easy reach. No one wants the law and its officers poking their noses into private business. . . . If manslaughter was done, a reluctant government would be forced to take action, but it is fairly plain that no one expects this to happen. Thus in civil disputes, and even in criminal cases where the motive is not robbery or banditry, the government remains passive and the law is allowed to slumber. The Chinese government, whatever the theory of the reformers, is in practice still actuated by the Taoist principle of "non-action," preferring to leave the people to govern themselves which they do very well, and which is all they ask.
>
> Even in cases where the crime is in no sense a family matter the action of the law is reluctant and the possibilities of compromise infinite.

The author of these passages appears as though speaking from plenty of data either available to him in statistics or obtained through long years of residence. But what are the facts cited in support of such assertions?

    1. A youth who is engaged to a girl eloped with another girl who is also engaged to someone else. The girl's family starts a chase. But they never intend to find the couple; all parties concerned will finally be pacified through negotiation. The law is indifferent to all of these happenings.

    2. A young man of good family and education impelled by some impulse committed a series of burglaries, not because he was poor and needed money, for the objects he stole were of little worth. On one occasion in a struggle to escape he stabbed the householder in the leg with a small penknife. He was arrested and put in gaol. Negotiations went on between his family and the victim's family. Finally the matter was settled in the following manner: The victim gave up prosecution; six men of substance were found to guarantee the young criminal's behaviour; the same guarantors would also undertake to provide the youth with some means of livelihood. (76–80)

This chapter was originally published in *The Far Eastern Quarterly*, III, No. 3, May 1944, pp. 211–21.

Any one who has glanced over present-day Chinese law will realize that neither fact proves the author's point. Present-day Chinese law would not of course interfere in the first case. In fact under Chinese law adultery by mutual consent is not criminal behaviour, and will only be a legal offence when the injured party (the woman herself, her husband or his wife or her parents) takes action, or if the woman is under 14 years of age. The treatment of the first case is, therefore, in perfect accordance with modern Chinese law.

The second case cited is equally irrelevant to the point in question. The author has not indicated the age of the young offender but even if he is not a minor, the result is again in harmony with the provisions in modern Chinese law, for it is stated in the legal code:

> For injury to other person's body or health, imprisonment or hard labour for three years or less, or a fine of one thousand dollars or less will be imposed.
>
> But this crime is only prosecuted when the victim takes legal action against the offender.   (Vol. II, chap. 23)[1]

II

During the years 1942 and 1943 the present writer undertook a period of research in the Tali area, where Mr. C. P. Fitzgerald, the author of the afore-quoted work, previously made his studies, and has been able to observe certain features of Chinese law in action, which is, in the main, governed neither by the principle of "non-action" nor by the principle of "face" as Fitzgerald would insist (77, 80), but primarily characterized by the fact that much of the law is at variance with the customary rules of conduct of the people. The spirit of modern law demands uniformity; the customs of a land so vast and so poorly equipped with means of communication as China are bound to be highly diversified. The law has abolished concubinage; the people regard concubinage as a matter of course. The law prescribes that no private individual has the right to commit violence against any other individual; the people regard beating of slave-girls and apprentices as something inherent in the order of nature. The laws says that social or sexual intercourse between unmarried adults is entirely their own concern; the people look upon any unrelated two persons of different sex having close contact with each other as having committed adultery and are to be treated as such, with violence sometimes endangering the lives of both parties.

The following is one of many cases in the writer's possession illustrating the distance between the spirit of law and ideas entertained by the people:

Case in Tali District Court, 1941
Plaintiff: Mrs. Yang, J.T., 27 years of age.

Defendant: Mr. Yang, J.T., farmer.
Plaintiff's Statement of Her Case:

This is an appeal for divorce. In the time of the Republic one husband can only have one wife, but Mr. Yang has five wives. The plaintiff is but the fourth wife. When Yang got his fifth wife from Hsiakuan he had apprehensions that the plaintiff would stop him, so he acted in advance by hiring men and women to lock up the plaintiff's bedroom and then pulled and pushed her back to her mother's home. Before the plaintiff married Yang, Yang told her that he had no wife. That was why the plaintiff married him. The plaintiff only found out too late, after having entered his house, that he had three other wives, and that she was merely the fourth concubine. The plaintiff then only blamed herself for her own fault and hoped that the preordained ill-fate would thus be worn off. But Yang's licentious desires were never satisfied and he went to Hsiakuan on the 17th of the seventh month (Lunar Calendar) to take a fifth concubine. Since the arrival of this licentious woman, Yang has completely ignored his wife and the other concubines and regards them as cattle and slaves. The wife, seeing the circumstances, divorced him at once. Even the third concubine also decided to divorce him because of the obvious inequality. . . . When he and his hired hands chased the plaintiff out of his house they did not allow her to take any of her belongings, like gold rings and luggage. The plaintiff is not "fermented fish or rotten meat" [meaning that she is still good for remarriage], there is no reason why she should stay with such a house. The plaintiff knows Your Honour's high sense of justice and hopes that you will have pity on her, will punish that Yang, J.T. and grant her a divorce, etc.

Defendant's Statement of His Case:

The defendant is now 30 years of age. . . . He appeals to Your Honor to punish a cunning woman who left her husband and forced him to be descendant-less, in order that the good customs of the country will be preserved. At thirty the defendant is still without a son. Under this pressure he married the niece of Mr. Li (i.e. the plaintiff) of the same village as the concubine in the year 1937. The defendant thought then that the good union would last forever. But her mother, who is cunning in nature and bloodthirsty at heart, had other plans. Her mother has four daughters one of whom was married to a Mr. Wang (C.T.) of T'ao Yuan village. Her mother then instigated her daughter to divorce that husband. Mr. Wang could not do anything but allow her to divorce him. Her mother was very pleased [implying that the mother could get more money by remarrying her divorced daughter] and then arranged to marry that daughter again to someone else. She has won once and she is now hoping for another victory. That was exactly why she had since sometime ago started quarrels with the defendant. She first sued the defendant at the village headman's office for a divorce. Her request was refused. It could not be otherwise. The headman realized that the defendant being heir-less, was perfectly right in taking a concubine in the hope of getting a son. But the defendant was powerless against this concubine's cunning and tricky mother who in the second month of this year took her daughter home and refused to let her come back to the defendant's house, in spite of his repeated requests for her return. Moreover, the same old woman induced the mother of another woman, H.H., whom the defendant married, to take H.H. away from the defendant too. Thus the defendant, from the position of being the husband of a wife and a concubine dropped to that of a bachelor. His feelings are hurt beyond measure and his pains are great, What is worse, the defendant has an old mother of sixty years of age who day in and day out hopes that the defendant will have a son. Her anxiety was so acute that she could not sit down or sleep well. Under such circumstances the defendant married a girl Y.P. from Shen Chi village outside the east gate of Tali, as a concubine. This marriage was arranged under the auspices of the defendant's father and certified by middlemen and gifts of good faith. Such a marriage is perfectly natural. The ancients said: "When one is thirty and is still son-less, one ought to marry a concubine." They also said: "One man married nine wives." The plaintiff not only left the defendant in the second month of the year but also accused him of having locked up her bedroom and chased her out in the sixth month of the year. What an absurdity. The defendant has the courage and purity of heart to face the heaven or gods and ghosts. Everybody in Yun Ch'ang village knows the reputation of the plaintiff's mother. Her by-name is "Secretly Retain Half Inch" [this by-name is not comprehensible to the present writer]. She is connected with any evil or mischief in the village and is an unspeakable woman. The defendant married her daughter but unfortunately did not know soon enough about this old woman's character. This is his own fault which has caused him great suffering. Fortunately Your Honour has come to this area. Your Honour loves the people and always insists on straightening out wrongs amongst the people, however remote they are situated from the central seat of your court. That is why the defendant has decided to appeal, in tears, to Your Heavenly Honour to pass the judgement of returning the plaintiff to her lawful husband, so that the defendant will again enjoy a harmonious union and a permanent peaceful family life. The cunning old woman will then fully realize that to create more trouble will be useless. . . . If this end is attained, not only the defendant will feel extremely grateful to Your Honour but his descendants in the generations to come as well . . . etc.

Three weeks after presenting the above statement the defendant, after having been admonished by the judges in court for his ignorance and illegal practice of taking concubines, became apprehensive and presented the following second statement:

The defendant *k'out'ous* three times before Your Honour, and kneels before Your Honour to wait for your honourable and quick judgment so that he will not be entangled . . . . In the last trial Your Honour asked for the presence in court of the defendant's concubine Y.P. [the fifth] for information. But my concubine Y.P. wrote back to say that the case did not concern her and she therefore could not come to court. The defendant begs Your Honour not to take offence at this refusal. The defendant has lately conferred with his own parents, and after careful thinking over has come to the conclusion that it will probably be useless to force the plaintiff's return to him. The defendant married that woman because of the need of an heir. Maybe her refusal to return is preordained fate. Under the circumstances any further pressure applied may result in serious and unforeseeable consequences. The defendant is a foolish peasant who knows nothing about the law. If according to the articles of the law he should be divorced from his wife he is willing to obey. If according to the legal articles he should not be separated from this concubine he in the same way does not dare to go against the law. He only wishes that Your Heavenly Honour will pass judgment and he will never dare go against your judgment. In this way the woman who has deliberately run away from her husband and the woman who hopes to extinguish a family line will know the power of the law. The defendant and his whole family as well as his sons and grandsons and great grandsons, etc. in the generations to come will forever feel grateful to you. . . . etc.

These statements speak for themselves. The makers of these statements have no thought for consistency of the facts or arguments. Secondly there is over-statement of one's own case on each side. Thirdly, litigation is taken in the manner of a face-to-face quarrel, as seen by the use of abusive language throughout these legal statements. Fourthly both parties praise the judges in the hope of obtaining personal favour. (This practice was prevalent in traditional China, before the fall of the imperial dynasties.) And lastly, most important of all, neither party had a very clear view of the law in force. In other words, between the law of the legislators and the law as the people conceive it there is a wide cultural and psychological gap. This gap is not peculiar to this case. Similar cases may be added almost indefinitely from the records of the court and prison of the Tali District Court. For example, the traditional Chinese family ideal is everywhere being shaken, but in the minds of the majority, many of the traditional rules of sexual conduct are still intact. In the minds of many, the penalty which a woman having committed adultery deserves irrespective of circumstances is death. The following case illustrates this attitude:

CASE:
Y., a native of Chien Ch'uan, West Yunnan, was married at 17. His wife lived with his parents before marriage as *T'ung Yang Hsi,* a custom prevalent in many parts of China among poorer people. She was liked by his father. Relations between the young couple after marriage were good. In the year when Y. was 24 came the family's downfall. The building of a motor road by the government required the commandeering of most of the family's land. In the same year his wife gave birth to a son. His mother asked in the house whose son it was, his father's or his? (implying that his father committed adultery with his wife). There had been a quarrel of long standing in the family all round. Y. suspected that his father in fact committed adultery with his wife. One day the young couple went together through a pine wood. He killed her and threw her body in the hills. Y. returned home telling the family that he told his wife to walk ahead while he stopped to gamble in a street, but that when he had finished gambling he could not find her. Several days later his wife's body was discovered and his father-in-law sued him. Y. was arrested and has already been in prison for nine years.[2]

Another case, while similar in some ways to the above, illustrates also the strength of kinship:

CASE:

Mrs. X., a young widow, behaves rather loosely with men in the village. Her uncle (father's brother) is the headman of the village. Although Mrs. X is in charge of an independent household (her husband had no living parents), such behaviour on her part lowered her uncle's social prestige beyond repair. Her uncle hired some one and murdered her. The old uncle was arrested for murder.

Another case involves a man and wife who killed his younger brother's fiancée.

CASE:

The family consists of two brothers and the older brother's wife. The younger brother is betrothed to a girl in the village. The girl, on the other hand, maintains adulterous relations with another man. The villagers gossiped so much about this matter that she eloped with her love to Kunming. Her fiancé went to Kunming and found her and persuaded her to return to the village. She returned to the village with her fiancé but her own parents declined to take her in their house. The fiancé asked his own brother and sister-in-law to take her in, but this request was also met with refusal. Seeing the difficulties ahead the young fiancé left for Kunming again without having obtained a solution of the problems. The fiancée had nowhere to go. No one would take her in. Finally she went back to the house of her fiancé's brother. He and his wife told her to go away but she would not. They beat her with clubs, still she would not leave the house. Then one evening after severely beating her, they cut her nose off with a knife, and she bled to death. The criminals did not attempt to keep their crime a secret. During the court hearings they told everything in clear and concise language, but they did not recognize that they had committed a crime. They insisted that they had done the right thing. Their sentence at the District Court was five years imprisonment for each, but they are [appealing] to a higher court for a mitigation of the sentence.

Such severity is sometimes applied to an adulterous man:

CASE:

T. is a graduate of the lower primary school in the village. His father was an illiterate peasant. T. himself stayed on the farm after his graduation. He was married when he was eighteen. Relationship with wife was very good. During the seventh month of one year his wife went to stay with her blind mother for a few days. The only other member in her blind mother's family is a young nephew. One evening a young man came into her mother's house and attempted to rape her. The blind mother sent the young nephew to fetch T. who ran to the scene of trouble at once, and saw the young man wrangling with his wife. The young man, seeing his arrival, fled from the house. T. started to chase him. At a point about one mile from the house the young man tumbled on the ground after hurdling a ditch. T. followed up and without another word, stabbed him with a knife, and that killed him. T. then presented himself at the office of the district governor for judgment. He was very angry when he learned that he was sentenced to imprisonment for five years for manslaughter, because he thought he was without any fault. "Such a man ought to be killed," T. reiterated again and again.

In a country where divorce or dissolution of engagement was a male prerogative the desire to obtain it on the part of many a female produces crimes which at first sight will be incomprehensible to the Westerner, as the following case shows:

CASE:
This case involves two sisters, R. and S. Their father was a minor clerk in the district government, who because of debt incurred through gambling, sold all the family's property and ran away. Since the father's desertion their uncle (the father's younger brother), who lived in the same courtyard but who maintained an independent household, began to interfere with affairs in this family. R. married a coolie at the age of sixteen. S., the younger sister was betrothed to someone but not yet married. When S. was sixteen she came to know a middle school student and loved him very much. One day her uncle saw a photograph given her by this student. He beat her severely before sending her to her fiancé's parents' house. Her uncle, by so doing, was upholding the good name of his family. When S. first got to her fianceé's family her relation with the family was cordial. But soon her uncle's wife went along and gossiped about her relation with the middle school student. Her fiancé's parents chased her out of the house. S. then went to her sister's family to take refuge. During this time S. became more familiar with the middle school student and was more determined to marry him.

But how could this be done? In the village if S. was to marry the middle school student she could only wait for her fiancé's death. S. and her older sister made a plan to kill S's fiancé. One evening S. induced her fiancé into the house of R. The two sisters strangled him with a rope and threw his body into the river under cover of night.

A few days later the body was discovered not far from the bank of the river. With the body was also found S's apron.

Both sisters were arrested. At the Tali District Court R. was sentenced to life imprisonment and S., the death penalty. Both sisters are now appealing at a higher court.

The judge at the Tali District Court told the author that when S. was chased out by her future mother-in-law and her fiancé did nothing about it, she could either sue her future mother-in-law for re-entrance into the family or for dissolution of the engagement. In either suit she would probably have won her case. The judge further pointed out that according to the law, even if she just went ahead and married the middle school student before having obtained dissolution of the engagement she was at the worst liable to a sum of compensation and at the best free from any legal disabilities. But neither she nor her sister were aware of the law; nor had the opportunity to consult it. What is more in the eyes of the other villagers they were misbehaved women all right, but by no means foolish women, for to them the death of the fiancé was the only right way in which to bring about the dissolution of the engagement.

The problem of using violence against persons is a very serious one. Some of the afore-quoted cases bear out this point. The stronger party in any dispute, emotional or otherwise, always tends to take the law in his or her own hands. "To beat him up" is a phrase that is not rarely heard in the daily life of the people. A case like the following is indeed not unusual, although the actual consequences may not always be fatal.

CASE:
W. belongs to a farmer's family, Mohammedan in faith. His father had a tutor to teach him the classics for a few years. One day while he was working in the fields he saw some youths from a neighboring village trying to stop a stream for catching fish. The stopped water ran into his field. He attempted to stop them and started a quarrel with them. The other youths attacked him *en masse.* He made use of a scythe in his possession and fatally wounded one of them. The wounded young man died in a few days. W. is sentenced to five years imprisonment for manslaughter.

Even feuds are not unheard of:

CASE:
N. is the only son of a well-to-do farmer. He is a graduate from a higher primary school. In 1934 his father's family had a feud with his father's older brother's family. The two families quarrelled over a piece of land of about 18 *mu.* When the quarrel was at its height, each of the two families sent out forty or fifty armed men. N.'s mother's brother and the latter's two sons also joined the fight on the side of N.'s father. Both of the sons of N.'s mother's brother were killed during the engagement. There were numerous other casualties. (This feud happened in a village in the District of Ch'eng Kiang, south-east Yunnan. The District Government intervened, but the details are not available). Shortly after the fight his father's older brother put a price of a hundred thousand dollars on N.'s head. (N. being the only son, if dead his father's older brother's children will be the legal heirs to all N.'s father's property). When a price was placed on N.'s head N. fled to Kunming, where he entered the police service. Later he changed his employment and entered the army. His plans were to become a commissioned officer and then return to the home village to obtain revenge. Shortly afterwards he became a corporal. One day he was reproached by a superior officer for failure to discharge his duties well. He deserted. His superior officer found him and persuaded him to return to the camp. But he stabbed the officer and fled and entered a machine-gun corps.

He is now in prison for having participated in a looting affair.

As may be clear from the last quoted case the higher one's position the easier it will be to take revenge; or in other words, the easier it will be to take the law in one's own hands. This fact is closely related to the very common practice of making public announcements of gratitude to officials, military or civil, who have done their duty (or the most ostentatious part of it) or who have been able to protect one party from being molested by a stronger party. Such announcements may be found today in any newspaper in interior China. The following is a quotation from *West Yunnan daily news,* published at Tali, in 1943.

Chief Directing Officer Mr. C. T. C. of XX Area Army Corps, who is now stationed at Hsiakuan, is an officer who is very strict in regulating his soldiers and is loved by both merchants and the people. This fact is so well-known that the undersigned does not have to mention it once more. During the past spring the undersigned, because of his not too cordial relations with one or two worms among the population, was anonymously accused of some serious crime (political) at this army corps headquarters. Fortunately enough Mr. C. took swift action and abided by the strictest procedures of law. He sent officers to investigate the truth of the case and was able to catch the real culprits behind the scene. Mr. C. then handed the case to Military Judge L. Judge L. is well-learned in law and shows deep insight in human affairs. The case was cleared up in one hearing. . . . The undersigned is a poor man and has always been serving in impoverished educational institutions. Had Officer C. not been straightforward and dutiful the undersigned would have sunk low by a crime never committed, which would be what the terrible intriguers desired. The undersigned is extremely grateful to these officers, but is sorry that he has nothing to offer in the way of a return. He can only make this public announcement to express his gratitude. Will people of all walks of life please note.

Signed (by the principal of XX Primary
School, of XX District)

III

There are other problems pertaining to court procedures which are no less vexatious to the keepers of law. We have previously seen the trouble of over-statement of one's own case. Another common trouble is that some plaintiffs accuse as many people as possible, giving the impression that they do not know whom they want to accuse. It is not, however, that they really do not know whom they want to accuse, but it is the common idea that the more people they get entangled in the suit the more difficult it will be for the real defendant to escape judgment. Another trouble is that some plaintiffs think that somehow they can get the better of the law by suing at different official offices, as though visiting different shops to get a more favourable price for the same commodity. The following case came to the writer's notice just before he left Tali:

A peasant woman was beaten by a neighbour. She sued him at the sub-district headman's office and got the judgment of damage in her favour of three hundred dollars. She did not take the money, and sued him again at the district governor's office. This time she took the damage of four hundred dollars but several days later she sued him again at the Tali District Court. On being asked by the judge why she sued again she retorted: "Do you think that 400 dollars would have healed my wound?" (She had no wound and was perfectly well during the court hearing). The judge asked her for a bill of expenses from the doctor who treated her as evidence, but she did not have one, nor had she the faintest idea what it was. The judge then had to spend about twenty minutes in explaining to her what such a bill was and its importance for this case. But when she turned up for the next hearing she had failed to bring this piece of evidence just the same. Yet she argued left and right that she was wronged and so forth. It turned out that she never understood in a real way the judge's instructions during the previous hearing.

Probably education and better communication will gradually reduce some of these problems. All of the judges in interior courts have to do a certain amount of educational work, as the last quoted case shows. There is no conclusive evidence elsewhere that these factors (education and better communication) reduce criminality as such, but education will make more people conscious of the existence and significance of the law while easier communication will foster contact and bring people together so as to develop a greater unity of psychological and cultural background. They will gradually bridge over the difficulties which arise from the fact that modern Chinese law has not grown out of the life of the people, but is in a large measure given to the people.

At least as far as the Tali District Court records are concerned there are indications that rustic folks commit more crimes of violence than all other classes of persons put together. The writer has tabulated the background of and crimes committed by the ninety-nine prisoners kept in the Tali District Court jail between the years 1939 and 1941, and has found that of the ninety-nine prisoners seventy-nine were registered as "farmers," (as differentiated from laborers, merchants, soldiers, officials, etc.). He has further found that of the 79 farmers kept in the gaol thirty-five committed manslaughter or murder and twenty-eight committed physical violence against others and caused serious injuries.

One reason for the preponderance of farmer-prisoners is, of course, the fact that the Tali district contains more farmers than other classes of persons. There is also the possibility that farmers have less opportunity of evading the law, or of appeal to a higher court, than other classes of persons. But with the inflation of the national currency as it stands today (prices are now two to four hundred times their pre-war level), money as a deterrent factor against litigation is largely gone. The fees charged by the courts today have only slightly increased above their pre-war level but the average farmer's income, unlike that of the university professor or of the small official, has roughly risen with the prices. The following table compiled from three years records of the Tali District Court and the Branch Higher Court situated at Tali tells a certain interesting, though inconclusive, story.

New Cases That Have Appeared at Tali District Court and the Branch Higher Court Situated at Tali

Jan. 1939-Dec. 1941

	A. Tali District Court		B. Branch Higher Court	
	Civil	*Criminal*	*Civil*	*Criminal*
1939	171	45	315	66
1940	364	91	529	112
1941	301	96	415	114

The increase in the number of new cases is evident, but the facts are not conclusive for several reasons: First, it is not known how many of the criminal cases are ones involving crimes which are not automatically prosecuted; that is, crimes which are only prosecuted when the victims take legal action. Secondly, the effect of increase of population in the Tali area since the opening of the famous Yunnan-Burma Road in 1939 is a factor which can only be evaluated through a comparative study of many areas in interior China.

NOTES

1. In contrast to this article the spirit of the law towards crimes involving "serious injury" is totally different. "Serious injuries" are: "Disability of one or both eyes; of one or both ears; of the faculties of speech or smell; of the functions of one or more limbs; of the function of reproduction; and other injuries which are incurable or difficult to cure, and have severe effects on health" *(Legal Code,* Vol. 1, Chapter One, Article 10). Crimes involving one of these injuries will be prosecuted without action on the part of the victim.

2. Information concerning this and several of the cases which follow was obtained through interviews with prisoners and judges by Mr. James C.S. Yang, one of the author's students at Hwa Chung College.

18

A Cholera Epidemic in a Chinese Town

THE PROBLEM: THE COMMUNITY IGNORES WESTERN MEDICINE IN FIGHTING CHOLERA

In the spring of 1942 a serious cholera epidemic struck the community of Hsi-ch'eng, a rural market town of 8,000 inhabitants in Yunnan Province, southwestern China. Unlike many similar communities in this area, Hsi-ch'eng lacked neither the facilities nor the trained personnel that would make possible the use of the best techniques known to western medical science for fighting the disease. Some years prior to the epidemic several of the wealthiest families had supported the establishment in the community of a hospital and three modern schools. The hospital had about 20 beds, one graduate nurse, two fully qualified medical doctors, a number of assistant nurses, and a nursing training class. The three schools, two of which were coeducational, had a total enrollment of approximately 1,400 from Hsi-ch'eng and other communities. In addition, there was a missionary college, with a Chinese and western faculty, which had moved to this area from a part of China devastated by the war with Japan.

Immediately after the first cases of cholera were detected, these agencies went into action. The schools made up and distributed posters and other informational material detailing measures for limiting spread of the disease. The hospital offered its facilities to all stricken inhabitants, and announced that bed space would be free for those too poor to pay.

The inhabitants were deeply disturbed by the epidemic and expended a tremendous amount of energy in measures to fight it. Nevertheless, practically no one took advantage of the modern services freely offered by the hospital. Nurses even went out into the streets urging people to adopt certain preventive and curative measures; yet they found few people willing to follow these measures. Meanwhile the death rate mounted. Between the tenth of May and the tenth of June, when the epidemic abated, nearly two hundred men, women, and children died of the disease in Hsi-ch'eng—an alarming fatality figure.

Why did the people of Hsi-ch'eng fail to avail themselves of medical services that were readily available and freely offered, in the face of so dire a threat to their lives and health? What measures did they adopt? What does their choice of methods reveal about the role of culture in affecting a population's response to a crisis?

The Situation

Hsi-ch'eng Combats a Cholera Epidemic[1]

Hsi-ch'eng is located within a day's journey on foot or horseback from the Burma Road and lies about 6,700 feet above sea level. It is bordered by a lake on one side and a mountain rising to 14,000 feet on the other. The general occupation of the entire area is agriculture, rice being the staple crop. However, trading in various forms is also very common; it represents the backbone of Hsi-ch'eng economy. Trading in this community includes both local exchanges in periodic markets and large-scale commercial adventures into the outer world.

The town of Hsi-ch'eng proper is not walled. There is only one continuous thoroughfare, which leads from the north to the south. Into it at irregular intervals run other streets in east-west direction. Some years ago four gates were erected, one at each end of the main thoroughfare, one at the end of a street running into it from the east, and one at the end of a street from the west. In this way a large section of the town is shut off from the outlying areas at night, when a town watchman patrols the streets with a gang. However, Hsi-ch'eng's population is not confined within these gates. Outside are at least nine clearly marked clusters of houses, each called a village. Within the four gates, each street, or each section of a street, is also designated a village.

The racial origin of the inhabitants is open to question. Both the town and the district seat as well as their satellite villages have legends about the migration of their ancestors from some central provinces into Yunnan. The place most frequently given for the original habitat is "Nanking," a place which bears, however, little semblance to the former national capital. A few genealogical records indicate that their ancestors were from Anwhei Province. However this may be, the inhabitants today are proud of their claimed Chinese origin.

The people of Hsi-ch'eng emphasize the difference between the sexes. They zealously guard the virginity of unmarried women and the chastity of married women. The cult of ancestors is deeply institutionalized. Not only the very powerful and wealthy clans but also some ordinary ones establish a separate clan temple. Every family tries hard to assure good sites for its graveyards according to geomancy, a system of divination to determine whether a burial site is favorable or not. The nature of the site is supposed to affect the rise or fall of future descendants of the family group. Old imperial honors granted from Peking continue to be highly valued. When real honors are lacking, imaginary ones are often substituted. By these and other tokens the people of Hsi-ch'eng are not only Chinese in culture but also, by their own insistence, more Chinese in some ways than the residents of many other parts of China.

Hsi-ch'eng is distinguished from most rural Chinese towns in having a disproportionately large number of wealthy families. Some of these families are outstanding not merely locally but even in the larger provincial cities and in Kunming. Thus, Hsi-ch'eng includes the three usual social classes of China, a small upper crust, a somewhat larger middle group, and a rather large lower class. But class distinctions are blurred. For one thing, the rich and the poor meet and join in conversation as a matter of course at community functions. For another, many poor people claim remote common ancestry with some of the rich. The importance of the cult of ancestors overshadows the significance of the class difference.

How the People Dealt with Cholera

Cholera is known and dreaded in all parts of China. When the disease struck Hsi-ch'eng in the spring of 1942, the face of the village was profoundly changed. Funeral processions became a common sight. At first, some processions were as elaborate as the families of the dead could afford. Later, all processions became hasty and comparatively simple. During the evenings the streets, crowded before the onset of the epidemic, were virtually empty. Except for the carpenters' shops, darkness and silence prevailed. Even during the day the streets were nearly deserted. Men and women became reticent and gloomy. There is no question that all were deeply disturbed by the epidemic and would do nearly anything to eliminate it.

Cholera is a disease for which western medicine has at its command fairly effective methods of diagnosis and prevention. The etiological agent, *vibrio comma,* is known. The primary source of infection is fecal contamination; diagnosis can be made by direct microscopic examination. The mode of transmission, the incubation period, and the period of communicability are known. Methods of control center on instituting stringent sanitary measures to prevent communication of the disease and involve detection and isolation of carriers and thorough disinfection of all contaminated materials.

Western methods for combating cholera were at the disposal of the people of Hsi-ch'eng through its modern hospital and schools. At the onset of the epidemic, the physician in charge of the college infirmary, who was an American missionary and a graduate of Harvard Medical School, gave a special lecture to the entire student body on the cause, prevention, and treatment of cholera. The college authorities advised the students to take stringent sanitary precautions and to refrain from eating raw food or food exposed to flies, and from drinking unboiled water. In addition, arrangements were made to have students and faculty receive injections, a measure generally believed at that time to be effective.

The hospital and the local schools also went into action. At first, the hospital administered injections on the premises. Later, nurses were sent into the streets to give free injections. Hospital beds were made available for stricken patients, free of charge for those too poor to pay. The number of beds was limited, but even these were not used to capacity.

The local schools did things in a much more dramatic manner. They exhibited large posters everywhere in town. One poster displayed pictures of several food peddlers with their retailing stands of sweets, pea-curd, and the like. These stands were covered with flies. Several customers were pictured eating the food. Another poster pictured an open-air toilet in use. Several people were seen in the act of vomiting. Flies swarmed on their stools and on the material ejected from their mouths. The caption below the picture read: "The flies in both places are the same and carry cholera germs from the one to the other." A third poster showed in enlarged form the structure of a fly and of some cholera germs, with detailed scientific explanatory notes on how these germs could be communicated and by what means such communication could be prevented.

The inhabitants of Hsi-ch'eng reacted vigorously to the cholera threat, but they responded according to their own ideas of its cause and of effective countermeasures, and not the ideas of the school and hospital authorities. The popular explanation of cholera was that it was brought by epidemic-carrying spirits sent by the gods and might be withdrawn by the gods, provided they were propitiated by moral behavior and prayer. The spirits, meanwhile, could be kept off by charms. The first and most important measure the people undertook was to stage prayer meetings, one after another. These prayer meetings were elaborate and costly. They were staged in different neighborhoods and were primarily the work of hired priests and other religious specialists. The shortest one lasted one day and one night, and the longest, six days and seven nights. Thousands of gods were invoked. During the course of the epidemic, 19 such prayer meetings took place. Money for the prayer meetings came from a multitude of small donors as well as from the leading families.

The prayer meetings, though most colorful and certainly occupying the central place in Hsi-ch'eng's mode of dealing with the epidemic, were not the only steps taken. Along with the prayer meetings, in which the priests prayed to the gods to forgive misconduct and exhorted the populace to be moral, the inhabitants also resorted to a number of other measures designed to protect the individual or the community from the ailment.

Native cures and prescriptions were offered by individuals as a public service by means of handwritten or printed posters displayed in various parts of the town. Some of the prescriptions consisted of herbs cited in *The Codex of Chinese Drugs,* a volume prepared by Chinese doctors with western training. Other prescriptions advised the consumption of certain ready-made drugs in pill or powder form as well as acupunctural practices. These public notices were signed by actual names or by such designations as "a retired oldster" or "a famous physician in the army."

Moral injunctions from priests and others, exhorting the populace to abstain from sex and otherwise purge themselves of evil thoughts and deeds, were posted throughout the town. These posters emphasized the need for keeping streets and alleys free from animal droppings and household refuse. The bases for the exhortations were made explicit: "What you see means more to the gods than what you hear; what you think means more to the gods than what you eat." People were reminded: "Flat earth has no waves; all trouble begins with the human heart." But the inhabitants did not limit themselves to words. In conjunction with the local police, leaders made strong efforts to bring about general cleanliness in the community so as to please the gods. Taboos were place on many varieties of food, from pea-curd and potatoes to meat and fish.

Palm-shaped cacti were hung on gates, lime powder lines were drawn on walls to connect the lintels of the family portal, and amulets of yellow paper with drawings were carried around by individuals. The Chinese name for palm-shaped cactus is fairy-palm, and since the epidemic was believed to be caused by evil spirits, the sign of hands of fairies or of superior deities would ward off the disease-making spirits. The drawing of lime powder lines was a recent innovation. Residents had observed people of the missionary college and hospital spread lime powder on the floor to disinfect wards and outhouses and had adopted this practice without much knowledge of its practical function. Amulets have been used by the inhabitants of Hsi-ch'eng and all China since time beyond memory.

People secured medicine from the gods and drank what they described as "fairy water" for prevention or cure. The medicine was generally a package of sandy material composed of ashes of burned incense sticks obtained in a shrine after a request for help made by an applicant or by the priest acting on his behalf. The contents of the package were then taken home and administered with water. The bulk of Hsi-ch'eng's fairy water came from a rock located about ten miles south of the community. The rock, known as Nine Goddesses Spring, was said to gush water only when an epidemic struck and to remain dry at all other times. All during the cholera epidemic this water was carried to Hsi-ch'eng on pack horses and sold at 50 cents a cup. Not all fairy water came from that particular rock. Residents also drank water from a fountain-like arrangement in an incense burner located in front of a temporary shrine. This was also considered fairy water by virtue of its association with the abode of the gods.

From a western viewpoint, the effectiveness of indigenous methods for coping with the epidemic varied greatly. For example, the taboos on a large number of foods, though imposed for supernatural reasons, might actually have restricted the spread of the epidemic. The taboo on fresh fruits and vegetables was helpful because fruits were usually eaten unwashed and unpeeled, while vegetables were as a rule cleaned in the contaminated public streams before cooking, and sometimes were consumed raw. The taboo on meat and fish can be seen in a similar light, especially because meat, broth, and potato are all suitable media for the growth of cholera bacteria.

Other indigenous measures such as the prayers, the various rituals, and the moral injunctions, while they might have helped to reassure and stabilize the disturbed community, had no demonstrable effect on the epidemic. Furthermore, some measures might actually have led to effects diametrically opposed to the desired ones. For example, one of the indigenous cures for cholera directed the victim to open up his finger tips to let out blood. This could lead to serious infection and complicate later treatment. Drinking fairy water from unclean containers might have resulted in increasing the rate of infection to a considerable extent.

The indigenous practices for dealing with the epidemic can be grouped into three categories: those which could have beneficial effects, those which could produce results with no direct bearing on the epidemic, and those which tended to be harmful. Below are classified the various measures according to these categories.

Measures Taken and Their Results

Measures taken	Local rationale	Effects according to western medical theory
Taboos on eating potatoes, string beans, turnips; all sour fruits, confections, new wheat flour, fresh meat, fish, pumpkin, egg plant, etc.	To please the gods To avoid making the abdomen cold	Taboos on meat and potatoes would limit the growth and spread of the bacillus; other food taboos neither harmful nor beneficial
Taboo on dirt and on animal and human soil in streets	To make the air and ground clean for gods	Improvement in general sanitation, which might mitigate the epidemic
Emphasis on morals	To purify the heart and thus please the gods	Without demonstrable connection with the epidemic
Prayer meetings and scripture-elaboration sessions	To beg forgiveness of the gods through a collective appeal	Congregating might contribute to spreading the disease
Hanging cactus stalks on gates; making hand prints on walls and doors; drawing lime powder arcs in front of house gates, etc.	To ward off epidemic-giving spirits	Without demonstrable connection with the epidemic
Medicinal prescriptions	To cure cholera To prevent cholera	Some prescriptions harmful, some good, others indifferent
Drinking fairy water	To cure and prevent cholera	Possible increase in the incidence of infection

There is no doubt that some of the local practices were based on valid knowledge. However, since people indiscriminately employed the three kinds of measures and resorted to some of them under what medical science would regard as false assumptions, it is clear that they made no distinction in their own minds between "nonscientific" and "scientific" practices. This conclusion is further underlined by the attitude of Hsi-ch'eng toward the modern measures. For example, local police made sure that the inhabitants kept the streets much cleaner than before, but they also enforced the taboo on meat as well as taking part in the prayer meetings. Similarly, some of the prescriptions offered by local people as a public service were evidently compounded of both western and indigenous specifics, mixed together. But most of the local people either failed to utilize modern precautions and remedies or used them concurrently with all the indigenous practices for the same purpose.

The People Explain Their Actions

Following the epidemic, the writer, at that time an instructor in the local college, interviewed 31 residents of Hsi-ch'eng in an effort to discover the reasons behind the pattern of response to the epidemic. The basic idea shared by all informants was that modern measures were evidently useful in fighting the epidemic but that they were neither the only devices nor the most important ones. A majority of those questioned had contributed substantial sums to the prayer meetings; several were important officers at these meetings; and many had also employed amulets, indigenous prescriptions, and other traditional devices. One man who had received an injection and required all his children and grandchildren to be immunized also served as an official at a prayer meeting, explaining: "After all, nobody knows which spirit he might have offended unintentionally." Another man who received injections explained that he also served as an officer in a prayer meeting because his parents wanted him to be there. One man who took his son for an injection after the youngster became ill claimed that the boy got well as a result. On the other hand, scores of men and women, whether or not they were parents of school children, refused the injections and paid virtually no attention to the other modern measures available to them.

Some men and women refused injections on the ground that it was "too painful." In fact, this was the most frequently used reason for refusing the injection. This reason was apparently a polite excuse for avoiding something which did not appeal to them, for most local men and women, when seriously ill, would not hesitate to allow native acupuncture practitioners to insert long silver pins deep into their bodies. These pins were not sharp and certainly not disinfected. Other reasons given for not taking the injections were that the informant had "no time," or that the injections were inconvenient.

Limited Appeal of Western Techniques

Why did the inhabitants of Hsi-ch'eng mix modern measures with ancient practices or even refuse the newer methods outright? It is not an adequate answer simply to say that these Chinese farmers were "irrational" or "prelogical" as is sometimes asserted. In Hsi-ch'eng, as in all societies, the individual's perception is guided by the traditional tenets of his culture. As the average individual in Hsi-ch'eng grows up, he learns to view the world as it is seen by the people around him. In the minds of most of these people, no clear separation is made between that which is "natural" and that which is "supernatural." Supernatural forces are seen as operating in everything; it is only in certain segments of western or westernized society that people consistently call one kind of cause "natural" or "scientific" and another kind "supernatural" or "magic."

This does not mean that the people in Hsi-ch'eng possess a different order of mentality from people in societies that do make a distinction between these two kinds of causality—that they are "illogical" while people in western societies are "logical." In both cases an individual will judge any practice to be reasonable or "logical" not on the basis of his own pure, abstract "rational" analysis, but on the basis of the fundamental premises about the nature of cause and effect provided for him by his culture. If his culture stresses the "scientific" nature of cause and effect, he will tend to judge things by this standard; if his culture assumes that there are supernatural forces at work in all happenings, he will inevitably see things in this way. In either case it is the culture and not the individual that plays the determining part.

The residents of Hsi-ch'eng, in dealing with the cholera epidemic, relied but little on injections and other scientific measures because they were reared in a cultural milieu to which the western practices were totally alien. Under such circumstances, even the select few who might have been skeptical of indigenous usages because of western education and contact had to follow suit, or at least not be drastically different, in order to maintain their status and respectability in their community. This was why those who sponsored and supported the modern institutions also contributed much to the indigenous practices.

Thus, to the man of Hsi-ch'eng, in dealing with the cholera epidemic, the taboos and prayers were as logical in terms of his own culture as injections and hospitalization would be to one whose outlook had been conditioned by modern science. In either case the diagnosis made and the means resorted to are culturally given. Brought up in their cultural setting, the people of Hsi-ch'eng had acquired ideas about ghosts, epidemic-giving spirits, gods, punishment, and personal fate. They left the bulk of the work of prevention and cure to the specialists of their culture—the priests. The Euro-American and western-trained personnel in Hsi-ch'eng had also acquired, under similar circumstances but in a different cultural environment, ideas about bacteria, hospitals, medicine, and injection. They felt that the burden of cure and prevention should rightfully fall upon those designated by their culture as specialists—doctors and public health officers.

In each case it was the culture and not the individual that had a magico-religious bias, or a leaning toward the scientific. In each case individuals acted according to their cultural conditioning. The fact that many western medical personnel in 1942 believed implicitly in the efficacy of anticholera injections—a measure which today is considered of less value—documents the determining quality of culturally reinforced beliefs, independent of their ultimate objective validity.

Neither the people of Hsi-ch'eng nor any other population invariably reject all new elements. But whenever people borrow from other cultures they tend to reinterpret the new elements and to alter them to fit their own framework of expectations. This was why the villagers either refused modern scientific measures or mixed them with indigenous practices. Modern medicine and its practitioners had no definite place in their own cultural tradition—a tradition in which a cholera epidemic or any other emergency, such as a drought, was dealt with by using *all* available measures. Taboos on fruits, meat, and fish were maintained during the epidemic, not out of consideration for the preventive measures of modern science, but as a means of pleasing the gods. The lines drawn with lime powder on the walls of family homes and semicircles drawn in front of the lintels of others may be seen in the same light. Elders of Hsi-ch'eng had noted the first appearance of such designs some ten years before, after residents saw lime powder used as a disinfectant. It was only natural for a spirit-wary people who had been using cactus leaves to ward off cholera-giving spirits to turn this new product to a similar purpose.

IMPLICATIONS

Science in Chinese Life and Magic in American Life

It is widely held that western societies put a high premium on "rational" explanations and behavior. A little reflection will show that magic in its various forms is still prevalent in many parts of the western world. Even in contemporary American life "scientific" thinking characterizes the thought-processes of only a small minority. Peasant peoples in Europe and rural American communities still maintain practices and beliefs properly called "magical." The prevalence of magical thinking is attested by the tremendous circulation of horoscope magazines, the prosperity of the Spiritualist churches here and in Europe, and the utilitarian expectations of church-goers in Mexico and other Latin countries.

However, the relative importance of magic or science, especially on a conscious level, differs widely from culture to culture. In this, Hsi-ch'eng and the cities of America contrast sharply. In Hsi-ch'eng the place of honor is reserved for spirits and priests, benevolent or malicious, and for traditional prescriptions and herbs. In such a culture, modern medicine, to enter into local consideration, has to compete with spirits, fairy water, and herbs.

On the other hand, the culture of America is one in which scientists and technicians are believed to provide answers for everything. In America these occupy the place of honor enjoyed by supernatural forces and priests in Hsi-ch'eng. Consequently, Americans who believe in luck, charms, talismans, and horoscopes have to do so apologetically. They will either announce that they do it for fun, dismiss these things as insignificant, or use them with great discretion. But Americans who work with science are under no such handicap regarding their work.

In the light of this picture, it is understandable why so many advertisements in America, offering toothbrushes with a curvature resembling that of the dentist's mirror or cigarettes that have been endorsed by "doctors in a nationwide survey," and so on, try to cash in on the name of science. While some of these advertising offerings are undoubtedly honest and sound, many are not. For example, the Vrilium Products Company in Chicago in 1948 sold about 5,000 of their "healing pencils" at about $300 each. According to the company's literature, each pencil contained "vrilium catalytic barium chloride," guaranteed to "emit healing rays for the relief of burns, sprains, aches, sinus trouble, blood disturbances and a number of other ailments." Among the customers were many prominent people. During the trial of the company's officials in 1950 under the Pure Food and Drug Act, about 70 witnesses from many walks of life were willing to testify for the defense. After the company's officials were convicted, an entrepreneur offered the sum of $10,000 to purchase the firm's name and stock.

To most Americans, mysterious phenomena must be given acceptable explanations in terms of atoms, neutrons, magnetic power, or other concepts of modern science. In contrast, when flying machines first passed over my native village at night in north China, the villagers concluded that these represented terrible appearances of the gods, and they prostrated themselves in worship. This is not to deny that Chinese even in the old days had empirical knowledge, nor that many modern Americans still maintain belief in the occult. An example of an American counterpart of Hsi-ch'eng's appeal to the supernatural was found in the continued and concentrated prayer meetings held by Texans during a recent drought. But such efforts are no longer a nationwide matter in America, while resort to western science continues to concern only a few Chinese.

The basic similarity between Hsi-ch'eng in China and a town in the United States, along with the basic contrast between them, is thus obvious. Their similarity comes from the fact that both peoples react to new stimuli by reinterpreting them or altering them to conform with known practices. Their difference is in what constitutes the "known practices." In Hsi-ch'eng, scientific measures must be put in harmony with local notions about spirits, taboos, and herb doctors which customarily figure in healing and prevention of diseases. In America, on the other hand, chemical compounds, healers, and new ideas and goods, whether sound or otherwise, become most marketable when put forward as the brain child of "scientists," or as products of some laboratory where accuracy is allegedly measured in one millionth of an inch. It is thus not too far-fetched to say that to achieve popular acceptance, magic has to be dressed like science in America, while science has to be cloaked as magic in Hsi-ch'eng.

Introducing Western Techniques to Nonwestern Peoples

The magico-religious way of coping with disease is as firmly entrenched in the culture of Hsi-ch'eng as is the scientific way in the culture of Americans. In the face of this how and under what circumstances can we expect communities to be receptive to new medical techniques or other ideas of foreign origin?

The possibility of such changes seems to depend upon a variety of circumstances. In the first place, there is no doubt that an individual separated from his native society can change much more readily than a community. A native of Hsi-ch'eng, if removed to an American metropolitan center, will tend to fall in line with the ideas held by the Americans about the nature and cure of disease. He will not change all of his previous ideas and customs in this area, but he will be more receptive than his people at home to ideas about the effectiveness of scientific precautions against disease. And as soon as he is convinced, he can go ahead and act in accordance with these new beliefs without fear of losing the respect of his neighbors.

In the second place, products of science which do not involve vital matters tend to be more readily accepted, on a trial basis, than others. For example, Chinese peasants definitely prefer trains or buses, when available, to horsecarts, or the telephone and post office to divination as a means of communication. On the other hand, a new and scientifically developed agricultural technique will not be readily trusted by farmers whose entire livelihood depends upon the success of next year's crop. The smaller the economic margin, the smaller will be the desire to experiment with new techniques.

In the third place, new elements which do not interfere with the existing social organization, or can be easily fitted into the framework of existing practices will generally encounter little resistance. Thus, articles of ornamentation go freely from one culture to another, and few peoples have been known to prefer their native weapons to western firearms once the latter are made available to them. On the other hand, mechanized pumps did not make any headway in Chinese villages principally because their use would have necessitated a type of cooperation to which Chinese farmers are not accustomed.

In the fourth place, some western technological improvements require organized enterprise and operation on a scale that is beyond the capacity of individuals or even a number of communities. The droughts and famines that periodically plague the Chinese could no more be controlled by a few Chinese communities than the Mississippi River rampages can be remedied by any single county or even state in the United States. In such a connection a strong central government, capable of coordinating and cementing local differences, can be a positive factor. Past differences between China and Japan in the pace of industrialization are certainly related to the existence, in the latter country, of a strong centralized government, as contrasted with its much weaker counterpart in China.

In the fifth place, it makes a good deal of difference whether a people have been exposed to foreign contact voluntarily or as the result of political pressure or military conquest. In the latter case, the impact of contact may be very different from any instance thus far discussed, because the "selectivity" of the people is affected. This may happen within a society, when an autocratic government is bent on forcing westernization, or between two societies where one is under the thumb of the other. At one time the Board of Health of the Yunnan provincial government in China compelled all individuals seen in the streets to be inoculated against typhoid and cholera. In this case the villagers evaded the order by staying away from all markets. These strongarm tactics were later abandoned because they had failed. By contrast, the British authorities in Africa have frequently required that bushes be cleared by compulsory labor or that whole villages in the tsetse fly area be moved, so as to eliminate the sickness which the fly causes. In this case the method is still being used because it has apparently succeeded.

However, the differences in ultimate outcome may not be so great as the immediate success or failure would seem to indicate. The immediate results may have been brought about with such brutality or such total disregard for indigenous culture patterns, that the changes themselves, though apparently beneficial, may have produced emotionally disturbing effects. Then, later, when voluntary action becomes possible, even beneficial changes may be psychologically identified with the disturbing and unpleasant aspects of the former contact situation, and negated. Changes undertaken voluntarily have a better chance to persist than forced changes.

This brings us to two considerations concerning the relationship between change and emotional factors. No human behavior is free from emotional content and all cultural practices are invested with emotional significance. It follows that changes tend to be easier to introduce where the emotions of the recipients are least disturbed. On the other hand, where strong emotional involvement is inevitable, change may be expedited if these emotions can be mobilized for and not against the program.

The second consideration follows the first. Although positive emotions may be helpful when they support desired changes, they may ruin the chances of successful change when those who urge change are overexuberant, overmilitant, or extreme in their expectations. People all over the world find changes distasteful or, at the least, troublesome. Urban westerners are no exception. It is true that most westerners consciously seek change in science and industry. But attempts to bring about changes in family life, religious institutions, patterns of government, or even their recreational and dietary habits, would encounter considerable lack of enthusiasm, if not firm resistance. The desire for change in science and industry is part of their way of life, deeply rooted in the very social, religious, political, and personal habits which they would be highly reluctant to change.

Westerners who are engaged in effecting changes in the non-western world must remember that a reluctance to accept changes even in cases of severe problems of economic underdevelopment, malnutrition, and famine, or disease and epidemics, is also deeply rooted in local social, religious, political, and personal habits. In such circumstances any frontal attack on traditional usages, or an insistence that the native peoples give up their accustomed practices and champion only the new technique, tool, or idea, is doomed to failure.

While serving as a medical social worker in the Peking Union Medical College Hospital between the years 1934 and 1937, the writer observed many instances of such failure in respect to medicine. This college has produced some of the best medical doctors trained in the western tradition that China has ever known. But it failed to train its men to be aware of their patients as human beings with a given way of life which could be upset by the ideas and procedures of the foreign treatments the doctors tried to introduce. In Chinese tradition, and in the traditions of a vast majority of mankind, a sick individual will try any and all cures. If he cannot do so himself, it will be the duty of his kin to do so on his behalf. It is not at all unusual for a Chinese to consult three or four doctors simultaneously, while at the same time petitioning several gods. Consequently, when patients were persuaded to come to a western-trained doctor or to a modern hospital, they did not feel bound to that doctor or hospital in the same way as western patients would be. If the modern clinic could clear away their ailment in one visit, fine. If not, they had no compunction about seeing another man or visiting a temple, with the full intention of trying the western-trained doctor again, later on. However, the American-trained Chinese doctors often got furious with such patients, giving them a severe scolding, or even refusing to see them again. The doctors failed to realize that their job was to employ western modes of treatment insofar as possible, but not to convert the patients to a western outlook. Such an outlook would involve a drastic reorganization of the patient's social and psychological orientation that could not possibly be achieved in short order, nor within the context of the doctor-patient relationship.

People who are used to resorting to a variety of practitioners or sources of help in any emergency, medical or otherwise, will find the idea of concentrating on one doctor or one type of cure strange and disturbing. By insisting on all or none, modern medical workers do a disservice to their own cause, inducing social and ideological conflict. When this happens, people will either withdraw altogether or fight back with determination. In either case, the effort to introduce something new has backfired.

What is true with reference to the acceptance or rejection of western medicine by individual patients is equally true in a situation which involves favorable or unfavorable reactions to new public health measures by whole communities. If the innovators will promote their cause with a degree of modesty and humility, and present their ideas to the natives as one of the alternatives but not as the only true road to salvation, they will find their chances of success materially improved.

Summary

When a serious cholera epidemic struck the rural Chinese market town of Hsi-ch'eng in 1942, the inhabitants expended most of their efforts to combat the disease in measures based on their traditional understandings of the nature of disease and the methods of cure. Western medical facilities available in the town were for the most part ignored or utilized inconsistently. The behavior of the residents becomes comprehensible if we realize that the distinction made by westerners between "magical" and "scientific" practices is not relevant to rural Chinese. Their culture has taught them that supernatural and moral considerations play an intimate part in cause and effect, and they trust this belief. The average American, on the other hand, has been taught to have an equally strong and implicit faith in science, and will subscribe to nearly any sort of idea or technique so long as it is represented as scientific. Any attempt to introduce new knowledge or new techniques in a foreign setting will benefit from the realization that all communities respond to these attempts according to premises implicit in their own cultural traditions.

NOTE

1. The factual material in this case study is extracted from Hsu (1952a). Hsi-ch'eng (West Town) is a fictitious name.

19

Chinese Kinship and Chinese Behavior

Observers of China have often polarized their views: before the Communist Revolution the theme of the unchanging East predominated. Even when some changes were noted, the difficulties in effecting those changes were underlined. Since 1949 the Western view has tended to converge on the opposite pole. All traditional Chinese ways are supposed to have been swept away by the new regime in one stroke.

Neither of these views is in accord with what we know about human behavior. Over the centuries every culture has changed to a greater or lesser extent—the problem is that some cultures have changed much faster than others. Chinese culture as a whole has changed much more slowly than its Western counterpart as a whole. Thus, though Marco Polo (1254–1324?) was greatly astonished by the cultural achievements of China, by the first half of the 19th century the Middle Kingdom could neither match Western power of production nor find any answer to Western encroachment. Whether we think of science and technology, or of modern government and education, or even of art and literature, the West and not China holds world leadership since then.

The problem of why some cultures have undergone astonishing changes while others have not is by no means easy to solve. However, so long as we keep thinking in terms of complete change or no change, instead of beginning to scrutinize—on a comparative basis—how far each culture has changed and in what ways, we shall never even come close to solving that problem.

Similarly, if we concentrate all our attention on details and do not rise above them, we can perhaps see the immediate causes and the superficial meaning of a few events, but we can never discover the fuller pattern of change and continuity in culture.

In the following pages I shall analyze certain aspects of Chinese behavior under communism and relate them to each other as well as trace their genesis in the Chinese kinship system. In this I have been stimulated by a number of papers presented at this Conference. In his analysis of the present Red Guard movement in China, Franz Schurmann (1968) concludes that its object of attack is the party elite, and not the army and the

---

This chapter was originally published in *China in Crisis,* Vol. 1, *China's Heritage and the Communist Political System,* Ping-ti Ho and Tang Tsuo, eds., Chicago: University of Chicago Press, 1968, pp. 579–608.

bureaucracy. He is correct as far as he goes, but he merely tells us that the Maoists have taken action X and not Y or Z. He does not ask the more important questions: What is the relationship between X and Y and Z, or between X, Y, and Z on the one hand and A, B, and C (which are prominent factors in the larger picture) on the other? It is important to gain some idea as to the immediate target of so spectacular a phenomenon as the Red Guard, but unless we also attempt to assess happenings in conjunction with the larger and relatively more permanent objective of the regime, our interpretations will remain unrelated to each other or to the central characteristics of Chinese society and culture.

Moreover, Schurmann dismisses the problem of kinship as a major concern of the Chinese leaders in Peking. He writes:

> Kinship is an organizing principle for the perpetuation of authority. If it should turn out that the "rich peasants" of a certain county are related and actively pursue the achievement of kinship ties (through intermarriage), and if it should be that the party functionaries of a province are similarly related, then familism, that most ancient of China's sociational principles, still remains a strong force and China has indeed not changed that much. We obviously do not know. Yet, to my knowledge, cliquism based on kinship has not been raised by the Communists as a target for revolutionary action, at least not since the early 1950's, nor has it been raised now during the cultural revolution. (541)

I cannot agree with the narrow conception of kinship which underlies these observations. I believe that the present attack on the party elite is itself a phenomenon which must be seen in a much wider context. That context has to do with the overwhelming importance of kinship in the fabric of Chinese society, and the Communist leaders are determined to change that society. The larger and therefore relatively more permanent objective of the Chinese mainland authorities is to reduce the power of kinship in order to build a modern nation through rapid organization and industrialization. The present attack on the party elite by the Red Guards is, therefore, but an immediate step in the same direction.

Contrary to Schurmann, I believe that the problem of kinship is still very real in China today. The fact that "kinship has not been raised by the Communists as a target for revolutionary action, at least not since the early 1950's, nor has it been raised now during the Cultural Revolution" is no evidence that kinship is not part of the picture. Appearances are deceptive. The burden of this article will be that in spite of the facts mentioned by Schurmann, important ingredients of kinship origin *are* at work. Our task is to identify these ingredients and to demonstrate their role, so as to relate the more recent developments in mainland China to those which preceded them and, thus, to be in a better position to anticipate future developments. To do this, of course, is only to follow a basic axiom of science: to explain the unknown by way of the known.

Structure and Content

My first point of departure is that major determinants in human affairs are to be found in human relationships. Whether in politics, economy, or even religion, the primary objective of human action is the initiating, building, maintenance, or destrution of human relationships. The basic human relationship is the dyad. Complex human relationships are multiplications and permutations of the basic dyad. Thus a biological family consisting of parents and unmarried children has a smaller and a different structure than a joint family with several married couples under the same roof, just as a factory with assembly lines has a larger and more complicated structure than a household workshop in which the managers and the workers are all members of the same family.

Structure is an organization of dyads. Every class of dyads has a pattern of interaction that is usually peculiar to itself. Thus the pattern of interaction in a husband-wife dyad is different in essential ways from that in a mother-son dyad. And both are different from that in an employer-employee dyad. These different patterns of interaction are called attributes. When more than one dyad is involved, their respective attributes affect each other through combination, co-ordination, modification or elimination so as to form an overall pattern which we term content.

Content is an organization of attributes. Every organization, be it a biological family, a factory, a university, a labor union, has a structure with many sets of dyads and a content with a variety of attributes. Contents can differ where the structure is the same. Structurally, the Japanese husband-wife dyad is the same as its American counterpart, especially if we take, for example, suburban Tokyo, where the household is likely to be composed of parents and unmarried children. But the content of the Japanese husband-wife dyad (whether we find it in a Tokyo suburb or a Nagano village, where parents-in-law are more likely to be present) is very different from its American counterpart. Structurally, a factory in India and in Japan could be the same, each with its board of directors, president and vice-president, manager, foremen, and workers. But the contents (ways in which the officers interact with each other and in which the foremen treat the workers) can be demonstrably different (Hsu 1959). Conversely, content may be similar where structures are different.

Yet structure and content can also lead separate existences. China's two houses of parliament, at different points of time during the warlord period, were little more than rubber stamps of the warlords. This was an example of structure without content, or at least of a content vastly different from what the structure would have led us to expect. A married couple who live apart and do not see each other is another example of structure without corresponding content.

The possibility which concerns us most in the present exercise is a situation where content operates in the absence of the corresponding structure. This possibility can be illustrated in a variety of ways. For example, the dream of every wife is that her traveling husband behaves as if she were present at all times, just as the highest hope of most parents is that after they have passed away or their children become independent, the youngsters will still conduct themselves according to the philosophy of life which the elders had tried to instill. In both instances the content may continue when the structure is temporarily or permanently absent. This is the aim of all education. The hope of teachers is that their students will carry from the classroom not only what they have been taught—the three R's, for example—but also something of the "school spirit." On a more scientific level, the task is to attempt to pinpoint the interactions which took place before the parents passed away or while a student was still in school (when the family and the school structures were still existent) to see in what specific ways these interactions bear on the behavior of the products of the family and of the school after the structures have been eliminated.

My view is that the main objective of the Communist authorities has been to transform Chinese society from its kinship foundation to a political (non-kinship) one. To accomplish this, they have not only to propel a majority of the Chinese from their kinship base (structure) but also to disengage them from ways of thinking and interacting rooted in kinship (content). The difficulty is that ways of thinking and interacting rooted in kinship content may not bear any obvious resemblance to such things as "the achievement of kinship ties (through intermarriage)" or "cliquism based on kinship," which are matters of structure. Consequently, an observer unfamiliar with the real difference between structure and content is likely to conclude that kinship has nothing to do with present-day events, since he does not see activities usually associated with kinship.

In three previous publications I have (1) detailed the differences between structure and content (1959); (2) explicated the relationship between content and attributes; (3) introduced the terms "dominant relationship (dyad)" and "dominant attributes"; and (4) laid out a basic scheme for viewing a number of kinship systems in the world (Hsu 1965, 1966). The details of my hypothesis and how they may help us to deal with the relationship between kinship systems and sociocultural patterns and developments on a worldwide scale need not concern us here.[1] The most relevant part of my hypothesis for the problem at hand is how it can enable us to see the forces of kinship in the Chinese scene today even when conventional elements of kinship are absent. Although our immediate concern is with the Chinese case, we need to examine its American counterpart in order to reveal the role of kinship content in either one of them.

According to my hypothesis, the Chinese kinship system is dominated by the father-son dyad, the United States kinship system by the husband-wife dyad. The main attributes of the father-son dominated Chinese kinship content are as follows:

1. Continuity   3. Authority
2. Inclusiveness   4. Asexuality

In contrast, the main attributes of the husband-wife dominated American kinship content are as follows:[2]

1. Discontinuity   3. Volition[3]
2. Exclusiveness   4. Sexuality

The Characteristics of Chinese Kinship and Behavior

While every human being may be related to other human beings on the basis of a variety of principles—kinship, contract, hierarchy, ideology, etc.—the kinship principle comes first everywhere. In the course of growing up, an individual may discard the kinship principle for other bases of relating to others, but the Chinese individual is less likely to do so because one of the attributes of his kinship system is continuity. Furthermore, the Chinese individual tends not only to be reluctant to leave his first principle of human relationship—no matter how old he becomes—but he is also reluctant to replace it or sever connection with it even when he assumes relationships with other people on other principles. Thus, when he is married he will still tend to maintain close ties with his parents; and when he has to make career decisions his elders' wishes are likely to figure largely in these decisions. This pattern of behavior is also an intrinsic expression of the attribute of inclusiveness in the Chinese kinship system. According to this attribute, relationships tend to be additive rather than to supersede one another. There is a minimum tendency toward breaking relationships, and a maximum tendency toward blending them or blurring them.

Of course not all Chinese kinship ties are of equal intensity. There are closer ties and more remote ones. But the characteristic is that the closer ties tend to last for life and beyond, while the more remote kinship ties can always be readily called into service when circumstances permit or dictate.

The longer the vertical ties last, the more inclusive the horizontal ties become. If parents and unmarried children alone have to maintain their ties, a nuclear family will be the result. But if parents and their married sons and the sons' children maintain close ties, the pattern naturally becomes more commensurate with a joint family. By the same token, if there are close ties between lineal ancestors of many generations past and their descendants of many generations to come, then the number of collateral relatives involved will be large and some kind of clan or other forms of kinship-related larger grouping must necessarily come into play. In other words, inclusiveness also tends to be a function of continuity *and is a form of continuity itself.*

The attributes of discontinuity and exclusiveness inherent in the American kinship system mean that human ties are likely to be less long-lasting among Americans than among Chinese, that their boundaries will be more clearly defined, and that they will tend to supersede each other rather than be additive. As soon as it is physically and socially possible, Americans are encouraged to replace their kinship ties with other ties.

Of course not all Americans discard their kinship ties with equal facility. But those who do are praised with such terms as "mature," while those who do not are described as "poor marital risks." Consequently the American parent-child relationship legally comes to an end when the youngsters reach 18 or 21. The American household is characteristically one where even the husband and wife maintain individual privacy which cannot be intruded upon except by invitation, and where the parents alone can discipline their children—efforts at discipline by grandparents and others are resented and likely to be regarded as interference. Finally, marriage for any American means drastic reduction (if not total elimination) of psychosocial involvement with one's own parents.

The attributes of continuity and inclusiveness tend to cause Chinese kinship relationships not only to perpetuate themselves but also to expand their influences even when no kinship ties can be traced. For example, Chinese employees often make themselves "dry sons" or "nephews" of their employers. On the other hand, discontinuity and exclusiveness not only cause American kinship relationships to terminate themselves relatively soon in an individual's life, but even when kinship ties are indubitably in operation the tendency is to transform such ties into non-kinship form. For example, American parents have to try to make a point of establishing and maintaining friendship even with their grade-school children.

The attribute of authority in the Chinese system makes it relatively easy for the father and mother to exercise their authority. In fact, the authority of any superior relative tends to be as readily exerted as that of the father. Conversely the problem of the authority of the American father in his family is legendary and is rooted in the fact that volition and not authority is an intrinsic attribute of the American kinship system. The American father has so much of a problem with it precisely because the attribute of volition leads sons and daughters to challenge authority—everyone is to think for himself.

Some sociologists have tried to differentiate between authority and power. In my opinion, power is only one of three bases of authority. First, authority may be enforced by brute power of the physical or economic kind, but this is the least reliable base, for the authority will immediately become untenable when the force is withdrawn or weakened for any reason. Second, authority may be exerted by "charisma." My use of the term "charisma" is not entirely confined to the political sense in which Max Weber uses it. To me, charisma simply means a kind of attraction to a multitude of people for any reason whatever—technical, sexual, oratorical, etc. In this sense Marilyn Monroe and Babe Ruth had charisma just as did Franklin D. Roosevelt and Abraham Lincoln. A person enjoying charisma has influence and can command the voluntary following of a very large number of people. Such authority is easier to maintain than brute force but it is also subject to change because charisma fluctuates and does not last forever. The third basis for authority is tradition. Here the most important consideration is whether one should obey another person's commands for no other reason than that it is one's place to do so. Thus, where a system of slavery is prevalent the master does not have to explain to the slave why he must obey. The fact that the master holds the place of master and that the slave is in the place of a slave is enough reason for the slave to obey the master's commands. In the same way, in a caste society the duties and obligations between members of the higher and lower castes also do not have to be explained on any rational basis.

The Chinese father's authority was based on tradition, since authority is a deeply embedded feature of the Chinese kinship system. The Chinese son had to obey the father by virtue of the positions respectively occupied by the father and by the son. Hence the Chinese dictum: "No parents are wrong (vis-à-vis their children)" (*tien-hsia wu pu-shih chih fu-mu*). Contrariwise, in the American system the father can command the son, or the son is more likely to obey the father, only if the father's command seems agreeable or reasonable to the son. Otherwise, the son can challenge the father's command—and will get much sympathy from others for standing up to his father's unreasonable authority. Volition but not authority is a deeply embedded feature of the American kinship system, hence the American emphasis on child development and understanding. In America, authority is chiefly based on charisma with brute force lurking somewhere in the background (for example, parents can threaten recalcitrant children with disinheritance), never on tradition. In China, authority is chiefly based on tradition with brute force lurking somewhere in the background (for example, fathers could report disobedient sons to the authorities and secure immediate arrest and punishment). Occasionally charisma might expedite authority in some Chinese circumstances, but it has never been the most important basis for authority in China.

If tradition is the basis, authority is less likely to be challengeable, discontinuous, or temporary than if authority is based upon charisma or brute force. Hence, the attributes of continuity and authority are commensurate with each other, just as are the attributes of discontinuity and volition.

The attribute of asexuality in the Chinese kinship system finds expression in the custom of assigning sex to a restricted place. A woman has no business demonstrating her sex appeal to any except her husband (unless she wants to be considered "bad"), and then only for continuation of the family line. The strictures were so narrow, for example, that a mother-in-law was not supposed to conceive again if her married son already had a child. This custom was more or less prevalent throughout China, but more strictly observed in some localities than in others. In West Town, a community in southwestern China where I did a series of field studies between 1941 and 1943, I collected cases in which the mothers died as a result of abortion attempts undertaken because their daughters-in-law had already given birth to children. When the primary function of the continuation of family line is already being assumed by the younger woman, there is no reason for the older woman to engage in sex.

Conversely the attribute of sexuality in the American kinship system expresses itself in the generalization of sex into all sorts of relationships. The customary American aversion on the part of young men to going out with their sisters (and vice versa), and the exaggerated fear on the part of American males of any kind of physical intimacy with each other are just two indications of this generalized sexuality.

INFLUENCE OF KINSHIP CONTENT ON NON-KINSHIP BEHAVIOR

In the foregoing analysis we have already seen at some points how the Chinese kinship system affected Chinese behavior beyond the kinship organization. Now let us look for further evidence. The first and foremost is the scarcity of secondary and non-localized groupings in Chinese society as a whole. For example, the Chinese never developed an organized bar of lawyers, even though they always had many lawyers. There have, in fact, been few cause-oriented groupings on any voluntary basis. In their long history the Chinese have never been known for large-scale cause-promoting or cause-preventing organizations, the kind of organizations so common in the West. The Chinese have not been interested even in seeking the "truth," holding the "truth" to be either relative or self-evident.

There were, however, some non-kinship groupings in China. One of these was the "society for giving away free coffins." With the enormous Chinese emphasis on continuity, those who died without the care of heirs deserved much sympathy. Stories extolling filial piety such as one in which a daughter sells herself into slavery in order to bury her father are well known in China. Another non-kinship grouping was the "society for the preservation of papers bearing written characters." Viewing all written characters as having been handed down from ancient sages, and therefore respected objects, this society hired men to roam the streets collecting any and all pieces of paper bearing written characters. At the end of the day the man went to the local Confucian temple and burned his collection. He did not collect trash or litter, only pieces of paper that bore written characters—the object being to save the written characters from being trampled on.

However, even these organizations always remained localized affairs. The Chinese never had a *national* federation of the society of free coffin givers or of the society for the preservation of papers bearing written characters, or national conventions to discuss ways and means of improving the societies' work. In fact most of the local societies were not even organized; they were simply the pet projects of energetic and well-to-do individuals.

A very interesting Chinese non-kinship organization was the *hui-kuan,* which according to Ping-ti Ho is best translated into the German *Landsmannschaften.*[3] Professor Ho's use of the term *Landsmannschaften* is indeed sound, for these organizations are based on the Chinese idea of *tung-hsiang,* or fellowmen of the same local area, and are truly illustrative of the Chinese pattern discussed here.

Each *Landsmann's* group was an organization of local people in another area. In American terms, for example, there might be an organization of Chicago traders in New York called "Chicago Hui-kuan," or of North and South Dakota traders in Miami, Florida, called "Two-Dakotas Hui-kuan." A *hui-kuan* would usually have a house with some dormitory space and offices. A Chicago trader or office seeker arriving in New York would find in it a convenient place to live and some facilities for contacts for his own purposes. Throughout China, as Ho has demonstrated, there were many hundreds of such organizations. Some were organizations in the provincial capital for travelers from a district or several districts. Sometimes they were organizations in the national capital for travelers from different provinces or a section of a province. But their purpose was the twofold one of lodging and contacts, and no others. Furthermore, none of these organizations was consolidated on a national scale. The growth or decline of each was generally dependent upon the increase or decrease of the need of the local travelers. They were not cause-promoting organizations with a kind of ideal toward which they worked, and there were no all-China or even regional conventions of *Landsmannschaften* to discuss ways and means for better fulfilling their functions or enlarging their memberships.

In the light of the absence of cause-promoting or cause-preventing groupings, it becomes relatively clear why, in modern Chinese military history, commanders could be so easily and so often bought over by rival leaders, a phenomenon Martin Wilbur has so eloquently reported on.[4] Not being committed to any kind of abstract and non-kinship causes, those commanders tended to make their decision on the basis of what it would mean to their families and larger kinship groups. When the price was right they naturally saw nothing wrong with switching sides.

The second major correlate of the Chinese kinship system is the lack of centrifugal tendency on the part of the population in general. Being tied not only to his kinship structure but also to his kinship content, the Chinese individual was unwilling to leave his home community, or would return to it if he had to make his fame and fortune elsewhere. An old Chinese saying goes: "A man who has reached fame and fortune but does not return to his home village (town), is like one who wears the best of silk, but strolls on the street during a pitch-dark night."

Since the Communist assumption of power in China, there has been an eruption of talk and writing in the United States concerning the alleged threat of millions of Chinese outside of China, especially in Southeast Asia. It is, of course, true that there are sizeable Chinese communities in many Southeast Asian countries. Forty per cent of Malaya's population is Chinese; about 10 per cent of the population of Thailand is Chinese. But had the Chinese been as inclined to leave China as were the Irish and the Swiss, or all Western Europeans, one should not find it difficult to perceive the possibility that a majority of Southeast Asia territories and many other parts of the world would have been dominated by the Chinese instead of by Westerners.

The objective fact is that, in spite of poverty, dynastic changes, and invasion by tribal peoples from the north, very few Chinese—in proportion to the total Chinese population—have ever left China. The Chinese population in Southeast Asia was drawn overwhelmingly from the coastal regions of two Chinese provinces: Fukien, the province directly opposite Formosa, and Kwangtung (including Hainan Island), the province of which Kwangchow is the capital. Ninety per cent of the Chinese population in Hawaii (which forms less than 6 per cent of the total population of that state even today) came from one district in Kwangtung province which happens to be the birthplace of Dr. Sun Yat-sen. More than 80 per cent of the forebears of the Chinese in mainland United States came from four districts, which are located next to that one. Chinese in other areas simply did not have this tendency to emigrate from their ancestral land. Here and there on continental Europe are infinitesimal groups of Chinese merchants from Chekiang province who went to France and Germany as part of the labor force contributed by China to the Allies in World War I.

Historically a few Chinese explorers achieved great renown. In the Ming dynasty, a eunuch admiral commanded a large fleet, collected vassals Chinese-style in various parts of Southeast Asia and reached as far as the east coast of Africa. (At one point Admiral Cheng's forces captured the King of Kandy in the highlands of Ceylon and brought him back to China a captive, where he eventually passed away.) In this regard, the developmental trends of Chinese immigrant groups abroad and European immigrant groups abroad have presented a sharp historical contrast. It was people of European origin who set up the independent countries of the United States, Mexico, and all the Latin American republics as well as Australia and New Zealand. No Chinese colony ever decided to declare itself a new nation in some new territory independent from China except once briefly for a span of about 10 years in Borneo. The Chinese were too much oriented toward their "homes."

Finally, the contrast between Chinese centripetality and European centrifugality (of which the American case is an extreme version) is nowhere shown more clearly than in the history of proselytism. Practically all the missionaries of the world are European or American, not Chinese.[5] Once in the T'ang dynasty about 3,000 devout Chinese monks went separately over a period of several hundred years to India *in search of the true teachings of Buddha for the purpose of bringing them back to China*. To the best of my knowledge only one Chinese monk ever went to Japan for the purpose of proselytism. Even in this case he went at the repeated urging of some Japanese monks who were in China on a pilgrimage first (Reischaver 1955).

A third correlate of the Chinese kinship system is the desire to seek authority in all interpersonal relations outside of kin. In fact, Chinese scholars and officials and others always made use of actual kinship ties or teacher-pupil ties whenever these could be traced. In the absence of such actual ties, they would not hesitate to initiate pseudo-kinship or pseudo-teacher-pupil ties through which the seeker of influence always took the part of the inferior. Those who have read the Chinese novel, *The Golden Lotus* (Egerton 1954), can readily call to mind the case of Hsi Men Ch'ing, the main character, who enjoyed enormous powers because of his alliances with various officials. In one instance Hsi Men Ch'ing scored a major advancement by getting himself accepted by the Imperial Tutor as a ritual son. His success was preceded by a great deal of help on the part of the Imperial Tutor's household manager and twenty loads of extraordinarily extravagant gifts as Hsi Men Ch'ing's offering in celebration of that high official's birthday. In fact, Hsi Men Ch'ing even referred to himself as "your pupil" in conversation with the Imperial Tutor's household manager. Hsi Men Ch'ing is an imaginary character, but his action patterns are normal for China.

Richard H. Solomon of the University of Michigan has gathered a very interesting piece of evidence which supports our analysis of the characteristic Chinese approach to authority. He points out that "the notion that people relate to authority in very different ways has not been well recognized in political science—primarily because of the lack, until recently, of cross-cultural and comparative studies" (Solomon 1966). Solomon's findings, based on intensive interviews and the use of some specially constructed TAT pictures in Taiwan and Hong Kong, indicate that in the traditional Chinese educational process

> parents and teacher both tended to discourage a child's efforts at autonomy and self-expression in terms of what they saw as a higher goal of group solidarity. The discipline of a traditional male's childhood centered about restraining his own impulses for action and "holding in" emotional frustrations that came from confrontations with harsh and manipulative authority. [The traditional Chinese child] developed a sense of self-control primarily in matters of emotional discipline, rather than in discipline of his body and physical behavior. Guidance in his actions, he learned, was to come from authoritative adults.   (389)

I think the latter part of Solomon's observation contains a misreading of the Chinese personality configuration. For in making a rather sharp contrast between emotional discipline and physical discipline he has given the impression that the Chinese have little physical discipline. The fact is that when Chinese college students are compared with their American counterparts they tend to be less spontaneous and less active—that is, in a certain sense, more physically disciplined. (This difference is at least in part responsible for the stereotype of Chinese inscrutability.) What really distinguishes the Chinese from the Americans—a comparison Solomon seems to be making even though not explicitly—is their lesser emphasis on individual autonomy and self-expression and greater expectations from and receptivity to authority.

Another correlate of the Chinese type of kinship system comes from the attribute of asexuality. Sex tends to be restricted to a corner of the Chinese social and cultural world and not generalized into diverse aspects of it as in the West. For the Chinese, sex is relegated to where it belongs—so to speak—that is, to marriage or to prostitution. It does not operate in other areas where it is not directly relevant. Therefore, even today the Western term "sex appeal" tends to have an undesirable connotation when translated into Chinese. On the other hand, in the American culture, sex is so ubiquitous that it tends to appear in the most unexpected quarters, whether it is a question of buying one kind of soap or another, or smoking one kind of cigarette or another.

The Chinese have never had the problem of sexuality disguised as art. There has simply been no attempt at injecting sexuality into the arts; consequently, there is no body of Chinese literature devoted to explaining or defending sex-infiltrated products as art. (Thus there can never be Chinese counterparts to the case of Greek statues found unacceptable for museums in Texas.) At different times the Chinese have had a great deal of pornography circulated—now surreptitiously, now openly; but these have been works solely of pornographic intent, not artistic.

If my observations are correct, then the so-called "puritanism" observed by many non-Chinese visitors to mainland China today must be regarded as a result of Western projection into the Chinese scene of a point of view rooted in the Western kinship system where sexuality is a prominent attribute.

Chinese women of good families have never worried about their sex appeal to the general public, even when they appeared in public. Their clothing was designed to conceal rather than to reveal their forms. Consequently the kind of blue and formless uniforms which have struck non-Chinese observers in mainland China so forcibly was not due to any particular Chinese Communist attempt to promote "puritanism," but simply a continuation of something that has always been Chinese. The Communist administration has now induced or enabled a much larger number of Chinese women than ever before to participate in public activities, whether in government, commerce, industry, schools, or public demonstrations. The Communist administration may have accentuated an age-old pattern to a certain extent, but it did not create it. Formless blue work clothes or uniforms are perfectly in keeping with the Chinese attribute of asexuality.

With their kinship attribute of asexuality, Chinese females who achieve professional competence or political prominence tend to be treated in terms of their professional competence or political prominence, but not of their sex. On the other hand, no matter how much equality of the sexes is discussed and emphasized in the United States, the female professional will always be subjected—either covertly or overtly—to discrimination by males. American males tend to see female professionals as always posing a threat, because members of the fair sex are automatically regarded as being able to offer something other than their professional competence which—inevitably—puts the males at a disadvantage. Sexuality being generalized, it is impossible for most American males to see females entirely free from that attribute.

This does not mean that the Chinese like to have female leaders. Their tradition is very clear and emphatic on this point: males are superior to females; males should handle affairs outside of the home, females should handle those inside it. Only a few times in Chinese history have empress dowagers actually usurped the imperial power. One empress even ruled as "emperor," but the point is that when and if such women succeeded, Chinese males tended to accept them, more readily than most American males, in terms of their power or talent. Even when Chinese eunuchs became powerful—as they did during parts of the Ming dynasty—they were accepted and obeyed by members of the bureaucracy in much the same way as were emperors or powerful ministers. The question of their being "sexless" did not seem to influence their functioning as administrators or authority figures. The only limitation was that, since female rule was not part of the Chinese tradition, Chinese female rulers were prevented by their countrymen's unwillingness to part with tradition—an expression of the kinship attribute of continuity—from making their rule permanent. Any such usurpation could not, therefore, be legitimatized and was always temporary.

A fifth correlate of the Chinese kinship system is to be found in the peculiar nature of Chinese bureaucracy. Bureaucracy everywhere has certain universal characteristics, but in addition to these, Chinese bureaucracy had some characteristics of its own. The members of the lower echelons of the Chinese bureaucracy have always looked up through a particular line of affiliation to the members of the higher echelons—either along kinship, pseudo-kinship, or teacher-pupil lines. Therefore, the programs for "self-strengthening" initiated in the late Ch'ing period by the four outstanding men—Tseng Kuo-fan, Tso Tsung-t'ang, Li Hung-chang, and Chang Chih-tung—were not coordinated with each other. Instead, they tended to undercut each other's strength because—since the groupings were organized on specific affiliations, and not on more abstract causes—it was not possible for them to join forces on any permanent basis. The primary lines of affiliation could not be disregarded, and such dividing lines always prevented generation of overall strength for overall causes necessary to do the job. The lines of human affiliation always stood in the way of the issues.

This analysis adds a new dimension to the fact that Chinese society in the late Ch'ing period possessed no secondary elite to serve as an effective force for modernization and as an effective link between the general population and the power center. The infrastructure of the society could not deal with the conditions created by the impact of the West. In terms of my analysis, the kinship content of the Chinese made the kind of divided affiliation under able men like Tseng, Tso, Li, and Chang inevitable, and in turn such divided affiliation made the absence of an effective link between the general population and the new power center inevitable. The "self-strengthening" activities under these leaders could not spread into the general population in any overall way. Old people were always in command in China because the lower echelons always looked up to their own particular elders for guidance. The old people in each grouping were in command because the younger men, being products of a kinship system in which the attribute of authority was dominant, gave them that command.

The last distinguishing feature of Chinese bureaucracy is that it pigeonholed the individual even more than bureaucracies in the West would have done in the normal course of events. Bureaucracy means pigeonholing, and all bureaucrats anywhere are interested in "holding the line" and "doing the right thing" and therefore are somewhat more negative than positive in approach. But Chinese bureaucracy has excelled in this regard. For example, the Chinese idea of *te jen* mentioned by Philip Kuhn is an essential expression of this tendency (Kuhn 1968), and reminds us of what Solomon found in his interviews among Chinese refugees in Taiwan and Hong Kong. In the West the prevalent emphasis is on the development of the individual and on improving the society so that it provides additional opportunities for the individual. The Chinese concept of *te jen* is not aimed primarily at individual development but, rather, stresses the need to find the right individual for the right pigeonhole so that affairs of the state (or of the village) can be run smoothly in terms of the needs of the larger organization.

Corresponding to the concept of *te jen* in the case of bureaucracy, a common Chinese concept in the kinship sphere is *hsing chia*. *Te jen* means that you find the right man for the public office; *hsing chia* means that you find the right member to prosper the kinship group.

In the light of the foregoing analysis we can also understand why the Chinese have always shown a lack of concern for organized religion. The history of religion in the West has been marked by great turmoil, population movements, persecution, and wars. The history of religion in China is singularly uneventful—at least, so far as the extent to which religion has made any difference in Chinese history. The fact is, in the first place, the Chinese never had the idea of a congregation, that one "belonged" to a particular established religious faith and temple. The Chinese approach to temples is essentially like their approach to stores. Whichever store gave them the most satisfaction they would return to. And they would not hesitate to switch their patronage or to deal with several stores at the same time.

The lack of specific affiliation to particular faiths and temples is indicative of the absence of deep commitment on the part of the Chinese to such causes and organizations. It is not hard to see how this Chinese approach to various religions would supply little impetus for persecution. The usual analysis of persecution concentrates on those who persecuted, or were bent on doing so, neglecting the role of the persecuted. In my view, intensive and extensive persecution requires not only persecutors but also people who invite persecution because of their commitment. The Chinese lack of commitment to religion has made religious persecution unnecessary.

Some scholars may regard the persecution of Buddhists in the T'ang dynasty as contrary to the last observation (Yang 1961). But this is a misreading or exaggeration of the Chinese facts. A few T'ang emperors persecuted Buddhists, but not because they disliked the new faith; rather, primarily because of their suspicion that treasonable elements were using monasteries and monkhood as a cover or temporary refuge. Consequently the persecution by the emperors took three forms. First, the monasteries and temples, as well as monks and nuns, were to be registered and regulated to make sure that no dangerous elements were disguising their rebellious activities. Second, in the so-called Great Persecution of 845–846, the Emperor Wu-tsung decreed that "only two temples with thirty monks each were permitted to stand in each of the two capitals, Changan and Loyang. Of the 228 prefectures in the Empire, only the capital cities of the 'first grade' prefectures were permitted to retain one temple each with ten monks" (Hu 1953).

Compared with their European counterparts, such forms of persecution can only be described as perfunctory. If the Chinese authorities were really interested in the elimination of Buddhism as a religious faith, they would never have given Buddhist monks and temples regulated recognition and existence. They would have aimed at extermination, as did European kings and popes, even to the extent of detecting by inquisition or witch-hunting traces of the undesirable faith in persons who otherwise had already professed some form of government-accepted religion.

The third form of Chinese persecution of Buddhists was to require monks and nuns in excess of the authorized number to return to civilian life. The interesting thing is that none of the hundreds of thousands of monks and nuns forced to return to civilian life seemed to have resisted the order; the persecuting T'ang Emperor got his wish without having to resort to execution or imprisonment. It is hard to find better and more direct proof of the Chinese lack of desire to invite persecution.

It is small wonder then that the Chinese persecution of Buddhism was short-lived, limited to four occurrences up to A.D. 955 and completely absent since. C. K. Yang, who, I think, has not perceived the significant difference between the Chinese and Western patterns of religious persecution, comments on the above facts as follows:

After 955, there were no further major persecutions of the Buddhists, but Buddhism as a nationally organized force intimately linked to political issues also came to an end. From this period on, Buddhism became acculturated to the Chinese social milieu both in its theology and its organizational relationship with the secular authority. (1961:122–123)

In view of the continuous history of religious persecution and strife in the West, one finds it difficult to accept such an observation. How did Buddhism in China become so *easily* "acculturated to the Chinese social milieu both in its theology and its organizational relationship with the secular authority" while Judaism, Protestantism, and Catholicism continue even today to be sources of trouble and to divide Westerners? The Chinese lack of commitment to particular faiths and, hence, their custom of having no firm memberships in particular congregations are the obvious answer.

Even the Chinese emperors, each of whom always had the absolute power of life and death, could not (or found it impractical to) force the people to worship their and their ancestral souls in separate public temples. According to Ho, the founder of the Han dynasty had his ancestral temples erected in every province of the empire:

From his death in 195 B.C. to 40 B.C., every deceased Emperor had his temples in the capital city and provinces. From the third Emperor to the eighth, each erected his temples during his lifetime. By about the middle of the first century B.C., there were 176 imperial temples and 30 temples for empresses and crown princes throughout the empire, which required 24,455 victuals and sacrifices annually, 45,129 temple guards, and a government staff of 12,147 in charge of sacrificial ceremonies and music. (1968:17)

In spite of such obvious desire on the part of the rulers to deify themselves, and the tendency for them to proliferate their own temples, the custom of individual temples for individual emperors was shortly abolished, and the trend turned into consolidation of these separate temples into a single clan temple for each dynasty. "As a result of the debate of 40 B.C., imperial temples in the provinces were abolished. From eastern Han (A.D. 25–220) onward there was usually only one temple erected for the dynasty founder after his death to which all later emperors of the same dynasty were posthumously attached."

Professor Ho gives a functional explanation of this trend, from greater proliferation of individual temples to the consolidation of all the temples into one for the entire dynasty: "Since western Han time, the emperor's charisma had been generally taken for granted and an elaborate system of imperial temples was no longer needed" (Ibid). I disagree with this interpretation. The tendency of autocratic or despotic rulers everywhere is the glorification of the ruler's person. There is simply no evidence that the emperor's charisma in China had at any time been so generally taken for granted. In fact, more symbols (such as prostration in audience) were added to the court rules to sanctify the Emperor's augustness as Chinese history unfolded. The clear trend was from a relatively more equalitarian approach to the emperor to a more hierarchical one. No Chinese emperor was ever known voluntarily to reduce external signs of his augustness.

My interpretation is that the consolidation of the individual emperors' temples into one dynastic temple was an expression of the strength of Chinese kinship in two ways. On the one hand, the people could not be induced to take the many temples as seriously as the emperors had wished. On the other hand, even for the august person of the emperor the kinship solidarity of his clan overruled his need for individual expression of his own power and prestige. The precedence of collectivity over individual prominence was the Chinese rule among commoners, and this rule obviously was strong enough even to overcome the desire and necessity on the part of the emperors to make themselves each a separate and final symbol of authority.

All Chinese prominent families used to eulogize their particular ancestors by the expression *tsu-te tsung-kung* ("ancestors' merits and efforts of the lineage") by which was meant "our prominence today is a result of the cumulative merits and efforts of our ancestors and clan members." How could the extreme power, prestige, and wealth enjoyed by any single emperor be due to his own merits and efforts only? It is from this angle that we can also understand why, as pointed out by Herrlee G. Creel, even though King Wu was really the de facto founder of the ancient Chou dynasty (*ca.* 1500 B.C.) because he conquered or subdued rival feudal lords, the official inscriptions always gave his father King Wen the greater place of honor (Creel 1968). All subsequent founders of Chinese dynasties, including that of the Manchu, pursued the same course of *chui feng* to their forebears; that is, posthumously conferring upon them greater places of honor.[6] This is the true way of the ancestors' shadow.

In a similar light we can now understand why, since later Han times, the ancestral temple of the ruling dynasty was the sole concern of the imperial descendants and not of the people. The emperor's ancestors were the concern of the emperor and his kinsmen alone, just as among the common people the ancestors of each clan were the concern of the members of that clan alone. There was no common worship of a common ancestor between members of different clans among the commoners, and there could not be any common worship of the same between the emperor's kinsmen and the ordinary people.[7] The kinship principle was so strong in China that it even separated the ruler and the ruled.

The unimportance of religious affiliation also explains why Chinese dynastic rulers seemed also to be very generous toward the ancestral temples of the previous dynastic rulers. For example, instead of having them destroyed in order to eliminate symbols of previous power, most Chinese dynasties preserved them even to the extent of allowing regular offerings and sacrifices, though naturally on a reduced scale compared to those made to their own temples. When the Emperor K'ang-hsi of the Ch'ing dynasty visited Nanking, the original seat of the Ming dynasty where the tomb of the founder of the Ming dynasty was located, he did an unusual thing. He prostrated himself and kowtowed before the shrine of the founder of the Ming dynasty.[8]

To sum up the analysis so far, Chinese kinship content bred a kind of centripetal orientation in the individual, so that he tended not to leave or forsake his kinship base as he went through life. He could cooperate best among non-kins by creating pseudo-kinship ties, but he would find it extremely difficult to commit himself to groups or causes outside of his kinship base, especially if such commitments conflicted with it or required severance from it. Furthermore, and this is particularly important in our present connection, if and when he left his kinship base entirely, his ways of relating to his fellow human beings retained their roots in what we designate as Chinese kinship content and its component attributes.

The concrete expressions of these attributes are often so different from the usual kinship and pseudo-kinship ties that they tend to obscure the vision of even acute scholars. As early as the 1920's and 1930's, Chinese and Western observers spoke about the changing Chinese family when they saw some educated Chinese young men and women dating each other or choosing their own mates, living in nuclear households, or talking about independence from their parents. What they did not see, and what most observers still fail to see, is that such structural changes in Chinese kinship, even if they became more widespread than they actually have been, did not automatically alter the true influences of the Chinese kinship content in the Chinese society at large; these influences have been over two thousand years in their entrenchment and proliferation.

A number of scholars have observed that the Chinese have the longest continuous civilization of the world. In fact, both Creel and C. P. Fitz-Gerald feel that the Chinese civilization is unique. While I do not necessarily consider Chinese civilization unique, I do believe that it is because of the nature of the Chinese kinship structure and content that the system has lasted so long and developed in essentially the same terms for more than two thousand years. The stable and resilient cornerstone is the Chinese kinship system which, on the one hand, has kept a majority of Chinese busy with their relatives and their local groups, and, on the other hand, has kept them away from strong or absolute involvement with larger organizations and causes which might alter or seriously challenge their kinship roots. The authority of the ruling dynasty was not challenged except when natural forces such as famine or population growth, or human forces such as external invasion or excessive bureaucratic corruption so tipped the scale as to threaten the bare existence of large segments of the people. Then, relatively temporary chaos ensued until some enterprising new man, aided by a decrease in population pressure through civil disorder and natural disorder, was able to restore balance by setting up a new dynasty. In so doing, he was bringing about no successful revolution but only a successful rebellion. He and his heirs would rule the country according to the same institutional framework and in the same spirit as before. So long as the larger factors were undisturbed, even an idiotic heir could run the country, for the emperors ruled by the negative acquiescence of the people rather than from their positive support. The people tolerated the emperors as long as the emperors knew how to play their part by not interfering actively, or too much with the private activities of their subjects.

This was a negative stability, based on a live-and-let-live policy, but not a positive stability with a high degree of active political integration and national solidarity, such as is found in either the democratic or the authoritarian West. At any given point in time, the number of Chinese who actively participated in governmental affairs, or who were even interested in governmental affairs, was very small. The primary concern of a majority of Chinese was how to protect and enhance their private kinship interests. They could do this by becoming the most favored bureaucrats or subjects of the rulers. If that did not prove possible, they would not greatly resist retirement to their primary kinship spheres where they would at least receive the adulation of their descendants.

Once this sophisticated and well-developed society and civilization (as Creel put it) was toppled, it fell with great force. It fell with such great force precisely because it was sophisticated and well-developed in its particular pattern of mutual adjustment between the rulers, the bureaucracy, the local gentry, and the common people, each with their own particular kinship sphere for psycho-social needs such as sociability, security, and status. Had it not been so sophisticated and well-developed, it would have been more open to large changes. It was not open to such changes because the Chinese were too tied to their kinship structure and content, finding too many satisfactions in them to be easily disengaged from them and assume absolute commitments to groups and causes unrelated or contrary to them.

This gave the Chinese society no suitable infra-structure for drastic breaks with the past. There was simply no across-the-board secondary elite which could serve as a link between the common people (with no reference to kinship affiliation) and any possible new centers of innovative power. Having developed so sophisticated a civilization, and having been reared in their kinship attributes of continuity, inclusiveness, and authority, the Chinese simply had too many answers from the past which they thought could deal with the new problems. When some answers were not effective in dealing with the new problems the Chinese could either retreat to their kinship sphere, or—too immersed in their kinship content to see its inadequacy—easily find other answers from the wealth of their sophisticated and well-developed past.

When the Chinese repeatedly failed in their attempts to deal with the impact of the West, they finally went into a number of convulsions beginning with the Taiping Rebellion, through the Boxer Uprising of

1900, the Revolution of 1911, the Northern Expedition of 1926–28, and finally the Communist Revolution which culminated in the establishment of the Peking regime in 1949. Throughout the century of turmoil, there were intellectuals and leaders who thought the correct answer was complete Westernization, or a revitalization of Chinese traditional values, or a compromise between the two. But the real problem was how to entice a majority of the people away from not only their traditional kinship structure but also its content.

THE OBJECTIVES UNDERLYING THE CULTURAL REVOLUTION

Now we are in a position to return to Schurmann's analysis of the aim of the Red Guard movement. The twin goals of any modern Chinese government—Nationalist or Communist—are national greatness and industrialization. The second goal will, of course, raise the general level of living, but it especially will serve as the sinew of national greatness. But so long as the Chinese are embedded physically in their traditional kinship structure and psychologically immersed in its kinship content, they are not likely to move very far in the desired direction.

As noted previously, the attack on Chinese traditional kinship structure began long before the Communist Revolution and lasted all the way down to the early 1950's, as Schurmann correctly observed. The inciting of some children to denounce their parents, recruitment of youngsters for youth corps and political activities, the assignment of college graduates to work in rural or border areas, the relocation of ancestral tombs and the discouragement of the continuation of the age-old custom of family and clan graveyards—these and others were means of getting the people out of their kinship structure. But the attack on Chinese traditional kinship content was much less obvious before, and only intensified since the early 1950's. The reason is that the stumbling block posed by Chinese kinship structure was much more obvious than that posed by Chinese kinship content. The latter is more difficult to identify than the former. Once this is understood, we can easily see that the Red Guards are simply one of the instruments for attacking the many underlying psychological legacies of Chinese kinship content characterized by, according to our analysis, the attributes of continuity, inclusiveness, authority, and asexuality. The unleashing of the Red Guards seems bizarre only to those who do not understand this.

However, not all attributes of the Chinese traditional kinship content are equally dysfunctional to the desired changes. The attribute of continuity was related to the fact that the Chinese were resistant to breaking with the past, so that there were only rebellions and no revolutions. What the Chinese Communists want, as did the Nationalists before them to a lesser extent, is a revolutionary break with the past and not merely a replacement of leadership personnel. This was why they have had public confessions, compulsory autobiography-writing, work-study programs, and extensive rectification campaigns (*san-fan, wu-fan,* etc.) even before the Red Guards upheaval.

Similarly, inclusiveness, another attribute of the Chinese kinship system, is also dysfunctional. This attribute was characteristically expressed in such Chinese behavior patterns as never allowing politics or religion or other non-kinship matters to divide human beings. For example, Chinese have never allowed religion to be a bar to marriage, or politics to separate children and parents. What the Communist leaders wish to bring about is a condition in which *only* those who share the same correct political views come and work together. Hence, divergence in political views has recently become, unlike former times, a bar to marriage, to association, and to friendship. The aim is to replace the age-old tendency of inclusiveness rooted in kinship with a tendency toward exclusiveness based on sharply drawn ideological lines.

The Communist leaders do not want to eliminate all attributes (or all aspects of them) of the Chinese kinship system. Some are being redeployed for achievement of new goals. It has been noted that in China, even under the Communists, old leaders keep command, regardless of how old they become. This seems highly consonant with the attributes of continuity, and especially with that of authority. In practical terms, this means that those who had authority tend to continue holding it, so long as they seem to be able to deal effectively with all or at least the most urgent problems. This was the substance of the age-old Chinese concept of Mandate of Heaven. It is difficult to imagine why the Chinese leaders would want to attack this aspect of the attribute of authority.

We have already noted how the alleged "puritanism" in mainland China today is a Western misreading of a traditional Chinese pattern, one rooted in their kinship attribute of asexuality. For Chinese girls to appear at work or in the streets wearing formless blue, or otherwise seemingly unmindful of their sex appeal, or for Chinese couples to converse unromantically about locomotives or commune production, these are in perfect keeping with Chinese custom. A popular Chinese love song in the 1930's depicted two lovers parting. The girl was seeing her sweetheart off by going a last extra mile with him. They were both enchanted by the beautiful scenery but saddened by the impending separation. And she went on: "For you I am willing to share the same pillow and mat." But he responded: "A gentleman must be moral in his conduct; how dare he follow his own private desires?" An American girl in similar circumstances would undoubtedly have found his response upsetting, to say the least, but the Chinese girl saw no cause for annoyance or worry.[9]

Since the revolutionary goals require that more Chinese become involved in non-kinship activities more intensively than ever before, any lowering of romantic fever in the interest of these larger goals is welcome.[10] In this we should remember that in essence early Christianity also tried to divert romantic energy to devotion to God. That was why St.

Paul thought celibacy to be much better than the marital state. The difference is that the Chinese under Communism do not have to expend so much effort repressing their sexuality. The attribute of asexuality already characterized their pattern of husbanding their total energy so that sex did not have to be deposed; it never occupied a central place in their scheme of things as it did in the West.

Beside the measures which are relevant to specific Chinese kinship attributes, there is a whole series of others that aim at reducing kinship involvement and increasing social and political integration in general. But most of these have not been well understood by students of China.

Take the "Great Leap Forward," for example. There is no doubt that economically it was a failure. The backyard furnaces produced iron and steel that could not be economically and efficiently used. Agricultural production suffered terribly because of diversion of manpower and energy to non-agricultural objectives. Although the severe crop failure of 1959–61 could not entirely be laid at the door of the Great Leap, the latter had a great deal of bearing on the former. But the Great Leap was psychosocially a good thing and must be considered a success. For the first time in Chinese history, the common people were made to become aware of some relationship, some intrinsic and positive relationship, between what they did as individuals and the overall purposes of the state.

Another example is the commune. The Western press has often tried to feed the public's desire for cheap sensationalism by concentrating on the greatly exaggerated report of separation between husbands and wives or the breaking-up of the family. Several important aspects of the commune are particularly commensurate with our analysis, but only one of them will be dealt with here. This is its work-point system.

The system operates more or less as follows. Every member of the commune receives a number of work points in the total work accounts of that commune for one full day's work according to previously agreed upon criteria differentiating men, women, and adolescents. No one is paid daily, but everyone accumulates work points in the commune's accounts. The accounts are settled at fixed intervals and the total proceeds of each period are usually settled in the proportion of something like 40 per cent for the commune as a whole (to go to group benefits and improvements) and 60 per cent for the individual. The details of the accounting of work points vary from place to place, as does also the period of settlement.

There is no question as to what the work point does in terms of its possible effect on interpersonal relationships. For example, some women prefer to earn work-points instead of having more children who tend to tie them down, in spite of crèches and nurseries. Even more important, for the first time, women have come to appreciate their own labors in terms of some standards other than as wife, mother, or daughter-in-law, so that the importance of their contribution is economically, and therefore more objectively, measurable. This to me is a most important device for individualization, for loosening of kinship bonds, with corresponding possibility for increase in involvement in larger groups on non-kinship bases.

Curiously the mechanism indicated here is revealed in a letter to Ann Landers by an American lady. This lady said that in all of her married years she had "felt like a nobody because I was only a 'housewife.' " Her husband made her feel that she should be grateful to him for putting food in her mouth and clothes on her back. However, she now felt better because the home economics department of her state college had published a leaflet in chart form which showed "what a housewife is worth in dollars and cents per week on today's labor market." According to this chart's very moderate wage scale, her work came to something like $7800 a year. So she says,

> Believe it or not, this leaflet gave me dignity. I am no longer feeling like a parasite. Tonight when Mr. Greatheart comes home I am going to greet him like a woman who earns about $8000 a year, because that's what I am.[11]

In my view, this American lady's grievance and her way of redressing it explain very eloquently one of the most basic possible effects of the work-point system in Chinese communes. In both cases the question is the change of the woman from being an appendage of her husband or of a kinship group into an independent, valuable unit of production in the larger frame of reference. The difference is that the American lady, living in a civilization that is already individual-centered, has taken the matter in her own hands to make her man see the light, while her Chinese sister, living in a society which has always subordinated the individual to a place in a kinship network of privileges, duties, and obligations, is being ushered by way of the work-point system into a new view of her place in the national scheme of things.

The present Red Guard movement must be seen in the same light. I have no quarrel at all with the thesis that this movement is primarily aimed at the party functionaries. But it is unmistakable that this attack on the party functionaries came *after many different movements attacking bureaucrats from the previous regime, intellectuals, landlords, industrial and commercial leaders.*

The party people, since the revolution of 1949, have constituted a new elite. They have enjoyed seventeen years of special privileges and power. These people are not a single entity, any more than is the army. A multifarious party elite have to be, from time to time, made more uniform according to the overall ideology, just as a multifarious army has to undergo the same process. Furthermore, what is achieved in one generation needs not only to be enlarged in the next generation, but even the gains that have already been made need also to be maintained through a constant process of re-examination and reintegration. Under Chiang Kai-shek, a nationally publicized slogan consisted of two lines from Dr. Sun Yat-sen's last will:

> *The revolution is not yet a complete success,*
> *Comrades must persevere still more.*

Can we not see Mao's Red Guards as an attempt to encourage comrades to persevere still more?

But Mao's China is much better organized than that of his predecessor; Mao and his oligarchy also have much greater power and they have taken more drastic steps than their predecessors. Chiang's New Life Movement organization sent Boy Scouts and other New Life Movement workers to separate pedestrians on the sidewalks of Nanking, so that all should proceed forward on the left, according to Chinese traffic rules. In terms of Chinese history, that kind of "missionary" effort was already a departure from tradition. Mao's Red Guards are much more zealous and violent. Depending upon one's point of view, Mao's Red Guards are comparable to American White Citizens Councilors, the Ku Klux Klansmen, or frontier vigilantes; or they may be likened to prison reformers, protestant evangelists and revivalists, or Women's Christian Temperance Union members led by Carrie Nation, who, with hatchet in hand, busted up many saloons. In any case, they are even more drastic departures from China's past. But in the Chinese leaders' view what the country needs most is a sharp break with the past, a reduction of the attribute of continuity, a modified use of the attribute of authority, a greatly modified version of the attribute of inclusiveness, and an accentuation, at least for the time being, of the attribute of asexuality.

CONCLUSION

The hypothesis presented here does not attempt to negate the importance of other factors such as (1) Western invasion of China (for example, what would have happened in China if the West had not actively knocked down her doors and kept up its intrusion?); (2) population pressure (for example, would the Communist leaders have chosen other courses if man-land ratio were more favorable?); (3) the condition of the Chinese economy (for example, did the economic difficulties of 1959–61 determine the subsequent policies?); (4) the wisdom, or the lack of it, of unleashing the Red Guards at this time; (5) the wisdom, or the lack of it, of the present near break with Russia.

This is a working hypothesis, to be further refined and tested. In presenting my thoughts, I hope to see if we may acquire new insights by looking at some of the facts presented by others from a different point of view. At the same time, I am inviting criticism so that the formulation of this hypothesis and its implications may be improved. Many problems pertaining to the hypothesis have not been worked out. Some of these will be treated in a forthcoming book, already referred to, and need not detain us here.[13]

It is not my intention to try to explain everything with this hypothesis. What I do emphasize is that there are certain discernible forces in the Chinese kinship system which may be linked, by means of this hypothesis, with certain regular patterns of activities and developments in the larger Chinese society. I maintain, therefore, that we can achieve a more complete and better understanding of what is going on in China today with this hypothesis than without it.

NOTES

1. An international symposium on this hypothesis was held August 20–29, 1966, at Burg Wartenstein, Austria. The nineteen participants (sixteen anthropologists and three sociologists) each contributed a paper criticizing, revising, or substantiating the hypothesis. The results have been published in Hsu (1971d).

2. The derivations and definitions of these attributes are given in Hsu (1965).

3. Ping-ti Ho, "Salient Aspects of China's Heritage," (Ho Ping-ti and Tsou Tang, 1968:34). Extensive data can be found in Ping-ti Ho, *Chung-kuo hui-kuan shih-lüeh* [An Historical Survey of *Landsmannschaften* in China] (Taipei: Student Publishing Co., 1966).

4. Martin Wilbur, verbal comments in this Conference.

5. The Arabs had one big outburst of proselytism linked with their military conquests, accompanied by forcible attempts at conversion.

6. In Western usage, an honor awarded posthumously is a reward for merit or achievement on the part of some one who did not live to receive it. According to Chinese custom, *chui feng* means either a posthumous award in the Western sense, or a posthumous award for merit or achievement not on the part of the deceased recipient but for merit or achievement on the part of his descendant. When the founder of a dynasty conferred this honor on his deceased father (usually also on his deceased mother) the underlying assumption was that he owed all he had accomplished to his parents. The latter was the most essential element of *hsiao* ("filial piety").

7. This is in sharp contrast to the Japanese custom, according to which the emperor's ancestress—especially the first ancestress—was regarded as being the progenitor of all Japanese and hence the imperial ancestral temple at Ise was, and is, a place of worship for all Japanese.

8. I am indebted to Ping-ti Ho for this information.

9. The Chinese-American contrast between patterns of man-woman relationship is extensively analyzed in Francis L. K. Hsü, *American and Chinese: Two Ways of Life* (New York: Abelard-Schuman, 1953). (Revised and updated third edition: *Americans and Chinese: Passage to Differences,* Honolulu: University of Hawaii Press, 1981.)

10. Ezra F. Vogel has made an excellent analysis of this transition in terms of one from friendship to comradeship in his "From Friendship to Comradeship: The Change in Personal Relations in Communist China," *China Quarterly,* no. 21 (March 1965), pp. 46–60.

11. *Chicago Sun-Times,* Feb. 9, 1966.

12. See Footnote 1 above.

20

Iemoto *and Industrialization*

Not recognizing or refusing to admit the primacy of man's relationship with his fellow men, the power of particular cultural traditions to shape and sustain that relationship, and the resultant differing patterns of PSH for the individual in various societies, many scholars have tended to treat the spectacular economic achievements of Japan with the same sort of explanations they have used concerning developments in their own societies. Their arguments proceed along two directions: on the one hand, the same economic achievements must be rooted in human values similar to those prevailing in the West, or, that even if the Japanese did not begin with the same human values, the conditions of modern industrialization must have necessarily forced them into Western ways of seeing themselves and reacting to the world around them.

The patterns of kinship, *iemoto* and the kin-tract principle are commensurate with the Japanese pattern in religion and social stratification. The net result of the *iemoto* pattern in religion and caste-ism is essentially conservative. Changes are relatively superficial. Some structural rearrangements in the form of suburbia, *Eta* imvrovement organizations, or foreign missionary ventures have occurred, but the content of human relations, the way the individual feels about himself, about each other, and about the world around him has not.

We are now ready to show that what is true for other aspects of modern Japanese development is equally applicable to her economic miracle, a subject with which we began our present inquiry. In this chapter we shall take a look at the Japanese employee and show how his approach to his work and his relations with his employer are different from those of his American brethren. We shall then show that such differences are possible because the Japanese economic miracle is rooted in the *iemoto* pattern and not in those Western values commonly associated with Western industrialization.

THE JAPANESE WORKER

The Japanese worker operates, even today, at some disadvantage in comparison with his U.S. counterpart. The economic facts are obvious. More than half of the workers in Japan's manufacturing industries

---

This chapter was originally published in *Iemoto: The Heart of Japan,* by Francis L. K. Hsu, Cambridge, Mass.: Schenkman Publishing Co., 1975, pp. 201–38.

(compared with about a quarter in the U.S.) are employed in factories with 1 to 99 workers, while only 20 percent (compared with twice that many in the U.S.) are employed in factories with 1,000 or more workers. Those in smaller factories not only have to contend with less efficient tools of production, but they must also accept wages lower than those paid in larger factories. The wage disparity between large factories and small workshops is still considerably greater in Japan than in other industrially advanced countries. For example, in 1949 the wages in small British workshops were only 16–17 percent lower than those in very large factories with 1,000 or more workers. But in 1958 Japanese wages in workshops with less than 100 workers were two-thirds to one half lower than those in factories with 1,000 or more workers. However, by 1967 this disparity was considerably reduced (Rō Dō Shō 1967:18–19).

Japanese wages, moreover, are still lower than those offered in most industrially advanced countries. In 1967 Japanese hourly wages were less than one-fourth the amount of wages paid to U.S. workers, half of those for British workers, and 5 percent lower than those of French workers. In spite of these disadvantages, the index of productivity of Japanese labor has consistently risen faster than the rise of real wages. For example, the productivity rose by 50 percent from 1965 to 1968, while the real wages during this period rose by only 27 percent.

This high productivity is due primarily to the average worker's loyalty to his employer, who reciprocates in his turn. For both parties the economic facts are not unimportant, but their importance is overshadowed by other factors.

The Japanese worker relates to his peers, employer, and work in ways that are very different from his American counterpart.

To begin with, a very substantial number of Japanese workers are recruited by the factories through the labor boss, on whom the factories depend for labor supply, and on whom workers in search of work depend for finding employment.

The relationship between workers so recruited and their labor boss is that of *oyabun-kobun* (parent-child or boss-follower), a system well described for the English reader by Bennett and Ishino (1963:40–85). The labor boss may recruit workers for a short term project, in which case the *oyabun-kobun* relationship is temporary. Or he may recruit workers for on-going work, in which case the relationship is permanent. Whichever the case, the commencement of the relationship was marked by definite ceremonies and such ceremonies were reported as late as the 1950's. The labor-boss is responsible not only for locating jobs for workers, but also for helping them in their private lives, as though they were his children.

Traditionally the *oyabun-kobun* relationship extended horizontally into elder-younger brother ties, grandfather-grandchild ties, and even uncle-nephew ties. Military occupation authorities and other U.S. inspired reform bodies discouraged the labor-boss system and even made exaggerated claims about its destruction. They saw it as purely exploitative (Bennett and Ishino 1963:121). But its main features, centering in paternalism, a term full of negative connotations for Americans, have persisted to this day. This paternalism is still welcomed, not resented, by most contemporary Japanese workers (Rohlen 1974:91). In fact the term paternalism is not often used in Japanese. It is definitely a Western term, but when it is used in Japan, it is most appropriately translated as *onjo shugi,* or "kind treatment of employees."

Consequently, while not all regular workers in factories are under the labor-boss system (some would say not more than ten to fifteen percent), all Japanese workers operate within a highly paternalistic system unheard of among, and intolerable to, their American brethren.

For example, many (I think most) workers and *sarari men* (salary men) live in company dormitories (for single employees) or in company apartments (for married employees) near their places of work (Whitehall and Takezawa 1968:265). They participate in a variety of company sponsored activities and social events and enjoy numerous company provided extra-curricular facilities such as sports fields, equipment and various other courses including English conversation and flower arrangements.

The Japanese employer is not just someone who impersonally pays his employees for work. He is a sort of senior relative, friend and counselor. Of course, the presidents or their senior lieutenants in large establishments must of necessity be physically remote from thousands of employees. When a labor-boss is not involved, the person to whom the Japanese worker looks for a paternalistic relationship is his supervisor, through whom he maintains a positive identification with the company at large. His general foreman is his formal "guarantor" upon his entry into the company. If he is a minor and charged by the police with a traffic offense the general foreman, as a rule, accompanies him to the traffic court as a parental substitute. Immediate supervisors of Japanese companies vividly report and discuss their concern with and sense of responsibility for the men in their shops.

A panel discussion among immediate supervisors found in *QC to Ningen Kankei* (Quality control and Human Relations, Tetsujiro Kato 1966), the fourth book of a series entitled *Genba QC Tokuhon* (The Workshop Quality Control Reader), leaves no doubt as to the depth and width of this concern. The panel discussion was entitled "Support from the Top and the Bottom," and its eight participants included supervisors from Shin Mitsubishi Heavy Industries, Kawasaki Iron and Steel Works, Takeda Pharmaceuticals, Matsushita Electric Co., Komatsu Manufacturing Co., and Sumitomo Rubber.

The chairman of the panel discussion began with a list of indicators of low morale among workers such as, "lack of concentration on work," "production of defective work," "failure to obey rules governing work-shops," signs of "insomnia and alcoholic smells," "objecting to new machinery for the sake of objecting," "no smile, dishevelled hair, no greeting (in the case of women)," and others. He then proceeded to give a list of common causes of workers' poor performance such as "poor health," "indulgence in gambling and leisure," "family problems," "troubles in romantic relationships," "oversensitivity and inferiority complex," "friendship, religious, and ideological problems," and so forth (Kato 1966:14–15).

The participants then related some of their own successful experiences in dealing with the poor morale of workers in their charge. Only a few samples are given below.

> One of my subordinates was engaged to a woman in his home town. Some time ago he went home to arrange the wedding date. But upon his return to the factory he would not engage other workers in conversation nor look at us in the face. He also produced many defective products. (Previously his products had been 100 percent acceptable.) So I gave him a psychological test. . . . The result confirmed that he was not in an ordinary state of mind. . . . I asked him if something was wrong at his home. He then told me that his marriage plan broke up because his ex-fiance had a boy friend. . . . I (temporarily) transferred him to an easy job so that he could relax. In addition, I told him about my own (similar) experience. Successfully overcoming this problem, he not only was married to another woman last spring but also passed the national government license test (for some sort of certificate).   (Kato 1966:15)
> . . . I also made use of our company newspaper. I would put an ad in it which read: 'The young men in our shop are looking for brides.' Seeing this our workers began thinking 'Well, our supervisor is very demanding about job performance, but he is concerned with our attaining happy marriages.' In this way our men started feeling very positive about their relationship with me. If there is this kind of trust between the supervisor and his men things generally work out very smoothly.

> The worker's awareness that if he talks to the supervisor he will understand him; and the supervisor who kindly (like a parent) takes care of his men for example, by finding a future spouse for him (or her): These are both important. These in essence suggest that the workers trust in the supervisor. ("If I talk to the Oyaji [father][1] he will take care of it.") is indispensable for a good morale. (Kato 1966:17)

> Unless the employees feel 'Our supervisor is concerned with even very personal matters about me' it is impossible to educate present young people into respectable workers.   (Kato 1966:18)

The chairman of the panel discussion concluded the session by making the following observations:

> The shop supervisor needs support both from the top and the bottom. To attain this he must lead an orderly life.

> The shop supervisor must be involved in his subordinates' personal life. For example, if the workers feel 'My Oyaji (supervisor)[2] understands me, he even tries to find a bride for me,' this is an indication of his deep trust in the superior.

> Thus, it is our conclusion that if these two conditions are satisfied the shop enjoys good morale and the workers develop genuine willingness to do a good job. (Kato 1966:22)

Some recent findings of Masako Osako in a Japanese automobile factory illuminate particularly well Japanese workers' attitudes towards work, towards superiors and towards the company (Osako 1972). This is a plant employing modern mass-production techniques comparable to the best in the United States. It exhibits all six of the main characteristics of mass production jobs as specified by Charles R. Walker and Robert H. Guest (1952) namely (1) mechanically controlled work pace, (2) repetitiveness, (3) minimum skill, (4) predetermination of tools and techniques, (5) minute sub-division of production and (6) surface mental attention.

Western scholars, being obsessed with the economic factor, generally link the worker's loyalty to his employer with wages or the nature of modern technology (Blauner 1964 and Goldthorpe et al. 1968). To her question "When do you feel a sense of satisfaction from your immediate job?" Mrs. Osako received mostly negative answers. That is to say, most of the respondents experienced little or no satisfaction from the performance of their immediate jobs. The workers' feelings about their wages were equally negative. Mrs. Osako asked the following questions: "What do you think of the salary you get in this plant in relation to (1) your company's ability to pay wages and (2) your work load?" Eighty-three percent of the sample viewed their wages as low in relation to the company's ability to pay and ninety-five percent thought that the salary they received was low in relation to their work load.

Yet, in spite of such negative or lukewarm views about their job satisfaction and material rewards, the Japanese automobile workers in question overwhelmingly feel positively about their company. Only 18 percent of Mrs. Osako's respondents say the company "does not do much of anything" for its workers, while 84 percent view their company as "better" or "just about the same" "compared to other places of work." Finally, to the question, "Would you mean to stay in this plant until your retirement?" 48 percent of the respondents gave a positive answer, 34 percent were ambivalent, while only 18 percent answered "no." Mrs. Osako notes that since several respondents in the last group "intended to return to their home because they were the eldest sons," the actual number of those unequivocally negative toward their present job was obviously even smaller.

In an attempt to reconcile the negative attitude concerning job satisfaction and material rewards with the positive attitude towards the company, Mrs. Osako suggests that the Japanese workers differentiate between the job as assembly line men and employment as members of a large company. She draws this conclusion especially in view of the fact that what her respondents liked about their occupation mostly had to do with the prestige of the company, the welfare and recreational activities, good co-workers and friends in the plant community, etc., while what they did not like about it mostly had to do with night shifts, monotony of the job, the heaviness of the job, etc.

I think Mrs. Osako's effort to reconcile the contrasting responses has unnecessarily compartmentalized the Japanese worker's perception of himself and the world. What every living individual seeks is a satisfactory level of PSH according to the cultural orientation transmitted to him through the kinship system. For the PSH of Western individuals, job satisfaction and wage levels have priority over relationships with superiors, co-workers and friends in the plant community. Consequently dissatisfaction with the former means dissatisfaction with the entire work situation.[2] But for the PSH of the Japanese, the human relationships are primary and the order of priority is reversed. Consequently, dissatisfaction with the job and wages is greatly overshadowed by a much more important satisfaction with employer-employee links and with membership in a big company.

In this light we can understand why many Japanese workers and employees do not mind traveling long distances every day to maintain the same employment in the same plant.

The longest commuting I know of is done by an employee of a Tokyo company who lives in Shizuoka. He commutes four hours each way every day. The plant used to be nearer his home, but when it moved away the worker did not want to find other employment.

But even more spectacularly congruent with our analysis and Mrs. Osako's findings is the way Japanese labor is organized. Superficially, Japan has three major unions, each having more than a million members. The Sōhyō (General Council of Trade Unions of Japan) is the largest, with over four million members. The Dōmei (Japanese Confederation of Labor) has nearly two million members, and the Chūritsu Rōren (Federation of Independent Unions) has one million members.

In fact, only the All Japan Seamen's Union is a union in the Western sense. Most other unions are organized strictly within *units of individual enterprise*. Applying the Japanese pattern to the American situation we would have a union for GM plant #354 in Flint, Michigan, and another for plant #24 in Harvey, Indiana. These are not called locals. Each is an independent union with its own powers of settlement.

There is, therefore, much closer contact between union leaders and workers and between employers and employees in the Japanese situation than in its American counterpart. The Japanese employee is rarely fired and less easily laid off than in America. By and large, automation and rationalization have not led to industrial contraction and mass unemployment. The Japanese unemployment rate has been consistently lower than that of the United States, the United Kingdom, West Germany, or Italy, even during recent years. Japanese employers see lay-off or firing as the last resort, never as the first steps, in any adverse economic development.

This reduces the possibility of impersonality since each side sees the other as individual human beings with human feelings and needs; the situation cannot but encourage a positive attitude on the part of labor towards management. In addition to the infrequency of intentional damaging or pilfering of plant property, this positive attitude has led to three outstanding results: (a) greater increases of labor productivity than wages (a fact we noted before), (b) the small labor turnover, especially in the big factories (a fact also noted earlier), and (c) the scarcity of strikes and their resulting destructive effects.

Japanese workers engage in verbal and written arguments and exposés against their employers, but strikes are usually averted by amicable settlements. Every May and every November employees of all large and medium-sized concerns engage in what they call the "Spring Offensive" and the "Autumn Offensive," respectively. These are times when the size of the summer and winter bonuses are decided upon. There will be slogans on the walls, sporadic speeches to small and large gatherings and leaflets denouncing the employers in strong terms. Even if a strike occurs, it will be short. Often the employees of a plant or organization will engage in token "strikes"—during the lunch hour or after closing time. In some instances, the "strikers" sing international labor songs. And symbolic of the *positive* attitude of the workers towards employers and place of employment is the fact that not infrequently a vase with a flower arrangement is found at the entrance of a workshop or next to an oily and smelly engine, brought by some worker from his home.

THE WHITE COLLAR EMPLOYEE

The Japanese *sarari man* (salary man or white collar worker) identifies even more with his company than the blue collar worker does. He has more reason to do so.

He is recruited shortly after graduation from high school or from college. This commences a life-long career. As the official statement of one bank puts it: "When a person is accepted into the bank as a member, he is not chosen for his skill; nor is he selected to do a predetermined task. Rather, he is regarded as someone with the potential to learn and to be trained to do increasingly difficult work throughout his career with the bank. It is assumed that his stay will be a long one. . . ." (Rohlen 1971:45).

Beginning with a rigorous initial training period lasting anywhere from six weeks to three months, the employee is progressively integrated into the community of his employers and colleagues through ceremonies, company papers, fringe benefits, welfare facilities and company sponsored or oriented activities. The central theme of the initial training usually concerns *seishin,* or spirit, often involving Zen meditation, group living, and twenty-five mile endurance walks.

After this training period, the new employee settles down at his new place of employment, where his life at work overlaps largely with that at play, and where his devotion to the company is thoroughly reciprocated by the company's to him. If he is single he usually lives in a company dormitory. If he is married he is still likely to reside with his family in a company-owned apartment house.

The company hires instructors in English conversation, flower arrangement, judo, and other arts for any dweller of its dormitories who wants to take advantage of them. The company also provides sports facilities such as basketball, baseball, track and field, tennis, and fencing, for its employees.

If he is looking for a wife, he is often assisted in the effort by one or another of his superiors. At the wedding of a *sarari man,* the chief of his department is likely to be asked to take a place of honor. Often the chief sits as *nakodo* or (matchmaker) in the ceremony, whether he in fact was instrumental in bringing the couple together or not. After the wedding the *sarari man* and his bride can have an inexpensive honeymoon in one of the company-owned resort facilities.

Americans are familiar with office Christmas parties, but Japanese office sociability goes much farther. They have one-day office picnics and week-end office excursions. Employees of a department in a bank, government office, or hospital, sometimes numbering thirty or more, will go by train or in chartered buses to spend the week-end in a resort or hot springs hotel. In such excursions the Japanese will go with his office superiors and subordinates, leaving his wife behind.

Two conclusions can be drawn from these facts. On the one hand, the Japanese employee's life with his family is very much segregated from his life with his co-workers. His spouse has little or nothing to do with his work-connected activities (Vogel 1967:102–103). On the other hand, the Japanese factory hand or office worker maintains close personal ties with co-workers, superiors and subordinates in his work unit far beyond his work requirements. Participation in and maintenance of work-connected social ties is voluntary, not compulsory. But non-participation is regarded as abnormal and as a sign of dissatisfaction.

In both respects, the Japanese worker differs significantly from his American counterpart. The American's personal affairs and recreational activities are his own. They are unconnected with his employment. And the American's spouse has much to do with his business-connected travel and entertainment.

Most Japanese corporations reinforce their employees' identification with the company through daily and periodical ceremonies. For example, before starting each day's work, workers and employees in every factory of Matsushita Company get together and sing the following song:

> *For the building of a new Japan*
> *Let's put our strength and mind together.*
> *Doing our best to promote production,*
> *Sending our goods to the people of the world.*

> *Endlessly and continuously,*
> *Like water gushing from a fountain.*
> *Grow, industry, grow, grow, grow!*
> *Harmony and sincerity!*
> *Matsushita Electricity!*

This kind of song is not unique to a particular corporation called Matsushita. Compare it with the song sung by all the employees of a medium-sized bank in northern Japan to which Thomas Rohlen, the ethnographer, gave the fictitious name Uedagin:

> *A falcon pierces the clouds,*
> *A bright dawn is now breaking.*
> *The precious flower of our unity*
> *Blossoms here.*
> *Uedagin Uedagin*
> *Our pride in her name ever grows.*
>
> *Smiling in our hearts with glory.*
> *For we carry the responsibility for tomorrow's*
> *Independent Japan.*
> *Our towns and villages prosper*
> *Under our banner of idealism raised on high.*
> *Uedagin Uedagin*
> *Our hopes inspired by her name.*
>
> *Marching forward to the new day*
> *With strength unbounded.*
> *We continue forward step by step.*
> *Oh, the happiness of productive people.*
> *Uedagin Uedagin*
> *Brilliantly radiates her name.*[3] *(Rohlen 1974:36)*

Such employee devotion is not mere wishful thinking on the part of the company. The Japanese employees respond by acts which certainly help achieve the company's objectives. For example, most Japanese workers, and especially white collar employees, tend to work overtime without demanding compensation. The clock watching syndrome is generally absent. Many employees, especially new ones, but old ones as well, tend to work long after the normal office hours just to complete what they think should be finished before they leave the office or shop. It is not uncommon for a majority of the members of a given office to work until nine or ten in the evening three or four times a week.

The turnover among white collar workers is even lower than among blue collar workers. The seniority system assures a salaried man not only a permanent place in a company, but automatic promotion as well. A

Japanese diplomat-author compares the position of a Japanese salaried man to one who has found himself on an escalator. All he has to do is to stand still and he will automatically get to the top (Kawasaki 1969:97–98). Consequently there is far less mobility from one company to another in Japan than in the United States. Japanese companies do not raid each other for talent, however desirable, no matter what the competition is. For the Japanese employee, leaving one company to join another is even more risky than trying to switch escalators in the middle of a ride. A man who changes from one company to join another is likely to be an object of some ostracism. He will not easily find a new place to go to. If he does, he is less likely to be trusted than before. One anthropologist rightly observes that termination of a job other than by retirement, or resignation because of marriage for women employees, carries an extreme sense of failure. It is an "embarrassing and unhappy affair similar in atmosphere to marital divorce" (Rohlen 1974:74).

I am aware that while these observations agree with those of Abegglen (1958), they differ somewhat from those of others. For example, Marsh and Mannari (1970:795–812) criticize Abegglen on two main grounds. First, the pattern of lifetime commitment, which Abegglen regards as the central aspect of Japanese factory social organization, is more characteristic of factories with over 1,000 employees, yet such factories employ only one-fifth of Japan's manufacturing labor force. Second, even those employees who exhibit lifetime commitment behavior by remaining in the same firms "often do so not on the basis of lifetime commitment values but for a variety of reasons extraneous to these values" (Marsh and Mannari 1970:810–811).

I think neither of these criticisms should deflect us from the reality that the Japanese employee is considerably less likely than his American counterpart to leave his firm, a fact which Marsh and Mannari do not deny (Marsh and Mannari 1970:811). This point is confirmed by many other observers, including Whitehall and Takezawa (1968:151–153). In view of our extensive analysis of the importance of the *iemoto*-pattern in Japanese life, we have no reason to suppose that the more pronounced lifetime commitment behavior of the Japanese employees in large firms is an anomaly. To the contrary, we must regard the large Japanese firms as being more capable than their smaller counterparts in providing the conditions for the realization of behavior patterns central to the Japanese way of life. Furthermore, as the industrial process moves further ahead in Japan, is there any good reason to believe that the proportion of large firms will not increase?

Intensifying the sense of identification with the place of employment are several other features. One of them is the fact that the white collar employees of each company, and especially of each department or section of the company, are sometimes products of the same colleges. For example, most officers of the Bank of Tokyo in Osaka are graduates of the prestigious Tokyo University, and a few other national universities. I know an officer who felt out of place there because he came from a missionary institution, Sophia University. The fact that this man's father was a vice-president of the bank and one of its directors did not make too much difference. Another friend of mine began his life as a *sarari man* in a major trading company in Osaka after graduation from Osaka Foreign Language University. Although he had only been with this large company of over a thousand employees for less than two months when we first discussed the subject of school ties, he was able to give me the following rather precise list of particulars:

1. The President of the corporation graduated from Osaka University;
2. The Vice-President of the corporation graduated from Kyoto University;
3. A majority of the white collared employees in the corporation graduated from Keio University;
4. The next largest group of white collared employees in it graduated from Waseda University;
5. About five or six were graduates of Kobe University and Kansei Gakuen University;
6. A small number graduated from Tokyo University, but among them are three heads of departments;
7. A few graduated from Osaka Municipal University among whom was a director of the company;
8. A few are graduates of Konan University. (My informant commented: "The university is not good, but the parents of its students are 'good'—they are usually wealthy. Also a former president of the company was once a professor at Konan University"), and no one was from Doshisha University (a missionary institution).

My informant proudly mentioned that two department heads of the company were from his own alma mater, namely Osaka Foreign Language University, though the total number of its graduates in this company was among the smallest.

However, a year after I left Japan this informant wrote to me in a state of great consternation and unhappiness. His trading company decided to merge with another to become truly a giant concern, but the few graduates from his alma mater were now like a "few grains of sand in a giant ocean." He actively considered resigning from the company, and for the next two years, this was a sentiment reflected in every one of his letters. He only decided to stay on after that because, I suspect, a change of employment, which would involve much social readjustment, was far less attractive than the prospect of keeping a position in which he already had some seniority.

This highly vertical organization and strong seniority system combined with closed origin ties would seem to be detrimental to the selection and use of talent. But here Japanese industries and business are helped by two factors.

On the one hand, there is the continuing devotion of the Japanese employee to his superiors and to his company, already pointed out, which makes him work harder and for longer hours than his Western counterpart.

On the other hand, there is the operation of the *ringi* system, unique to Japan. The *ringi* system typifies the group nature of Japanese management decision-making processes. It consists of five steps:

a. A proposal written up by middle management;
b. Cautious horizontal consideration of the proposal;
c. Cautious vertical consideration of the proposal;
d. Formal affixture of the necessary seals to the *ringisho* document, which contains the proposal;
e. Deliberate final ambiguity with respect to authority and responsibility for the proposal. (Glazer 1969:88–90)

The Japanese thus reduce the chance of incompetent decision-making by the top executives who arrived at the top merely by way of the seniority route. The devoted young talents do the brain work. They are secure in the knowledge that they do not risk their own individual careers by wrong individual decisions and that they too will eventually be promoted through the seniority system. Executives on the highest level of prominence are also protected from risking their individual careers. This in part accounts for the fact that Japanese businesses are "run" by old men over 60 or even 70.

In a Tokyo office a *sarari man* let me witness a gesture of devotion to his office superior which I had never experienced in the Western world. We were at the end of an interview in his office which, being that of a lower-middle ranking officer, was small and sparsely furnished. But the size and nature of his office were never part of our conversation. As I was preparing to take my leave, he said, "Let me show you the office of my section chief." He took me to an office three times as big as his, very well furnished, pointed to the empty chair behind the big desk ornamented with lots of bric-a-brac and proudly said: "This is the desk of my section chief."

The pattern of permanent bond between inferiors and superiors even exists among corporations and between corporations and the government. The *zaibatsu* Mitsubishi illustrates this point well. By 1963 this extended corporation had 21 manufacturing companies with 103 factories, plants and mines all over Japan. Imported iron ore is processed in one of her iron and steel works in Tokyo. It is made into a cracking tower in her factory in Kawasaki, consumed in her petro-chemical plant at Yokkaichi. The latter uses the oil she imports to make synthetic fibers which are woven into cloth in Nagoya and exported by her trading company in her own ships made at one of her yards in Nagasaki, Yokohama, Kawasaki, Tokyo, or Hiroshima.

Two other giants, Sumitomo and Mitsui do their business in much the same way. Sumitomo is Japan's largest producer of chemicals. She has

200,000 people in her employ. Mitsui was responsible for nearly ten percent of all of Japan's imports and eight percent of her exports in 1963. She deals with everything from bridges to buttons and cars to canned goods.

Various *zaibatsu* compete with each other. In view of the fact that each of them comprises so many enterprises in the same or similar lines of endeavor, some Japanese scholars have become alarmed by what they describe as excessive competition among the *zaibatsu*. One of these scholars, Professor Shuji Hayashi of Tokyo University even likened this competition with that between the Japanese Navy and Army during and before World War II. For example, the two military arms of the Japanese government each developed its own separate air force without coordination with each other and no exchanges of technical know-how. "The Navy developed the world famous Zero fighter and the Army, the Hayabusa fighter, quite independently" (Hayashi 1965).

Americans are likely to see monopolistic practices and price fixing in the Japanese *zaibatsu,* and may think some anti-trust laws are in order. In fact the Occupation under General McArthur ordered the *zaibutsu* disbanded. But one by one they were revived as American authority in Japan diminished. In the Japanese context, not only are the American fears of monopoly unnecessary, but the *zaibatsu* are unavoidable. For *zaibatsu* too are an expression of the *iemoto* pattern of doing business. The *zaibatsu* not only cooperate with each other in some instances (for example, in the new petro-chemical industry), but also with the Japanese government. The *zaibatsu* willingly put government plans into action. This cooperation between government and *zaibatsu* is not realized by force of law but through the close, subtle *iemoto*-like relationship linking the government, the central bank, and the *zaibatsu*.

Thus, at the core of the phenomenal Japanese economic development is the mutual and nearly permanent bond between vertically placed individuals (the master and his disciples, or the boss and the workers, etc.), a bond similar to that found in the *iemoto*. This is the bond on which the Japanese individual lavishes most affection and which is the central ingredient of his PSH. Hence, quitting a company is rare and, if and when it occurs, is an "embarrassing and unhappy affair similar in atmosphere to marital divorce."

The groups formed through this bond compete with each other (there is competition among departments, among factories, among *zaibatsu,* etc.), but there is no competition within each group. In this way, devotion to superior, to place of work, and to higher authority is generated and nurtured while danger to personal security is minimized and eliminated. These establishments or groups and their branches or divisions or offshoot companies *(kogaisha)* are not called *iemoto*. But they all partake of the *iemoto's* basic features. For each factory or division or unit of a company is like an *iemoto,* linked with the larger *iemoto*. In a similar manner, the different component companies of a *zaibatsu* relate to the *zaibatsu,* and the different *zaibatsu* relate to the government. Being accustomed to the hierarchical way of relating to one another, in which the business world and the personal one are not rigidly segregated, the Japanese are more free than Americans and other Westerners to work and cooperate with their equals and unequals without fearing charges of "authoritarianism" or "dictatorship" or the onus of "bootlicking" or "submissiveness."

Some Western students have said that the Japanese economy has succeeded so well because the Japanese government has played so large a hand in encouraging and subsidizing business and industry. The truth is that such government aid would have been deeply resented as "interference" in America. Americans, as members of corporations or as individuals, are not averse to obtaining fruits from the government preserve if they can get them on their own terms. They will milk the government in the same way that they will exploit the natural resources. But in doing so they do not want to appear subservient to the government. On the other hand, strong government planning, regulations and support in India and a host of other countries have not led those economies out of their apathetic states. There is an old proverb which says you can lead a horse to water but you can't make him drink it.

The secret of Japan's economic success is the human factor, not what goes on in the individual Japanese, but how the Japanese seek their satisfactory level of PSH through their particular way of relating to and working with each other.

SINO-JAPANESE CONTRASTS IN PERSPECTIVE

Robert Bellah in his *Tokugawa Religion* (1957) set forth a systematic theory for Japan's rapid economic development, especially as it contrasts to what happened in China. According to Bellah, "China was characterized by the primacy of integrative values where Japan was characterized by primacy of political or goal-attainment values. . . . A society characterized by the primacy of integrative values is more concerned with system maintenance than with, for example, goal attainment or adaptation; more with solidarity than with power or wealth." On the other hand, in Japan "the central value system which was found to be present in the Tokugawa Period remained dominant in the modern period, in perhaps an even more intense and rationalized form. The adaptation of that central value system which had been worked out as the status ethic of the various classes proved very favorable for handling the new economic responsibilities which fell to each class" (188–89). In my view this explanation of Japan's rapid economic (and military) rise, in contrast to China on the basis of differing values, is inconsistent with the facts. China and Japan did not have fundamentally different values. Instead, it was the differing nature of the social groupings through which the same values expressed themselves that seems to have made the difference. Perhaps Bellah is not totally unaware of this fact when he observes: "The rationalism inherent in the Confucian ethic seems to need to be linked with a value system in which political values have primacy if it is to have an influence in the direction of modernization. This was the case in Japan and perhaps of present-day China" (Bellah 1957:192).

But seeing the need for such a link and demonstrating how such a link can become reality are different matters. Bellah fails to appreciate that political values, too, are powerless unless they find themselves in the fertile soil of human groupings. What we have done in the foregoing chapters is to detail how the dynamics of PSH requirements for the individual, institutional arrangement, and cultural orientation conjointly made that link possible in Japan but not in China.

Our starting point is kinship—that fundamental social structure and content in which all human life begins. Like that of the Chinese, the Japanese kinship system is father-son dominated; but unlike the Chinese, its structure is made more flexible and its content is considerably altered by unigeniture and the markedly hierarchical and sometimes binding relationship between the heir and his other brothers. Those Japanese who have to leave the kinship group of their origin must find the fulfillment of their PSH needs elsewhere. In doing so they do not free themselves entirely from kinship. They are merely propelled by a more flexible kinship structure and are strongly conditioned in the particular composition of their kinship content. That is why they devote themselves and are bound to their secondary groupings such as *dozoku* and especially *iemoto* based on the kintract principle, the essence of which is found in religion as in occupation, in government as in the military, in intellectual pursuits as in artistic endeavors. Japanese kinship content, in contrast to its Chinese counterpart, enables the Japanese to expand his kinship-like *iemoto* almost indefinitely.

When the Japanese individual is freed from the structural restrictions of the *iemoto,* as, for instance, when he is born and raised in the United States, the content of the *iemoto* remains operative. What Caudill and DeVos say about the Japanese Americans' success in the American business and industrial world bears on this:

A simile is useful in pointing up the similarities and difference between Japanese American and white middle-class *achievement orientations;* the ultimate destinations or goals of individuals in the two groups tend to be very similar. But Japanese Americans go toward these destinations along *straight narrow streets lined with crowds of people who observe their every step,* while (white) middle class persons go toward the same destinations along wider streets having more room for maneuvering, and lined only with small groups of people who, while watching them, do not observe their every movement. In psychoanalytic terminology, this means that the *Japanese Americans have an ego structure that is very sensitive and vulnerable to stimuli coming from the outer world, and a superego structure that depends greatly upon external sanction.* This tends to be true of middle class Americans as well, but not nearly to such an extent. For example, individuals in both groups are interested in acquiring money in amounts suffi-

cient to be translated into the achievement of social class presitge; however, every move of a Japanese American toward amassing money is carefully watch-ed, and the way he does it, *and the ultimate use he makes of it in benefitting the community are equal in importance to the financial success itself.* This is less true of the American middle class, where an individual can make his money in a great variety of ways and, so long as these are not down-right dishonest, the ways are sanctioned because of the end product—the financial success.
   (Caudill and DeVos 1956:1117:italics mine)

   The notion of achievement motivation is rooted in the American indi-vidual-centered way of life. It may be useful in gauging how well minority groups in the United States perform according to white American stan-dards but this has no true intersocietal validity. What is more important here, is the way the Japanese Americans, according to Caudill and DeVos, perceive themselves and relate to others. They work toward their destina-tions "along narrow streets lined with crowds of people who observe their every step," they have "an ego structure that is very sensitive and vulner-able to stimuli coming from the outer world," and the "ultimate use" the successful Japanese Americans make of the wealth they have acquired "in benefitting the community are equal in importance to the financial success itself." These are all intrinsic expressions of the content of the *iemoto,* even though the social atmosphere among the Japanese American is not orga-nized on the *iemoto* model (e.g. with the *iemoto's* generational seniority and rigidity of personal affiliation) and is not called "iemoto." But it is among Japanese Americans that we find such clear distinctions between *issei, nisei,* and *sansei* (respectively first, second and third generation Japanese Americans), just as in Japanese corporations we find such clear distinc-tions between *sempai* and *kōhai* (respectively upper and lower generations of employees).
   The age old content of the *iemoto* has given the Japanese a goal orienta-tion and a pattern of obedience to authority that fit extremely well with American corporation needs. If present trends continue, I expect many American employers to prefer Japanese employees to Americans. In fact many American employers in Hawaii already do so.
   Chinese Confucianism and Indian Buddhism did not give rise to the Japanese type of blind obedience to authority and religious commitment which link the family with the nation. Japan received Confucianism and Buddhism from China but made use of them through Japanese kinship structure and transformed them in accordance with Japanese *iemoto* con-tent. It was the Japanese who changed the meaning of the Chinese word for scholar *(shih)* into *samurai,* thereby transforming the four ranked classes of Japanese society into *samurai,* farmers, artisans and merchants. (In China, the scholar, not the warrior, headed the social order.) It was the Japanese who placed devotion to Buddha (or master) higher than that to parents. It was the Japanese who merged the ancestral souls with Buddha and worshipped the same ancestress as the ruling imperial house.
   Therefore, while we do not disagree with Bellah that "a great deal of

Chinese society can be seen as the symbolic extension and generalization of kinship ties" (Bellah 1957:189), we must note that this is not what basically differentiates the Chinese from the Japanese. Our analysis reveals that most of Japanese society, too, can be seen as "the symbolic extension and generalization of kinship ties." The most significant difference between China and Japan lies in the fact that most of Chinese society is a symbolic extension of the father-son dominated kinship system while Japanese society is a symbolic extension of a similar kinship system complicated by mother-son sub-dominance, unigeniture and an intensified hierarchy. The latter propel a majority of Japanese males into much wider circles of relationships than the Chinese, but these wider relationships are kinship-like in structure and especially in content, as we see clearly in the *iemoto* system.

The Japanese did not develop universalism any more than the Chinese, in Parsons' terms, in these wider circles of human affiliation symbolized by the *iemoto* system. On the contrary, "particularism remained unchallenged. Japanese nationalism remained peculiarly particularistic due to its focus on the imperial family . . . the main family of which all Japanese families are branch families" (Bellah 1957:181), and the Japanese *iemoto* system remained peculiarly particularistic due to its focus on the person of the founder or the big master, who was the fountainhead of all wisdom and discipline for all members of each system. But while the Chinese kinship system provided for no more extension than the clan (the size of which is always limited because it is founded firmly on the principles of birth and marriage), the Japanese kinship system provided for affiliation of men into much larger groupings across kinship lines, each founded primarily on the kin-tract principle. Combining kinship and contract, the kin-tract principle provides for voluntary entry into any grouping, as in contract relations, but once entered, departure from it becomes far more difficult, as in kinship relations.

Having already been loosened from the primary kinship bonds, the Japanese were, more easily than the Chinese, drawn into larger enterprises (economic, political, religious, military) whose objectives were not those of the narrowly defined kinship ones. Long before intensive contact with the West, they already had established among themselves a system, as Marion Levy put it, of "tight control over the vast majority of . . . individuals" (Levy 1953:195). In the light of our analysis so far, Levy's use of the words "tight control" is not appropriate. What really occurred was that, through the *iemoto*, a vast majority of Japanese found themselves affectively linked in relatively larger arenas, and that those links more easily adapted themselves than the traditional Chinese human links to certain requirements of modern industrialization and nationalism.

Compared with the Chinese *tsu,* based on the kinship principle, the *iemoto,* based on the kin-tract principle, has two outstanding advantages in the modernization process. First, it allows the introduction of new blood whenever necessary. This fact has two consequences. On the one hand, the size of the establishment, once it is freed from the restriction of agriculture, may be expanded indefinitely. And the sizes of many Japanese *iemoto* are enormous, unmatched by any comparable grouping in China. Being centrally based on the kinship principle, wider Chinese affiliation was always strictly dependent upon the biological facts of birth and death within the narrow limits set by that principle.

On the other hand, the selection of unrelated individuals for inclusion more readily fits in with the criterion of performance, and this nurtures goal orientation of the achievement motive to an extent that cannot be matched by groupings primarily based on the kinship principle, as among the Chinese. The achievement motive is not absent among the Chinese, but the kinship principle was so strong that the sons and grandsons of wealthy or prominent fathers, being assured from birth of their wealth or position, usually turned out badly. As a result, the prominence of a Chinese family name and the integrity of its wealth or business never lasted beyond two or three generations (Hsu 1949:256–278). The sons of prominent or wealthy Japanese fathers have not been subject to the Chinese type of unfavorable educational influences. The custom of un-igeniture and the hierarchical relationship among siblings reduced the unfavorable influences of parental wealth and power on the younger sons. The resulting pattern of stress on performance cannot but have affected sons fortunate enough to be heirs. The long histories of prominence of most Japanese *iemoto* and business establishments stand in sharp contrast to Chinese non-kinship groupings.

The other Japanese advantage in the modernization process is that the *iemoto,* like its rural counterpart, is a corporation consisting of many branch corporations in which the individual enjoys permanent membership and to which he has made permanent commitment. This is the arena that provides him with his basic source of PSH.

The head *iemoto* commands extreme obedience from the branch *iemoto,* but the former does not interfere with the internal affairs of the latter. In particular, the former cannot replace the latter or any one of the latter's disciples. Since performance is a main criterion for one's place in the hierarchy, and since each branch corporation has autonomy, the whims and personal predilections of the superior have much less chance of affecting the organizational regularity of the whole. The individual on a lower rung of the hierarchy cannot rise above his senior, but his own rank cannot arbitrarily be lowered or taken away, nor can the conduct of his duties be significantly altered by order of the "big boss."

The importance of the *iemoto* for the PSH of the Japanese and the extension of the content of the *iemoto* into Japanese government is what, in my view, has prevented widespread corruption in Japanese government in sharp contrast to what occurred in the pre-1949 governments in China. Since kinship and locality ties were the objects of individual affect for the Chinese, giving them their basic sources of PSH, bureaucratic considerations stood generally outside their PSH needs. The common Chinese expressions to describe a man just appointed to a post are *shang t'ai la* (gone up the stage) and a bureaucrat just resigned or who has been dismissed from his post, *hsia t'ai la* (gone off the stage). The Chinese truly regard government work as mere role performance. Consequently, the Chinese in the bureaucracy had neither fixed places in it nor any permanent committment to its hierarchical organization or goals. Any Chinese could move up or down, due to either his own actions, or to the arbitrary actions of his superiors or his superior's superiors. It was well known that competitive bribery (not fixed dues as in the Japanese *iemoto*) was an indispensable means for maintaining a position in Chinese officialdom or for promotion in it.

These factors were responsible for the spectacular and speedy Japanese advancements after contact with the West, just as their absence in China was responsible for Chinese stagnation and chaos during an entire century of Western domination. The Japanese advantages had their roots in the *ie* and in the *dōzoku,* just as their extension literally enables us to regard, at least figuratively, the entire Japanese nation as one huge *iemoto*.

However, the Japanese have reached modernization and industrialization via a very different psycho-social route than that found in the West. Japanese non-heirs were not, as were their Western counterparts, encouraged to seek, or bent on seeking, their own fame and fortune on their own terms. Their kinship system encouraged them to look for mutual dependence instead of independence. They developed newer and larger groups with non-traditional objectives, without feeling a need for significant changes in their traditional pattern of human relationships. That pattern is based on the attributes of the father-son relationship modified by unigeniture and a hierarchical relationship between the heir and his brothers. The structure, but especially the content, of the *iemoto* system has provided modern Japanese enterprises with their most important sources of organizational loyalty and strength. The widespread *oyabun-kobun* or *oyabun-kobun*-like relationships in modern Japanese industries and commerce is only the most formal expression of this fact.

In the *oyabun-kobun* relationship we find the emphasis on vertical affiliation with an establishment or interest group *(batsu)* and seniority (continuity), yet a disregard for actual kinship (discontinuity); the overwhelming importance of being a product of a certain school (exclusiveness) but the relative lack of discrimination among individuals on the basis of talent (inclusiveness); and finally, the intensification of the most explicit pattern of superordination and subordination (authority).

For the Chinese the transition from the traditional to the modern was more difficult. Levy puts his finger on a crucial element in this contrast when he says:

> The new forces in Japan undercut many of the old patterns just as they had in China, but they did not simultaneously undercut the sole or the major sources of control over individuals as they did in China. (Levy 1953:194)

Again we must object to Levy's use of the term "control." What the Chinese traditional social organization lacked was provision for strong non-kinship and non-local secondary groupings in which individuals could find sources for PSH.[4] Consequently, when new objectives (development of nationalism and industrialization along Western lines) arose under Western impact, the traditional Chinese human framework was unresponsive to its new organizational requirements. Instead, most Chinese floundered about and were unable to unite in strength in the wider arena once they had left their kinship or local moorings. They retained their basic kinship attributes, some of which could have been utilized to good advantage in the new situation as they were in Japan. But there was no traditional structure to which to harness them for the new ends.

A useful analogy may help us to understand this better. Bravery is an admirable virtue in many societies. Bravery is also a necessary attribute for winning a war. However, poor leadership and inefficient organization, not to speak of inadequate and inefficient equipment, can render this quality fruitless. The deciding factor is not the existence or non-existence of the attribute of bravery, but the organizational channels by means of which the potentials of this quality can be realized.[5] The Chinese may have been brave, to pursue this analogy, but they did not have the structure through which they could make use of this attribute of bravery. The Japanese, as we have shown, had both the attribute and the structure which enabled its realization.

Social Organization, Cultural Ideal and The Individual: The Dynamics of Mutual Escalation

Our basic hypothesis which runs through this book is that, if the individual cannot, because of the nature of the kinship system in conjunction with a particular type of cultural orientation that shapes the direction of his ideal life, find the fulfillment of his PSH in the basic kinship group, he must join or form other groups for this purpose. In doing so, the patterns of his search for a group and of his conduct in that group are very much governed by the kind of content his initial kinship group has imparted to him. The diagram below is a sketch of the dynamics of the interrelationships linking the cultural orientation, the individual PSH needs, and the social grouping in the Japanese situation.[6]

The Japanese have the same starting point as the Chinese : mutual dependence. Between the parents and heir (often the eldest son) there is complete community of interests and automatic sharing of honors and responsibilities. His interpersonal relationships may also be described by the term situational determinism as in the Chinese case which, though characterized by Benedict as the ability to turn suddenly about face without embarrassment, is in effect the tendency to be more sensitive to the requirements of one's place in a network of interpersonal relations than to one's own personal predilections.

Diagram 1: Japanese Pattern of PSH

Kin-tract Relationship Supplements and Replaces Kinship Ties

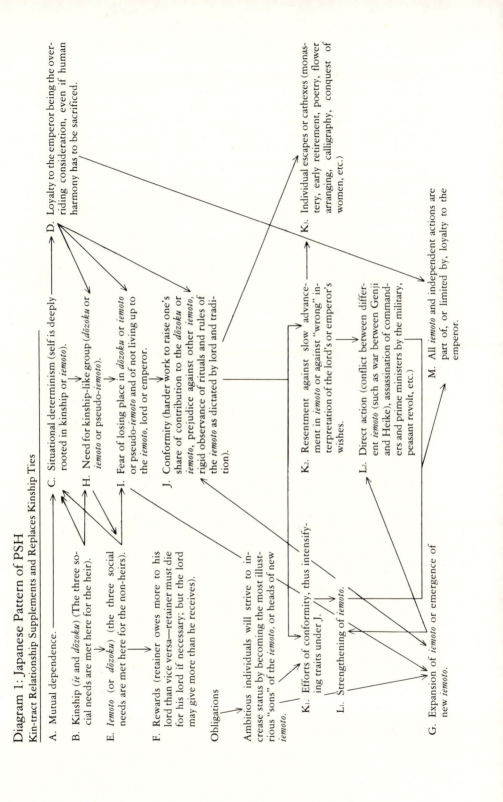

A. Mutual dependence.

B. Kinship (*ie* and *dōzoku*) (The three social needs are met here for the heir).

E. *Iemoto* (or *dōzoku*) (the three social needs are met here for the non-heirs).

F. Rewards (retainer owes more to his lord than vice versa—retainer must die for his lord if necessary; but the lord may give more than he receives).

Obligations

Ambitious individuals will strive to increase status by becoming the most illustrious "sons" of the *iemoto*, or heads of new *iemoto*.

K₁. Efforts of conformity, thus intensifying traits under J.

L₁. Strengthening of *iemoto*.

G. Expansion of *iemoto* or emergence of new *iemoto*.

C. Situational determinism (self is deeply rooted in kinship or *iemoto*).

H. Need for kinship-like group (*dōzoku* or *iemoto* or pseudo-*iemoto*).

I. Fear of losing place in *dōzoku* or *iemoto* or pseudo-*iemoto* and of not living up to the *iemoto*, lord or emperor.

J. Conformity (harder work to raise one's share of contribution to the *dōzoku* or *iemoto*, prejudice against other *iemoto*, rigid observance of rituals and rules of the *iemoto* as dictated by lord and tradition).

K₂. Resentment against slow advancement in *iemoto* or against "wrong" interpretation of the lord's or emperor's wishes.

L₂. Direct action (conflict between different *iemoto* (such as war between Genji and Heike), assassination of commanders and prime ministers by the military, peasant revolt, etc.)

D. Loyalty to the emperor being the overriding consideration, even if human harmony has to be sacrificed.

K₃. Individual escapes or cathexes (monastery, early retirement, poetry, flower arranging, calligraphy, conquest of women, etc.)

M. All *iemoto* and independent actions are part of, or limited by, loyalty to the emperor.

Since the kinship group is the basic source of the Chinese individual's PSH he can ignore the world outside. Hence the Chinese ideal of harmony among men as described by Confucius and as depicted in Chinese literature is one of live-and-let-live rather than one of positive action to maintain or change anything in the name of it except within the kinship sphere. He would disturb the ideal of harmony among men only if his kinship group was threatened or violated by another kinship group. For example, if his father was murdered by someone, he must avenge it at all cost. Or if his mother desired something difficult to obtain, he would be justified in going to all lengths to secure it. The kinship group is the beginning and ending of his immutable world.

The Japanese cannot rely on his basic kinship group to satisfy his PSH requirements. Instead, he has to leave it and secure them in a larger, yet kinship-like, group which we term *iemoto* (E in Diagram 1.). Since the boundary of the *iemoto* is not limited by kinship, it is more flexible than the Chinese *tsu* and it allows far more room for large scale expansion. In its widest extension the imperial house is something of the *honke* heading a giant *iemoto* comprising all Japan.[7] This gave Japan but not China the basis for patriotism and nationalism under Western pressure in modern times. The resources for development in the Japanese human situation are easily mobilized for various objectives: political, artistic, military or industrial.

The reward-obligation ratio (F in Diagram 1) is unequal, but unlike the Hindu situation, individuals situated on the lower rungs of the hierarchy owe the superior lords more obligations than vice versa (they must die for their lords but the lords need not die for them). On the other hand, the lord may also voluntarily give to his subordinates more than what he receives in return, although this never works automatically (the lord's honors do not automatically go to his subordinates), in contrast to the relationship between the Chinese father and his son.

However, every way of life has a tendency of escalating itself. That is, though sharing the same culture with others, some individuals are more ambitious or active than others. If the culture says adventure is a desirable goal, some members want to travel farther and make more difficult journeys than others. If the culture says there should be taboo against eating pork, some members want to surpass other by avoiding even the mention of the word pork in their conversation. If the culture says filial piety is a good thing, some members want to honor their parents in ways calculated to outshine all other filial sons in the past.

Ambitious individuals will not stop at merely doing the right thing according to the accepted rules. They want to do more according to those rules. How far such ambitious individuals can and will go is dependent upon the limitations set by the size of the arena within which he has been conditioned by his culture to derive the resources for his PSH. Since the Chinese PSH is confined to the kinship group, the ambitious Chinese is most likely still to define his ambitious acts within that group. He will give bigger weddings for his children than his neighbors, stage more colossal funerals for his deceased parents to outshine others, and reach for higher places in officialdom or perform more spectacular acts to glorify his ancestors or ensure the welfare of his descendants yet unborn. He may even lavish a good deal of money to improve his home town by repairing roads, building bridges and giving donations to schools.

Not so in Japan. The ambitious Japanese will try to become the most illustrious "sons" of the *iemoto*. But as they have escalated their individual contributions to the cultural ideal, their exalted statuses will necessarily provide a stamp of approval so that the generations which follow them are bound to find in their acts sources of inspiration and models for imitation. The results of following such patterns of ambition cannot but have a major or minor impact on the social organization in part or on the whole. Thus the individual, social organization and the cultural ideal escalate each other.

How do ambitious individuals in Japan help in this mutual escalation process? If they are already heads of *iemoto,* they will try to obtain more disciples or retainers, or to be masters who have more secret formulae that are the envy of other masters. If they are only members of *iemoto,* they may try to achieve eminence in their *iemoto* or become the most illustrious branch *iemoto* under the grand master. If they are not affiliated to some master already they may start new and bigger *iemoto.* We use the word "new" here not to denote anything drastically different in design or aim, but in the sense of a freshly begun *bunke*-like establishment, with a more ambitious representation and the same aim as the *honke* establishment, with the same old social design and the same old social aims. Here is where the ambitious Japanese and their Chinese counterparts will differ. They differ in the extent to which their ambitious acts affect society as a whole.

For one thing, whether their ambitions may drive them to expand their existing *iemoto* or to start new *iemoto* (G in Diagram 1), the number of Japanese involved is likely to be large, much larger than what their Chinese brethren can do since the kinship principle severely curtails the latter's efforts for recruitment. Even more important is the almost unlimited variety of objectives of the Japanese *iemoto* in contrast to the extremely limited objectives of the Chinese *tsu.* Consequently, the ambitious Japanese not only can affect more of his countrymen but can steer them into a larger variety of goals not previously embodied in the traditional Japanese culture and society. The Japanese who follow them are swayed not so much because they are convinced of the importance of the new goals but because their relationship with the leaders of their *iemoto* or pseudo-*iemoto* is necessary for their PSH.

The forces for conformity in the Japanese situation combine those operating in Hindu India and in China. On the one hand, there is the fear of not living up to the ideal of devotion to the master lord or emperor (corresponding to the fear the Chinese have of not living up to ancestral names, etc.). On the other hand, there is the fear of losing place in the *iemoto* or pseudo-*iemoto* (corresponding to the Hindu fear of losing caste; I in Diagram 1). The answer to such fears in the Japanese interpersonal context of situational determinism (C in Diagram 1) is the Japanese way of conformity (J in Diagram 1). In this case conformity means harder work to raise one's share of contribution to the *iemoto*, prejudice against other groups or *iemoto*, rigid observance of rituals and rules of the *iemoto* as dictated by lord and tradition.

But the more flexible nature of the kin-tract principle does not only enable the ambitious Japanese individual to expand the old *iemoto* and begin new *iemoto*. He can also intensify conformity (K_1 in Diagram 1), or resent slow advancement in his *iemoto* (K_2 in Diagram 1). The two courses of action will of course strengthen the hold of the existing *iemoto* on the individual (L_1 in Diagram 1). But the resentment against slow advancement under the circumstances is conducive to direct action (L_2 in Diagram 1). Japanese history provides numerous examples of direct action: not only conflicts between different *iemoto* such as the war between the Genji and the Heike, but also assassination of military commanders and government ministers, in the name of the divine will of the emperor. Superficially, the latter type of Japanese examples of direct action appears to be similar to that also found in Chinese history, but that is not the case. Chinese rebels mostly aimed at replacing the dynastic ruler (no matter what they publicly proclaimed); but Japanese rebels, as a rule, acted on behalf of the emperor, with or without his consent or knowledge, since no new imperial dynasty ever emerged (M in Diagram 1). For although *iemoto* is capable of enormous expansion, its greatest expansion is via the pseudo-kinship ties which proceed from the great shrine at Ise to the Japanese nation as a whole, as all Japanese have a common ancestress, Amaterasu. Therefore, although the immutable world of the Japanese is his *iemoto*, which secondary group is capable of linking the individual with Japan as a whole, in contrast to the Chinese secondary group *tsu* which provides no comparable foundation.

As we noted before, neither the Chinese nor the Japanese developed universalistic approaches to ethics or religion or any other major social and cultural objective. Both Chinese and Japanese were particularistic when compared with Westerners. The real Chinese-Japanese difference is that the particularistic approach of the Chinese was narrower in application than its Japanese counterpart. In the Chinese scene, the particularistic approach is confined by the kinship principle, but in the Japanese scene it enjoys a wider scope of opportunities because of the more flexible kin-tract principle. Through the *dōzoku* system the Japanese individual has already been lifted out of his immediate kinship roots which would have put a low ceiling on his wider involvements. At the same time, the attribute of continuity from the father-son relationship prevents him from going too far afield; he incorporates himself in a kinship-like *iemoto*, with the imperial house as his ultimate limit.

Compared with Westerners, the Japanese have never been truly universalistic in their thinking. The ultimate confirmation of this observation is found not only in the non-acceptance of non-Japanese in Japan, but in the Japanese scheme for the world at the height of their power and conquest before and during World War II. Their Greater Asia Co-prosperity Sphere was not a model for present or future universal egalitarianism, even at the conceptual level. What they wanted was a world hegemony in which all would live in harmony if they would accept their proper (inferior) places below the Japanese in a graded hierarchy of races and peoples—a sort of world establishment in the *iemoto* model.

Our analysis so far leaves no doubt that the Japanese way of life is considerably different from that of the Chinese and both are very different from that of the Americans. The question is, is it quite similar to that of Hindu India? My answer is no. The reason is that the role of mother-son relationship is the dominant one in India, but its importance in Japan is greatly overshadowed by the father-son relationship, unigeniture, and markedly hierarchical and binding ties between the heir and his brothers.[8]

The attributes of diffuseness, dependence and libidinality originating from the mother-son relationship are at most points held in check by, or greatly subordinated to, those originating from the father-son relationship. Though sharing the Hindu view of the impermanence of life and the all-embracing nature of the universal God, or Buddha, the Japanese confine themselves to specific creeds originating from particular ancestral father figures, buttressed by their pseudo-kinship relationship to the emperor through the Shinto shrines. Though dependent upon the master or the imperial supermaster, blind devotion for the Japanese demands not *passive* following, as in Hindu India, but *active* carrying out of the will (actual or supposed) of the father figure of his *iemoto* (or of the super-*iemoto*, the national state). It is a relationship in which diffused dependence takes a secondary place to more specific actions commensurate with the attributes of continuity and authority.

In *Clan, Caste and Club* (Hsu 1963) I concluded, from my analyses of the interrelationship between social organization, cultural ideal and the individual in the Chinese, Hindu and American ways of life that the Chinese way was the least dynamic and generated the least amount of internal impetus to change; the American way is most dynamic and generates the most internal impetus to change; while the Hindu way leads to a society remarkably dynamic in appearance which in the long run undergoes little real change. Now we must observe that the Japanese way, though it is basically Chinese, has led to more dynamic results because it always had a wider human field in which to play.

The Japanese scholar Hayashi, whom we quoted before, wants the Japanese to develop a new concept of work. According to him, instead of their present unshaken faith in the group (corporation, university, government department, etc.), Japanese about to begin working careers should "select their specialty carefully" as American students do; and instead of devoting their time and energy in analyzing "the financial conditions of the nation's leading enterprises" in the hope of entering one of them for life regardless of what jobs they will be obliged by the company to accept, they must aim at becoming professionals who take pride in their chosen professions as individuals. Otherwise, in Hayashi's opinion, ". . . there is a long way to go for Japanese society to be democratized" since it is composed of human clusters, not individuals equal to each other as in the West, where social status differences have "nothing to do with the value of those engaged in certain professions because of the Christian idea of 'anyone is equal before God' " (Hayashi 1965).

In view of our analysis, Hayashi's exhortation to Japan that "clusters must go" and that his countrymen "must do away with their faith in their group" is simply unrealistic. It is as unrealistic as if he were to ask Americans to forget their individualism. In both cases the visible values sprang from deep historical and psycho-cultural roots, and they cannot be altered for the asking. On the other hand, Hayashi needs to examine more closely the Christian West, especially the differences between what it does and what it professes. Had he done so, especially in the light of our PSH formulation, he might also have realized that not only have Christian ideals failed to eliminate social inequality based on work in the West but that the very individualism which he wants his fellow Japanese to develop has much to do with the genesis and maintenance, by force if need be, of that very inequality in the Christian West and in the attitude of the Christian West toward the rest of mankind. As long as the Western way of life continues to make the PSH resources scarce for the individual, the strife for superiority (either by advancing or by keeping and pushing others to a lower place) will be intensified rather than otherwise. Furthermore, is Professor Hayashi not aware of the fact that all the totalitarian ideologies no less than those of democracy and individual freedom were creatures of the West (see Hsu 1970:422–440)? In fact, American scholars like Edward T. Hall favor the Japanese culture over its American counterpart "in any race to solve both environmental problems and human problems" (Hall 1970:234).

Most recently another Japanese scholar, Professor Shōzaburo Kimura, of Tokyo University, expresses concern in a somewhat similar vein. He acknowledges that Japan has indeed gone far in the contemporary world and he agrees with our conclusion that the *iemoto*-pattern with its kin-tract principle of human organization is principally responsible for it. However, he feels that the same characteristics in human relations which propelled Japan to such great success today are truly stumbling blocks to Japan's future participation in a cosmopolitan and rationalized world and that they will forever prevent Japan from becoming a true member of a United Europe or of a United World. According to Kimura, in that larger world, America included, the trend is from national enterprises towards multiplenational enterprises, even towards international enterprises unhampered by narrow, national interests (Kimura 1972:35).

I think Professor Kimura, too, has misread the future of a world still dominated by the West. Those who are impressed by the recent European

Common Market developments need to remember the West's numerous efforts for an universal Christendom. The fact is that, not only the Christian West as a whole but within each individual Western nation, Christian unity is nowhere in sight. Instead, what we witness is numerous ecumenical calls combined with perpetual divisiveness among the professed Western believers of Christ. To go back to our PSH formulation again, as long as the resources for PSH are scarce most human beings will suffer from insecurity which cannot lead them to cooperate with each other except temporarily in face of some real or imagined common crisis. The scarcer the resources for PSH, the higher the interpersonal tension within the society, the lower the level of its rationality and the harder it will be for such societies to unite with each other for any length of time. I am by no means a pessimist, but the objective evidence points to more intense separatism and nationalism rather than greater world unity, at least in the foreseeable future.

The Japanese are fortunate in that they have in their traditional *iemoto* pattern of human relationship no lack of PSH resources, and at the same time it also provides them with the psycho-cultural wherewithal for military or economic capabilities to defend themselves against genuine threats from without.

Under the stimulus of Western expansionism during a shamelessly colonial era, the Japanese imitated the expansionist and colonial minded West and lost. Should the Japanese not consider a different destiny in which they can make the best of all possible worlds?

NOTES

1. Here and again below the term *Oyaji* ("father") refers to the supervisor who is generally considerably older than the men he supervises.

2. As I write these passages I notice an article in the current issue of *Life* magazine (Sept. 1, 1972, pp. 30–38) entitled "Boredom on the Assembly Line," which deals with job dissatisfaction among Detroit auto workers. The author claims this to be a new industrial revolution with which the factory will have to contend. Typically, some American auto makers have thought of what they call "Job Enrichment," which would enable workers to exercise their creativity. But no real, economically feasible solution for this American problem is in sight.

3. These songs are sung by all employees together, male and female. However, Japanese society and culture is, of course, male-centered. Nearly all the important positions are occupied by males. Consequently, all the exuberance and enthusiasm towards the corporation described here is primarily relevant to male employees. As early as the 1920's some female factory workers voiced dissatisfaction with their conditions of life to which the following song of *Joko* (female worker) bears witness:

Joko's Song

The life in a dormitory is more trying than the bird's
    life in a cage and the prison living
The factory is a hell, the supervisor, a demon;
    and the machine, a fire wheel.

How I wish I had wings to get out of here and fly
    over to the other side of the water.
Senior Residents behave so arrogantly,
    but they too used to be the same jokos.
Working a factory is just like serving in a prison:
    only difference is that we do not have metal chains.

I am a *joko,* a vain bird.
I cannot fly in spite of my wings.
I cannot fly in spite of the open sky.
(Because) I am in a cage even though I can see the sky.
I am a small bird, but with the wings broken.

As my parents were unsuccessful,
no, they were not unsuccessful, but as I was shiftless,
I was deceived by a tail less fox,
and brought to this place.

Rather than working in this dreadful mill,
I would run away to the end of the Manchuria border.
I would rather experience hardship in the strange land.
(Even the work at Manchuria must not be as dreadful
    as it is here.)

Please listen to me——(name) *san*
Because of my wish to be loyal to my parents,
I am going through such a hardship, hundreds of miles
    away from home.

Filling up the pockets with gravel.
I prepared myself to be drowned.
—But if I die, it would be a disgrace to the company.
—But if I return home, it would be a disgrace to
    my parents.
Only bitter tears come out when I think of my situation.

Really this is a terrible world for *jokos.*
What kind of people their parents are,
if they brought them to this world
knowing their fate to be *jokos.*

How I wish to treat my parents to a cup of *sake,*
with joyful tears in my eyes.
When I imagine their saying
"When is our daughter coming home (it can be very soon)?"
my mind is flooded with tears of agony.

I wish I would be a wall board in the company office
so that I could read the letters from my home.

How can we spin well when we eat nothing but vegetables
for the three meals.   (Collected by Hosoi 1922)

It is important to note that the song writer, instead of rebelling against the exploitation, laments her own fate. In fact, even under such distress she is concerned with the company's reputation and her parents' face.

With economic prosperity and American influence, especially after World War II, more women have entered into the business and industrial world (Rō Dō Shō 1967:78–84), the lot of female workers has improved and more females have been admitted to white collar ranks. But the female employee's position remains inferior to that of her male counterpart in wages and as a matter of hierarchy. For example, in 1966, in the non-agriculture and non-forestry trades, female temporary employees hired on a daily basis still outnumbered female regular employees hired on a permanent basis, while the picture was totally reversed among the males. Far more males were hired on a permanent than on a daily basis (Rō Dō Shō 1967:85). As another example, female clerks in the same office as a rule serve tea to their male office mates, but not vice versa. In recent years faint noises of female rebellion are occasionally heard and the posted demands of one such female rebellious effort I knew as early as 1965 stated: "no more pouring tea for male colleagues." But these rumblings of female dissatisfaction have not yet made serious inroads into male dominance.

4. The provincial and occupational "guilds," which have been noted by many students of China, were no exception to this statement. (See Hsu 1968.)

5. Exactly the same thing holds true for natural resources, the abundant presence of which in many regions of the earth never assures their effective utilization unless the requisite skills, tools, capital, and human organization are at hand.

6. This analysis follows that given in *Clan, Caste and Club* (Hsu 1963:162–191 and 204–224), where the Chinese, Hindu and American situations are compared and contrasted with each other.

7. Of course, the great importance of the emperor was built up by the Meiji reformers. But if Japan did not have the *iemoto* type of human organization based on loyalty to *daimyō* etc., and the Japanese did not have their particular *iemoto* type of approach to religious affiliation, such reformers would have found it impossible to glorify the emperor by reviving State Shintoism for modernization purposes. The *iemoto* structure and content were the true foundation which made such developments possible. The Chinese reformers in the 19th century never put their thoughts in that direction, and even if they did, they would not have succeeded.

8. After the publication of *Hikaku Bunmei Shakai Ron* (Hsu 1971c) Dr. Tsurumi Kazuko wrote in a review: "The author argues that the Japanese family system is a synthesis *(nuiawase)* of Chinese and Indian (Hindu) types, whereas the *iemoto* combines Chinese and American types. Yet, if the author's postulate that the

secondary grouping in a society is determined by its family system is correct, then the Japanese *iemoto* should be a mixture of Chinese and Indian (Hindu) type of secondary groupings instead" ("Nihon kazoku no genri o saguru." Shūkan Gen Ron. Jan. 28, 1972).

I think Dr. Tsurumi has misunderstood our position and her misunderstanding comes from two sources: (a) the term kin-tract which we describe as the basic principle governing *iemoto* is derived from an abbreviated combination of the terms kinship (the basic secondary grouping in China and contrast the basic principle of secondary grouping in the United States), and (b) the notion that one system as a whole could simply be a cross between two other systems as wholes. No suggestion is made that the basic principle of Japanese *iemoto* organization combines that of the Chinese clan with that of the U.S. club. Instead, the term kin-tract denotes the fact that the criteria for recruitment to the *iemoto* is more flexible than to the kinship group but that once the relationship is entered into it becomes as binding as in kinship. However, no term can encompass all the reality it is designed to call attention to. This superficial difficulty is easily reduced by realizing that the important *guides* for our comparison and contrast are the attributes, not the systems as wholes. For example, authority (part of the principle of the hierarchy), is as prominent an attribute in the Japanese situation as it is uncharacteristic of the U.S. system. Except for the element of volition connected with entry into the *iemoto* or *iemoto*-like relationships, the latter has little else in common with the U.S. club or club-like organization. This conclusion is inevitable once our attention is focused on attributes. Our analysis should leave little doubt that in kinship system and in secondary grouping, the U.S., the Hindu and the Chinese stand apart, each from the others. However, to the extent that father-son dominance and mother-son dominance offer no attribute leading to rejection of kinship, the Chinese and Hindu systems are more similar to each other than either is to the U.S. system. The Japanese system, being primarily a variation of its Chinese counterpart, is therefore, closest to that of the Chinese, less close to that of the Hindu, and farthest apart from that of the U.S.

21

Roots of the American Family: From Noah to Now

Much has been said about the many problems which beset us today, such as crime and violence, and their causes. The quality of television, drugs, economic fluctuations, and even weather changes have been blamed. More recently, a finger has been pointed at the family. That is, at least in part, why the august Smithsonian Institution is elaborating the theme of "Kin and Communities" in its bicentennial celebration.

But what is the link between the American family and our basic problems? I suggest that the key is to be found in the highly discontinuous way in which we relate to each other. Here an analogy may help.

In physical matters glue is used when we want to join objects together. There is the usual household paste which is a mixture of flour and water, and there is Elmer's glue, which is supposed to hold diving boards together. Objects stuck together by household paste can be separated by soaking in water. But Elmer's glue is stronger than the power of tractors: the objects it holds together cannot be pulled apart without destruction.

If we transfer the glue analogy to the human scene, we might say that the glue which glued Romeo and Juliet together was some kind of Elmer's glue, while that which bound the Midnight Cowboy to any of his clients was no more than the thinnest of household paste.

In all societies human beings relate to each other by two kinds of glue: role (or usefulness) and affect (or feeling). We understand role in terms of skilled or unskilled labor, white collar or blue collar, dentists and diamond cutters, housekeepers and politicians, customers and salesmen. As our society has grown in complexity, the number and variety of roles have grown with it. In fact, role differentiation is the major concomitant of the growth in societal complexity. For example, in today's conditions, giant corporations often have more diverse personnel and more workers and specialists on their payrolls than do many small member states of the United Nations.

On the other hand, while our roles have evolved in number and proficiency with the complexity of our industrial society, our affect has not. We still have the same kind of feelings as our ancestors had many thousands of years ago: love, hate, rage, despair, endurance, hope, anxiety, forbearance, loyalty, caring, betrayal, and so forth. The list is not long, and

This chapter was originally published in *Kin and Communities: Families in America*, Allan J. Lichtman and Joan R. Challinor, eds., © Smithsonian Institution, Washington, D.C., 1979, pp. 219–36. Reprinted by permission of the Smithsonian Institution Press.

many of the terms describing them are partially or wholly subsumable under each other.

That is why, in contrast to old books on science and technology, which are useless to us except as curiosities or as material for histories of science and technology, great literature (fiction, poetry) and great art (painting, sculpture) and even great philosophy and ethics survive the ages, for we moderns experience the same agony and joy and the same loyalty and duplicity as the ancients. We can relive their lives through what they have written and they, too, were they alive today, would have been able to discuss with us our problems with our children, parents, friends and enemies, employers and employees, sweethearts and spouses.

To return to the glue analogy. Role works like household paste. Humans linked by it are easily pulled asunder and can be replaced. Affect is like some more tenacious Elmer's glue. Humans linked by it cohere to a far greater degree, and replacement cannot be made without psychic cost or disturbance.

CULTURE AND AFFECT

However, the *patterns* of affect which operate among Americans are different from those which motivate people of other cultures, such as the Chinese and Japanese. Americans and Asians may experience the same love, hate, and despair, but the ways in which they express love, hate, and despair, and especially what makes them love, hate, or despair, differ greatly.

Literature is one of the best evidences for this. I will not detail the spectacular differences between Western novels, drama and art, and their Chinese and Japanese counterparts. I have done this elsewhere (See Chapter 12. Also Hsu 1975). Briefly, the two outstanding psychological characteristics of Western and American novels and drama are: freedom of the individual to the extent of egotism and preoccupation with sex. The former expresses itself in characters in search of identity such as Holden Caulfield in *The Catcher in the Rye;* in those who go it alone to prove themselves by conquest, such as Captain Ahab in *Moby Dick* and the old man in *The Old Man and the Sea;* or in those striving to be something they can never be, such as Herzog in *Herzog.* More extreme manifestations of egotism are found in *Papillon* or *On the Road* or *Easy Rider.*

Freedom of the individual has given Western men their singleness of purpose and their absolute zeal in pursuing many objectives of which they may justifiably be proud; conquest of space, exploration of the high seas, spreading social benefits through their missionary spirit, elimination of poverty and disease via science and technology, and many more. But it has also led to the shrinkage of affect and the tendency to substitute role for affect altogether.

THE SHRINKAGE OF AFFECT

Shrinkage of affect takes many forms: loyalty becomes scarce, friendship turns shallow, people refuse to consider each others' needs or to be involved in their affairs. It is also linked to the fact that American males have a strong aversion to contact with each other, except in emergencies (such as mouth-to-mouth resuscitation) or in certain sports (such as wrestling). This aversion is the external symptom of an inner inability to form deep friendships. American men will combine to conquer the external world but they must shun lasting and undying attachment to each other.

Why? Could not the answer lie in a fear of homosexuality? If sex is everywhere, then the only safe area for intimacy is between members of the opposite sex. This is why Holden Caulfield, the young hero of J. D. Salinger's *The Catcher in the Rye,* bolted out of his favorite teacher's apartment with haste when he found the older man sitting on the edge of the couch and stroking his hair. This is also what the other itinerant farm laborers suspected when, in John Steinbeck's *Of Mice and Men,* they questioned Lenny and George as to how long they had been traveling together. The more our culture is preoccupied with sex, the less persons of the same sex have been able to develop and maintain *affective* relationships with each other. At first this inability was confined to males, but our females have been catching up. They too are seldom to be seen walking hand in hand with each other.

We have then an atomistic situation in which humans become emotional islands to themselves. The individualist may need others for his rise to power or fame or fortune, but he cannot afford to be slowed down by affective baggage in his quest for success. In order to make breaks with the past more clearly and easily, he must have few affective involvements. In such a context, one man's gain is necessarily viewed as another man's loss. Our news media and popular publications make much of the exploits of many successful individuals. But for every girl who is crowned Miss America there will be thousands or even hundreds of thousands of disappointed and heart-broken damsels. A psychological climate favoring driving individualists bent on cut-throat competition will hardly enable them to develop genuine and lasting friendships with each other. This is the root of what Philip Slater speaks of as *The Pursuit of Loneliness* (1970).

EXTERNALIZATION OF HUMAN RELATIONSHIPS

An affectively atomistic situation leads to more than individual loneliness. It necessitates the escalation of role, and of externalized inducements or restraints, at the expense of affect.

Externalization of human relationships finds expression in diverse ways. Our principal approach to crime and violence is one example. We rely on surveillance, detection and control: more secure locks and fences, more hidden cameras, more guards, more electronic alarms. We develop mugger-proof public vehicles, vandal-proof schools, shoplifter-proof supermarkets, and rapist-proof co-eds, all the way to child-proof medicine bottles and crash-proof automobiles. Yet crime and violence continue to increase year after year so that it is an elaboration of the obvious to quote statistics on the subject. The ingenuity of the externalized means for stopping crime and violence will surely be outmatched by the creativity of those bent on more ingenious means for breaking the law.

Externalization of all relationships has inevitably changed the nature of discipline in our society. It is often cried that America lacks discipline. This is not true. There is ample evidence of discipline in American life. Take a look at our super-highways and the thousands of cars which ply them at high speed twenty-four hours a day. This would be impossible without discipline. Our huge hotels, offices, water works, mines, air lines, and atomic plants cannot be run without discipline.

What is wrong is that this discipline is increasingly externally imposed and is less and less due to a desire to respect or care for others: their rights, their safety, and their happiness. Driving within a speed limit because cops are there to catch me is one thing, while doing so because I do not want to injure someone is quite another. Operating a machine strictly according to instructions for fear it will blow up in my face is one thing, while doing so because I do not want to harm my fellow employees is quite another. We emphasize rules of survival, not rules of morality.

KINSHIP AND BEHAVIOR

Roles are first learned in the family, but the individual's capacity for role mastery continues in schools, in work shops, in factories and offices, and through diverse other networks and situations of life. An old Chinese proverb says: "He who works throughout old age, learns throughout old age."

That is not, however, the way we acquire our patterns of affect. The real hothouse for such patterns in every society is the kinship system, at the core of which in America is the nuclear family. The kinship system is the first web of human relationships for the individual. It sets the basic feeling tone and establishes the affective foundation for all subsequent interpersonal patterns because it comes first, because it catches the individual *tabula rasa,* and because it conditions the individual when his or her cerebral development is faster than at any other time. The family is the arena through which the individual develops feelings about himself, about his fellow human beings, and about the rest of the world. Such feelings, in turn, determine what roles he or she chooses and how well he or she is motivated to perform them throughout life. In the broadest sense the kinship system is the psychic cell of every society. It holds the key to social and cultural development in the same sense that the germ cell holds the key to the adult biological organism yet to appear (See Chapter 13).

Many observers speak of the decline of the family in America. High divorce and separation rates, generation gaps, prevalence of single parent households, increasing numbers of couples living together without marriage, unwed mothers, abused children, runaway fathers, juvenile delinquents, children returning to empty homes because their mothers are working: these are among the symptoms of it. These symptoms led scholars such as Urie Bronfenbrenner to say that "the family is falling apart" (Bronfenbrenner 1977:41), and Dr. Margaret Mead to urge the need "to redesign the whole social structure with the family at the core" (Mead 1976).

However, when we come to the question of why "the family is falling apart" and how to reconstruct our family for a better America of the future, I am at variance with a majority of other social scientists. For example, Bronfenbrenner says: "What's destroying the family isn't the family itself but the indifference of the rest of society. The family takes a low priority" (Bronfenbrenner 1977:42).

My question is, is not the society which is so indifferent to the family run by Americans who are products of that very family? What transformed them into such monsters who want to destroy the social grouping of their origin?

Others are more specific and claim industrialization or modernization to be the prime mover of social and cultural change, including changes in the family. I think this view is a misapprehension. It is based on the Western fallacy of another era, that Christianization of the world was the means to free mankind from greed, violence, and war. Christianity has not merely failed to free the Western peoples, who took to it in droves, from greed, violence, and war; it has failed, despite Western pressure, to gain many converts among the rest of the world, especially in Asia.

In the first place, I do not agree that the American family was once very different from what it is today. American fathers certainly seem to have exercised more authority over their wives and children in the frontier days, but how did they themselves become so independent of their own parents to begin with?

Besides, the "extended family of several generations, with all its relatives" (Bronfenbrenner 1977:41), never really existed on any grand scale in America. Mary J. Bane, in a piece of recently published research, shows that only 6 percent of households in America contained grandparents, parents, and children, and that the percentage of such households remained the same in 1970 (Bane 1977). Bane also opines that it is doubtful that Americans move more often today than they did in the last century. If mobility is decimating America's family and social fabric, she concludes, it has been doing so for a long time, unrelated to the extent of industrialization. Whether industrialization or mobility is compatible with some sort of extended family has been the subject of sociological debate (see, for example, Parsons 1949:191–92 and Litwak 1960:385–94).

What I wish to point out, in the second place, is that American society is not, as many would claim, a "young, rambunctious society, only 200 years old" (Bronfenbrenner 1977:42). Every society consists of three basic elements: cultural heritage, social organization, and individual behavior. The first consists of everything handed down from the past, from ethics, myths and ideas about gods to games, artifacts, and skills. The second refers to the way the individual members of society are organized into groups, such as families, clubs, classes, and castes, both to act and to transmit the cultural heritage from generation to generation. The third element, individual behavior, is generally so strongly influenced by the cultural heritage transmitted through the social organization that it is predictable on a probability basis.

Once this is understood, it will be easy to see that American society is not merely two hundred years old. In fact it is much older than Chinese society. Its cultural heritage came from the Chaldaeans, the Sumerians and the Babylonians, not to mention the ancient-Israelites, the Greeks and the Romans. The American social organization descends directly from Anglo-Saxon and Teutonic Europe. Most of American society's individual members speak English, and those who were native born were socialized by immigrant parents who rambunctiously claimed their society in America to be new because they had rejected the societies of their origin and because their old cultural heritage and social organization encouraged them to be adventurous and to seek the new.

The germs of this Western development, allegedly brought about by industrialization, were inherent in the Western psycho-cultural orientation long before the appearance of the Industrial Revolution. In fact we can go straight to the myth of Noah and the flood which we already touched on in Chapter 16.

To punish the wickedness of men, God decided to flood the earth and kill all except the chosen man Noah and his family. Noah made an ark into which he packed his wife, his three sons and their wives, together with seven pairs of all "clean" animals and one pair of all other animals. After they had floated around for some forty days, the flood subsided and the ark landed on Ararat, where Noah at once thanked the Lord by appropriate rituals. Next, Noah drank the wine he had made and, while under the influence of liquor, he masturbated in his tent. Ham laughed at his father's condition and called in his two brothers. They all expressed disgust toward Noah but covered him up. Some kind of quarrel ensued. Noah then cursed Ham and condemned his son Canaan and future descendants to be eternal slaves but blessed Shem and Japheth and told them to disperse in their separate ways to people the earth.[1]

We have in this most celebrated of Western myths, still being taught in churches and schools, dramatized on the stage and screen, thematized in literature and serialized in comics, all the ingredients which some of our social scientists claim to be the results of industrialization and therefore of recent origin. Ham's lack of reverence for his father did not originate with him, for when the flood came Noah left his own parents to perish. And his son's lack of reverence for him was more than matched by Noah's vindictiveness toward his own flesh and blood. The evidence for mobility is equally strong. Not only did Noah and his family escape the disaster by boat but they never returned to their old home after the flood waters subsided. Despite the fact that they were the only eight people left in the world, Noah and his kin could not stay together.

There is even in this myth clear indication of Western absolutism, in which role approach has erased all affect considerations: a God who decided on his own final solution, a solution that another notorious dictator was later to attempt on the Jews. Myth is not, of course, reality. But myths, like art, inform an audience of traditional values, reflect the fantasies of the people, and may consciously or unconsciously give direction for future courses of action. That is why President Carter, in response to public objection, recently had to amend his remarks concerning who killed Jesus (reported in *Chicago Sun-Times,* May 14, 1977). That is why Black Muslim leader Wallace D. Muhammed is trying to convince black Christian churchmen that depicting Christ as a Caucasian is harmful to non-Caucasians (reported in *Chicago Sun-Times,* May 27, 1977). The contents of such myths are, at the very least, as reliable indices of how people feel about themselves, each other, and the rest of the world, as are the results of the public opinion polls or even some of our scholarly questionnaires.

The significance of this myth becomes even clearer when we realize how the contents of its Chinese counterpart point to another totally different pattern of affect, also under no industrial or modernizing influence. In the reign of the Emperor Yao (said to be about 2357–2258 B.C.), a terrible flood devastated China. Yao appointed a certain Kun to control the flood but the latter, after nine years of work, was unsuccessful. Yao took full responsibility, resigned from office, and offered the throne to Shun (said to have reigned between 2258 and 2206 B.C.). Emperor Shun executed or exiled Kun for his failure but appointed the executed man's son Yu in his place. Yu worked all over the country for thirteen years, during which time he passed by his wife's door three times. Being absorbed in his official duties Yu did not once go in to see his wife. After Yu's success, Emperor Shun gave Yu his throne. Yu became the next emperor, thus exonerating the name of his father, and the Chinese lived happily ever after.

The Chinese myth reveals how differently they felt about themselves, about each other, and about the rest of the world. For one thing, the Chinese legend named no chosen man. Instead all Chinese suffered from the disaster together. It did not provide for an escape by boat to a new world. Instead all the Chinese stayed where they were born and raised and did the best they could. There was no question of sons going in different directions from their parents. Instead the son worked hard to succeed where his father failed. In his toils Yu did not visit his wife even when convenient, for larger duty took precedence over matters of his own heart. Finally it is most significant that the supernatural had no place in this

Chinese story: no Chinese god would impose the final solution on all Chinese as punishment for their faults.

In both cases, the myths contain the basic psycho-cultural germs which were to grow, unfold, spread, and proliferate in their respective kinship systems independent of economic developments. In both cases the central themes of the myths and the perceived solutions of the problems are consonant with the two societies' broad, historical development.

I am aware of the fact that there is variation in kinship patterns among Western peoples. There is zadruka in Yugoslavia. The French pattern of dowry is absent in the United States. The German father is more stern than his English counterpart. The Spanish and Italian style of chaperoning their daughters before marriage is inconceivable to most American parents. But if we take a broader and longer historical view, it should become clear that Western society as a whole is centrifugal or outward looking, and that centrifugality is rooted in a kinship situation that was centrifugal long before the Industrial Revolution. The society did not destroy the family. Instead, the family nurtured individuals with an affective pattern which threatened to dismantle itself and the society with it.

The Chinese society, on the other hand, has always been centripetal or inward looking. That too was rooted in a centripetal kinship pattern since ancient times. That is why there are today more people of European origin outside than inside of Europe, while less than 3 percent of Chinese are outside of China. To many, the Chinese appear to be the largest racial group in the world, but this is only because most ethnic Chinese are still in one contiguous area, whereas Europeans are scattered over all parts of the globe.

Noah's power over his children looks excessive to us today, but if parental power were really that absolute, Noah would not have been able to condemn Canaan and his future descendants to eternal slavery *without permission from his own elders*. The facts that Noah left his own parents to perish in the flood and had such a free hand in dealing with his own progeny are clear indications of discontinuity between the generations and of freedom of the individual. In such a context, figurative children of Noah would naturally be moved to escalate the same discontinuity and individual freedom even further. What has happened in the American family is the inevitable growth of the Western kinship roots. Those roots explain why the American family, though different in spectacular ways from its European ancestry, remains part of the same psycho-socio-cultural development.

CAN WE SAVE OUR FAMILY?

I do not think we need to worry about the disappearance of the American family as a physical fact. Unisex marriages, cohabitation without marriage, generation gaps, and singlehood notwithstanding, Americans living in matrimony still constitute the majority. Even increasingly high divorce rates do not threaten the family with extinction. For example, divorced and widowed persons are most likely to get married again. The desire to possess the loved one is so pervasive that most young people will still seek the marital contract as a way of securing a predictable affective relationship, especially in a society where other relationships are subject to change without notice.

What we must ask ourselves instead is, what can we do to reshape our kinship system so as to make our families less centrifugal and to give future Americans more, rather than less, trust in each other?

I am aware that some scholars regard the present woes of our society as the necessary price to be paid for "the limitless opportunities of the future" (Slater 1966:94). To them, the instability of our primary group is a necessary condition of more creativity and imagination and of maximum commitment to larger groups and issues.

To some extent I agree with this position. For example, the Chinese, who were oriented to seek their security and their life's satisfaction in human involvement, failed to develop industrialization, in spite of their considerable and varied achievements in science which are reported in the monumental works of Joseph Needham.

But perhaps the temporariness of our family and the de-personalization of our human relationships have gone beyond the point of no return.

Given the foregoing analysis it seems clear that one fundamental task is to reevaluate the boundary, content, and worth of our value of privacy. Privacy is an essential attribute of individualism. It can mean many things, physical, social, or psychological, and have many degrees, from keeping one's health problems secret to making career decisions by oneself.

In the parent-child context the American way in privacy expresses itself as follows. Before the children come of age their parents have exclusive powers over them and tend to shield them from intensive interaction with all others. Even when grandparents live in the same house, they are only guests, with no jurisdiction over their grandchildren. Parental authority among the poor may be more diffuse. Recently I met a student who was born and raised in the small Alabama town of Mount Vernon. He told me that when he was a child his grandfather or a non-family member could punish him for such wrongdoings as stealing watermelon from another's field. When his own parents learned of his misdeeds they would give him another thrashing. However, this pattern no longer obtains in his home town today. My informant says it is because strangers have moved in who do not share the same standard of judgment. He finds no explanation for why grandparents today are also excluded from the authority to discipline their grandchildren.

Certainly among most middle class Americans everywhere today the custom is for the mother to write out a list of do's and don't for any baby sitter to follow, whether or not the sitter is a relative. In short, whoever else is allowed a hand in the child's upbringing is merely acting at the command of the parents. Recently a fourth grader who asked her mother about her grandparents because they were doing genealogies in school received the reply: "Tell your teacher it's none of her business." Teachers, too, are supposed to deal only with areas that parents have given permission for and nothing else.

At the same time children begin to guard their own privacy early. They learn more from what their parents do than from what their own elders say. Their parents also give them encouragement in that direction since training children for independence is the American thing.

In pre-school years the situation is manageable. Parents have the last word and children can express their demand for privacy and independence in limited areas. But, as children move into pre-teen and teen years and demand larger and larger spheres for privacy and independence, a conflict between the generations is inevitable. The more exclusive parents' control over their children, the less likely the parents are to contemplate with pleasure their children's freedom. This often leads to strong adverse feelings between parents and children which preclude rational management.

This conflict has far-reaching consequence. It has been repeatedly observed that peer pressure is great, so great that much of the juvenile delinquency and drug problems are attributed to it. What we must see is that submission to peer pressure is not universal, as some social scientists would have us believe, but a function of the separation of parents and children. The greater one's need to separate from one's parents, the greater one's need to belong to peer groups.

Thus the exclusive parental control is at the root of generation gaps and peer tyranny; it prevents the cultivation in the young of the affective need for a mixing of ages which so many authorities see as desirable. In the circumstances efforts to turn us into our own family historians will lead to no more than a new form of pastime. Unless the interest in our own genealogies is matched by affective links with our own forebears, it will have no bearing on the actual shape of our families to come.

We ought at least to try some truly revolutionary ideas. In an earlier connection I have already explained the importance of a society's literature as evidence of its pattern of affect. I now wish to say that literature is also the main carrier of that pattern and transmits the pattern from generation to generation. We need, of course, to inform our young of the traditional pattern of feeling about ourselves, about each other, and about the rest of the world, the pattern which is central to the cultural heritage of Western man. We need also to offer them the knowledge that the traditional Western affective pattern is not the only one possible. We need to see, for example, that there are alternatives to unconditional surrender or absolute victory, to total *individual* failure to total *individual* success, and to leaving home as a way of solving life's problems.

How many Americans know that there is no counterpart of *Moby Dick* or *The Old Man and the Sea* in Chinese literature, or that the Chinese did not have first person novels like *The Sun Also Rises, The Great Gatsby* and *The Deere Park?* Or again, how many know that relatively few Chinese novels dealt with sex or romance, and that those that did always let the social requirements overshadow the pursuit of individual happiness? How many know that the hero in the Chinese equivalent of *Gulliver's Travels* was not alone, but accompanied in his adventures by a friend and a brother-in-law? Finally, how many of those here knew, prior to today, some other version of the flood myth and its totally different solution? Do we even know that the Sumerian and Babylonian versions of the myth, from which the Hebraic version was derived, differed from the latter in important aspects?

These are not mere exotica. They are expressions of other basic approaches to men, gods, and things. Few Americans know about such matters because Americans have been brought up so exclusively on Western literature that they are led to see the struggles and problems of a Captain Ahab or an Elmer Gantry or an Achilles as pan-human. How can they feel otherwise? Their writers, critics and instructors are accustomed to speak of the human condition when, in fact, they are merely dealing with the condition of Western man.

One revolutionary idea I wish to propose is not merely the introduction of non-Western literature and art into our schools, museums and galleries. To a certain extent this is being done. What I envisage is that they will be introduced not as separate segments of the curricula or exhibits, but as part of the general program of instruction and research. They should be incorporated in our basic readers and nursery rhymes. At the high school and university levels, black literature or Japanese art should be taught not only in Black Programs or Japanese Studies. Instead they should be required, for example, by English departments, which teach Homer, Melville, Hemingway, and Joyce.

Another revolutionary idea I wish to propose is addressed both to our government and to our universities. In our universities we have departments of economics, government, and business management, but none of the family, except when it is subordinated to home economics or some other low prestige subject. Our government has Departments of Health, Education, and Welfare, the Treasury, and Justice, but none of the Family.

If the family is so important to us, why not create an independent and prestigious unit devoted to the family? Such a unit would examine not only the questions already posed in the preceding paragraphs, but also whether, as some journalists report, counter-culture lifestyles (such as unisex marriage, cohabitation without marriage, and so forth) are truly correlated with a decline in competitiveness and individualism.

"If America can send men to the moon she can do anything" is an often-aired sentiment. In view of my analysis, such a sentiment is highly misleading. Sending men to the moon is a technical matter and therefore in the role domain. I have no problem in predicting even more spectacular achievements to come in that domain.

But in the affect domain where change of patterns of human feelings is required, we have yet to make the first major breakthrough. I am proposing that we aim at such a breakthrough by rethinking the way we feel about ourselves as individuals, about each other, and about the rest of the world.

May I conclude with my encounter with some land snails in Brittany, France, some thirty-five years ago. I was a first-year graduate student at London and took my first spring vacation in France. At a spot where two small farms were divided by a low ridge, I saw several land snails, barely on one side of the ridge, burned to a crisp. The stumps on that side of the ridge were burned but those on the other side were not. Had the snails been able to move but a quarter of an inch farther from the burning side they would have saved their lives. Unfortunately, they failed to do so.

Are we land snails on a French farm or Americans of the twentieth century?

NOTE

1. The passage concerning Noah's self-eroticism is generally deleted or changed into more neutral statements in the modern versions of the Bible or the Torah. However, if we hold such neutral statements to be correct, it is puzzling why Noah should be so angry with Ham. There are other versions of what happened in the tent. One of them even had Ham committing sodomy on Noah.

Part VI

Intercultural Understanding

Introduction

In "Role, Affect and Anthropology" (Chapter 11) I suggested the possibility that the cultural tree is not unlike the biological tree after all, except that different societies, in contrast to the biological species, often try to make friends or ally with each other.

That is an extreme possibility that we do not believe, or wish to believe. Yet once we admit the great importance of affect in human affairs, we cannot but note that most views of intercultural understanding as well as culture change are overly optimistic. Many aspects of cultures have changed from the time when man first used the digging stick, but the affect-dominated fundamental direction of each culture seems to persist over time. Distant peoples can easily come together for conferences and socials and instantly talk with and send pictures and messages to each other via phone, television, or satellites, but the question remains as to how much they really understand or care about each other's loves and aspirations, fears, anxieties, and sensitivities. Furthermore, an obvious conclusion from some of the foregoing chapters is that societies steeped in rugged individualism are less capable of, or inclined toward, intercultural understanding than others imbued with a sociocentric view of man.

Having said this, I must ask, should we passively accept it? A most vital characteristic of all mankind is its resiliency in the face of impossible odds. We have so far seen this resiliency in our fight against physical obstacles. Why should we not deal with our psychocultural obstacles likewise?

"Intercultural Understanding: Genuine and Spurious" (Chapter 22) examines some common pitfalls and suggests some remedial measures. This is followed by "The Cultural Problem of the Cultural Anthropologist" (Chapter 23), which shows how the field worker can break the psychocultural barrier to improve the quality of our ethnography for us all.

22

Intercultural Understanding: Genuine and Spurious

Some months before President Nixon's visit to China in 1972, an evening television newsman commented on the Venice Film Festival in which the exhibitors from Peking received much attention.

They received so much attention, he said, not because of the quality of their films, but because this was their first time around. He wryly noted that the general level of the Chinese films shown at this festival was not particularly good anyhow.

The station then showed an excerpt from a Chinese film, a kind of operatic ballet, entitled *Red Detachment of Women*. It featured many body gyrations not dissimilar to traditional Western ballet, but the men and women wore uniforms and acted and danced to a theme replete with patriotism, anti-imperialism, defeat of Kuomintang forces, and class struggle efforts. Not without obvious sarcasm, the reporter concluded that the Chinese were offering exchange programs with the Americans and, with luck, we would be able to see Chinese films in our neighborhood theaters.

The reporter was not alone in his low esteen of Chinese films. During the week of President Nixon's visit to China, that same operatic ballet was released over one of the TV networks in its entirety. I made an informal poll among my students, colleagues, and friends who saw it and found most of my respondents thought it boring or unattractive. Even Joseph Alsop, a reporter who had turned after his 1972 tour of China from a vehement critic of the new regime into a high praiser of its achievements, concurred in the low opinion of the arts in new China. "Furthermore," Alsop concluded, "the official art and . . . the official literature are awful beyond imagining."

The reasons are obvious enough. Although there are exceptions, such as *Man for All Seasons, Gone with the Wind, Sound of Music,* and *Cabaret,* most American box-office successes today seem to be films bearing such titles as *Bonnie and Clyde, Last Tango in Paris, In Cold Blood, Deep Throat, Easy Rider, Midnight Cowboy, Adrift, Night of Dark Shadows, The Love Machine, Lovers' Ecstasy, Without a Stitch, School for Love, Free in Marriage, Lolita, The Wild Bunch, The French Connection, The Godfather, Exorcist, The Sting, In the Realm of the Senses,* to name but a few. Many—in fact most—of these films deal with sex, violence, and individual adventure. It is these films and

The substance of this chapter was first delivered in a speech at Cubberly Conference, School of Education, Stanford University, June 28, 1973. It was revised and published in the *Anthropology and Education Quarterly*, November, Vol. VIII, No. 4, 1977, pp. 202–209.

others like them that our advertisers acclaim in such terms as "a sublimely erotic work of art," "a legend, a success, irresistible," "the most exciting experience," "after which sex will never be the same." Advertising *The Long Goodbye,* the film's director Altman says in *The Plain Dealer* of Cleveland, Ohio: "This film is full of fun—murder, maiming, drunkenness, infidelity, topless yoga freaks, four-letter words, everything, like my first big success M*A*S*H. It's got the same ingredients." The new Chinese art simply does not measure up to the high artistic standard of such American fare.

Without arguing about the relative merits or demerits of the films themselves, two things are nevertheless clear: the American filmmakers have sold their products well to the U.S. public, and the Chinese films have not played to empty houses in China.

Some may, of course, cynically retort that the Chinese audiences like their kind of entertainment because they have no choice or have been ordered by a totalitarian government to do so. And others may, with equal facility, suspect that American audiences patronize their kind of entertainment because merchants of filth have led them down the garden path. There is probably some truth in both observations. But do they explain it all?

The White-Haired Girl

One of the earliest Chinese operatic ballets created under the new government is *The White-Haired Girl,* which has since also appeared on the screen. Probably many Americans have seen it since it, too, was not long ago on U.S. network television. The plot is said to be based on an actual fact that occurred in a small village in a north China province between 1935 and 1939. It dramatizes the struggle of the farmers against oppressive landlords, ending in the liberation of the oppressed with the arrival of the Communist Eighth Route Army.

A widowed farmer was compelled to sell his 17-year-old daughter to his landlord for payment of a debt, following which the father committed suicide. The young girl was subject to constant abuse, raped, and made pregnant by the landlord. Seven months later the villain decided to sell her to a brothel. After an unsuccessful suicide attempt she was helped by a servant to escape to a hidden cave where she gave birth to her child. She kept herself alive by stealing the food offered to the deities in a lonely mountain temple. After some time her hair turned white because of diet deficiency and because she rarely saw daylight. In the meantime the Japanese invaders occupied the area and the villainous landlord became a Japanese puppet official. The Communist liberators came, heralded by a characteristic marching song, the white-haired girl was rescued, the landlord and his henchmen were dragged away to their execution. The curtain falls after the bright sun rises from the east with the jubilant civilians and soldiers singing the praises of the new era in a grand finale.

Communist propaganda—some Americans would say! In a sense, yes. It was written, produced, and shown for political purposes. But the enthusiasm of the Chinese audiences could hardly be a mere artifact of totalitarian authority. Derk Bodde of the University of Pennsylvania who saw this operatic ballet in Peking during the first year of communist rule had the following to say about the reaction of the Chinese audience:

> Emotionally, they were completely one with the play and, during tense moments, roared their disapproval of the landlord, shouted advice to the heroine, and cheered the arrival of the Eighth Route Army. "Let her get him!" shouted my neighbor—a mild-looking youth two seats away, who before the play had been reading a pamphlet entitled The Chinese Revolution and Chinese Communist Party—during one exciting episode in which the heroine is restrained by her comrade from attacking the landlord.   (Bodde 1950:168)

The White-Haired Girl has since become a classic in China. Over 20 years later, in the summer of 1972, I saw it twice, once on film in Shenyang in Manchuria and later on the stage in Shanghai. The Eighth Route Army has now been changed to People's Liberation Army (PLA). The film version is less animated than the stage production, but on both occasions the audience roared disapproval of the villains and bravos at the heroine and her rescuers, led by her one-time boyfriend, now turned soldier. In fact, in the Shenyang theater, a three- or four-year-old girl, held on her mother's lap not far from us, shouted "bad eggs" as soon as the villain and his cohorts appeared on the screen. Probably she had seen this piece before, but the spontaneity of her reaction was unmistakable.

Why are the Chinese so excited by such a plot? Has the communist government created here something totally new in China? Have the Chinese people been so brainwashed by their new leaders that they accept whatever is fed them?

It is more likely that such new dramatic products are not totally new to the Chinese—indeed that the Chinese common man was emotionally tuned in to *The White-haired Girl* as early as 1949 and has continued to be tuned in.

Suffering under oppressive landlords and corrupt officials was a common theme in Chinese novels and legends—as was the punishment of such villains by "Robin Hoods" or good kings and just officials or benevolent supernaturals. A characteristic villainous act was the abuse of young daughters of helpless parents. There are many Chinese novels based on invasions and ravages by foreign hordes and Chinese victories over them. Other themes common in Chinese drama and literature are poverty, good deeds and their reward, filial sons and daughters risking their lives to save or avenge their fathers or mothers. Love affairs are not absent, but in most part they are not central; and in the end they are usually subordinated to peace, justice, propriety, and glorification of ancestors.

The concept of patriotism and anti-imperialism arose with the coming of the West. They are new—but they did not begin with Chinese communism. College and high school students used to demonstrate in the streets against an impotent government, in the name of patriotism and anti-imperialism, and often volunteered in organized groups to educate the illiterate peasantry and semiliterate merchants on these and related subjects. Furthermore, the psychological distance is not that great from the old dependence on and submission to the benevolent elders and the rare but incorruptible officials to a new reliance on well-disciplined cadres and liberation forces under a fatherly political leader. What is new is the fact that the incorruptible official has become the rule rather than the exception and that the ability to rise against centuries-old oppression is now a firmly established trend. Naturally Chinese audiences respond enthusiastically to their kind of entertainment.

From *Iliad* to *Last Tango in Paris*

What is true of the Chinese is equally true of the Americans. I do not mean that the two peoples are undergoing the same stages of development. But I do mean that, just as the new Chinese developments in the arts since the Communist revolution are not that new, American events since the late 1950s have their deep roots in the American past.

Since the 1950s American scholars have been talking a great deal about the changing American national character and the changing American values and society. In view of the heated racial problems, the intensified polarization between the left and the right, the exacerbated generation gap, the appearance of youth communes, riots in and out of prisons, women's liberation, gay liberation, and many other new developments of the 1960s and 1970s, this is understandable.

Certainly the pioneers who came to America from Europe held the notion that they were creating a new world. Ever since the beginning of the United States as a nation, Americans have prided themselves in having established a republic totally new. Americans like to claim that whatever they do or produce—whether it be merchandise or sociological theory—is revolutionary.

There is indication, however, that all of this is not so new. All that claim to change—revolutionary change—seems no more than expressions of a desire to change because it has been the American fashion to want to change, to believe that change, any change, is good. Change is an American Sacred Cow. But do the new movies, novels, and theatrical arts in which sex and violence and four-letter words have become commonplace represent something new for the Western man—new in spirit, new in objectives, and new in the way that man treats the world around him and goes about solving his problems?

Of course, they do not. What America has done is to escalate values, attitudes, and aspirations held dear by Western man from the beginning of Western history, thereby magnifying their strengths and their weaknesses, their rewards and their punishments. The ultra "modern" American movies are closely linked with more traditional Western fare such as *Moby Dick,* the semitraditional work *The Old Man and the Sea,* and both of these with ancient Western masterpieces, such as the *Illiad,* the *Odyssey,* and *Agamemnon.*

The *Illiad,* the *Odyssey,* and *Agamemnon*—especially the first two—are among the most widely read treasures of Western literature. They are taught in high schools and colleges. They are annotated and interpreted and published in numerous editions. They have been presented in films and on stage under diverse guises. I have been to several contemporary American social gatherings where those assembled recited them very much as they were recited at the Panathenaea among ancient Greeks in accordance with a law attributed variously to Solon, Hipparchus, or Peisistratus. What do they tell their readers?

To secure the return of his seduced sister-in-law, Agamemnon amassed a formidable fleet of some 1200 ships by twisting the arms of many less powerful princes and convincing them to become his allies; sacrificed his first-born daughter to get a suitable wind; sailed to far away Asia Minor and besieged the city of Troy for ten years until the stubborn enemy was vanquished and the city laid to waste. However, not only were the conquerors beset by weather and quarrels among themselves on their return journey, but those who made their way home were met by treachery greater than the initial abduction of Helen and hostility on the part of those they had left at home years before. Shortly afterwards, the returning heroes and their people, known as Achaeans, were driven out of their homelands by northern invaders, such as the Thessalians and the Dorians.

Furthermore, the manner in which American scholars and teachers of English have approached these Greek tragedies is interesting. They do not as a rule discuss the social and political implications of the Trojan War. Instead they speak of the *Iliad* as "the tragedy of Achilles," dwelling on "the sufferings of the Greek forces in his absence," "the story of a great man who through a fault in an otherwise noble character (and even the fault is noble) brings disaster upon himself, since the death of Patroklos is the work of free choice on the part of Achilles," "the vengeance taken by Achilles on Hektor," and the resolution of Achilles' anger "in a grudging forgiveness by the return of the body of Hektor to the Trojans" (Lattimore 1951:17).

Illicit love, romantic or other intrigues, personal mistakes, personal suffering, personal anger, personal invincibility, personal triumph and personal freedom—and more along the same line—these rather than the individual's role in society, are the central substances of these dramas intended by their authors and accepted by their audiences. The same emphasis has held sway in the West ever since.

The art, literature and drama that Westerners appreciate most are those that succeed in vivid, moving portrayal of the individual's emotions and struggles and adventures, even when the subject matter is military campaigns, pure and simple.[1] Since the focus is on the individual, the reason for the emotions, the legitimacy of the struggles, and the social consequences of the adventures are not the concern of the authors nor that of their audiences. The current money-makers from American filmdom are merely the latest escalated expression of the same traditional Western values, just as the revolutionary operas and operatic ballets in present day China have not departed from the same old Chinese view that the individual is significant only as part of a larger social network. In pre-1949 China, the kinship network had prior claim over the individual; in post-1949 China, the new aim is for the national network to replace the narrower kinship network. In either case individual wishes and aspirations take second place.

Drama and literature may not always be true to life, but they certainly reflect how each people feel about themselves, about each other and about the world around them. And the pattern of such feelings cannot but steer the pattern of their actions over time. It is interesting to read how Sasha Davis, the heroine of a best seller *Memoirs of an Ex-Prom Queen* (Shulman 1972), actually resorted to Emerson's words for strength, inspiration and guidance in her meanderings and search for independence. "We must go alone; . . . I must be myself. I cannot break myself any longer for you, or you. . . . Nothing is at last sacred but the integrity of your own mind. Absolve you to yourself, and you shall have the suffrage of the world." And Sasha boarded the train from Cleveland, Ohio, to Lake Placid, New York, on the first leg of her freedom quest.

PSYCHOCULTURAL CONTINUITY

From this point of view the continuity between the modern and the traditional drama and literature in both China and the West takes on added importance. In each case drama and literature are a key to past events and future directions. For how a people feel about themselves, about each other and about the world around them cannot but determine the priorities in the way they tend to conduct themselves, relate to each other and to the world around them.

Like the heroes of the Trojan War, Western men have always been eager to commit themselves to distant campaigns with or without provocation. Since they are individual-centered, they have been accustomed to define their roles, their problems, and their solutions to their own satisfaction, with little reference to how others see and feel about their roles, their problems and their solutions. Does it require great flights of imagination to see a psychocultural pattern that links the Trojan War, the medieval Crusades, and the American intervention in Vietnam?

In each case, the leading campaigners were obsessed with one objective. In each case, tremendous amounts of armed might were mobilized to achieve an objective, the significance of which was either questionable or far outweighed by the expenditure of life and resources. In each case, willing or unwilling allies were pressed into service. In each case, victory on the battlefield did not lead to peace or happiness abroad or at home.[2]

The Chinese drama and literature are equally reflective of the way the Chinese feel about themselves, about each other and about the world around them. One characteristic was that the Chinese have always looked inward, fighting primarily to secure their borders or to ward off actual or potential invaders. Their life style was conservative, and they taught their children to look for contentment, to be worthy of the shadow of their ancestors. Their Great Wall does not even have a symbolic counterpart in the West, even though European rulers liberally made use of the fortified castle. T'ang, Yuan and Ch'ing emperors did embark on some wars not purely defensive, but one singular fact is that few if any of their subjects ever followed in the footsteps of their conquests to colonize the new territories. The fleets of the Ming Admiral Cheng Ho (a contemporary of Leonardo da Vinci) sailed seven different times in the South Seas and conquered their way as far as East African coasts. Few Chinese ever left China and settled away from their homeland.

The world population distribution today bears witness to these diverging Chinese and Western ways revealed in their drama and literature. The population of Europe minus Russia stands today at about 450 million. But the white population of the two Americas alone comes to over 500 million. In other words, there are at least as many whites outside of their home continent as within it. By contrast, only less than 3 percent of persons of Chinese origin are outside China today. The Chinese population in China today is about 750 million (a conservative estimate) while the Chinese outside of China (including the South Seas, Caribbean, and the two Americas) comes to between 15 million and 19 million (estimates vary greatly).

Understanding the events and behavior patterns of another society may be compared, to be trite, with assessing an iceberg on the high seas. We can easily see what is on the surface. But to deal effectively with what we see on the surface depends upon our ability to gauge what is below. The top of the iceberg is analogous to what many observers see in a society today. But unless the observers know something about the submerged portion of the iceberg, consisting of the psychocultural patterns deeply rooted in what went on before, they are likely to be superficial in what they see or, much worse, to misunderstand what they see.

They are likely to be superficial in what they see (especially if they do not know the language) because they will fail to evaluate what is important and what is marginal. They are likely to misunderstand what they see because, in searching for meaning, they cannot but project the psycho-cultural premises rooted in their own past into the alien events.

I am not suggesting that some cultures like those of China and the United States are so different that mutual understanding is impossible. Besides, the problem just outlined is not peculiarly American but is one of intercultural communication in general. What I have been doing is to dwell on particular facts at some length so that they will elucidate the problems involved.

EYE-WITNESS ACCOUNT

The problems cannot be solved by more eye-witness accounts. Now that travel to China is more possible than before, will Americans achieve a greater understanding of what the Chinese are all about? Not necessarily so, even for those with extended Chinese experience. Joseph Alsop, whom I mentioned before, wrote how he and his wife discussed a question that puzzled them most, as they rode the train from China to Hongkong. Both of them found the Soviet Union and other European Communist countries depressing, in contrast to their month long trip to China, which they found "neither suffocating nor depressing." "Rather than thanking God to be crossing the border (which is standard post-Russia trip response), we wished we could have had several months more." Alsop and his wife asked themselves, "Why?"

Alsop's question was well posted, I think, for I had the same feeling about Russia when I was leaving her in the summer of 1964. But I think Alsop's answer to it is quite confused.

On the one hand he said that "this new China *works* in Chinese terms," and that, in spite of the failures of the Great Leap and the devastation of the Cultural Revolution, "everywhere, you see the strong foundation for a better future being boldly, laboriously, intelligently laid. Whether in agriculture or industry, you find eye-popping achievements. So I suppose it is this sense of forward movement that answers the question we argued on the train to Hongkong."

On the other hand he could not but also note that "there was no hint of the more free life that goes on, under the surface, in the Soviet Union. A Chinese Solzhenitsyn is unimaginable. There is no underground art or literature. All march to the same drum, or they have their 'thoughts reformed.' " (*Washington Post,* January 10, 1973)

I suspect that neither of these reasons was what made the Alsops feel the way they did in that train leaving China. Achievement-wise we could say the same things about the Soviet Union. If we contrast Russia before and after the Revolution, don't we also see eye-popping achievements? Don't we also see a sense of forward movement? In fact, Sir Alexander Eggleston, the Australian Ambassador to China during World War II, once explained to my satisfaction in Chungking that he thought the Soviet Union *worked* because the Russians were Russians. The Australian envoy was not alone in this.

As to underground art and literature, why don't they exist in China? Why do all Chinese march to the same drum? Isn't it paradoxical that the Alsops found their journey in a society where there is "no hint of the more free life" neither suffocating nor depressing, while they thanked God each time they left another one where there is not only "the more free life" but which also produced writers like Solzhenitsyn whom Alsop and his countrymen have come to lionize?

The paradox will remain a paradox as long as we only see China and the Chinese through the colored glasses of individualism. I think it is the human element that distinguishes the Chinese from the Russians as well as the Americans. I think China's forte, regardless of what else she is doing, is the way the people relate to each other and how that way of relating has been mobilized from the traditional to the new scheme of things.

The Alsops were not totally unaware of this. "Our countless hosts were friendly, interesting and forthcoming. Our interpreter-manager, Yao Wei, was the most ideal traveling companion that either of us had ever encountered." But in the end the Alsops chose the typically American reason, the "sense of forward movement," as answer to the question why they wished to stay when they had to depart.

Had the Alsops really understood the importance of that Chinese characteristic, they would have appreciated that the paradoxical facts sprang from the same source, that the lack of underground art and literature in China is an expression of the same human pattern where their "countless hosts were friendly, interesting, and forthcoming."

A group of American psychologists, educators, and clinicians who visited China more recently also seem to have missed the same point (Kessen [ed.] 1975). They found a number of features in the Chinese preschool and school scene that puzzled them. (1) How were the "immobile, shy and almost expressionless toddlers" in nurseries transformed into the "expressive, well-organized, socially adept four-year-olds?" (Kessen 1975:63); and (2) why were the Chinese children "far less restless, less intense in their motor actions, less crying and whining [sic] than American children in similar situations?" (Kessen 1975:69). To these they added two more questions at the end of their book: (3) "How do children learn the remarkably precise and by American standards advanced forms of dance, sculpture, and music?" (4) "And how do Chinese parents and teachers manage the first signs of conflict among children?" (Kessen 1975:220).

The American visitors only speculated about the third of these "puzzles." They thought that Chinese teachers must have "developed procedures for early education in the domains of dance and figural representation that would be profitable for us [Americans] to understand" (Kessen 1975:221). But they ventured no speculation about the other "puzzles." I think that the answers to all of them do not reside in some particular "procedures" but in the fundamental nature of the Chinese cultural heritage and the shape it has given to the relationship between the Chinese individual and his society. The American visitors themselves caught a glimpse of that relationship when they observed:

> Sparsely furnished by American standards, the Chinese kindergartens seem to emphasize interaction among adults and children rather than the child's impact upon, and reaction to, things. (Kessen 1975:79)

Here is the key that would have made these "puzzles" less puzzling to the visitors, had they understood the implications of this one observation by themselves, which they passed over lightly.[3]

THE MUSEUM APPROACH

Another common way of dealing with intercultural understanding revolves around what I call the museum approach. We stage East-West Philosophers' Conferences. We organize symposia in which the participants describe patterns of family, death customs, religion, rites of passage, relationships between the generations in a variety of societies. We have libraries that can boast of hundreds of thousands of books and papers on and from the non-Western world. We have a galaxy of Asian studies or non-Western studies programs in our universities.

But the books and papers remain unread except by specialists or students under the compulsion of class assignment. At various universities where I lecture, I make it a point to ask those in the audience who have read a Chinese or Japanese novel in English translation to raise their hands. The result: sometimes one or two persons raise ther hands, sometimes none, and at no time more than 1 percent.

Even more discouraging is that, as yet, I see little or no evidence that any non-Western thought patterns have benefited American thinking with reference to any of our major social problems. The results of our investigations, and the cures or preventive measures they have led to, however sophisticated methodologically, inevitably suffer from the intellectual myopia of their designers and executors. Some of our scientific investigations are not unlike counting, classifying and "computerizing" pebbles on the beach to determine the causes of rising and ebbing of tides.[4]

If this sounds too absurd, consider our approach to violence or to drug abuse. Air piracy is surely a major form of violence. In an hour-long television program by CBS (October, 1972) on hijacking, a psychiatrist, Dr. David G. Hubbard, Director of the Aberrant Behavior Center in Dallas, Texas, gave his conclusions after interviewing 48 culprits in jail. These men are schizophrenic paranoics, he says. They are suffering from a sense of failure, inadequate masculinity; they have dreams of glory forever, and they are interested in death but do not wish to die by their own hands. Furthermore, they consider any of the following four outcomes of their actions as success: (1) touching the $100,000 (or whatever amount) even though losing it five minutes later; (2) death after causing another's death; (3) landing in a foreign jail after having forced the plane to land where they command it to; and (4) even taking the plane out of its authorized ramp.

Given this kind of approach it is but natural that our major attempts to prevent air piracy have been chiefly in the form of detection, force, and hoped for elimination of sanctuaries for hijacked planes. The astonishing thing is that the aforementioned psychiatrist, after concluding that "the hijacker is unique, he should be treated as such" in a *Life Magazine* interview earlier (August 11, 1972) which gave his views on the subject wide publicity, now admits there are an estimated 8 million Americans possessing the psychiatric syndrome he describes. We may be able to stop air piracy by some of the methods of external control currently in use, but do we seriously believe that creative Americans bent on antisocial acts will not find other areas of criminal enterprises?

Is it not unrealistic to think we can successfully deal with such a large number of potential air pirates in the population by electronic detection and guards? Is it not time for us to scruntinize some of the fundamental and cherished premises of the U.S. culture to see why we have such a large number of potential air pirates?

Being confined by the traditional American line of thinking about social problems (and I do mean "traditional"—the usual American way is to relegate the patterns of thinking in other cultures into the category of "traditional" while equating, openly or implicitly, American ways with "modern"), it is also not unnatural for America's top research men in the universities concerned with the air piracy problem to be as intellectually myopic as some clinicians and the general public. Thus a professor of psychology from Wisconsin, on the same television program mentioned before, concluded that news reporting of air piracy cases stimulates more hijacking. We do not dispute the notion that "how to" reporting may have some escalating effects in all areas of crime. What I am appalled by is the low level on which our scientific talent and support is focused."[5]

However disrespectful it may seem to compare the dignified work of our eminent scholars with the opinion of a suburban Chicago police chief after a rash of 1972 murders, their similarity strikes us with some force. The "theory" of the police is that heavy and continuous rains drive some unbalanced individuals berserk, hence the high frequency of murders.

A look at our prevailing approaches to drug abuse and we find the same picture: punishment of the pushers, explanation of the pitfalls of addiction to our young, treatment of addicts by physical or psychological means, but nothing about the more fundamental causes of the persistence and spread of the problem in our society. For example, under the impact of the West, China did have a drug problem for over half a century. But American scientists dealing with the drug problems have so far not been interested in or even noted the fact that Chinese drug addicts were mostly adults and old while their American counterparts today are predominantly young. That difference surely says something about the systems as causes, not the individual.

ANTHROPOLOGICAL MYOPIA

Some readers might say that this is to be expected since psychiatrists, sociologists, and suburban police chiefs are not cross-cultural in their views. What about world traveling anthropologists? Have they not gone to many societies and observed and recorded diverse cultural ways for our edification? Have their efforts not helped us to advance the cause of intercultural understanding?

Unfortunately my answer to this question is, as a whole, not as positive as I hoped it to be. Elsewhere I have documented how the intellectual myopia of white American anthropologists has prevented some of them from formulating universally valid theories in a variety of subjects, from the meaning of witchcraft and caste studies to the role of the economic factor in human behavior and the so-called changing American character (Hsu 1973a). In spite of its cross-cultural protestations, American anthropology will remain white American anthropology with cross-cultural decorations unless it takes a more open-minded approach to other competing assumptions—rooted in other cultures—about man and what makes him run.

For purposes of this presentation, I will give but one example. This concerns a phenomenon that I term "Neo-Instinctivism."[6] If we behave the way we do not because of economic factors, then it must be because of biological endowment,[7] for the individualists wish to avoid focusing on man's relationships with other men at all costs. Some of the relevant publications are as follows: *The Human Animal* (La Barre 1954), *Men in Groups* (Tiger 1969), *The Imperial Animal* (Tiger and Fox 1971), *The Hunting Peoples* (Coon 1971), and, of course, *The Naked Ape* (Morris 1967).

I shall deal only with one of them, *Men in Groups*. Tiger's thesis begins with the assumption that male bonding is universal from prehistoric hordes to complex modern communities. This male bonding, which is a "spinal cord" of the human community, is probably biologically based. It is still evident among primates. It provides a "definite genetic advantage" *(Ibid.:* 99) in hunting. Since the "hunting phase" occupied about 99 percent of human history, and since the evolution of the "hunting hominid was well under way 14 million years ago, the selective pressure on human populations existing during [that phase was] of particular and crucial importance in determining the human genotype" *(Ibid.:* 98).

Up to this point, Tiger's arguments seem reasonable. What becomes untenable is that he proceeds from here to show that this "biologically" programmed male bonding is the basis of behavior patterns of today's man in politics, in play and work, in religion, in age-grading, and in voluntary associations many of which involve bloody initiations, aggression, and war.

To prove his thesis, Tiger's data concern Western man 99 percent of the time. The few non-Western facts he uses are incidental or contradictory. For instance, Tiger points to Madame Sun Yat-sen as an example of one of those females who could only acquire high office "by being politically active relatives *of senior politicians who die"* *(Ibid.:*73). But he does not mention the high positions of Madame Binh at the Paris Vietnam Peace talks, Madame Chiang in Taiwan, and Madame Mao in mainland China before her downfall. We do not know the power position of Madame

Binh's husband, but we do know that Mrs. Chiang and Mrs. Mao were exercising great authority while their husbands were alive and in power.

Furthermore, these Oriental women did not even gain power by any of the "constitutional and other legal restraints" which, according to Tiger, might "permit successful dominant females an effective role" (*Ibid.:*75).

A more basic flaw is Tiger's use of William Golding's *Lord of the Flies* as very important evidence of male bonding and aggression. A less ethnocentric anthropologist might at least have inquired as to whether comparable novels could be found in China, Japan or India. The author would have received a negative answer, not even in India and certainly not in Japan or China.

It is not possible here to detail the many differences between Western novels and Asian novels and what they signify. I have treated them elsewhere (See Chapter 12 and Hsu 1975). The total absence of *Lord of the Flies*-type of literature in Asia is basic and critical and must be faced by Tiger if he is to make his point. As it is, Tiger takes English public school culture and its ethics of violent mastery, hierarchy, and concern about a monotheistic God to be universal human nature.

This procedure of taking an example of the Western behavior pattern to be the universal human pattern is followed by all the others in the neo-instinctivistic veiUnithey see violence and aggression as inevitable. They echo the psychologist B. F. Skinner (1971)—all mankind is headed toward self-destruction. Somehow the real cultural differences in which the anthropologists have been claiming to be specialists for so long have been lost. When the chips are down, Western anthropologists are so immersed in their own civilizations that they mistake their own cultural ways for the ways of the rest of mankind.

Human beings are not subhuman apes. The lack of human trust, the proliferation of aggression and violence in some societies that some anthropologists have mistaken for subhuman behavior are also cultural. They are manifestations of one variety of culture and are certainly not universal. For example, there are many societies, industrialized or other-wise, where it is still safe to walk the streets after dark, where employees are still devoted to their employers, and where friendship among men is still lasting because they are unafraid of being sentimental toward each other. Japan is one such example (Hsu 1975).

Human beings everywhere associate primarily with other human beings: they rub shoulders with each other, confide in each other, and compete against each other. We are produced by human beings and mentally shaped by human beings. The major key (though never the only key) as to why we behave like human beings as well as to why we behave like Americans or Japanese is to be found in our relationships with our fellow human beings, not in our instincts or our relationships with animals or things.

THE PUBLIC AND INTERCULTURAL UNDERSTANDING

Under the fad of cultural pluralism, two phenomena have come about among the general public. First is the popularity of many Asian and African items, from clothes to artifacts, which adorn American bodies and embellish American homes. Second is the increase of non-white participation in formerly all-white preserves, such as exclusive clubs, desirable residential locations, entertainment, and business and industrial establishments. I note with interest that even the Chicago *Sun-Times* has recently added a daily column in Spanish. At the height of the troubles in Chicago's West Side there was a public clamor for more Spanish-speaking police officers. But what has happened is no more than the opening up of opportunities for non-whites to assume white roles and white goals but strictly in white psychocultural terms.

In this context we can understand what our filmmakers have recently found to be "black power at the box office." As one newspaper reports: "Black films, produced by the major studios in most cases written, directed by and starring blacks, are earning lots of green." Often the black films are but old white film stories colored black. Thus *Cool Breeze* is a black version of *Asphalt Jungle, Shaft* features James Bond in black face, *Blacula* is the first black vampire, and so on *(Parade* magazine, Sept. 17, 1972). Not unnaturally, these and other black films prompted Julius Griffin, leader of the Hollywood chapter of NAACP, to declare the films to be another form of "cultural genocide," that the U.S. blacks

> must insist that our children are not constantly exposed to a steady diet of so-called black movies that glorify black males as pimps, dope pushers, gangsters and super males, and that we will not tolerate the portrayal of black women on the screen as women of loose morals who climb in and out of bed. *(Ibid.)*

In the same context, too, we can understand why, though stories bearing Chinese themes have increased in popularity in TV and motion pictures, the actors and actresses who portray the main Orientals are white, such as the television series *Kung Fu,* just as in the old Charlie Chan series several decades ago. A common defense of their use of whites to act the role of non-whites is the claim by the studios and producers that they have searched hard for non-whites for leading roles but failed because the non-white actors and actresses don't seem to have the necessary charisma. I think the truth was probably that the Oriental actors and actresses were turned down because they looked and acted too Chinese, Japanese, or whatever; they did not fit the image the American directors and the American public had of what Chinese and Japanese should look like and how they should act.

SOME CORRECTIVE MEASURES

What can be done to generate more genuine intercultural understanding within the United States and between Americans and people of the non-Western world?

First, we need to greatly increase the non-Western content in our curriculum on all levels, but especially the grade and high school levels. This means not only rewriting many texts in history and social studies but also reference works such as encyclopedia where the life and events of people of non-European origins are concerned.

For example, even an excellent and widely used text such as *A Global History of Man* (Stavrianos et al. 1964), produced with the support of the Carnegie Corporation of New York with the aim of providing American children with a more adequate coverage of the societies around the world, contains basic and obvious prejudices. Here World War II was made to begin in September, 1939, when Germany invaded Poland, instead of in July, 1937, when Japan began her full scale aggression against China. This position cannot be defended by the assertion that July, 1937, only marked the beginning of war between the two Far Eastern countries. For the 1939 date merely ushered in conflicts among European nations, while the United States officially stayed out of the European and the Pacific conflicts until December, 1941.

With such a view of the world it is easy for the same authors to see the entire course of World War II as a *Western* accomplishment (Stavrianos, op. cit.: 206–214). Not only is China scarcely mentioned in the text, but she and her leaders are also absent from the pictures. Besides plates of some bombed out cities, there is one showing Churchill, Roosevelt, and Stalin at Yalta, one of Churchill, and one drawing with an American girl offering milk to a Greek child. Chiang Kai Shek, who fought aggression before any of the Western leaders went into action, and who, by his refusal to come to terms, tied down 3 million Japanese soldiers on the mainland, did not even make a group picture.[8]

As to reference works, the *Encyclopedia Britannica* (14th edition) not only gives 143 pages to its United States section against 41 pages on China, but the U.S. pages are replete with beautiful landscapes and the magnificence of the Library of Congress and the White House, while the China pages feature a land where coolies, fortune tellers, opium smokers, and primitive waterwheels predominate—a picture in America's popular misconception of that Asian land. By contrast there are no pictures of American slums, ghettoes, Negro sharecroppers, Mexican migrant workers or even common factory hands.[9]

Second, we not only need more curricular and reference materials on the non-Western world but also must have a stronger emphasis on comparative studies. In human affairs exact measurements are difficult. For example, in Lucian Pye's study of China's politics it is said:

> Since it is central to our hypothesis that their culture has repressed aggression to an extreme degree, it follows that the Chinese are likely to have very complicated and extremely ambivalent feelings about everything closely related to the force of aggression. (Pye 1969:126)

We have no way of evaluating such a statement. How repressed is "repression to an extreme degree?" Yet this observation on the Chinese approach to aggression is, by the author's own admission, the basis of his entire work.

Furthermore, even if exact measurements are obtained in some instances, their scientific significance is often not easily settled. For example today we have about 5 percent of the employables in the United States unemployed.[10] Yet the so-called "acceptable" level of unemployment, according to economists, keeps changing. In the early 1950s the "acceptable" or even "healthy" level was put at 2 percent or at most 3 percent. Later in the Kennedy years the figure was pegged at 4 percent.

What we must do is to make systematic comparisons of whatever society or culture we study with American society and culture. Only through such an approach can we compensate for one-sided statements, which confuse rather than elucidate intercultural understanding. Psychoanalysts have to undergo analysis as part of their training in order to analyze their clients. Why not analysts of culture?[11]

Third, human beings in any society are not automatons. They do and make things but they have feelings about what they do and how they relate. It is not enough to know that the Chinese use chopsticks, the Hindus wear saris and the Japanese have flower arrangements, or the sizes of Balinese families, the customs governing Malayan employment and the ways Navajo Indians dispose of their dead. If we are truly interested in the human individual—and this interest is reiterated often enough—we must attempt to unravel how different people feel about the self, about each other and about the rest of the world. These to me are at the very heart of intercultural understanding, for it is these feelings that motivate human behavior, regulate the differing cultural premises which make human beings behave differently in different societies, and determine the individual's happiness or satisfaction in the long run.

Without waiting for the result of elaborate inquiry and testing by the behavior scientist, results which often obscure the forest for the trees, we have a ready but so far unused source for gaining insight into human feelings. That source is literature, especially novels and poetry. How many Americans know that there is no counterpart to *Moby Dick* or *The Old Man and the Sea* in Chinese literature, or that the Chinese did not have first person novels such as *The Great Gatsby, The Sun Also Rises,* or *The Deere Park?* Or again, how many know that relatively few Chinese novels dealt with sex or romance and that those that did always let the social requirements overshadow the pursuit of individual happiness? Finally, how many know that the hero in the Chinese counterpart of *Gulliver's Travels* was not alone but accompanied in his adventures by a friend and a brother-in-law?

These are not mere exotica. They are expressions of some other basic approaches to men, gods and things. But few Americans know about such exotic matters because Americans have been brought up so exclusively on Western literature that they are led to see the struggles and problems of a

Captain Ahab or an Elmer Gantry or an Achilles as pan-human. How can they feel otherwise? Their writers, critics and instructors are accustomed to speak of the human condition when in fact they are merely dealing with the condition of Western men.

There would have been nothing unusual about this state of affairs were America a closed society with its citizens interested only in following in the footsteps of their ancestors. But it is no foundation on which to build a pluralistic and democratic society. My third and final proposal is, therefore, that we increase non-Western literature not as a separate segment of our curriculum but as part of our general program of instruction and research. Instead of teaching black literature or Japanese literature only in Black Studies or Asian Studies, we should also require them, for example, in departments of English, where we teach Homer, Herman Melville, Hemingway and Joyce.

NOTES

1. For a fuller examination of the thematic contrast between Chinese and Western art and literature through recent times, see Chapter 12.

2. According to news reports around September 14, 1971, General Creighton Abrams told visiting Senator George McGovern that his five big problems in conducting the war had nothing to do with the enemy. These five problems were as follows: (1) racial hostility in the armed forces, (2) the use of drugs in the armed forces, (3) the dislike of the war by our soldiers, (4) the poor morale of our soldiers, and (5) the hostility against American forces and Americans in general on the part of the South Vietnamese.

3. For a fuller review of *Childhood in China*, see my review of it in the *American Journal of Sociology*, September 1977.

4. The following paragraphs on our approach to violence were first published in *The Center Magazine* is an article entitled "Kinship is the Key," which has become Chapter 13 of this book.

5. After writing these pages I became aware of an article by Nathan Caplan and Stephen D. Nelson, two psychologists at the University of Michigan, entitled "On Being Useful: The Nature and Consequences of Psychological Research on Social Problems" (1973). In this article they analyzed the six months' issue of the 1970 *Psychological Abstracts* (44:1–6, plus the semiannual index). Their findings bear out the conclusion that there exists "a person-centered preoccupation and causal attribution bias in psychological research which, when applied to social problems, favors explanations in terms of the personal characteristics of those experiencing the problem, while disregarding the possible influence of external forces" (p. 209). Both the psychiatrist and the psychologist just discussed are apparently doing the in-thing in American psychology today.

6. The following paragraphs on "Neo-Instinctivism" were first published in the *American Anthropologist* (Hsu 1973a:14–15).

7. Or biological condition. Recently I saw a television report of probation officers in one area who help parolees to reform by changing their diet.

8. See Francis L. K. Hsu 1981, pp. 98–102, for more evidence of ethnocentrism in this and other publications.

9. In its 15th edition (1974) nearly all photos have been omitted in both articles.

10. This statement was made long before the onset of Reagonomics.

11. For a fuller statement of the comparative approach and methodology thereof, see Hsu 1969b.

23

The Cultural Problem of the Cultural Anthropologist

From the moment when Malinowski arrived at Port Moresby, New Guinea, he was fascinated by its scenery.

> Feeling of sheer delight at being in so very interesting a part of the tropics. We climbed fairly steeply . . . I walked to the top, which gave a lovely view of the interior . . . I rode down past fenced-in native gardens and along a little valley, turning into a transverse valley, with grass higher than my head on horseback . . . Fires had been kindled in a few places. Red, sometimes purple flames crawled up the hillside in narrow ribbons; through the dark blue or sapphire smoke the hillside changes color like a black opal under the glint of its polished surface. From the hillside in front of us the fire went on down into the valley, eating at the tall strong grasses. Roaring like a hurricane of light and heat, it came straight toward us, the wind behind it whipping half-burned bits into the air. Birds and crickets fly past in clouds. I walked right into the flames. Marvelous—some completely mad catastrophe rushing straight at me with furious speed.   (Malinowski 1967:11–12)[1]

Such moving and skillful descriptions are found throughout the 298 pages.[2] The diary contains no other negative reaction to the local geography other than an early entry that "the extreme beauty out here does not affect me so strongly" and that he found "the region right around Port Moresby rather dismal" (p. 13).

THE CULTURAL PROBLEM OF MALINOWSKI

Raymond Firth says in his introduction to the diary: "My reflection on this is to advise anyone who wishes to sneer at passages in this diary to be first equally frank in his own thoughts and writings, and then judge again" (p. xix). I think Firth's point is well taken. And Firth's caveat should also absolve all of us who, for scientific purposes, probe Malinowski's diary with an analytic eye.

My aim in this paper is threefold: What can we learn from Malinowski's reaction to his field context? How far have we gone in our fieldwork and understanding of the diverse human ways of life since his days? And

This paper was first delivered as Presidential Address at the American Anthropological Association's annual convention at Los Angeles in 1978. It was then published in the *American Anthropologist,* Vol. 81, No. 3, 1979, pp. 517–32.

finally, in light of the above, are there steps we can take to improve our role as fieldworkers and as trainers of future anthropologists?

Some of Malinowski's personal problems may or may not be relevant to other fieldworkers. His preoccupation with sex, which kept troubling him in lecherous thoughts and dreams, even led him to paw native women (p. 256). In Part II of the diary, a hankering for E.R.M., whom he eventually married in 1919 (after New Guinea), appeared nearly every time he made an entry in the diary. But Malinowski was certainly not the only fieldworker troubled by the sex problem.[3] And we can only guess whether a stronger sex drive than that of others is the reason that he is the only anthropologist who has given us a whole book with the most clear details on sex among an non-literate people (Malinowski 1929).

Another of Malinowski's personal problems was hypochondria. He was always beset by physical troubles and was constantly resorting to hot compresses or enemas or taking medicines: calomel and salts, arsenic, quinine, iodine, and others. I frankly do not know how this peculiarity can be related to his writings.

The next problem, namely that of racial and cultural superiority, was more basic to the fieldwork situation then than today. In spite of his hostility toward Christian missionaries, Malinowski's sense of racial and cultural superiority over the natives in his field came through loud and clear. He frankly called them savages, niggers, boys, not once but repeatedly. I have counted some 69 entries in which he expressed various degrees of aversion toward them, from irritation to anger and hatred.[4] At one point he said:

> I handed out half-sticks of tobacco, then watched a few dances; then took pictures—but results very poor. Not enough light for snapshot; and they would not pose long enough for time exposures . . . . At moments I was furious at them, particularly because after I gave them their portions of tobacco they all went away. On the whole my feelings toward the natives are decidedly tending to *exterminate the brutes*.   (p. 69; emphasis in original)

or

> The natives irritate me, particularly Ginger, whom I could willingly beat to death.   (p. 279)

Malinowski did write favorably of the natives on some occasions.[5] But not only were such entries few, they were mostly a few positive words about the despised. For example, he wrote: "The women's faces pleasant, not the perennial whorish expression of the Kiriwina women" (p. 225). Other favorable entries occurred merely at times when the natives were useful, as in the following: "Then I went to the village and collected material. Very intelligent natives. They hid nothing from me, no lies" (p. 33), or "Talked with natives from Tunowada. Wonderful men—I at once felt the difference in the quality of their information" (p. 147).

Other statements, at first seemingly neutral, on closer inspection turned out to be unfavorable:

> After breakfast, Tomaya Lakwabulo, his little stories about the other world. The *baloma* language. When I ask him a question, there is a short pause before he answers, and a *shifty look in his eyes*. He reminds me of Sir Oliver Lodge.   (p. 160; emphasis in original)

Malinowski had little regard for Sir Oliver Lodge, a British physicist who devoted much of his later life to spiritualism.

Only on two occasions (pp. 51, 153) Malinowski used the word *friend* in connection with particular informants. In another book *(The Sexual Life of Savages)* Malinowski spoke of Tokulubakiki as "my best friend," but in the diary he merely referred to him without comment (p. 291). But the ratio between the unfavorable entries and favorable ones and other evidence do not support the idea that Malinowski ever felt genuine friendship in the affective sense for any of the natives.

First, while he specified names for some natives, he used only anglicized nicknames that he or other Whites gave them (Janus, Sixpence, Ginger, etc.). For most of them, he used no names other than "niggers," "boys," and "savages." Second, while he made numerous records of having breakfasts, lunches, dinners, and teas with Whites, including the governor of New Guinea and his wife, missionaries, traders, and other officials, he scarcely ever mentioned sharing meals with any native.[6]

Third, Malinowski was intolerant of any exchange on equal terms with the natives:

> On this occasion [Malinowski was discussing a new house with some informants] I made one or two coarse jokes, and one *bloody nigger* made a disapproving remark, whereupon I cursed them and was highly irritated. I managed to control myself *on the spot,* but I was terribly vexed by the fact that this *nigger* had dared to speak to me in such a manner.   (p. 272; emphases in original)

Finally, on several occasions when he was erotically attracted by some particular native female, feelings of racial superiority stopped him cold:

> At 5 went to Kaulaka. A pretty, finely-built girl walked ahead of me. I watched the muscles of her back, her figure, her legs, and the beauty of the body so hidden to us Whites, fascinated me. Probably even with my own wife I'll never have the opportunity to observe this play of back muscles for as long as with this little animal. At moments I was sorry I was not a savage and could not possess this little girl.   (p. 255)

By contrast, in the numerous entries on his lecherous feelings and actions vis-à-vis white women, including his landlord's wife (p. 165), Malinowski never once thought sexual intercourse with them was impossible and only referred indirectly to one of them (Toska) as "whore" (p.

297). Yet, in spite of his lack of positive feeling for the natives, he unrealistically expected some natives to have positive feelings toward him:

> Gomaya; I gave him some tobacco; he *cadges* more . . . Knows nothing about Vakuta. With his doglike face, Gomaya amuses and attracts me. His feelings for me are utilitarian rather than sentimental.   (pp. 142–43; emphasis in original)

It is in this context of his aversion to "inferior natives" (in his view) with whom he had to deal often that we can understand why Malinowski devoted so much space in his diary to the wonders of nature. To concentrate on things was one way of escaping from the hated human connections. Writers such as Thoreau who extolled the virtues of solitude invariably dwelt effusively on the beauty in trees, rivers, mountains, insects, and animals. It was Mark Twain who, in exasperation, said something like, "The more I look at human beings, the more I like dogs!"

The other escape route for Malinowski was Western literature and music. At various times he submerged himself in Shakespeare, Zola, Kipling, Conan Doyle, Jane Eyre, de Maupassant, Thackeray, Dumas, as well as in magazines such as *Punch, Graphic, Life, Papuan Times,* and *English Man.* He often found himself so addicted to the novels that he could not stop reading. At other times, he resolved not to read "trashy" novels anymore. As to music, quite a few times the scenery moved Malinowski to song.

> I went for a walk along the foot of the hill. There was a fairy-like view on the mountain side, now filled with the rosy light of sunset, and on the bay. Overcome by sadness, I bellowed out themes from Tristan and Isolde.   (p. 52)

or

> Behind the promontory, a rain cloud. I felt a curious desire to be caught in a real rain without any protection. I began to roar out a Wagnerian melody.   (p. 230)

Other entries mentioned that he was stirred by the "Prize Song," "Marche Militaire," and "Rosenkavalier." Malinowski even sang the words "kiss my ass" to a Wagnerian melody "to chase away" flying witches when he was a little nervous walking with some natives at night (p. 157). There is only one entry in which Malinowski expressed pleasure at a native melody, *tselo,* accompanying a dance (p. 37).

Role, Affect, and Culture

In all societies, human beings relate to each other by role (usefulness) and by affect (feeling). The role-affect difference is not, as one of my colleagues warned me, a standard distinction made in anthropology, but to me it is at the heart of human existence. It holds the secret of what we intend by "the meaning of life." We know role in terms of skilled or unskilled labor, white collar or blue collar, dentists and diamond cutters, housekeepers and politicians, and many others. As our society has grown in complexity, the number and variety of roles have grown with it. In fact, role differentiation is the major concomitant of the growth in societal complexity. For example, each candidate for national office today is supported by an army of experts including speech writers, public-relations men, technicians, and foot soldiers beyond the imagination of small-town politicians of yesteryear. Giant corporations often have more diversified personnel on their payrolls than many small member states of the United Nations.

This development in role differentiation is inevitable as a large society becomes more industrialized. The number and variety of laws have increased as ways of fleecing the public and corruption have become more creative and bureaucratic departments and problems of production have escalated.

On the other hand, although our roles have evolved in number and proficiency with the complexity of the industrial society, our affect has not. We still have the same kinds of feelings as our ancestors who lived many thousands of years ago: love, hate, rage, despair, endurance, hope, anxiety, forbearance, loyalty, betrayal, and so forth. The list is not long, and many of the terms used to describe the feelings are similar to each other, or may be partially or wholly subsumed under each other. That is why old books of science and technology are useless to us except as curiosities or material for histories of science and technology whereas great literature (fiction, poetry) and great art (painting, sculpture) and even great philosophy and ethics survive the ages, for we moderns experience the same joy or agony and the same loyalty and duplicity as the ancients. We can no longer get along with their digging sticks and outhouses and horsecarts, but we continue to experience and seek similar solutions to the same old problems that they had with their children, parents, friends and enemies, employers and employees, and sweethearts and spouses.

However, the *patterns* of affect that operate among Westerners are different from those that motivate people of other cultures, such as the Chinese, Japanese, and Melanesians. Westerners may experience love, hate, and despair the same as the others, but how they express love, hate, and despair, and especially what makes them love, hate, and despair, possess distinct characteristics that are not universal.

Elsewhere, I have demonstrated some of these differing patterns of affect among Chinese, Hindus, Japanese, and Euro-Americans, by the use of their respective art forms, novels, dramas, and plays (Hsu 1963, 1970, 1971b, 1975. See also Chapter 12 of this book). What their characters struggle for, what their problems are, what solutions they look for, the extent to which the authors delve into the mental processes of the characters—in these and other respects the literature of each society reveals how the patterns of affective involvement and yearnings of its members are unlike those of the others.

Malinowski's diary makes it clear that he was so deeply imbued with the Western pattern of affect that he and his natives completely parted ways in this respect. That was why he would often bury himself in Western novels, even ones that he called "trashy." The diary contains quite a few entries in which he "longed" for "civilization," for "culture" (e.g., pp. 150, 155, 214).

Consequently, Malinowski never seemed to relate to his natives as human beings who might be his equals or trusted colleagues, much less as intimate friends or affectionate partners in pursuit of common goals. Instead, he was irritated by them and upset by their inaccurate answers to his questions; he hated them for their lack of attention to what he wanted and for their consequent failure to cooperate with him in his quest, and he despised them for their "cruel" customs.

The conclusion is inevitable that Malinowski never had any positive feeling for the native, for the natives had no part in his dreams—manifestations of some deeper layer of his unexpressible conscious (See Chapter 13; according to Freud, preconscious). The dreams were about autoerotic homosexuality (p. 12), Cracow (p. 233), his girlfriend N. S. and his mother in Poland (p. 202), fraternization with two crippled German cavalry officers (p. 203), his Polish chemist friend and his inventions (p. 70), marriage with T. and traveling (p. 71), a white friend C. R. (p. 195), etc. The only two dreams that might be seen as relating to the natives were: (a) "about the possibilities of research in New Guinea" (p. 73); and (b) a near-dream in which E. R. M. (his fiancee in Australia) figured intensely but "suddenly right into the golden dreams, comes in the leper's face" (p. 240).

For Malinowski's truly positive feelings, we must go to his fieldwork and its rewards. The following entry leaves us in no doubt on this matter:

> As for ethnology: I see the life of the natives as utterly devoid of interest or importance, something as remote from me as the life of a dog. During the walk, I made it a point of honor to think about what I am here to do. About the need to collect many documents. I have a general idea about their life and some acquaintance with their language, and if I can only somehow "document" all this, I'll have valuable material.—Must concentrate on my ambitions and work to some purpose. (p. 167)[7]

At this point you may raise the following questions, as did one of my colleagues: Is it possible for an anthropologist who hates his natives to understand their ways of doing things? Conversely, is it also possible for one who is so enamored with his natives that he merely romanticizes their ways?

There is, indeed, the danger of overemotionalism in fieldwork. But what we are speaking of here is not so much strong love or hate, but Malinowski's inability to relate to the natives on anything like their own terms. As my friend Lee Sechrest puts it: He was unable to relate to them in terms of their own views of things . . . their own activities, customs and the like. Instead he was continually disappointed by the fact that they were not Europeans (personal communication).

How this lack of relationship with the natives on their own terms may affect an observer's perception is clarified by the startling results of a recent experiment under the direction of Stanford University psychologist D. L. Rosenhan:

Eight sane people gained secret admission to 12 different hospitals, located in five different states on the East and West coasts. The quality of the hospitals varied from old and shabby ones to quite new research-oriented and well-staffed ones. All but one were supported by federal, state, or university funds. One of the eight pseudopatients was a psychology student in his twenties. The other seven were older and "established": three psychologists, a pediatrician, a psychiatrist, a painter, and a housewife. Except for alleging hallucinatory symptoms to gain admission and falsifying name, vocation, and employment to avoid identification, no further alterations of person, history, or circumstances were made. Upon entering the psychiatric ward, each pseudopatient "ceased simulating any symptoms of abnormality" (Rosenhan 1973:251).

In spite of their show of sane behavior in the ward, in 11 of the 12 admissions, the experimenters were each diagnosed as "schizophrenic." In one admission that pseudopatient was diagnosed as "manic depressive." The perceptions of hospital staff, including psychiatrists, were so controlled by the psychiatric setting and by what they expected that they failed to differentiate any of the pseudopatients from the real patients (Rosenhan 1973:250–58).[8]

How Far Have We Gone and How to Improve Future Work?

Given a field situation in which the anthropologist feels racial and cultural superiority over the people who are the subject of inquiry, can we not see the possible skewing of the anthropologist's insights into the alien ways of life? Of course, we no longer have the colonial situation that obtained when Malinowski was in the field. Except for a few remnants, such as Namibia and Hong Kong, practically all former colonies have become independent. It is not easy to call natives of Nigeria or Sri Lanka "niggers," "savages," or "boys" when our government and theirs maintain diplomatic relations on the ambassadorial level. But prejudices die hard, and Western technological superiority still nurtures in many the illusion of Western racial and cultural superiority in general.

Positive Ethnocentrism versus
Neutral Ethnocentrism

Ethnocentrism is not confined to Westerners. But what distinguishes theirs from that among the Navajo, the Tikopia, and the Chinese is positive ethnocentrism, in contrast to neutral ethnocentrism.

The significance of the emergence of positive ethnocentrism in the cultural sphere, which in my view is comparable to that of the emergence of the vertebrae in the biological world, has yet to be understood in anthropology.

Peoples with neutral enthnocentrism tend as much as those with positive ethnocentrism to "see one's in-group as always right and all out-groups as wrong whenever they differ" (Kroeber 1948:266). But neutral ethnocentrists tend to have no desire to change the ways of those whom they see as inferior or wrong. Military conquest of one society by another was common to all known human history. But proselytization to let the only truth prevail everywhere was confined only to people with positive ethnocentrism. That is why all the world's missionaries and missionary movements were and are of Western, and secondarily Arab, origin. On the other hand, even when the Chinese empire extended far and wide under Han, T'ang, and Ming, no Chinese court had ever attempted to spread Confucianism or any other form of Chinese beliefs or ethics, and no individual Chinese ever received a call from above to do the same.

In fact, the evidence points to the contrary. In 730 A.D., during the T'ang dynasty, a Tibetan king and son-in-law of the emperor asked for various Chinese classics and histories. The request was refused. When the request was refused a second time and after the death of his queen, the Tibetan king even invaded China with a force of four hundred thousand. During the same T'ang dynasty, some three thousand Chinese Buddhist monks went on foot in small groups to India, not to spread the wisdom of Confucius or some Chinese holy man, but to learn and to bring back to China the teachings of Buddha in their original.

The sharp differences in the psychology of positive ethnocentrism and its expansiveness, in contrast to neutral ethnocentrism's lack in expansionist tendencies, express themselves in myths. In the ninth century, an Arab traveler named Ibn-Wahab made his way by sea from Bossarh to India and thence to China. He obtained an audience with the emperor. During a long conversation the emperor showed the Arab a casket containing images of the prophets. As soon as the Arab saw the images, he muttered benedictions upon them. The Arab explained to the emperor that he recognized the prophets by the attributes with which they were represented. Pointing to one figure, the Arab said, "This is Nuh in the ark; he has been saved with those who were with him whilst God submerged the whole earth, and all that was on it." Thereupon the Chinese emperor, according to the Arab, responded,

It is Nuh, as thou sayest, but it is not true that the whole earth was inundated. The flood occupied only a part of the globe, and did not reach our country. Your traditions are correct, as far as that part of the earth is concerned which you inhabit; but we, the inhabitants of China, of India, of es-Sind, and other nations, do not agree with your account; nor have our forefathers left us a tradition agreeing with yours on this head. As to thy belief that the whole earth was covered with water, I must remark that this would be so remarkable an event that the terror would keep up its recollection, and all the nations would have handed it down to their posterity.   (Frazer 1919:I, 215–16)

How the Arab traveler tried and failed to change the mind of the emperor is immaterial here. I cannot help but note two things. First, the Chinese ruler rejected the universality of the Western flood myth but did not doubt its veracity for the West. Second, he also refrained from claiming any universality for the Chinese food myth (see Chapter 16).

INTERNAL IMPETUS VERSUS EXTERNAL IMPETUS TO CHANGE

I do not know the origin of positive ethnocentrism and missionary movements in the West. And my dominant Kinship Dyad hypothesis (see Chapter 14) is designed only to investigate how, once a given way of life has begun, it is continued and escalated from generation to generation. But I think the reason that positive ethnocentrism and proselytization are Western characteristics is the same as the reason that capitalism and free enterprise sprang from Europe. Missionary movements are expressions of the spirit of free enterprise applied in the religious field. Both are rooted in individualism. Merchants seek bigger and better markets and material gains to beat other merchants, missionaries—the religious entrepreneurs—wish to win more souls and build grander churches to outshine other savers of souls.

One evidence for this thesis is that, even before the appearance of Christianity, Westerners already exhibited a tendency to combine military conquest with proselytization. One of the acts of Alexander the Great (B.C. 356–23) during his retreat from the west bank of the Indus River is described by the anthropologist Prince Peter of Greece and Denmark:

Undeterred, yet deeply shaken by the incomprehension surrounding him, Alexander persisted in his views. After the ordeals of retreat from the Beas and the terrible crossing of Gedrosia (the Baluchistan desert), on arrival in Susa he organized the marriage of ten thousand of his followers to Iranian maidens. And at Opis, in Mesopotamia, on his way to Babylon and his premature end, he gave one last, vast banquet, in which all joined him in a symposium and the drinking of a "loving cup" to the union of mankind and universal *amonia* (concord).   (Peter 1965:7; emphasis in original)

Need we observe that no non-Western conqueror throughout the centuries did anything even remotely resembling what Alexander did and hoped to accomplish?

Today there is no scarcity of anthropologists who deal with social and cultural change because of the impact of the West, its industrial ways, its democratic or communist ideologies, or its Christianity. Malinowski wrote in his diary that "contact between two cultural spheres must have had a great deal to do with the change in custom" (p. 37). But a point so far unclarified in most anthropological literature is that changes may come from within the society (internal impetus to change) or primarily from pressure from without (external impetus to change) (Hsu 1961:400–56). In this, Western societies and cultures as a whole, especially those of northern Europe and the u.s.a., by their incessant internal impetuses to change, contrast sharply with the rest of the world, including China, Japan, and India, where internal impetuses to change were and are negligible. For them, contacts with and pressures from other societies and cultures were the main forces for change.

Once that is understood, we can see that the monotheistic nature of the religious creed (whether Judaism, Islam, or Christianity) is not the cause for internal impetuses to change and for proselytization. Societies and cultures with strong internal impetuses cannot but be expansionist, and religious proselytization is simply another avenue for their expansionist tendencies.

The contrasting histories of proselytization between Islamic Arabia and Christian West speak volumes. Arabs, under the strong leadership of Mohammed and his heirs, strongly proselytized as they expanded their political domain; at one time the Arab missionary Ibn Fadhln even worked among the "primitive" ancestors of modern Scandinavians, the Vikings, whose habits so disgusted the Islamic missionary that Fadhln said they were like "asses who have gone astray" (Coon 1948:410–26). But, as Arabian political and military powers waned, Arab interest in proselytizing abroad decreased. Arabs, like Chinese and Hindus, might be efficient traders in some foreign countries, such as East Africa, but a majority of them in their homelands are not noted for their spirit of enterprise. The peoples from Italy, England, Germany, Holland, the United States, and even Portugal, Spain, and the Scandinavian countries, have, on the other hand, continued their missionary endeavors, either by individual volunteers at the grass-roots level or by governments, in spite of their governments' loss of status as colonizers.

THE ANTHROPOLOGIST'S NEED TO STUDY HIS OWN CULTURE

Adherents of positive ethnocentrism have brought benefits as well as disasters to many societies and cultures of the world. For example, foot binding prevailed in China for some ten centuries. Such was the lack of internal impetus to change that only three scholar-officials seem to have raised feeble voices against the custom during that long period. It was not until the coming of the missionaries that its abolition was forcefully initiated and eventually accomplished. The spread of Western public-health measures, Western notions of universal education, Western ideologies of democracy and socialism, Western movements of equality between the sexes, and individual freedom, etc. are other benefits of positive ethnocentrism. In fact, but for the Western way of life, we would not have the science of anthropology or this association under whose auspices we periodically gather to eat, to drink, and to advance our knowledge of mankind.

In my view, if one of the worst manifestations of Western ways of life was its long history of Inquisition in Christianity, its most brilliant manifestation is its aggressive, sustained attempts at global proselytization in religion and in other fields. Just as the Inquisition has had no counterparts outside Europe (except Goa, in India, under the Portuguese), so, nearly all of the world's Christian missionaries were and are white.

In this we have a clear-cut body of data that Malinowski, like all other anthropologists before or after him, failed to take into consideration in theorizing about religion. This is as true of *Anthropology Today* (the 1953 volume edited by Kroeber and subtitled *An Encyclopedic Inventory*) as it is of the latest *International Encyclopedia of the Social Sciences* (1968; see articles by Argyle 421–28, Bellah 407–14, Dittes 414–21, Vallier 444–52, Wilson 428–37, and Yalman 521–28). Consequently, the difference between true monotheistic religion and those creeds that merely have a supreme deity lording it over other gods and ghosts remains confused in introductory texts (e.g., Ember and Ember 1973:424) and in works on religion (e.g., Wallace 1966:88–101).

Why have Malinowski and our fellow anthropologists failed to see the obvious—that proselytization was and is an outstanding characteristic of Western positive ethnocentrism in religion, in contrast to the patterns of religion in the rest of the world? I would like to venture two interrelated conjectures.

Having come from a culture heritage in which monotheism and proselytization have been intrinsic for so long, anthropologists probably took such characteristics as part of the order of nature. With their positive ethnocentrism, most Western anthropologists probably feel it in their bones that the rest of the world must eventually see the light. That is one side of the picture.

The other side is that most anthropologists, having seen something of the non-Western ways of life, must at times feel ambivalent, consciously or unconsciously, about those very "superior" Western characteristics that also found historical expression in the Inquisition, the Crusades, and the colonial subjugation or enslavement of nearly half of mankind. Could it be that this ambivalence was why Western anthropologists have failed to study their own culture in the way they tried to analyze natives having other ways of life?

The failure is understandable although not scientifically defensible. By meticulous observation and note taking and diary keeping we may be able to understand the role aspects of the society and culture we study: we record the methods of diaper control or count the number of times people interact with their mothers in contrast to their fathers. But can we begin to understand others' affective needs or feelings when we do not have an objective understanding of our own? Don't psychoanalysts have to subject themselves to prolonged analyses before being able to analyse their clients? Malinowski said of the natives, "But their information was vague, and they talked without concentration, just to 'put me off' " (p. 146), or "The fellows are unpleasant and answer my questions with obvious reluctance" (p. 227). Is it possible that his informants were without "concentration" because what the ethnographer asked was not what they were interested in?

Furthermore, when Malinowski found his informants "vague," "reluctant," or otherwise uncooperative, did he have any idea (probably never occurred to him) how "vague," "reluctant," or otherwise uncooperative the natives of England or Poland would have been to a foreign inquirer—especially if the foreigner asked about their family troubles, their sexual practices, their financial dealings, and their taboos?

One American anthropologist was in China in 1949 when the communist forces gained control of the area where he was working before he was able to leave. His work stopped; he was evicted; and his field notes were confiscated. In his report to the foundation and to the profession, he bitterly denounced the new officials of China as ignorant of science. My question is: Did he know whether the officials of either faction in the U.S. Civil War or of any of the participating nations in World War II would show more understanding of science had some foreigner been caught in comparable circumstances? Did he ever reflect on how well comparable American officials would "understand" the scientific purpose of an Asian or African investigator in the United States even when no war was in progress?

We have no way of addressing some of our questions to Malinowski. But we can ask ourselves how many times we were in the same ethnographic boat as Malinowski and how we handled the situations. As for me, I know about some of the "vague" answers I received and the "reluctance" to respond on the part of "my natives" in England when I tried to study English family life after I completed my graduate education at the London School of Economics.[9] I also know how "reluctant" American corporations are toward researchers. My son-in-law, Dr. Richard Balzer, a lawyer who studied the life of American blue-collar workers from within the factory, was turned down by some 50 big corporations before he was finally accepted by the Western Electric Company. In 1973 he worked for five months as a participant observer on the assembly line in the company's Merrimack Valley Works in North Andover, Massachusetts. Before beginning the fieldwork, he signed an agreement with the plant manager;

one of the provisions was, "The Company reserves the right to review material prior to publication and suggest corrections, resulting from misunderstandings, . . ." (Balzer 1976:3).

I also encountered "vague" answers to my questions, "reluctance" to discuss what I was most interested in, and uncooperativeness in general from quite a few of "West Towners" in southwestern Yunnan. There were unpleasant moments, one of which was when I was given the local census to copy, but an official asked for it back after a single day. Someone higher up had evidently changed his mind. As a result, I got figures for only one of the ten census divisions (see Hsu 1971a:110–13).

But even when I was most annoyed by some "West Towners," I could never have developed the feelings toward them that Malinowski entertained at times toward his South Seas islanders, for the simple reason that they and I were both Chinese—this in spite of the fact that I was, to West Towners, a "downriver man," a term applied at the time to all non-Yunnanese, who, for the most part felt superior to the Yunnanese. I suspect that, had Malinowski been studying the English or the Poles, he also would never have reacted to *all* English or *all* Poles so negatively for whatever reason. Instead, he would have reacted to them more selectively, as individuals.

There were other reasons that Malinowski could not have been so sweeping about the Whites. While he hated, disliked, and despised some Whites, whom he terms "rascals" who "harassed" him, he obviously enjoyed and sought the company of most other Whites and was thoroughly in tune with their ways, their literature, and their music. In addition, Malinowski's diary shows that he often discussed the natives with his white friends and acquaintances, though never vice versa. Had he worked among the English or the Poles, the chances are that he would have had occasions on which to discuss some English or Poles with other English or Poles. How far did this fact influence the results of Malinowski's study? I do not know. But it is a methodological question worth researching.

I firmly believe that systematic study of the ethnographer's own culture is the first order of business in his or her training.[10] It should be required of every graduate student working for the Ph.D. degree in anthropology, or it can be made the first intensive field experience. So equipped, every anthropologist later working in an alien field must then ask himself or herself: Do I have some real friends here among my informants, to whom I relate, affectively and on terms of equality, as I do to some of my real friends at home?

The Need for Comparison

There is another reason why the anthropologists should seek systematic understanding of their own culture. No matter what single society (or village) anthropologists study, they cannot help but make some sort of comparison with the society and culture whence they came. They will necessarily view the other ways of behaving, thinking, and feeling through the filter of their own. Many ethnographers have had occasions to feel compelled to make a point by comparing or contrasting some "primitive" custom with "our own" (which can mean French, American, English, Hungarian, Western as a whole, or whatever). Elsewhere I have given many such examples from the works of scholars who primarily studied "primitive" societies (Hsu 1969b:53).

There is a way to use such offhand comparisons—as a teaching device or to elucidate a difficult point. But such comparisons are unsatisfactory because "our own" part of the data is not systematically studied and is generally taken out of social and cultural contexts. More important, implicit comparison through the filter of the anthropologist's own ways of behaving, thinking, and feeling may lead to even greater fallacies.

For example, Maurice Freedman argued that ancestors are not feared in China as in some West African societies because the living are not conscious of having displaced their ascendants from coveted positions of power (Freedman 1966:143–54; 1967:90–102). Arthur Wolf disagrees with Freedman and offers "a simpler explanation": "Chinese ancestors are not feared because they are not conceived of as powerful beings" (Wolf 1974:168). I cannot see how Wolf's explanation is simpler, but I think both are wide of the mark because they are interpretations through Freedman's and Wolf's Western cultural filters; they are not consonant with Chinese cultural postulates.

A major Chinese cultural postulate is father-son identification and continuity of the generations. The father automatically bequeathed his wealth to his sons and was duty bound to see all his children married and well placed. In turn, sons were responsible for the pleasure and welfare of the parents in life and after death. Socially, the mutual sharing of their status was even more automatic. "First thirty years, respect the son because of his father; second thirty years, respect the father because of the son." In other words, the father's prestige determines the son's social position when the son is young; the order is reversed when the son comes of age. In dynastic days, parents were awarded high honors, even posthumously; because of their son's high achievement in government; eldest sons would be eligible for the equivalent of certain degrees without having to take the imperial examinations.[11] Because of such manifestations of the Chinese premise of father-son identification, I concluded that Chinese did not have to fear harm by the spirits of their ancestors. The mutual bond between them was culturally defined as too automatic to leave room for such harm (Hsu 1971a:8–9, 240–41; 1963:45). In 1942 during a major cholera epidemic that counted within a month some two hundred dead among the "West Town" population of eight thousand, the local people invoked and pleaded with all sorts of major and minor gods and spirits, including Jesus Christ, Mohammed, and gate gods, in a whole series of public rituals lasting many days and involving prayers, offerings, sacrifices, and exorcising maneuvers; but none of these was aimed at deceased ancestors, who were not sources of harm (Hsu 1952).[12]

Rooted in a culture pattern where the young are encouraged to become independent of their parents and are supposed to find their own identities since parental fame and fortune are considered to be some sort of disability that they must strive to overcome, and where father-son rivalry, Oedipus complex, and generation gap are regarded as self-evident truths, Freedman and Wolf, not unnaturally, saw naked power struggle as all-important in the Chinese situation.[13] I can easily give other examples to substantiate the same fallacy.

One way to avoid interpreting alien patterns of culture through the implicit cultural filter of the ethnographer is to make explicit and systematic comparison. In explicit comparison the student at least puts him or herself on record so that others can objectively evaluate the comparison. The first step toward improving the quality of our results is conscious and systematic comparison of the society and culture we study with that from which we came.

There is, in addition, a second and equally important reason for comparing at least two societies and cultures in any ethnographic work. Unless we can reduce all statements about human behavior to quantitative terms, our qualitative statements about human affairs must be comparative to have any meaning. There simply are no exact measurements that will enable us to see them in absolute terms. For example, how do we measure despotism? How do we measure sibling (or any other) rivalry? How many fights or quarrels or lawsuits must we see for a relationship to be termed rivalrous? And we have to remember that despotism and rivalry are relatively easier entities to gauge than others such as religiosity and prejudice.

Systematic comparison will enable us then to say, for example, that political oppression would seem to be greater in society X than in society Y because the incidence of escapism seems to be higher in the former than the latter, or that people A seem to be more prosperous than people B because the percentage of unemployment is lower in the former than in the latter. Had students of man really compared the incidence of religious persecution in the West and the non-Western worlds, we might have had a more sharpened scientific understanding of exactly how religion and religious ways differ with differing patterns of culture, instead of being satisfied with such generalities in our introductory texts or learned treatises as "religious persecution is universal," or "religion functions importantly in reinforcing and maintaining cultural values."

The Importance of National Character Studies

Not so long ago I had a conversation with a fellow anthropologist on the subject of national character studies. Without going into its merits or demerits, he simply said, "That's obsolete. No one is doing it anymore."

I think my friend's response was a typical expression of what Erich Fromm terms the "market personality." The essence of that personality is, "Give the customers what they want." Politicians have to master that art by way of survival. But will it not be deleterious to the future of our discipline if we, too, cannot rise above that psychology? In a society where business, industry, and politics are in command, we scholars alone have the peculiar and legally binding custom, called tenure, that protects us from market fluctuations. Are we going to strengthen the moral basis for that privilege? Or are we going to do what a Chinese proverb says, "Advertising mutton, sell dog meat"?

I don't mean to suggest that we should keep pursuing some line of research even if it leads us to a blind alley. But national character research is not one of these, even if it has not won a popularity contest lately among anthropologists. One of the basic contributions of anthropology is our attempt to see and deal with the fields of our study as wholes. In the case of an isolated small tribe such as Tikopia, a relatively thorough knowledge of its ways may be sufficient for the ethnographer to speak of the Tikopia as a whole. But, in the case of a village community in a large society, especially a literate society with many thousands of village communities, can we stop at one or two single village communities? Yet, whether the anthropologist likes it or not, he will, even if he has studied one village in India or Japan or Indonesia, be called upon to teach courses on Indian Culture, Japanese Family, and Indonesian Political Institutions. From time to time, too, for either scientific or practical reasons, he will be forced to comment on these societies as a whole.

There is a new urgency for studies of national character. Not only have most of the former colonies become independent nations, but, thanks to the Western ideology of equality and freedom, many ethnic groups within larger societies are seeking or aspiring to independence so as to erase their minority status. The growing demand for ethnic studies is another expression of this. Are we going to study the life of a single hamlet in Malaya or Brazil without reference to what motivates its leaders and civil servants in their respective national governments? Are we going to close our eyes to the diverse ways in which the Bretons in France, the Catholics in Northern Ireland, the Basques in Spain, and the Nagas in India strive toward their objectives, and to the ways in which the French, the English, the Spaniards, and Hindus separately deal with their independence demands? These problems cannot be understood by descriptions of the marriage customs or age-grading practices in single villages or tribes, any more than either descriptions of the neglect of children by Alorese mothers can shed any light on the nature and the pattern of political and social struggles in Portuguese Timor or descriptions of the ancestor cult of the Ovimbundu can shed light on the emergence of socialism in Angola.

THE NEED FOR A NEW LOOK AT KINSHIP

In view of today's world developments, I see national-character studies as a more important, not less important, area of anthropological work for the future. At the same time, I think such areas of study as cross-cousin and parallel-cousin marriages and the Crow, Omaha, Hawaiian, and other kinship systems, etc., to which most introductory texts or social organization works devote much space, all belong to the paleontology of cultural studies. They were traditionally anthropological subjects, but I have yet to see any substantive observations on how the behaviors of peoples with matrilocal and matrilineal arrangements differ significantly from those with patrilocal and patrilineal arrangements, except for Malinowski's modified Oedipus complex in the Trobriand Islands.

Yet, the primary importance of kinship in social and cultural development is undeniable. For that is the group in which nearly all human beings begin their earthly existence and spend quite some years (although variable) of their early lives when their affective patterns take definite shape. But the secret of its primary importance cannot be revealed to us as long as we continue to be preoccupied with traditional anthropological concepts and categories such as kinship terms, residence rules, marriage preferences, and descent lines. We can even make complicated mathematical games with them, but what is their relevance to the growth of nationalism, the development of and responses to urbanization, industrialization, Christianity, Islam, socialism, democracy, or even the culture of poverty? Shouldn't we abandon them in favor of more productive concepts and categories, just as biological anthropologists today have moved away from head and nose and other anthropometric measurements, toward genes and blood groupings?

EPILOGUE: A PERSONAL NOTE

Some readers of this article may think that I have been too hard on Malinowski. I wish to state unequivocally and with all sincerity that I received more intellectual stimulation and personal guidance from Malinowski than from any other teacher that I have ever had, undergraduate and graduate—in spite of the fact that I had the good fortune of knowing him for only a single academic year, 1937–38.

Of the many unforgettable moments and events that I experienced during that period, one thing stands out in my mind. I would write out the first draft of a paper and he would invite me to his house. There, in his study, he lay down in a disheveled daybed, a pair of pajama pants wrapped around his head, covering his eyes. Sitting in a chair at a nearby table, I would read the paper aloud, paragraph by paragraph. As soon as he found a flaw in any sentence or paragraph, he raised questions, brought up contrary evidence, and usually convinced me that his views were better.

Once, he let several paragraphs pass without making a single comment. Suspecting that he had dozed off, I purposely inserted two sentences that were *non sequitur*. At once he blurted out: "What did you say? What does that have to do with the subject?" After that, I realized he never missed a word I read to him.

Sometimes I disagreed with his objections. These, he considered with care, and eventually, if one of my counterarguments proved to be more meritorious, he would gracefully say, "Yes, Lang Gwa, you are right." Lang Gwa was his best pronunciation of my Chinese given name, Lang Kwang. He thought I should not have a name like Francis, and insisted on addressing me by my Chinese name.

It was during one of those sessions that he taught me the importance of documentation in all my observations. I was describing the rituals to ancestors in my north China village. I said that many Chinese paid homage to their ancestral spirits "as though the spirits were actually there." Malinowski asked me, "How do you know, and how do you document this statement with facts?" Up to that point, I had taken the statement as self-evident. Under his pressure, I eventually found many factual items from my notebooks that satisfied him. One of them was: When making rice and wine offerings, the Chinese worshipper places the bowls or cups from the side of the ancestral tablets, as a living son would when placing a bowl or cup before a living parent.

Since the appearance of Malinowski's diary, some have questioned the propriety of its publication. When I first learned about the diary from some reviews, which made much of its sexuality, I, too, wondered if Malinowski would have approved of its publication.

Having studied the diary with some thoroughness, I now feel that Malinowski, being the great teacher that he was, would not have minded. Malinowski was a man of strong loves and hates, and strong opinions. The diary might very well have been his selfconscious catharsis for the ethnocentrism that he, as a normal member of the Polish or British tribe, could not wholly repress but, as a scientist, attempted to keep from distorting his ethnography.[14] I think that Malinowski would have been pleased to learn, were he alive today, that his diary may enable us to take a giant intellectual step forward.

Advancement through human generational succession requires that those who come later learn from the actions and thoughts of those who have gone before. Essential to this continuing process is careful analysis of both their merits and their defects.

The world today is in such a sorry state largely because mankind as a whole has been slow or has refused to learn from mistakes of our forebears. The future of our particular discipline will indeed be dim if we find no hard lesson in the performance of our predecessors.

NOTES

Acknowledgments. I am greatly indebted to Donald T. Campbell, Klaus F. Koch, Lee Sechrest, Joseph C. Berland, and Robert Textor for reading the manuscript and giving valuable criticism that materially improved it.

1. In the following pages, numbers in parentheses refer to the page or pages in Malinowski's diary. All other references begin with the author's name.

2. See, for example, pp. 5–6, 8, 10, 13–14, 22, 25, 31–33, 35, 38, 40, 42, 46, 49, 52–53, 62, 64, 67, 71, 82, 85, 87–88, 93, 95, 97–98, 115–16, 125, 137, 140–41, 155, 170, 173, 226–29, 231–37, 247–48, 250, 256, 258, 260.

3. For example, George Stocking, Jr., in a review of Malinowski's diary, says: "More specifically, several anthropologists have indicated to me in conversation that their own sexuality had been a gnawing problem for them in the field" (Stocking 1968:193).

4. Pp. 13, 35, 37, 48, 57–58, 62, 67, 69, 70–71, 85, 92, 111, 125, 130–31, 144–46, 154–56, 160, 162, 167, 173, 175, 178, 188, 191–92, 208, 214–16, 220–21, 225–28, 230–31, 233–34, 236, 238–40, 250, 253, 260–62, 264, 267–68, 271–73, 276, 279, 282–84, 286–87, 291.

5. Pp. 33, 35, 37, 45, 51, 58, 83, 142–43, 147, 153–54, 195, 220 ("the niggers came and were friendly"), 225, 229, 230, 235.

6. Pp. 9, 15, 17, 19–22, 26, 36, 43, 45, 47, 52, 58, 61, 71, 77, 82–83, 89–91, 96, 115, 167, 248–50, 262, 267–68.

7. This or a similar pattern of thought is repeated quite a few times in the diary, e.g., 227, 229, 277, 278, 291.

8. The results of Rosenhan's experiment remind me of what another psychologist, Nevitt Sanford, said on another occasion: "Academic colleagues after going to administration begin to lie" (1975). A number of articles critical of Rosenhan's results followed the Rosenhan publication. Four of them together with a rebuttal by Rosenhan appeared as a symposium in a single 1975 issue of *Journal of Abnormal Psychology* (see Crown, Milton, Spitzer, Weiner, and Rosenhan in References Cited. Also see Robins 1975). But the point that preconception and context color both expectation and perception, which centrally concerns us here, remains valid.

9. Eventually I completed the study and wrote a manuscript of 280 pages, entitled *The English Wife*. But it was never published. The several English publishers who saw the manuscript did not want to publish it. They thought what I said was too uncomplimentary to the English men vis-à-vis their wives, and therefore it was untrue. One major American publisher was interested. But its editor told me, "The book is about the English, and you are Chinese. Where does America come in?" His solution was, without securing my consent, to ask a well-known white American anthropologist to write an "Introduction" in which the American family would be brought in to make the book acceptable to American readers. Then I became too busy with other projects.

10. Milton Singer expressed the same view, for somewhat different reasons (Singer 1967:8).

11. The official Chinese term for this usage was *yin* (shadow).

12. Of course, there could be individual Chinese who hated their fathers, but they do not negate the spirit of filial piety of the Chinese society as a whole any more than white supremacists can negate the principles of freedom and equality inherent in the U.S. society as a whole.

13. Although Freedman was English and Wolf is American, the differences, if any, in their cultural roots with reference to the questions here are slight.

14. George Stocking made a similar point in a review of the diary (Stocking 1968).

Bibliography

Abegglen, James C.
   1958   The Japanese Factory. Glencoe, Ill.: Free Press.
Abel, T.M., and F.L.K. Hsu
   1949   Some Aspects of Personality as Revealed by the Rorschach Test. Journal
         of Projective Techniques 13(3):1–16.
Adams, Charles J.
   1965   Islam. In a Reader's Guide to the Great Religions, Ch. VIII. New York:
         Free Press.
Africa
   1935   8(4) A special issue of the journal containing articles on witchcraft
         culture change by E.E. Evans-Pritchard, G.St.J. Ordre-Browne, F.
         Melland, and A.I. Richards.
Alexander, Franz
   1952   Development of the Fundamental Concepts of Psychoanalysis. In Dyna-
         mic Psychiatry, Franz Alexander and Helen Ross, eds. Chicago: Univ.
         of Chicago Press, 3–34.
Anonymous
   1966   My Secret Life. New York: Grove Press.
Argyle, Michael
   1968   Religious Observance. International Encyclopedia of the Social Sciences
         13:421–28.
Bales, Robert F.
   1950   Interaction Process Analysis: A Method for the Study of Small Groups.
         Cambridge, Mass.: Addison-Wesley.
   1953   The Equilibrium Problem in Small Groups. In Talcott Parsons, Robert
         F. Bales, and E.A. Shils, Working Papers. Glencoe, Ill.: Free Press.
Balzer, Richard
   1976   Clockwork: Life In and Outside an American Factory. New York:
         Doubleday.
Bane, Mary Jo
   1977   Here to Stay. New York: Basic Books.
Bateson, Gregory
   1942   Some Systematic Approaches to the Study of Culture and Personality.
         Character and Personality 11:76–82. Rpt. in Personal Character and
         Social Milieu, Douglas Haring, ed. (1949), 110–16. Syracuse, N.Y.:
         Syracuse Univ. Press.
Beals, Ralph L., and Harry Hoijer
   1965   An Introduction to Anthropology. 3rd ed. New York: Collier-
         Macmillan.
Beck, S.J.
   1946   Rorschach's Test. New York: Grune and Stratton 11:25.
   1952   Rorschach's Test III: Advances in Interpretation. New York: Grune and
         Stratton.

Bellah, Robert N.
  1957   *Tokugawa* Religion. Glencoe, Ill.: Free Press.
  1968   Religion: A Sociological Study. International Encyclopedia of the Social
         Sciences 13:407–14.
Benedict, Ruth
  1934   Anthropology and the Abnormal. Journal of General Psychology
         10:59–80.
  1946   The Chrysanthemum and the Sword. Boston: Houghton Mifflin.
Bennett, John
  1969   Northern Plainsman. Chicago: Aldine
Bennett, John, and Iwao Ishino
  1963   Paternalism in Japanese Economy. Minneapolis: Univ. of Minnesota
         Press.
Bennis, Warren G., and Philip Slater, eds.
  1966   The Temporary Society. New York: Harper and Row.
Benson, P.H.
  1960   Religion in Contemporary Culture. New York: Harper.
Bergler, Edmund
  1949   Conflict in Marriage. New York; Harper.
Blau, P.M., and W.R. Scott
  1962   Formal Organizations. San Francisco: Chandler.
Blauner, Robert
  1964   Alienation and Freedom. Chicago: Univ. of Chicago Press.
Bodde, Derk
  1950   Peking Diary. New York: Henry Schuman.
Bohannon, Laura and Paul
  1953   The Tiv of Central Nigeria. London: International African Institute.
Bohannan, Paul J.
  1963   Social Anthropology. New York: Holt, Rinehart, and Winston.
Bohm, Ewald
  1958   Rorschach Test Diagnosis. Anne G. Beck and Samuel J. Beck, trans.
         New York: Grune and Stratton.
Boswell, James
  1950   Boswell's London Journal, 1762–1763. New York: McGraw-Hill.
Boyer, Ruth M.
  1964   The Matrifocal Family among the Mescalero: Additional Data. Amer-
         ican Anthropologist 66:593–602.
Brandon, S.G.F.
  1962   Man and His Destiny in the Great Religions. Manchester: Manchester
         Univ. Press.
Brickner, R.
  1943   Is Germany Incurable? Philadelphia: Lippincott.
Bronfenbrenner, Urie
  1977   Nobody Home: The Erosion of the American Family. Psychology To-
         day, May:41–47.
Browne, C.R.
  1929   Maori Witchery. London: Dent.
Burton, Roger V., and John W.M. Whiting
  1961   The Absent Father and Cross-Sex Identity. Merrill Palmer Quarterly of
         Behavior and Development 7(2):85–95.

Cannon, W.B.
  1942   Voodoo Death. American Anthropologist 44:169–81.
Caplan, Nathan, and Stephen Nelson
  1973   On Being Useful: The Nature and Consequences of Psychological Research on Social Problems. American Psychologist 28(3):199–211.
Caudill, William, and George DeVos
  1956   Achievement, Culture, and Personality: The Case of the Japanese Americans. American Anthropologist 58:1117.
Chapple, E.D., and C.M. Arensberg
  1940   Measuring Human Relations: An Introduction to the Study of the Interaction of Individuals. Genetic Psychology Monograph 22:3–147.
Ch'en, Kung Lu
  1935   *Chung Kuo Chin Tai Shih* (Recent History of China). 2 vols. Shanghai: Commercial Press.
Ch'en, Shou-yi
  1961   Chinese Literature: A Historical Survey. New York: Ronald Press.
Chiao, Chien
  1981   Cognitive Play: Some Minor Rituals Among Hong King Cantonese. *In* Bulletin of the Institute of Ethnology. Taipei, Taiwan: Academica Sinica.
Chin, Ai-li S.
  1966   Modern Chinese Fiction and Family Relations: Analysis of Kinship, Marriage, and the Family in Contemporary Taiwan and Communist Stories. Cambridge, Mass.: MIT Press.
Clark, Kenneth
  1963   The Blot and the Diagram. Encounter (Jan.).
Clark, W.H.
  1958   The Psychology of Religion. New York: Macmillan.
Cohen, Yehudi
  1964   The Establishment of Identity in a Social Nexus: The Special Case of Initiation Ceremonies and their Relation to the Value and Legal Systems. American Anthropologist 66:529–52.
Collis, Maurice
  1943   The Land of the Great Image: Being Experiences of Friar Maurique in Arakan. New York: Knopf.
Confucius
  1960   Chinese Classics, Vol. I. Rpt. Hongkong: Univ. of Hongkong Press.
Coon, Carlton S.
  1948   A Reader in General Anthropology. New York: Holt.
  1971   The Hunting Peoples. Boston: Little, Brown.
Creel, Herlee G.
  1953   Chinese Thought from Confucius to Mao-Tse-tung. Chicago: Univ. of Chicago Press.
  1968   Comments on Ping-ti Ho's Salient Aspects of China's Heritage. *In* China in Crisis: China's Heritage and the Communist Political System, Ping-ti Ho and Tang Tsou, eds. Chicago: Univ. of Chicago Press.
Crown, Sidney
  1975   On Being Sane in Insane Places: A Comment from England. Journal of Abnormal Psychology 84(5):453–55.

Dennis, Wayne
    1947   Does Culture Appreciably Affect Patterns of Infant Behavior? *In* Read-
           ings in Social Psychology. T.M. Newcomb, E.L. Hartley, et al., eds.
           New York: Holt, 40–46.
Dittes, James E.
    1968   Religion: A Psychological Study. International Encyclopedia of the So-
           cial Sciences 13:414–21.
Dollard, J.
    1937   Caste and Class in a Southern Town. New Haven, Conn.: Yale Univ.
           Press.
Dollard, J., N.E. Miller, L.W. Doob, O.H. Mowrer, and Robert Sears
    1939   Frustration and Aggression. New Haven, Conn.: Yale Univ. Press.
Doré, Henry
    1914–1938   Researches in Chinese Superstitions (trans. from the French). 13
           vols. Shanghai: T'usewei Printing Press.
Drake, St. Clair, and Horace R. Cayton
    1962   Black Metropolis: A Study of Negro Life in a Northern City. New York:
           Harper and Row.
DuBois, Cora
    1944   The People of the Alor. Minneapolis: Univ. of Minnesota Press.
Eberhard, Wolfram
    1952   Chinese Festivals. New York: Henry Schuman.
Egerton, Clement (Translator)
    1954   The Golden Lotus. 4 vols. New York: Grove Press.
Eggan, Fred
    1950   Social Organization of the Western Pueblos. Chicago: Univ. of Chicago
           Press.
Ekvall, Robert B.
    1964   Religious Observances in Tibet. Chicago: Univ. of Chicago Press.
Ember, Carol R., and Melvin Ember
    1973   Anthropology. Englewood Cliffs, N.J.: Prentice-Hall.
Erikson, E.H.
    1950   Childhood and Society. New York: Norton.
Evans-Pritchard, E.E.
    1937   Witchcraft, Oracles and Magic Among the Azande. Oxford: Clarendon
           Press.
    1940   The Nuer. Oxford: Clarendon Press.
    1965   Nuer Religion. Oxford: Clarendon Press. (First published, 1956)
Fei, H.T., and T.Y. Chang
    1945   Earthbound China. Chicago: Univ. of Chicago Press.
Fenichel, Otto
    1945   The Psychoanalytic Theory of Neurosis. New York: Norton.
Firth, Raymond
    1936   We, the Tikopia. London: Allen and Unwin.
    1954   The Sociology of *Magic* in Tikopia. Sociologus 14, New Series, 103,
           113–15.
    1959a Social Change in Tikopia. London: Allen and Unwin.
    1959b Problem and Assumption in An Anthropological Study of Religion.
           Huxley Memorial Lecture (1959). Journal of Royal Anthropological
           Institute 89(2):129–48.
    1967   Tikopia Ritual and Belief. Boston: Beacon Press.

Fitzgerald, C.P.
1941 The Tower of Five Glories. London: Cresst Press.
Fortes, M.F.
1959 Oedipus and Job in West African Religion. Cambridge: Cambridge Univ. Press.
Foster, George M.
1965 Peasant Society and the Image of the Limited Good. American Anthropologist 67:293–315.
Frank, L.K.
1950 Society as the Patient. New Brunswick, N.J.: Rutgers Univ. Press.
Frazer, James
1919 Folk-lore in the Old Testament: Studies in Comparative Religion, Legend, and Law. London: Macmillan.
Frazier, Edward F.
1966 The Negro Family in the United States. Rev. and abridged ed. Chicago: Univ. of Chicago Press.
Freedman, Maurice
1966 Chinese Lineage and Society: Fukien and Kwangtung. London: Athlone Press.
Freedman, Maurice, ed.
1967 Social Organization: Essays Presented to Raymond Firth. London: Cass.
Freud, Sigmund
1943 A General Introduction to Psychoanalysis. Rev. ed., authorized English trans. Joan Riviere. Garden City, N.Y.: Garden City Publishing Co.
1962 Civilization and Its Discontents (trans. from the German and ed. James Strachey). New York: Norton.
Fries, M.E.
1947 Diagnosing the Child's Adjustment Through Age-level Tests. Psychoanalytic Review 34.
Fromm, Erich
1949 Psychoanalytic Characterology and Its Applications to the Unerstanding of Culture. *In* Culture and Personality, Sargent and Smith, eds. New York: Viking Fund.
Galbraith, John Kenneth
1958 The Affluent Society. Boston: Little, Brown.
Gillin, John
1948 Personality from the Comparative Cultural Point of View. *In* Personality in Nature, Society, and Culture, C. Kluckhohn and Murray, eds., 169–72. New York: Knopf.
Goldfrank, Esther
1945 Socialization, Personality, and the Structure of the Pueblo Society. American Anthropologist 47:516–39.
Goldthorpe, John, et al.
1968 The Affluent Worker: Industrial Attitudes and Behavior. Cambridge: Cambridge Univ. Press.
Goode, William J.
1951 Religion Among the Primitives. Glencoe, Ill.: Free Press.
Gorer, G.
1943 Themes in Japanese Culture. Trans. New York Academy of Science 2:106–24.
1948 The American People. New York: Norton.

1949   The People of Great Russia. London: Cresst Press.
Grover, Robert
1961   The One Hundred Dollar Misunderstanding. New York: Grove.
Gunther, John
1950   Roosevelt in Retrospect. New York: Harper.
Hall, Edward T.
1971   The Paradox of Culture. *In* In the Name of Life, Bernard Landis and
        Edward S. Tauber, eds. New York: Holt, Rinehart, and Winston.
Hallowell, A.I.
1942   Acculturation Process and Personality Changes. Rorschach Research
        Exchange 6:42–48.
Harris, Frank
1925   My Life and Loves. New York: Grove Press.
Hart, C.W.M.
1954   The Sons of Turimpi. American Anthropologist 56:242–61.
Hart, C.W.M., and Arnold R. Pilling
1960   The Tiwi of North Australia. New York: Holt, Rinehart, and Winston.
Hayashi, Shuji
1965   The New Japanese Concept of Profession. *Chuo Koron* (Central Forum),
        Tokyo, May Issue. As reported by Takeo Nakeo, in Mainichi Daily
        News, Tokyo, May 14, 1965, p. 7.
Helfer, Ray E., and C. Henry Kempe
1968   The Battered Child. Chicago: Univ. of Chicago Press.
Hendricks, Ives
1934   Facts and Theories of Psychoanalysis. New York: Knopf.
Herskovits, M.J.
1948   Man and His Works. New York: Knopf.
Herskovits, M.J., and Frances Herskovits
1959   Sibling Rivalry, the Oedipus Complex and Myth. Journal of American
        Folklore 72:1–15.
Hertz, M., and H. Margulies
1943   Developmental Changes as Reflected in the Rorschach Test Responses.
        Journal of Genetic Psychology 62:189–215.
Ho, Ping-ti
1966   *Chung Kuo Hui Kuan Shih Lueh* (A Historical Survey of Landsmann-
        schaften in China). Taipei, Taiwan: Student Publishing Co.
1968   Salient Aspects of China's Heritage. *In* China in Crisis: China's Heritage
        and the Communist Political System, Ping-ti Ho and Tang Tsou, eds.
        Vol. I, Book I. Chicago: Univ. of Chicago Press.
Hoebel, E.A.
1960   Man in the Primitive World. 2d ed. New York: McGraw-Hill.
1966   Anthropology: The Study of Man. New York: McGraw-Hill.
Hogbin, Ian H.
1934   Law and Order in Polynesia. London: Routledge and Kegan Paul.
Holy Bible
1952   Old Testament Section. New York: Thomas Nelson.
1946   New Testament Section. New York: Thomas Nelson.
Homans, George C.
1941   Anxiety and Ritual: The Theories of Malinowski and Radcliffe-Brown.
        American Anthropologist 43:1964–72.
1954   The Human Group. New York: Harcourt, Brace.

Honigmann, John
1949 Culture and Ethos of Kaska Society. Yale University Publication in Anthropology, No. 40.
Horney, Karen
1939 New Ways in Psychoanalysis. New York: Norton.
Hosoi, Wakizo
1922 Tragic History of *Jokos* (female workers). Tokyo: Kaizosha.
Hostetler, John A.
1976 Hutterite Society. Baltimore: Johns Hopkins Univ. Press.
Hostetler, John A., and Gertrude Enders Huntington
1967 The Hutteries in North America. New York: Holt, Rinehart and Winston.
1968 Communal Socialization Patterns in Hutterite Society. Ethnology 7(4):331–55.
Howard, John Addison
1968 Foreword, *In* Unto the Generations: The Roots of True Americanism, by Daniel L. Marsh (see Marsh).
Howells, W.
1948 The Heathens: Primitive Man and His Religions. New York: Doubleday.
Hsia, Chih-ts'ing
1961 A History of Modern Chinese Fiction, 1917–1957. New Haven: Yale Univ. Press.
Hsu, Francis L.K.
1948a Under the Ancestors' Shadow. New York: Columbia Univ. Press. (See also Hsu 1971a.)
1948b American and Chinese Adolescence: Their Theoretical Implications. Unpubl. paper read at Toronto meetings of the American Anthropological Association, 1948.
1949a China. *In* Most of the World, Ralph Linton, ed. New York: Columbia Univ. Press.
1949b Suppression *versus* Repression: A Limited Psychological Interpretation of Four Cultures. Psychiatry 12(3):223–42.
1951 The Chinese of Hawaii: Their Role in American Culture. New York Academy of Sciences 12(6):244–50.
1952a Religion, Science, and Human Crises: A Study of China in Tradition and Its Implications for the West. London: Routledge and Kegan Paul.
1952b Anthropology or Psychiatry: A Definition of Objectives and Their Implications. Southwestern Journal of Anthropology 8:227–35.
1953 Americans and Chinese: Two Ways of Life. New York: Henry Schuman. (See also Hsu 1970, 1981.)
1954 Cultural Factors. *In* Economic Development, Principles and Patterns, H.F. Williamson and J.A. Buttrick, eds. New York: Prentice Hall, 318–64.
1959 Structure, Function, Content, and Process. American Anthropologist 61:790–805.
1960 A Neglected Aspect of Witchcraft Studies. Journal of American Folklore 73(287):35–38.
1961a Psychological Anthropology: Approaches to Culture and Personality. Homewood, Ill.: Dorsey Press.
1961b Kinship and Ways of Life: An Exploration. *In* Psychological Anthro-

pology: Approaches to Culture and Personality, F.L.K. Hsu, ed. Homewood, Ill.: Dorsey Press.

1963 Clan, Casto and Club. Princeton, N.J.: Van Nostrand-Reinhold.

1964 Rethinking the Term "Primitive." Current Anthropology 5:3.

1965 The Effect of Dominant Kinship Relationships on Kin and Non-kin Behavior: A Hypothesis. American Anthropologist 67:638–61.

1966 Rejoinder: A Link Between Kinship Structure Studies and Psychological Anthropology. (A reply to Stratherns' critique, 1966.) American Anthropologist 68:997–1004.

1968 Chinese Kinship and Chinese Behavior. In China in Crisis: China's Heritage and the Communist Political System, Ping-ti Ho and Tang Tsou, eds. Vol. 1, 579–608. Chicago: Univ. of Chicago Press.

1969a Japanese Kinship and Iemoto. (Being the three new chapters added to the Japanese translation of Clan, Caste and Club, 1963; see Hsu 1971.)

1969b The Study of Literate Civilizations. New York: Holt, Rinehart, and Winston.

1971a Under the Ancestors' Shadow. 2d ed., with a new chapter. Stanford: Stanford Univ. Press. (1st ed., Columbia Univ. Press, 1948.)

1971b Psychological Homeostasis and Jen: Concepts for Advancing Psychological Anthropology. American Anthropologist 73:23–41.

1971c Hikaku Bunmei Shakai Ron (The Sociology of Cultures). Consisting of the Japanese translation of Clan, Caste, and Club and Japanese Kinship and Iemoto. Three new chapters specially written for the Japanese version of this book. (Trans. Keichi Sakuda and Eysun Hamaguchi.) Tokyo: Baifukan.

1971d Kinship and Culture. Chicago: Aldine.

1973a Prejudice and Its Intellectual Effect in American Anthropology: An Ethnographic Report. American Anthropologist 75(1):1–19.

1973b Kinship is the Key. Center Magazine 6(6):4–14.

1975 Iemoto: The Heart of Japan. Cambridge, Mass.: Schenkman Publishing Co.

1977 Review of Childhood in China, William Kessen, ed. American Journal of Sociology 82(2):521–24.

1979 The Cultural Problem of the Cultural Anthropologist. American Anthropologist 81(3):517–32.

1981 Americans and Chinese: Passage to Differences. 3d ed. Honolulu: Univ. Press of Hawaii. (1st ed., 1953; 2nd ed., 1970).

1984 Exorcising the Trouble Makers: Magic, Science, and Culture. Westport, Conn.: Greenwood Press.

Hu Shih

1953 Ch'an (Zen) Buddhism in China: Its History and Method. Philosophy East and West 3(1) April.

Hucker, Charles O.

1957 The Tung-lin Movement of the Late Ming Dynasty. In Chinese Thought and Institutions, John K. Fairbank, ed., 132–62. Chicago: Univ. of Chicago Press.

Hughes, E.R.

1943 The Great Learning and the Mean in Action (English translation of the Confucian classics Tsa Hsuch and Chung Yung). New York: Dutton.

Institute for Research, Indiana University

1953 Sexual Behavior in the Human Female. Philadelphia: Saunders.

Isaacs, Harold R.
    1958   Scratches on Our Minds: American Images of China and India. New York: John Day.
Jones, James
    1951   From Here to Eternity. New York: Scribner's.
Josselyn, Irene M.
    1948   Psychosocial Development of Children. New York: Family Service Association of America.
Kahn, R.L., and D. Katz
    1960   Leadership Practices in Relation to Productivity and Morale. *In* Group Dynamics, D. Cartwright and A. Zander, eds. Evanston, Ill.: Row, Peterson.
Kardiner, A.
    1945   Psychological Frontiers of Society. New York: Columbia Univ. Press.
Kato, Masaaki
    1959   *Noiroze: Shinkeishō Towa Nanika* (Neurosis: What Is It?). Tokyo: Sogensha.
Kato, Tetsujiro
    1966   *QC to Ningen Kanke* (Quality Control and Human Relations). Vol. 4, *Genba QC Tokuhon* (The Workshop Quality Reader). Tokyo: Nikkagiren.
Kawasaki, Ichiro
    1969   Japan Unmasked. Rutland, Vt.: Charles E. Tuttle.
Keesing, Felix
    1958   Cultural Anthropology. New York: Rinehart.
Keoskemet, P., and N. Leites
    1945   Some Psychological Hypotheses on Nazi Germany. Library of Congress, Experimental Division for the Study of War Time Communications, Document No. 60.
Kessen, William, ed.
    1975   Childhood in China. New Haven: Yale Univ. Press.
Kimura, Shōzaburo
    1972   *San Shi Shū Dan to Ie no Ko Shū Dan* (Warrior Grouping and Iemoto Grouping). *In Bun Gi Shun Ju* (Literary Spring and Autumn). March, 22–35.
Kinsey, Alfred C., W.B. Pomeroy, and C.E. Martin
    1948   Sexual Behavior in the Human Male. Philadelphia: Saunders.
Kirk, Grayson (as told to Stanley Frank)
    1960   College Shouldn't Take Four Years. Saturday Evening Post, March 26.
Kittredge, George L.
    1929   Witchcraft in Old and New England. Cambridge, Mass.: Harvard Univ. Press.
Kluckhohn, C.
    1944   Navaho Witchcraft. Papers of the Peabody Museum 22:2.
Kluckhohn, C., and D. Leighton
    1947   The Navaho. Cambridge, Mass.: Harvard Univ. Press.
Kluckhohn, C. and Henry A. Murray, eds.
    1949   Pesonality in Nature, Society, and Culture. New York: Knopf.
Kracauer, Siegfried
    1947   From Caligari to Hitler. Princeton, N.J.: Princeton Univ. Press.
Krige, J.D.
    1947   The Social Function of Witchcraft. Theorea: a Journal of Studies of the

Arts Faculty, Natal Univ. College 1:8–21. Rpt. *in* Reader in Comparative Religion, William A. Lessa and Evon Z. Vogt, eds. Evanston, Ill.: Row, Peterson, 1958.

Kroeber, A.L.
1948   Anthropology. New York: Harcourt, Brace.

Kroeber, A.L., ed.
1953   Anthropology Today. Chicago: Univ. of Chicago Press.

Kuhn, Philip
1968   *Comments on* Nineteenth Century China: The Disintegration of the Old Order and the Impact of the West. *In* Ho and Tsou, eds. Vol. I, Book I. Chicago: Univ. of Chicago Press.

La Barre, Weston
1954   The Human Animal. Chicago: Univ. of Chicago Press.

Lattimore, Richard
1951   Introduction. *In* The Iliad of Homer, Richard Lattimore, trans., 11–15. Chicago: Univ. of Chicago Press.

Lea, H.C.
1939   Materials toward a History of Witchcraft. 3 vols. Philadelphia: Univ. of Pennsylvania Press.

Lee, Rose Hum
1952   Official Cases for Delinquent, Neglected and Dependent Chinese Boys and Girls, San Francisco Bay Region. Journal of Social Psychology 36:15–31.

Leighton, D., and C. Kluckhohn
1947   Children of the People. Cambridge, Mass.: Harvard Univ. Press.

Lessa, William A., and Evon Z. Vogt
1958   Reader in Comparative Religion: An Anthropological Approach. Evanston, Ill.: Row, Peterson.

LeVine, Robert A., and Barbara B. LeVine
1966   Nyansongo: a Gusii Community in Kenya. Vol. 2, Six Cultures series. New York: John Wiley.

Lévi-Strauss, C.
1949   Les Structures Elementaires de la Parenté. Paris: Presses Universitaires de France.
1953   Social Structure. *In* Anthropology Today, A.L. Kroeber, ed. Chicago: Univ. of Chicago Press.

Levy, David
1948   Anti-Nazis: Criteria of Differentiation. Psychiatry 11:125–67.

Levy, Marion J., Jr.
1953   Contrasting Factors in the Modernization of China and Japan. Economic Development and Cultural Change 2:161–97.

Lewis, Oscar
1953   A Mexican Village. Urbana: Univ. of Illinois Press.
1959   Five Families: Mexican Case Studies in the Culture of Poverty. New York: Basic Books.
1966   La Vida: A Puerto Rican Family in the Culture of Poverty. New York: Random House.

Lindesmith, A.R., and A.L. Strauss
1950   A Critique of Culture-Personality Studies. American Sociological Review 15:587–600.

Linton, Ralph
  1936 The Study of Man. New York: Appleton-Century.
  1949 The Cultural Background of Personality. New York: Appleton-Century.
Little, K.I.
  1948 The Negroes in Britain. London: K. Paul, Trench, and Trubner.
Litwak, Eugene
  1960 Geographic Mobility and Extended Family Cohesion. American Journal of Sociology, 385–94. Rpt. *in* Society and Self, Bartlett H. Stoodley, ed. New York: Free Press, 1962.
Liu, James T.D.
  1957 An Early Sun Reformer: Fan Chung Yen. *In* Chinese Thought and Institutions, John K. Fairbank, ed., 105–31. Chicago: Univ. of Chicago Press.
Look (magazine)
  1958 Youth Without a Delinquency Problem. April 29, pp. 22, 75–78.
Lowie, Robert H.
  1924 Primitive Religion. New York: Liveright.
Lu Hsun
  1941 Ah Q Cheng Chuan (The True Story of Ah Q). Trans. by Wang Chi-chen *in* Ah Q and Others. New York: John Day.
Malinowski, Bronislaw
  1922 Argonauts of the Western Pacific. London: Routledge and Kegan Paul.
  1925 Magic, Science, and Religion. *In* Science, Religion, and Reality, J. Needham, ed. New York: Macmillan, 1948.
  1929 The Sexual Life of Savages in North-Western Melanesia. New York: Harcourt, Brace, and World.
  1967 A Diary in the Strict Sense of the Term. Norbert Guterman, trans. New York: Harcourt, Brace, and World.
Mannari, Hiroshi
  1965 *Bizinesu Erito* (Business Elite). Tokyo: Chuokoron Sha.
Marcus, P.M.
  1960 Expressive and Instrumental Groups: Toward a Theory of Group Structure. American Journal of Sociology 66:54–59.
Marsh, Daniel L.
  1968 Unto the Generations: The Roots of True Americanism. New Canaan, Conn.: Long House.
Marsh, Robert, and Hiroshi Mannari
  1970 Lifetime Commitment in Japan: Roles, Norms, and Values. American Journal of Sociology 76:795–812.
Mauss, Marcel
  1923–24 Essai sur le Don, Forme Archaique de l'Echange. Annee Sociologique V 91:1.
  1954 The Gift: Forms and Functions of Exchange in Archaic Societies. I. Cunnison, trans. Glencoe, Ill.: Free Press.
McIlwraith, Thomas F.
  1948 The Bella Coola Indians. Vol. 1. Toronto: Univ. of Toronto Press.
Mead, Margaret
  1928 Coming of Age in Samoa. Rpt. *in* From the South Seas. New York: Morrow, 1939. (First published in 1928.)

1930   Growing up in New Guinea. New York: Morrow.
1964   Anthropology, A Human Science (Selected papers, 1939–1960).
        Princeton, N.J.: Van Nostrand.
1976   Speech given June 15, 1976, at the St. John's Church, Washington, D.C.
        Reported by Mary Ellen Perry *in* The Washington Star, June 16, 1976.
Meggitt, M.J.
1965   The Lineage System of the Mae-Enga. Edinburgh and London: Oliver
        and Boyd.
Middleton, John M.
1960   Lugbara Religion: Ritual and Authority among an East African People.
        Published for the International African Institute by Oxford Univ.
        Press.
1965   The Lugbara of Uganda. New York: Holt, Rinehart and Winston.
Middleton, John M., and David Tait
1958   Introduction. *In* Tribes Without Rulers, John M. Middleton and David
        Tait, eds. London: Routledge and Kegan Paul.
Middleton, John M., and E.H. Winter, eds.
1963   Witchcraft and Sorcery in East Africa. London: Routledge and Kegan
        Paul.
Miller, Henry.
1961   Tropic of Cancer. New York: Grove Press.
Million, Theodore
1975   Reflections on Rosenhan's "On Being Sane in Insane Places." Journal of
        Abnormal Psychology 84(5):456–61.
Monez-Kyrle, Roger
1951   Some Aspects of State and Character. *In* Germany: Psychoanalysis and
        Culture, G. Wilbur and W. Muensterberger, eds. New York: Interna-
        tional Universities Press.
Morris, Desmond
1967   The Naked Ape. New York: McGraw-Hill.
Mowrer, O.H., and C. Kluckhohn
1944   Dynamic Theory of Personality. *In* Personality and the Behavior Dis-
        orders, McV. Hunt, ed. New York: Ronald Press.
Murdock, G.P.
1949   Social Structure. New York: Macmillan.
Murphy, Gardner
1947   Personality. New York: Harper.
Murray, Margaret
1921   The Witch-Cult in Western Europe. Oxford: Oxford Univ. Press.
Nadel, S.F.
1954   Nupe Religion: London: Kegan Paul.
Nakamura, Hajime
1960   The Ways of Thinking of Eastern Peoples. Tokyo, trans. from the
        Japanese by Japanese National Commission for UNESCO. Japanese
        version: *Toyojin no shi yi ho ho,* Tokyo, in four vols., Vol. 1 (1961), Vol.
        2 (1961), Vol. 3 (1962), Vol. 4 (1962).
Naroll, Raoul
1956   Social Development Index. American Anthropologist 58:687–715.
National Government of China
1936   Ministry of the Interior Yearbook. Shanghai: Chinese Government
        Printing Office.

Norbeck, Edward
1961   Religion in Primitive Society. New York: Harper.
Nordenskiöld, Erland
1938   An Historical and Ethnological Survey of the Cuna Indians. Göteberg,
          Sweden: Comparative Ethnographical Studies, vol. 10.
Northrop, F.S.C.
1946   The Meeting of East and West. New York: Macmillan.
Opler, Morris
1941   An Apache Lifeway: The Economic, Social and Religious Institutions of
          the Chiricahua Indians. Chicago: Univ. of Chicago Press.
1965   An Interpretation of Ambivalence in Two American Indian Tribes. *In*
          Reader in Comparative Religion: An Anthropological Approach,
          W.A. Lessa and E.Z. Vogt, eds., pp. 421–31. 2d ed. New York: Harper
          and Row.
Orlansky, Harold
1949   Infant Care and Personality. Psychological Bulletin 46:1–48.
Osako, Masako M.
1972   Auto Assembly Technology and Social Integration in a Japanese Fac-
          tory: A Case Study. Ph.D. diss., Sociology Department, Northwestern
          Univ.
Otterbein, Keth F.
1965   Caribbean Family Organization: A Comparative Analysis. American
          Anthropologist 67:66–79.
Parsons, Talcott
1949   The Social Structure of the Family. *In* The Family: Its Function and
          Destiny, Ruth Nanda Anshen, ed. New York: Harper.
1955a Family Structure and the Socialization of the Child. *In* Family,
          Socialization and Interaction Process, Talcott Parsons and Robert F.
          Bales, eds. Glencoe, Ill.: Free Press.
1955b The Organization of Personality as a System of Action. *In* Family,
          Socialization and Interaction Process, Talcott and Parsons and Robert
          F. Bales, eds. Glencoe, Ill.: Free Press.
1971   Kinship and the Associational Aspect of Social Structure. *In* Kinship and
          Culture, Francis L.K. Hsu, ed., 409–38. Chicago: Aldine Publishing Co.
Pearson, Gerald H.J.
1958   Adolescence and the Conflict of Generations. New York: Norton.
Peter, Prince of Greece and Denmark
1963   A Study of Polyandry. The Hague: Mouton.
1965   The Importance of Alexander the Great's Expedition for the Relations
          between East and West. A paper delivered at Amsterdam Institute of
          the Tropics.
Peters, V.
1965   All Things Common. Minneapolis: Univ. of Minnesota Press.
Pierson, A.T.
1886   The Crisis of Missions. New York: Fleming H. Revell.
Piotrowski, Z.A.
1943   Formulae for Educational and Vocational Guidance in Adolescence.
          Rorschach Research Exchange, Jan. 7, pp. 66–26.
Pye, Lucian
1968   The Spirit of Chinese Politics: A Psychocultural Study of the Authority
          Crisis in Political Development. Cambridge, Mass.: MIT Press.

Radcliffe-Brown, A.R.
  1924   The Mother's Brother in South Africa. South Africa Journal of Science
         21:542–55. Rpt. *in* Structure and Function in Primitive Society. 1952.
         Glencoe, Ill.: Free Press.
  1939   Taboo. Cambridge: Cambridge Univ. Press.
  1945   Religion in Society. Journal of the Royal Anthropological Institute
         75:33–43.
Radhakrishnan, S.
  1948   The Bhagavad Gita, with an introductory essay, Sanskrit text, English
         trans. and notes. London: Allen and Unwin.
Reay, M.
  1959   The Kuma: Freedom and Conformity in the New Guinea Highlands.
         Melbourne: Melbourne Univ. Press for Australian National Univ.
Reischauer, Edwin O.
  1955   Ennin's Travels in T'ang China. New York: Ronald Press.
Richards, I.A.
  1932   Mencius on the Mind: Experiments in Multiple Definition. New York:
         Harcourt, Brace.
Richards, T.W.
  1954   The Chinese in Hawaii: A Rorschach Report. *In* Aspects of Culture
         and Personality, F.L.K. Hsu, ed., New York: Abelard-Schuman., pp.
         67–83.
Riesman, D.
  1952   The Lonely Crowd. New Haven: Yale Univ. Press.
Rō Dō Shō
  1967   *Rō Dō Haku Shō* (Labor White Paper). Tokyo: Okura Shō Insatsu Kyoku.
Robins, Lee, N.
  1978   A Critique of the Labelling Theory Paradigm. Paper presented at the
         Conference on Critical Evaluation of Behavioral Paradigms for
         Psychiatric Science. Gleneden Beach, Ore.
Rodnick, David
  1948   Postwar Germany: An Anthropologist's Account. New Haven: Yale
         Univ. Press.
Roheim, Geza
  1950   Psychoanalysis and Anthropology. New York: International Universi-
         ties Press.
Rohlen, Thomas P.
  1974   For Harmony and Strength: Japanese White-Collar Organization
         in Anthropological Perspective. Berkeley: Univ. of California Press,
         1974.
Rorschach, Herman
  1942   Psychodiagnostics. New York: Grune and Stratton.
Rosenhan, D.L.
  1973   On Being Sane in Insane Places. Science 179(4070):250–58.
  1975   The Contextual Nature of Psychiatric Diagnosis. Journal of Abnormal
         Psychology 84(5):462–73.
Sanford, Nevitt
  1977   Loss and Discovery of Moral Character. *In* We, The People: American
         Character and Social Change, Gordon J. DiRenzo, ed., 80–94. West-
         port, Conn.: Greenwood Press.
Schapera, Isaac, ed.
  1937   The Bantu Speaking Tribes of South Africa. London: Routledge.

Schneider, David M.
 1961 Introduction: The Distinctive Features of Matrilineal Descent Groups. *In* Matrilineal Kinship, David M. Schneider and Kathleen Gough, eds. Berkeley: Univ. of California Press.

Schulze, Franz
 1967 Scotch Broth, Chicago Chrome. Chicago Sun-Times, Oct. 14, 1967.

Schurmann, Franz
 1968 The Attack of the Cultural Revolution on Ideology and Organization. *In* China in Crisis: China's Heritage and the Communist Political System, Ping-ti Ho and Tang Tsou, eds. Vol. I, Book I. Chicago: Univ. of Chicago Press.

Sen, K.M.
 1961 Hinduism. Baltimore: Penguin Books.

Shih, Nai-an
 Ching Dynasty (1644–1911) *Sui Hu Chuan,* (trans. in full by Pearl S. Buck *as* All Men Are Brothers. New York: John Day, 1948.

Shulman, Alix Kates
 1972 Memoirs of an Ex-Prom Queen. New York: Knopf.

Singer, Milton
 1967 On Understanding Other Cultures and One's Own. Journal of General Education 19(1):1–23.

Skinner, B.F.
 1971 Beyond Freedom and Dignity. New York: Knopf

Slater, Philip E.
 1966 Some social Consequences of Temporary Systems. *In* The Temporary Society, Warren G. Bennis and Philip Slater, eds. New York: Harper and Row, 77–96.
 1970 The Pursuit of Loneliness. Boston: Beacon Press.

Smith, Raymond T.
 1956 The Negro Family in British Guiana. London: Routledge and Kegan Paul.

Solien, Nance L.
 1959 The Consanguieal Household Among the Black Carib of Central America. Unpubl. Ph.D. diss., Univ. of Michigan.

Solien de Gonzales, Nancie L.
 1961 Family Organization in Five Types of Migratory Wage Labor. American Anthropologist 63:1264–80.

Solomon, Richard H.
 1966 The Chinese Revolution and the Politics of Dependency: The Struggle for Change in a Traditional Political Culture. Unpubl. Ph.D. diss., Univ. of Michigan.

Snow, Edgar
 1962 The Other Side of the River. New York: Random House.

Spitzer, Robert L.
 1975 On Pseudoscience in Science, Logic in Remission, and Psychiatric Diagnosis: A Critique of Rosenhan's "On Being Sane in Insane Places." Journal of Abnormal Psychology 84(5):442–52.

Stavrianos, Leften S., et al.
 1964 A Global History of Man. Boston: Allyn and Bacon.

Stocking, George
 1968 Empathy and Antipathy in the Heart of Darkness. Journal of History and the Behavioral Sciences 4(2):189–94.

Stout, David
  1947   San Blas Cuna Acculturation: An Introduction. Viking Fund Publica-
          tions in Anthropology, no. 9. New York: Viking Fund.
Suchman, Edward S.
  1958   The Values of American College Students. *In* Long-Range Planning for
          Education. Washington, D.C. American Council for Education,
          119–20.
Summers, Montague
  1926   The History of Witchcraft and Demonology. London: Paul, Trench,
          Trubner, and Co.; rpt. New York: University Books, 1956.
  1927   The Geography of Witchcraft. London: Paul, Trench, Trubner; rpt.
          New York: Knopf.
Sutherland, Edwin H.
  1949   White-Collar Crime. New York: Dryden Press.
Swanson, Guy E.
  1960   The Birth of the Gods: The Origin of Primitive Beliefs. Ann Arbor:
          Univ. of Michigan Press.
Sweetser, Dorrian Apple
  1966   Avoidance, Social Affiliation and the Incest Taboo. Ethnology 5:304–
          16.
Tatje, Terrence A.
  1967   The Chinese and Gusii Kinship Systems: A Comparative Analysis in
          Terms of Hsu's Dominant Kinship Relationship Hypothesis. Unpubl.
          MS.
  1974   Mother-Daughter Dyadic Dominance in Black American Kinship. Un-
          publ. Ph.D. diss., Northwestern Univ.
Thetford, William N., Herman B. Molish, and Samuel J. Beck
  1951   Developmental Aspects of Personality Structure in Normal Children.
          Journal of Projective Techniques 15:58–78.
Thomas, Elizabeth Marshall
  1958   The Harmless People. New York: Knopf.
Thompson, Clara
  1950   Psychoanalysis, Evolution, and Development. New York: Hermitage
          House.
Tiger, Lionel
  1969   Men in Groups. New York: Random House.
Tiger, Lionel, and Robin Fox
  1971   The Imperial Animal. New York: Holt, Rinehart, and Winston.
Toynbee, Arnold
  1947   A Study of History. Oxford: Oxford Univ. Press.
Tsao-Chan
  17th Century *Hung Lo Meng* or The Dream of Red Chamber, trans. C.C. Wang.
          Garden City, N.Y.: Doubleday.
Turnbull, Colin M.
  1961   The Forest People. New York: Simon and Schuster.
United States Government
  1931, 1932, 1933 Uniform Crime Reports, 11(4)
Vallier, Ivan A.
  1968   Religious Specialists: Sociological Study. International Encyclopedia of
          the Social Sciences 13:444–52.

Vogel, Ezra
  1963   Japan's New Middle Class. Berkeley: Univ. of California Press.
Walker, Charles R., and Guest, Robert H.
  1952   The Man on the Assembly Line. Cambridge, Mass.: Harvard Univ.
         Press.
Wallace, Anthony
  1966   Religion: An Anthropological View. New York: Random House.
Weber, Max
  1963   The Sociology of Religion, trans. from the German Religionsoziologie,
         1922, by Ephraim Fischoff with an Introduction by Talcott Parsons.
         Boston: Beacon Press.
Wedge, B., and S. Abe
  1949   Racial Incidence of Mental Disease in Hawaii. Hawaii Medical Journal:
         337–38.
Wegrocki, Henry J.
  1939   A Critique of Cultural and Statistical Concepts of Abnormality. Journal
         of Abnormal and Social Psychology 34:166–78. Rpt. *in* Personality in
         Nature, Society and Culture. New York: Knopf, 1948.
Weiner, Bernard
  1975   "On Being Sane in Insane Places": A Process (Attributional) Analysis
         and Critique. Journal of Abnormal Psychology 84(5):433–41.
White, Harrison C.
  1963   An Anatomy of Kinship: Mathematical Models for Structures of Cumu-
         lated Roles. New York: Prentice-Hall.
Whitehall, Arthur M., Jr., and Shin-ichi Takezawa
  1968   The Other Worker: A Comparative Study of Industrial Relations in the
         United States and Japan. Honolulu: East-West Center Press.
Whiting, John W.M., and I.L. Child
  1953   Child Training and Personality. New Haven: Yale Univ. Press.
Whiting, John W.M., Richard Kluckhohn, and Albert Anthony
  1958   The Function of Male Initiation Ceremonies at Puberty. *In* Readings in
         Social Psychology, E. Maccoby, T.M. Newcomb, and E.L. Hartley,
         eds. New York: Holt, Rinehart, and Winston.
Whyte, William H.
  1956   The Organization Man. New York: Simon and Schuster.
Williams, Jay
  1957   The Witches. New York: Random House.
Wilson, Bryan R.
  1968   Religious Organization. International Encyclopedia of the Social Scien-
         ces 13:428–37.
Winch, Robert
  1950   The Study of Personality in the Family Setting. Social Forces 28(3):310–
         14.
  1971   The Modern Family. 3d ed. New York: Holt, Rinehart, and Winston.
Wolf, Arthur P.
  1974   Gods, Ghosts, and Ancestors. *In* Religion and Ritual in Chinese Society,
         131–82. Berkeley: Univ. of California Press.
Wolfe, Alvin W.
  1954   The Institution of Demba Among the Ngonje Ngombe. Kinshasa, Zaire
         [Belgian Congo] Review 8:853–56.

Wright, Arthur F., ed.
    1953   Studies in Chinese Thought. Chicago: Univ. of Chicago Press.
Wu, Cheng-en
    (1500–1582) *Hsi Yu Chi.* (Partially trans. by Helen M. Hayes *in* The Buddhist
        Pilgrim's Progress. New York: Dutton, 1930. Also partially trans. by
        Arthur Waley *in* Monkey. New York: John Day, 1943.)
Yalman, Nur
    1968 Magic. International Encyclopedia of the Social Sciences 9:521–28.
Yang, C.K.
    1961   Religion in Chinese Society. Berkeley: Univ. of California Press.
Yan, Lien-sheng
    1957   The Concept of *Pao* as a Basis for Social Relations in China. *In* Chinese
        Thought and Institutions, John K. Fairbank, ed., 291–309. Chicago:
        Univ. of Chicago Press.
Yang, Martin C.
    1945   A Chinese Village. New York: Columbia Univ. Press.
Yinger, Milton
    1957   Religion, Society and the Individual: An Introduction to the Sociology
        of Religion. New York: Macmillan.

Author Index

Subject Index

Achievement: American, ix–x; of Chinese in the U.S., 49 et seq.; of Japanese in the U.S., 372–73

Adolescence: Chinese transition from to adulthood, 81–90; the drawbacks of Chinese pattern, 89–90; *see also* Generation gap

Air piracy: American ideas about, 411–12

Alorese, 132, 134–35, 139

American factory workers: Detroit auto makers' dissatisfaction with jobs, 207

American family, 305; alleged causes of its decline, 391–93; the centrifugality of, 393–95; extended family in America, 391; future of, 394–98; kinship and behavior, 390–94; lack of long term change, 391; roots of, 387–99

Ancestor worship, 215, 246; and dominant dyad, 251 et seq.; Han emperors' failure to make the people worship imperial ancestors, 347–49; misinterpretation of Chinese, 433–34; types of, 250–51

Arabs, 97

Art: Chinese and Western differentiated, 176 et seq.; culturally different reactions to pornography, 106; pornography, 106; as revelation of life, 105–107; and sex in, 177–78; in Taiwan and the People's Republic of China, 181; variety in American, 178–79

Art and literature: durability of in contrast to scientific theories and technology. 168

Asexuality and art, 343

Association: lack of free in Chinese society, 284–85; *Hui-kuan* locality organization, 340

Authority: Chinese way in, 342–43

Bellah, Robert N.: on industrial development of Japan, 372–75

Bureaucracy: Chinese and Western compared, 345; peculiar characteristics of Chinese, 344–45

Buddha, 427

Chiang Kai-shek, 39, 354

Childhood experiences: in China and Japan compared, 124–25; contrary facts, 131–37; early versus later experiences, 131–37; its importance, 130–31; maternity care, 132–35; socialization, 104–105; solution to contradictions, 138 et seq.; in U.S. and Germany compared, 126–27

China under Communism: commune, 353–55; cultural revolution, underlying objectives, 351–55; fallacy of the individualist view, 409–11; goal

Rugged Individualism Reconsidered is set in ten point Garamond type with one-point spacing between the lines. Garamond is also used for display. The book was designed by Judy Ruehmann. The book was composed by Williams of Chattanooga, Tennessee, printed by Thomson-Shore, Inc., Dexter, Michigan, and bound by John H. Dekker & Sons, Grand Rapids, Michigan. The paper on which the book is printed bears the watermark of S.D. Warren and is designed for an effective life of at least three hundred years.

THE UNIVERSITY OF TENNESSEE PRESS : KNOXVILLE